DEATH MARCH

DONALD KNOX

DEATH MARCH

THE SURVIVORS OF BATAAN

Harcourt Brace Jovanovich, Publishers
New York and London

Library of Congress Cataloging in Publication Data

Knox, Donald, 1936-
Death march.

1. World War, 1939–1945—Prisoners and
prisons, Japanese. 2. World War, 1939–1945—
Personal narratives, American. 3. World War,
1939–1945—Campaigns—Philippines—Bataan
(Province). 4. Bataan (Philippines : Province)—
History. 5. Prisoners of war—United States—
Biography. 6. Prisoners of war—Japan—Biog-
raphy. 7. Prisoners of war—Philippines—
Bataan (Province). I. Title.
D805.J3K59   940.54′72′52095991   81-47555
ISBN 0-15-124094-9   AACR2

Printed in the United States of America

First edition

B C D E

To Kathleen

CONTENTS

MAPS

Photographs are between pages 166-167 and 326-327.

PICTURE CREDITS

SECTION I
Page 1, top, John Falconer, bottom, Leon Beck; page 2, top, Norman Matthews, bottom, National Archives 208 AA 287 J-1; page 3, U.S. Army Photo SC 202648; page 4, top, U.S. Army Photo SC 334301, bottom, U.S. Army Photo SC 131315; page 5, top, U.S. Army Photo SC 131305, bottom, U.S. Army Photo SC 131284; page 6, bottom, National Archives 208 CN 5602; pages 8 and 9, Gasei; pages 10 and 11, Wide World Photos; page 12, top, U.S. Army Photo SC 282340, bottom, National Archives 208 AA 288 BB-1; page 13, top, National Archives 208 AA 288 BB-2, bottom, U.S. Army Photo SC 282346; pages 14 and 15, U.S. Army Photo SC 282345; page 16, Gasei.

SECTION II
Page 1, top left, John Posten, top right, John Falconer, middle, Leona Gastinger, bottom, Hattie Brantley; page 2, top, Leon Beck, bottom left, Hadley Watson, bottom right, Marie Wohlfeld; page 3, top left, Cletis Overton, top right, Victor Mapes, bottom, William Wright; page 4, top, Theodore Bigger, bottom, John Mamerow; page 5, top, Robert Brown, middle, Wilburn Snyder, bottom, Frank Stecklein; page 6, top left, Michael McMullen, top right, William Wallace, middle left, Andrew Aquila, middle right, Roy Diaz, bottom, Stanley Sommers; page 7, Stanley Sommers; page 8, top, John Mamerow, bottom, John Falconer; page 9, bottom, Michael McMullen; page 10, John Falconer; page 11, top left, William Wallace, top right and middle, John Mamerow, bottom, John Falconer; pages 12 and 13, Norman Matthews; page 14, John Mamerow; page 15, National Archives 80-G 700767; page 16, Leona Gastinger.

Memory is a strange bell
Jubilee and knell.

—Emily Dickinson

PREFACE

Lost in the seemingly unending written history of World War II is the story of the American servicemen who surrendered to the Japanese on Bataan Peninsula in the Philippines. Only in the memories of the survivors does that story remain alive. Nearly 10,000 American troops became prisoners when Maj. Gen. Edward P. King, Jr., surrendered Luzon Force on April 9, 1942. At the time, this surrender represented the heaviest numerical reversal ever suffered by an American force in a single engagement with a foreign foe. Blanketed by the larger national disaster of Pearl Harbor, Bataan has drifted into the shadows of defeat. Also relegated to obscurity is the fate of the American captives who spent three and a half years surviving their imprisonment. Today, if you are curious, you can hear their stories only if you attend one of the conventions and reunions held each year by the survivors. What you will hear is not pleasant; many of the stories still tear deeply into memories, still cause outrage. Even thirty-nine years later, the cruel deaths of friends and comrades are not easy to think about.

The 6,000 to 7,000 who died in captivity are represented in this book by the living. And to stay alive required luck. If you had your malarial attack on one day instead of another, if you volunteered for the wrong detail or were put on the wrong ship, if you didn't have a buddy, if you got beaten instead of slapped—such chance moments decided whether you lived or died. One survivor said, "I doubt anyone remembers an average day. What sticks in our minds are the funny days or the horrible days. The ones in between just blur together. If you got through a day without any trouble you forgot it. Just sort of mental preparation for the next day. We lived them one at a time. There were lulls. If it stayed as rough as some days there wouldn't have been any survivors."

Because death became commonplace, it is the horror of what it took to survive that is remembered. Little is forgotten, yet much is not spoken of. To give voice to these memories is to relive many of them. Some men choose not to remember anything. Others cannot. My questions often reminded survivors of harrowing moments just over the borders of their memories. Actual incidents often could not be recalled, though the pain lingered. Thus some of the events that took place between April 1942 and August 1945 will never be known.

Attending a reunion of The Defenders of Bataan and Corregidor is like walking into the village found at the conclusion of Ray Bradbury's *Fahrenheit 451,* where the escapees keep alive in their memories complete books that have been destroyed. Some Bataan survivors remember the names of men who died thirty-nine years ago, and many stories are told about them. Nostalgia played an insignificant part in the storytelling process.

In the following pages memory becomes a passport to a world so terrible that none but a few could imagine it, let alone actually live in it. These Bataan men—most in their late teens or early twenties when the war began—entered a wilderness that had no rules. What a prisoner did to stay alive one day might cause his death the next. There were no maps to show a prisoner how to get from sunup to sundown alive. Every emotional and physical path had to be explored afresh each day. Men who did so successfully lived; those who didn't died.

Today these men re-enter this memory world because it has become a place, no matter how repellent, they know they can leave alive. But I believe there are deeply personal stories that were not told to me, stories that lay behind a wall, guarded by emotions these men do not want to share. Occasionally I would hear a story that would end in mid-sentence. Gentle probing would not take the story further. It was as if, once remembered, the survivor decided to seal off from the curious this new part of his memory as quickly as he had shown it. Other survivors will not talk about what happened because they feel no one will believe them. In today's world of Toyotas, Sonys, and Nikons their stories can sound exaggerated. Even I, especially at the beginning of this project, listened incredulously at times to what I was being told.

Like Daumier's drawings, many of the stories contain enough dramatic narrative and characterization in a few lines or pages to fill several novels. Some of the stories are only fragments, others have no endings. I have written them as they were told to me. They are presented in straight narrative line or by thematic content. I have sifted through the accounts, examined the evidence, and brought, I hope, some common sense to sometimes contradictory information. At all times I have tried to present an accurate and balanced account of what it must have been like to be held prisoner by the Japanese.

When the Emperor of Japan announced his country's surrender in August 1945, there were 4,000 Bataan survivors—a little more than a third—still alive. As might be expected, after the war these men lived diverse lives. Of the people who speak in this book one became a general, another a millionaire, another the mayor of a small Texas town, and one a space program administrator. Others taught school, farmed, worked in factories, ran their own businesses. There is a college professor here, a house painter, a Baptist preacher, two doctors, and a mailman. A large group, when they could find no work after the war, re-enlisted. Several saw service in Korea. One even served in Vietnam. Now they are in their sixties and early seventies. If they share anything besides the comradeship of having survived a common ordeal it is their love for the United States of America. They also share nightmares, scars, and sick bodies. The effects of malnutrition, physical abuse, and hard labor show on most of them.

I found many survivors disliking the Japanese, and some hating them. It is surprising perhaps that so many carry no feelings at all. Yet none that I know drives a Japanese car.

Beyond these brief observations I think it is useless to speak for these survivors. It is from their own stories, from their own words, that readers can draw conclusions about them.

There are no heroes in this book. The survivors do not see themselves in heroic guise. It is common nowadays to be told that Americans are too confused, too sophisticated, or too spoiled to have heroes. But even in 1945, when the survivors of Bataan returned home, they arrived quietly, anonymously. Not much was done to recognize their sacrifice. Perhaps Americans had too many heroes then. There were winners everywhere. It was the wrong time to recognize men who had lost, men who had surrendered. But the life-and-death struggle recorded in this book tells about more than survival. Heroism, the Caucasian mountaineers say, is endurance for one moment more. For the 10,000 young Americans who, not too many years ago, surrendered to the Japanese on Bataan, life became almost more terrible than death. Perhaps the truest valor then was to have lived.

D. K.
Eagan, Minn.

THE SURVIVORS WHO CONTRIBUTED TO THIS BOOK

NAME	RANK	UNIT	BRANCH OF SERVICE
Austin Andrews	Seaman First Class	USS *Oahu*	US Navy
Andrew Aquila	Private First Class	192d Tank Battalion	US Army
Leon Beck	Private	31st Infantry	US Army
Theodore Bigger	Captain	48th Matériel Squadron	US Army Air Force
Jack Brady	Private First Class	228th Signal Operations Company	US Army
Hattie Brantley	2d Lieutenant	Army Nurse Corps	US Army
Robert Brown	Private First Class	17th Pursuit Squadron	US Army Air Force
James Caire	Tech. Sergeant	27th Bombardment Group (L)	US Army Air Force
James Cavanaugh	Staff Sergeant	28th Bombardment Squadron	US Army Air Force
Charles Cook	Sergeant	27th Bombardment Group (L)	US Army Air Force
Ishmael Cox	Corporal	31st Infantry	US Army
Ferron Cummins	Sergeant	34th Pursuit Squadron	US Army Air Force
Lee Davis	Private First Class	30th Bombardment Squadron	US Army Air Force
Kenneth Day	Corporal	5th Air Base Group	US Army Air Force
Roy Diaz	Private First Class	194th Tank Battalion	US Army
Lewis Elliott	Private	60th Coast Artillery (AA)	US Army
John Falconer	Private First Class	194th Tank Battalion	US Army
Harold Feiner	Staff Sergeant	Provisional Tank Group	US Army
Nicholas Fryziuk	Sergeant	192d Tank Battalion	US Army

NAME	RANK	UNIT	BRANCH OF SERVICE
William Garleb	Corporal	31st Infantry	US Army
Leona Gastinger	2d Lieutenant	Army Nurse Corps	US Army
Hubert Gater	Corporal	200th Coast Artillery (AA)	US Army
Fred Gifford	Corporal & 2d Lieutenant	21st Pursuit Squadron	US Army Air Force Philippine Army
Benson Guyton	Captain	60th Coast Artillery (AA)	US Army
William Hauser	Corporal	192d Tank Battalion	US Army
Mark Herbst, M.D.	1st Lieutenant	57th Infantry (Philippine Scouts)	US Army
Thomas Hewlett, M.D.	Captain	Medical Corps Philippine Department	US Army
Eugene Jacobs, M.D.	Major	14th Infantry	Philippine Army
Forrest Knox	Sergeant	192d Tank Battalion	US Army
Eddy Laursen	Private First Class	93d Bombardment Squadron	US Army Air Force
Marion Lawton	Captain	31st Infantry	Philippine Army
Kermit Lay	2d Lieutenant	I Philippine Corps	US Army
Victor Lear	Private First Class	27th Bombardment Group (L)	US Army Air Force
Ralph Levenberg	Sergeant	17th Pursuit Squadron	US Army Air Force
Wayne Lewis	Corporal	31st Infantry	US Army
Mel Madero	Tech. Sergeant	194th Tank Battalion	US Army
John Mamerow	Major	Adjutant General's Office Philippine Department	US Army Air Force
Victor Mapes	Private First Class	14th Bombardment Squadron	US Army Air Force
Norman Matthews	Private First Class	27th Bombardment Group (L)	US Army Air Force
William Mattson	Sergeant	194th Tank Battalion	US Army
Charles McCartin	Corporal	803d Engineers	US Army
Jerome McDavitt	Captain	24th Field Artillery (Philippine Scouts)	US Army

NAME	RANK	UNIT	BRANCH OF SERVICE
Michael McMullen	Private First Class	27th Bombardment Group (L)	US Army Air Force
Loyd Mills	Captain	57th Infantry (Philippine Scouts)	US Army
Cletis Overton	Private First Class	27th Bombardment Group (L)	US Army Air Force
John Posten	2d Lieutenant	17th Pursuit Squadron	US Army Air Force
Blair Robinett	Private First Class	803d Engineers	US Army
Paul Sarno	Corporal	20th Pursuit Squadron	US Army Air Force
Bernard "Chick" Saunders	Corporal	27th Bombardment Group (L)	US Army Air Force
Alfred Schreiber	Tech. Sergeant	27th Matériel Squadron	US Army Air Force
William Sniezko	Tech. Sergeant	31st Infantry	US Army
Wilburn Snyder	Private First Class	31st Infantry	US Army
Stanley Sommers	2d-Class Carpenter's Mate	USS Finch & Naval Battalion	US Navy
John Spainhower	Captain	57th Infantry (Philippine Scouts)	US Army
Frank Stecklein	Staff Sergeant	USAFFE Headquarters	US Army
Daniel Stoudt	Private First Class	192d Tank Battalion	US Army
Charles Thornton	Private	27th Bombardment Group (L)	US Army Air Force
Robert Taylor, Chaplain	Captain	31st Infantry	US Army
Houston Turner	First Sergeant	31st Infantry	US Army
Michael Tussing, Jr.	Private First Class	27th Bombardment Group (L)	US Army Air Force
H. G. Tyson	Sergeant	3d Pursuit Squadron	US Army Air Force
Gerald Wade	Corporal	93d Bombardment Squadron	US Army Air Force

NAME	RANK	UNIT	BRANCH OF SERVICE
William Wallace	Private First Class	27th Bombardment Group (L)	US Army Air Force
Hadley Watson	2d Lieutenant	57th Infantry (Philippine Scouts)	US Army
Robert Wolfersberger	Corporal	27th Bombardment Group (L)	US Army Air Force
Mark Wohlfeld	Captain	27th Bombardment Group (L)	US Army Air Force
William "Cowboy" Wright	Tech. Sergeant	17th Pursuit Squadron	US Army Air Force
Eunice Young	2d Lieutenant	Army Nurse Corps	US Army

ACKNOWLEDGMENTS

In writing this book I have received most generous help. I should like first to record my gratitude to Dr. Stanley L. Falk, Chief of the S. E. Asia Branch of the U.S. Army Center of Military History, who first suggested the idea for this book to me. His continued encouragement was essential and deeply appreciated.

I owe a special debt to Ben Guyton, who always found the time to introduce me to his fellow survivors at the annual conventions held by The Defenders of Bataan and Corregidor, and to Wayne Carringer for the hospitality shown me at the Fontana Dam, North Carolina, reunions.

I am also indebted to Stan Sommers, National Sr. Vice Commander and MedSearch Chairman of the American Ex-Prisoners of War, Inc., who supplied me with much needed information about prison life. Gen. Harold K. Johnson also took time from a busy schedule to answer questions about camp existence. I owe a special obligation to Frances Worthington Lipe, who answered what must have been, for her, elementary questions. Her original work in identifying camps and her map of Japanese Prisoner of War Camps published by the Medical Research Committee were of immense value.

I have been fortunate in being given permission to use a number of private papers. I should like to thank Kenneth Day, for allowing me to use excerpts from his excellent unpublished manuscript; John Posten, who shared his wartime diary with me; and William "Cowboy" Wright, who made available his valuable work in progress on the 17th Pursuit Squadron. I should also like to thank Brig. Gen. Curtis Beecher, U.S. Marine Corps (Ret.), for permitting me to read his superb unpublished account of his captivity. From it I was able to unravel many of the mysteries of prison life in Cabanatuan and to restore some order to the horror of the *Oryoku Maru* voyage. George B. Abdill, Director of the Douglas County Museum in Roseburg, Oregon, took the time to supply me this manuscript. Rudolph Clemen, Jr., of the American Red Cross, supplied much information and I am grateful for his sharing with me a copy of Volume XXII from the American Red Cross's unpublished historical monograph series "Relief to Prisoners of War in World War II" by Arthur Robinson. Col. Eugene C. Jacobs, U.S. Army (Ret.), has given me permission to use many of his excellent drawings of Camp No. 1 at Cabanatuan. Of the dozens of memoirs I was able to read, Brig. Gen. Steve Mellnik's *Philippine Diary 1939–1945* and Brig. Gen. W. E. Brougher's *South to Bataan, North to Mukden* proved to be particularly useful.

In matters of geography I received valuable assistance from Lynne Anderson of the Map Division, O. Meredith Wilson Library at the University of Minnesota. John Riley at the Ship History Branch of the Navy History Center always cheerfully located the names of Japanese freighters and American submarines.

While writing this book I received helpful suggestions from friends who took a kind interest in my efforts. For their suggestions and support I am grateful to Paul Bosner, Peter Bradley, Marty Robinson, John Rahmann, and Frank Liebert, as well as my colleagues at KTCA-TV. To Jim Russell, who by shouldering much of my work allowed me to finish the manuscript, I am especially indebted.

John Hochmann provided as always many helpful suggestions, and for editorial assistance and support I am grateful to Peter Jovanovich.

I owe more than I can ever tell to the hundreds of Bataan survivors and their families I met and spoke to. I am very grateful for their friendship and for their sharing still-painful memories with a stranger.

I should also like to thank Diane Koppy, who translated hundreds of difficult tapes into legible transcripts, and Marjorie Nugent for providing me with much needed research.

Lastly, I owe so much to my sons, Neil and Alexander, whose love and energy suffuse their Dad's life. I am also profoundly grateful to Kathleen Rucker for her patience and for her generous and untiring collaboration in all phases of the preparation of this book.

INTRODUCTION
by Stanley L. Falk

On the morning of January 28, 1944, Americans awoke to find their newspapers filled with shocking reports of the fate of nearly 10,000 of their fellow countrymen captured by the Japanese almost two years earlier on Bataan Peninsula, in the Philippines. With unbelieving eyes they read an incredible account of cruel atrocities inflicted by an unfeeling enemy on sick and helpless captives. The story of the tragic movement of American prisoners out of Bataan—which came to be known as the Bataan Death March—and of their subsequent bitter incarceration in grim Japanese prisoner-of-war camps came as an ugly surprise to a nation previously unaware of what had befallen the brave defenders of Bataan.

Until this time, there had been no public inkling of events in that distant place seized so early in the war by the conquering Japanese. When Bataan surrendered on April 9, 1942, most Americans realized that its stubborn defenders would probably remain prisoners until the end of the war. No one assumed that this captivity would be particularly pleasant, but few had any idea of just how cruel and bitter it would quickly become. There had been, of course, some shocking tales of Japanese atrocities in China, but hardly anyone considered that such a large group of Americans could be so grossly and systematically mistreated. That the prisoners would be beaten, starved, denied water, tortured, and murdered as a normal part of their captivity was unthinkable and, for many months after their surrender, unheard of.

The first reports of what had actually happened in the Philippines reached the United States approximately a year after Bataan's surrender. In April 1943, a small group of Americans being held in the former Philippine penal camp at Davao, in the southern Philippines, managed to elude their captors and escape. With the help of Filipino guerrillas, the escapees were rescued by submarine and soon reached General Douglas MacArthur's headquarters in Australia. The 2,000 prisoners at Davao had been engaged in growing food for the Japanese army, and life was somewhat better than in other prisoner-of-war camps. Yet as the testimony of those unfortunate enough to be held there revealed, the Davao prison camp was a grim and brutal place, where death was common and torture and deprivation even more so. One of the men, Captain William B. Dyess, had been captured on Bataan. And it was his account of the Death March and of the savage treatment that followed that first alerted the United States government to the extent of Japanese cruelty.

Dyess's testimony was similar to the dramatic accounts in the pages of this book. It told of harsh mistreatment, deliberate torture, and unprovoked horrors. Although our government feared that publishing this news would lead to retaliation and further cruelty to prisoners still in Japanese hands, it was not too long before the story was common knowledge in many quarters of the American press. By the early weeks of 1944, journalistic pressure was extreme, and a joint War and Navy department announcement revealed the facts to a stunned world.

A combination of shock and outrage gripped the American public and led to the desire for revenge, for punishment of the Japanese, though few could begin to comprehend what had happened on Bataan and in the prison camps. Even fewer had the slightest notion of why it had occurred. Not until many years after the war did the story of the American captivity begin to emerge. Here, in Donald Knox's moving presentation, portions of the story are being told for the first time. Yet the question of *why* it happened may never be completely understood.

A partial explanation lies in the type of army that surrendered on Bataan. There were roughly 78,000 troops: some 66,000 Filipino soldiers led and supported by about 12,000 Americans. For more than three months after forming their stubborn defensive line in the jungles and mountains of Bataan, they had lived on a drastically reduced daily ration of perhaps fifteen ounces of rice, a tiny portion of flour, salt, sugar, and canned meat and milk, and an occasional monkey, snake, or lizard. Near the end, they were eating less than a thousand calories a day. It was a diet that barely kept men alive, and certainly left them in no condition to fight.

Even worse, it increased their susceptibility to disease in the hot, malarial conditions on Bataan. Dysentery, diarrhea, and beriberi were the inevitable results of malnutrition, vitamin deficiency, and poor sanitary conditions. Malaria spread rapidly as the supply of quinine diminished and soon exceeded all other diseases in the number of its victims. By the eve of the final Japanese offensive, nearly one-third of the entire Filipino-American army was sick or wounded.

Weighing heavily, too, was an overwhelming depression, brought on by the grim awareness that, whatever had been promised, no help could be expected from the United States. There would be no escape from Bataan save through death or capture. Such a combination of physical and mental exhaustion made it all but impossible to resist the final Japanese assault. Worse, it left the men of Bataan in no shape to withstand the rigors of captivity.

The Japanese were less concerned with their new prisoners than with taking the island of Corregidor, which blocked the entrance to Manila Bay. The stubborn defense of Bataan had delayed them too long. Thus the first thing they wanted to do was clear the peninsula in order to launch their assault on Corregidor. Their plan was to assemble the prisoners in southern Bataan for a phased movement by foot, truck, and rail to an internment camp in central Luzon. It called for proper food, water, and rest, and, in accordance with Japanese army regulations, directed that the prisoners be treated with a "friendly spirit." None of this came to pass. The Japanese bungled badly.

The initial assembly of the prisoners was unco-ordinated and disorganized. The phased movement to follow never took place in any reasonable or systematic form. There was inadequate food, water, and medicine, and the captives were denied most of what was available. No provision was made for the sick and the wounded.

Strangely enough, many of the prisoners traveled in relative comfort, with little harassment, and reached their planned destination relatively unscathed. But for the majority of the unfortunate captives, the movement from Bataan was indeed a death march. Instead of a carefully organized military movement, the exodus from Bataan, with some notable exceptions, was a series of torturous marches, of needless exposure to a merciless sun, of crowded, filthy assembly areas stinking of disease and human refuse, and of beatings, torture, and arbitrary execution.

The Japanese had tragically underestimated the size of the army they faced on Bataan, and hence the numbers of prisoners they would take. They had based their plan of evacuation on 40,000 captives. In addition to this, they had little knowledge of the terribly poor physical condition of the American and Filipino soldiers on Bataan. While low on food and medical supplies themselves, they nevertheless failed to recognize how much worse off the Bataan defenders were and the special provisions for receiving thousands of sick and wounded prisoners that would be necessary.

The Japanese soldier into whose keeping fate had delivered the Bataan defenders was the product of a stern and coercive society. He was part of a hard and brutal military system, where physical punishment was routine and arbitrary. He endured his lot stoically and without question, and treated his subordinates with the same routine callousness that he experienced from his superiors. Fiercely indoctrinated never to surrender, he held in contempt anyone who did. To this deep-seated revulsion was added the ancient samurai tradition of revenge, reinforced by the heavy casualties suffered by the Japanese in capturing Bataan.

The Japanese soldiers charged with guarding the prisoners were confused, uncaring, and inconsistent. Some were reasonably kind and humane. Others displayed a sadistic cruelty as shocking as it was fatal to their captives. Certainly neither General Homma, the Japanese commander, nor his officers seem to have shown any great concern over the fate of their captives. They made little effort to improve the difficult and chaotic situation following the surrender in southern Bataan, and they were indifferent to the suffering of the prisoners and the harsh brutality of their troops. This failure of Japanese leadership was the ultimate factor in condemning the Bataan defenders to a cruel fate.

As the testimony in this book so clearly shows, the Death March from Bataan was a tragic nightmare, without form, reason, or mercy. The words of the survivors, though calm and almost matter-of-fact, forty years after their ordeal, reflect the horror of the torment still clearly fresh in their minds.

Although the Death March may have ended with the arrival of the prisoners at Camp O'Donnell, the remainder of their captivity was to offer no surcease from the brutality of their ordeal. Numbed, exhausted, and bewildered, they entered a prison no less horrible than the march itself. At O'Donnell the cumulative effect of the grim movement from Bataan and the continued brutality and indifference of their captors took an ever-increasing toll. Nearly twice as many Americans died in the first two months at prison camp as had perished on the march. This mortality rate signaled the beginning of a hell that would last for over three more years.

Donald Knox has spent years finding and interviewing hundreds of Bataan veterans in all parts of the country to set down their stories in this moving book. With careful and deliberate skill, he has organized this material and woven it together into a dramatic and effective tapestry. From the first days of war, through the heroic fighting for Bataan and the savage Death March to O'Donnell, he has brought these men, of all ranks and ages, through the numbing change from simple peace to bitter captivity. He unveils their stories of the harsh life in the prison camps, the attempts to escape, the hard labor and cruel punishment, the agony of the death ships that carried prisoners to Formosa, Manchuria, or Japan, the final days of brutal captivity, and, at last, liberation and return to America.

Much of the story in these pages has been told before, but never so personally and so eloquently. There is also much detail that is new. The last days of the struggle for Bataan are made clearer. The strange and difficult personal relationships within the prison camps emerge in sharp perspective. The dangerous, abrasive life of the Philippine guerrillas, as witnessed by those American prisoners fortunate enough to escape, is convincingly revealed. Perhaps the most effective and touching portion of this testimony comes from descriptions of the depressingly low-key, almost indifferent, reception that awaited the liberated prisoners when they returned from their years of captivity. The final pages of this book stand as a sharp indictment of how the United States has treated its veterans.

Death March: The Survivors of Bataan is a poignant and moving tribute to courage and the will to survive. The men of Bataan deserve nothing less.

PART I

DYING

1
WAR

Across the international date line in the Philippines, at midnight of December 7, 1941, the United States of America continued to be the world's only major power still at peace. In the preceding year Denmark and Norway, then Holland, Belgium, and France had been invaded and conquered by Nazi Germany, and the Battle of Britain had begun. It was the time of the Maginot Line, the Ardennes and Dunkirk, of the Blitz and the Spitfire. Then a year later, in June 1941, Hitler turned eastward and invaded Russia.

In the Pacific, 1941 saw Japan enter the tenth year of its endless war with China. After earlier signing the Tripartite Pact with Nazi Germany and Fascist Italy, that summer Japan seized French Indochina and immediately saw its relationship with the United States worsen. President Franklin Roosevelt froze all Japanese assets in the United States and then, along with Great Britain and the Netherlands, placed an embargo on her oil supply. These economic sanctions cut deeply into Japan's ability to continue the war with China and threatened the country's industrial might. Japan's moderate Prime Minister was replaced by a former War Minister, Hideki Tojo. A country smaller than California, with a population of 74,000,000 people, Japan constituted a dynamic force in the Pacific. Expansionism figured largely in her plans. Now, in mid-1941, Japan saw itself possibly withering away to a second-class nation. To break out of this economic stranglehold, Japan determined to go to war with the United States. To win that war, it was essential

for her to smash America's naval strength in the
Pacific. An audacious plan was proposed which
would destroy America's battleships at their anchorage in Pearl Harbor. If this plan could be
accomplished, Japan saw itself in a position to
gather up all of Southeast Asia. This plan included
the conquest of America's Pacific possession, the
Philippine Islands.

As the threat of war became more real that
summer, the U.S. War Department recalled Gen.
Douglas MacArthur to active duty and assigned
him command of all Army forces in the Far East.
Almost at the same time the largely untrained and
poorly equipped Philippine Army was called to
active service and placed in MacArthur's new
command structure called the U.S. Army Forces,
Far East (USAFFE). The largest United States Army
unit in the islands was Maj. Gen. Jonathan Wainwright's Philippine Division. All the enlisted men in
this unit were Philippine Scouts except for the
31st Infantry, which was composed entirely of
Americans.

Summer turned to fall. The United States began
to seriously increase its shipments to the Philippines of troops, planes, and other materiel. The
initial plan of defense for the archipelago's main
island, Luzon, was for the troops to fall back into
the mountains of the Bataan Peninsula, across the
bay from Manila, and there hold out until the fleet
from Hawaii arrived. With the steady arrival of
men and equipment, this plan was replaced with
a decision to fight the enemy on the invasion
beaches. Optimism infected the military planners
in Washington and Manila. Much of this feeling
centered around the offensive potential of the
Army's new heavy bomber, the B-17. In the beginning of December there were thirty-five of these
Flying Fortresses on Luzon, at Clark Field. In addition, the total military force in the Islands was

appreciably larger than it had been five months earlier. The U.S. Army garrison's total strength had grown to 31,095 officers and enlisted men. The ten reserve divisions of the Philippine Army had been nearly completely mobilized and, although still poorly equipped and trained, they made up a force of some size. Projections of a Japanese offensive had it taking place in the spring of 1942. By then the untrained Filipinos would be ready.

As December 7 gave way in Manila to December 8, none of the people who are about to tell their stories were aware that the events of that day would so thoroughly and drastically affect their lives.

Manila, Monday, December 8, 1941 (AP):

United States Army bombers and pursuit planes roared into the air and headed northward at dawn today soon after word reached Manila of the outbreak of hostilities between Japan and the United States. This is the only sign of war here at 5:25 a.m.

Manila, December 8 (North American Newspaper Alliance):

A Japanese air attack is expected momentarily. . . . Air raid precaution spotters are on all roofs.

Shanghai, December 8 (monitored radio broadcast):

Super dive bombers came in at terrific speed and, before anyone could realize what was happening, bombs were dropped and heavy damage was caused. Manila Army and Navy bases were heavily attacked by dive bombers and bombers of the heaviest type. Terrific destruction followed.

Manila, Tuesday, December 9 (New York Times):

Fort Stotsenburg, sixty miles north of Manila, and the adjoining Clark Field, an Army air base, were pounded in the afternoon. Military buildings were reported set afire and 200 casualties were estimated. It is understood that planes took off from Clark Field and pursued an undetermined number of raiders.

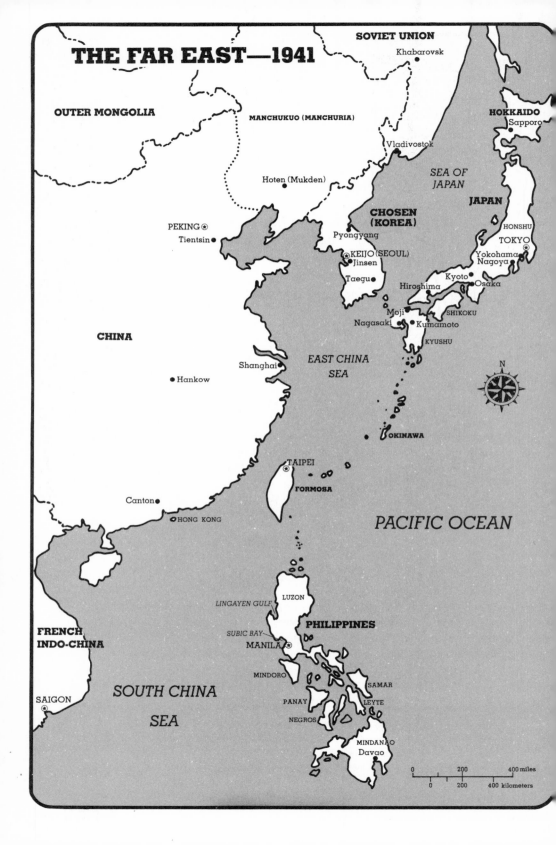

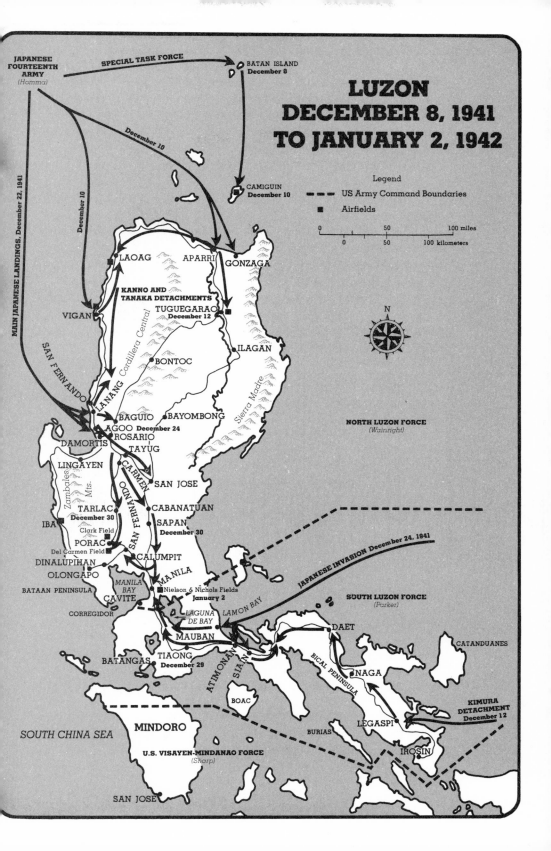

LUZON
DECEMBER 8, 1941
TO JANUARY 2, 1942

JAPANESE
FOURTEENTH
ARMY
(Homma)

SPECIAL TASK FORCE

BATAN ISLAND
December 8

December 10

CAMIGUIN
December 10

Legend

━ ━ ━ US Army Command Boundaries

■ Airfields

0   50   100 miles

0   50   100 kilometers

MAIN JAPANESE LANDINGS, December 22, 1941

December 10

LAOAG

APARRI   GONZAGA

VIGAN

KANNO AND
TANAKA DETACHMENTS

TUGUEGARAO
December 12

ILAGAN

SAN FERNANDO

BONTOC

Cordillera Central

N

BAGUIO   BAYOMBONG

Sierra Madre

NORTH LUZON FORCE
(Wainright)

LANANG

AGOO December 24
ROSARIO

DAMORTIS

TAYUG

CARMEN

LINGAYEN

Zambales Mts.

SAN JOSE

SAN FERNANDO

TARLAC
December 30

CABANATUAN

IBA

Clark Field

SAPAN
December 30

PORAC

Del Carmen Field

CALUMPIT

JAPANESE INVASION December 24, 1941

DINALUPIHAN

OLONGAPO

MANILA

BATAAN PENINSULA

MANILA
BAY

Nielson & Nichols Fields
January 2

SOUTH LUZON FORCE
(Parker)

CAVITE

LAMON BAY

CORREGIDOR

LAGUNA
DE LAY

DAET

CATANDUANES

MAUBAN

BATANGAS

TIAONG
December 29

ATIMONAN

SIAIN

BICOL PENINSULA

NAGA

BOAC

KIMURA
DETACHMENT
December 12

MINDORO

BURIAS

LEGASPI

SOUTH CHINA SEA

U.S. VISAYEN-MINDANAO FORCE
(Sharp)

IROSIN

SAN JOSE

After a day of widespread aerial attacks throughout the Philippines, Japanese bombers swept in over Manila Bay early this morning and attacked Nichols Field, the United States Army air base on the outskirts of this capital. . . . The damage was believed to be light.

War Department communiqué, December 10:

Reports from the Far Eastern Command indicate a definite attempt of the enemy to invade the island of Luzon. Actual landings were effected along the northern coast of Luzon. The Japanese attacks are in considerable strength. Military and naval installations on Luzon have been subject to intermittent Japanese air attacks throughout the day, that on the naval base of Cavite being particularly heavy.

War Department communiqué, December 11:

There were no further developments in the situation in Northern Luzon. Enemy detachments who landed on the Lingayen coast are being disposed of and mopping up operations are in progress.

USAFFE communiqué, December 15:

The enemy effected unopposed landings in limited numbers. . . . The situation both on the ground and in the air was well in hand as the first week of military operations came to a close.

★ ★ ★

Pfc. JACK BRADY, 228th Signal Operations Company:

At 5:30 in the morning [of December 8] I was aroused by our first sergeant awakening the man next to me. He told him to take his weapons and stand guard at a transmitter because we had just gotten involved in a war with Japan. I knew that was just absolutely ridiculous. I laughed like hell and went back to sleep.

Pfc. BLAIR ROBINETT, Company C, 803d Engineers:

I was sleeping off a drunk at Nichols Field* when one of the guys came in and woke me up to tell me that we were at war. I said, "You crazy stupid ass, get away from me. Nobody's at war." That's when he showed me the newspaper headline of Pearl Harbor being bombed. I remember wishing that the Japs had sunk the goddamned place. I despised Hawaii. I'd been

---

* Nichols Field, the principal fighter base on Luzon, was located just south of Manila.

stationed there before being shipped to the Philippines. Soldiers, Sailors, Dogs: KEEP OUT!

I'd been in the sack only four hours and hadn't had a chance to sober up. That newspaper headline sobered me fast.

Sgt. FORREST KNOX, Company A, 192d Tank Battalion:

Pearl Harbor ruined the best joke we ever had cooking. Our little bit of Army was different from the regular Army. Ours was a family, a National Guard unit.* Everybody had a nickname. A big fat Swiss captain, Fred Bruni, we called "The Sow." Another captain, Walter Write, who was smaller than I, we called "Peewee," and only if he addressed me as sergeant would I address him as captain. I was known as "Knocky." We all knew each other from school or the neighborhood and it just made sense that we'd constantly have little jokes working. We had one guy in the company, Bernard Shea, who was known as "One Horse," who took the brunt of many of our jokes. He was a little different from the rest of us and it was a dirty rotten shame they ever took him overseas. He was used as an officer's dog robber and in that capacity he functioned fine. But I knew, because he didn't have enough smarts to survive, Bernard was dead the day the war started.

Outside of Clark Field,† where we were, we could walk to a barrio called Sapangbato. We called it "Sloppy Bottom." Most evenings we'd go down and get into these little Filipino bars. In them we could get little duck eggs called *balóts*. Just before the duck is ready to hatch the Filipinos hard-boil the egg. To the Filipino this is a great delicacy. The joke was that you were a true native if you knew which end of the egg to break to avoid biting the duck's ass. Well, One Horse went completely apeshit the first time he saw someone eat a baby duck. Of course the next night we coaxed him over to a corner table. When we had him pinned in there and everybody had some drinks, we brought over the barmaid who began eating *balóts* in front of us. Well, a joke is a joke, but poor Bernard was frantic. They wouldn't let him go and everybody just leaned on him while the barmaid ate baby ducks. Finally, he wiggled loose and crawled out under the table. Well, we couldn't pass this up. So we bought two *balóts* and on the next morning, which was December 8, the cook, who was of course serving hard-boiled eggs, was going to put the two *balóts* on One Horse's mess kit. I'll tell you there wasn't a soul in the company who was going

---

* Company A came from Janesville, Wis.
† Clark Field, where most of the B-17s were based, was sixty miles northwest of Manila.

to miss Bernard cracking open his hard-boiled baby-duck eggs. Then those rotten sonovabitchin' Japs bombed Hawaii and we didn't have breakfast. You know what our reaction was to Pearl Harbor? We were furious with the Japs for ruining the best gag we ever thought up. It seems now like a silly reaction.

Sgt. RALPH LEVENBERG, 17th Pursuit Squadron:

The war found me hung over. I was a young kid and it was no big deal to get me drunk, probably a few rum and cokes and a San Miguel beer and, plop, I'd be out. The night before Pearl Harbor was bombed I had had my promotion party at the N.C.O. Club. The bill for it turned out to be the only one I never paid. I signed a chit for $75.00, but before I could pay it the Japs blew up the club.

Pvt. LEON BECK, Antitank Company, 31st Infantry:

Each Friday the training schedule was posted on the company bulletin board. This told us what the coming week's training schedule would be. If, for example, the schedule showed a class on military courtesy and customs, it would tell who the instructor was, what the required uniform would be, where it was going to be held, and for how long:

On Monday our training schedule showed that after reveille and breakfast we were going to have instruction in extended-order arm-and-hand-signals in the field. And on the morning of December 8, that's exactly what we did. Since we had no orders canceling this exercise we went into the field just as if nothing had happened.

Sgt. FORREST KNOX, Company A, 192d Tank Battalion:

To help us get over the disappointment of losing our duck gag, we were immediately ordered to scatter our tanks in the brush outside the Clark Field perimeter. We realized we didn't have any ammo loaded, and when they couldn't find our machine-gun belt loader they told us to load the damn stuff by hand. I avoided that duty for a while and instead was told to clean the cannons. "Christ," I said, "you have fifty-four tanks and only one rammer staff. Besides, I don't even know where the staff is." They said, "Clean them damn cannons!" "O.K., O.K.," and I went and cut a piece of bamboo and wired a chunk of burlap to the end.

An absolute no-no in the Army—the one thing you never do—is wash a barrel with gasoline, because it removes the oil, permitting the barrel to rust. By God, I cleaned seventeen cannons that morning. Just zip, zip with a bucket of gasoline and my piece of burlap. Each tank commander yelled at me, but I told them I was cleaning out the cosmoline so they could fire the cannons. It was up to those jackasses to put the oil back in so they wouldn't rust.

2d Lt. JOHN POSTEN, Fighter Pilot, 17th Pursuit Squadron:

Early in the day my flight was on alert at Nichols Field, where news came through about the attack on Pearl Harbor. Around ten o'clock we got orders to send a couple of flights to patrol north of Clark Field. There were supposed to be some bombers on their way south from Formosa. The Japs bombed Baguio, but our patrol missed them.

Pfc. ROY DIAZ, Company C, 194th Tank Battalion:

My company commander drove up in his jeep and told us to get all the fifty-gallon aviation gas drums away from Clark Field because the Japs were headed our way. This was about 10:30 in the morning. We got all the drums on our trucks and headed for the bamboos.

Pfc. ROBERT BROWN, 17th Pursuit Squadron:

Monday, because I had a dental call all the way up at Clark, I was at the airstrip at Del Carmen.* Before leaving with a small group of other men who were also going for medical treatment we had heard from some tankers that Hawaii had been hit. We got to Clark midmorning and all their B-17s and P-40s were in the air. While my tooth was being fixed the planes started coming back in. I had a radio operator friend in the hangars so I dropped down to see him. He told me that orders had come through that MacArthur had grounded our planes and that we were not to fire on the Japs until fired on. So here were all these B-17s and P-40s lined up on the runways. They were trying to keep the P-40s hot, though. While they were sitting there they'd start 'em up, shut 'em down, start 'em up, shut 'em down. We couldn't figure out why we hadn't been hit yet. On the way over to Clark, I noticed that the Filipinos in Sloppy Bottom and Angeles had already begun boarding up their windows and doors.

---

* Del Carmen Field was fifteen miles south of Clark Field. The 34th Squadron based there was equipped with P-35s.

Maj. JOHN MAMEROW, Adjutant General's Office,
Philippine Department:

I knew about Pearl Harbor at 5:30 in the morning. I was awakened at Fort William McKinley by a telephone message that
the war had begun and that I was to report to headquarters at
Nielson Field.* I thought it was nuts. A car came and picked me
and the air officer up and delivered us to Nielson. A short time
later Major General Brereton† arrived from MacArthur's headquarters and gave us as much of the story about the bombing
at Pearl Harbor as he knew. He didn't know the full extent of
the damage there, but knew we were on a full war alert. Headquarters anticipated that a declaration of war would be made
the next day. We were told to stand by for orders. General
Brereton also told us he had requested permission to bomb Formosa and that we were to begin to draw up that plan. I was told
by the General's chief of staff‡ to sit on the telephone and keep
the war diary. The next thing I knew we got a call from General
Sutherland,§ MacArthur's chief of staff, saying the Formosa
plan had been disapproved, but to make sure our airplanes were
secure.

   The B-17s at Clark Field were sent off a couple of times that
morning and orbited, until they were finally brought in before
noon to refuel. There was talk of keeping them ready in the
event the raid on Formosa might be approved at a later time.
Around noon we began sending a message to Clark—three
sentences had been sent when our teletypes went out.

Pfc. JOHN FALCONER, Company A, 194th Tank Battalion:

Around chow time I walked over to Clark Field, which is right
next to Fort Stotsenburg, and when I looked up in the sky I saw
all those nice beautiful planes coming over. They started dropping something. To me it looked like pepper coming from the
planes.

Pfc. ROBERT BROWN, 17th Pursuit Squadron:

Just about the time we began to get ready to return to Del
Carmen, we heard the drone of aircraft. Looking up, here's a
"V" formation of bombers coming over and all our planes still
on the ground. I was right off the end of the field when the
bombs started down. When the big guys got through, the fighters
started raking us, pulling up right over the top of me. Scared

* Far East Air Force's headquarters, on the outskirts of Manila.
† Maj. Gen. Lewis H. Brereton, the Army Air Firce commander.
‡ Col. Francis M. Brady.
§ Maj. Gen. Richard K. Sutherland.

and amazed! I couldn't believe someone was attacking the United States. Absolutely unreal! All these Zeros so close I could see the big red dot on their wings. Hell, who could believe this? Us? And here's our planes all sitting on the ground.

Pfc. VICTOR MAPES, 14th Bombardment Squadron:

About noon the B-17s came in to re-gas. They lined them up on the runway and the crews cut out for chow. I was listening in the barracks to a very loquacious radio commentator named Don Bell, when all of a sudden he said that Clark Field was being bombed. As far as I knew, and I was there, nothing was happening, but just to make sure some of us went outside to the back of the barracks. Coming in over the mountains from the China Sea, up in the silvery clouds, were these two beautiful "V" formations of twenty-seven planes each. Someone commented about a beautiful Navy formation. I remembered Don Bell. "Attack!" I yelled. "Japanese!" We ran for a small bamboo revetment and dove into a little hole. We had our gas masks with us and were trying to get them on when the bombs began walking up the runway, like a big giant stepping down the line. One of the bombs hit right nearby. We made a mad scramble, trying at the same time not to suffocate in these old gas masks, and crawled into a cement latrine. The fighters came in next and their machine guns were going through the air, cutting all around. I saw a guy throw his shoe at a plane, another was firing his .45. Everything was a holocaust. It seemed like it went on forever.

Sgt. FORREST KNOX, Company A, 192d Tank Battalion:

All of a sudden there's just a hell of a burst of smoke coming up from down on the hangar line. Christ, it looked like gasoline had exploded because of the black smoke. I'm still looking at the field when the sound got to me. Well, it didn't take but just a fraction of a second to know what the hell that was. The guy with me and I popped inside a tank and closed the turret. We're sitting in there and this guy says, "What do we do now?" "Well," I said, "I don't think we do anything." "We can't stay here," he replied. I said, "Sure we can." After a while I decided to have a look and I tipped the hatch back. I had no more than got out of there when the Zeros started coming. I grabbed the machine gun, jerked the pin from the mount, and yelled for a box of ammo. Once I hooked it on the side, flipped the lid, and worked the bolt one more time to get a round in the chamber, I was ready to go. I knew we had some P-40s on the field, and when these fighters started coming over I had no idea they were Zeros. I was under actual attack and didn't realize they were Japs. The first one came by real close. He made a sweep across that field, and there isn't much mistaking them once they get within a hundred feet of you. They stand right out. They've got this big flaming ass hole on the fuselage. I said, "For heaven sakes!" I'd never been trained for antiaircraft fire and the .30s had no AA sites. They called it an "antiaircraft" mount, but it was like a lot of things the Army did. Once they wrote the name on it, that was what it became. Ridiculous! But anyway, I started shooting at the next fighter that came by. All of a sudden they were all around like a bunch of hornets. I hollered down into the tank, "Jesus Christ, they're all over the place. Come up here and help me. Hell, I can't look both ways at once!" We worked out a system which let him stand on the tank's front deck and look in the opposite direction from where I was firing. If he saw a plane coming he'd tell me and I'd wheel around and try to shoot the fool thing. I was firing so much that the empty ammo cases kept building up on the deck. As I was trying to depress the breech down into the open hatch, in order to get enough elevation on the barrel, I had to lean over and my feet would slip on the empty casings. I'd start to go nose down into the turret. To push myself up I'd have to let go of the gun. I don't think I hit anything. They never bothered to explain how far you had to lead an aircraft in order to hit it. I found out later. But at this particular time, when it should have been duck soup because they were so close, I was missing them by fifty feet.

Pfc. ROY DIAZ, Company C, 194th Tank Battalion:

When the bombers got through with us, their fighters came in. My buddy and I set up a .50-caliber machine gun right out in the rice paddy. I worked it around and said, "When we get one coming by real close, you feed this thing. I'm going to knock him down." About then here comes this darn Zero, no more than 500 feet away. I'm about to touch my .50 off when this tank officer starts screaming. "Don't fire. You'll give our position away." He's in a tank and we're out there in the wide open rice paddy. I don't know what position we'd give away. We didn't have a position. Anyway, this Zero came over and we watched him. He was so close I saw that the pilot wore a white scarf. I could have knocked him down with a shotgun.

Pfc. LEE DAVIS, Medical Corpsman,
30th Bombardment Squadron:

After the bombing I hollered, "Anybody need medical aid?" Some guys started yelling, but before I could get to them the

Zero fighters came in and started finishing off anything running or burning or untouched. Men were firing rifles, machine guns, anything they had. But as soon as any gun opened up, the Japanese, who seemed to be aware of all our emplacements, would attack it. They knew where every plane was. And in just the short time they were there, they destroyed everything.*

After the attack, to get back to my 30th Squadron billeting area, I had to cross where the motor pool used to be. There were bodies lying all over under the trucks. Men had sought refuge under gas trucks and these had immediately blown up. It was chaos all over.

Pfc. VICTOR MAPES, 14th Bombardment Squadron:

Afterwards there were explosions and heavy smoke and someone still had a radio playing. They were playing beautiful music in Manila, just like nothing had happened. Then the wounded started coming in. Most were cut up and bloody. All of them should have been in the hospital, but some stayed to fight the fires and carry the dead.

Capt. JEROME McDAVITT, 24th Field Artillery,
Philippine Scouts:

About three o'clock in the afternoon I was summoned to headquarters and told to take my battery personnel and equipment to the bombed area of Clark Field. There we were to sneak out the dead bodies and place them in the morgue. That afternoon four other American officers and myself, along with our Philippine Scouts, put many men into the morgue.†

2d Lt. LEONA GASTINGER, Army Nurse Corps:

My friend had a bowling ball that was the most gorgeous thing you ever saw, aquamarine with her name written on it in gold. The day Pearl Harbor was bombed she and I had the morning off and since she'd left this bowling ball over at the Army-Navy Club we decided to go over and get it. When we got there we bowled a few games and had lunch. When we tried to go back to Sternberg [General Hospital] we couldn't find a cab, so while we waited for a bus we bought a *Manila Tribune*. That's how we learned Clark Field had been bombed.

---

* Far East Air Force lost eighteen of thirty-five B-17s, fifty-three of 107 P-40s and three of fifty-two P-35s. An additional twenty-five or thirty miscellaneous aircraft were destroyed. Many planes listed as operational were also heavily damaged.
† At Clark Field fifty-five officers and men had been killed. Total casualties for the first day of the war were eighty killed and 150 wounded.

Sgt. H. G. TYSON, 3d Pursuit Squadron:

At Iba* I had just finished eating lunch and was fixing to get a piece of pie when somebody hollered, "Get out of the mess hall. Here they come!" Everybody jumped up and started for the door, where our helmets were setting on a table. When I got to the table I couldn't find my helmet. Finally there was only one left and I was the only one left indoors, so I grabbed it and ran outside. I crossed over to the garbage pit and dove in. I watched the attack from there. Our P-40s had been up for quite a while and were coming back in to land when the Japs hit them. Some were shot down by the Zeros and some crash-landed in the bomb craters on the runway. We lost all twelve that had been in the air. The first flight of twin engine bombers that hit us had fifty-four planes. Then the Zeros came back and strafed. The garbage pit was large enough that the Zeros could fire into it and hit the opposite bank. So during this time I kept jumping from side to side, depending on which direction the fighters were coming in from. Then a flight of twenty-seven bombers came up from the south and bombed us again. They pretty well wiped us out. We lost about forty-five men out of 160 and sixteen out of eighteen fighters. We managed to patch up two of them and they flew off to Nichols Field. I don't know what the Japs thought our little squadron had, but they sure made sure we didn't have it when they got through with us.

We had a radar warning unit that was stationed with us. They called it RDF [Radar Directional Finder]. I never knew for sure, but it was claimed by some of the guys that when the Japs were spotted these men panicked and ran, leaving the set on. The Japs rode that beam right into us. The first bomb hit right in the middle of that outfit, so it sounded reasonable that this might possibly have happened.

Tech. Sgt. WILLIAM "COWBOY" WRIGHT,
17th Pursuit Squadron:

Sometime between 4:00 and 5:00 p.m. on the 8th, our fighters on Nichols Field took off for another airstrip. All the aircraft got off. One came back, however, and landed. My line chief told me to go over and see what was wrong. As soon as I got up on the wing I knew what the trouble was. The pilot was shaking like a leaf. I asked him if anything was wrong. He didn't answer. He hadn't shut off the engine, so I told him to hold the brakes. Then we ran it up to takeoff RPMs, then tried both mags.

* Iba Field was on the west coast of Luzon, thirty-five miles from Clark Field.

They checked out O.K. I told him to shut it down if he wanted to, that we would find something wrong with it. He then asked if I thought he could find the rest of the flight. I asked him if he knew where they were supposed to go and he said yes. I told him I thought he should not have any trouble, because it would take a few minutes for them to land, as the strips were not large enough for more than two or three to land or take off at a time. He took off and eventually landed with the rest of the squadron.

2d Lt. JOHN POSTEN, Fighter Pilot, 17th Pursuit Squadron:

Just before dark we received orders to move to Clark Field, because they figured Nichols would get it that night. Around noon we heard that the Japs had done a nasty job on Clark Field. They had bombed and strafed for forty-five minutes, which is a plenty long time!

When we got to Clark Field I couldn't see how we were ever going to land; everything in sight was burning and the field was covered with bomb holes. What men were left on the ground marked the holes for us and we finally could see a place about big enough to land in. I landed with the rest, but found I was with the 21st Pursuit Squadron [also from Nichols Field] instead of the 17th, which was my outfit. The 17th had received orders over the radio to go to Del Carmen. My radio was not working.

Pfc. VICTOR MAPES, 14th Bombardment Squadron:

All afternoon at Clark we stayed to feed the firefighters and wounded until dark. When we limped back to our barracks, our clothes were hanging from the rafters. There was a big hole where the Japs dropped one right through the roof. We couldn't find anyone from our unit, so we wandered away. We saw a man in his '38 Ford lying there, shot. Looked like he was trying to get off the base. Then there was a dead pilot in the cockpit of a B-17. We could barely see him by the fires that were still burning. When we got to the edge of the jungle there was firing and yelling. Everyone was trigger happy. It was dangerous to be moving. We spent the night at the edge of the jungle behind two logs.

2d Lt. JOHN POSTEN, Fighter Pilot, 17th Pursuit Squadron:

That night everything was confusion. The hangars were still burning and every once in a while a lot of ammunition would go off that had been stored there. Automobiles, trucks, and planes were wrecked and burning all over the place. All the wounded had been taken away, but the dead were still lying where they fell. There was a whole B-17 crew lying dead next to their burning ship. They had been hit by a bomb before they could reach cover. The 20th [Pursuit Squadron] got only three ships off the ground; the rest were riddled before they could get the motors started. That's how much warning they had! Three of them tried to take off as the bombing was going on, but were killed before they could leave the ground. A friend of mine reported seeing a pilot burn to death just a few feet from him, when a bomb landed close and set the ship on fire. He could see the pilot trying to fight his way out, but not quite be able to move. A gang of workers ran into a gasoline shed when the bombing started, and the whole place was blown up about a mintue after they got inside. Some of the crewmen were on the field and were killed before they could reach cover. After the bombers went over, a group of pursuits strafed the field and killed as many as the bombs did. The 3d [Pursuit Squadron] was just about wiped out over at Iba, too. They got a few planes off, but most of them, including pilots and men, were killed or wounded on the ground. That night we all went back into the hills to sleep. We didn't do very much sleeping, though.*

Cpl. FRED GIFFORD, 21st Pursuit Squadron:

I hadn't been off the assembly line at Nichols Field since noon servicing our remaining P-40s.† We did not want to be caught like the fighters at Clark. I left about 3:30 that morning [December 9]. I was very hungry because I hadn't taken any time to eat before we finished. The first place I went was to the kitchen tent. The cook told me they had a big GI can full of pork chops cooked up and that I should help myself. I fixed myself a big sandwich and laid it down on the table, when I heard some bombers coming over.

The next thing I knew they were dropping bombs. I forgot my sandwich. I forgot about being hungry. I grabbed my rifle and took off out of the tent. The streets were full of confusion, so I ran down between the ropes. A bomb landed so close to me I felt its heat. I ducked into a rice paddy and stepped in a carabao hole. I thought I'd broken my leg. The

---

* The first day of the war also saw successful Japanese invasions of Malaya and Thailand.
† The 21st Pursuit Squadron's P-40Es had arrived in the Philippines on December 7. As the fighters had just been uncrated, much work still needed to be done on them.

planes went on over. I was in misery. I thought for sure my leg was broken. About then I noticed I could hear our machine guns still chattering. The tracers made the sky look like a circus was in town. So I got up and hobbled over to the gunners and ordered them to cease fire. They were all manned and operated by real young Filipino boys. They didn't have the brains, or else were too scared, to release the triggers on their guns. I was as scared as anybody else.

When I looked out onto the field I could see in the firelight that the Japs never missed a target. They were very good. They must have had us mapped out perfect, bcause they didn't miss anything. Not one bomb hit an empty hole. Every one hit a gasoline storage tank or one of our remaining airplanes.

Pvt. LEON BECK, Antitank Company, 31st Infantry:

We were first bombed before dawn on December 9 as the Japs went in on Nichols Field. I found it very exhilarating. I mean this is what it's all about. But with no way of retaliating, it got old real quick.

2d Lt. JOHN POSTEN, Fighter Pilot, 17th Pursuit Squadron:

At Clark on Tuesday, December 9, we took off before dawn. The fellow in front of me took off and hit the wreckage of a B-17 on the edge of the field and burst into flames just like he had been hit by a bomb. We yelled to him over the radio that he was getting too close to the edge of the runway, but I guess he didn't hear us. It sure was a horrible sight. I was next in line for takeoff and you can bet I stayed clear of that spot. At the same time we were taking off, my own squadron was taking off from Del Carmen and Lodin, one of the fellows I lived with, was killed the same way. They were the only two pilots killed that morning, but we lost eight ships, all on the takeoff, so you can imagine the condition the fields were in.

Pfc. VICTOR MAPES, 14th Bombardment Squadron:

At daylight we awoke at Clark to one of the few remaining P-40s winding up. When he began to take off he hit a demolished B-17, the one with the dead pilot in it. Both planes blew up. That was the second day of the war.

When I walked down what was left of the flight line later in the day, I noticed from the bullet holes that the Jap fighters had strafed our planes both ways. First they strafed the length of the fuselages, then they turned around in a figure eight and came down the wings. That's how neat a job it was.

2d Lt. LEONA GASTINGER, Army Nurse Corps:

I was assigned to a medical ward at Sternberg General Hospital. Many of my patients had TB or other sicknesses and they were all waiting to be shipped back to the States for further medical treatment. When I entered my ward Tuesday morning I expected it to be full of patients. To my astonishment it was empty. All my patients had gone back to their units. They had gotten their clothes, dressed, and reported back to duty, because they knew there was no way to get back home now.

Pfc. WILBURN SNYDER, 3d Battalion Medics, 31st Infantry:

On Tuesday two other medics and I were sent down to Port Area so that we could hold sick call for the MPs who were stationed there. I suppose they knew Port Area was going to be hit and we should be there. Sure enough, on the 9th the planes came over and bombed Nichols and Nielson Fields and Port Area. They knocked the naval base at Cavite plumb into the Bay.

2d-Class Carpenter's Mate STANLEY SOMMERS, USS *Finch:*

Just before Cavite was bombed I saw flashes of silver way up in the sky. Then the bombs came down. First thing they hit was Sangley Point, which is where we had our oil dumps. Black smoke just billowed out. Most of the Navy yard was constructed of wooden buildings which went up right away. People kept running around, not knowing what to do. It was a bad raid.

Cpl. PAUL SARNO, 20th Pursuit Squadron:

Cavite took a terrible beating. The bombs just completely demolished it. I'm not ashamed to tell you that I was assigned to go out and bring the dead in. My lieutenant gave me some whiskey first, and then told me what had to be done. We took everyone we could find, and after a bombing many men were just in pieces. We used the Jai Alai Frontón Pavilion as a morgue. They were stacked all over the place. I don't know how I did it. I couldn't do it today, but in 1941 I was a kid and didn't know any better.

Pfc. ROY DIAZ, Company C, 194th Tank Battalion:

When our tanks were ordered south we went right through Manila and up past Cavite. What a mess that Cavite was. It was just a rumble of nothing. Stinking bodies all over, and nothing stinks worse than a dead human being. Everything was still on fire.

Pfc. WILBURN SNYDER, 3d Battalion Medics,
31st Infantry:

When we got out of our foxhole, we rushed to Port Area in our ambulance. Many of the people working the docks were caught in the open just looking at the planes when the bombs fell. By the time the bombs started falling, it was too late. They got conked. First we tried to separate the dead from the wounded, leaving the dead for last since there was nothing we could do for them. There was a young Filipino girl and by the time we got to her, her father was standing over her, weeping. We threw her into the ambulance and brought her to the aid station. This was the first trip I made. She had shrapnel all in her, especially in her chest. I started to rip off her blouse and she said, "No, no, no, no!" Her daddy finally talked her into letting us treat her. She was bleeding all over. It was horrible. Finally, so many wounded came in that it just became a process. You see, after a while it dawned on me that what I was doing was nuts. It was just not a place to have feelings. Instead, it was a place to do what I was trained to do. Well, that worked for a while. It worked until I picked up a dead American. People can say what they want about loving everyone alive, but when you pick up your own, there's a mixture of feelings, a mixture of sorrow and pity and anger that just almost blows your mind.

Pfc. ROBERT BROWN, 17th Pursuit Squadron:

On December 10 our P-35s from Del Carmen went up to strafe some Japanese transports which were reported north of Lingayen.* We got seventeen aircraft into the air. Sixteen came back. As soon as they had all landed we began to refuel and rearm them. About ten mintues later the Japs came in. They must have followed our pilots back. They caught us out on the runway. About ten Zeros strafed us in turn, just in and out, in and out. We radioed for help. A P-40 already in the air responded. He got right in at the end of the Japanese strafing line and when the last Zero pulled up our guy jumped him. That was the first Jap plane I saw destroyed.

---

* The first Japanese landing was at Vigan where, on the morning of December 10, they put ashore 2,000 men. The town, which is the capital of Ilocos Sur Province, lies on the South China Sea nearly 220 miles northwest of Manila. On the same day, Guam surrendered and Wake Island continued to be bombed.

2d Lt. JOHN POSTEN, Fighter Pilot, 17th Pursuit Squadron:

All the planes we had left were sent out on the 10th to see what they could do. I patrolled over Clark Field most of the morning. That afternoon the Japs came over in clouds, bombers and pursuits together. We had a little warning so we got into the air and tried to stop them, but they outnumbered us five or six to one. Holbrecht was shot down and killed. Feallock bailed out, Glover bailed out, Phillips bailed out, also White, Krueger, Woodside, and several more. They were strafed by the Japs on the way down, but made it O.K.

I got in a fight before I got halfway to Manila and I was really scared because this was the first combat I had had. My right tire was shot, one gas tank was shot, and both wings and the tail had holes in them. The motor cut out about five minutes after the gas tank was hit and I was about to bail out, but it caught again when I changed to another tank. I headed for a cloud bank and lost the two Japs that were on my tail.

During this time we really took a beating. We had only a few planes left and one or two remaining fields to land on. This whole time I was very tired, dirty, hungry, and uncomfortable. Towards the end of the first week we did not fly at all as we tried to reorganize. Seventy-five percent of our fighters and bombers were destroyed in the first four days.

One day I was on the ground when Clark Field got bombed again. It was the first raid I'd been through on the ground. I was never so scared in all my life. You can read about them all you want, but you will never realize what it's like unless you actually go through one.

2d Lt. LEONA GASTINGER, Army Nurse Corps:

Several days after the first bombing raids on Manila, my roommate and I decided that we had better make some emergency preparations. We went off to the PX and each bought a camera case. Then I sat down and cut out my favorite snapshots of each family member and put them in the case along with some jewelry. I wore this case on my uniform belt all the time.

During this period my roommate and I decided that at no time would we both be undressed at the same time. If one wanted to shower, the other one sat with our gas masks and other emergency equipment, ready to help the other one dress in the event of an air raid. This decision came about during one of our first air-raid alerts. We'd been on duty all day and were fixing to take a shower and change our clothes. My roommate was in the lavatory brushing her teeth, wearing nothing but her ankle bracelet, and I had just dropped my uniform when the air-raid siren sounded. Well, in that split second we froze. I was trying to think, do I put my uniform on or do I grab something out of the closet. My roommate just stood there with the toothbrush in her mouth. Finally, we relaxed and did what was necessary, but it was then that we decided we'd never be undressed at the same time. Rather a weird thing, but we were in our own way working out what would make us feel the safest. We were trying to work with this situation.

Pvt. LEON BECK, Antitank Company, 31st Infantry:

There wasn't enough transportation to move us out of Manila, so the authorities commandeered all the Pambusco [Pampanga Bus Company] buses they could lay their hands on. To the best of my knowledge, on December 12 my company of the 31st Infantry was moved to Bataan, where we immediately began constructing fortifications around a sugar cane plantation named the Abucay Hacienda.

2d Lt. JOHN POSTEN, Fighter Pilot, 17th Pursuit Squadron:

On top of everything else it began raining. I tried to make a shelter out of banana leaves, but it leaked and everything got wet. While we were trying to fix up what planes we had left, I managed to take a bath in a small brook. It was for the first time in the week since the war began. On Saturday, December 13, our C.O., Buzz Wagner, made a one-man raid on Aparri, which the Japs were using as a base.* He got two in the air and five on the ground.

2d-Class Carpenter's Mate STANLEY SOMMERS,
USS *Finch*:

On December 11 my mine sweeper, the *Finch*, was on duty station in Manila Harbor. We saw a formation of Japanese horizontal bombers coming over. You damn well knew anytime they were up there, going overhead, they were after you. We always expected it, but this day was different. They really were after us! As soon as the bombers were spotted, the *Finch* began zigzagging Manila Bay. I was on a three-inch dual-purpose antiaircraft gun. We did a lot of firing, but they were so high we couldn't reach them. It was more of an idea to do something, to

---

* At the mouth of the Cagayan River, Aparri is a port 275 miles north of Manila. Here the Japanese made the second of their two preliminary landings on Dec. 10, and it was in response to this invasion that the war's first hero, Capt. Colin P. Kelly, Jr., made his legendary flight.

be occupied—that way you had no time to think. When you're waiting for them to come in, you're scared to death. But when you're actually in action you don't have time to think about that. I've seen bravery in people I didn't expect it from, and people that I thought would be real military, weren't. They were the first you'd find on the "double bottom."* On the other hand, those sailors who were always in trouble with dirty uniforms, or for coming back late from liberty, turned out to be the best sailors we had. They stayed cool and kept firing. The first string of bombs straddled us. As we were in shallow water, the bombs exploded on the coral, and shrapnel from that sank us.† Everyone got off all right. The skipper managed to get her close to shore and we went off in lifeboats. When I left her I felt like my home had been destroyed.

Sgt. RALPH LEVENBERG, 17th Pursuit Squadron:

We were concerned with what we were going to do now. The older sergeants were very comfortable in this situation. Their philosophy was, "Hell, you're just one little spot on the ground. They're not going to hit you." I spent my time in the orderly room where there was more confusion than anything else. I wasn't really scared yet. It was a little bit exciting. Something new's happening. I hadn't understood yet the severity of my situation.

Pfc. WILBURN SNYDER, 3d Battalion Medics, 31st Infantry:

Manila continued to get plastered. The bombing was very heavy. Once they put some sailors on top of Pier 7 in a sandbag machine-gun nest. Why they wanted to get those poor fellows killed I don't know. After a raid we ran in to the pier and found a Filipino standing there. He wasn't scared, he was angry. "These goddamn Japanese. We need to kill these goddamn Japanese!" Then he looked real stern and said, "I don't believe God will punish me for cussing the Japanese." "Well, Joe," I said, "we need to get up on top and get the wounded sailors off the roof." He said, "Joe, they're not wounded, they're dead. When they stopped firing, they were dead." Sure enough, when we got up there they were both dead, without doubt.

Pfc. JACK BRADY, 228th Signal Operations Company:

I was assigned to a courier service. After Clark and the other airfields had been bombed and we lost all our aircraft, we be-

---

* Hiding in the bottom of the ship.
† USS <u>Finch</u> was sunk near Caballo Island (Fort Hughes).

gan wondering what would happen to the Air Force people. To answer our question, several of them appeared at our barracks and said that they had been ordered to report to us. Along with these Air Force officers, we got some enlisted men from the 200th Coast Artillery who were no longer needed to man the antiaircraft guns at Clark Field. The enlisted men became the drivers and the officers became the couriers. Six of these pairs made our various message runs. They'd pick up a batch of things at one headquarters and deliver them to another. We called our barrack the "Pony Corral."

We worked twenty-four hours a day. I kept up the dispatch logs. I never had a chance to see what was happening to the rest of Manila. We subsisted on sandwiches and coffee. There was nothing else. In fact, there was no time to eat because we were extremely busy.

One day we were shorthanded and, since I was available, I went with an Air Force lieutenant to deliver a message to General Wainwright's headquarters, which was north of Manila. The roads were nearly deserted. When we arrived at Fort Stotsenburg two MPs told us they didn't know where the General was, but that we had better get out of there because they were going to blow the place. After driving a lot we found General Wainwright in a shack beside a plantation. He was taking a break on the front porch and listening to his Filipino valet playing "La Paloma" on the guitar. I didn't see him that clearly, but I remember he looked like everybody else, except maybe a little thinner than most.

Pfc. JOHN FALCONER, Company A, 194th Tank Battalion:

During the middle part of December my tank platoon was constantly on the move up in northern Luzon, around Lingayen Gulf. I rarely knew where I was. I was the driver of an M-3 tank.*

During the war my tank commander was a sergeant named Hyatt. He was a very stable, quiet person, but he knew what was going on all the time. But mostly, I had a higher commander. Being a Christian I carried a Bible with me and could always reach it while in the tank. I don't know how many people believe this, but I feel that it gave me a great deal of protection.

One night, having withdrawn all day, we were ordered

---

* Nicknamed the "General Stuart," the M-3 Light Tank carried a crew of four, weighed fourteen tons and carried one 37-mm cannon and five .30-caliber machine guns. The 192d and 194th Tank Battalions were each equipped with fifty-four M-3s. Besides being used in the Philippines, the Stuart saw service with British and Commonwealth units in the North African desert, where it was known as the "Honey."

off the road into a field. Before shutting down the engines we turned our tanks and aimed them down the road. During the night our battalion commander challenged some movement on the road. When he didn't get the proper response back he ordered us to open fire. I can still see it to this day, it was like a spectacular fireworks display. We raked the field and road with tracers. In the cross-fire it wasn't possible for anyone to survive. It was beautiful. It was brutal. But it was either them or us. A very good friend of mine found the next morning that the reason his .45 jammed was that it had taken a Japanese bullet down the barrel. He planned to save the bullet as a souvenir of the war. He didn't though. He died at Cabanatuan.

Most days we just chugged up and down dusty roads. Once, on an emergency night march, we plowed through some low-hanging branches. Unfortunately for us these branches contained hundreds of ferocious biting ants. Even more unfortunately, our hatch was open. They became, for a while, far worse than the Japs.

2d Lt. JOHN POSTEN, Fighter Pilot, 17th Pursuit Squadron:

A week and a half after the war began, Buzz Wagner and two other pilots, Strauss and R. M. Church, went out at dawn to strafe and drop bombs on the airport at Vigan which the Japs were using as a base. Strauss stayed up at 15,000 feet as a lookout while Buzz and Church went in. On the way down some Jap AA set Church's ship on fire. He kept right on and dropped his bombs before he crashed and burned. Buzz got another fighter. We used to get a lot of laughs from Church. He was short and stout and always had a big cigar. The night before he left for the raid on Vigan, we had been kidding him about his cigars.

But all the news wasn't grim. The day after Lieutenant Church crashed, one of our pilots, Sheppard, came back O.K. He'd crashed four days earlier. That was one of the troubles bailing out around the islands. It would always take several days to find your way out of the jungles. We all began carrying jungle kits and automatics.

On the 20th we moved to San Marcelino,* where the living was worse than at Clark Field. The first meal we had was a chunk of half-rotten beef and a cup of coffee.

Sgt. H. G. TYSON, 3d Pursuit Squadron:

It wasn't so much that we were so ill prepared. It was the fact that our high command had put our Air Force completely out

* A pasture-like emergency field west of Clark.

of commission by saying, "Keep those planes on the ground and wait for the enemy to strike first." Of course, we had twelve fighters in the air at Iba and it was just the worst luck that they were landing to refuel when the Japs attacked. I don't know what difference it would have made, though, to the bombers, since our fighters didn't have any oxygen in the cockpits which would have allowed them to get high enough to get to the Japs. The P-40s were equipped for a pilot to use oxygen, but we didn't receive the oxygen.

While we were still at Nichols Field we got the first two or three P-40Bs that were shipped into the islands. The ones we received at Iba were P-40Es and they brought them in without any guns on them. We spent the days before the war arming them. The pilots could get little gunnery practice in them. As a matter of fact, before the war began they had very little experience in flying the P-40s. We had had P-35s with their radial engines prior to that. There's a big difference between them. The P-35s have short noses and the P-40s long ones. The pilots, accordingly, had a lot of trouble with the center of gravity on the P-40s, especially flying off grass runways. If they'd had cement runways, they'd have been all right. The P-40s were sluggish taxiing, and just a little tap on the brakes and the pilots would send the planes over on their noses. They did some damage to their own planes.

The pilot training time on these planes was also lessened by another example of how goofed up things can get. We had those first P-40s ready to go except we had no coolant for the engines. When we put a tracer on the coolant we found out what had happened. There was a colonel in San Francisco who couldn't understand why so much Prestone was needed for the Philippines, so he sent it to Alaska. It took us quite a while to get our Prestone.

It was a crying shame, once we got our P-40s in the air, to see them shot down by the Japs like sitting ducks. Their pilots were real good. They flew those Zeros like they knew what they were doing. The P-40 was a better airplane than the Zero. It was faster. It just wasn't as maneuverable. The strategy at the beginning of the war was for our pilots to dogfight the Japs. We'd try to get on a Jap's tail, stay there, and shoot him down. The problem was that a Zero could turn inside a P-40 and get on its tail. Later in the war the strategy changed and our pilots learned that the best way a P-40 could fight a Zero was to hit and run. Make your pass and then run like hell. Of course, Claire Chennault and his Flying Tigers had been fighting the Japs for some time. Chennault had learned and his P-40s had handled the Japanese better than ours did. Somehow no one thought it important to tell our pilots in the Philippines what Chennault's pilots in China knew.

We, of course, knew about Chennault. In fact, sometime in '41 the Flying Tigers had come through the Philippines recruiting pilots, mechanics, and armorers. We could get discharged if we enlisted with them. Three hundred dollars a month sounded mighty good in comparison to the seventy-two a month I was making. So I volunteered, but not being twenty-one I had to have my mother's permission. A day or two after the last boat sailed from the Philippines for the States, I got the telegram from my mother giving me permission. By then it was too late.

Before we got our P-40s we had older P-35s. Our government diverted a shipment of them to us which had been intended for Sweden.* They had the Swedish insignia on them and all the tech orders were in Swedish. We had some time learning about that airplane. None of this contributed to us preparing for war quickly.

2d Lt. JOHN POSTEN, Fighter Pilot, 17th Pursuit Squadron:

Our P-40s were faster than the Jap's, but not near as maneuverable nor could they climb away from them. Another thing is that we had an awful lot of trouble with the guns, they hardly ever worked! A lot of men had planes in their sights but nothing happened when they pulled the trigger.

Tech. Sgt. WILLIAM "COWBOY" WRIGHT, 17th Pursuit Squadron:

The P-40s we flew had some interesting quirks. For example, if one of the .50-caliber machine guns jammed, it couldn't be cleared until it got back on the ground. When you're firing a machine gun you may get a bad shell now and then that doesn't fire. If it doesn't fire it's got to be taken out, and the only way to get it out was to recharge the gun. It's just like a .22 automatic. If the bullet doesn't fire, you have to kick it out by moving the bolt. It's the same thing with a machine gun. Our machine-gun ammunition had a lot of duds. If a pilot found that his guns jammed, he'd have to get out of the air. He couldn't just push a button and get his guns recharged. They were supposed to recharge hydraulically, but we didn't have it hooked up and had been told not to hook it up. Our landing gears were hooked to the same system, so if we blew the end out of a gun

---

* In Oct. 1941, forty-eight P-35s scheduled for shipment to Sweden were diverted to the Philippines.

it would damage the landing gear. The only way we had to clear the guns was, when they landed, to go under the wing and charge them with a wire cable.

Our ammunition was so bad that the pilots could only shoot a few times before their guns jammed. I remember one flight one of our pilots made. It was a good thing he hadn't seen any Japs. I found out that none of his guns would have fired.

It should be remembered that the P-40 was much heavier and less maneuverable than the P-35. I knew that some of our pilots wanted to go up to practice their dogfight tactics, but weren't always able to get someone else to go up with them. As a result, the war started with about half our pilots being very inexperienced. Some of them were almost afraid to go up.

Sgt. FERRON CUMMINS, 34th Pursuit Squadron:

The pilots were under enormous strain. None of them had any experience in having someone shoot at them. You could tell how much pressure they were under, because of the tone in their voices. It was two or three octaves higher than usual. They would land, get into another airplane, and go right back up. As long as we could keep the planes serviced, they went up all day. There was no rhythm to it.

It was very hard on the pilots learning to fly the P-40s. Most of them hadn't been out of basic long enough to lose their touch on the little trainers they used. At Del Carmen, on the second morning, a pilot from another squadron started to take his P-40 off. He was going out on patrol. When he varied just a little bit down our runway he took out three P-40s and himself. We had no fire-fighting equipment. I was close enough to hear him scream. Those are things that went against us all the way. Most everyone was just inexperienced.

Pfc. WILBURN SNYDER, 3d Battalion Medics,
31st Infantry:

I'm not being critical of them because I love the Filipinos, but the Philippine Army was the most ill-prepared bunch of men you can imagine. They were still drilling with wooden rifles when the war started. If you understand the Filipino people you know they are not a fighting people. They love everybody. Suddenly they were expected to transform their character, and when you couple this with their being ill equipped and untrained, you can understand why they couldn't do anything to help us in the fighting. When the Japs hit the beaches they just broke and ran. Now, the Philippine Scouts were different. They were part of the American Army and they were tremendous fighters. Men who saw it told me that a unit of Scout Cavalry once rode up alongside the blind side of a Jap tank column and threw hand grenades down the open turrets. I don't know whether this is true or not, but I wouldn't doubt it because later I saw these Philippine Scouts fight.

Sgt. FORREST KNOX, Company A, 192d Tank Battalion:

The M-3 tank, as we knew it, had a couple of serious flaws. Number one: riveted construction. The lightest hit blew the rivet heads off. The rivet did more damage to the crew than shell fragments. Number two: the track had a bad habit of coming off. A skilled driver kept the power on in turns. A poor one took his foot off the throttle and threw the track. On a withdrawal any breakdown was serious. Number three: the guns were not figured out right. The AA mount needed a higher post and an AA-type barrel for rapid fire. The cannon had armor-piercing ammo only, and when we did meet Jap tanks it just bounced off. We should have had HE [High Explosive]. We made our own by pulling the projectiles out of World War I ammo and stuffing it in ours. It worked to perfection.

1st Lt. MARK HERBST, M.D., 3d Battalion,
57th Infantry, Philippine Scouts:

At Fort McKinley, before we were sent north to Olongapo to try and stop the Japanese invasion, I was issued a case of medical instruments that had been used by the 31st Infantry in their 1918 Siberian expedition. The instruments were in cosmoline and the medications were in hard-rubber bottles. Some we tried to use but found them too old to be effective.

Pfc. WILBURN SNYDER, 3d Battalion Medics,
31st Infantry:

The rifles we had, the first M-1s, looked good but weren't worth a hoot in the field. We got tired of pulling the trigger and having nothing happen. Most of the 31st Infantry traded them off to the Filipinos for their old Springfields. We knew when we pulled the bolt back on an '03 Springfield and shoved it forward, there'd be a bullet in there ready to fire. You'd take an M-1 out of its rack, hold it carefully in the truck that took you out to the range, get out, shoot, and it would be great. But take it out in combat where it got misused and dirty, and it became highly undependable.

We found later on Bataan that our 3-inch Stokes mortars were also almost hopeless. The first night at Abucay our mortar men were in a rage. They'd fire five rounds and only two would explode. We'd hit right in amongst the Japs and nothing would go off.

But the worst part of being unprepared was that it destroyed our strategy of holding the Japs on the beaches. Right away that didn't work. So MacArthur put Plan Two into effect, which was the original plan before the war began: establish lines across Luzon north and south of Manila. These would hold the Japs long enough to get us into Bataan. We never had enough time, though, to establish these new defensive lines. We never stopped them. They crashed on through and came in straight for Manila.

2d Lt. JOHN POSTEN, Fighter Pilot, 17th Pursuit Squadron:

On Tuesday, December 23, I drew the morning reconn with Kiser. We went up to check on a landing party at Lingayen. We saw eighty or one hundred ships in the Bay!

New York Times, Tuesday, December 23:

JAPANESE ATTACK LUZON COAST NORTH OF MANILA.*

New York Times, Wednesday, December 24:

JAPANESE LAND STRONG FORCE SOUTH OF MANILA.†

New York Times, Thursday, December 25:

The Army's High Command tonight considered the possibility of removing military headquarters and Philippine Commonwealth government offices from Manila and declaring it an "open city" . . . in an attempt to save it from further Japanese bombardment.

Field Headquarters, U.S. Forces on Northern Luzon Front, December 27 (UP):

Japanese forces tonight advanced slowly against stubbornly resisting American and Philippine troops in a huge north-and-south pincers upon Manila. Both the Japanese thrusts were regarded as dangerous. In all,

---

* Under the command of Lt. Gen. Masaharu Homma, the Japanese 14th Army was assigned the task of capturing the Philippine Islands. The main Japanese landings began on the morning of Dec. 22 along Lingayen Gulf. By the end of the day Homma's 43,000 troops had linked up with the Japanese force which had landed at Vigan on Dec. 10. The defense of this sector was given to Maj. Gen. Jonathan A. Wainwright's North Luzon Force.

† On Dec. 24 the Japanese landed 7,000 men at three locations on Lamon Bay, 70 miles southeast of Manila. This force was opposed to Brig. Gen. Albert M. Jones's South Luzon Force.

the Japanese may have between 150,000 and 200,000 troops ashore on Luzon.

A correspondent who inspected the Southern front, reported that United States tanks engaged the Japanese . . . and then fell back, fighting a delaying action.

War Department communiqué, December 29:

The Commanding General, United States Army Forces in the Far East, has consolidated the majority of his troops in Pampanga Province and shortened his lines.

War Department communiqué, January 1, 1942:

Despite heavy enemy attack attempting to break up our troop movements, the maneuver designed to regroup the two forces of American and Philippine troops opposing the Japanese in the north and the southeast has been successfully accomplished.

War Department communiqué, January 2:

Advanced elements of Japanese troops entered Manila at 3:00 p.m. American and Philippine troops north and northwest of Manila are continuing to resist stubbornly attacks which are being pressed with increasing intensity.

New York Times, Saturday, January 3:

General MacArthur appeared to have centered his defenses in the highly rugged section of Bataan, a peninsula province west of Manila Bay.

★ ★ ★

Maj. JOHN MAMEROW, Adjutant General's Office, Philippine Department:

Before Christmas everyone was ordered out of Manila and everything and everybody went to Bataan.* General Jones came up from the south and General Wainwright's bunch came down from the north. How they got into Bataan I'll never know. All those trucks and men converging on a few bridges and then swinging into the Bataan Peninsula. And the Japs let us do it.

2d Lt. HATTIE BRANTLEY, Army Nurse Corps:

We were scattered about Manila on the night of 23 December, but our Fort William McKinley unit was somewhat intact, and

---

* The decision to fall back to Bataan was reached on Dec. 23, and the withdrawal began the next morning. On this same day Wake Island surrendered.

Colonel Duckworth, the hospital CO from McKinley, held Officer's Call. He announced that we would be going to "the field" the next morning. We were to take one lightweight case with white duty uniforms only. Nothing else, he emphasized. "The hospital where we are going is all set up." Most of our group was quartered at the Spanish Club and we were assured our luggage would be safely cared for and sent to us at a later date.

Pfc. WILBURN SNYDER, 3d Battalion Medics, 31st Infantry:

We were told that Manila was to be declared an open city and we were pulling out. I packed all my possessions, girlfriend and family's pictures, all the things that meant so much to me, in my footlocker. Now I learned we were only going to take our packs. While we waited to board the island buses, our first sergeant says, "This is going to separate the men from the boys," and he looked down at me because I was just a kid of eighteen. He stopped and looked at another fellow. "I imagine this'll separate the boys quick, don't you?" This other guy didn't say anything. Nobody was saying anything to him. We started out in a caravan.

The next day we stopped at noon for chow. While we were eating, some high-flying Japanese bombers came over. We lost our sergeant right then. He literally went crazy. "They're coming to get us! They're coming to get us!" He jumped up and started to run. We never saw him after that. I learned later that he had a Filipino wife in Manila and the Japs interned him as a civilian.

2d Lt. JOHN POSTEN, Fighter Pilot, 17th Pursuit Squadron:

We were told to clear out. Things had gone pretty bad and the Japs were pushing our forces back around Lingayen Gulf. Then we heard there were about fifty more transports around Alabat Island and some more at Legaspi and Batangas. We left at night in a convoy of trucks. We moved what planes we could and burned the rest along with all the food, bombs, and ammunition we didn't have room for. On the way to Bataan we met convoys from Manila, Cavite, McKinley, and Olongapo. We moved without lights and the roads were choked with wrecked trucks and cars. It looked like a small Dunkirk.

Pfc. ROBERT BROWN, 17th Pursuit Squadron:

We left in convoy and headed towards Bataan. The roads were thick with Filipino civilians. It was hell trying to move our tugs and trucks down through this mass of retreating humanity. It was so dusty I couldn't see the road. If the Japs had any brains they'd have come down and strafed the roads. My God, we were lucky. There was no place to go. We were out on the flats. All those people and no place to hide.

Sgt. H. G. TYSON, 3d Pursuit Squadron:

On Christmas Eve we got word the Japs had landed just east of us at Lamon Bay and were heading in our direction. If we didn't want to be cut off we knew that we'd better get away fast. After scrounging some transportation we traveled to Manila, where we stayed overnight at Santo Tomas. The next morning they took us down to the piers. There was a little interisland steamer there and a lot of .50-caliber ammunition on the dock. We went through an air raid while we were loading the ammunition. Soon after that we took off. Nobody told us where we were going. This little boat just chugged across Manila Bay to Bataan and when we got there they said, "Here you are, boys. You're in the infantry now."

2d Lt. HADLEY WATSON, Company H, 57th Infantry, Philippine Scouts:

Nichols Field was burning and the smoke and flames lit up the whole sky. On Christmas Eve three of us took the flag down at Fort Santiago* for the last time. I'm not ashamed to admit that I cried. Then we got on our motorcycles and rode down to Port Area and up the gangplank of some small old vessel which took us over to Corregidor.† The following morning we rode the motorcycles back up that gangplank and sailed over to Bataan.

2d Lt. LEONA GASTINGER, Army Nurse Corps:

Christmas Eve day we went out to Bataan. The night before, they told us we were going to another hospital. I envisioned a great big brick building like we were used to. So we packed very important things like our white uniforms. As luck would have it, half my uniforms were at the laundry, so I packed some material which I intended to make new uniforms from. We also

---

* Headquarters of the Philippine Department.
† Corregidor, the largest of the American fortified islands at the entrance to Manila Bay, was the wartime garrison for nearly 10,000 men, mostly American. Known as "the Rock," the island had a bombproof headquarters, a hospital, and storage areas buried inside the Malinta Tunnel. After Manila was evacuated, General MacArthur moved USAFFE Headquarters to Corregidor. Although heavily fortified, the island was dominated by Mount Bataan, just two miles away on the Bataan Peninsula.

had around a little scotch, a couple of bottles of rum and a can of peanuts, all of which we took. The buses and trucks picked us up the next morning.

2d Lt. HATTIE BRANTLEY, Army Nurse Corps:

We had known from the beginning of the war we would retreat to Bataan. Roosevelt would send ships in two or three days, our supplies were there, the hospitals were all ready, and all we had to do was go over there and hold out. So we were prepared when we were told we were going to a hospital that had been all set up for us. We all had this beautiful mental picture of a big building with flowers around it and all the other things we were accustomed to seeing at an Army hospital. So we went in buses and our white starched uniforms. Several times on the trip, because of enemy bombings, we ended up in ditches.

2d Lt. LEONA GASTINGER, Army Nurse Corps:

We rode all day and finally stopped in Bataan at a little place called Limay and our destination, Hospital No. 1. Instead of finding a fine standing hospital we found an empty camp with some Filipinos hanging around. I wasn't used to native country. Having been over there less than six weeks, I hadn't gotten around. I didn't even know what a nipa hut was. Now I was surrounded by a large number of them on each side of a compound. They were quite large, had wooden floors, were roofed with nipa palm and, when it rained, didn't leak. Jap planes had been coming over all day. We watched all kinds of war equipment try get down this road on Bataan, and when we left the buses we were relieved to have finally arrived. But we all thought, "This is a hospital?" Frankly, we were numb; I don't think much went on that first day except our trying to get organized. Early that evening my roommate and I remembered that we'd seen a little store with a Coca-Cola sign outside the compound. We walked up there and, believe it or not, we got a cold Coke. Sitting out on the railing of this little store reminded me of being in an old country store in the back country of rural Georgia. That was the last Coca-Cola I had for a very long time.

2d Lt. HATTIE BRANTLEY, Army Nurse Corps:

Somebody took one look at us—bedraggled, dirty, dispirited females—and shortly a truck came to the door of the building with some new clothes. Air Force coveralls, all size 42. The belts were stitched across the back from side to side. And the front is best described by the modern day adage of "hang loose!" Letha McHale, who weighed about eighty-nine pounds, got lost and wasn't seen for quite a while when she tried on a pair. On Rosemary Hogan they looked tailor-made. And the rest of us in between—we hung loose.

We sat on the beach that night and stared across at Manila, wondering what was happening at the Army-Navy Club, the Manila Hotel, and other familiar spots. We also wondered what was happening to us. But let me quickly say, the main theme then, there, and forever after was, "Help is on the way!" We evidenced faith, hope, and trust—in God, in General MacArthur, in FDR, and the USA. In fact, anytime anyone looked in the direction of the Bay and did not see a convoy steaming in it was with disbelief. And the assurance that this convoy would arrive at least by tomorrow!

On Christmas Day all available hands went into the warehouse and dug out the gear for the hospital. There were old iron cots, rusty and dirty, and I'll swear they were packed in 1918 newspaper. We uncrated and distributed, setting up about eighteen of those nipa buildings with thirty to forty beds [cots] each.

2d Lt. LEONA GASTINGER, Army Nurse Corps:

Those of us who were assigned to the operating room started looking for the instruments we needed to take out a man's appendix. We went to a warehouse which was full of boxes, crates, and cases. It doesn't take too many instruments to take out somebody's appendix, but it does take things like knives, hemostats, and retractors. The boxes were supposed to be coded, so we would know what was in them without opening them. They weren't. We opened box after box and instead of finding simple surgical instruments, we always found things like instruments needed to do very delicate eye operations. When we finally found the nitty gritty of what we needed, we thought we'd just wipe the stuff off. You see, each instrument was covered in what looked like shellac. Well, we thought we'd just wash that off with green soap. So we made a solution and put our instruments in while we finished our unpacking. When we lifted them out we expected the covering to be all loosened up. It wasn't even gummy. It was as hard as before. We decided to try something a little stronger, alcohol. But alcohol wouldn't take it off either. The only thing we hadn't tried was ether. So I sat all day in front of a bucket of instruments cleaning them with ether until I was practically anesthetized. At the moment we were doing this no one thought how awful it was to use ether this way, because it was going to get very scarce in just a few days. But we couldn't use the instruments the way they were, so priorities were set.

Capt. ROBERT TAYLOR, Chaplain, 31st Infantry:

I celebrated Christmas at the Abucay Hacienda drinking a can of tomato juice and eating field rations. Our colonel was a very patriotic and conscientious man, and he called for a meeting of all officers and senior noncoms in the old burned and bombed-out church of the hacienda. He told us that it was Christmas Day and that in a few hours people in America would be worshiping and celebrating this day. Then he said, "Around the life of this Christ whose birthday we celebrate revolves the spiritual and moral principles upon which our country was built." Then he added, "May the day never come when our people will forget that fact." So we took time off from our preparation of the defensive line to observe Christmas, because of its importance to the men and to our country. I thought that was quite significant.

Sgt. RALPH LEVENBERG, 17th Pursuit Squadron:

It's normal for every outfit to have a scrounger. You know, the guy who can get everything. We had a gentleman in our organization, Paddy Clawson, who was the company carpenter with twenty-seven years in the service. On our way over in the boat from Manila to Bataan on Christmas Day he said to me, "Stick close because we're going to have lunch before we go anywhere." I didn't know what the hell he was talking about. When we arrived at Mariveles there was no continuity, no anything.
    "Oh, you're Air Force. Up the hill."
    "Up the hill, where?"
    "Just keep going up the hill."
    It was a rout. We knew we had to go to Pilar where we had a couple of P-40s left, but no idea how to get there. But I followed Paddy Clawson and he took me out of the crowd and we went behind a building. From his musette bag he pulled out a big loaf of GI baked bread and a Virginia baked ham. I'm Jewish and never had ham in my life. But I'll never forget that Christmas dinner. Later, we started up the highway heading towards Pilar any way we could. We arrived at KP #118 [Kilometer Post 118] and found that we had also arrived at Pilar with the rest of our squadron. We sat around or dug foxholes. We didn't even know what an order of battle was. We

weren't trained for anything like that. We were trained for making airplanes fly. Problem was, there weren't a lot of airplanes around.

2d Lt. JOHN POSTEN, Fighter Pilot, 17th Pursuit Squadron:

I spent Christmas Day looking for my outfit. Our car broke down and I had to hitch a ride on another convoy. No one knew where anyone was or where they belonged. I could see Manila and Cavite burning, where we had blown up everything we couldn't move.

Pfc. JACK BRADY, 228th Signal Operations Company:

On Christmas Day I had to make a run out to McKinley. On the way back the road was closed by a fire and I couldn't get through. When I finally arrived in Manila my original group had already left for Bataan. I couldn't do a damn thing about it. I was completely separated from the rest of my outfit.

I grabbed a ride in a truck with a sailor and a fellow from the air warning company. Everyone was trying to get back into Bataan. There was one road [Route 7] from San Fernando to Bataan. It was a two-lane highway with a four-foot shoulder on either side that dropped straight down to a ditch. Both lanes were covered with Army trucks, Pambusco buses, and civilian automobiles. Anything that had an engine, or could possibly roll, was on the road headed for Bataan. The civilians and the troops were walking on the shoulders going the same way. Every few hours the Japs would come over and strafe us.

The heat was tremendous, especially when packed in as tight as we were. We were a tremendous mass of confusion. Outfits were strung out for miles. Once in a while I'd see an outfit that had stopped and was waiting for its stragglers to fall in so that it could regroup. Then they'd fit back into the crowded road and get separated all over again.

Once, several hundred yards in front of us, we were blocked by a burning truck which had just been bombed. All traffic came to a halt. We just stopped and sat there. It was really fantastic! All those people waiting could easily have tipped that truck over and gotten it off the road. But no one did anything. I don't want to make a hero out of myself or the people I was with, but we saw that something had to be done. Especially with the Japs flying overhead. We decided we weren't going to stay on that hot road any longer than we could help. So we went up to that truck and tipped it off the road. Just five of us against that two-and-a-half-ton truck. Of course, when you're scared you can do lots of things you couldn't do otherwise. Everyone just standing around made me mad! I was as scared as anyone. I'll clue you, I was scared the whole time. I knew the Japanese were not aiming at me personally, they were just shooting at the uniform, but I was inside it. That was enough to scare the daylights out of me.

When I finally found my outfit a week later, my first sergeant was very unhappy. He had already changed his morning report to show that I was dead. Now that I showed up he had to pick me up again and redo all his paperwork.

Pfc. LEE DAVIS, 30th Bombardment Squadron:

When we got to San Fernando, La Union,* we ran across an area full of food supplies that had been collected for Christmas dinners. In the rush of the retreat the food was just sitting there. We pulled in with our ambulance. We noticed there were none of our officers around. So two of our enlisted men, a private and a corporal, took off the insignias that would identify them as enlisted men and began calling each other colonel and major. They marched up to a supply sergeant and told him they needed Christmas supplies for one hundred men. "Major, have that sergeant standing there load this ambulance immediately. Be quick, because we have to move out." "Yes, sir!" So, our "major" told the sergeant to double-time his men in the loading of our ambulance. When we got to Bataan we were received as heroes. Our mess sergeant made up a Christmas dinner exactly like the one we would have had in the States, turkey and all the trimmings. As we passed by with our full mess kits, there were tired, dusty troops coming down the road, troops who hadn't eaten for some time. At that time I didn't feel guilty about eating in front of these troops or not sharing it with them, because I was quite hungry myself. Only now can I realize how they must have felt, tired from fighting and retreating, and here they find a bunch of Air Force men eating a complete Christmas dinner.

Pfc. VICTOR MAPES, 14th Bombardment Squadron:

In Bataan I got the first inkling that this was going to be a funny kind of war. See, I thought everybody done a war alike. We were all tired and hungry when we arrived. Then it dawned on us that we didn't have anything to carry water with. Our sergeant told me to go over to a neighboring Air Force outfit and borrow some cans. They had some big milk cans, lots of

---

* There are two San Fernandos in northern Luzon. This one is in La Union Province and on Lingayen Gulf. The other is the capital of Pampanga Province and the gateway to Bataan.

them. I asked if I could borrow one to get some water. They said, "You silly son of a gun. If you haven't got sense enough to bring your own cans down here, tough on you!" Boy, they gave me a hard time. I finally bargained with some natives and got some dirty old five-gallon oil cans.

In looking around wherever I went, I noticed everyone had beds and footlockers and stuff like that, but no one had food. We began worrying about all the food we'd left behind at Clark Field. Our CO was up in San Fernando [Pampanga], so I got two or three gung-ho types—I mean they were daredevils—to go with me in one of the big wheelers back to Clark. Christmas Day we went up in daylight the same road we'd come down. Several times we had to get off to the side of the road while the Japs flew off.

When we got to San Fernando we ran across our CO, who was loading bombs at the rail head and who wanted to know what in the hell I was doing in San Fernando. "Well, we're going back," I said, "to get some field ranges we left behind, along with food." He said, "Good luck, but I've never seen ya."

We clicked up on the edge of Clark Field and listened a little. There wasn't a soul around. Everything was so doggone neat. We located our rations and found that the big roast ovens were still warm from the roast beef dinners still in them. The meat was done just right.

Once we loaded the trucks we had a terrible drive back in the dark. Pure havoc! We couldn't use our lights, and on both sides of the road were halftracks and trucks and all kinds of wrecks, everything imaginable run off into ditches. It was a dead giveaway that something was happening. All the time everybody was telling us, "strategic withdrawal." Strategic withdrawal—it looked like a complete screw-up.

We hit Guagua around midnight and didn't know which fork of the road to take. A Philippine Scout came up and pointed us to the right road. Then he yelled, "Merry Christmas." It was the only Merry Christmas I heard all that time, 'cause everything was going all to hell!

Pfc. MICHAEL McMULLEN, 27th Bombardment Group (L):

I drank a lot. Believe me. I drank a lot before I got to the Philippines, and I drank a lot after I got to the Philippines. However, I did my job and my particular job at that time was to drive a tank truck loaded with airplane gasoline. On Christmas Day a colonel came through from up north. I don't know what he was so shook up about, but shook up he was. "You've got to move the hell out of here, now! The Japs are right behind me." We were set up in a temporary airfield north of Manila.

So the orders came down from the old man to go down to Manila, where we would meet a boat that would take us to Mariveles on Bataan. Our Christmas dinner of chicken was on the stove and naturally I'm my usual self—higher than a kite. But when the word passed down that we had to leave, we went out and confiscated all the available transportation we could lay our hands on. We waited for night so the Japs wouldn't strafe us, and then took off in convoy for Manila. I had two men with rifles riding the tank and a sergeant from the motor pool with me in the cab. We were the last truck in line and in the darkness we got lost. My old sergeant kept handing me this gin bottle every now and then and naturally I'd take a drink. The night was so black I couldn't see where I was going. Before long I pulled over and got out to scrape the paint off the headlights. Once in a while after that I'd flick the lights on and off to make sure I was still on the highway. The two boys on the back of the truck kept beating on the cab and hollering, "For God's sake, Mac, slow this damn thing down." My sergeant would give me another swig of gin and say, "Here, Mac, take a drink and pour on the oil."

Finally we pulled into the Manila Port Area with our lights on, because I didn't know where we were. Someone hollered, "Shut those damned lights off"—those weren't his exact words —"before you get us all killed." I stopped right there and a man walked up to the other side of the cab and really began chewing out my old sergeant. I couldn't see who it was because I was driving a cab over engine job, but I could see my sergeant sliding down in the seat. When I had enough of this bawling out I said, "Hey, buddy, you get the hell out of our way or I'll run you down." I put the truck in gear and took off down the street. The sergeant looked at me and said, "You know what you just done? You chewed out a colonel back there."

Anyhow, we were in the Port Area and we couldn't find the rest of our convoy, the boat that was supposed to meet us, or anybody who knew anything about us arriving. So I said, "Well, Sarge, what are we going to do?" "Let's take a nap," he said. So we went underneath the truck and fell asleep.

All of a sudden someone's shaking me and it's our old man. He said, "How'd you get here?" Hell, I didn't know except I was on a gravel road most of the time. Then he went off to find out what we were all going to do. When he came back a little while later, he told us to gas up and drive to San Fernando by the same route.

I got into San Fernando at six o'clock that morning and stopped at the Pikes Hotel to have a drink. While I'm there, who shows up but the old man with the rest of the convoy. He said to me, "Mac, when this war's over with I want you to show

me how in the hell you went into Manila and back ahead of me,
when you never passed me."

Pfc. ROY DIAZ, Company C, 194th Tank Battalion:

We were on the road south of Manila, outside Piis, when we
were ordered to attack the Japanese. Our platoon commander,
Lieutenant Needham, wanted to first make a reconnaissance. A
major from the 1st Infantry [PA] kept insisting that the Japanese
had nothing but small arms in front of us. Lieutenant Needham
kept arguing, but this major said, "No, no! There's nothing in
there." They got it around the first bend. Never had a chance.
Not a chance. The Japs had antitank guns hidden off the side
of the road. Needham got it in the turret. The first shell cut him
right in half. These were the first men in our outfit killed. The
whole company was out of Salinas, California. We knew everyone. We were like brothers.

We covered the retreat from the south all the way to
Bataan. Soon as the Filipino Army would move out, we'd cover
for them. We'd stay there until the last officer came through, and
then we'd pull back and cover the next area. Then the Filipinos
would go through and we'd do it all over again.

One night on the retreat I really got snockered. It was at
San Pablo. Our company commander called me over to his
halftrack:

"Hey, Diaz, come on over."
"Yes, sir, I'll be right over."
"Where's Bernard?" (That's my maintenance sergeant.)
"I don't know, but he's around."
"Get him over here."
"What's up, Captain?"
"Have a drink."

I don't know where he got it, but he had two bottles of
scotch and a couple of boxes of cigars. All night long we killed
these two bottles and smoked cigars.

The next morning I wasn't feeling very good. Oh, boy! All
of a sudden here comes a Filipino truck full of cigarettes. Pied-
monts. We hijacked the whole thing. Gave the cooks the cigarettes, so they could distribute them to the men.

2d Lt. JOHN POSTEN, Fighter Pilot, 17th Pursuit Squadron:

The day after Christmas I found my outfit more or less intact.
Things were sure in a mess. They were getting ready to move
when I found them. It had been three days since I washed my
face, let alone taken my clothes off. I was filthy. I found a
Philippine barber and had him cut my hair off. It sure was a lot
cooler and cleaner that way, even though it looked like hell.

The Japs bombed the shipping in Manila Harbor. There was a column of smoke over the capital that almost hid the sun.

Pfc. MICHAEL TUSSING, Jr., 27 Bombardment Group (L):

The sad thing was we ended up in Bataan without any food. But in Port Area there was shipload after shipload of stuff that never got moved out of there. There was just acres and acres and acres of crates and boxes. Once you got back there, it was no problem to load up. Somebody just forgot to organize the movement of these supplies to Bataan. They got the men in all right, but they forgot the food.

Pfc. JACK BRADY, 228th Signal Operations Company:

The first thing you found out when you arrived on Bataan was there wasn't any food. We knew there was food of all kinds back in Manila so the same bunch that I arrived with decided we'd go back to Manila in our truck to get a load of food. It was simple. We traveled at night when the roads were not as crowded. It took us a whole night to make the trip, load up, and be back by morning. We lost our truck on the third trip. On our way back we were stopped by some tankers who told us to be careful because of Japanese patrol activity. We didn't know any other road to use, so we just became more cautious. I can't remember now why we didn't cross the bridge, maybe there was too much traffic on it, but anyway, we took the road that cut off along the river and planned on crossing at a ford we'd been told about. We had gone several miles when we ran into a Japanese patrol. Actually, we ran them down. As soon as we spotted them the driver said, "I'm going to run through them." And he did. We just went right through them, shooting at the same time. As soon as we got out of range, we decided to forget the ford and cross the river wherever we could. When we found a place with a nice low bank we started to cross. Somewhere in the middle the engine went underwater. We swam the rest of the way. Had to leave that truckload of chow behind. Too bad.

Sgt. WILLIAM MATTSON, Company A,
194th Tank Battalion:

My halftrack was coming through the barrio of Guagua and we were in a line with trucks carrying Filipino Regular Army troops. Any time they heard planes or bombs they'd just jump out of their trucks and run off. This, of course, kept backing up the road. Finally I had enough, and when a Jap plane began strafing the road at Guagua and the Filipinos left their trucks, I hopped out of my halftrack and got in the Filipino truck right in front of us and drove it down to Bataan. There I found it was full of gas, ammunition, and flour. It just happened we had a first sergeant who'd been a bricklayer, and when he found I had driven in a truck of flour, he scrounged around some and built us an oven. Once we found the yeast, we began to have fresh bread. We were the envy of the other outfits.

Pfc. MICHAEL McMULLEN, 27th Bombardment Group (L):

I took it upon myself to drive to Manila and load up whatever food I could get at Port Area and drive it back to Bataan. No one ever gave me an order or tried to stop me. When we would be bombed we'd leave the damn truck and hit a ditch. When we got into Manila smoke was everywhere. We took things anywhere we could. If I found a dump somewhere and needed to sign my name, I signed. It didn't make any difference to me. In all honesty, my trucks were loaded with two-thirds food and one-third booze. The last time I was in Manila was December 31. The Japs were on one side of the city and I was on the other. The city was on fire and smoke made driving very bad. We loaded that truck strictly with chow. We also found some calico cloth and a few cuckoo clocks which we bartered for some booze at a barrio on our way back to Bataan.

2d Lt. JOHN POSTEN, Fighter Pilot, 17th Pursuit Squadron:

I went back to Manila for New Year's Eve. About nine o'clock they blew up all the oil and gas supplies in the city! They blew up what was left of Nichols, McKinley, Port Area, and Cavite. It looked like the whole place was going up. We were told to get out at once because all the bridges were to be blown up. We went to a show first and just caught the tail end of the last convoy. We could hear them blowing the bridges behind us. On our way back we passed a dozen or more villages laid flat by dive bombers. We passed a railhead filled with ammunition cars burning. The ammunition was going off all around. I don't know how many cars we saw wrecked and burning on the road. It took us till dawn to get back, the roads were so choked with wrecks and retreating forces.

Pfc. ROY DIAZ, Company C, 194th Tank Battalion:

New Year's Eve we pulled into Manila and were the last ones in the column.* It was pitch dark. We came across one of our tanks which had crashed into a big statue of José Rizal. When he clobbered it he bent the idler. Maintenance should have a

---

* This was the tail end of one of the retreating columns of Jones's South Luzon Force.

truck full of parts. We didn't have extra track, let alone an idler. We stayed all night to try to get that darn thing fixed. We'd take the track off, try to straighten the idler, put the track back on, start the engine, track would fall off. Did this three or four times. Meanwhile thousands of Filipinos are moving past us all heading for the mountains or Bataan.

Around daybreak we got real discouraged. A Filipino came over to us, "Hey, Joe, you better take off. The Japs are right behind me."

We immediately loaded whatever we could in our half-track, shot a hole through the tank's engine, and took off. Now we didn't know where we should go, or how. Our outfit was way ahead of us and all we had were SOCONY Motor Oil Maps, you know, service station maps. I'm thinking, "What in the hell did our reconnaissance do all this time before the war?" I thought they were making maps. So, heck, we kept going. None of the bridges had been blown yet, and we ran into our company way up around San Miguel. We were lucky.

Sgt. NICHOLAS FRYZIUK, Company B,
192d Tank Battalion:

New Year's Eve I was guarding a road at the Concepcion-Tarlac road intersection. San Fernando was blowing up in every god-damn direction. Nobody knew what the hell was going on and I'm scared shitless. I'm a tank maintenance sergeant, but right then I'm on the ground guarding my position. With me is a boy from Texas. I don't know who he was but he was a big guy and he had a submachine gun and two .45s. Typical cowboy. I had two bottles of Canadian Club whiskey which I got from one of the barrios we went through. So he and I were going to celebrate New Year. Well, we celebrated. All of a sudden a big staff car comes roaring down the road with its headlights on. So we stop it. A Filipino gets out. I start giving him a hard time. He tells me he's a colonel. I say, "I don't give a shit who you are, turn them goddamn lights off." Well, he keeps arguing and telling me he isn't turning them off. The Texas boy then steps into the middle of the road and shoots out both goddamn lights with his machine gun. We had orders. Nothing was to come down that goddamn road with its lights on and that was it!

2d Lt. JOHN POSTEN, Fighter Pilot, 17th Pursuit Squadron:

January 1 I was on alert, but did not fly. I spent most of the day sleeping. I heard the Japs were in Manila,* and some of the

* Although two Japanese divisions could have entered Manila New Year's Day, it wasn't until the following day that General Homma allowed the capital to be occupied.

roads we had come over the night before were now in Jap hands. They must have been right behind us. North of us, where the troops continued to come into Bataan, we could now see and hear artillery fire at night.

Cpl. WILLIAM HAUSER, Headquarters Company, 192d Tank Battalion:

There wouldn't have been no Bataan if the retreat hadn't been covered by the tanks. You can't say anything derogatory about the Philippine Scouts. Those guys were excellent. But the Filipino Army troops were something else. Once a line had been set up with Filipino troops, you could forget it. Those guys would bug out and the only thing keeping the Japs back would be the tanks.

Sgt. FORREST KNOX, Company A, 192d Tank Battalion:

It was rather nerve-racking. The native infantry had a bad case of the runs, so you could never tell for sure if the troops passing you in the night were friendly or not. Only sure test was when they seen you if they waved or shot at you. I passed up several chances to shoot Japs. I thought they were our troops. I had been assured the men in front of me were Filipinos. But our infantry screen would simply melt away. They had a million excuses, to see the captain, to get more ammo, to find some medics, to get water. When they said, "I go to seek my companions, Joe," it was the last of them and we were on our own. They would hold up two fingers as they passed us and say, "V for Victory, Joe." We would do the same and answer back, "V for Vacate, Joe."

Pfc. ROY DIAZ, Company C, 194th Tank Battalion:

Finally, we were ordered back to the Calumpit Bridge,* but we stopped on the wrong side; we didn't cross it. If you're going to go into Bataan you have to cross this bridge. Then the bombers came over. "My God," I said, "I'm just a Pfc. This can't happen to me. If they hit that bridge I'm going to be stuck on the wrong side." They never did bomb it and we crossed shortly afterwards.

---

* The Calumpit bridges carried the Manila Railroad and Route 3 over the Pampanga River, and were the key to getting all of General MacArthur's forces east of the river across and on to San Fernando, where Route 7 ran south into Bataan.

Cpl. WILLIAM HAUSER, Headquarters Company,
192d Tank Battalion:

We went down to cover the Calumpit Bridge but found that a
Jap force coming down from the northeast would bisect one of
the roads we were using for our retreat.* So a platoon of our
tanks from Company C was sent over to the town of Baliuag
with orders to hold it at all costs. The next day we reconnoitered
the whole area, looking for fords across the Angat River which
the Japanese might use. At one point a local Filipino showed
one of our tanks where it could cross. When they tried, it sank
to the turret.

In the early afternoon we began trading fire with the Japs,
who had begun to hit us with some machine guns. The highway
that crossed the bridge turned at right angles about four blocks
down and then went into the town square. When we pulled
back we left one of our tanks at this road crossing. The Japs
sent some tanks down the road and before they made their turn
our tank would blast them broadside. The rest of us set ourselves up in different places.

Our lieutenant pulled his tank real gently into a nipa hut
so that it covered him. Then he aimed his barrel out one of the
windows. I was in the headquarters communications halftrack,
listening on the radio set. For a while everything was relatively
quiet except for some machine-gun fire. About four o'clock the
shit hit the fan and they began shelling our position. The radio
woke up. We'd hear reports of tanks coming across the bridge,
coming down from the north, and reports of "Got him!" The
battle lasted a while and we kept going back and forth, up and
down the streets. Once we were a couple of feet from the lieutenant hidden in the shack. He got four goddamn Jap tanks. He
radioed our colonel, "You want a goddamn Jap tank? I'll put a
line on one and drag it in by the ass."

Finally, when it got to be dusk, my halftrack was told to get
out of there and move back to Plaridel.† We knew the Jap infantry would begin to move in.

When we finally crossed the Calumpit Bridge the engineers
blew it right behind us.‡ That afternoon the Japs hit some cans
of ammunition at the railhead at San Fernando and for hours
it was like Fourth of July. We didn't stay there but continued
towards Bataan. There was confusion everywhere.

---

* This was Route 5 which, seven miles south of Baliuag, ran into Route
3, the road that carried General Jones's retreating South Luzon Force.
† Near the intersection of Routes 3 and 5, and five miles from the Calumpit
bridges.
‡ The bridges were blown at 6:15 a.m. on Jan. 1, 1942.

Pfc. JOHN FALCONER, Company A, 194th Tank Battalion:

Towards the end of the retreat things became chaotic. At one
point we were rear guard and were supposed to hold a bridge
until some infantry pulled back through us and crossed over
the bridge. When it became our turn to cross, we found the
engineers had already blown it. Having had no time to reconnoiter other crossing possibilities, we dismantled our guns, left
the tanks on the road—seventeen of them in a row right before
the demolished bridge—and waded across the river. Later we
found out from another tank company who came down behind
us that, by going another block to the right, we could have
driven our tanks across a shallow ford.

Pfc. ROY DIAZ, Company C, 194th Tank Battalion:

I didn't stay in the rear echelon very long. I don't think I was
there two hours, when we got the call that one of our tanks
needed maintenance. So here we went up to the front lines, up
to Guagua.* What a nightmare that was!

  We were in one of these big six-by-six trucks and we just
kept driving down the road looking for our tanks. We went
right through Guagua. We couldn't find them no way. A mile
the other side of Guagua, here's an officer in the middle of the
road flagging us down. "Where in the hell are you going?" I
said, "We're looking for our tanks." "You won't find them down
here," he said. "You go down here another mile you're going to
find Japs, man." So we turned around and we're beating along
back to Guagua and I happened to look. I said, "Hold it!" I saw
one of our 37-mm's sticking out of the camouflage. You'd think
those damn guys in the tanks would come out and say something where they were. Well, we stopped. I said, "What the
hell's wrong? Which tank?"

  "Eaton's."

  "Forget it. Call the ordnance! I don't even want to look at
it." I knew what had happened. He'd already wrecked three.

  All around us the Philippine Scouts were firing their self-
propelled 75-mm's at the Japs down the road. At that time the
Japs weren't firing back. A Filipino came over to us with a
bunch of chickens. We started to cook them late in the afternoon [of January 3]. All of a sudden, "Boom, boom, boom!"
"Geez," I said, "them 75s still firing out there?" Our sergeant
said, "That's Japs. This is incoming." One minute we were

* During the first week of January the retreating forces from both ends
of Luzon continued to pour into Bataan. In order to give these troops
time to prepare their final defenses, General MacArthur established a
defensive line, fifteen miles from the base of the Bataan Peninsula, between the barrios of Porac and Guagua.

sitting around a fire cooking chickens, and the next one artillery is hitting all around. One of the shells raised the nipa right off the roof of the shack alongside us. The shrapnel sounded like a bunch of quail going over. I headed for a hole I'd spotted at the back of one of the houses. I dove in right on top of my company commander. He started cussing me out. "Goddamn, get off of me." I said, "How in the hell did you get down here so fast, Captain?" But nothing funny. They just flattened Guagua. One kid got killed in a halftrack, another had both legs shot off.

That night, when the firing stopped, they put me and my buddy on guard up in the turret of one of the tanks. I had a sub-Thompson and he was on the .30. We were so damned tired. Just sitting on the bench I dozed off. All of a sudden that .30 rips over me. I was in a stupor. I'm trying to get the safety off my Thompson. "What the hell did you shoot at?"

"Over by that shack, there's a whole bunch of Japs."

"Shoot that damn shack. Set it on fire."

Our tracers would do that. We just kept pumping our fire in there. My Thompson was no damn good. They were too far away. You could see them running. I don't know how many we killed, we never had the chance to investigate, but we kept pumping that .30 right where we saw them.

When it became daylight the only thing I saw standing was the church, and it had a shell through the roof. I thought, how in the hell do I survive in this thing?

Our captain came over to us: "You're maintenance. You better get the hell out. It's getting too damn hot here." So we went down the road ten or fifteen miles, when we saw an artesian well just pouring out water. We were so dirty we decided to take a bath and change into our clean fatigues. We had just finished bathing and had our new fatigues on when, hell, we look down the road and here comes the Filipino Army in buses, one after another. When they saw us out in the field, they stopped right in the middle of the road. In the meantime we could see Jap dive bombers flying back and forth. A Filipino captain came up: "Hey, Joe, what are you going to do?" That's what they used to always say. They thought American troops were gods. They never had an idea of what to do. This captain hadn't a clue now of where he was going or what he was supposed to do. He came over and wanted me to tell him what to do. I said, "You better get those goddamn buses out of here."

"Oh, but sir, those are not my orders."

"Don't 'but sir' me," I said, "get the hell out of here. Don't you see those planes? They're going to knock the hell out of you."

"Oh, but sir . . ."

And with that I pulled my .45. "Listen, Joe, get in that damned bus and get them under the trees because you're going to get it." Sure enough, last bus, before it hit the mango grove, *patooom*, right dead center. Jap dive bomber had spotted them. These Pambusco buses were all gaily painted red and yellow and were hard to miss. Meanwhile I dove into a carabao wallow. That's mud. I landed on my back and I'm looking up and I see the next bomb coming down, right straight at me. "Oh, my God," I said, "it's got my name on it. I hope it's got the wrong address." I went right on my belly, face down, and I kept my mouth open because I knew the concussion was going to be bad. *Boom!* It threw up clods of dirt. "Oh, God!" All the dirt landed on me. I knew I wasn't hit, though. I shook my head and looked at the other kid that was with me. He was right out in the open, lying flat on the ground. I walked over to him. Blood was coming out of his nose and ears, but he wasn't hit. I thought, "Hell, we're alive, but dirtier than when we started." I revived him, put him on the truck, and headed for the rear.

Cpl. WILLIAM HAUSER, Headquarters Company, 192d Tank Battalion:

At one point my halftrack was ordered north, towards Lubao, to reconnoiter. About midday, learning nothing, we returned on the same road. All of a sudden we came across this terrific cross-fire a little bit down the road. Now we knew it couldn't be Japanese firing because they were still north of us, so we figured that it was coming from two Philippine Army units which had panicked and were firing at each other. One had probably taken a short round and that started them firing across the road. Anyway, these guys are shooting back and forth and we have to go down the road between them. A confused situation. There was no cover for us. Filipinos or not, we decided if they shot at us we'd shoot back. We set up our machine guns and poked our nose down the road. Well, both sides recognized an American halftrack, so they stopped firing and let us roll through. Soon as we got past, damned if they don't start shooting at each other all over again.

Pfc. WILBURN SNYDER, 3d Battalion Medics,
31st Infantry:

We got back to Layac Junction late in the evening and Captain Graham told us to dig foxholes.* "How deep?" we wanted to know. "Deep enough to get your head under," was the answer. We established our aid station at the bottom of a small hill where most of us dug our foxholes.

Around 9:30 the next morning they opened up on us. Some of our aid men who had dug holes on the side of the hill to be closer to the line got caught real bad. When it started smacking in there, I couldn't figure out how they'd get out. All of them did, though. As soon as the Jap artillery began, a Philippine Scout battery opened up behind us and it soon became an artillery duel over our heads. The bombardment went on steadily, poom, poom, poom, poom, all morning long. We got quite busy tending the Filipino wounded. Most of our guns were in the open so we took a pounding. All the Japs had to do was locate one of the Scout 105s [howitzers] and pang!

We got orders in the afternoon that as quick as their artillery let up we were going to pull out. Word was we had been cut off and were going to have to fight our way back, and we did. We counterattacked. They let up. We moved out.

There was a kind of glory in this morning. It was the first time, we felt, that the Japanese had been stopped since they started the war.

* At Layac Junction all the roads to Bataan joined. To permit the troops holding the Guagua-Porac Line sufficient time to safely withdraw into the peninsula, it was vitally important that the road junction be held. The Japanese began their attack along the Layac line on the morning of Jan. 6 with an artillery barrage. Withdrawal of the line began that night.

2
BATAAN

Bataan Peninsula juts south into Manila Bay like a fat thumb. Twenty-five miles long and twenty miles wide at its base, the peninsula features rugged mountains and heavy jungle. Two extinct volcanoes, Mount Natib in the north, Mount Bataan and the Mariveles Mountains in the south, dominate Bataan's central spine. Facing Manila Bay, the east coast, which in the north is flat and swampy, turns hilly the farther south it goes. The western coastal plain is narrow and broken by numerous claw-like promontories which reach into the South China Sea. The entire peninsula is crossed by small streams and deep ravines and gullies. A single all-weather perimeter road begins halfway up the west coast, at Moron, then runs down and around Mariveles in the south and up along the entire length of the east coast. In the middle of Bataan the peninsula's only east-west road runs across the saddle separating Mount Natib and the Mariveles Mountains and connects the barrios of Pilar and Bagac. Bataan was considered by American planners to be a perfect place to wage a defensive battle.

Facing the Bataan Defense Force was General Homma's reorganized 14th Army. Underestimating the size of MacArthur's forces and expecting light resistance, Homma gave the mission of taking Bataan to the recently arrived and poorly trained 65th Brigade. The brigade was reinforced with supporting artillery, armor, and air units, as well as an infantry regiment.

The defense of Bataan was conceived as a

defense in depth. The first battle line stretched from Mauban in the west across Mount Natib to Abucay in the east. Beaches along both coasts were guarded to prevent Japanese amphibious landings behind the main battle line. To organize this defense, General MacArthur drew a line down the center of the peninsula. West of the line the defense was entrusted to General Wainwright's I Philippine Corps, east of the line, to Maj. Gen. George M. Parker, Jr.'s II Philippine Corps. Both were under MacArthur's USAFFE Headquarters on Corregidor.

Into Bataan had fled, in the last week of December and the first of January, nearly 80,000 troops, 13,000 of whom were Americans, and 26,000 civilians. Of critical importance to the defense of Bataan were available supplies. Immediately an inventory was taken to see what had arrived during the rush of retreat. It showed a satisfactory supply of ammunition on hand but, more important, it revealed an acute shortage of rations. Drastic action was required and on January 2, 1942, General MacArthur ordered that the 106,000 troops and civilians be placed on half rations.

Hunger notwithstanding, the defense of Bataan began with the morale of the American forces high. They had helped successfully execute an extraordinarily difficult retreat and were now dug in behind a strong line of defense. The running was over. They waited for the Japanese to attack, confident they could hold out until the American fleet arrived and rescued them.

2d Lt. HATTIE BRANTLEY, Army Nurse Corps, Hospital No. 1:

We soon had a routine—it consisted of work, work, and more work. We went to the wards as soon as it was light, left later

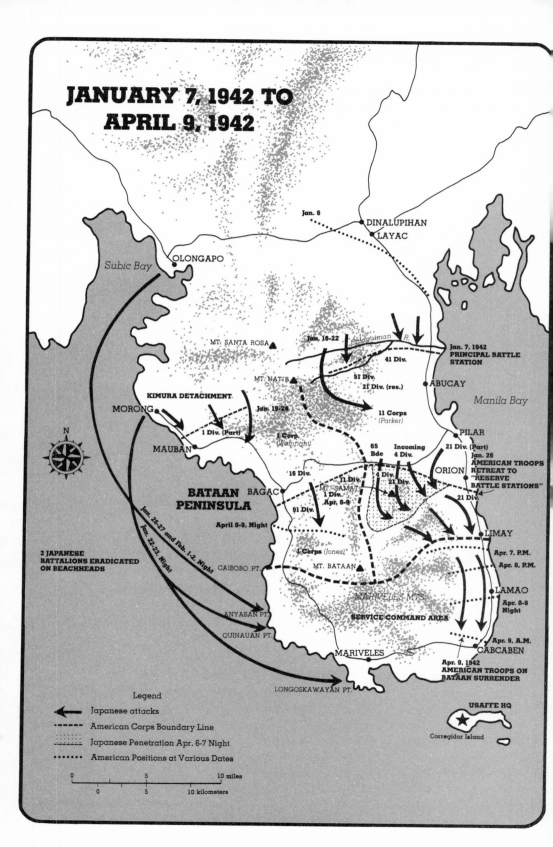

JANUARY 7, 1942 TO APRIL 9, 1942

Jan. 6

DINALUPIHAN
LAYAC

Subic Bay

OLONGAPO

MT. SANTA ROSA ▲

Jan. 16-22   Calaguiman R.

41 Div.

Jan. 7, 1942
PRINCIPAL BATTLE
STATION

MT. NATIB ▲

51 Div.

21 Div. (res.)

ABUCAY

Manila Bay

KIMURA DETACHMENT

MORONG

Jan. 19-24

1 Div. (Part)

II Corps
(Parker)

PILAR

21 Div. (Part)

Jan. 26
AMERICAN TROOPS
RETREAT TO
"RESERVE
BATTLE STATIONS"

MAUBAN

I Corps
(Wainright)

65
Bde

Incoming
4 Div.

ORION

16 Div.

11 Div.
21 Div.

Div.

BATAAN
PENINSULA

BAGAC

MT. SAMAT
1 Div.
Apr. 6-9

21 Div.

91 Div.

April 8-9, Night

LIMAY

Jan. 26-27 and Feb. 1-2, Night

Apr. 7, P.M.

Apr. 8, P.M.

Jan. 22-23, Night

I Corps (Jones)

MT. BATAAN ▲

2 JAPANESE
BATTALIONS ERADICATED
ON BEACHHEADS

CAIBOBO PT.

LAMAO

MARIVELES MTS.

Apr. 8-9
Night

SERVICE COMMAND AREA

ANYASAN PT.

QUINAUAN PT.

Apr. 9, A.M.

CABCABEN

MARIVELES

Apr. 9, 1942
AMERICAN TROOPS ON
BATAAN SURRENDER

LONGOSKAWAYAN PT.

Legend

← Japanese attacks

------ American Corps Boundary Line

:::::: Japanese Penetration Apr. 6-7 Night

•••••• American Positions at Various Dates

USAFFE HQ

★

Corregidor Island

N

0   5   10 miles

0   5   10 kilometers

to eat breakfast, then returned, and worked throughout the day until too dark to continue. We never seemed to get through. At dark we'd leave the wards to a skeleton staff of a nurse or two for the compound and a corpsman on each ward, and go sit on the beach and watch for the convoy that was coming.

Tech. Sgt. WILLIAM "COWBOY" WRIGHT,
17th Pursuit Squadron:

They took my crew of repairmen, cooks, and equipment north a short distance to an airstrip we called "Little Pilar." It had been a rice paddy. The next day the ground crews arrived and early in the morning our three remaining P-35s began coming in.

2d Lt. JOHN POSTEN, Fighter Pilot, 17th Pursuit Squadron:

We took off from Lubao before dawn and got to Little Pilar as it was getting light. Our AA did not recognize us and shot O. D. Wyatt down in flames. He had been with us in Manila on New Year's Eve. We could find nothing left of him. All we found were some small pieces of his plane.

Tech. Sgt. WILLIAM "COWBOY" WRIGHT,
17th Pursuit Squadron:

Our own antiaircraft guns shot one of the planes out of the air, killing the pilot. Another pilot was so shaken up that he overshot the runway and when he hit the soft dirt stood his plane on its nose.

As a result of this mistake it was decided that some of our officers should be assigned to the antiaircraft batteries surrounding our field. Lieutenants Page and Majors were selected for that duty. A few days later a shell blew up in the muzzle of a gun and, along with the regular crew, Page and Majors were killed.

Pfc. MICHAEL TUSSING, Jr.,
27th Bombardment Group (L):

Most of the time at the front was spent stringing barbed wire and digging foxholes. At night we slept an hour and had guard duty an hour. You can imagine how much sleep you got, lying on the ground without mosquito nets in rat-infested bamboo thickets. An hour on and an hour off, and all day working hard. It was rough.

I had an attack of malaria and our medical corpsman moved me back of the front to a small aid station he'd set up in a bamboo thicket. There, he and a nurse took care of a lot of men.

One of the nights I had a temperature of 106 degrees. I remember when the fever broke I got up to pour the water off the canvas cot I was sleeping on. I went back to the line shortly afterwards.

Pfc. VICTOR MAPES, 14th Bombardment Squadron:

Everyone on Bataan was hungry. For some, though, it was worse than for others. We had all the supplies we'd brought back from Stotsenburg. Some nights hungry guys from other outfits, hearing about our bunch of groceries, would try to filch them. To keep them away we'd fire over their heads.

Pfc. MICHAEL McMULLEN, 27th Bombardment Group (L):

It got to be a case where it was survival of the damn fittest and I was going to survive. When I brought a truckload of chow into Bataan before Manila fell, you can be sure it had booze on it. Having it gave many of us a feeling of courage. False courage would be putting it in its proper perspective. Whatever you call it, I know a lot of men lived by it until it gave out.

But something worse than the booze giving out also happened. I don't really know how many truckloads of chow I brought in from Manila that we hid back in what we called "Happy Valley." But there were a lot. Somehow the quartermaster got word of our cache and they came in and confiscated all of it. I felt like shooting everybody.

War Department communiqué, January 8:

Fighting of varying intensity is reported from all sections of the front. These operations are probably preparatory to a large scale general attack by the enemy.

Tech. Sgt. WILLIAM "COWBOY" WRIGHT,
17th Pursuit Squadron:

We hadn't been at Little Pilar long before the Japanese started looking for us. We had the airstrip pretty well camouflaged. For example, after our aircraft took off we'd rearrange the rice straw in wind rows. The planes themselves we hid in the wooded areas to the north and south of us. We would also keep two or three men busy most of the night watering the strip, which kept the dust down.

On January 6 three Jap dive bombers came over the hill out west of us. Our work area was at the west end of the runway, so they were on us before we could do anything. I had a dugout about 100 feet away and as I ran by our kitchen hut I had to laugh, because the foxhole close by was already packed full of men.

Earlier some high-altitude bombers had come across and we had taken hits on some aircraft and a gasoline truck. I had gotten a bite to eat and had decided to take a look at the bomb damage. About the time I began to saunter down the runway I heard aircraft approaching, and when I looked up I saw three dive bombers heading directly towards me. Before I could reach a nearby ditch the bombs started falling. I figured my time was up as the bombs behind me kept coming closer. It sure was a relief when they started falling in front of me. The bomb that landed the closest to me cut off a six-inch tree just above the ground. I returned to the kitchen area and postponed my walk to the other side of the airfield until the next day.

2d-Class Carpenter's Mate STANLEY SOMMERS,
Naval Battalion:

After the *Finch* sank I was stationed at Mariveles. To make ourselves less of a target, one of the first things we did was take our Navy whites and stain them with coffee. They came out kind of mustard yellow. We were put in the Naval Battalion. This was made up of men without commands, sailors without ships, and Air Force people without planes. Strays is what we were. My platoon commander was a first-class gunner's mate. We had a lot of mess stewards who were Filipinos. They didn't even know which end of the gun to fire. The rest of us didn't know how to fire a gun if the safety was on. A lot of us were scared.

Staff Sgt. JAMES CAVANAUGH, 440th Ordnance
Company, 28th Bombardment Squadron:

I was given a rifle, an Enfield which had been in cosmoline since 1922. Frankly, I didn't know a thing about them. I was raised in the city and never hunted. Luckily, I had a fellow from Texas in my squad who was used to handling rifles. He got the cosmoline off for me.

Tech. Sgt. WILLIAM "COWBOY" WRIGHT,
17th Pursuit Squadron:

On January 8 we got orders to abandon our little airstrip. Our few P-40s were flown to Cabcaben Airfield and Bataan Field. We had one flyable P-35, but because the guns had been taken off and it had no armor plating, none of the pilots wanted to fly it. When we got ready to leave, we destroyed it.

We joined the rest of the squadron and moved south, ending up in the hills and jungles along Bataan's west coast. Our job was to protect the bays from future Japanese landings.

2d Lt. JOHN POSTEN, Fighter Pilot, 17th Pursuit Squadron:

They took a few pilots from each squadron, including Raymond Sloan, and a few of the best crew chiefs along with the enlisted men. Each squadron had to make up an infantry company now. They made Sloan a company commander. I knew it must be getting serious when they took those trained Air Force men and made infantry out of them.

Pfc. VICTOR MAPES, 14th Bombardment Squadron:

I ended up near Cabcaben Airfield and when the Jap planes would come over the antiaircraft batteries on Corregidor and Cabcaben, would open fire. Because the bombers were too high they'd fire short, and we'd get all the shrapnel falling on us. You'd hear *whooosh* and this big old piece of shrapnel would come tearing down through the trees. *Whooosh!! Whooosh!!* All day long, every day, down through the trees. Boy, it'd make your tail end horsewhip. I mean that sound puckered you. The joke was, you'd say, "I'm really shook up down here," and our old first sergeant would say, "So are the trees."

All of a sudden, after running up and down all these hills and dodging this shrapnel, and not having enough sleep because of the continuous havoc, we were ordered to Mindanao on the *Mayan*. She was an ancient interisland steamer. Fact is, she was the boat that took President Quezon of the Philippines to Corregidor just before Manila was abandoned. They boarded us at night. There were 600 men scrambling to get on a boat built to handle 250 passengers. It was pandemonium. Six hundred hungry and tired men all crowding on, yelling. It reminded me of mad dogs. They told us we were going to Mindanao, south of Luzon, to prepare airfields for the planes which were supposed to reinforce Bataan.

Staff Sgt. JAMES CAVANAUGH, 440th Ordnance Company, 28th Bombardment Squadron:

I had the job, for a while, of carting Filipino soldiers up to the front lines. They'd load fifteen or twenty on my truck and I'd drive them up. When they went up to the front they'd carry a sack of rice, a live chicken, and maybe a bicycle.

Once in a while a Japanese plane would come over and strafe us. The Filipinos would scatter in all directions and it would take two hours to get them back together. Once we had them reassembled, we would always have fewer than when we started. They were never soldiers. They didn't really want to fight.

2d Lt. LEONA GASTINGER, Army Nurse Corps,
Hospital No. 1:

Now we used to get some Filipino soldiers who had been wounded in the back while running away from Japanese planes strafing the roads. They'd cry and be feeling real sorry for themselves. So to cheer them up I'd always remind them that they weren't wearing their helmets in the right place. That usually got a laugh out of them.

2d Lt. HATTIE BRANTLEY, Army Nurse Corps,
Hospital No. 1:

Early one morning there was a gas attack alarm. We had been warned the enemy would probably use poison gas and this was why we had to wear those gas masks all the time. Well, it was just beginning to get light, and it seems the alarm was given in the medical officers' quarters. Dr. Weinstein was from Atlanta, a brilliant surgeon and a very fastidious person. He was one of those persons who never expected anything to happen to himself—others, yes, but he was going to be a great surgeon and live a normal life. This point of view made war a little bit more trying on him than to some others with more relaxed personalities. Well Dr. Weinstein, in his hurry and fright, put his gas mask on, and as it was the first time he had even looked at it, much less put it on, the cardboard was still covering the isinglass eye holes. He got the mask on and in the bare daylight found he couldn't see. He caused quite a commotion screaming that his career was ruined, his surgical ability was forever lost, he was blind. Needless to say, his fellow officers enjoyed the episode for the next few days.

2d Lt. JOHN POSTEN, Fighter Pilot, 17th Pursuit Squadron:

Life was not without its little jokes. Once White went to Iloilo* to bring back some liquor and candy. We'd all developed a sweet tooth because there weren't sweets to be had anywhere. Two of our other pilots, Dyess and Brown, decided they'd take off and "intercept" White on his return. They scared the hell out of him. White did not see them until he had his wheels

---

* The principal city on Panay Island in the central Philippines.

down. He thought for sure they were Nips. He pulled up so quick I thought he was going to stall out.

That technique was how those slant-eyed bastards worked. They'd hang around our fields waiting to catch us as we took off or landed, and we didn't have enough planes to do anything about it. Once in a while we'd get even, though. In the middle of January, during a recon, Glover and I shot down a Jap seaplane. He dropped his bombs when he saw us coming, but we both nailed him.

That day I also sent home my monthly allotment check of $115. Figured someone might as well use the money I was making.

2d Lt. LEONA GASTINGER, Army Nurse Corps,
Hospital No. 1:

Sometime in early January, while I was still at Hospital No. 1, the Japanese bombed the village of Limay, which was right up the road. The patients began hearing planes, so I went out to see if I could see anything. My ward was at the right-hand edge of the whole complex, and as I stood on the little stoop which led to the porch, I saw a fighter with a great big red circle on it make a low pass over the hospital. The Jap pilot looked right at me and grinned. I was petrified! For a minute I couldn't move.

Several more came over and bombed the village. That's when I got the baby. As they began to put the dead in a pile, a young Filipino man came through the back of my ward carrying a bundle. He was a man that worked in the compound and he was carrying this absolutely new baby. He said to me, "I give the baby to you." To me! Good heavens, I thought, I can't . . . But I said, "Yes, I'll keep it." I couldn't actually keep this baby for my very own, that couldn't be, but while I could I took care of it and was responsible for it. When I looked at it I saw it was a girl and that she had shrapnel wounds. There was a deep gash down the leg that wound onto the foot. There were also little marks on its head which, thank goodness, were not deep.

My friend and I took care of this little girl baby. We cleaned the wound and bandaged it each day. Later we learned that her entire family, including grandparents—everyone except the father—had been killed in the raid.

I asked my doctor friend what we should call her. He said that when he was in medical school the doctors named all newborn girls Bridgette. So Bridgette she became. In the month we had her she got well and began growing. We fed her milk out of a medicine bottle and one of our corpsmen—Lord knows where he found them—brought us some nipples.

The funny thing was that everybody around the hospital

who heard about the baby wanted to do something for it. I took some white material that I carried into Bataan, which I thought I'd never use when I got there, and made some little sack garments and her diapers. All the patients wanted to feed her. We'd bring her to the beds of the wounded soldiers and they'd give her a bottle. Most were Filipino soldiers and it was like they were taking care of their own sister or child. Another young Filipino who I'd never seen before did her laundry. Every day he'd wash her soiled diapers and hang them on a line to dry, and bring us clean clothes from the day before. I don't remember his name or where he came from or where he went.

New York Times, January 10, 1942:

The anticipated assault by heavily reinforced Japanese forces on United States and Philippine units on Bataan was unleashed with tremendous force yesterday.

The terrain on which the enemy action was begun is hilly and, in spots, densely wooded. The American-Filipino Forces, although inferior in numbers of men, tanks, and planes, had previously prepared positions in anticipation of just such a Japanese attack.

New York Times, January 13:

General Douglas MacArthur reported a heavy artillery battle along his entire front and bombing attacks on his fortifications.*

Pfc. VICTOR LEAR, 27th Bombardment Group (L):

We had a good line of defense set up at Abucay. We had our machine guns in position and felt good about the area we were defending. But the Japs did not choose to hit us with frontal attacks. They hit, instead, the Filipinos. The Japs kept dropping fire bombs and submitting the Filipinos to constant punishing artillery fire. They just demoralized them. We did take incoming artillery barrages, but not like the Filipinos.

Pfc. WILBURN SNYDER, 3d Battalion Medics, 31st Infantry:

We lost six men out of twenty-nine at Abucay. We lost them quick. Soon after the Japs launched their big attack against our defensive line at Abucay, we were told that we were going to

---

* The Japanese opened their assault on Bataan Jan. 9 with an attack on the Philippine Army divisions holding the Abucay Line. On Jan. 16 one of these Philippine divisions, the 51st, counterattacked in order to restore positions lost the previous day. After it had achieved some success initially, the Japanese applied severe pressure and the 51st fell back in confusion. The U.S. 31st Infantry, moving from the area around the Abucay Hacienda, was ordered to counterattack. Vicious fighting went on for the next five days.

move up to fill a gap. One of the Philippine Scout groups moved up before daylight. We didn't even know they were going to come up with us, till they started falling in the foxholes with us. When we got to the gap, all we found were the dead Filipinos that had stayed, and a wounded American second lieutenant who had recently been a noncom. During the fighting our officers would come by offering commissions to American corporals or sergeants, if they would go to one of the Philippine Regular Army units. What they were doing was taking a corporal and sending him up to command a company of raw Filipino recruits. Most of these fellows were killed when their companies deserted. When we arrived to block the hole caused by the Filipino desertions, we found this American lieutenant near death. It dawned on me then, for the first time, that this thing was futile. My energy and enthusiasm began waning.

Cpl. WILLIAM GARLEB, Company H, 31st Infantry:

Most times everything was in confusion. Once I heard firing behind me and then some rounds came over. It was a machine gun and it was going *pow-pow-pow*. I thought the Japs had gotten behind us. So I took my rifle and laid it back of the foxhole and clicked off the safety. Soon I saw some bushes move and as I took aim, two American officers who were with the Scouts stepped out into the clearing. They were out catching snipers, just spraying the bamboo. They had no idea they were firing right into the back ends of their own troops. In no uncertain terms I got them out of there.

The fighting was terrible! The Abucay Line was open because the Philippine Army had run off, leaving us on our own. Companies F and H got pinned down. I was to run back to headquarters to tell them of our situation. I ran back, I don't know how, about fifty feet and rolled into a foxhole. I laid in this hole and pretty soon another rifleman fell in on top of me. He takes his gun and throws it to me. He can't stand it. Men were being killed all around us. He says, "Shoot me through the hand. I can't take it." This really made me mad. I was trying to keep my own fears under control.

Pvt. LEON BECK, Antitank Company, 31st Infantry:

The hardest thing in combat is to learn to control your emotions. If you can stay on top of them so that you don't let fear or panic take over, and if you can fall back on the training you've received, why then you can settle down and become a combat soldier. The emotional stress is terrible. Terrible! I think you make a psychological adjustment in shooting an individual in combat that you could never make in civilian life. I was trained that it was honorable, even glamorous, to kill an enemy. Combat is very confusing. It seemed like to me, almost immediately, when a fire fight broke out, we'd lose our chain of command. In action everybody kind of acts on their own.

Cpl. WAYNE LEWIS, Company D, 31st Infantry:

Fear is not a problem when you're active in hand-to-hand fighting. It's in the quiet spells that the fear comes.

Cpl. WILLIAM GARLEB, Company H, 31st Infantry:

There's subliminal fear—not the fear of imminent death which is always there—but that underlying gnawing tension that makes you so tired, so bone tired that even your hair gets tired.

Cpl. WAYNE LEWIS, Company D, 31st Infantry:

The first Jap I met face to face was a lot bigger than I had expected. I was walking through a clump of bamboo and I walked right into him. As a matter of fact, I had to look up to see his face. Luckily for me, he had an automatic rifle and as he started to swing it up, I shoved my .45 in his face and pulled the trigger. That big bullet caught him right under the chin and blew half his damn neck away. He scared the hell out of me.

Pfc. WILBURN SNYDER, 3d Battalion Medics,
31st Infantry:

You can't describe combat. It's like trying to describe the taste of an orange. Once the Japs hit our barbed wire, they stacked up to where you couldn't see the wire. They were piled so high our machine guns didn't have any more field of fire. We killed them with pistols as they came over. It was horrible. They came with these shrill cries. The only way we were going to stop them was to kill them. You killed them or you didn't stop them.

I remember one night at Abucay. We were sent out by a captain to bring back a man that was wounded. His platoon had not brought him back. We kept going forward. Finally we ran into a group who pointed us a little further out. We went where they pointed. Boy, were we dumb. It never dawned on us that we had just passed our forward observation point and that we were now crawling into the Japanese lines. They could have reached out and killed us. The only thing that saved us was the fact that they were planning an attack. We reached the fellow and put him on the litter. He'd been dead from go because his throat had been cut. We took him back anyway. We had no more than returned than the battle broke out. The Japs started hollering and coming. Our lines repelled the attack.

As soon as things got quiet our CO went to the officer that had sent us out and told him, "Don't ever do that to my men again. In the first place, you should have brought your own wounded back when you withdrew. Secondly, you knew your man was dead and, lastly, you risked the lives of four men to bring back a corpse. Don't ever do that again."

Sgt. FORREST KNOX, Company A, 192d Tank Battalion:

One halftrack we could hear on the net, who was on the north side of the line, came under artillery fire. He kept calling battalion headquarters, asking what he should do. First, he said the shells were falling just short of his position. A few minutes later he called that the shells were falling just behind his position. The next call, he was frantic, they were all around him. Headquarters finally got back to him, "Shut your damn mouth, the Japs are monitoring your radio."

2d Lt. JOHN POSTEN, Fighter Pilot, 17th Pursuit Squadron:

Five of us went out on the morning of the 16th to keep the Jap artillery spotter out of the air for an hour, while our lines at Abucay filled a hole where the Japs had come through. We saw only one plane and he stayed clear of us. I acted as lookout and lost the others when they went into an overcast.

I saw a lone Jap plane about 2,000 feet below me. I missed the first burst, and when he got in position for a second shot, I pulled the triggers, but the guns didn't work. I didn't know whether to get mad at the guns or myself.

War Department communiqué, January 16:

Ground fighting continues all along the front line. Enemy shock troops with special training are attempting aggressive infiltration. Attack planes and dive bombers are being used incessantly by the Japanese against our front line troops.

Cpl. WILLIAM GARLEB, Company H, 31st Infantry:

Jesus, they strafed all day long. At night, all night, they pounded us with artillery.

Cpl. WAYNE LEWIS, Company D, 31st Infantry:

They once sent up an artillery officer to act as a spotter. When things would get quiet he'd raise up out of his foxhole and look around. I told him to keep his damn head down. Eventually, a sniper got him. The bullet hitting him sounded like a wet piece of bread slapping a wall. He put his hand up over his face and

I saw the blood running down over his thumbs. He sat down, cross legged, and kept saying, "Oh, Mother," until he died.

1st Lt. MARK HERBST, M.D., 3d Battalion,
57th Infantry, Philippine Scouts:

I think the most tragic thing I saw on Bataan was the day they brought in two fellows with exactly the same wound. Everyone was wearing these old World War I doughboy helmets. These two boys each had taken the same 25-mm hardnose Japanese rifle bullet in the same place on the helmet, in front where the brim met the crown. One was a Filipino. His bullet had gone through the helmet and then rolled around the inside and went out the back. He didn't have a scratch. Scared the hell out of him, of course. The other boy, an American, had the bullet hit his helmet the exact same place, but he had a hole as big as a quarter through his skull. Same kind of bullet, hitting the same place. One man walked away, the other we buried.

Pfc. WILBURN SNYDER, 3d Battalion Medics,
31st Infantry:

The sugar cane at the Abucay Hacienda was tall enough to gather. It was also tall enough to hide the Japs who used to infiltrate our lines. So one of our officers, a major, decides to burn down the cane fields and he gets himself some gasoline and starts to burn them down. Now this major was a good officer, he doesn't say, "Private, you go out there and set the cane field." Instead, he does it himself. He always wore two .38s. Well, he spreads this gasoline all throughout the cane field so he can really get it burning. Whether he banged two cans together causing a spark, or what, I don't know, but while he's in the cane field it starts on fire. Huge conflagration. We all knew he was in there, but no one could go in to get him. The fire was so hot. Then, all of a sudden, he steps out of the flame and all he's wearing are those two .38s. He done had all his clothes burnt off. Man, we ran up to him and said, "Major, we've got to get you back to the hospital." "Hospital?" he said. "All I need is some new clothes."

Cpl. WAYNE LEWIS, Company D, 31st Infantry:

We used to get rations off dead Japs. They always carried a little bag of what looked like oyster crackers which were mixed with teeny balls of white sugar. We also found sticks on them that looked like resin. We found out later it was solidified fish soup. We'd break a hunk of that off and throw it in a canteen cup of water.

One time I ate some raw turnips I dug up. I got dysentery so damn bad that they had to carry me off the front line. No one would get in a gun position with me. They'd just throw me the ammunition. I was crapping all over the place. Finally, they sent me back to the hospital. They filled me with paregoric and sent me right back.

Cpl. WILLIAM GARLEB, Company H, 31st Infantry:

I know I had pains in my stomach all the time. After the first couple of days your stomach shrinks and it's not as much a problem as it is at first. Of course, with stomach pains you're never sure if it's really hunger or fear. Particularly when you're in and out of heavy hand-to-hand combat, being hungry is really not the point. First off, the stench of rotting bodies is so awful that it kills any hunger pains.

Pvt. LEON BECK, Antitank Company, 31st Infantry:

The hunger began for me on the Abucay Hacienda Line. They'd send us one can of rations which had to be divided between four men. If you were lucky you got a can of salmon. If you were unlucky you'd get a can of tomatoes. A solid packed can of salmon had some substance. But after you shared a can of peeled tomatoes four ways, there wasn't much left. The cans varied. You might get anything—a can of peaches, for example. They tried to get these cans to you twice a day; sometimes they didn't make it. If you were lucky, you got issued mule meat or a ration of horse. We were hungry all the time and worried about being hungry. We were physically and mentally sick as well. I was nineteen years old when the war started and combat's a hell of a load to put on a hungry nineteen-year-old.

If they had taken everyone who had malaria out of the lines there wouldn't have been anyone left to hold the Japs. We didn't have preventative medicine for malaria in those days. If you got anything for malaria it was liquid quinine taken out of a shot glass.

When you were so far down physically that you could no longer function is when they put you in the hospital. As soon as you got back on your feet you went back to your unit.

War Department communiqué, January 23:

The Japanese are continuing to launch heavy attacks on General Mac-Arthur's positions. During the past twenty-four hours the fighting has been extremely heavy. Apparently the enemy has adopted a policy of continuous assaults, without regard to casualties, hoping by great superiority in numbers to crush the defending forces.*

Cpl. WILLIAM GARLEB, Company H, 31st Infantry:

Down the road a little from the front lines and across a little trail was the first-aid station. I had been laying on a stretcher for several days with amebic dysentery and a fever of 106. Then one evening somebody stuck their head in the tent and said there was increasing activity at the front and that they expected to take a lot of casualties. All around me you could hear the various companies of the 31st moving out. Mess kits were rattling and men began to move forward. All around me in the aid station, men who were totally physically unfit, men who hadn't had enough food for weeks, men who simply could not fight again, began to go towards the front. I promise you, these men could not walk, let alone fight. But they went.

Pfc. WILBURN SNYDER, 3d Battalion Medics,
31st Infantry:

I can remember the day Abucay fell. I don't remember the date, but I can remember what happened. They shelled and shelled us. I was a litter bearer that day and I had just gotten back to the aid station late in the afternoon, when we were told that the line broke and we were ordered to pull back. Of course, by that time the line was right back with us. We got some infantrymen to help us and we began carrying all the wounded we had back to the next line. As we pulled back our artillery covered us. The Japs were so close that our own artillery was dropping near enough to jar us. About the time it got dark, one of our tank outfits came from nowhere and set a roadblock just after we went through. They gave us the breathing room to get everyone back to Orion. The tanks rolled in later and them old boys came back shouting, "Man, we had a field day! We ate them up!" We spent the next few days digging into a new defensive line.†

2d Lt. LEONA GASTINGER, Army Nurse Corps,
Hospital No. 2:

When the front line broke they moved Hospital No. 1 further back down the road to Little Baguio. Before we pulled out, we

---

* On Jan. 22 heavy Japanese artillery and air attacks drove the weary American and Philippine Forces back to the line they had held at the beginning of the counteroffensive.
† On Jan. 22 General MacArthur ordered the withdrawal of the entire

gave baby Bridgette to the local Red Cross. I never saw her again.

I didn't make the move with No. 1 because I was reassigned to Hospital No. 2. The first thing I realized on coming into Hospital No. 2 was that it was out in the jungle. Once a fellow came down looking for somebody and he said, "Gosh, I thought I'd never find you." He told me that this was one of the remotest places on Bataan. I said, "Well, trust our medics to find it!" If you went off into the wildest part of the jungle and brought along a bunch of bunk beds and set them up by a little stream and supplied yourself with a few pills, you'd have an idea of what Hospital No. 2 was like.

They'd dug foxholes for us and cleared the area by cutting down the underbrush. I was assigned to Ward No. 10, which had 150 beds in it—that is, beds lined up under the trees. We took our area and divided it up so we could get in the maximum number of beds. Had to make use of the topography, you know, where the hills were, where the trees were, and where the rocks were. The hospital took a lot of room and it was connected by paths, not streets. I used to get lost in the area. Once, when I was returning from the OR [operating room] to my ward, someone told me about a shortcut which, instead of taking me along the straightest path, would take me across the creek, up a hill, then down a trail which would lead me directly to my ward. Half an hour later I ended up in the Bachelor Officers' Quarters.

When we first moved in, all we had was a shelter half, you know—a little piece of canvas, which we stretched over our mosquito net bars to protect us from the elements. Several weeks later they began to worry about what would happen to us in the monsoon season. So they brought in some old Manila buses that had been used in the evacuation. They tore out the seating and gave them to us to use as quarters. These buses are not made like ours. You could board them from the sides, so the seating went sideways. They reminded me of San Francisco cable cars, only larger. We put one GI bunk across the rear, then another along one side, and the third bunk was near the steering wheel over the gas tank. When they drove in and parked them, they still had gas in the tanks. This caused a lot of humor. We used to kid about having our own bus to leave in as soon as the war ended. Wouldn't that have been nice. The buses were not perfect, but they sure were more permanent and a little bit more secure than a mosquito net between us and the elements.

Mauban-Abucay Line southward. By morning of the 26th, both I and II Corps were behind the new defensive line which, roughly paralleling the Pilar-Bagac road, extended from Orion westward to Bagac.

It used to be awful before they gave us the buses. We had rats and snakes and other things that crawled all over the place. I was scared to death. They'd crawl over your feet. We never saw them in the daytime, but we surely saw them at night. I remember one time I was sitting on my bed writing a letter to my mother, when I heard this rattling and scrambling underneath me. I looked down and there was the biggest lizard I'd ever seen in my life. This one had come up into my territory. "Now, look," I thought, "how am I going to get rid of you?" I figured I'd see who would frighten the other the worst. If I squealed loud enough, I'd frighten him enough so he'd run. Otherwise I was going to have to get up and chase him. So I just let out a scream. He took off for the river bank and I never saw him after that.

2d Lt. HATTIE BRANTLEY, Army Nurse Corps, Hospital No. 1:

Little Baguio, where we relocated Hospital No. 1, was an old motor-pool site of a few frame buildings and a huge shed with a corrugated roof covering a concrete floor. It was built in three levels and each level was an ideal place and size for a ward. Again, beds were set up and we continued to run Hospital No. 1 —or vice versa, it ran us. Frances Nash had surgery working before anybody took a deep breath.

Ambulances came off the road to a tent where the wounded were sorted. The patients were checked and directed as needed —on to surgery, the gas gangrene ward, medical wards, or on to Hospital No. 2.

We also had a Japanese prisoner ward and although the census was never high, they were given care and treatment as human beings in need.

One of our first acts after moving Hospital No. 1 was to use a number of white sheets, which we couldn't spare as there was always a shortage, and fasten them with wooden stakes out on the hillside in the form of a huge white cross. This was to plainly mark our site as a hospital and noncombatant facility.

2d Lt. JOHN POSTEN, Fighter Pilot, 17th Pursuit Squadron:

Once, six of us took off on a night mission. Because of the rough and narrow field we used, Ibold ground-looped on the takeoff and hit a rock with his right wing, which set his bombs off. It blew the hell out of his ship, but he survived.

I went down to Hospital No. 2 to see him, and it almost made me sick to see how the other patients were shot up. Some had arms or legs missing, others were blind, and still others were shellshocked. One fellow had only half a face. The beds were right out in the open with not even a tent covering them. There were also quite a few civilians there. The bombings used to get more natives than soldiers, because the natives didn't know enough to lay down. On the way back to the field I passed a cemetery with 100 new white crosses all lined up in even rows.

Tech. Sgt. WILLIAM "COWBOY" WRIGHT,
17th Pursuit Squadron:

We were moved from Pilar Field, which is on the east coast, way over to Kilometer Post No. 205, on the west coast. From here we moved into position along the shore of "Bobo" [Caibobo] Point. We didn't have too much action in this area. We were well dug in and had the bay fairly well covered with .50s. We had cleaned the area of underbrush, hoping that snipers wouldn't sneak in on us. One night I was guarding a path, with Sergeants Morgan and Sauer looking after an open area near me. About two in the morning they came over to me, white as sheets. Morgan told me, "We were watching a stump in the moonlight when we noticed it was turning." I decided it must have been a python. Morgan and Sauer turned their post over to the snake and spent the rest of the night with me.

One night we got word that Jap barges had been sighted moving towards shore in our area. Later, three barges loaded with Japs moved in just north of the point. The .50s opened up on them. When the barges turned away we threw enough lead to sink one of them. The men on the guns that were doing all the damage said the barrels of their machine guns got cherry red while they were firing.

The Japs did, however, succeed in getting about 1,500 troops ashore south of us. We went down there the next day and joined up with some more Air Force guys.*

Cpl. FRED GIFFORD, 21st Pursuit Squadron:

Now, instead of being in the Air Force, which I loved, I was marching in the infantry, which I hated. They told us that about twenty-five Japanese had landed behind our lines over on the west coast and they wanted some of us to go over there and

* The first of several Japanese amphibious forces landed Jan. 23 at two points along Bataan's rugged southwest coast. The Battle of the Points, as these engagements were collectively known, raged for the next three weeks.

clear them out. So they took the fellows from the 21st and 34th Pursuit Squadrons and we went over to clean them Japs out. We got over there and found that a whole division of Japanese troops had come in behind our lines.* So we got stuck!

War Department communiqué, January 25:

A heavy enemy attack was made on the left flank of General Mac-Arthur's troops in the Bataan Peninsula. . . . Among the hostile troops participating in the assault were many who landed at night . . . on the west coast of the peninsula. There were heavy enemy infiltrations along the beaches and in the mountains. Defending troops were forced to give ground with considerable losses.

2d-Class Carpenter's Mate STANLEY SOMMERS,
Naval Battalion:

On January 23 we received orders to go to Longoskawayan Point, which is just around the bend from Mariveles, and where there were reported some Japanese snipers. Later we learned there were a lot more than snipers. So down the jungle trail we went, walking along in our coffee-colored uniforms, when all of a sudden we ran into a strongly defended and entrenched Jap position. Right away our guys started coming back with their legs shot away. Then, suddenly, we had Japs firing in back of us. We didn't know where in hell they were, but they had us pinned down. We couldn't get at them. I was scared to death because I couldn't see anybody to shoot at. I heard them, though. At first the guys were trigger-happy, just shooting into the bush. They didn't hit anybody. We spent the night pinned down. The next day, they called in the Philippine Scouts to help us out.

Capt. JOHN SPAINHOWER, 57th Infantry
Philippine Scouts:

The Nips made a landing at Longoskawayan Point and a lot of Navy cooks and bakers and some pick-up Air Force people were holding them off. They sent my battalion in to help them out. We got some artillery support and then the minesweeper *Quail* came in and was able to fire point-blank into the Japanese positions. We left around 300 dead Japs. The one prisoner we took died later. As soon as we had finished there, we were ordered further up the west coast where the Japanese had made several more major landings.

* It was actually two battalions of infantry.

War Department communiqué, January 27:

Picked Japanese groups executed simultaneous attacks at several points along the west coast line of Bataan. There was savage fighting in the underbrush.

Sgt. RALPH LEVENBERG, 17th Pursuit Squadron:

All of a sudden one morning we were all lined up and our first sergeant says, "O.K., we've got a mission to perform. We're going to join up with other units in the jungle over on 'Quinine' [Quinauan] Point, because they found fifteen or twenty what they think are infiltrators and snipers. It will take us till five o'clock tonight and then we'll be back. The cooks will keep our chow hot for us." Twenty-one days later we got back.

I think as Americans we were lulled into the fact that nothing could ever happen to us. I mean we really believed we were going to go into the jungle and wipe those Japs out. We stretched out, eighty or ninety men, an arm's length apart, where possible, and we walked through the jungle. We didn't crawl; we walked. We didn't sneak; we made all kinds of noise. We walked through a valley leading to the beach as if we were on a picnic.

When we got to the beach everything was quiet. Not a thing around. To break the tedium of just waiting around, one of the men put his rifle in the crook of a tree and fired at an imaginary target far out of his range. As quick as that shot, the hills came alive and the Japs opened up on us with everything they had—and that was a lot! They had sat there and watched us for a while.

I dug a foxhole with my hand and I ate sand for three hours. It was frantic at first. Then it got scary. I mean I was frightened. Our CO was a major, an Air Force administrator who didn't have the first idea of what to do. We stayed pinned down for hours and nobody came to help us. Fortunately, we had a couple of prior servicemen in our outfit who had been in the infantry. One of them was Paddy Clawson, the sergeant who had given me my first ham on Christmas, and he began telling the major what to do. In fact, he took over. The major followed his instructions and, thanks to these ex-infantrymen, we managed to escape from the trap by working our way to a ravine. We spent that first night huddled quietly in the jungle. We were in shock.

Sgt. FERRON CUMMINS, 34th Pursuit Squadron:

The first night in the command post I was assigned to a telephone. We had a Jap sniper nearby. Every time my telephone rang, he'd start shooting in the direction of the sound. This went on all night. At first I tried to keep them from calling in. Then I tried to smother the bells by holding onto them. Finally, every time they rang and the Jap would shoot, I'd move to a new location. All night the phone would ring, the Jap would shoot, and I'd move. This went on every fifteen minutes.

The next morning, as soon as it became daylight, we got the sniper. It was like hunting a rabbit, except we were looking in the trees.

Cpl. FRED GIFFORD, 21st Pursuit Squadron:

There was the time that the Japanese tried to land reinforcements from a barge. We pulled up one of these old cannons—looked old enough to have been in the Civil War—and we shot up that barge full of Japanese. They all jumped out and started to swim back out into the China Sea. It was target practice for us. We sure did like to use our rifles this way. I don't think there was one of them Japanese got away. Without reinforcements we pushed the Japs back to the cliff.

We was trying to eradicate them but none would surrender, not even after we forced them over the cliff. They found caves to hide in and they wouldn't surrender. We even tried to dynamite them out. We'd put about twenty-five sticks of dynamite with a detonator on a rope and then let it down the cliff face till it reached a cave and then tried to swing it into the Japs. We still couldn't get them. So our squadron commander—he was a man that loved to fight—decided to go down there and see just how strong them Japanese were. They came around asking for volunteers and I thought, "Well, better than to stay in this stinking jungle," so I volunteered. They sent us volunteers back to the command post where they passed around cigarettes, which we hadn't had for a long while. We lounged around in the shade until all the volunteers had been collected. There were twelve Air Force men and two officers. "All right, men," we were told, "board the truck. We're all going down to Mariveles." That's where we had built a new airstrip to receive all them planes what they'd promised us from the United States that we never got. While our CO was in the radio shack trying to get our orders, we parked in the shade of a mango tree and smoked our captain's cigarettes. He came back a half an hour later and told us we were going down to the naval base, which was also at Mariveles. Them sailor boys down there just welcomed us like long lost brothers. I couldn't figure out what the score was because one fellow said to me when we got to the billeting area, "Here, take my bed. I've got an innerspring mattress." I hadn't slept on a bed since the war started. He practically forced it on me. I didn't know then that the Japanese had slipped troops into the area and they used to come in and raid during the night. That night I slept on that innerspring mattress and slept right through a small raid. I never got touched and I never woke up.

When our CO got us up it was still dark. He said, "Now, fellows, I'm going to give you all a chance to back out of this thing honorably, or you can go along with me. You should know there's a thousand-to-one chance you'll never make it back." We all stood there like a bunch of mummies. We was pretty much under discipline during the days of the old Army, and we didn't talk in rank while we was being talked to. "Well," he said, "I'm glad you decided to follow me in. I never did like to lead people who would start to follow me and then back out."

After the captain got done speaking, this one boy that was aside of me said, "Boy, I wish somebody would have stepped out. I don't want to go in there." I said, "Why didn't you step out then?" He answered, "I wasn't going to be the only one to step out and leave the rest of the men to go in."

Shortly after that, twelve sailors and two Navy officers joined us. They operated what they called armored launches.* What they actually had was a whaleboat with a quarter-inch piece of steel wrapped around the front of it. While we were sailing over, before we went in and landed with them Japs up in the caves, our squadron commander gave us a little talk. "Now, fellows, it's against the rules of convention to plunder these Japs. But anything you get I won't see none of." This stimulated our urge to get in there because, boy, there was a great demand for battle flags and swords and those Lugers the Japanese had, which they must have gotten from the Germans. You could really sell souvenirs for a lot of money or trade them for food, which was the big deal.

As we were about to land, the Japanese sent a dive bomber strike against us. "Head this boat in for shore," the sergeant said, "I'll take them Japs any day before I'll take them bombers." When we got on shore the Japanese raked us over, killed more of their own than they did of us. We lost some men out of the Navy, but they stayed with them boats.

We had been given little submachine guns which had a sling that went over your shoulder. We also had an asbestos glove for the left hand, which we needed when we operated the gun. We'd thrown away our gas masks and had taken extra ammunition and put it in the empty pouch.

* These three boats were the forty-foot motor launches off the submarine tender USS Canopus.

We completely eradicated them Japs. Our commanding officer told us, "If anybody wants to surrender, you know what to do with them. You just have to make up your own mind. You can't take them back with you and you can't leave them here. You know what to do with them." So that's the way we did them when we went in.

Pfc. ROBERT BROWN, 17th Pursuit Squadron:

The Japs kept making landings at different points along the west coast. I had been transferred to the 17th Pursuit's sector of the coast, which was between Anyasan and Silaiim Points and a little north of where the other points battles were going on. Soon as I got there the Japs made their landing in our area [the night of January 27]. The morning after the landing we felt we were going to wipe them out on the beach and be back for supper. Well, we were there three weeks.

We started down off the ridge towards the beach and we're coming down through the jungle and here, all of a sudden, we come on a deserted Filipino Constabulary camp. Here's these tents all set up and not a soul anywhere. They'd left everything. I changed clothes right there. We'd been sleeping on the ground and we couldn't get a bath or anything, so if you could find something that fit, you just changed clothes. Hell, they had shirts, pants, and everything. I put on a pair of pants that had blue stripes down the sides of them. And there was a monkey they'd left tied between two trees. The poor old guy hadn't any water or anything else, so we cut him loose.

The Constabulary had taken off when the Japanese landed. I'm telling you, these people, you could be with them and the next thing you'd be all by yourself. They just didn't hang around when there was any danger.

As soon as we had changed clothes, we started going down the ridge towards the beach and the Japs. We were disorganized. We were not an infantry unit in the first place and we were split up, because of the jungle, into three units—the left, the right, and the middle.

"Bring up the left flank."

"Hell with you, bud, bring up the right flank."

We hadn't gotten far when we started picking up some sniper fire. By then we had lost contact, believe it or not, with both our flanks. Suddenly, some Filipinos came up the trail and our CO, Captain [Raymond] Sloan, stopped them.

"Where are you going, Joe?"

"Our companions are all wounded . . ."

See, most of the Filipino soldiers would drop their guns

and grab their mess kits and take off. Not the Scouts, but the Regular Army.

Sloan says, "If you got friends wounded down there, go back and get them."

I went down the trail maybe 100 yards when we picked up some heavy sniper fire. The Filipinos dove to the right side of the trail and I went to the left. They ended up behind a tree with big sweeping roots. I found myself lying behind a tree the size of a toothpick. I wasn't hidden at all. I found this all very, very spooky because fighting in the jungle you can't see anything. I began looking through the trees, trying to pick up where the sniper fire was coming from. You could hear the *pop* of the rifle, but it was hard to distinguish where it came from. I heard two more rounds. *Pop! Pop!* I asked, "Joe, you O.K.?"

"No."

When I look, one of the Filipinos has taken it right through the head, and his friend is taking his .45. That's always the first thing they did.

I thought, "My God, what's going on here?" I'm the only American and I'm getting scared. Pretty soon I heard somebody down to the left of me speaking English. I shouted to them and we began talking back and forth. There were six or seven other people from the 17th Pursuit pinned down just like me. I finally crawled through the jungle and got to them. We then tried to throw some hand grenades into the jungle, but this proved ineffective. Our grenades were all 1918 jobbers and if two out of ten went off, we'd be lucky.

Since it was getting late, we decided we'd make a run for it. We had lost contact with everybody, but we felt if we ran down the trail we'd run into our left flank. They had to be down there somewhere. So we picked up one at a time and ran like hell. Then we'd dive into the jungle. Then we'd pick up and go again. Finally, after going like this for a while, we ran into a larger group from our squadron. We decided to take off and continue down to the beach. We went single file and just before we reached the beach, the Japanese opened up from both sides with machine guns. This is a big thrill! So here we are, pinned down again, but now it's getting dark and to retreat we have to climb up the ridge we just came down. Well, when you're scared you get a lot of strength, and we just climbed up that ridge like we were on motorcycles.

We got back on top and joined some more of our unit at five minutes to eight. The reason I remember the time is that a sniper above our command post shot a Filipino. The bullet went across his watch, through the head of his penis, and lodged in his leg. The bullet stopped his watch at 7:55. One of our boys who later died a horrible death—dysentery at O'Donnell—fired a .30-caliber air-cooled machine gun from the hip and knocked the Jap right out of the tree.

A jeep came down shortly afterwards with our meal that day, if you want to call it a meal. We had half a peanut butter sandwich and half a cup of coffee.

War Department communiqué, February 3:

Two Japanese attempts to land troops on the west coast of Bataan were broken up during the night of Feb. 2. A serious attempt was made at midnight. A large number of barges under naval escort approached the coast. The raid was discovered by a few of our night flying pursuit planes.

2d Lt. JOHN POSTEN, Fighter Pilot, 17th Pursuit Squadron:

We had just gotten to bed when we were awakened and told again to hit another landing party of thirteen boats and 1,000 men over on the west coast around Anyasan Bay. We really gave them hell. We went over in ones and twos. As soon as one flight finished, we would load it with ammunition and bombs and send it over again. We kept that up till about 3:00 in the morning. Some four planes were shot up, but we all got back O.K. Between us and the beach forces we got nine of the thirteen and badly damaged a couple more, so they landed less than 500 men. The ground forces mopped up the mess we left.

War Department communiqué, February 4:

Our troops continue to mop up tattered remnants of the Japanese who had previously landed on the west coast or who had infiltrated behind our lines.

Sgt. FORREST KNOX, Company A, 192d Tank Battalion:

Each day the tanks went into the pocket spread out on a single front. Most of the time we were hub to hub, maybe ten feet or less between vehicles. The combined fire of all machine guns and cannons was fierce. The brush lay right down and would straighten back up as the fire slackened. We gradually cut down all the trees and brush about the size of a football field. Some of the machine-gun barrels I replaced had the rifling wore right out of them. They would be smooth at the breech. There was always some rifling left at the muzzle. We were burning eight to ten thousand rounds a day in our tanks. Supply officers screamed like mad. We were way over our allotment. The crews fighting just couldn't believe anyone would deny them ammo when they were in action.

Each night the Japs pushed back and each day we recovered the same ground. Our infantry, which were Scouts [45th], would follow right behind the tanks, but those Japs never quit coming back to the killing ground.

Pfc. ROBERT BROWN, 17th Pursuit Squadron:

The Japanese were well dug in. We got word once that Corregidor was going to fire across to see what they could do with their big 12-inch mortars. We could fire shells all day and never hit anybody because our shells would either explode in the trees or not reach the Japs who were dug ten to fourteen feet into the ground. Corregidor fired at least thirty-five rounds across. We'd sit there and count them. They sounded like boxcars going through the air because these babies were big hunks of iron.

But we still couldn't really get at them. They just had a lot of running room. The Japs kept trying to reinforce them, too. Once they sent in a little put-put with more men and supplies. They made a mistake because around dawn is when this put-put tried to come in. One of our 155s up on the point fired a round over, a round under, and then blew her right out of the water.

As time progressed and we began to get a better hold of this situation, thanks mainly to the arrival of units from the 45th and 57th Philippine Scouts, the Japanese began sending airplanes over to drop food to their surrounded troops. Their planes would come in over the tree tops and drop their stuff. We got more of it than the Japs. We wanted food, too.

One day we had just put a machine gun back on the trail below the West Road when, by God, if it doesn't begin firing. A few minutes later they brought down a Jap prisoner. This was our first contact with a live Jap. He was shot through the nose when a bullet went across and cut his cheek. His leg was also banged up. We took several photographs of him and then sent him back with a Filipino Scout to a POW compound we had established. But hell, they'd been gone only an hour when the Scout came back alone.

"Hey, Joe, what happened?"

"He tried to escape. I had to shoot him."

That was the end of that ball game. I don't think too many Jap prisoners made it back to the compound.

Finally the Philippine Scout units who were in with us circled the Japs, pursuing them down on the beach. A Japanese plane came through and began laying smoke. When he did that the Japs came charging out, and if it hadn't been for the Scouts we'd probably have been wiped out. We lost our commanding officer, Raymond Sloan. He got three bullets through the belly. What a shame, these high-paid Air Force pilots down there fighting as infantry.

The Scouts set up another line and caught the Japs in a cross-fire in a gulley and we had dead Japs everywhere. When we mopped up we had Japanese swimming out there in the water for five days. Master Sergeant King saw one out on a reef and he went out to try to talk him in. He kept saying to him, "Come on in, son. Come on in. You're O.K. Come on in." King got within twenty yards of him, but the Jap never did come in. He'd rather drown than let himself be captured. That's how fanatical they were. I mean, he wouldn't be captured!

Sgt. H. G. TYSON, 3d Pursuit Squadron:

We actually didn't get in on any of the real fighting other than some of the spillover as the Japs were trying to get away. One day I was on patrol duty guarding a cliff trail above the beach. Seven Japs came down the trail and right into the sights of my machine gun. But I had a hand grenade and since they were all bunched up, I decided the easiest way to get rid of them was with the grenade. I pulled the pin and threw it. When it went off it sounded like a firecracker. Of course the Japs scattered like a covey of quail. Six got away in the jungle. The only one I got was the one who jumped off the trail and broke his leg when he landed on the beach. After that I had no faith in hand grenades at all. Threw all I had away. The whole incident I found rather disappointing.

War Department communiqué, February 5:

With reference to the fighting on the west coast, General MacArthur said: "All enemy thrusts on the west coast have now been completely mastered. The enemy troops employed in this desperate venture were his best. They have been entirely destroyed."*

Pfc. ROBERT BROWN, 17th Pursuit Squadron:

In a matter of a day or two all the dead Japs were swollen up three times the size of your body. There were all kinds of dead smells. We didn't bury them because there were too many. After we pulled out for a rest I heard rumors that they brought a bulldozer in and covered them up. I never saw it, though, and I didn't really give a damn.

---

* It wasn't until Feb. 13 that the last of the Japanese amphibious forces were destroyed. Two days later the Malayan campaign ended with the surrender of Singapore.

2d Lt. FRED GIFFORD, Philippine Army:

When we finished up with that "Battle of the Points" deal we
went back up topside. We were told that they were in very
bad need of men up on the front line. They told me that the
Philippine Army was open and that there was a second lieutenant's commission for anybody who volunteered. So I said,
"I'll take it!" I took it for a couple of reasons. First, I wasn't
family with any of the outfits over there. I figured, too, that
going with the Filipinos I would have a better chance of survival because they knew all the holes and crevices there was
to crawl into when the crawling-in time came. The trouble of it
was that on the front the Japs pinned us down so bad with
shelling and all the aircraft they threw at us, we never had a
chance to get away.

When I arrived on the line it didn't take long to figure out
why they needed officers in the Philippine lines. The fact was
that the officers were being killed as fast as they were replaced. The Japs zeroed in on the officers. It was just like anything else. If you can get the leader to stop, you don't have
no troubles stopping anybody else. We also weren't in too good
of a condition. We were poorly equipped with fighting tools
and the rations were terrible. I remember some days we would
get rations that was supposed to be served to horses, because
it was raw rice with the husk still on it. We took it and boiled
it, then flavored it with a little bit of soybeans and some kind
of canned fish. Sometimes we'd get one bowl of that in a day,
sometimes we wouldn't. When a hunting party would catch a
wild boar, or we'd get a part of a cavalry mule, we could make
a sandwich of that.

We used ammunition, hand grenades, and rifles which was
issued during World War I. Much of the time we were almost
within spitting distance of the Japanese. Then we used our
hand grenades. We'd play ball with them. They wouldn't detonate. You'd throw it to the Japs and the Japs would throw it
back. So we got smart. When we pulled the pin we'd bang that
grenade on our heel until we could hear that little pin snap.
When we heard that we knew to get rid of it, because it was
going to blow up. We learned the hard way.

About a third of the time, we was in hand-to-hand combat. Now them Japanese should not be underestimated, because
they were good soldiers. I would never hesitate to have an
army as good as they were. My young troops were not well
trained, but the Constabulary was. Some of these men were
old enough to have served in the Spanish Army. They must

have had fifty years of experience. These old men were strewn among the recruits to give the young Filipinos more courage. The thing about the Filipino Army is just about like all the other armies. You have to get up front and holler, "Come on!" You can't get behind and holler, "Go on!" If you did they'd turn around and come back at you. Make one mistake that way and you'd end up being a victim of circumstances.

The first night I went up to the line, my raw troops deserted me. After spending one whole day getting out from behind the Japanese lines, I went back to the command post. I went in and told my CO that I was not going to fight two armies at one time. I just wasn't going to fight both the Japanese and the Filipinos. It was out of the question. He politely put his hand on my shoulder and said, "You should have learned a good lesson from this. Now get the hell up there and use it!" So I started back, wondering what he meant about learning a good lesson. By the time I got there I had it all figured out. I ordered my men to dig in right before dusk, because when it gets dark in the jungle it gets dark quick. What I figured out was that I was supposed to control the men, and for the men not to control me. So, I got on the machine gun and after everyone had dug his hole I said in a voice loud enough for all to hear: "Now, everyone get in your holes and stay there unless you come out to take care of the Japanese. If the enemy does not come across but I hear a twig snap, or if a man takes a step, I intend to stop him with a machine gun. You fellows better stay put." One of them spoke up, "When do you sleep?" I said, "I forget about sleep because I have a job to do and sleeping is not a part of it." From that point on I never lost another man from deserting at night.

War Department communiqué, February 15:

Fighting in Bataan was limited to local unimportant patrol skirmishes. Forces of the enemy are evidently being regrouped for a resumption of the offensive. Japanese units on the front lines . . . are being relieved by fresh troops.

War Department communiqué, February 26:

Fighting has lessened in Bataan, with operations limited to relatively minor patrol skirmishes. The Japanese are still holding their main battle positions. A period of positional warfare seems indicated.*

---

* Unable to crack the new Bagac-Orion defensive line, General Homma ordered a general withdrawal of his battered forces northward. There the Japanese rested and reorganized and awaited reinforcements.

2d Lt. LEONA GASTINGER, Army Nurse Corps,
Hospital No. 2:

We had friends who would just disappear and we would wonder what had happened to them. Then all of a sudden somebody would drop by and tell us about someone and we'd be
terribly surprised. There was a young pilot who I'd met one
time in Manila. One day I was in my ward when a soldier came
up to me. "Are you Lieutenant Gastinger? Well, Sam told me
the next time I saw you to say hello and to tell you he went
to Australia." That's the kind of message you'd get.

One boy I knew in Fort Benning before I was sent to the
Philippines; I don't think I'd had three dates with him. He was
a sweet person and always just proper, never smart alecky. I
never knew how much he liked me until I saw him again in
Manila just before the war broke out. I said to him, "You never
said you cared for me back at Benning. We were just friends
running around in a crowd." He said, "Yes, but you were dat-
ing somebody else." "Well," I replied, "you were too." I only
saw him twice again before we went to Bataan. Then one day a
friend of his came by and told me he had gone down to Iloilo
and how I could get in touch with him if I needed anything.
Once I received a radiogram from him, but then that was the
last I heard of him. I have never been able to find anybody
who remembers where or how he died.

2d Lt. HATTIE BRANTLEY, Army Nurse Corps,
Hospital No. 1:

All the battle casualties came to us in Hospital No. 1. We did
all the surgery and took care of the wounded for the first recovery period. Then as soon as they were able to travel—and
many before they were able—they were sent to No. 2, which
was being used partly as the convalescent hospital. We had to
find beds for the new casualties which were arriving all the
time. The worst thing for me was each morning when the doctors and I had to go down the line deciding which patients
would be taken out. Some of the guys we sent back had been
hit only two or three days before. But we needed the beds.

I was head nurse in a couple of wards and took care of
the post-op surgical patients. We worked from daylight until
we could no longer see. It was just a day-to-day grind. Of
course, when there was a huge influx of casualties, surgery
would work around the clock.

When we began to run out of things our commanding
officer, Colonel Duckworth, asked me to make out a list of items
that we were short of and which we urgently needed. My ward

officer and I ordered lots of line, which we used for traction. When it got to the CO he scratched that off the list and told us to use jungle vines instead.

Our patients were also on half ration. We were, however, able to give them something at noon, like soup or a cup of hot tea. They had a little something to break the monotony and to give them a little more nourishment.

1st Sgt. HOUSTON TURNER, Company B, 31st Infantry:

I was in the hospital a couple of weeks with malaria. I nearly starved to death there. They didn't feed you any food to speak of. We had wounded and sick in the company that refused to go back to the hospital facilities. In the company maybe you had a friend who was taking care of you. You were always better off with a buddy, because at least that way someone would take care of you. That way you had a better chance.

Well, I went because my malaria was so bad. They just put me on a bed in the open. I was so damn sick I didn't know one end from the other. They told me I was going to have to dig a foxhole next to my bed. I said, "The hell with it. I can't." I was too sick.

The most interesting thing that happened was I got to see a couple of fights between the stray dogs that were roaming around also looking for food.

Hell, I was fed there once with canned tomatoes and shredded coconut! Especially with a fever, you know that's not going to help you. Fortunately, I ran into a fellow there that I'd been in the service with before the war, and he told me to eat with him. He had managed to steal some food. I did. He didn't have a lot either. So I could see my best bet was to get out of there and get back to my company, 'cause there I had friends who were scavenging all the time.

I went up to the nurse and told her I wanted to leave. She asked me whether I thought I was well enough to leave. "Sure . . ." I said. "Give me back my weapon and I'll be on my way." She told me she didn't know where my rifle was. They'd lost it. So I said, "Well, I'll go back without it then." And so I did. I went out and caught a truck going back to where my company was and that was that. Food wasn't much better, but I was amongst friends.

Pvt. LEON BECK, Antitank Company, 31st Infantry:

The first few days on Bataan, of course, we talked about booze and women. Later, it turned to food. Still later, not only did you talk about food, you dreamed about food, you fantasized about food. In February, food became an obsession.

Sgt. H. G. TYSON, 3d Pursuit Squadron:

Our rations had gotten so low that we were on a starvation diet. Finally, our commander put out the word for us not to do anything that we didn't have to do. That way we saved our strength and energy. So we spent days just lying around the western beaches of Bataan. For a while, too, we went fishing with dynamite. We'd put rocks and nails and other scrap metal into a little old milk can, put a fuse and a blasting cap on it, and begin fishing. We'd drop this homemade grenade off the cliff and when it would detonate in the water, the dead fish would float to the surface. Then we'd swim out and collect them. Did this for a few days. Then the blood from the fish attracted sharks. When they started coming in, we quit fishing.

Cpl. WAYNE LEWIS, Company D, 31st Infantry:

When we got it, we ate rice. Earlier, as long as they lasted, we ate off the pack mules and the horses out of the 26th Cavalry. After that we killed and ate snakes, cats, monkeys, and anything else that had meat on it. The horse meat, I thought, was very good. I remember the first time I ate carabao, it tasted just like the mud it used to wallow in.

Pvt. LEWIS ELLIOTT, 2d Battalion, 60th Coast Artillery:

The 26th Cavalry corral was right up the road. We always said we ate the 26th Cavalry right out of the saddle. And we did. Horse meat is surprisingly good. It's a little coarser than beef. Once I came back off the front line and on the trail ran across three guys with a pot on the stove. I lifted the pot lid to see what they had and I saw a little old bleached hand that looked exactly like a baby's. It was a monkey. "Come on," they said, "stay for dinner." I seen that little hand. "No thanks, I'll see you later."

Seaman 1st Class AUSTIN ANDREWS, USS *Oahu:*

We had Filipinos swimming out to us on the *Oahu,* trying to trade their rifles for food. We'd give them what we could and send them back, because they needed their guns more than we did.

2d Lt. LEONA GASTINGER, Army Nurse Corps, Hospital No. 2:

Between my two roommates and myself we had friends who would sometimes bring us a jar of peanut butter or a jar of jelly. Most times we had sardines and rice for breakfast and rice and sardines for supper. We usually ate at eight o'clock and four o'clock.

We sometimes got bread baked by our field baker. I knew this doctor, who I got to be friends with, a nice young fellow, a young bachelor and smart as a whip, and he'd come over to my ward before he went to the operating room. He'd bring his little piece of bread around in the morning and ask me to fix him a sandwich. Most times I'd carry that half sandwich around, wrapped up in a cheap paper napkin, in my hip pocket. Then, around two or three o'clock he'd get out of the OR and come around to pick up his sandwich. It was always kind of beat up, but anything tasted good.

Once, somebody gave us some coffee. We'd make a fire out in a little pit, boil our water, and make our coffee. We used the grounds three or four times, or as long as we could get any color or taste out of it. Then somebody would ask dibs on it when we were through, and they would take the grounds and boil them again.

2d Lt. HATTIE BRANTLEY, Army Nurse Corps, Hospital No. 1:

One of the nurses received her boyfriend, who brought her a package. She quickly opened it, thinking surely it was food. She found a bracelet. "Well," she said, "you can't eat a bracelet." The look on his face made her attempt to rectify the situation with, "You can't beat a bracelet."

Sgt. RALPH LEVENBERG, 17th Pursuit Squadron:

Rumors were rampant. One we all believed was that two shiploads of colored troops had already landed in Manila and they were on their way to get us out. We were going to be evacuated and, since we fought the war, were to be returned immediately to the States. And we believed this. We had nothing to counter these stories and we were very naive. This was the day when soldiers did what they were told and never questioned senior noncoms or officers. We had no newspapers. We had no radios. We had no telephones. I think the rumors were good, though. It gave us something to believe in. When morale is so bad and there's nothing more to do, rumors help.

Pvt. LEON BECK, Antitank Company, 31st Infantry:

Oh my God, rumors were everything! There were going to be paratroop drops, and convoys were always going to dock the next day. When the Japs began to shell Corregidor from Cavite, some of the ships around Corregidor changed anchorage. A rumor that the fleet had landed with reinforcements made the rounds immediately. People lived on rumors. That was the only hope we had, so the rumor mill was quite active. We believed them even though, if we'd stop to analyze them, we knew they couldn't possibly be true. But we wanted to believe them and so we ended up actually believing them. Some rumors were even published. Once I saw a pamphlet announcing reinforcements were on the way and that our food was going to be increased. Not one rumor ever came to pass.

2d Lt. HATTIE BRANTLEY, Army Nurse Corps, Hospital No. 1:

Of course we had lots of bull sessions. We used to just live for bull sessions and rumors, my land, the rumors were just fabulous. Tomorrow everything was going to be all right, things were coming, and we talked about what was going to be. And we believed every word of every rumor. I think, now, it was part of the psychology of survival. If you had known that you were going to be a captive of the Japs for three and a half years, you wouldn't have existed. You would have given up right then.

2d Lt. LEONA GASTINGER, Army Nurse Corps, Hospital No. 2:

I guess my twenty-sixth birthday was about the worst I ever felt on Bataan. On this day I always used to get presents from my family and especially from my mother. On my break, feeling somewhat solemn, I went down to the creek, sat on a rock, put my feet in the water to cool off, and wrote my mother a letter. After I finished it I reread it and all of a sudden I started crying like an idiot. Eventually, I got control over myself and thought, "For heaven sakes, what in the world is the matter with you? If I'm crying over this letter and feeling sorry for myself, can you imagine how my family will react to it? Oh my goodness, I can't send this letter." So I tore it up and wrote a more pleasant little note about how I was all right and in one piece and that sort of stuff.

That was as bad as it got. It didn't get down to screaming

or anything like that. But it wasn't like this all the time. We did our job and put up with the bad, but in the meantime if there was anything funny, well, we laughed about it.

Many a night a few of us nurses would sit around in the dark and imagine we were going on picnics. There were a lot of us from down South, and one of the old things we did back home was go on an all-day "singin' and dinner" on the picnic ground. We'd all fantasize about what we would take. See, everybody would bring a covered dish. I would have probably taken a medium-sized platter of fried chicken. Now the way things changed on Bataan, when we talked about what we'd bring, it was always in huge amounts. I thought of a huge GI platter of chicken. Another person wanted to bring buckets of lemonade, and another said she was going to bring a great big GI dishpan full of potato salad. I'll tell you, by the time we thought of everything to have on that picnic, we weren't quite as hungry as when we started.

We'd also set out there and sometimes, well—we'd sing. Mostly we'd do "Camp Town Races," or "Someone's in the Kitchen with Dinah," or "Oh, Suzanna," or just anything we could think of. We'd also make up parodies. A few weeks before Easter we began singing the "Easter Bonnet" song. Then someone would yell, "Oh, yes, but this year's Easter bonnet is a helmet." Darn, if we didn't get on that and try to rewrite the song with our own words: "This year's Easter Bonnet/Is an Army helmet/With dust all upon it . . ."

As bad as things were, there was always someone in the group who would be bubbly and who would come out with something and like to make you giggle.

2d Lt. HATTIE BRANTLEY, Army Nurse Corps,
Hospital No. 1:

There was a dearth of mail during this time. One of the nurses did, however, receive a package from home. It was a sparkling, shiny, beribboned straw hat, and just before Easter! Everyone who heard about that hat and came to the hospital area for any reason asked if they could see it. The crown jewels of England were never viewed with any more solemnity than was that hat.

2d Lt. JOHN POSTEN, Fighter Pilot, 17th Pursuit Squadron:

Someone found a piano, so we decided to invite some of the nurses and have a dance. It was quite a party. Best time I had since the war started. A few of the guys got hold of some alcohol and made punch. Everyone was unconscious by twelve o'clock except the few of us who didn't drink. We got to take the nurses home. The girl I danced with came from Philadelphia, Mississippi. I really think it did us a lot of good. We decided then we'd try to have two parties each month, to see if we could enjoy that damn war. When we ran out of alcohol a few weeks later, the parties stopped.

War Department communiqué, March 17:

General Douglas MacArthur arrived in Australia by plane today. He was accompanied by Mrs. MacArthur and son and by his chief of staff. . . .

On February 22 the President directed General MacArthur to transfer his headquarters from the Philippines to Australia.

There is nothing to report from other areas.

New York Times, March 18:

Maj. Gen. Jonathan Mayhew Wainwright, now commander of the American-Filipino forces in the Philippines, is regarded as one of the most brilliant tacticians in the regular United States Army.*

2d Lt. HATTIE BRANTLEY, Army Nurse Corps, Hospital No. 1:

Amazingly, and truthfully, our patients for the most part all had hope. They knew it was desperate, but there was not a day that you didn't hear that ships were on the way, and somebody would climb a tree and pretend to look out on the Bay to see if the flotilla was in sight. Of course, when General MacArthur left Corregidor and claimed, "I shall return," we joked about it a lot.

I had a very young GI who had lost all four of his limbs. We called them basket cases in those days. There was never enough time to do all the things you needed to do, but one day I sat down on this GI's cot to talk to him, and smiling from ear to ear he said, "What's a nice girl like you doing in a place like this?" Now just imagine what chance, what hope, had he of getting out of here alive, and yet he was thinking about me. Most of the GIs were. The corpsmen were particularly thoughtful and protective of us. When the bombing started they would

---

* As early as February, Washington decided that any attempt to relieve the Philippine garrison would be doomed. To save General MacArthur, President Roosevelt ordered him to Australia. Reluctantly MacArthur, along with his family and some staff, left Corregidor in four PT boats on Mar. 12. On arriving in Mindanao, he was flown to Australia.

The War Department designated General Wainwright as commander of U.S. Forces in the Philippines (USFIP), which replaced USAFFE. Maj. Gen. Edward P. King, Jr., was assigned to command the forces on Bataan, which were now called the Luzon Force.

insist I find shelter—if nothing else, to get under the duty desk. But I would not; I couldn't. I would not have had the courage to climb under the desk while my patients were exposed. It's not that I'm any great, brave person, I'm scared on a second-floor balcony, but I just couldn't do it, and I didn't. During the raids I would go and sit on their beds and talk to them. And I must say that a lot of people ran for foxholes, which is fine. We were encouraged to do so because we were vital personnel, but everybody did his or her own thing. Eventually, the bombs really came into our area. We were down, but not out, and not under.*

2d Lt. LEONA GASTINGER, Army Nurse Corps,
Hospital No. 2:

I'll tell you the truth, the morale of the troops was great! They came in to us and always told us we were going to win and that a convoy was coming in the next day. I guess the time that everybody felt the worst was when we heard on the radio that a convoy of our troops had gone to Ireland instead of coming to us.†

2d Lt. JOHN POSTEN, Fighter Pilot, 17th Pursuit Squadron:

March was relatively quiet. Some missions, but nothing much to talk about. After a raid on Subic Bay on March 2, we cracked up three of our five P-40s on landing. The fourth never returned and we were left with one. The ground crews managed to patch one of the planes up with parts from the others. So in March we had two P-40s which we could use. To give us something to do, we painted death's head insignias on both of them. We used the 0-1‡ when we could to bring supplies in from Iloilo [Panay Island]. Once we took turns flying some medical officers so they could collect their flight pay. Mostly we got hungrier and hungrier.

Things began to pick up, however, in late March. The Japs began sending in waves of from nine to twenty-seven planes. These were the big boys. Of course we didn't have anything to send up after them, so they had things pretty much their own way. They bombed us steadily. Mariveles got its share. They bombed Hospital No. 1 on the afternoon of March 30 and killed quite a few people.

* The Japanese began intense air and artillery bombardment of Bataan on Mar. 24.
† The first convoy of U.S. troops arrived in Northern Ireland on Jan. 26.
‡ This Curtis Falcon was a small early-model observation plane.

2d Lt. HATTIE BRANTLEY, Army Nurse Corps,
Hospital No. 1:

A light plane visited us each morning—"Tojo," we'd say. We felt secure with the white cross we'd placed on the hill. But one day several bombs fell in the area. A direct hit on a foxhole adjacent to the hospital killed several persons. And the cross was blasted. Dust flooded the place, the wounded moaned. Everybody was numb, frightened. Father Cummings entered the hospital area and climbed upon a big steel desk. He began aloud, "Our Father, who art in heaven, hallowed be thy . . ." The planes returned, but his voice was lifted over the roar and they zoomed overhead without further damage. His voice lent an atmosphere of peace and hope to those of us in this unreal situation.

2d Lt. JOHN POSTEN, Fighter Pilot, 17th Pursuit Squadron:

We were bombed or strafed every day. The Japs had planes in the air all day, every day. I was on alert to move our P-40 to Mariveles if the Japs broke through. American planes kept coming up from the south every night and taking pilots and men out. The lines were catching hell and Corregidor looked like it was continuously on fire. They caught most of the hell.

Earlier in March the Japs had dropped a message to General Wainwright saying if he didn't surrender by March 22, they were going to take Bataan and everyone on it. They had dropped several of these messages before, but had not done much about it. Now they seemed to mean it.

PROCLAMATION

Bataan Pensinula is about swept away: important points of southern Luzon between Ternate and Nasugbu are in the hands of Japanese forces and mouth of Manila Bay is under complete control of the Japanese Navy. Hopes for the arrival of reinforcements are quite in vain. The fate of Corregidor Island is sealed.

If you continue to resist the Japanese Forces will by every possible means destroy and annihilate your forces relentlessly to the last man.

This is your final chance to cease resistance. Further resistance is completely useless.

Your commander will sacrifice every man and in the end will surrender in order to save his life.

You, dear soldiers, take it into consideration and give up your arms and stop resistance at once.

Commander-in-Chief of the
Imperial Japanese Forces

War Department communiqué, March 23:

The Japanese commander issued a manifesto addressed to General Wainwright demanding that he surrender by noon today or suffer the consequences. No reply was necessary and none was made.

2d Lt. JOHN POSTEN, Fighter Pilot, 17th Pursuit Squadron:

Towards the end of March the food situation was at its worst. The men walking around looked like the walking dead. Over fifty percent of the men were sick at our field and the rest of us were so weak we could hardly do the necessary work. I was in very poor shape to fly, and if I did go up I hoped it would be a short mission. I have never been so hungry in my life. Men were getting desperate. I had a bottle of vitamins, but they didn't take the place of real food. I kept wanting some of my mother's stew. There were times that I could see a plate of it in front of me. My voice changed to a very high pitch. It sounded funny as hell. Some of the men ate monkeys and reported it wasn't bad. We ate all the lizards until you could hardly find one.

Then on March 27 they started a training table for the remaining twenty-five pilots. We began getting all the extra food there was around, so we'd be in shape if we got some extra planes in. If they expected us to fly without killing ourselves, they had to give us more food. The new chow was plenty good. I couldn't help feeling sorry for the men that didn't get it and had to watch us eat. I could hardly look them in the face. Some men were so weak, their food had to be carried to them. It was not unusual for men to keel over waiting in the chow line.

2d-Class Carpenter's Mate STANLEY SOMMERS, Naval Battalion:

At the end of March we were hungry and dirty and sick all the time. We'd have rice and a fish which had to be divided into our squad of men. I had malaria and never got any quinine. I would alternate between fever and chill. I would lay on my cot and sweat. Then everybody I knew got dysentery. We were running constantly. It was a bad dysentery, too, because we had a bloody mucus discharge. We were weak, we had no food or medicine, we had fever, and we had the runs. We were in pretty bad shape.

Sgt. FORREST KNOX, Company A, 192d Tank Battalion:

One day our CO got on the radio and told our tank crews that the mess sergeant had a big pan of baked beans waiting for them when they came back. Everyone on the net heard him and those rear-area officers came flocking in like flies on a turd. That talk of hot baked beans must have driven them hogs about half crazy. Our CO, course, invited the colonel to help himself. Then it was seconds, thirds, and fourths. The tanks came in around 4:00 p.m. There were a few beans left in the pan where they had burned onto the side so hard the officers couldn't scrape them loose with their spoon. Funny thing, a man's reaction to an outright insult like that. The crews looked at the pan and just walked quietly away. I never heard one of them swear. That was the part that fascinated me. Hunger was a nagging thing that never went away. You could ignore it most of the time, when it hurt was when you realized some hog had taken advantage of you and eaten your rations. Well, our CO paid as high a price as you can go a month later on "The March."

Tech. Sgt. WILLIAM "COWBOY" WRIGHT,
17th Pursuit Squadron:

We knew that our officers were trading cartons of our cigarettes to some of the boat crews for sugar, fruit juices, and jam. None of this, however, was ever seen on our table. Eventually, a discussion came up as to why this was the case. One of the officers finally admitted that they had eaten some of it and the rest was in their tent. He said further that before they would let us have it, they would dump it in the Bay. Paddy Clawson laid his .45 on the table and told the lieutenant to think a little about that before he did it. The rest of the food was divided with us soon afterwards.

We had another kind of trouble with officers as well. One of our gun crews on the 30-caliber Lewis was in the Talaga Bay area. An officer had tried to sneak in on them a couple of times to see if he could catch them dozing. The crew asked me what they should do the next time this happened. I obliged and told them exactly what to do. The next time it happened, when the gun crew challenged the officer and the officer failed to respond, the gunner pulled the bolt back on his Lewis and let it slam forward. They got an answer real quick. Matter of fact, no one bothered that gun crew after that.

War Department communiqué, March 27:

In Bataan there were a number of sharp clashes between patrols. There were troop and truck movements behind the enemy lines, which indicated that increased activity may be expected.

2d Lt. JOHN POSTEN, Fighter Pilot, 17th Pursuit Squadron:

Just before the Japs started their big push I got the chance to leave Bataan. Captain Dyess told me I was going south as a passenger to Del Monte [on Mindanao] to bring back a P-35. I was squeezed into the back seat and shared the flight with a .30-caliber machine gun. At 2:00 a.m. on April 1 we took off in an old Navy "Duck" [a Grumman J2F-6] that the 20th had fixed. It did ninety-five miles per hour. It took us four hours and thirty minutes to get to Cebu and then two more hours to Del Monte, which we made in daylight. Twice over the mountains of Cebu our engine cut out, and when we landed we had a flat tire.

The food down there sure was good. I was supposed to take off for Cebu the same day I arrived, but my orders were changed, so I didn't leave until the 2nd [April]. I hated to think about returning to that hellhole I'd left.

When I got back to Cebu I was ordered to wait over another day, which didn't make me mad. Donaldson came down the same night. He reported that things were really breaking up on Bataan.

In Cebu I spent the day in a wonderful big house. I had a room and bath all to myself! I had coffee in bed and a hot shower when I got up, and a shave and shoeshine when I got downtown. Those people didn't know a war was going on. It seemed impossible that 400 miles north of where I was, about 70,000 men were starving to death. There was so much of everything on Cebu.

I returned to Bataan and found that the front lines really caught hell while I was gone.*

War Department communiqué, April 4:

In Bataan the enemy laid down a heavy artillery fire. . . . From the intensity of the fire it was assumed that it was preliminary to a ground attack.

---

* Two months behind their victory schedule in the Philippines, Imperial General Headquarters in Tokyo was concerned at General Homma's inability to finish the fighting on Luzon. Throughout late February and March Japanese reinforcements poured into the Philippines. Twenty-two thousand fresh troops arrived, as well as many more guns and sixty twin-engine bombers. Naval air units were also attached to the 14th Army. By the end of March Japanese forces opposite the Bagac-Orion Line were rested and reinforced, and on April 2 they were ready to open an all-out offensive. The first objective was Mount Samat, the high ground just behind the center of the Bagac-Orion Line. At 10:00 a.m. on April 3, Good Friday, the Japanese opened the final battle with a five-hour artillery barrage.

Seaman 1st Class AUSTIN ANDREWS, USS *Oahu*

On board the gunboat we didn't know how in the hell Bataan held up. We sat in Manila Bay and watched. At night you could see the artillery duels with the tracers going back and forth. We were right even with the line and I'd never seen such fire power. Then, during the day the dive bombers and bombers would work the guys over. I'll tell you, they were taking one hell of a pounding.

War Department communiqué, April 5:

Furious fighting raged along the right center of our line in Bataan. The enemy launched a heavy infantry assault supported by an intense artillery concentration. Large numbers of shock troops were massed opposite our positions and succeeded in making some small gains.

Pvt. LEON BECK, Antitank Company, 31st Infantry:

When the Japanese started their big offensive they just pounded us with artillery. Thousands of rounds an hour falling in an area not more than a mile in depth. There wasn't a minute that we didn't have Japanese airplanes over us. They were either coming in or pulling away. They wanted us and they were going to get us. We lost every gun, every truck, and every piece of equipment we had.

As soon as the Japs broke our lines the men in my antitank squad, as well as some rifle squads, pulled out in a group and during the night crossed Mount Samat. Once we tied up with a unit of 26th Cavalry and another time we established a line with a battery out of the 200th Coast Artillery. We'd form new groups and try to reestablish a line of resistance. We'd hold until the line would break somewhere else, and to avoid being flanked we'd pull back again and try to reestablish another line further back.

The artillery was murderous. Their planes came and went at will. They could bring in air strikes any time they wanted. They kicked our butts good. When we pulled out the right hand didn't know what the left was doing. Units kept running over each other. Things were hectic. Hectic is a pell-mell movement with people acting on their own, without orders. At first, it was every unit for itself. Later, it boiled down to every man for himself.

The day we fell back was the day we were supposed to advance three or four miles. We had been assembled the day before and were shown what our objective was going to be. Come nightfall we were in position, but we never made the attack. Their artillery tore us up too bad.

2d Lt. FRED GIFFORD, Philippine Army:

We were slaughtered. Everyone was a replacement. On Mount Samat I never got to know a man's name. I might have a machine gunner five minutes or I might have him five hours, but I never had him longer than a day.

Our machine guns were off the P-40s because we salvaged them when the planes couldn't fly. They were air-cooled, which means they had no water jackets to cool the barrel. We were only supposed to fire short bursts to prevent the barrel from overheating. But there were times when the Japanese came in so strong that we had to hold the trigger down. When the gun jammed we didn't try to unjam it. We just pulled off the heated barrel and stuck on a cool one.

The Japanese, after they captured or killed a Filipino, would put on one of their uniforms and infiltrate our lines. I couldn't tell the difference between a Japanese and a Filipino, so I left it up to the Filipinos to make that distinction. See, I wasn't trained to be infantry, but it didn't take long for me to learn to duck when something was coming in. Other things, too, I just picked up. Sometimes when we got overrun we had to play possum. There was a possibility that you might get a bayonet through your back, but if you had your head and shoulders covered, the chances were they'd pass you by. Then you had to figure out how to get back to your own lines by passing through the Jap lines, or how to attack them from their rear. This last step usually depended on getting enough men together to do it. Sometimes we just butchered them and went right on through them. Knowing how we'd play possum, we never let them do it to us. If a fallen Jap didn't have blood all over him, we shot the back of his head off.

We got into bayonet fights with the Japanese quite a bit. I never had bayonet training and the Philippine Army's training never extended to nothing. The Japs had years of training. They'd use the old screaming bit, which was supposed to scare you. It's like when they break a board with a karate chop. Every time they stuck us, they always screamed and carried on.

Pfc. MICHAEL TUSSING, Jr.,
27th Bombardment Group (L):

We were sent up to Mount Samat to plug a hole. It was a precarious situation. We tried to form a line in this heavily wooded jungle. Everything was strictly unorganized. We were there two days before we learned that we had plugged only one sector of the hole and that our flanks were in the air. We were pulled out immediately.

Cpl. ISHMAEL COX, Company C, 31st Infantry:

On the retreat off Mount Samat we dodged around. We heard the Japs and saw the Japs. Hell, one morning I killed seven of them jokers myself. Somebody had to hold the line so the rest could get out. My unit was picked to hold. I was laying down in the best place you ever seen. Got behind a little rise and I just sat there waiting for them. When they came over the rise I knocked them off like picking off ducks. I know I got them because I was the only one around. I laid there and I just pumped them. I was so hungry that after a while I went over to where they lay. Yes, siree. I took my foot and rolled them over and took all the food they had on them. I ate their rice and they had these brown Slim Jims. It wasn't no Slim Jim, but it's as near as I can come to describe it. I also ate some rotten fish all rolled up and a few little candy sugar balls. That's how I ate my first Japanese meal.

Pfc. WILBURN SNYDER, 3d Battalion Medics, 31st Infantry:

The retreat at Mount Samat was very disorderly and not at all like the withdrawal from the Abucay Hacienda. On Good Friday (April 3) we were going down a mountain trail. The mountain rose up one side and the Japs had their artillery across a little valley from us. We had no place to hide and were set up for them like a duck shoot. All we were trying to do was get out. One of our officers came by asking for volunteers to fight a delaying action. I was astonished he got his volunteers, because it was going to be a suicidal situation. The astounding thing was he got those men when our morale was as low as a snake's belly. We used to sing a song all the time, "The Battling Bastards of Bataan"—"No father, no mother, no Uncle Sam . . ." This depicted our bitterness towards the government. I didn't volunteer. You see, I'm not a brave man. The volunteers who fought that delaying action on this mountain trail saved us for the time being.

Being in the medics, I was really not supposed to volunteer unless it was necessary. 'Course, now it came to when it was a necessity. Coming off Samat there were no cooks, mechanics, or medics. We were all riflemen. We would now have to either fight or swim. My regimental commander laid right next to me. A few hours later I tagged him dead. An artillery shell hit right at us. I rolled one way and when I managed to look around I saw my CO lying there. I crawled over to him and saw his arm hanging just by the muscle. I finished cutting it off and put a tourniquet around what was left. Then I rolled him over to look at him and that man was dead. A little later we fell back some more and spent the night wherever we laid down. The next morning in this new line my CO came up to me and said, "I believe this is your tag." I thought I was seeing a ghost. He told me that he had been unconscious and when he came to, he managed to crawl back to our new line. "Well," I said, "I'll tell you one thing. You won't be nearer dead without needing to be buried." He didn't get angry. He just laughed about it and handed me back the tag. 11:30 that morning I put it back on him. No mistake. I was laying right by him and he was hit just as smooth between the eyes as you'll ever see.

2d Lt. JOHN POSTEN, Fighter Pilot, 17th Pursuit Squadron:

I left Bataan for good at 2:30 the morning of April 6. Reported to Del Monte. All the planes evacuated Bataan about then. Hank Thorn came down with two men in his baggage compartment. We all felt that Bataan was on its way under. I sure felt sorry for the poor devils left behind, particularly Glover and Shorty, who just missed the last plane. I remember the men expecting help right down to the last minute. They couldn't believe that the U.S. would let them down after what they had been through.

War Department communiqué, April 7:

Superior enemy forces, supported by tanks and artillery, continue to attack the center of our line in Bataan. The Japanese have thrown fresh reserves into the fighting and have made some additional progress. Heavy losses have been sustained by our forces. . . . Japanese dive bombers are assisting in the attack, dropping bombs and machine gunning our front line soldiers.

Pfc. BLAIR ROBINETT, Company C, 803d Engineers:

We moved into a ridge line between the 57th Infantry and the 31st Infantry east of Limay. In back of us we were bolstered by some 75-mm guns on halftracks. We came under heavy fire and there was fighting going on back and forth. The 57th was ordered to pull out. We pulled off across the back of the 31st and onto the road. Then they pulled through us. We were the last to come down the road. With everything burning, it was a scene which would describe Hades. It was a miserable damn time. Because of my bad back, which I got when I was knocked off a truck, I was given light communications duty. But now, instead of sitting in front of a switchboard, I was carrying a damn field telephone. It was a heavy piece of trash. There was no way I could use it with all the wires shot up. So I tried to throw it away. I was told it was government property and that it could not be dumped. My back was bothering me, but I couldn't sit down and rest. If I had, I would have had a Jap sitting across my shoulders.

Pfc. WILBURN SNYDER, 3d Battalion Medics,
31st Infantry:

When the Japs broke our lines we came back through the foothills of Mount Samat. They were firing artillery. We stayed on this trail. There wasn't any other place to go. The Japs were firing pointblank, right into us. Most of our men were sick or wounded. Morale was so bad that I treated a guy who shot himself in the arm. Bang! Guys would do anything to get away from the artillery and planes.

We were ordered to counterattack. What we were going to counterattack with, I have no earthly idea. But those were our orders. Our officers met in a clump of trees and I was standing nearby. The Japanese put a round right in the trees. Plump! I don't know how many were killed. It blew me down and away. Whenever I got up, I got up running. They say you don't remember when you're shellshocked, but I remember I dove into a foxhole. I wouldn't budge. Finally, some of the medics came over and told me they were going to send me back to the hospital. I didn't want to go. I didn't want to leave the fellows I was with. Nothing to do with heroics. I was too scared to leave. I kept digging deeper down into the hole. Whenever they reached down to pull me out, I'd fight them off. Finally, my captain came over and coaxed me out by telling me he wasn't going to send me back. A few hours later I was normal again.

The Japs just pounded us. The worst day was April 8. The Jap bombers came over in waves. Then they'd send in the fighters to strafe us. The tanks came in to help us but they were slaughtered. Some things I can't no more remember than a goose, but this day is just vivid in my mind.

We were loading wounded on a bus. The shells were landing all around. An officer told me to get on too: "You might as well go, too. This is the last bus back. It's all hopeless." I refused. I wanted to stay with my group. So I didn't get on. That bus went fifty yards and got hit square. Blown to smithereens. Nobody knows how many men were killed those last days. They have no earthly idea. There were a lot. The dive bombers were over us so that we couldn't breathe. Flying like mosquitoes, knocking out our tanks, killing our men. I said, "This is it!" This was continuous. I lived through everything else, but I never felt I'd live through this. I became careless because I felt it was only a matter of time. I'd go out on the trail and bring back wounded with no thought of fear. We were defenseless. We had our rifles, but what good were they against dive bombers?

2d Lt. LEONA GASTINGER, Army Nurse Corps, Hospital No. 2:

Towards the end of the fighting we had run out of space. There were no more beds. One patient would sleep on the spring, one on the mattress, and one on the stuffed mattress covers. That's the way we anted up for bed space. They just kept bringing wounded in. By the time you got your roster made up, you'd have to make it all over again.

2d Lt. HATTIE BRANTLEY, Army Nurse Corps, Hospital No. 1:

I can remember doing dressings. Starting right after breakfast and continuing right throughout the day. I'd not go far along that line of cots before my back would not straighten up, and I'd get down on my knees, finally not even bothering to arise, but crawling to the next cot. My experience in a cotton patch back in East Texas stood me in good stead for this work.

With casualties mounting and the need for expansion, a load of 100 triple-deck bunks were delivered to our hospital. The chief nurse sent me out to arrange a new ward. A huge acacia tree was selected as the site. Planes approached and this time a 500-pound bomb was dropped directly on the hospital. Many patients and corpsmen were killed and wounded. Some nurses received shrapnel wounds. Dr. Weinstein cursed in Yiddish and operated all day, doing some spectacular orthopedic procedures, and later had no memory of that day.

Capt. MARK WOHLFELD, 27th Bombardment Group (L):

My main worry was the Jap planes. Fortunately, instead of working us over, they attacked the Philippine Army unit on our west flank. They persistently dive-bombed them and with the exception of one fighter who strafed us once, we were left alone. We moved out through a bamboo thicket. We didn't know who was in front or beside us. It was like walking about in the dark. About noontime I heard the crackle of small arms in the jungle in front of us. The sound was dim, but I could tell it was an engagement.

As we passed our regimental reserve line we heard what sounded like tanks. Someone yelled, "There's tanks! There's tanks!" Men began to run. Several of our noncoms had to stand on the trail and punch the ones running by. Anything to stop the panic spreading. Finally, we got some order and we moved out again. We kept going down the path until we came to some dead Japanese all covered with flies. I assumed they were in the fire fight I had heard earlier. That night we camped along the Alangan Ridge. I had no information from anybody of what to do. Our regimental command post was gone, the commanding officer of the battalion was gone, so all the responsibility was on my shoulders.

The men with me were not professional infantrymen. They were Air Force mechanics, technicians, or communications men. Some of the officers were pilots. The rest of the officers used to, back in the States, drill one night a week and spend two weeks in camp during the summer. The men, consequently, were confused. They didn't know what to expect. They were just remotely acquainted with the rifles they carried. They had been fed enthusiastic rumors from the rear that help was on the way, that General MacArthur was going to send thousands and thousands of men and hundreds and hundreds of planes. The men were debilitated. The water they drank was polluted. The water they washed in had dead bodies lying in it. They lived in trenches, and their latrines had to be covered every other day because of the flies and maggots which they drew. They saw their buddies blown apart and shot up. The same truck that brought whatever food there was up to them, carried the dead and dying back. For good reason, the men felt hopeless. They didn't resign themselves to all sorts of religious mumbo jumbo because they knew their lives depended on their trigger fingers and their officers.

The morning of the 8th of April I decided we'd make a line along the Alangan Ridge. We didn't have any shovels, so we began to look for a good natural defensive position. As we moved up the line of ridges which led to the main ridge line, the Japanese planes found us and began to work us over good. I gave the order to go beyond the ridge, which had practically no cover, and to, if possible, get to the wooded area beyond. The dead and wounded from the first bombing couldn't be moved because we didn't have litters. The whole battalion began moving over the ridge. While I waited for the rear guard to come over, we got a terrific dive bombing by six Japanese planes. They blew some of our men into fragments. Some of the trees were blown down. The grass was on fire. The officers kept hollering, "Get moving! Get across! Go! Go!" The smoke was everywhere. Some enlisted men were shouting, "Captain! You've got to come over here! Captain! Private So-an-So's got his arms around a big tree and he won't let go!"

"Oh, Jesus," I said, "pull him off!"

"No, you better come yourself."

They took off and I went to the tree and there he was with his arms around the tree. At first I thought he had a little bundle of something on the back of his neck. But it wasn't a bundle. His scalp had been blown off and his hair was hanging down on his neck. The back of his exposed skull looked like a baseball. I went up to him, "Jesus Christ, let's go, let's go! We'll get you down to an aid station." But he was incoherent. I yelled, "Let's go, for Christ's sake. I've got other things to do!" I tried to pull him off but he had a steel grip on that tree. He stood there in the smoke. No blood was coming from his skull, just white bone. Finally I told him, "All right. You'll just have to stay here till the day of doom. Good bye." And I left him hanging on that tree. I didn't even know his name.

I finally got everyone who could move off the ridge and by that evening we bivouacked near Trail 20. I took a muster and found seventy-five men and officers present. Four months earlier, to the day, we had mustered 770 men. The rest were scattered, had taken off, were wounded or were dead.

Before we settled down for the night, we tried to get some drinking water. We managed to find a stream nearby. Drinking water in the jungle when you have thousands of men around is like drinking urine out of a toilet bowl. As long as you don't see what's in the water, you drink it. So we filled our canteens in the dark. There was still a lot of shooting going on near us, but we were not engaged.

During the night a group of officers came through the heavy brush. Fourteen of them. I counted. Some were from my unit. They urged me to go with them to Corregidor. I told them I couldn't abandon, nor could they, the men we were leading. We argued back and forth, and I told them that if I survived the war I'd make sure that each of them was court-martialed. It made no difference, and they left before dawn to find a boat that would take them to Corregidor.

Pfc. MICHAEL TUSSING, Jr.,
27th Bombardment Group (L):

We ended up that night on top of the mountain, and the road that then descends in a zigzag to Mariveles. Earlier, in the afternoon, after coming out of a malaria attack, I was back in the kitchen area when the guys came back and told me the line had broken and we'd better get away. We started out straight through the hills. From where we stood now, in the dark above Mariveles, we could see the ammunition dumps blowing up. The Japs had dive-bombed all that afternoon, but in the night they were dropping flares. It must have looked like a circus from the air. We were so worn out that we just lay down right there and went to sleep. I was awakened by an earth tremor. The trees were bending over and the old recon [four-wheel truck] I was lying next to almost rolled over me. It seemed like it lasted for five minutes, but I'm sure it couldn't have been more than one.

Cpl. HUBERT GATER, 200th Coast Artillery (AA):

It was about an hour before sundown. A stranger walking in would have thought the men had gone crazy. They were destroying all the antiaircraft equipment. The Japs had broken through the front lines on the Manila Bay side of Bataan. The orders were for the 200th and the 515th Antiaircraft Regiments to destroy all their heavy equipment and to fall back to Cabcaben Airfield and form a defensive infantry line. It was after dark by the time the trucks had been parked behind the line that we were to form. We then started marching in single file down the ridge overlooking the runway. Our only interruption was an earthquake that I felt sure was a bad omen.

I don't believe the line we formed was much more than a mile long. There was less than 1,500 men to accomplish the order. Once in place, three men formed small triangles to protect one another by cross-fire. Each man dug his own shallow foxhole. There was a shortage of shovels, so most of us spent the night digging with our bayonets. To a man, we expected the night or next day to be our last on this earth. The Japs would naturally bring up their big field guns with a reported 30,000 troops. We didn't have a chance.

War Department communiqué, April 8:

The present Japanese attack is the longest sustained drive of the enemy since operations began in Bataan. Waves of shock troops have attacked almost continuously without regard to casualties which have been heavy on both sides.

Cpl. WAYNE LEWIS, Company D, 31st Infantry:

About 200 of us were sent up to see if we could stem the Japanese advance. It was my last battle. They turned all their artillery on us up there. They blew those big trees to toothpicks.

You had to see it to believe it. I was shot through both legs and the foot. Somehow I was carried down off the mountain and left at Hospital No. 2. I didn't know where I was. When I came to the last time, I was sitting in a stream with my feet in the cold water because it felt good. I was watching the bloody water run down the stream. A nurse who had come down to get a pail of water found me and yelled for some medics. They came and carried me up to where a whole bunch of guys were on the ground. I didn't even know where the hell I was. When my time came, they took me in the operating room. The doctor told me they were going to have to cut off one of my legs. I told them that if they did I was going to cut their goddamn heads off. While I was lying there they cut the legs off another guy. That scared the hell out of me. Finally, they began working on me and got my left leg in a cast. About the time they started on my right leg the word came around that the nurses had to leave, on account they were going to be evacuated to Corregidor. What I remember most about the nurses was that some of them were pretty damn nice-looking gals. 'Course, I'd been in the jungle a long time, too.

2d Lt. HATTIE BRANTLEY, Army Nurse Corps,
Hospital No. 1:

It was on the 8th of April, the evening, it had been a cruel, horrible day with lots of casualties, when we all went to officers' call and our colonel told us nurses to get our barracks bags because we were being evacuated to Corregidor. Our reaction was, "We can't go, we can't go. Our patients are here." Colonel Duckworth told us we were needed on Corregidor and this was an order. He told us we had to go and that we'd all see each other in a few days. It was just like "See 'ya tomorrow" when you know you're not. We all stood and talked and joked about it— "The Golden Gate in '48." Then we were hurried onto buses, and then some of the nurses jumped off to retrieve the rings and earrings which they had hidden. I had just washed my only extra pair of coveralls, so I left them behind. We moved out, inching our way through a scene of unbelievable activity. Ammunition exploded on all sides, the nighttime sky bright as day. Corregidor's guns roared over our heads, vehicles jammed the road, soldiers slogged along in choking dust.

2d Lt. LEONA GASTINGER, Army Nurse Corps,
Hospital No. 2:

Just before dark on the 8th, we began to hear a lot of mortar fire on the ridge back of us. I hadn't realized the Japs were that close. An hour later we got orders from our CO, Colonel Gillespie, to report for transportation. I don't remember how I reacted, but I know it was the same thing that had happened in Manila. You do exactly what they tell you to do. I packed a suitcase, then at the last minute a pillowcase. I had washed my hair so it was all rolled up in pin curls. I threw my wet laundry, a carton of cigarettes, and some other things in the pillowcase. I also gave my spare suitcase to one of the other nurses who had lost hers.

Capt. JEROME McDAVITT, 24th Field Artillery,
Philippine Scouts:

I had stopped in Hospital No. 2 to try to get a cup of coffee when Clint Maupin, the adjutant, asked me if I'd take a group of nurses down to Mariveles, where they would meet a boat that would ferry them across to Corregidor. They obviously didn't want the nurses in the field when the Japs came in. I told them I'd be glad to do it if my CO gave his permission. Within the hour Maupin had obtained that permission. They wanted to send me because the hospital had no doctors to spare and, additionally, Colonel Gillespie did not want to show any favoritism in his command. Maupin and I rounded up some rolling stock which included a paneled delivery van, a truck used to carry supplies and junk, and my own Hudson sedan.

2d Lt. LEONA GASTINGER, Army Nurse Corps,
Hospital No. 2:

We reported to the headquarters area where some trucks were waiting for us. I ended up riding in a fine sedan with a friend of mine and our chief nurse. There were about fifty of us and our orders were to go down to Hospital No. 1 and then to proceed to Mariveles, where we would board a boat for Corregidor. We were supposed to meet the boat after midnight. Somebody told me it was only about five miles to Mariveles. We left Hospital No. 2 between 10:00 and 10:30 p.m. Right away we ran into problems. We began to lose a lot of time because the road was so crowded with troops. Bataan was falling back. We knew the Japs were close behind. We crawled along for a while. Once, I saw a jeep with two men carrying a white flag. They were heading towards the Japs. The flag looked like a torn sheet.

Finally, the column ground to a halt. The road was just too clogged for anything to move. There were civilians and military people everywhere. You could hear them calling out their companies. They were trying to find out where they belonged. The lines of resistance were collapsing fast.

Capt. JEROME McDAVITT, 24th Field Artillery,
Philippine Scouts:

We crawled along the road in low gear with our lights off. It
wasn't much of a road to begin with, just two lanes, but now
it was also jammed with vehicles and people, mostly Filipinos.
Within a mile of Hospital No. 1 we were stopped by the Military Police. Then all hell broke loose. They began blowing the
ammunition depot at Little Baguio.

2d Lt. LEONA GASTINGER, Army Nurse Corps,
Hospital No. 2:

After we'd stopped for a while my friend and I got out of the
car. Just as we did the big ammunition dump farther down the
road started blowing up. I mean it blew! We wandered around
until our chief nurse said that we should wait where we were,
while she took the car to see if she could find someone to help
get her trucks moving again. So she took the car and drove
off. This other girl and I just kind of walked around. I saw this
fellow with a clipboard and a flashlight. Like a moth drawn to
flame, we walked over to him in the dark. I heard him say,
"Sergeant, it's not before dawn, it's not after dawn, but at dawn
every gun on Bataan is surrendered." I interrupted, "Major,
what in the world's going on?" I can see him even now almost
leave the ground. He jumped and looked around and saw me,
an American woman, standing there. He said, "Who are you and
what are you doing here?" And I just calmly said, "Well, I'm
one of the nurses," thinking he'd know all about us.
    "What are you doing here?"
    "We're waiting for the ammunition dump to blow up, so we
can get on down to Mariveles. Our car has gone somewhere
else and in the confusion we've been separated from the rest of
our unit."
    "Oh, my gosh! Sergeant, get my jeep and take these girls
down to Little Baguio as soon as you can and then come back
here."

Capt. JEROME McDAVITT, 24th Field Artillery,
Philippine Scouts:

We waited several hours for that ammo dump to cool off before we were allowed to go through. About 4:00 in the morning
we began rolling again and because there had been no traffic
in front of us the road was clear all the way to Mariveles. We
pulled in to what was left of the Navy installation. I looked and
saw that there wasn't any boat or anything around that would

take us to Corregidor. Of course we had arrived too late to make the arranged rendezvous.

2d Lt. LEONA GASTINGER, Army Nurse Corps,
Hospital No. 2:

It was close to dawn by the time the sergeant got us down to Hospital No. 1. When we arrived there wasn't anyone else around. The others had already gone on. My friend and I were so tired we just sat on the steps of one of the buildings and tried to figure out what we should do next. Colonel Duckworth, the hospital's CO, must have heard us because he called out, "Who's out there talking?" I told him it was Leona. "My God," he said, "what are you still doing here?" After we told him our long story, he called his corporal over and told him to take us down to Mariveles.

When we got down to the beach we found the rest of our unit. Of course the boat that we were to meet had long gone. We were just there on the beach. There were old cars and trucks and junk around, and the Jap planes kept coming in to strafe. We took cover as best we could. I spent a great deal of time in a big concrete culvert.

Capt. JEROME McDAVITT, 24th Field Artillery,
Philippine Scouts:

The nurses stayed hidden under some concrete wreckage while I began to look for some way to get to Corregidor. There were no telephones, but I did find a Navy lifeboat with two sets of oars. I got one of our drivers to help me get that boat in the water by telling him I'd take him to Corregidor. Then I went back to the gals and told them that I could only take a few of them this trip. Three stepped forward. To the remaining nurses I explained my plan of rowing to Corregidor to get them help. There really was nothing else to do. One of the nurses, Eunice Hatchitt, a gal from near my home in Caldwell County, Texas, came up to me and said, "Jerome"—she didn't call me captain or nothing—"Jerome, if you don't come back and get us, when I get back home I'm going to tell your Mama and Papa." And she meant every damn word!

Then the five of us got into the boat and started rowing for Corregidor. The Japs didn't have too many planes around that early in the morning, and besides, we must have looked pretty puny to them. About halfway across Manila Bay we ran into a small Navy patrol boat just put-put-putting along. They picked us up and took us over to Corregidor's North Dock. We checked the three nurses into Malinta Tunnel and I reported that the other nurses were at Mariveles and that someone had to go get them.

2d Lt. LEONA GASTINGER, Army Nurse Corps,
Hospital No. 2:

Hiding on the beach, it dawned on us that we had had nothing to eat or drink since the night before. We were tired and worn out. Someone remembered having seen some supplies on one of the trucks. So around 7:00 a.m. we were given a big can of peaches and asked to pass them around. We took half a peach at a time until the can was empty. They certainly were delicious.

Shortly afterwards a tiny little boat from Corregidor came into our area and laid a thin plank across some pilings, and we had to cross from the beach to the boat on this narrow board. The Japs kept coming in, strafing and bombing the beach around us. When the planes would get close the boat would move out into deeper water, and when the planes had gone she would come back in and pick up a few more of us.

Walking across that plank took courage. It's a wonder some of us didn't fall in the drink. I don't see why we didn't panic. Finally, my turn came to board. I never could walk across a creek on a little thing of a bridge without being frightened. Seeing the water when I looked down, I didn't know whether I could do it. The nurse in front of me froze on the plank. She couldn't move. The Jap planes were coming in and that boat was starting to back off. I realized that if she got her weight on the end of the board closest to the boat, they would get her on. Otherwise she was going to fall in, and the board with her. I don't know what propelled me, but I dropped my suitcase and jumped up on the end of the board and grabbed her hand and said, "Look to that man. Just look at him and take a step . . ." And I pushed her and he pulled her, and we both got across the plank at the same time and landed on the little deck.

When we were all safely on board, the little boat took off for Corregidor. The Jap bombers were hitting all around us. We just sailed around a while, zigzag, trying to circle away from the Japanese. Floating in the bay, we came across a Filipino whose ship had been bombed. He was very tired and near the end of his strength. We stopped to pick him up. As they began to pull him aboard, he saw all these American women watching him and he decided he didn't want to come on board. We couldn't figure out why. Finally some of the Filipinos convinced him and when they dragged him on deck, we saw he was stark naked. He hadn't realized we didn't care. We weren't going to be worried about modesty at a time like that.

Over on Corregidor, when we arrived, everybody was surprised to see us. They all knew we hadn't made the first boat, and consequently had given us up for lost. But we were welcomed back into the land of the living. It was a funny thing to have someone say to you, "Oh, gee, we thought you were dead."

Once I got myself together again, I realized that I didn't have my suitcase. When I dropped it to help my friend across the plank, no one had thought to pick it up. All I had, therefore, was that little camera case I'd bought in Manila after we went to war. I had enough clothes for three of us in that suitcase I left behind. I found out that one of the girls had carried an empty suitcase with her the whole way. I said, "Why didn't you take mine on board?" Times of distress, people do all kinds of crazy things. I had Navy friends who kept telling me to send some clothes to Corregidor, so I would be sure to have them if Bataan fell. Not believing that Bataan would fall, I didn't see any sense in doing it. I should have listened to them.*

2d Lt. EUNICE YOUNG, Army Nurse Corps, Corregidor:

They started bringing the nurses over during the night. They came in groups. The last ones arrived around 7:00 a.m. They were very tired. Some of them were worried about boyfriends or husbands they'd left on Bataan. No one was hysterical or crying or carrying on.

All night long the men kept arriving, too. They came over in every kind of boat you can imagine. The ones I saw who made it across the Bay didn't talk, they were in shock.

Cpl. ISHMAEL COX, Company C, 31st Infantry:

I ran into some other guys who also wanted to escape. We decided we was going to Corregidor. Finally, we had four officers and about fifteen enlisted men. That night we went down to the beach and one of the officers began signaling Corregidor with a flashlight. A little river boat saw us, but wouldn't come into the beach. So we all started swimming to her and then I liked to not make it. I got the cramps and I got to hollering, "Hey, I don't believe I'm going to make it." This old sailor swam over and got me. He said, "Now, don't get excited. Just hold on." He took me aboard that ship. I thanked God because I would have drowned out in the Bay with them cramps.†

---

* On May 3 the submarine USS Spearfish evacuated Lieutenant Gastinger and eleven other nurses to Australia. After Corregidor surrendered, the remaining nurses, including Lt. Hattie Brantley, were imprisoned in Manila's Santo Tomas University.
† An estimated 2,000 persons escaped from Bataan in small boats and barges the night of April 8–9.

Cpl. WAYNE LEWIS, Company D, 31st Infantry:

The night the nurses left, Billy Barnett from the company walked into my hospital ward. "Your brother's lying down the road, dead," he said. "The company's all shot to hell. There's nobody left." I said, "Well, hell, help me get up." My left leg had a pretty good cast on it, but the right one was put on in a half-assed fashion. Billy told me where my brother was lying. "He was stopping tanks." So I said, "I'm going down and get his body." Right next to where I was sitting in the ward was a little tanker from the 192d who had his legs badly burned. He was a little short guy. I grabbed his crutches and I started down the road to get on the main route, so I could find my brother's body. I kept passing out because the blood would rush down to my legs and they'd hurt like hell and I'd black out. When I got down the road, I couldn't find my brother.* I turned around and began heading towards Mariveles and away from the Japs. I got around to a bend where I ran into a bunch of guys who said the Japs were killing everyone up ahead. So we took off down this trail. We found an antiaircraft gun down there and some searchlights that had been blown up. But the gun looked like it was all right. We leveled it down, right at the trail. We sat there not knowing what the hell to do. The Japs came down so we fired two rounds. The third one blew up the gun. I guess the gun had been damaged or sabotaged by our own people. It killed one guy. In the confusion I limped into the jungle and ran into some more guys hiding out. We spent the night flashing SOS signals at Corregidor, hoping like hell they'd come after us. And no one ever came after us, see.

Seaman 1st Class AUSTIN ANDREWS, USS *Oahu*:

We felt a lot of emotion. We'd been sitting out in the Bay, in ringside seats, watching the whole show for nearly three months. Now Bataan was falling. The ammunition dumps were going up. It was one huge explosion after another. There would be one down the way, then another one a little closer, and another further away. There was smoke on top of everything. We knew Bataan was falling. There was a feeling on the ship that we were losing a part of ourselves.

2d Lt. HADLEY WATSON, Company H, 57th Infantry, Philippine Scouts:

It was a living hell. Planes were coming over all the time, bombing and strafing. Once we had a lull and I was given orders to

---

* The brother survived the tank battle, but died in Camp O'Donnell a few weeks later.

get what was left of my company together and to be ready to move back at dark. As soon as the sun set we started to move back to our next line of defense. We never got there. I mean they just ran over us so fast there just wasn't enough ammunition or weapons to hold them. They were all around us, just thick as ants. We managed to burn out three machine-gun barrels before they ran over us.

Capt. MARK WOHLFELD, 27th Bombardment Group (L):

Along about 2:00 a.m. on the 9th I got a message to make contact with the unit on my left flank. I sent two runners, but they never came back. An hour later I received orders to move out. After marching in the dark for an hour or so, we came upon some other troops in front of us. They were men from the 31st Infantry. An officer asked, "Who's in command here?" I told him I was. He said, "I want only white American troops. That's what I'm gathering. How many men have you?" The officer was Brig. Gen. Clifford Bluemel. He said he had about 600 men. Now, he had about 675.

Nearby I noticed a big radio truck with generators and batteries. It was a monster which could only be used in a rear area. Later I was walking by the truck and I overheard Bluemel talking to General Parker.* Of course I could only hear Bluemel's end of the conversation. He had sort of a New York accent. "You want me to do what?" Listens. "You want me to extend the line? Fuck you! I can't form a line that long with stragglers. Now look, I've got some dependable troops here. We don't have to worry about people running." Listens. "You go to hell. We're going to stand here!"

We were told to take cover in a thicket. While there we came under fire from some Japanese 70-mm mountain howitzers. The shell fragments coming through the bamboo made a very startling sound because it sounded like ten shots, not one. The bamboo began to burn. I moved the men onto the road, near Lamao, and then down into a valley leading to Trail 20. As the sun came up we started taking small-arms fire from the jungle. We shot back but couldn't see what we were shooting at. The fire fight went on for a while until I heard a whistle blown. The word to drop our guns and that we were surrendering passed down the line. It was about 11:00 in the morning. I looked around. The wounded in the ditch were just laying there waiting to die. The trees and cogon grass were burning and there were billows of smoke. Of course there were the

* Maj. Gen. George Parker, Jr., commander of II Corps and Bluemel's commanding officer.

clouds of flies hovering over everything. Everyone had an empty canteen and we were all thirsty. "Cease fire! Cease fire!" I had a real feeling of relief. It was like a heavy load had been lifted off my back. It was over! It was over!*

1st Sgt. HOUSTON TURNER, Company B, 31st Infantry:

There were nine of us left. Three were wounded. My CO was hit as well. He told us we could surrender here or we could take off and do what we wanted to do. I wasn't ready to surrender, so I thought I'd move on. More than a couple wanted to go with me, but I didn't want them with me. Finally, I let two guys go with me.

The first place we headed for was where we knew there'd been a supply dump. We found some chow and settled down to cook us a meal. Soon we heard some Filipinos running down the trail, so one of the guys with me got curious and went to have a look. He came running back: "Christ, come on, there's Jap tanks coming." We jumped up and as we ran across the road one of my buddies got hit right next to me. I kept on running into the brush, heading towards the mountains. I don't really know what happened next, but I remember hearing planes strafing behind me. The next thing I knew, I was waking up and it was dark. There were a few Filipinos lying around. I didn't know what to do, so I headed for the hills by myself. Then I ran into an old first sergeant I knew. I asked him if he wanted to go with me. He said, "No, I'm too damned old to go over the hills. I'm just going to give up right here." "O.K.," I said, and left by myself.

Later that day, in a big canyon, I ran into a Jap patrol. I quickly got in behind a tree and found two guys already hidden there. One of them was a Philippine Scout, the other a lieutenant. That night we somehow lost the lieutenant. The Scout and I decided then we would find a boat and sail across Manila Bay and hide out with his relatives in Batangas Province. Before we could, though, the malaria came back on me. I could see that I wasn't going anyplace. So I gave what money I had to the Filipino and told him to go off by himself.

Tech. Sgt. WILLIAM SNIEZKO, Company B, 31st Infantry:

I was back scrounging for food near Hospital No. 2 when I got the word we were pulling back. I was wondering why all

---

* At approximately 3:30 a.m. on April 9, emissaries of General King started toward the Japanese lines under a white flag to arrange for surrender. Nine hours later, Luzon Force surrendered unconditionally. Nine days later, sixteen B-25s led by Lt. Col. James H. Doolittle made the first air attack on the Japanese homeland.

the men were running back. The officers were trying to turn them around, but they wouldn't stop, let alone turn. Their spirit was dead. They were just too tired, too sick, and too hungry. Then our people began blowing up all the extra ammunition left on Bataan. It was like a regular Fourth of July. Then someone told us General King had surrendered. We weren't really scared, but our spirits were really down. We wondered what we were going to do now. So we just sat down and waited.

War Department communiqué, April 10:

A message from General Wainwright at Fort Mills on Corregidor just received at the War Department states that the Japanese attack on Bataan peninsula succeeded in enveloping the east flank of our lines, in the position of the II Corps. An attack by the I Corps, ordered to relieve the situation, failed, due to complete physical exhaustion of the troops. Full details are not available.

Clark Lee (Associated Press):

Melbourne, Australia—General Douglas MacArthur was informed late last night of the fall of Bataan, whose defense he directed until his transfer to Australia in March. Headquarters staff here was deeply affected by the news because, as one officer said, "All our friends are there."

Chicago Herald American, April 10:

Announcement of the fall of Bataan was made in a brief communiqué . . . followed later by a statement from Secretary of War Stimson that the fate of the encircled defenders is not known, although they apparently face death or surrender.

Capt. MARK WOHLFELD, 27th Bombardment Group (L):

We dropped all our guns and stuff on the ground. No fear. Relief. Standing in a file. There was a heavy concentration of Jap planes hitting the Filipinos off to the west. Here's the damned cease fire and they're still plastering the poor Filipinos on the other side of the ridge. In front of me was my battalion commander. I had run across him during the night. We were lined up on a dirt road. The day was beginning like all the others—hot!

Soon we heard a lot of hubbub at the forward end of the line, way ahead of us around the bend in the road, and we saw our first Japanese. The first ones were artillerymen carrying a mountain howitzer. They were cheerful looking little fellows and they smiled as they walked by. They were all covered in sweat and we were amazed at the weight they carried. One carried a wheel, another the tube, another the trail, another the packs of the fellows carrying the piece. They all had flies around their heads. Having been in the jungle for a while, they were filthy.

After them came the infantry and they were a lot more vicious. They started to go through our pockets. Some knew a little English and hollered, "Go you to hell! Go you to hell!" One of the Japs went over to Colonel Sewell and showed that he wanted the colonel to take off his wedding ring. Sewell kept refusing. About then a Jap came up to me and cleaned me out. Then he reached in my back pocket. Suddenly he jumped back and the bayonet came up real fast between my eyes. I reached into my pocket and found a rifle clip I'd forgotten about. Quickly I dropped it on the ground. The Jap took his rifle and cracked me across the head. I fell. My head was covered in blood. When I looked up I saw Sewell couldn't get his wedding ring off, and the Jap was about to take his bayonet and cut it off along with the finger. Sewell saw me and he reached over to get some of my blood which he used to wiggle the ring off. Then he was slapped and kicked.

Cpl. HUBERT GATER, 200th Coast Artillery (AA):

At the road a small group of Japs were waiting for us. Others were coming up the road in trucks and tanks. I was with the first fifty or so to be disarmed. Never had that rifle meant so much to me. It was like losing a good friend. Tears came into the eyes of many. One man, as if apologizing, said, "I feel so damned helpless." It was exactly the way I felt. Our rifles were tossed in a pile. We were searched and told to sit down.

Capt. LOYD MILLS, Company C, 57th Infantry,
Philippine Scouts:

Hiding in the jungle we began to run short of food, so my first sergeant and I began looking for a Negrito village where we thought we could find food. We ran into a few shacks and got some cashew nuts which we roasted. In the course of trying to find a stream we stumbled into a Jap observation post. The ones we ran into were big men, not the little people a lot of folks think of. Actually, I had seen them before, down on the Points. These Japs were bearded and dirty. Of course I wasn't a pretty sight either. They slapped us around a little bit. I still had my rifle and .45. Thought for a while, since I was still armed and this being after surrender, they might shoot me as a guerrilla. Treated us pretty rough. After relieving me of my weapons and taking my wristwatch and rings, this big Jap lieutenant asked, "Do you like Roosevelt?" And I thought, "Oh, Christ, what am I going to say now?" If I say the wrong thing I've had it. I told him that Roosevelt was my commander and that I did what he told me to do. He slapped me on the back. "You O.K.," he said. "You army, me army, too. Are you hungry?" We stayed with them all that day and night. They were front-line troops, so we got better treatment from them than we did from the service troops later who were our guards. The next day we were sent down into the valley and out of the jungle at Cabcaben.

Pfc. JOHN FALCONER, Company A, 194th Tank Battalion:

When the order to surrender came it was a great relief to me. I should have been very wary, very fearful, but I wasn't. I thought it was a beautiful day. We found some abandoned trucks and some food. I had, right then, one of the best meals I've ever eaten in my life. I had creamed peas on toast. While we waited for the Japanese we sang songs.

The first Japs we saw were bone tired. They marched right past us. One Jap infantry private was so exhausted that he stumbled and fell in front of us Americans. A Jap officer gave some command, two riflemen came up, picked up the fallen soldier, took him off the road where we couldn't see him. Then we heard a shot and the two Japs returned alone.

Pfc. WILBURN SNYDER, 3d Battalion Medics,
31st Infantry:

We were out in a little mountain clearing with our white flag when the Japs came up to us. Captain Brannon told the interpreter that we were a group of medics. Didn't make any difference to the Japs what we were. They immediately separated the Filipinos from the Americans. We had a Hawaiian in our outfit. He was on the same ship I was on when we came over in October. We tried to tell the Japs he was an American, but they didn't believe us. They put him over with the Filipinos. I never found out what happened to him.

Pfc. CLETIS OVERTON, 27th Bombardment Group (L):

About sunrise we noticed that not far up the rise we were all sitting on, there were Japanese soldiers. Stretching back over another line of hills were more Japs. We were surrounded. There were hundreds and hundreds of us just sitting and waiting. Everywhere you looked there were white flags—handkerchiefs, sheets, pillowcases—hung everywhere. They didn't make me feel any better. Inside of me was a real deep sense of fear. No one knew if they took prisoners or not. Rumor was they didn't.

Early in the morning the Japs moved down amongst us. Being behind the lines I'd never seen a Japanese soldier before. I don't know what I expected to see, but they were dressed in olive green. Their caps had a little star above the bill and they had flaps over their ears and down around their necks. They were rather odd looking; most were short, but not all. Their rifles had bayonets mounted on them. The thing that made the most impression was when they began barking orders. No one understood, but we did know they were loud and forceful. If you didn't move promptly they'd slam a gun butt against your head or side. There was no kidding at all—they meant business. It didn't take much for me to realize that they would just as soon kill you as look at you.

Sgt. RALPH LEVENBERG, 17th Pursuit Squadron:

The first Jap we saw spoke beautiful English. He said, "Gentlemen, welcome. Evidently you have been separated from your organization and don't know what has happened." We acted dumb. "Well, the Japanese have won the war and you are now our prisoners." Then he gave us each a cigarette. After we had finished smoking them, he proceeded to beat the living hell out of us. Then he marched us off, and hell, we weren't a half a mile from where we started the night before. We joined up with our guys and marched to Mariveles.

Cpl. PAUL SARNO, Hospital No. 2:

After we had been told that we had surrendered, I was ordered to go with Sergeant Miller up to the road and wait for the Japanese. Hospital No. 2 was set back from the main road, so we had to walk up a winding lane to get to where we would meet the Japs. To make sure we would not be mistaken, we wore our Red Cross arm bands. We waited for quite a while and then they came in. Using mostly sign language, we tried to tell them we were there to meet them and to bring them down to the hospital. It was pretty confusing until a tall officer came over to us. He said, "I can speak English very well, I'm a graduate of the University of Washington and you'll understand everything I have to say." I said, "Yes, sir!" So we took him and his troops down to the officers' tent. Most of the senior officers were there, and I stayed because I had brought the Japs down. Well, most of our officers were doctors, so they froze when the Japs began to explain the conditions of the surrender and what would happen to us.* None of our people had a word to say. Capt. Arthur Wermuth, who was a patient and a combat soldier, finally began to take over our side of the discussion.

The Japs went through the wards trying to loot everything they could. They didn't come away with much because we had nothing.

2d Lt. KERMIT LAY, I Philippine Corps:

They pulled us off into a rice paddy and began shaking us down. There were about 100 of us so it took time to get to all of us. Everyone had pulled their pockets wrong side out and laid all their things out in front. They were taking jewelry and doing a lot of slapping. I laid out my New Testament. In the Bible I had some pesos and a ten-yen note my first sergeant had given me. There was a captain in front of me and I whispered to him whether I should leave the Jap money out. He said, "Well, I guess so. They said to lay everything out." Something told me there was trouble, though. I don't know how it came to me, I guess the Good Lord was on my side, but when I could I reached down and picked up that ten-yen note, folded it up real small and tucked it in right behind my belt.

After the shakedown, the Japs took an officer and two enlisted men behind a rice stack and shot them. We got to inquiring why they'd been shot. The men who had been next to them said they had Japanese souvenirs and money.

Sgt. RALPH LEVENBERG, 17th Pursuit Squadron:

I had a pair of specially made tinted rimless glasses. I got pulled out of the line by this Jap guard who wanted my glasses. When he pulled them off I tried to motion to him that he wouldn't be able to see out of them, but he kept grunting and making it very clear that he was bound and determined to have a pair of American sunglasses. About then came along the tallest Jap I'd ever seen in my life. A lieutenant. He yelled, and this little guard froze at attention. The lieutenant came over and returned the glasses to me and indicated I should put them away. Then he turned on this private who was still at complete attention. The officer removed a small sword sheath from his belt and began beating this guard in the face with it, murmur-

---

* There were almost 7,000 patients in Hospital No. 2, most of them Filipinos, at the time of surrender. The hospital's commanding officer was Lt. Col. James O. Gillespie, and the Japanese officer was Major Sekiguchi.

ing Japanese comments to him the whole time. That guard never wavered until he dropped completely unconscious. His face was just absolutely like he'd been run over with a tractor. I got back in line and kept my glasses in my pocket.

Capt. LOYD MILLS, Company C, 57th Infantry,
Philippine Scouts:

At one stop a Japanese sergeant, who spoke beautiful Oxford-type English, came up to me. He wasn't one of our guards, but happened to be around. He said something to me that I've always remembered. "You are going to find a lot of bad Japanese and you are going to find a lot of good ones. Please don't think that all the Japanese are alike as far as the treatment you are going to receive." Then he opened up a can of sardines, and with some rice, gave them to me and the men around me. It was the first real food I'd had in days.

Pvt. LEON BECK, Antitank Company, 31st Infantry:

The first group of Japanese we surrendered to really weren't too abusive. They were combat troops. I think they had a mutual respect for other combat troops. They did search us and take our watches and toothbrushes, but they weren't hostile. They escorted us along the various little trails that ran down out of the mountains and began to accumulate us into groups near Little Baguio, on the road out of Mariveles. Then, they began to move us up the road in groups of 100 to 150 men.

3
THE DEATH MARCH

With the surrender of Bataan, General Homma still faced the problem of subduing the American garrison on Corregidor, a short two miles away in Manila Bay. Only when Corregidor surrendered could Japan claim her most valuable prize—the Philippines. For the Japanese 14th Army the campaign was not yet over. Before this decisive battle could begin, however, it was necessary for the Japanese to remove the enormous number of prisoners which General King had just surrendered. Obviously, it was important to General Homma to get them as quickly as possible off Bataan and out of his way. Anticipating this problem in late March, an evacuation plan was developed by Homma's staff. The plan was simple; the captives would walk out of Bataan as far as San Fernando. There, they would be shipped by rail to a prison camp in central Luzon. From Mariveles on Bataan's southern tip to San Fernando it is almost sixty miles. Plans to feed and care for the prisoners along the road were proposed and agreed upon. Unfortunately for the men of the Luzon Force, the Japanese plan for their evacuation was based on three assumptions, all of which proved false. The first miscalculation assumed the surrendered force to be in good physical condition; caring for sick, hungry men played no part in the plan. The second error was in not allowing enough time to work out all the details of a proper evacuation. Lastly, the Japanese made a faulty estimate in the number of troops they would have to move. They assumed the figure would be between 40,000 and 50,000 men.

Because of the chaos that followed the disintegration of the Luzon Force, it is impossible even today to give a precise number to the men who took part in the march out of Bataan. On Good Friday, as the Japanese offensive began, 78,000 troops made up General King's command, including 12,000 Americans. The biggest problem in determining the number of men on the march is not knowing how many were killed during the last battle. There is also no accurate way to know how many escaped by drifting into the jungle or to Corregidor, and how many were left behind in the field hospitals. An educated guess, however, puts 62,000 Filipinos and 10,000 Americans on the march.

In all the confusion and disorganization which went into the evacuation of the prisoners, still another factor played its role. On April 9, 1942, no one knew what the attitude of the Japanese guards would be toward their prisoners.

Sgt. RALPH LEVENBERG, 17th Pursuit Squadron:

Mariveles. Now that was confusion! It reminded me of what it might have been like when the Jews exited Egypt into the desert—no one knowing where they were going or what they should take or how long it would take to get where they were going. Mariveles—tanks, trucks, cars, horses, artillery—like a Philippines Times Square. Everybody going every way and nobody knowing where they were going. And everything buried in dust, horrendous amounts of dust being churned up by the tanks and trucks. You realized that Homma's shock troops were coming down Bataan on their way to taking Corregidor. The Japanese were just in a rush to get us out of their way. Our officers were milling around, trying to find out what was going on. The Japanese officers also seemed confused as to what they were supposed to do with this pack of hungry, sick, bedraggled men they had captured.

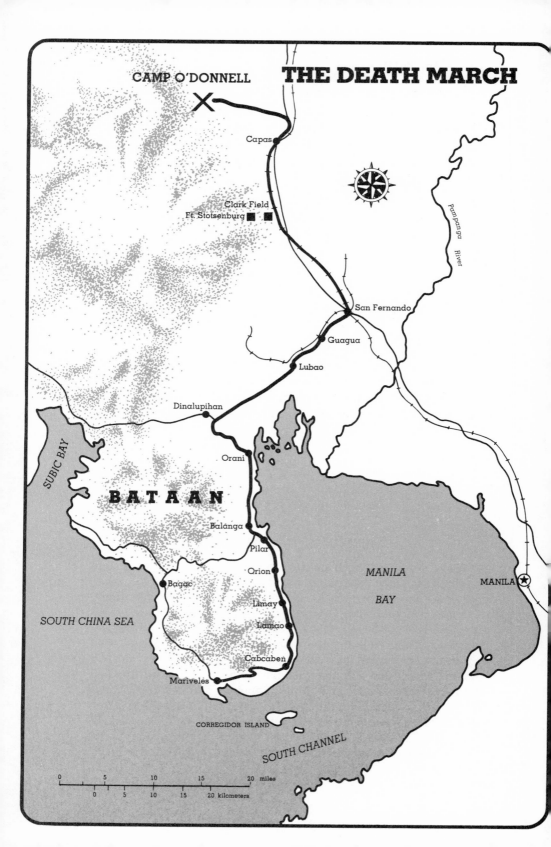

Cpl. ROBERT WOLFERSBERGER,
27th Bombardment Group (L):

There was continual noise! Mostly the continual barking of orders in Japanese, either wanting you to get off the road, or get back on the road, to speed up or to slow down, to stop or to start. The movement of people, trucks, artillery, and horses added up to continuous racket.

Pfc. BLAIR ROBINETT, Company C, 803d Engineers:

My group came up the road from Mariveles another half mile or so when a Jap soldier stepped out, came across, and took my canteen out of its cover. He took a drink, filled his canteen out of mine, poured the rest of my water on the ground, and dropped the canteen at my feet. I thought he was going to walk back to the line of Jap troops standing across the road, so I bent over to pick up my canteen. But he turned around and hit me on the head with his rifle butt. Put a crease in the top of my head that I still have. I fell face down on the cobblestones. I crawled back up to my knees, debating whether to pick up the canteen again. I figured the best course of action was to stand up and leave the canteen alone. Soon as the Jap troops moved off, I squatted down and picked it up. A little later a Jap soldier came over to one of the lieutenants out of our company, and when he found out his canteen was empty he beat the lieutenant to his knees with the canteen. Just kept slapping him back and forth across the face.

We moved down the ridge a ways when we saw this GI. He was sick. I figured he had come out of the hospital that was in tents out under the trees. He was wobbling along, uneasy on his feet. There were Japanese infantry and tanks coming down the road alongside us. One of these Jap soldiers, I don't know whether he was on our side or if he deliberately came across the road, but he grabbed this sick guy by the arm and guided him to the middle of the road. Then he just flipped him out across the road. The guy hit the cobblestone about five feet in front of a tank and the tank pulled on across him. Well, it killed him quick. There must have been ten tanks in that column, and every one of them came up there right across the body. When the last tank left there was no way you could tell there'd ever been a man there. But his uniform was embedded in the cobblestone. The man disappeared, but his uniform had been pressed until it had become part of the ground.

Now we knew, if there had been any doubts before, we were in for a bad time.

Capt. MARION LAWTON, 1st Battalion, 31st Regiment,
Philippine Army:

When we had marched several kilometers, we came to a large
group of prisoners who were all Americans. My little group had
increased to about fifty by then. There I found my commanding
officer, Colonel Erwin. He was a large fellow, a little over six
feet tall and weighed probably 240 pounds. He was the type
who believed in having an abundance of everything. I noticed
he had a heavy barracks bag with him. I'd thrown away everything except a change of socks, underwear, and toilet articles,
because I knew I couldn't carry a lot of stuff. Knowing how
heavy Colonel Erwin's bag was, I volunteered to help him, but
I warned him that I felt it was a mistake to carry that much.
"Oh, no," he said, "I might need this gear." He had extra shoes
and uniforms and who knows what else. Hadn't been looted
either.

The Japs put us in groups of a hundred, columns of four,
and marched us out by groups. I managed to stick with Colonel
Erwin. This was April 9, the actual day of surrender. It was as
hot as the dickens. The Jap trucks started coming in. And there
was just clouds of dust. We started marching. I can't remember
hours or specific days, but as we moved on it got hotter and
we got more fatigued. After a couple of hours people started
faltering. Thirsty, tired, some, like me, already sick. Most everyone was suffering from malaria and diarrhea, all hungry. I'd
been pretty well fed, but a lot of these fellows had been on half
rations since January and, on top of that, in the confusion of
the last few days they had eaten nothing at all. So we were
hungry, plus being under pressure of combat. We were emotionally spent, so horribly frightened and depressed and dis-
tressed, not knowing what was going to happen to us.

About midday Colonel Erwin, still holding his bag, started
slowing down and gradually dropping back. Soon I lost sight
of him. I got reports later of what happened. He finally dropped
back to the tail of the column and the guards back there started
prodding him. He drifted on back further still, until one of the
guards stuck him with a bayonet. I guess he was delirious and
fevered and exhausted. Finally, a guard pushed him to the side
of the road and put his rifle muzzle to his back and pulled the
trigger. He was one of the early casualties.

With this exception I didn't see many atrocities, other than
people being hit or bayonet prodded. See, I was among the first
groups out and all the killings and beatings took place in the
later groups, those who were one to three days hungrier and
weaker.

Pvt. LEON BECK, Antitank Company, 31st Infantry:

Almost immediately the group I was with was made to stop near some of our abandoned 155-mm cannons. They made some of us sit on a barrel, back to front, the whole length of it, and had photographers take pictures of us. The cameramen were from the Domai news service and spoke good English. They rubbed our nose in it by telling us they were going to use these photographs for propaganda purposes back in Japan.

When we arrived at Cabcaben Field, they lined us up with as many other prisoners as they could get on the air base. When I looked around I saw Japanese cannons lined up, row on row, gun positions dug right on top of each other, all pointed towards Corregidor. I'm sure the Japanese theory was that if Corregidor could see there were American troops masking their artillery positions, they would not counter battery. But they did. The Rock had some 12-inch mortars facing Bataan and as soon as the Jap guns opened fire, Corregidor fired back. And we were in the middle. But there is no threat so great that it will hold a man in position when there are 12-inch mortar shells falling on him. The Japanese found that out—they couldn't hold us. If you've ever heard the bands coming off 12-inch rounds, whirring through the air, and heard one burst near you, you know you're not going to stand around very long.*

Cpl. HUBERT GATER, 200th Coast Artillery (AA):

Suddenly the hill rocked under us. There was a roar to the left, to the right, and then several back to our rear. The Japs had moved their field guns into position around us on Cabcaben Field.

"Why the dirty bastards!" the man next to me said. "They're using us as a shield to fire on Corregidor." It was true. We should have realized then what to expect as their prisoners.

A flight of Jap bombers were flying over Corregidor. Our officers cautioned us not to watch them because if our anti-aircraft fire hit any of them we would cheer in spite of ourself. Our chief worry was, would Corregidor return fire on the guns that surrounded us?

* The Japanese placed a battery of 75s on the beach near Cabcaben during the afternoon of the 9th. The guns were clearly visible and return fire from Corregidor destroyed them. General Wainwright, aware of the plight of the surrendered troops, issued orders to his artillery to be aware of the areas around the hospitals and where prisoners could be assembled. On April 12, assuming all prisoners had been removed, he lifted this restriction. The next day fire from Corregidor again fell around Cabcaben, killing more prisoners.

Corregidor didn't, but a gunboat out in the Bay did. I don't know the size of the shells; they were some smaller than our 3-inch. The first shell was to our right. Apparently, a dud. It skidded through the grass and set it on fire. Some of the men flattened out; others stood up ready to run to cover. Our officers motioned us down. There were a lot of Japs around us now.

The second shell burst to the rear and center of us. At the time I thought it had hit some of our men. A Jap soldier got part of his chin tore off. He was a terrible looking sight running around, evidently half out of his mind. From chin to waist he was covered with blood.

A young Jap officer who had been silently watching us motioned with his hand for us to take cover. About 300 of us ran across Cabcaben Field to get behind a hill. The rest ran the other way, up the road.

Sgt. FORREST KNOX, Company A, 192d Tank Battalion:

Our CO's fright made him run on Cabcaben Airfield, when the big guns on Corregidor started shelling over us to get to the Jap batteries at the end of the runway. His lard ass was too much to carry. He collapsed of heat prostration before he reached the edge of the field. Sure, the men in our company could have picked him up and carried him, but you only did that for your friends. Somehow we were indifferent about him.

Cpl. HUBERT GATER, 200th Coast Artillery (AA):

Night came. We had moved across the road into a rice field. Jap soldiers, tanks, big field guns, and horses went by in a steady stream. Occasionally, a Jap would run out and hit one of us with his rifle. No one slept. Most of the night Corregidor was firing their big guns. The only way to describe it—it sounded like freight trains going through the air over our heads. They were firing into the area that the Japanese would use to invade Bataan. During the night a man was sent with some canteens for water. The canteens were taken and he was beat up.

The next morning a steady stream of Filipino civilians began to go by, moving out of Bataan. Old and young, many were evidently sick. I didn't realize so many of them had been trapped on Bataan.

Sgt. RALPH LEVENBERG, 17th Pursuit Squadron:

Eventually they started to systematically put us in groups of about 100 or so and marched us off. There were one, two, sometimes four guards, you never knew.

I was fortunate in two respects. First, I had a new pair of shoes, and second, I had some chlorine pills. The shoes I had kept with me ever since we left the barracks outside Manila, and the chlorine I had just managed to pick up. I don't know why, maybe because of my upbringing, I was taught to be protective of my physical being. I was therefore able from time to time, when we stopped near a creek which had dead bodies and horses floating in it, to get some water and purify it with the chlorine.

One of the tricks the Japs played on us—thought it was funny, too—was when they would be riding on the back of a truck, they would have these long black snake whips, and they'd whip that thing out and get some poor bastard by the neck or torso and drag him behind their truck. 'Course if one of our guys was quick enough he didn't get dragged too far. But, if the Japs got a sick guy . . .

The thing that burned itself into my mind for days and days was the imprint of a body in the road that had been run over, I don't know how many times. It was paper thin, but the shape was very clear. It was as if the guy was still pleading for somebody to reach down and pick him up.

Cpl. WAYNE LEWIS, Company D, 31st Infantry:

The day after I surrendered they put me in a group and started us marching up the road. And I was on these damn crutches. They were too short. They were rubbing the hell out of my sides because they didn't come up to my armpits. Rumor had it that the Japs were checking the numbers in the group, and if at the next check point the numbers didn't match, they'd kill people to even up the count. Then we heard for every guy missing at the next check point they were shooting ten guys.*

By the time I got to Kilometer Post 147 I knew I wasn't going to make it. I started lagging behind. I couldn't keep up. What was scaring me was that I figured they were going to kill me. I was at the rear of the column by then, and a bolt in one of the lousy crutches began to get loose.

When we got near Hospital No. 2, where I started from, I saw this guy wandering out of the jungle. He must have had malaria because he wasn't wounded. He was out of his head, but he had two good legs. So I told the sergeant who was staying with me to take this guy in my place. "I'm going back to the hospital." So I hit the jungle and managed to crawl back to Hospital No. 2, where I stayed until Corregidor was whipped.

* It was only a rumor.

Cpl. WILLIAM GARLEB, Company H, 31st Infantry:

I was in Hospital No. 2 at the time we surrendered. My ward, about fifty yards from the main road, was laying out under the trees close to a little stream. I was lying there a day or so later when a string of guys from the Death March came off the regular road and went down past me to the stream to get water. The guards allowed them to do that. Here they were, three feet from safety, right next to Hospital No. 2. All us wounded kept saying, "Come on, step in here." But these men didn't want any part of that. "I want to get out of Bataan." That's what they said. "We're getting out of this pest hole."

I knew what they meant. We were living in a world burnt to the ground. I was there on the night we retreated off the Abucay Hacienda, and the artillery had set the jungle on fire. We ran through a wall of flame. Jungle burned to the ground. Nothing left, even ground cover burnt. You can imagine living like that, and wanting to get out of there.

So they got their water, went back up to the main road into the dust, and joined their column. The Japs hadn't moved the patients in the hospital yet, and by pretending to be ill and staying with us some of these guys could have saved their lives. But not one of them did it.

2d Lt. HADLEY C. WATSON, Company H, 57th Infantry, Philippine Scouts:

They marched us in columns of fours, maybe thirty or forty to a column. We were all broken up into these groups. This Jap lieutenant got tired of walking along with us and he came up to all these motorcycles sitting by the side of the road. He thought he'd get himself one of these motorcycles with a sidecar, except he didn't know how to start it. So he kept looking around for somebody to start it for him. You have to see a Jap frightened and listen to him holler, to appreciate what happened next. Well, old Colonel Trapnell said, "Is there a man here who can ride that damn motorcycle?" So I went over there, motorcycle riding was my business, you know, and wound that little motorcycle up. It had one of them trip clutches on it, and I got that thing all wound up in first gear and showed him how to put his foot on the accelerator, and boy, he just took off lickety split. The thing is, he didn't know how to stop it, and he just rode the accelerator, thinking it was the clutch. He went down the road like a greased snake, yelling as loud as he could. I can still see him riding down the mountain, going faster and faster, with no idea how to stop it.

Capt. MARK WOHLFELD, 27th Bombardment Group (L):

We were all mixed up—privates, officers, Scout officers, 31st Infantry, 192d Tank Battalion, 200th New Mexico Coast Artillery—just a jumbled mass of humanity.

My group stopped at a small bridge up above Cabcaben to let some Jap horse artillery through. They were in a real hurry to get these guns in place and start on Corregidor. Right behind the artillery there arrived a great big 1942 Cadillac equipped with a freshly cut wooden camera platform attached to the roof. As soon as they saw us they stopped and the cameraman jumped out and placed his tripod and camera on the platform. He had his big box camera which he looked down into. A white-shirted Japanese interpreter staged us for the cameraman. He told us to line up and put our hands over our heads. We should look depressed and dejected. That wasn't hard. The cameraman took his pictures and started back down the road in his Cadillac towards Corregidor, while we started marching in the other direction. That picture eventually appeared in *Life* magazine.

An hour or so later we halted and fell out near a ditch where there were about five dead Filipinos lying around. They looked like swollen rag dolls. I used a handkerchief knotted at the four corners to keep the sun from my head. I asked the Japanese guard, part talk, part pantomime, "Can I have a helmet? Dead, Filipino. Sun, hot, hot." He finally gave in, but I wondered whether he'd shoot me when I got as far as the ditch: "Fuck it, I'll try it." There was this dead Filipino lying there, and because his face was so puffed up I could only barely manage to get the chin strap off. He was full of maggots and flies. I finally got the helmet off and wiped out the inside with a part of his uniform that wasn't soiled. Then I hung it from my belt so it would dry. Who cared for germs at a time like that? I came back from the ditch and sat next to Major Small. "Boy," he said, "could I stand a Coca-Cola now." I started thinking about my girlfriend then. She worked in Grand Central Station in a real estate office, and I knew she used to go downstairs on her break and get a nice Coke with lots of ice chips in it. I started to take the helmet off my belt and put it on my head, when I noticed the dead Filipino had scratched the name Mary in his helmet liner. The amazing thing was my girlfriend's name was also Mary!

After a column of trucks carrying landing craft passed us, we resumed our march. We fell in behind another group marching out. We'd gone a little farther when we pulled off to the side of the road again to let some trucks roll by. Some of our young guys started asking the Japs whether they could have a drink of water. I looked to my right and saw a buffalo wallow about fifty yards off the road. It looked like green scum. The guards started to laugh and said, "O.K., O.K." So all these kids, eighteen- or nineteen-year-old enlisted men, ran for the water and began drowning each other trying to get a drink. The Japs thought it was hilarious. I noticed at the end of the scum some others drinking through handkerchiefs, thinking that would filter the bacteria out. Finally, a Japanese officer came along and began shouting at the men in the water. There must have been fifty of them, and they scattered and ran back for the road. That wasn't the end of it. This officer found some Jap soldiers who had been watching us and ordered them to pull out of the line any Americans who had water stains on their uniforms. When we marched out, after a short while we heard shooting behind us.

That night when we stopped, most of us had had no water all day. Our tongues were thick with dust. We had come into this abandoned barrio and were now sitting in a field. My small group was made up of some senior officers, even a few full colonels. I noticed one, Col. Edmund Lillie, who had been my reserve unit instructor back in the States ten years before. I went up to him, but of course he didn't remember me. We started to talk and began wondering how we could get some water. There was an artesian well near us that had water dribbling out of it, but we were afraid that we'd be shot if we went to get any. Desperate as we were, Colonel Lillie asked a guard whether we could go and get water. The Jap agreed. Most of these officers did not have canteens, but I spotted an old pail, and since I was only a captain, I went over to get it. Inside the pail, stuck to the bottom, was some dried manure. "Maybe I can rinse it out," I said. Lillie told me, "Don't waste the water rinsing it, just fill it up." When I got to the well, one of the Jap guards kept urging me to hurry up. As soon as I got as much as I could, without running the risk of being bayoneted, I came back to the group. There wasn't much water in the pail, but it was something. Lillie told us we could each have only one full mouthful before we passed the pail to the next man. In those days an officer's word meant something, so that's just what we did. Each of us took one full gulp. That way there was enough for everyone.

Pfc. EDDY LAURSEN, 93d Bombardment Squadron:

I buddied up with a feller out of my organization. His name was Carl and even when we surrendered he wasn't well. When we first started out we had our canteens full of water. As we progressed on "the March," Carl wanted more water all the time. I ended having to carry his canteen as well as my own. If I hadn't, he would have drunk all our water the first day.

Another thing, Carl carried in his musette bag a huge Bible that his mother had given him when he enlisted in the service. It was a pretty good-sized book. About the second day on "the March" I discussed the problem of disposing of the Holy Book, which I respected, but I could see it was utter foolishness to try to carry it. We ended up giving it to a Filipino.

Tech. Sgt. MEL MADERO, Company C,
194th Tank Battalion:

I was very fortunate in that I had a buddy. We helped each other. I managed throughout the lootings to keep a bottle of iodine. Every time I got shook down by the Japanese they either missed or didn't want my iodine. Now, my buddy had some solvent coffee—you know, the old K rations had biscuits, a little piece of chocolate, and some coffee. So between us we had a combination that kept us going. Occasionally on "the March," when we were crossing a stream and the guards were not near, I managed to get some water in my canteen. Then we'd slip in my iodine to purify it, and my buddy would slip in his coffee to make it palatable. This way we avoided any dysentery. For the rest of the guys, however, it was murder.

Cpl. CHARLES McCARTIN, Company B, 803d Engineers:

We started up the road again with hundreds of other men, and the Japanese trucks, with soldiers standing up in the back of them, started to come down the road. I learned early to stay away from those trucks because every now and then the Japs would lean out and hit a guy who was within reach. They'd hit them with the butts of their rifles for no reason at all. They seemed to especially pick on Americans wearing steel helmets. Since I too was wearing a helmet, I stayed away from the trucks after I saw the first incident. We walked till evening, how far I don't know, and we were exhausted. We slept on a rocky section of the road. It was terrible, but we were so tired, we just laid right down.

The next day we walked again until we came to an artesian well where hundreds of men were filling their canteens with water. We got in line in a large field and it took about three hours for us to draw our water. We stayed there the night. The Japs used it as a collection point.

The following day we went out in a larger group. Gradually, as the day grew long and the heat took its toll, the bunched-up men just started to straggle out, so it ended up that just my friend and I and another friend were walking alone. There was maybe 100 yards or more between the various groups. We kept walking because we figured we'd all get together somewhere where we would be fed. We would pass stragglers and talk about where they were going to feed us. It was always "up ahead in the next town." Well, we walked to the next town and we'd hear somebody say it would be the next town. So we'd walk to that town, just hoping we'd find a place where they were going to feed us.

Pfc. CLETIS OVERTON, 27th Bombardment Group (L):

A lot of us in the unit tried to hang together, but in the confusion we were separated. Most men, if they had close buddies, were able to keep together, but anything more than two or three got all mixed up. Although we were in military-type formations, we didn't march, it was more walking along.

I don't know that we had a specific number of guards assigned to a certain group. All I know is that there were guards, maybe one walking fifty yards ahead and one walking fifty yards behind. Sometimes they walked along the side of us. It seemed that certain Japanese soldiers would accompany a group so far, and then another detail of guards would take over. Reminded me of a relay.

Well, it wasn't long—I don't remember the exact time, but I'd say sometime in the afternoon—I began to tire out. The heat was terrific and my duffel bag began to get heavy. I tossed my blanket away first. Then I began tossing everything else, until I kept just my toothbrush and toothpaste. Then I threw away the duffel bag.

Late that afternoon we met some Japanese horse-drawn artillery units coming down to Mariveles. My group had stopped to get out of their way when they too halted. Jap soldiers came up to us and began collecting our canteens, which they used to fill the large canvas buckets they used to water their horses with. Most of the guys got their canteens back, but in the melee of getting kicked back onto my feet and moving out again, I never had my canteen returned. Figured I was now at a real disadvantage. Of course they didn't serve water very often.

All along the road were artesian wells with water just flowing out of a pipe. Occasionally we were allowed to stop by the side of the road near one of these gushing wells. They'd make us sit there looking and listening to it for an hour or two. Then they'd move us along without any water, even though we'd sometimes try to talk a guard into letting us have some.

Those few times they would relent and let us at a well, we'd storm it like a stampede. Once it was so unbearable that we all broke for a well without permission and the Japs fired into the milling group of men. It was like shooting into a herd of cattle.

I went along about two days and was in real bad trouble. All I could get, whenever, was a cup of water, or maybe a buddy would share some of his canteen with me. On the third day we were waiting under some trees when I saw a Japanese civilian along the side of the highway, standing there with a quart bottle of water with a leather string around it. Now, I'd disposed of everything, but I did have a twenty-peso note rolled up and slipped into my hip pocket. I thought he might sell me his water, so I walked up to him and said, "Joe." I held out my twenty-peso bill and pointed to his water. He didn't say anything, but took the money and handed me the bottle. That's how I managed to get a quart of water and a bottle.

2d Lt. HADLEY WATSON, Company H, 57th Infantry, Philippine Scouts:

A Jap guard had taken one poor sick devil from the Air Force and had made him tote his field pack. After a while he couldn't tote it any further and he fell. When the Jap reached out to conk him, I stepped between them. That bugger hit me instead and told me to carry the pack. I never toted a pack as heavy as that one. So I started carrying that old Nip's pack. I went along there and some of the guys later started calling me an ass-kisser. I said, "That's all right, call me whatever you want, but I saved one guy's life." Later, the guard gave me a piece of cracker and some of that long-haired tea. Hell, I got to do something to survive. Later, we got down to a creek and this Jap guard let me go down and get some water. He gave me all kinds of privileges for toting his pack. Next day he was gone and I was back being on my own.

Pfc. JACK BRADY, 228th Signal Operations Company:

There were a couple of things that still bother me about the Death March. One of them was having to leave a friend behind because he couldn't go on and we couldn't carry him any longer. The other experience was when I tried to get some water. I guess you might say I was thirsty and I tried to get some water at one of those artesian wells. One of the Jap guards came up to me and with the butt of his rifle got me right between the shoulder blades. From the time I was hit until I got to O'Donnell I really don't remember a whole lot, because I just hurt too much.

Sgt. CHARLES COOK, 27th Bombardment Group (L):

By the second day I'd thrown my tent half away, my pistol belt away, and everything else extra. I had cut a piece out of my mosquito netting, just enough to cover my face and hands when I laid down. These little squares and my canteen are the only things I carried. Everything else weighed a ton. All I was interested in after a while was trying to take one step at a time. Along the side of the road people had thrown everything they didn't need to live with.

You didn't dare stop to get water. They'd bayonet you if you tried. I'll never forget or forgive them. Dag blast it, somebody gave orders to water their horses. Why not us?

I know one time I broke ranks to fill my canteen with water. I heard this Jap holler. He was running up to me. So I ran through the back of the barrio, jumping fences and scattering chickens. I came back to the column and just mixed in with the men. The guard never found me. I don't know which day this was, it was just on the walk.

Pfc. EDDY LAURSEN, 93d Bombardment Squadron:

Carl became more and more incapacitated the longer we walked. It reached the point that I had to enlist the aid of another soldier to help me carry him. One point we didn't have any Japanese soldiers around us and we were totally exhausted. I noticed a Filipino hut on top of a hill. I told the other two, "Let's go up this hill and maybe we can rest in that hut for a while." They thought that was a good idea, so we clambered up the hill. As we reached the top of it, lo and behold, we found six Japanese resting in the nipa hut. Today I get goosepimples thinking about it because they could have wiped us out right then and there. But they looked at us kind of startled as we looked at them kind of startled. Through sign language I indicated that one of my comrades was sick and that we wanted to lie down and rest in the shade. They said yes. Immediately though, they took whatever personal possessions we had managed to keep, but they let us rest. They also let us get all the water we wanted.

After a while, before we wore out our welcome, I decided we better pack up and leave, and when we got the chance joined another group on the road and got back out on the March.

Capt. MARK WOHLFELD, 27th Bombardment Group (L):

Midmorning one of the days, we boarded some trucks that were coming back from dumping their equipment down at the staging area for Corregidor. They jammed us on tight until we were like vertical logs. As the trucks went forward, we passed some marching American columns. When these men saw Americans on the trucks they tried to hang on to the sides and backs of the trucks. We were moving too fast and they fell off. If they didn't get to their feet fast enough, they were caught and beaten by their guards.

A few hours later we rolled into Capas, from where we walked an additional few miles to Camp O'Donnell. A week later I realized how lucky I was. Most of the men had walked, not ridden, out of Bataan. These men, when they began to arrive at O'Donnell, were in just terrible condition. It was hard to believe that these were the same men that I had surrendered with.

Capt. LOYD MILLS, Company C, 57th Infantry,
Philippine Scouts:

The nights were the worst times for me. We walked all day, from early morning until dusk. Then we were put into barbed-wire enclosures in which the conditions were nearly indescribable. Filth and defecation all over the place. The smell was terrible. These same enclosures had been used every night, and when my group got to them, they were covered by the filth of five or six nights.

I had dysentery pretty bad, but I didn't worry about it because there wasn't anything you could do about it. You didn't stop on "the March" because you were dead if you did. They didn't mess around with you. You didn't have time to pull out and go over and squat. You would just release wherever you were. Generally right on yourself, or somebody else if they happened to be in your way. There was nothing else to do. Without food it was water more than anything. It just went through me . . . bang.

I was in a daze. One thing I knew was that I had to keep going. I was young, so I had that advantage over some of the older men. I helped along the way. If someone near you started stumbling and looked like he was going to fall, you would try to literally pick him up and keep him going. You always talked to them. Tried to make them understand that if they fell they were gone. 'Course, there was nothing you could do about the people who fell in the back.

Pvt. LEON BECK, Antitank Company, 31st Infantry:

They'd halt us at these big artesian wells. There'd be a four-inch pipe coming up out of the ground which was connected to a well, and the water would be flowing full force out of it. There were hundreds of these wells all over Bataan. They'd halt us intentionally in front of these wells so we could see the water and they wouldn't let us have any. Anyone who would make a break for the water would be shot or bayoneted. Then they were left there. Finally it got so bad further along the road that you never got away from the stench of death. There were bodies laying all along the road in various degrees of decomposition—swollen, burst open, maggots crawling by the thousands —black, featureless corpses. And they stank!

Sometimes they'd make us stand at attention two or three hours. They'd just stop us and make us stand still. If you got caught sloughing off, shifting your weight from one foot to another, you'd get beaten. I remember very distinctly being beaten once. They hit me with a stalk of sugar cane, which is a pretty heavy instrument. Sugar cane grows anywhere from a half an inch to three inches in diameter and has a very hard skin on it. It doesn't wear out very easy. And they beat me all about the head and shoulders.

I can only remember being fed three times, and that consisted of walking past a gasoline drum that they were boiling rice in. You'd hold your hands out and a Filipino or a Japanese, depending on who was serving, would throw a spoonful of rice in your hands, and the next one would throw some salt on it, and you kept right on walking while eating out of your hands.

At night, when they put you in a barbed-wire enclosure, the Japs wouldn't let you dig latrines. Everybody had dysentery, and with no toilet facilities you'd just have your bowel movement wherever you were. So the nights were spent with people walking over you and around you, trying to avoid walking in the excrement which was everywhere. It just wasn't pleasant. No part of it. The days were worse than the nights though, because it was during the days that you caught the worst physical abuse.

And the weather was hot, hot, hot. The sun comes up hot, and it goes down hot, and it stays hot all night. It was just plain hell hot, the humidity was high, and the dust was everywhere, trucks moving alongside, raising more dust and confusion.

Sgt. FORREST KNOX, Company A, 192d Tank Battalion:

We were waiting in the sun. In an open rice paddy. We stayed there without water till a half dozen men had passed out from the heat. Then we were ripe. The guards put us on the road and double-timed us. Every kilometer they changed the guards because they could not stand to double-time in the sun either. After a couple of miles you could hear the shooting start at the tail of the column, as the clean-up squad went to work. The old Indian gauntlet with an Oriental twist.

While we were sitting there in the sun getting ripe, a Jap interpreter walked through the group. He was a 'Frisco Nip who could talk English like any American. He dumped out one officer's musette bag. It was packed full of money. He gave it a big kick and scattered it around. He said, "Where the hell do you think you are going, to whorehouse?" Then he laughed and walked away. He never even turned his head when we begged for water. That's when we started to double-time.

Capt. MARION LAWTON, 1st Battalion, 31st Regiment, Philippine Army:

We'd march all day, a continuous plodding along, just trying to keep up. I always tried to stay in the middle of the column rather than on the flanks. That way I was further away from the Japs and might avoid a random beating. I don't know how to explain a typical day except it was brutal, exhausting, hot, and your feet and legs just ached.

When we'd get to a little barrio or another convenient place, we might stop to change guards. Sometimes they'd pull us off the road to allow the truck convoys to go by. There weren't too many instances of people helping other people. You just didn't have any reserve strength to help anybody else. It was a matter of a person's survival. You could be generous up to a point, when there's plenty and you can share, but when you get down to the dregs there isn't much anybody can offer anybody else.

I believe once I was in a warehouse at night. Usually, however, I slept on the ground. Of course it was always crowded and always miserable. The ground would be hot and people would be milling around. Usually the faucet would have one spigot and there was always a line forming to get water. People were always stepping on or over you, people were cussing from being stepped on, and everybody was restless and frightened.

Pvt. LEON BECK, Antitank Company, 31st Infantry:

When it came daylight the Japanese would wake you up, make you form columns of four and stand at attention. Maybe once or twice they would allow an individual to collect a bunch of canteens so that he could go and get water. Then again maybe they wouldn't. It depended on the individual guards you were with.

First thing we would try to do is get all the men who were in the worst shape up to the front of the columns. That way as they got tired, and the men who were helping them wore out, we could pass them slowly back through the column taking turns holding them or helping them. We knew if a man reached a point where he couldn't walk any more, he was going to be killed. So we tried to take turns helping the sick and injured. Sometimes we would prevail upon the guards to let us regroup and we'd be able to put the sick back up front. Sometimes we couldn't.

The Jap guards wanted their little moments of glory. Sometimes they'd make you run at double-time. When you got all scattered out, and the guards couldn't adequately control you, they'd stop and bunch you up again. Then they'd make you double-time again until you straggled out some more, and the same procedures would happen again.

The most abusive guards I found were the Koreans. They looked different and wore a little different insignia. These Koreans had been conscripted into the Japanese Army and were used as service troops, because the Japs didn't trust them in combat. These guards hadn't seen any fighting and now they wanted to get a little blood on their bayonets—gung ho.

Staff Sgt. HAROLD FEINER, 17th Ordnance Company, Provisional Tank Group:

I don't know if the guards were Korean or Taiwanese. I was so miserable on that Death March that I couldn't tell you what they were. I know one thing about them, though—they were mean, sadistic, brutal. And yet, on "the March" I was befriended.

I had been hit at Cabcaben and had a piece of Corregidor shrapnel in my leg. It was the size of a piece of pencil lead and was laying along my shinbone. I had wrapped an old white towel around it and had managed to walk about fifteen miles, but I was getting weaker and more feverish the further I went. I was in bad shape. Guys had to help me. They would kind of hold onto me. If you fell, you were dead. They bayoneted you right away. No bullshit! If you fell, bingo, you were dead.

We finally stopped for the night near a small stream and I laid down. About an hour later this guy comes crawling along. He looked like an Italian, swarthy, kind of muscular. "Hey, fellows, any of you guys need any help?" he was whispering. "I'm a doctor." Didn't give us his name. When he got to me, he stopped and I told him about my leg. Just then a young guard saw us and came over. The first thing they did was hit you with their rifle butts. He spoke atrocious English and he yelled for us to separate. The doctor kept talking, and asked him would it be all right if he took the shrapnel out of my leg. "Wait, wait, wait," and he ran out into the road to see if anyone was coming. Then he came back and said, "Hurry, hurry." I remember the doctor saying, "Soldier, this is going to hurt. If you can take it, I'll get it out." He never had to worry about me hurting. As soon as he touched it, bam, I passed out. He took it out and wrapped a hand towel around my shin. When he left he said, "Yeah, well, I hope to God you make it. God bless you." He disappeared and I never got to know his name.

The Jap guard came up to me during the night and gave me a cup of sweetened chocolate, tasted like milk. I hadn't had any food and no water for days. I didn't speak one single word of Japanese then, but he could speak a little English, but with a really horrible accent. "Someday me go Hollywood, me going to be movie star." That's the way he talked. He made me laugh. All through the night he gave me something, because he knew I needed strength. In the morning he was gone. His squad had been replaced by another. The orders were given, "Everybody up, up, up." We got in line and I found I couldn't walk. My leg hurt so much. Some guys held me up and I was carried about 100 feet to the road. There we were told to stop and sit down. Then we were told to get up. We waited about a half an hour before we were permitted to sit down again. Then we were turned around and marched back to where we started. Wait . . . rest . . . wait . . . march . . . turn around . . . go back. We did this the whole day. I never had to walk, and by the time we started out the next day I had enough strength to limp along on my own. I'm not a religious man, but God said keep those men there, we want to save that man. I don't know what it was. I know I wouldn't have made it, if I had to march that day.

Maybe a day or so later we came to a river. I was still in fairly bad shape. There were a lot of little rivers, and because it was the dry season, they were shallow. The bridge had been knocked out and the Japanese had reconstructed an engineering bridge. Since their troops were crossing it when we arrived, we were made to march down the bank, cross the river, and march up the other side. Sounds simple. We were told not to touch the water. Some of the guys managed to drag their towels in the water and got some water that way. One man, however, reached over and tried to cup his hands and drink some. He was twelve feet from me. They shot him. Some guards on the bridge just popped him off. Going up the other side was hard for me with my leg. I kept sliding on the slimy clay. Finally some guys helped me up.

When we got to the top of the bank, there was a little bend

in the road before it crossed the bridge. At that point some Jap sentries were stationed and they were laughing at our struggles. When I got to the top—mind you, I was still crippled—for some reason, maybe because I needed help, one of the sentries took his rifle by the barrel and swung it at me and broke the ribs on my right side. Then I walked with broken ribs and a wounded leg. But I got to San Fernando. Had lots of help. But, hell, guys got there with less than me.

Pfc. CLETIS OVERTON, 27th Bombardment Group (L):

After the first couple of days I was sick, I felt feverish, thirsty, I didn't have anything to eat, and time became insignificant. Days and nights ran together. Certain things I can recall, though, but not the events that led up to them, or what happened later, or when they happened. I don't know why I remember things, but for instance . . . One night I knew we were crowded into a great big warehouse. They just crammed us in. It was a typical situation. There was no bathroom, no place to take a leak or have a bowel movement. So you just pulled down your britches for a bowel movement where you were. There was nowhere else to go. I don't know why I remember that, but that is something I remember.

Another time I saw a civilian woman bayoneted. Of course, on this March, the road was also full of civilians. They didn't know what was going on. There were times when we'd come up to a group of women and kids. I saw a Japanese guard by the side of the road knock a woman down, then slide his bayonet into her. That was the type of thing you saw going on.

Then, too, there was the time when we were stopped and in my group was an Italian-looking fellow who had a mustache. We were sitting, waiting for something. Well, some Japanese soldiers noticed this guy's mustache, and one of them came over and pulled it as hard as he could. They just laughed. Then another one came over and pulled it . . . and then another . . . and then another. Our guy just sat there and took it. He couldn't do anything.

I don't remember any food, except if you call it food, we passed a sugar cane field late one afternoon about sundown. Some of the boys broke through this sugar cane field and got stalks of cane and came back into formation with them. I had two or three joints of cane.

Like I said, time didn't mean anything, and most of the guys were sick, maybe near heat exhaustion, and I think some of us lost track of days. A lot of times if a fellow fell out, if he wasn't able to keep going or have his buddies help him, he was bayoneted. There's a couple of days I don't remember anything,

but I kept walking. I guess a couple of my buddies kept me
going.

2d Lt. KERMIT LAY, I Philippine Corps:

In our group there was a cavalry captain from Kansas City
named Miller who I had known before the war in Manila and
who I used to hang around with. When he was captured he still
was wearing Cavalry boots. During the March the boots got so
heavy that they began to rub huge blisters on his feet. He also
had dysentery and was real sick. A former MP company commander and I tried to hold him up. We were on either side of
him, but it was hard going on us and we began to fall further
and further back. Finally, one of the men at the rear of our
column, who kept watching for guards, yelled to us that a Jap
was coming. By now we were dragging Miller. When the guard
got to us he rammed his bayonet right through Captain Miller.
Naturally we dropped him and ran up and got into the middle
of the column.

Now some people think there was one Death March. There
were many Death Marches.

Pfc. EDDY LAURSEN, 93d Bombardment Squadron:

We were getting along pretty well when we came into a village
where we met a group of drunken Japanese soldiers. They were
drinking, laughing, and making fun of us. All of a sudden the
smallest one of the group jumped up and came into the line and
threw his arms up over my buddy Carl's neck and hung onto
him and wouldn't let go. We were now carrying Carl and the
Jap. We didn't dare fall down because no telling what would
happen. We proceeded this way for some time when suddenly
I felt a jerk. I don't know what happened exactly because my
entire concentration was on holding Carl up, but some of the
men behind told me later they had pulled the Jap off of us,
killed him, and rolled his body into a ditch. How they killed
him I don't know.

Cpl. WILLIAM HAUSER, Headquarters Company,
192d Tank Battalion:

I was sitting in this enclosure just numb by this time from the
heat, from the lack of food, and from the lack of water. We're
all sitting down in shit, because people had dysentery and
there was no place for them to go. There was one water spigot
for thousands of guys. If there was any shoving or pushing in
the water lines, the guards would come over and beat you. One

of the guys from our Headquarters Company got four inches of bayonet in his ass, and he didn't do the shoving. A Filipino did something, but our guy got picked out. He started to run but slipped and fell. A guard lunged at him with his bayonet. Then they dragged him over to a slit trench full of shit and kicked him in. This guy's arm kept coming out of the trench and the Japs kept pushing him back. If they didn't kill him with their bayonets, they made him drown in shit.

There were about 2,000 guys being kept in this enclosure at Lubao. If you played it smart you could remain there for a day or so while you rested. So we stayed there. We noticed that at some of the stops guys who had turned themselves in sick would get a truck ride to the next stopping point. We had a fellow with us who we'd been helping out, a guy named Emory. So Emory said, "I'm going to turn in sick and get a ride." We felt it was the best thing in the world, because we were pretty pooped ourselves from helping him. So, he turned himself in.

We spent another day in this compound when we decided, "Shit, we'll starve to death on the little bit of rice they're giving us." The next day we got in a column, and while I'm walking with a fellow from our outfit, I see a fellow drop out of line because he's got dysentery. He's off squatting with his pants down. I kind of recognize him and I kind of don't. When we got next to him, one of the guards walked over to him and started menacing him. To protect himself he put his hands up. I don't know what was in the guard's mind, maybe he figured the guy's fighting back, but anyway he stuck his bayonet in him, pulled it out, and stuck it in again. Only then did I realize the guy was Emory. I don't know why he didn't get on a truck. I saw them kill him.

Pfc. BLAIR ROBINETT, Company C, 803d Engineers:

There was something I couldn't figure out. Looking down, I saw one footprint in the dust. It was dark and it was a perfect footprint shape. Only one, though. Now, I couldn't imagine how a one legged man could be walking. Finally, I saw a man in front of me limping badly and his leg had blood running down it. Then I figured out how I could see one print. It was being left by the blood. A mile or so later his limp was so bad that he dropped out of the line.

Tech. Sgt. WILLIAM SNIEZKO, Company B, 31st Infantry:

I think it was the day before we got to Balanga. I was so weak and so sick, I just passed out on the road. If an individual defecated right before my face, I don't think I could have moved.

I was too weak to get up. Not only that, I didn't care whether I got up or not. I was just hoping somebody would kill me, put me out of my misery. I saw them do it to the others and I figured they'd do it to me. As I lay there I'd hear Americans talking to me as they went by, "Why don't you move out of there? Come on, get up." No one came over to help me up, though.

After I lay there for a while, a Japanese officer came up and moved me into the shade of a tree. He told me to rest. Then he had food brought to me, but because I was so sick I couldn't eat it. He let me rest there for two days before he came over again. I told him I was still sick. He said I'd better get up and walk. I was hoping he'd let me stay another day, although I was feeling better and stronger. Then he told me if I didn't move, he'd kill me. I got up and moved.

2d Lt. KERMIT LAY, I Philippine Corps:

I was real bad. This MP captain who had helped me hold up Captain Miller started looking out after me. I was getting weary. He said, "Come on, Kermit." I felt I couldn't take another step. "I'm going to fall out. I can't help it." He kept talking, "Come on, you can't do that." But I began to stagger, and as I went through one of the ranks I looked over and saw old Colonel Garfinkel. I really disliked him. I was over in the Philippines one time before, 1935, and had made corporal, and I remembered that Garfinkel had reduced me. When I saw him now I said to myself, "If that old gray-haired bastard can make it, so can I." He gave me incentive. So I managed to keep on chugging.

Cpl. ROBERT WOLFERSBERGER,
27th Bombardment Group (L):

I could see some artillery pieces by the side of the road and some Japs taking a break in the shade. Some of them had tied a big pole onto a tree so that it could swing back and forth. With this they were taking turns raking it through the column of men. It was a big game to them, seeing how many of us they could knock down with one swoosh of this pile driver across the road. Some guys would duck or fall down, and the guy behind would stumble. It created a lot of confusion.

Of course we had a grapevine that worked like a telephone. Word traveled pretty fast. If there was trouble up ahead the word would come back down the column, and those who could, would walk more lightly. When we saw the trucks carrying infantry, we learned to get as far off the road as we could. The Jap troops would carry bamboo sticks—rifle butts were heavy—and they'd lean out and swat you as they went by. If they didn't have sticks, they had stones or knotted ropes. They'd just swing whatever they had and see if they could hit you.

2d Lt. KERMIT LAY, I Philippine Corps:

There were things you didn't want to see. You tried not to see. There was this soldier that the Jap cars and trucks had rolled over. They'd run over this thing so many times that it looked like one of those small squashed animals you see on the freeway.

Another time there was a soldier sitting on a culvert with a stick in his hand. It looked like he was resting, but he was dead. The Japs had propped him up that way.

You tried to block everything out of your mind. You'd grit your teeth and say over and over, "I'm going to make it!" That way you would kind of block some things out. Some things got through.

Pfc. BLAIR ROBINETT, Company C, 803d Engineers:

They had all of us strip. We were strung out in long lines, jaybird naked. And they came along checking the clothes to see if there were any weapons concealed in them. This was around Limay. After we got dressed, an English-speaking Jap ordered all members of the Engineers to move off to the side. Whenever they specify a given branch that way, engineer means work. It means heavy work, bridge-building or road-building. Now, if he said, "Everybody six feet tall, brown hair, blue eyes, step out to the side," I'd more than likely step off to the side. But when he said, "Engineers," not on your damn life! It went through my mind the bastards wanted me to work. Nothing doing. To hell with them. I'll keep walking. Had I moved off to the side, there's a good chance I'd have had truck transportation. But there's a hell of a good chance I'd have died. The reason you find so few Engineers alive today is that most of them stepped out of line right there at Limay. The Japanese worked them to death. So when my column moved out, a lot of my buddies stayed behind on the side of the road.

Sgt. CHARLES COOK, 27th Bombardment Group (L):

The heat was terrible. Even the rocks were hot. I fell back towards the end of the column. This Jap just kept poking me with his bayonet. I knew what he wanted. He didn't have to put that bayonet at you but once. Somehow or other the passion to hate him kept me going. The hatred and the fear, a combination of both, gave me the strength to go on. I dug into this strength and got on up to the middle of the column.

Pvt. LEON BECK, Antitank Company, 31st Infantry:

On the march I was with four other men from my company. Already we had started to form little cliques that would look after each other. We would talk about food, the abuse we were getting, where we were going, and how long it would take before we were liberated. The consensus was that it would take six months before we'd be free again. That's one of the reasons I think I couldn't convince anyone to escape with me. There were too many uncertainties in an escape—where you're going, what are you going to do when you get there. You don't speak the language, you're sick, you're hungry, you're broke, and don't have any weapons and you don't know if the Filipinos are going to be receptive or not. But evidence had shown me that in every settlement we had gone through, the Filipinos would attempt to give us food and water. They'd take this old crude sugar which they cooked themselves, roll it into balls, and throw it to us. So I felt if I could survive the escape itself I had a pretty good chance with the people themselves, even if I couldn't speak the language. So I decided I was going to escape.

At the end of one day which had its usual number of head bangings and physical harassments, we got lined up in the town of Lubao. In front of us was a big corrugated tin warehouse called a *bodega*.* I knew we were in trouble when they began forcing the columns in there at bayonet point. So I worked my way to the edge of my group and snuck out and hid in an old burned-out building. I got back up into what was left of the tin roof and I hid out. I could just see the men being prodded into this building at bayonet point. When everyone was in they closed all the windows and doors and posted guards around the perimeter.

When I looked around my own roost, I found a jar of malt powder. I was so hungry I decided to eat it all right then. That way I didn't have to share it with the others. That was the point you reached, you got very possessive of little things. If you've ever tried to eat malt powder you know the first thing it does is form a ball when it gets wet, and it just sticks to the roof of your mouth. Gee, I got sick and threw up. I'd probably been better off if I'd not attempted to eat it all. But I was so hungry.

---

* This sheet iron warehouse in Lubao was owned by the National Rice and Corn Corporation. It was about 150 by 70 feet, and was located in a fenced-off area measuring 300 by 100 feet.

The next morning I saw that the Japs had a big hole dug across the road and they were throwing people in. Whoever couldn't get up off the *bodega*'s floor was being carried out and thrown in the ditch. Some would start to crawl out and the Japs would knock them on the head and throw them back in. Then they filled the hole—alive or dead, it didn't matter any.

2d Lt. KERMIT LAY, I Philippine Corps:

There was a big tin warehouse or granary somewhere along "the March" that they packed us into one night. You could sit or lay down, but there was no water and it was very hot. And it stank! The next morning across the road the Japs had dug a hole and had some Filipino soldiers burying some dead men, except not everyone was dead. One poor soul kept trying to claw his way out of the hole. The Jap guards really started giving these Filipinos a hard time, trying to get them to cover this man up faster. Finally a Jap came over, took a shovel and beat him on the head with it. Then he had the Filipinos cover him up.

Pvt. LEON BECK, Antitank Company, 31st Infantry:

As the groups reformed to continue the March after the night in the warehouse, I wiggled my way out from under the tin and joined a new group. The word had come down the line that if you didn't escape before you got to San Fernando, there would be no chance to escape because there they were going to put us into trains.

By then I was mentally to the point where I thought I was going to die, but I also knew, come hell or high water, I wasn't going to die a captive. Up till then I kept going, as sick and as weak as I was, out of sheer will power. There wasn't any magic formula other than will power.

In this new group I couldn't get anyone to go with me, so when I got to the town of Guagua, which was a few kilometers up from Lubao, they all helped me watch the guards, and I took off. I said, "Dear Lord, if you don't let my feet get stuck in the swamp, I'll keep pickin' 'em up and puttin' 'em down." It was all rice crops and fish ponds around me and I kept moving through a swamp, getting further and further away from the column.

Pfc. BLAIR ROBINETT, Company C, 803d Engineers:

One morning they moved us out into what I imagine was a *camote*, or sweet potato field. We were crowded up against one another, column after column moved in. Side by side we sat with our arms folded, heads bowed with the sun beating down on the back of our necks. I sat there three or four hours. The heat tore into the middle of the field. Some of the men passed out from heat prostration. I can't remember whether I collapsed, something runs in my mind that I did. What I remember next is a guard poking me with his bayonet trying to get me on my feet. I looked up at him and said, "Go ahead, you sonovabitch, do it." An American Air Force sergeant was standing alongside me, I don't know who he was, but he reached down and grabbed me and pulled me to my feet and into the line. He and somebody else held me between them when we began to walk. I couldn't manage to stand up. I told them they should leave me. "Oh, no," he said, "couldn't do that. You need something inside you." He had his blouse tucked into his pants and there was a bulge around his waist. He reached into his shirt and came out with a raw sweet potato. After I'd eaten one or two of them, I was back in business again.

Tech. Sgt. MEL MADERO, Company C,
194th Tank Battalion:

When my group got close to San Fernando, off to the right I spotted a sugar cane field in full bloom, looked like bamboo, but to men as hungry as we were we knew what it was. The words swept the ranks like wild fire. "There's sugar cane out there." Of course we couldn't remember when they'd fed us last. Many were near the end. No more hope for some. We knew the consequences—we broke ranks—took off for the cane. A vast army of locusts descending on a field to devour it. That was us. We took the Japanese guards by such surprise they didn't know what the hell to do. No one gave any orders, no one spoke, we just went into that field and tore it down. The guards finally rounded us up and got us back walking down the road. If someone had looked back at that field they would have seen nothing but nubs left on a hill. We gnawed on this sugar all day. We were told when we first arrived on the islands not to eat any native foods for sanitation reasons. They fertilized things differently. Here I had been so smart, using my iodine to purify my water. No dysentery. But polluted water was nothing compared to what pure sugar juice did to my innards. It got me to the trains at San Fernando, but it was a very unpleasant deal.

Cpl. HUBERT GATER, 200th Coast Artillery (AA):

Late in the day my group had been herded into a field surrounded by three strands of barbed wire. It could have been the town square or close to it. There were a number of Filipino and American soldiers already there. We were so tired, hungry, thirsty, and many so sick or wounded, that we didn't at first notice the condition of those that were there. We would never forget it by the time we left the next day. Fortunately, it was close to dark and we didn't have to sit under the tropical sun. It had been another long, hot day without food and very little water.

The night before, about 100 of us were crowded into what probably was a deserted two-room schoolhouse. We slept with heads on knees, not enough room to lay down.

Sometime after dark the Japs brought some cans of rice to the enclosure gate. A five-gallon can for each hundred men. These cans were not full. Who cared? Those close to the gate were fed. There was not enough to go around. There was no crowding or pushing. A friend helped a friend. Many didn't care. Besides being tired, many were in the last stage of malaria. Just to be left alone in the grass or dirt to rest, sleep, or die. To have at least one close friend, a buddy to hold you in his arms and comfort you as you died, was enough. The few that still had faith and courage would have lost it if they could have foreseen the future.

During the night, the Jap soldiers on guard had a game— for them. They would run in and act like they were going to bayonet a sick or wounded man, usually lying down. If the man had the energy to jump up to defend himself, he got bayoneted —not to kill, just to torture. Good, clean fun.

It was a long night. Too tired and hungry to sleep, but cautious enough to play possum. Morning came. Malaria, dysentery, and complete exhaustion was taking over. We discovered many in the field were dead. Some perhaps the day before that we hadn't noticed. Men with dysentery lay in their own filth. The sound of men moaning and gasping came from every direction. As the sun came up, so did the odor and the flies.

Later I talked to men at Camp O'Donnell who were behind us and arrived at San Fernando a day or two later. The dead had not been buried. The same terrible odor had doubled, and the sick and dying almost filled the area.

Capt. JOHN SPAINHOWER, 57th Infantry,
Philippine Scouts:

It was about noon. We had been herded into this compound and we were made to just sit in the sun. There was no shade. They saw to it that we had no shade. I came down with sunstroke. My buddies asked a Jap whether they could move me. He consented to this, so I was carried out of the compound and into a medical shack along with a lot of other Americans. This was at Orani. There was a Jap, I don't know who he was, brought me a sort of broth. It was kind of green and seaweedy.

The next morning an Air Force major lying alongside of me died. His groaning, in fact, awakened me. When I reached over, he was dead. I figured we were all going to die. I felt pretty fair, though, but not where I thought I wanted to rejoin my group. I saw them walk by around dawn going on another day. A few hours later a Japanese truck convoy, returning from Bataan where they'd taken artillery and supplies, stopped outside our shed. They loaded all the sick, the lame, and the lazy onto those trucks and moved us to San Fernando. Incidentally, at the time they loaded us on that truck I'll have to admit to being lazy. I wasn't sick any longer. I went past my group about twenty minutes later. They'd been on the road in the sun a couple of hours.

Tech. Sgt. ALFRED SCHREIBER, 27th Materiel Squadron:

With the exception of the railroad cars at San Fernando, I had a pretty straight march. In fact, there was a stretch of several miles when my group had no guards in sight. We could have taken off, I guess, but where would we have gone? I know we talked about escaping, but hell, there might be a bunch of Japs waiting for you. If you ran, you damn well knew you'd be shot if you were caught. As long as we were on the road, we figured we'd make it.

Pfc. BLAIR ROBINETT, Company C, 803d Engineers:

We'd come out of Lubao marching to San Fernando, had my life saved that morning, and we had almost reached the town of Guagua. We were stopped by a small bridge. I recognized where we were because I had helped blow this bridge four months before on our withdrawal into Bataan. The Japs had rebuilt only one span of it, so the traffic could go only one way at a time. We'd been pulled off the side of the road to let some trucks cross over first. We were on the north side of the road and there was a hot wind blowing from the south.

The road out of Bataan was covered with dust about up to your ankles. This day the dust was piling sky high. The Jap guards, in order to avoid having the dust blown on them, stepped to the other side of the road. My group was resting next to a high gardenia hedge. The trucks came down the road and the dust just covered us. We sat there eating grime. It got so bad we couldn't hardly see the trucks. Couldn't see the Jap guards, either. Suddenly my brain began to work. If I couldn't see the damn guards, they couldn't see me. If I was going to run, this was a good time to do it. I took off, jumped through the hedge, ran 150 feet, and dropped over the edge into a marsh. Father Duffy was right behind me. He made the break same time as me. We hadn't talked about it ahead of time. It was a good opportunity. We just instinctively went.

Duffy dropped down next to me and we lay back against the bank, hidden by an overgrowth. We lay there trying to catch our breath. About an hour later a Filipino boy, who must have seen us escape, came across to the edge of the bank and said, "Sir, can you hear me?" I debated whether to answer him or not, but at some point I was going to have to trust somebody, so I whispered back, "Yes, I can hear you." He told us to stay there and at dark he'd come back for us. About the time the sun started to go down this Filipino boy came back, picked up the two of us, and moved us across the marsh onto a creek. From there we were put into a dugout canoe and moved three or four miles into the fish ponds.

Cpl. CHARLES McCARTIN, Company B, 803d Engineers:

We came into a town with men standing in line waiting to be fed. We got in line. We hadn't stood there five minutes when some Japanese guards came over and ordered about 200 of us to start walking. We found out that the Japs had found someone with contraband, and they were going to punish our group for that by making us walk all night. So we walked most of the night. By midnight we were exhausted. We didn't know in which direction we were walking or which foot we were putting forward. We just went along blindly. The guards eventually got tired, too, and they gave us a little rest. We sat on the side of the road and my friend told me he couldn't go on. He was just too exhausted. I had taken his small pack to start with, and when I couldn't carry it any longer he agreed I could throw it away. After a while he started falling back towards the end of the group where the guards with the bayonets were. I could see he was about finished. He had gotten to the point where he didn't care whether they stabbed him or not. Luckily I was able to hold him on my shoulder long enough till we got to the rest spot.

As we sat there he got the idea that he would just roll over into the jungle. We all watched the guards. When they were as far away from us as they normally would get, my friend just rolled down the side of the road into the jungle.

Without having to carry him I managed to stick with the group, and we eventually did stop at a place where they gave us a plateful of mushy rice. We were allowed to sleep there and the next day we walked into San Fernando.

Pfc. EDDY LAURSEN, 93d Bombardment Squadron:

On the March Carl and I discussed escaping, pro and con. We finally decided to give up the idea, primarily because we'd have to run sometime sooner or later. And run like hell. We knew that. And Carl couldn't run ten feet if he had to, he was so weak. So we gave up the idea. The next day we got to San Fernando, where they run us into a huge compound with the dust and the dirt and the filth a foot deep.

Sgt. CHARLES COOK, 27th Bombardment Group (L):

The last night outside of San Fernando I walked all night. They changed guards from flatbed trucks. They wouldn't let us stop. All night long. Earlier that evening, when we arrived at the compound where we should have stopped, we found it so crowded that we couldn't get in. I said to myself, "Oh, I can make it down the road another 100 feet or so to the next compound." I didn't know that the next one, for me at least, was San Fernando.

It was then that I thought I might go, escape. Nobody around me talked about it. I remember saying out loud that if anybody would go with me, I was willing to take off. Nobody said anything. It was as if I was walking with a bunch of dead people. I was having an inner dream, marching, walking, straggling, escaping.

All night long we walked. Around dawn I began to feel that my shoes were full of sand. Somewhere we got a short break and I took my shoes off. They weren't full of sand, my feet were just burned up. I had about 10,000 teeny blisters, no bigger than a pin, on the bottom of my feet.

Cpl. ROBERT WOLFERSBERGER,
27th Bombardment Group (L):

My one night in San Fernando, waiting for the train, was spent in a cockfight pit.* The floor was bare dirt and at one end there were some wooden bleachers. People kept shuffling around, stirring up the dust. The heat was just unbearable. I mean, the heat from the men, mixed with the sun. They just jammed us in there. The misery was indescribable. The misery gave way

---

* Located in an open field, the cockpit was a large shed with open ends. Prisoners arriving in San Fernando were also assembled in an elementary school.

to hate and that built up inside me. I kept saying to myself, "I'll see you in the damn grave, not me."

Pfc. ROBERT BROWN, 17th Pursuit Squadron:

When I pulled into the bullpen it was full of people. It was at night. There was a lot of dust, dirt, filth on the ground. Everybody had dysentery. There were no toilets. It was absolutely horrible. I just fell down in the dirt and slept. But there wasn't much sleeping because people were going crazy. My God! They were screaming and going nuts. It was a nightmare. We were just jammed in there and we were all sick and we all had dysentery and we were hungry. It was like being in a cage with animals. I don't know how else to describe it.

Pfc. ROY DIAZ, Company C, 194th Tank Battalion:

The first time I defecated was in the cockfight arena in San Fernando. I hadn't had anything to eat and I was just constipated. God, how it hurt. My company commander was hollering so, trying to relieve himself. Finally, he got his fingers in and dug it out, so packed in was it.

Sgt. CHARLES COOK, 27th Bombardment Group (L):

I must have been one of the first groups that got into the boxcars, because I don't remember hearing a rumor about them. To know that we were there at the railroad station meant riding instead of walking. That was a good feeling, but it turned out worse than "the March"*

Pfc. ROBERT BROWN, 17th Pursuit Squadron:

They took us over and made us sit down by this railroad train. We were ordered to sit and cross our legs and to put our hands on our keees, and if we looked to either side we got beaten or bayoneted.

Cpl. HUBERT GATER, 200th Coast Artillery (AA):

Shortly after noon all that could walk were lined up outside the barbed wire and marched a few blocks to the railroad. In the months ahead we would realize that each time we left the sick they would never be seen again.

---

* The cars used by the Japanese to transport the prisoners were narrow-gauge boxcars made either of steel or wood. The larger steel cars were about thirty-three feet long, eight feet across, and seven feet high. The wooden cars were half as long and almost a foot shorter in height. Both had sliding doors on either side. The prisoners were placed in these cars and moved to Capas, twenty-five miles north of San Fernando.

There was a train and a few boxcars. The Filipino trains are smaller than ours and the boxcars about two-thirds the size we use. Our spirits rose. We were going to ride instead of more marching. In a few minutes we all wished we had continued to march. The boxcars had sat in the tropical sun with the doors closed.

The Japs divided us into groups of 100 men for each car. One Jap guard was assigned to a car. He pulled the door back and motioned inside. The heat from inside hit us in the face. We stalled for time but the Jap guard with his bayonet motioned us to climb in and he meant business. We all knew by now to openly resist them would be fatal.

We jammed in—standing room only. Into the oven we went and, protest be damned, the doors were closed. The three hours that followed are almost indescribable. Men fainting with no place to fall. Those with dysentery had no control of themselves. As the car swayed, the urine, the sweat, and the vomit rolled three inches deep back and forth around and in our shoes. Very little complaining.

Tech. Sgt. WILLIAM SNIEZKO, Company B, 31st Infantry:

They packed us in just as tight as you can be packed. In fact, I know there were people that never stood on the floor. They were being held up by their friends. The ones in the back, where there wasn't any air, passed out. I was about in the middle. Everyone at first started yelling and screaming. It was worse than anything that had gone on before. We decided we'd better save our breath and conserve our strength, because we knew they weren't going to open up the doors until we arrived at our destination.

Pfc. JACK BRADY, 228th Signal Operations:

It seems to me that once in a while our train would stop, and the Jap guards would open the doors so we could get some fresh air. Then is when we'd get the dead ones out. If we could, we'd lift the corpses and pass them over to the door. There was no way we could have passed them through. I never had much use for one character. When one of the men finally did die, this man cursed at him because he hadn't died sooner, so we could get him out the door and make more room.

Sgt. NICHOLAS FRYZIUK,
Company B, 192d Tank Battalion:

When they closed the doors it was like suffocating. It was hotter than a sonovabitch. I knew Paar, the guy I had helped all along "the March," was going to be a goner for sure. He stunk already. Another guy behind me began to holler and scream. He couldn't breathe. A lot of guys were in bad shape. I wiggled as best I could and got by the goddamn door and forced it open a little. Some guys said, "The Japs are going to shoot us." "Fuck 'em," I said. "Let 'em shoot me." The air hit us in there. It was hot air, but any air was welcome.

When we got to Capas, before we walked to O'Donnell, it was pandemonium. Japs and prisoners all milling around. What confusion! I got Paar under a tree and then began to look around for others I could help. I was trying to do my part the best I could. I looked for friends—well, everybody's your friend. You look at one guy, there's forty others. Hell, what could I do?

Cpl. HUBERT GATER, 200th Coast Artillery (AA):

We arrived at the small town of Capas. The boxcar doors were opened and we were ordered out. Sit down and be counted. Who could have escaped from that oven? While the Japs were making sure of the count, it gave us the opportunity to take off our shoes and pour the filth on the ground.

After a brief rest, we were told to get up and line up in a column of twos. Then we started marching down a dirt road the last five or six miles to Camp O'Donnell.

Some had marched all the way. A few had come by truck. Those that marched all the way suffered more. Many were back in Bataan, a day or two longer to march out. It wasn't the miles, it was the continuous delays along "the March." The change of Jap command and guards. Standing in place for two or three hours, waiting for the order to start marching again. The lack of food and water, the rundown condition of the men before the start. A combination of all these things would make O'Donnell just one big graveyard.

4
O'DONNELL

Camp O'Donnell was a partially completed American airfield eight miles west of the Manila Railroad line at Capas. It was here that the Japanese decided to imprison the men captured on Bataan, until Corregidor surrendered. Surrounding the camp, a high barbed-wire fence was strung and wooden gun towers built. Around this stockade in every direction, tall cogon grass grew on a brown, rolling, nearly treeless plain.

The camp consisted of nipa-roofed barracks, many still unfinished. During the American-Filipino retreat in December, an attempt was made to deny the Japanese use of the facility by destroying its water supply. The attempt was not completely successful, so when the American prisoners arrived four months later, there were, in their section of the camp, two partially functioning water pumps.

No medical facilities were supplied. Barracks were taken over and called a hospital. The doctors and corpsmen used only the medicine they managed to carry with them.

It was in Camp O'Donnell that the American prisoners first learned they would not be protected by any international agreement. Because of the confusion created in the handling of World War I captives, it had been suggested in 1921 that a diplomatic convention on prisoners of war should be held. Eight years of study by the International Committee of the Red Cross and interested governments led to the meeting of the Conference of Geneva, at which the agreement of 1929 Relative to the Treatment of Prisoners of War was drawn up. The final provisions of the Convention finally adopted by forty-three nations provide, first of all, a definition of the term "prisoners of war," and state that prisoners must be humanely treated. The articles further state that their honor shall be respected and the detaining power must provide for their maintenance. The Japanese government felt a fundamental objection to many of the articles and ordered its delegation not to accede to the proposed convention. Their point of view was summarized by the chief Japanese representative, Isaburo Yoshida, when he stated "that real improvement in the condition of prisoners depends, in the final analysis, on the humanitarian sentiments and good will of the belligerents." To help understand Japan's point of view towards prisoners, it should be remembered that the Japanese consider anyone who surrenders a traitor to their country and worthy only of contempt and of the harshest treatment at the hand of friend and foe alike. The Western idea of surrender simply does not apply to Japanese thought. Being taken prisoner while still able to resist was considered by the Japanese military to be a criminal act. Suicide, rather than surrender, was preferred.

Not wanting to stand out as one of the few nations not to agree with the articles of the 1929 Geneva Convention, the Japanese delegation signed the agreement. The Japanese government, however, failed to ratify it and at the beginning of World War II Japan stated they would apply it, withal "mutatis mutandis." This, in fact, they never did. In the absence of the Geneva Convention Japan's regulations for handling prisoners of war came from revised versions of Instruction No. 22, which had been issued to the Japanese Army in 1904.

By the end of April 1942, 9,300 Americans and perhaps 48,000 Filipinos had arrived at Camp

O'Donnell. How many men died on the trip will never accurately be known. Only crude guesses can be made. Probably between 5,000 and 10,000 Filipinos lost their lives. American deaths might conservatively be put between 600 and 700. What is known, however, is that the dying and suffering begun on "the March" did not end when the men arrived at O'Donnell. In fact, the Death March would not end for a very long time.

Pfc. JOHN FALCONER:

At the railroad station in Capas, the Japanese guards gave the Filipinos, who were around trying to help us, permission to pass us food. They had rice and meat or fish wrapped in banana leaves. I collected as much as I could carry. They then started passing out small, hard, caked sugar patties. I didn't have room for them, so I found a friend of mine from my home town. I told him that if he would carry all my banana leaves, I'd carry the sugar. Then, when we got to where we were going, we'd split what we had. This was a good deal for both of us, so we agreed to meet in the camp and divide the food.

Sgt. FORREST KNOX:

Down the road towards the camp, there were signs along the edge of the road which had one clear meaning: throw away Japanese money and souvenirs. The word was passed. It seemed that we marched in the east gate of O'Donnell to the inspection area. We spread out, about ten feet between men. All gear on the ground, pockets empty. The word was passed again, bury your Jap souvenirs. The area was loose sand. You could kick a small hole to drop something in and then drag dirt over it with your feet. The Jap reasoning was simple. You had to rob a dead Jap to get Jap money.

Cpl. HUBERT GATER:

A Japanese officer closely examined the possessions of each man. Three were told to step forward. A captain and an Arapaho Indian still had Japanese coins on them. My commanding officer, Captain Schultz, had a Jap fan. They were charged

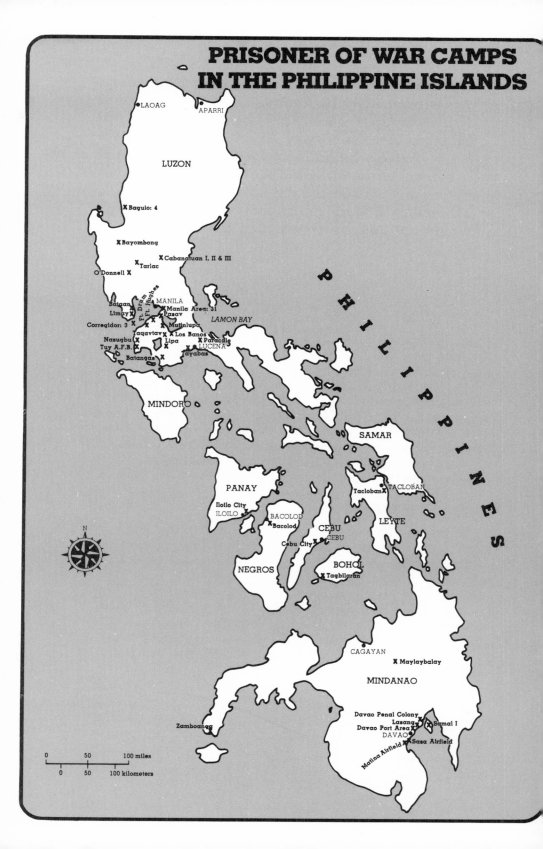

PRISONER OF WAR CAMPS
IN THE PHILIPPINE ISLANDS

●LAOAG   ●APARRI

LUZON

X Baguio: 4

X Bayombong

X Cabanatuan I, II & III
X Tarlac

O'Donnell X

Bataan MANILA
Limay X X Manila Area: 31
Ft. Drum X Pasay
Ft. Hughes
Corregidor: 3 X X Muntinlupa
Tagaytay X X Los Banos
Nasugbu X Lipa X Paracale
Tuy A.F.B. X X LUCENA
Batangas X Tayabas

LAMON BAY

MINDORO

PHILIPPINES

SAMAR

PANAY

Iloilo City Tacloban X X Tacloban
ILOILO

BACOLOD LEYTE
X Bacolod CEBU
CEBU
Cebu City X

NEGROS BOHOL
X Tagbilaran

CAGAYAN

X Maylaybalay

MINDANAO

Zamboanga

Davao Penal Colony
Lasang X X Samal I
Davao Port Area X
DAVAO
X Sasa Airfield
Matina Airfield X

0   50   100 miles

0   50   100 kilometers

N

with robbing dead Jap soldiers after battle. Of course this was a lie.

The morning of the surrender at Cabcaben Airfield, I was with Captain Schultz for the first few miles. A Jap soldier stopped Schultz and demanded cigarettes. In return, the Jap gave him a folding fan. It proved to be Captain Schultz's death sentence.

Sgt. FORREST KNOX:

Then we were marched to the area in front of headquarters. The commandant had a sort of table, or platform, he stood on. He was a little runt who talked in a high squeaky voice.* But no one laughed. We had just seen three fools led away to be shot. A word-for-word repeat of what he said would be difficult to recall. But I recall the message! The Japanese had not signed the Geneva Agreement, which regulated the way prisoners of war were to be treated. So we were not prisoners of war. We were guests of the Emperor. Then he worked himself into a frenzy. "You think you are the lucky ones. Your comrades died on Bataan. Those comrades are the lucky ones." He didn't make any mention of food or medical care. We thought it was an oversight. Later we thought it was deliberate.

1st Sgt. HOUSTON TURNER:

A Japanese officer gave us a little talk about what we could expect. He told us that Americans were dogs, that they'd always been dogs, and that they were going to be treated like dogs. He said that Caucasians had been enemies of the Oriental for 100 years and would always be enemies. He said these things real harsh. You might say, hysterical. Their way of expressing theirselves is a little different from us. He was jumping up and down like a duck on a hot plate. I didn't like the sound that Americans were dogs and that we were going to be treated like dogs. That's when I began to realize we had big problems.

Pfc. EDDY LAURSEN:

I still had Carl with me when we straggled into O'Donnell. On arrival they ordered us to sit out in the blazing hot sun. Carl asked me for some water. I always gave it to him, but I never gave him as much as he wanted. That was the point. He began gulping it. I said, "Take it easy, Carl." He said, "I'm going to drink all the water I want," and proceeded to empty the can-

---

* The Japanese camp commander was Captain Tsuneyoshi.

teen. In a minute he had passed out. Some of my buddies picked him up and the Japanese allowed us to put him in the shade of a nipa hut.

Eventually, the Japanese commandant came out and lectured us on how we should behave, now that we were guests of the Emperor of Japan. We listened to this boring lecture, laughing under our breath.

Afterwards, we were placed in O'Donnell. Carl came over to me and sheepishly apologized. I told him to forget about it, but pointed out that if he had done that on "the March," I would never have been able to carry him. We both knew what that would have meant.

Pfc. JOHN FALCONER:

When I got into O'Donnell, I had trouble finding the friend to whom I had given half my food. Finally I found him and he said, "Here, you take it all," and disappeared. I got all the wrapped packages that I had given him. When I looked in the banana leaves I found everything but the rice had been taken out. I learned later he had traded all the meat and fish for cigarettes. I don't know why, but I didn't get angry. I still had some rice left. God rest his soul, he didn't make it back. It taught me a very valuable lesson in survival, however: you looked out for yourself! You had to think very highly of yourself. You had to realize you were important.

Pfc. WILBURN SNYDER:

I remember when I first arrived at O'Donnell, General King telling some of the fellows that he felt he would stand trial for disobeying Wainwright's orders not to surrender. He said, "You men remember this. You did not surrender. You were surrendered. You had no alternative but to obey my order. I did the surrendering. I'm the one that has the responsibility, let me carry that responsibility."

Sgt. RALPH LEVENBERG:

The first thing we did was try to locate buddies. You'd walk through the camp asking whether anyone had seen or knew what happened to So-and-So. That way we tried to keep our squadron together. We talked of how long this would last— most thought three or four months at most. Then we counted the Jap planes from Clark Field that flew over and if fewer came back than went out, we'd wonder what happened to the missing planes. Then some guys would start to talk about home and tell stories about what they'd done before joining the Army.

You just marked time. You'd wait until they fed you. You'd stand for hours on the water line. Standing or sitting. Lethargic. I had a continuous dream. My favorite aunt, when I used to visit her, would always serve me my favorite breakfast of scrambled eggs and onions. For days at O'Donnell I'd wake up every morning waiting for this breakfast. All of us thought about family. Most of us were single and young. I was going on twenty-one. For most, it was the first time they'd been away from home. The weaker ones bawled. I mean like little kids wanting their mothers. We tried to help, but we learned from them one of the early rules of survival. When we found people who wouldn't help themselves, then, the hell with them.

I remember, in particular, one guy we tried to help. He was out of the squadron, an older man, married, and regular as a clock, if you know what I mean. Well, on the March and then at O'Donnell, he went nineteen days without a bowel movement. He had counted the days. Everyone, even the medics, explained to him the terrific changes his body was undergoing and that he shouldn't be surprised at his loss of regularity. But he didn't listen and he refused to eat. No way he was going to eat something he couldn't pass. We tried to force-feed him. Then before we got to him, he'd take his chow and dump it on the ground. Hell, we weren't going to let that happen, so we split up his chow. At this time most of us wouldn't take from another. Later, this happened. But even at O'Donnell, rather than see food wasted, we took. This was survival. The man died. Just starved himself to death.

Sgt. CHARLES COOK:

If I wanted a drink of water, I got up in the morning and headed for the water faucet. There would already be hundreds waiting in line. Just a water spigot. I'd have my own canteen and maybe someone else's. Seems like the only people who weren't in line were those who had already gotten their ration. I'd wait in line all day. The water would run a while, then they'd turn it off. So I just waited and took my chance.

Pfc. JOHN FALCONER:

Mostly, you stood with your canteen in line, waiting to get water. You stood for hours. I remember seeing men who had died while waiting in line. I don't claim to be a mathematician, but I knew if a certain number of men died each day, you knew sooner or later your own number was going to come up.

I'd sit by the fence and watch the bodies being carried out in blankets slung over poles. Endless movement. We sat and counted. Then there were so many we lost count.

Sgt. FORREST KNOX:

The odor in the camp gradually increased. I thought it was me smelling—no water to wash or bathe. Well, I finally snitched a canteen cup of water and took a bath. I only had a small bar of soap in my aluminum soap box, but I figured it would last a long time at the rate I was using it. I couldn't wash my clothes. Still, I made the attempt.

Cpl. GERALD WADE:

There was a creek just outside the camp. Before the war there had been a dam at one end, but this had been destroyed in the retreat. The American doctors decided they could use the raw river water to cook the rice ration in, but could not use it to drink from. Therefore the river was for cooking, and the pump for drinking. Everybody was dying of thirst. So the Japanese and the American doctors decided we could carry water from the river to the camp. Gilbert Neighorn and I decided, almost as soon as we arrived, to get on this detail.

After the Death March we were so filthy that on our first trip to the river Gil and I figured, the hell with it, we were going to take a bath. We got to swimming and noticed the only Japanese around were down a piece, working on the dam. "Goddam," I thought, "let's get out of here." So we swam across the creek. Because I was afraid the Japanese would come after us with dogs, we waded up another creek for about three hours. Then we broke out onto the plain. Then and there I had my first malaria attack. I just lay down out in the field and had my attack. It was one of the worst things you can go through. First, these very cold chills start up and down your back. You try to draw up as close as you can to keep warm. I shook like a leaf. Following this came a fever period where I was boiling hot. I was as weak as a damn kitten.

We stayed overnight, just laying in this field. The next day, around noon, we saw a Filipino who gave us what was left of his rice lunch. He spoke no English, but we traveled with him on a path that took us to a little group of huts back up in the hills. There we found a schoolteacher and a Philippine Scout sergeant who spoke English. I was very sick by the time I arrived. I couldn't even walk anymore.

Gilbert and I talked about getting to Mindanao. Sometime

the next day he decided he better try it on his own. So he went off and left me.

Sgt. FORREST KNOX:

This camp didn't have too good a fence, so the natives kept slipping out. Once outside the wire, who could tell a soldier from a civilian?

The Japs caught ten men outside the camp. Escapees or civilians, they didn't care. They made an example for everyone to see. Built a rack and hung them by their thumbs. The official verdict: guilty of escape, sentenced to be shot, sentence commuted to hanging by the thumbs in honor of the Emperor's birthday. His generosity was only exceeded by his good looks. I lived right across this road from where they hung. I wondered how long a man could hang in the sun without water. Well, after a number of days the Japs came by and cut them down. The incredible part was, one man was still alive. So they shot him. The Emperor's birthday was over and so was the Japanese lenience.

Pfc. JACK BRADY:

Unfortunately, there was no such thing as being laid up for a while at O'Donnell. There were people in much worse shape than I. Water had to be hauled, people had to be buried, wood needed to be brought in—all kinds of things needed doing. So in O'Donnell, if you could move, you did something.

The place was organized very simply. You picked where you wanted to lie down and that became yours. Officers or senior noncoms selected the men for work details. Those men selected, of course, weren't that many. Most of the men couldn't, or didn't, move. The first detail I went on was where I loaded wood onto trucks and carts for use in the camp. We needed wood to make the fire to boil the water to cook the rice in.

We had to have a water detail, too, because the only source in the camp of reasonably good water came from one pipe. The rest of the water had to come from the river. If it wasn't boiled before it was used, it would kill you. It would take a while, but you'd die. The stuff had more germs in it than it had water. We carried the water to the camp in fifty-gallon drums. It took eight men to carry each drum—four men carried and four men rested. Because there was constant need for water, this was a day-long detail. As soon as you made one trip, you'd go back for another.

The only thoughts I had at O'Donnell were of the flies.

They were so damn thick. At night they'd sit on the roofs and because there were so many of them, whole patches of thatch would fall down. What bushes there were we had stripped of leaves. But the branches were so thick with flies, they bent right down to the ground. Nowhere, absolutely nowhere, could you get away from those damned flies. All over. Everywhere. They were blue and green and they were all over the latrines and the food. When you ate, you had to keep waving your hand over the rice to keep the files from beating you to the chow. Still, sometimes, you'd get flies in your mouth.

I didn't go out on a detail every day because there were times that I went on what was called "sick call." I did not yet have dysentery, and it had been almost a month since I'd had a bowel movement, and I was getting a little bit concerned. Of course there wasn't anything to pass, but I didn't know that. For my constipation they just laughed and said I was lucky. Yes, I guess it's funny. It wasn't too long after that that I did get dysentery. I guess I ate too many flies.

The majority of men stood in the water line. The line stretched and curled around for hundreds of yards. A guard was somehow established on that line. Because the water just trickled out of a pipe, and to keep the line moving, they'd only let you fill half a canteen at a time. Otherwise it would take too long and fewer men would get water.

There was a time that several of us stood in line for days getting water to help Sergeant Couliss. He had become very ill with dysentery and anybody with dysentery becomes rather filthy. There's no way they can keep clean. We all thought he was dying. He sure did, and he told us that if he was going to die, he at least wanted to die clean. He was a good sergeant, so we stood in the line and got the water for him. Eventually, we must have gotten about two gallons. As soon as we cleaned him up, he recovered.

Dysentery was just terrible. They eventually separated the men with it from the other sick, by forming dysentery wards. You absolutely had no control, whatsoever, over your bowels. You just continuously eliminated feces mixed with blood and mucus. It's constant and it gets over everything and everyone. Eventually it killed you, unless you stopped running. Over all was the smell. Some people used handkerchiefs to cover their mouths and noses. It didn't do any good. You could still smell the stuff.

The graves detail was in two sections. There were those who dug the graves and those who carried the corpses. Each morning, as soon as we had finished eating what little chow we had, we'd go out to the burial grounds and start digging. We tried to dig three big graves at once, trying to get down as deep as we could. After the first group had gone out, the second would gather up the bodies that needed burying, usually picking the older bodies because they were most in need of burial. They'd be carried out and we'd try to have the graves ready so they could be put in right away and covered. Sometimes we were ready, sometimes we weren't. There were times when twenty to fifty bodies would lay in the heat, waiting for holes. We also tried to keep track of who was being buried. If they had dog tags on, we'd collect them. If they didn't, somebody would say who they thought it was and somebody else would write it down.

The corpses were carried in blankets strung over a pole. Then the poles were slipped out from the ends of the blankets and we'd pull the body out of the blanket. If it was at all possible we'd try to straighten the body out, because you could put more in a hole that way. Normally, we put them in head to foot. If they weren't straight they took up too much room and we had to dig many more holes that way. At one point we were putting in twenty to a grave. Because of the water table, some of the graves were only four or five feet deep, and when you stack two deep it doesn't leave much cover. It was completely mechanical. Once in a while, though, you found yourself burying a friend. Then that would be a little special. You might murmur a prayer. You just couldn't put your friend into a hole and cover him up without doing something extra.

Once I saw the opposite happen. There was a Corporal O'Brien and a Lieutenant O'Brien. For some reason Corporal O'Brien hated the guts of Lieutenant O'Brien. Something happened and the corporal promised the lieutenant that he was going to dig the lieutenant's grave and then piss on him before he covered him up. Two weeks or so later, Lieutenant O'Brien died and Corporal O'Brien kept his promise. A week later Corporal O'Brien also died.

Trouble with officers at O'Donnell was not unusual. The one thing that just really bothered me more than anything else was the absolute lack of control anyone had over them. And they apparently couldn't control themselves. I think they expected to have the same kind of consideration they got in peacetime. I think, too, that they thought they should have some extra privileges that nobody else had. For example, they expected somewhat better rations. The officers had better contacts with the Filipinos and through that were able to get better food. Once, when I was out on detail, I got four stalks of bananas. When I returned to camp they didn't go to the hospital. They went to the officers' mess. That's the kind of stuff I'm talking about. There were a large number of people who objected to this strenuously. They were going to kill the officers responsible. A large number of enlisted people began to take things into their own hands, and either they were going to get the extra food or get rid of the few who were eating it, one of the two. I think a couple of officers finally established control and the extra food in the officers' mess did stop.

Sgt. FORREST KNOX:

I was at the latrine. A man sitting at another hole was pulling the cheeks of his buttocks and straining. He was hurting. Finally, I asked, "Constipated?" He said, "No, I got bleeding hemorrhoids and I haven't shit in ten days and it has growed shut." My first thought was, "Just like a skin graft." He pulled and strained some more. I said, "Why don't you go to the medics?" His answer was pathetic. "I am a medic." The despair in his voice was too plain. I thought, "My God, they can't help themselves, how can they help the rest of us?"

Cpl. WAYNE LEWIS:

I always wondered when I was going to die. Every day was a different life. When I went to bed I never knew if I was going to wake up. When I woke up I never knew if I was going to see the sunset that night. I never knew, you see. I was always uncertain. In other words, I was always toned up for any goddamn thing. Everyone was under tension. No one ever got used to it. But we learned to live with it.

Sgt. FORREST KNOX:

The Filipinos were dying like flies. Carried in a tent-half buttoned up to form a tube, their bodies went by in an endless column. It never ended. Day and night the bodies were carried to the cemetery. I was kind of stunned by the death rate.

Cpl. HUBERT GATER:

Each morning, on the road separating us, the Filipinos would line up to take their dead away. Between two men, on a bamboo pole, wrapped in a blanket, was a Philippine Scout who had been on our side. Each day we would count how many of them died. If there were 400, we knew about forty Americans had died.

I went on the water detail. We had to go through the Filipino side of Camp O'Donnell. It was terrible. The Japs treated them as traitors.

We stopped by a small hill to wait for the Filipino water detail. On the side of the hill, later called Monkey Hill, was a Philippine Scout—probably an officer. He was chained to a post with about twenty feet of small chain. He had had no food or water, we were told, for five days. The tropical sun can make you mad, and mad he was. He ran to the length of his chain on all fours, like a chimpanzee, barking and chattering. The Filipinos who were with us just grinned. They were used to death. It was no funny matter to us.

We marched down the hill to a stream covered with green filth—just a carabao water hole. To my amazement, the Filipino soldiers, contrary to their teaching by American officers, fell face forward and drank, pushing back the green moss and brush. Our American group pleaded with them not to drink until they were back and could boil the water.

I didn't feel too proud of our own group. Three or four did just the same. A man dying of thirst or hunger is going to satisfy that desire and ask questions after. The cans were filled and we returned to camp.

Sgt. CHARLES COOK:

I was too sick and weak to go out on a detail. I remember one day, though, trying to carry a sick feller to the hospital. There were four of us and we were using one of the barracks's doors as a stretcher. We started carrying him, but found we were too weak. We went as far as we could before we told this guy he could die right there or he could walk, but that we couldn't go no more carrying him. He got off and made it close enough to the hospital so that we could carry him the rest of the way. I think he had malaria. I'm sure he died.

Pfc. ANDREW AQUILA:

In O'Donnell our boys were dying forty, fifty, sixty a day. We couldn't bury them fast enough. We'd dig a big hole, about three or four feet deep. It couldn't be deeper because water would seep into it. In the afternoon the bodies would be brought out. They were nude because their clothes, after being boiled, had been passed on to other prisoners. We grabbed them by the legs and their flesh would stick to our hands. There was tall grass around and finally we made short ropes from it to use in lifting the bodies off the litters. At first we didn't know enough to do that. Then we'd put them in this watery grave. While we shoveled dirt on them we had to hold them down with poles. Otherwise they'd float. At night the dogs went wild. They'd dig up the graves to get at the bodies.

Pfc. WILLIAM WALLACE:

The further we went into captivity, the worse it became. It gets to the place where it's unbelievable to the imagination of a person who was not there. You will eventually say, "Well, you could not possibly have endured the inhumane treatment that you were given and still survive." But, I learned the human body can suffer nearly everything and still survive.

Cpl. ROBERT WOLFERSBERGER:

I was in a semistate of shock or semiunconsciousness because of the overwhelming obstacles I was up against. Not only did I feel it individually, but I could see and feel it all around me. I saw it in guys' eyes and heard it in their voices. It was despair. Like a bad dream. What took place minute by minute, day by day, was so unreal, but nevertheless, there it was. In all ways it was all around me.

Pfc. DANIEL STOUDT:

We were given this wormy lugaw* in the mornings. Tried to eat it in the dark, if you could, so you wouldn't see the worms. If you ate one you could taste it. Picked them out, if you wanted to look. Other than that, you shut your eyes and ate, because you had to eat. I knew one guy, and there were a lot, who wouldn't eat. He always wanted to have a white shirt and suit on. He died gradually because he gave up eating.

Pfc. ROBERT BROWN:

Not eating was the easy way out. I buried so many of my friends and I couldn't understand why they were there. I'd see them stacked up like cordwood at O'Donnell. Guys out of my squadron. People I'd known. The shock of it was hell. I know one kid from our outfit, God we slapped him and cussed him and kicked him. Anything to try to make him want to fight. But I found when a man gives up, you're not going to get him back.

The food they gave us—that was a tough thing because there's nothing worse than boiled rice that's like water with no salt. When you got malaria hitting you every other day, with a temperature of 105 degrees, you're certainly not in much of a food-eating contest. But you also knew if you didn't eat you were going to die. I'd sit by the side of a shack and it might

* A watery rice soup which became a staple in the American prisoners' diet.

The luxury liner *President Coolidge,* turned troopship, tied up to Manila's Pier No. 7, Fall 1941. Three years later American prisoners embarked for Japan from this pier.

Antitank company of the 31st Infantry photographed in the Philippines, November 1941. Pvt. Leon Beck is seventh from left, top row.

Members of the 91st Bombardment Squadron on their way to Manila, October 1941.

Standing formation on Bataan, 10 January 1942.

Mariveles and Mount Bataan from Corregidor.

Don't wait to die

Before the bombs fall, let me take your hand and kiss your gentle cheeks and murmur ...

Before the terror comes, let me walk beside you in garden deep in petalled sleep ...

Let me, while there is still a time and place, Feel soft against me and rest ... rest your warm hand on my breast ...

Come home to me, and dream with me...

(Top left) Japanese artillery going into battle. (Bottom left) Japanese propaganda leaflet. (Top) Avoiding shrapnel from an exploding ammunition dump following a Japanese air raid on Lamao. (Bottom) Japanese air attack on a barrio on Bataan.

(Top left) Surrender. "They started to go through our pockets. Some knew a little English and hollered, 'Go you to hell.' " (Bottom left) "An interpreter staged us for the cameraman. He said, 'Look dejected.' That wasn't hard." Mark Wohlfeld is in the center of the photograph, arms raised, no helmet. Hadley Watson is behind him, arms raised, wearing helmet. (Top) Waiting for "the March" to begin 9 April 1942. (Bottom) "The Japs would lean out of passing trucks and hit us with their rifle butts. They seemed to particularly pick on guys wearing steel helmets."

The Death March. "We started marching. I can't remember hours or specific days, but as we moved on it got hotter and we got more fatigued."

"We stayed there in the sun without water until half a dozen men passed out. Then the guards put us on the road and double timed us." Notice that the steel helmets have been discarded.

"There was continual noise! Mostly the barking of orders in Japanese . . ."

"I had dysentery pretty bad but there wasn't anything I could do about it. You didn't stop on 'the March' because if you did you were dead."

Camp O'Donnell. "The Filipinos were dying like flies. Their bodies went by in an endless column. I was stunned by the death rate."

"I always wondered when I was going to die. When I went to bed I never knew if I was going to wake up." A Japanese propaganda photograph.

"You just marked time. Standing or sitting. Lethargic."

Corregidor surrenders.

take me an hour and a half to eat that rice. But I'd cuss myself and I'd make myself eat it. I'd gag and throw it right back down. You had to do it if you wanted to live.

Pfc. WILBURN SNYDER:

Not everyone that died died because they gave up, but many did. I spent much of my time trying to get two of my buddies to eat. That was the big problem. Many just said, "Well, phooey, what's the use?" It's kind of the way people rationalize sinning. They feel the temptation and think that they're going to do it sooner or later anyway, so why fight the temptation? And that's the way a lot of the fellows felt. No one could imagine how long this condition would go on, and if I'm going to die before it's over, why spend all my time fighting it and then die?

My biggest fear in prison camp was not the fear of dying, but the fear of dying in vain. See, I wanted to die for a purpose, and that's how I kept myself alive. I kept reminding myself that there was no more useless death in the world than to die in a rotten prison camp.

Sgt. FORREST KNOX:

Wesley Elmer came close to dying of dysentery. One old medic gave him the bamboo stick treatment every day. When you didn't have medication, sympathy was no help. So he beat Wesley every day with a stick. If you could make someone mad enough to fight, they would not die. These guys were so weak they couldn't help themselves, but if they promised themselves they were going to live long enough to kill that medic, they would live. You had to learn to hate with a passion. If you hated hard enough, you would not die. Turned out the man who beat him every day was his uncle. Kindness didn't make you live.

Our sergeant major, supposed to have been the most intelligent man in the battalion. He could quote regulations word for word without opening the book. Had an IQ of 160. He died because he couldn't eat rice. He said, "I can't eat that stuff." Man, you ate anything. I didn't care if it was shit, I ate it.

Nothing got throwed away at O'Donnell. The kitchen had some leftover rice that went sour. They said anyone who wanted some could have it. So I got a mess kit full. A smart man told me, "That stuff will give you the shits." "Well," I said, "maybe my system will get a little good out of it on the way through." It took more than smarts to survive. Stubbornness, maybe, was a better characteristic in this place.

Cpl. HUBERT GATER:

The theory of self-survival would bother me many times. Not only for myself, but for others. Can a man will himself to die in a two or three-week period? Mahatma Gandhi could go on a thirty-day hunger strike and survive. Some of our men seemed able to give up and die in three weeks or less.

1st Lt. MARK HERBST, M.D.:

They would die forty a day on our side and 100 a day on the Filipino side. We had trouble burying them. The water level was so high that you'd dig down three feet and half the grave would be flooded. You've heard the stories of the bodies in the grave being held down by poles until they got enough mud on them to hold them down. Or occasionally, seeing a hand or foot sticking out of a grave. This is true.

So many died of dysentery. If you had it you needn't bother pulling up your pants. You'd just go, go, go. It's cramps, colic, gas, bloating, running off of the bowels of blood, mucus, and fecal material. There were two different kinds, ameba and bacteria. The symptoms are essentially the same, but with amebic dysentery there's a little more blood. We tried to put everyone who had dysentery into separate wards. They were foul places. Stink and slop were the characteristics of these wards. The dysentery at O'Donnell had the most fetid odor around it. It was also a matter of morale. The men would see their buddy who couldn't do anything but sit and vile the place up. This just made it bad for the rest of the men, who were trying to stay alive.

Of course, everyone was emaciated as well. Many were suffering from malnutrition. They were all skin and bones. What they ate didn't have time enough to become absorbed. It was just burned up before it got a chance to do anything. Simply, no one had enough to eat to match anywhere near what they used. Plus, if you got sick, you used so much just fighting the fever.

Capt. LOYD MILLS:

Death was all around. A thousand or more died because of dysentery and malaria. There was no medicine, no quinine. If you got something—that was it. They had something called a hospital. It was not a hospital, it was a place to put the guys that were going to die.

I tried not to become pessimistic. I know now that if I stopped to realize the odds, I never would have made it. As time went by I realized it was going to be survival of the fittest. I was young and not married, which might have had something to do about making it back. I found a lot of married men had more problems than I. Thinking of their families made it more difficult for them. It was necessary to stop thinking about the niceties of life, to stop thinking of yourself as a gentleman. You had to get to be more of an animal.

Pfc. EDDY LAURSEN:

I was, eventually, separated from Carl. Almost immediately in O'Donnell I was put on a burial detail. I was on this for many weeks until I thought I was going to lose my mind. I begged an American officer to take me off it because I couldn't take it any longer. He told me he couldn't do that. A few days went by and I asked him again. A few more days, I asked again. Finally, he got tired of my begging and he let me off. The next day men on the detail came back to camp and told me they had buried Carl. I do believe that if I had had to bury him, I would have lost my mind.

2d Lt. FRED GIFFORD:

I was still walking, but not too strong. I got on the burial detail and I buried. I'd take a crew of men out and we'd dig a hole in the morning big enough to bury sixteen men, side by side. I worked on this detail for two weeks before I told our commanding officer I couldn't do this thing no more and that I had to have relief. I had gotten to the point where I was sick of it. We had no water to wash in. You'd climb through that dysentery, it was all over the place. You had it on your hands, your feet, in your hair. Men crawled under the barracks and died, just like animals. You had to crawl underneath to drag them out and there was all that shit and slime on your hands with no water to wash it off. You wiped it off the best you could. You couldn't dig the grave deeper than three feet, on account of the water coming in the hole. The water was so filthy you couldn't use it to wash in. It was polluted so bad that even handling it gave you dysentery, just like the men that died. That's how they got it.

Pfc. EDDY LAURSEN:

One of the rules I learned in keeping myself alive was to keep as clean as possible. It was virtually impossible, but you had to do every possible thing. The flies were so thick. You'd get your mess kit of boiled rice and you had to fan it as fast as you could to keep the flies off. All the way to your mouth you had to fan to keep from swallowing flies. One day I was watching one of these big blue bottle flies. He landed on a dry spot and when he flew away he left a wet mark. He had come from one of the slit trenches full of human feces. Now if he had landed on my food and I had eaten it, I would catch a disease. At O'Donnell there was no medicine.

1st Sgt. HOUSTON TURNER:

I damn near died in O'Donnell from malaria. I got an attack there. Somehow I must have lost consciousness and I woke up in the morgue, what they called zero ward. I was laying on a woven sawali grass mat, like a shutter that come off the windows of the barracks. There were stiffs all around me. I crawled over to a medic who was sitting around and asked him what I was doing there. He told me because I was supposed to be dead, that I had already been counted as dead and was on a list. I got up and he asked whether I could make it back to my company area. I sure tried. Of course I had to sit down and rest about five times before I got back to my buddies. They were surprised to see me. Shortly after that, a friend of mine came in off a work detail and he had been able to find some quinine. Just a quirk of luck that he happened to see me, because I had just about had it.

Pfc. JACK BRADY:

I remember one day, just before we left O'Donnell, when we actually had no bodies left to bury for the next day. The only ones who were buried that day were the ones who had died the preceding day. We had none left over from any of the days before. That was a good feeling. We knew we didn't have to dig as many holes. That was always a primary consideration.

Sgt. FORREST KNOX:

Well, they finally announced work details out. I tried getting on the mechanics detail. They were to go back to Bataan to pick up abandoned equipment—trucks and such. Well, they only wanted fifty men and I didn't go. Of this bunch only a few survived. Malaria killed nearly all of them—no quinine. The next group was to rebuild one of the bridges blown up on the retreat to Bataan. I made this work detail.

My brother Henry was also at O'Donnell. I went to him and asked if he needed me to help. He said no, that as an officer he probably had a better chance. I told him I wanted out of camp and could make the bridge building detail. I said, "Only a fool puts all his eggs in one basket." He said, "O.K. Good luck." I was trying to get one of us home. It didn't need a lot of explaining. Everyone with any smarts at all could see our percentage was going to be bad. Well, our education had started. Our little joke—we went to the "Far East University," majored in psychology.

PART II

SURVIVING

5
DETAILS

Pfc. ROY DIAZ:

O'Donnell was a mess. I was there only four or five days when the Japs called for mechanics. I volunteered and the next day I was back on Bataan. The detail was to get all the trucks that had been demolished in working order. We used to get ten or twelve trucks a day working. When we first arrived, Corregidor was still holding out and the Japs were mean. We had one guard who carried one of our .45s, his saber, rifle, and a bunch of grenades. All for us guys.

Seems, though, that he wanted to learn English, but he didn't know how to ask. Our maintenance sergeant got to making gestures with him. Pretty soon they start, "How do you say Japanese?" . . . "How you say English?" Soon as the guard began to learn some English, he'd take us to work without a gun or anything. Totally left us alone.

Then there was another guard who one day picked an old discarded Enfield rifle out of the sand. He spotted a big old carabao. Boom. Boom. Firing, trying to hit the carabao. Finally he knocked it over and he shared the meat with us. Another time this guard found a BAR in the jungle. He started to fire it. Man, everybody hit the deck! After that a Jap officer came over and gave this guard hell. He was afraid he was not only going to kill us but him, too.

We did some hard work down there, but we had plenty of rice to eat. But what knocked the devil out of us was malaria. Oh, boy, that killed a lot of people.

Pfc. VICTOR LEAR:

Of course you didn't know where they were going to take you, but the detail that I volunteered for ended me right back down into Bataan. They took about 100 guys down in two trucks. Once a week they'd have to replace one of these truckloads. The rest would be dead or dying from malaria. I got malaria, too, but I made it. I was lucky. We had a Jap lieutenant who was in charge of my detail. He was a sissy, but one of those high-class Japanese who'd screwed up somewhere, so he was put down to Bataan on a guard detail. He had malaria, too.

Somehow I got stuck cooking and that's how I survived. The Jap lieutenant would only take half his quinine and throw what he hadn't used under his bunk. I'd steal it. It was enough to keep me alive and I made it back.

Pfc. ROY DIAZ:

When this detail ended they shipped all the drivers back to O'Donnell, but they took the maintenance people to Manila. On our way we had an accident on one of the Pasig River bridges and the convoy was forced to stop. A Filipino kid was standing around watching, twelve years old maybe, and when he saw some of us were Americans he gave us a V sign. One of the Jap officers saw him do it. He went up to him and, with a bayonet, damned if he didn't cut the kid's two fingers off.

The convoy started again and after driving a while it stopped and the guards went into a store that sold candies. They came out with lots of stuff and gave us jars of strawberry jam. I'll never forget it—strawberry jam.

★ ★ ★

2d Lt. FRED GIFFORD:

When I run out and volunteered to go on a detail, because I was an officer, they called me a collaborator. I figured, well, forget that Philippine Army commission, dump it down the drain. I didn't want to be charged with collaboration, if I ever made it through. I just quit it right there in O'Donnell. I also didn't figure I was collaborating. I was going to help myself, because I was ready to take one of them sixteen places in the burial hole and I didn't want that.

This was one of the first details the Japs put together. Nobody knew what they should do. When some saw that I'd volunteered, they joined up, too. It wasn't very long till the Japs had their quota on the truck and were driving us heaven knows where. We wound up with the Japanese Air Force at Clark Field and they treated me real good. I got the detail of mowing the runway and dragging the bombs out before they were loaded on the bombers. We put a bar through the fins at the back of the bomb, and with four men on each side we'd drag these bombs over to the planes. It was hard work and the Japs used to give us rest periods along the line. We would sit down next to the bombs and whenever we could, with our heels, we'd kick them tail fins out of alignment. We'd bend them in all directions. I'm sure most of them bombs landed in the Bay and missed Corregidor.

★ ★ ★

Tech. Sgt. WILLIAM "COWBOY" WRIGHT:

In early May I went in a 100-man detail to Capas to help rebuild a bridge across the river. We were housed in a schoolhouse about a quarter of a mile from the bridge.

Several weeks later Corporal Williams perished, I would tend to say, of a broken heart. When he had come on this detail he still had his wristwatch, which had been a gift from his family. Someone told the Japs about him having a watch. I don't remember whether he got anything for it or not. Up until this happened, he seemed to be in pretty good spirits. Afterwards, he had no desire to continue on. He seemed to feel the whole world had turned against him. I felt sorry for him.

For about ten days I was unable to work after three of the men helping me carry a 3″ × 12″ × 12′ bridge plank decided to let it drop before I had a chance to get my end off my shoulder. I went down with the plank on top of my right shoulder. My main thought as I fell was to try to keep it from hitting my head. Three or four times while I was laid up the Jap that guarded us at the bridge came to see me. He'd bring me food and medicine. He was a baseball fan, so if he wanted a short rest he would start talking about the game to me. Some of the Japs were human. But you always had to watch your step, because if you got too far out of line there was always someone to take care of you.

★ ★ ★

Tech. Sgt. MEL MADERO:

I was called by the Japs to join a large Signal Corps detail which was going to return to Bataan to recover all the telephone lines we had laid between outposts. Telephone line was something they must have needed very badly. This whole detail of nearly 200 men consisted of communications people— radio operators, repairmen, telephone linemen, and other jobs of this nature. The Japs had a list of our names, ranks, and serial numbers and they called us up in O'Donnell by name. How they obtained this list I don't know. Supposedly, all our records were burnt before we surrendered.

The group down on Bataan that I became attached to consisted of George Dietrich and two Filipinos—a Scout lieutenant and a master sergeant. We had a truck and our guard was a Jap corporal. Back in Japan this guard apparently owned a garage, and his main concern on Bataan was for us to find him complete sets of auto tools and socket wrenches. So instead of recovering telephone wire, we spent our time on the various trails trying to find abandoned American motor pools. Before the surrender the orders were to destroy all our trucks, gasoline, and oil. Tools were not included in this order. One day we happened on an American depot where we found all kinds of tool kits still intact. When we gave them to him it was like we'd given him a million dollars. After that he really tried to repay us with kindness.

Once all the line and cable had been recovered, we were sent as a group to Fort William McKinley. There we would load telephone wire on our truck and drive it to the Port Area in Manila, where we would unload it. On our way back, this Jap corporal would nearly always stop and park near one of the Filipino markets. Then he would disappear, leaving us four sitting in the back of the truck. The Filipinos would see us there and flash the V sign. Others would throw us bits of tobacco, sugar cane, little rice cakes, and pieces of chicken wrapped in banana leaves. These people were very sympathetic towards us and tried to help every way they could. When our corporal thought we had enough he'd come back out of an alley, making all kinds of noise, swinging his sword and scaring the children. He'd look back at us and smile. Then we'd take off back to McKinley, where we shared our loot with the rest of the men.

On one particular Saturday some confiscated whiskey was distributed to the Jap officers who were stationed with us at Fort McKinley. A lieutenant who was in charge of our whole detail got hold of a little more than he should have and got high enough to want to go down to Manila to fulfill some of his amorous fantasies. His thought was that the Filipino lieutenant, who was in my section, would know where he could find a cabaret where he could drink, find some girls, and have himself a good time. So he came into where he was going to pick up the Filipino. I jokingly asked him if Dietrich and I could also come along. Apparently he was drunk enough to agree to anything and he agreed that we too could come along. Now it happened that we were imprisoned in the same barracks where the American troops were stationed before the war. Once the war broke out, most of the men were not able to return to get their personal gear out of the footlockers. So when we got there after our Bataan detail, with our fatigues falling apart, we picked up some pretty good clothes—sharkskin slacks, Filipino shirts and hats. Dietrich, the Filipino lieutenant, and I, along with the drunk lieutenant and his driver, all got in a car. Dietrich looked German and I of course looked Mexican, and the way we were dressed we actually didn't look like POWs. Our car had little Japanese flags flying from the fenders, so as we drove out the gate at McKinley the Jap sentries saluted us. Dietrich and I nearly fell over. We drove until the Filipino lieutenant thought he had found a respectable cabaret down near the Bay. After we had all taken our seats, we looked over the girls who were going to be our dancing partners. The Jap kept saying, "Go dance. Go dance." So, I picked a girl and began dancing. Soon as I had her on the floor I told her, "You won't believe this, but I'm an American prisoner." Well, she didn't believe me. So I danced with another and another until I found one who believed me. She had been out with Americans before and she knew I talked like one. Then the word got around to the rest of the ladies in the dance hall. Soon each of them was waiting in line to dance with me. They were hungry for information. They wanted to know if I knew what had happened to Sergeant So-and-So or a guy they knew out of the Navy. They all wanted to know if they were alive and whether I could take messages back to them. Suddenly I remembered where I was and what I was doing. All around me Japanese officers were also dancing. God, if we had been discovered, I'm sure we would have been shot right there. Our Jap lieutenant was now drunker than before and becoming very belligerent and very loud. He expected me to find a girl that would perform for him right there. Dietrich slipped out and brought in the poor Jap driver, who was worried out of his mind. Then all of us almost picked up the lieutenant and carried him to the car. He passed out on the trip back to McKinley so we got into our quarters without further problems.

Later I had reason to think more about that evening. While I was dancing with one of the Filipino hostesses, she suggested that I escape by just leaving with her right then. I began to think about hiding in Manila for the duration of the war. Two things prevented me from doing it, though. First, I could speak no Spanish and I was afraid of being caught. Second, the Japs had us in groups of ten and the bond was that if one escaped they'd shoot the other nine. I decided I couldn't take that chance. But eventually others did take that chance and I found myself the victim.

One Sunday, which was our rest day, three American officers asked me to be a fourth in a bridge game. During the game a roving guard came through. He watched us for some time before he moved on. In all that afternoon of bridge playing, the three officers never once mentioned to me they were planning to escape that evening. That night we weren't dismissed after nine o'clock roll call and no one understood why.

We stood around and waited. Soon a small force of Japanese, including that afternoon's roving guard, came back into my barracks. They marched up to me and dragged me to a room where I was interrogated. Over and over they asked, "Why didn't you go with them?" Knowing nothing of the plan, all I could say was, "I don't know anything about it." The more I repeated this line, the more infuriated the Japanese became. They began beating me. Just hauling off, whacking me across the face. They kept yelling, "Liar!" "Liar!" The officer in charge then took his sword, which fortunately he kept in its sheath, and hit me a blow across the back of my neck which brought me to the ground. Then I was taken to Bilibid Prison, which I knew had a terrible reputation.* I was put in the dungeon. It was a narrow cell without windows. Because of the seepage, the cell was very wet. I sat there many days in the dark without food, with only my thoughts for company. I never did figure out whether the three American officers had used me intentionally or unintentionally to further their escape plan. To make things look natural they needed another card player. One thing, though; they never told me of their plans, so I could go, or at least refuse to be left behind for the Japs to pick on.

I was interrogated several times. Finally I was told the Americans had been found and executed. I was on the next trip out of Bilibid to Cabanatuan. Dance halls and the easy times were left far behind.

★ ★ ★

1st Sgt. HOUSTON TURNER:

I was on a detail which had ten-man shooting squads. If one ran away, the other nine got shot. If all ten ran away, they had you on a bigger scale—100 would be marked out. That way they didn't have to watch us so close. We had a guy in our detail who most of the guys felt was a risk. They wouldn't have him in their shooting squad because they felt he'd run at the first chance. The Japanese couldn't understand why nobody wanted him. He began to worry that the Japanese would figure out what was happening and, to avoid the risk of his escaping,

---

* Bilibid Prison, near Manila's old walled city of Intramuros, was built at the time of the Spanish occupation. Inside twenty-foot-high walls, which covered a city block, the cement cell blocks were arranged as spokes in a wheel. The facility was used by the Japanese as their primary prison hospital, with its administration handled by captured American naval personnel from the Canacao Naval Hospital. From May 1942 to December 1944 the Japanese also used Bilibid as a central clearing house through which there was a continuous movement of prisoner work details. At times, between the hospital and the prison, there were as many as 2,000 prisoners quartered in the old prison.

shoot him. I have no doubt in my mind that's what would have happened. So he had to get on a shooting squad and quick. Because he used to be in my outfit, he came to me and begged me to talk to the other guys. He got on his knees and pleaded with me. Finally he convinced me he wouldn't run. I talked to the fellas and they felt he'd be all right if I said so. We took him into our group of ten. A little lesson I learned, know someone before you start recommending him. One of my first lessons. A few weeks go by and one night we come in from the fields for our count and this guy isn't there. The Japs hauled our asses down and put us in cages. Then they marched us out to the graveyard. I couldn't realize that I was gonna get shot. The Jap commander read us the riot act, but told us that he had received orders that there were to be no shootings. Like I say, I never did feel I was gonna get shot. I don't know why, 'cause people actually did.

★ ★ ★

Capt. THEODORE BIGGER:

The reason I got interested in going out on a detail was to get away from the death at O'Donnell. I thought there surely must be better places. We knew the Japs were in the process of cleaning up after the battles and were looking for men to do a lot of heavy labor. Once I decided I wanted to get out of O'Donnell, I went down and congregated near the main gate. There the Japanese would come in and count off the men they needed for a specific work detail they were forming. I was finally selected to go in a group of 150 men. We were put in closed trucks and driven south through Manila, then around Laguna de Bay to the little town of Lumban. There we were told we were going to help the Japanese repair a bridge that had been blown during the American retreat.

Tech. Sgt. JAMES CAIRE:

We were billeted in the building that had served the barrio as a theater. The balcony had benches arranged like steps and were wide enough for some of the men to sleep on. The theater floor was dirt, so the rest slept there or on the stage. On arriving in Lumban we were divided into three groups of fifty with an American officer in charge of each group.

Capt. THEODORE BIGGER:

I was the ranking American officer in the detail. Of course I wasn't issuing any orders. Japanese privates had more authority

than I did. Each group of fifty men was given its own identifying arm band—white, red, and green. We were told the first
night that if any American escaped the Japanese would shoot
ten of us.

Occasionally I would hear from the men that had gone up
into the mountains to cut timber for the pilings, that the guerrillas in the area were active. I didn't pay much attention to
this, because I couldn't see how it would affect us.

Pvt. CHARLES THORNTON:

A Chinese couple had a small store in the barrio. One day the
store was raided by the Japanese and a hidden radio found.
All day long the Chinese man was beaten. His wife was re-
peatedly kicked. That night the guerrillas in the area got even.

Tech. Sgt. JAMES CAIRE:

We were awakened the night of June 11–12 by loud shouts and
shooting. It was a dark night and we didn't know what was
going on, but we figured the local guerrilla band was attacking
our guards. The guerrillas began shouting for us to go into the
mountains with them. Because of the large number of sick men
we would have had to carry, it was decided we would remain
together and not make a run for it. At this time we did not
know that some Japanese guards had been shot.

Capt. THEODORE BIGGER:

The next morning the Japanese brought in a regular infantry
outfit to supplement our small detail of guards. We learned
that three or four guards had been killed. I was questioned
along with the two other American officers. Then the Japanese
took a head count of the prisoners and found we were one man
short. I didn't know what to expect.

Along about 2:00 p.m. all the Americans who were not too
sick to walk were marched to the barrio school building which
the Japanese used for a headquarters. The Japanese lined us up
in several rough lines. We were surrounded on three sides by
Japanese rifles and machine guns. We didn't like the circumstances at all. We didn't close ranks very well and there was
a good bit of mingling—men trying to move out of the way.
Something we had all learned on the Death March. Finally, a
Jap sergeant came along and began randomly pulling men out
of the line. I saw a good bit of this out of the corner of my eye.

Tech. Sgt. JAMES CAIRE:

I slept almost next to the man who had escaped and whether this was the reason or not, I don't know, but I was in the group of ten that the Japanese pulled out of the line.

Capt. THEODORE BIGGER:

There was a bit of confusion on the part of the Japanese. Some of the men who had been pulled out were wearing red and white arm bands. The Japs knew that the guy who had run wore green.

Tech. Sgt. JAMES CAIRE:

When the Japs saw that I was not wearing a green arm band they threw me back into the main group. Four others who were wearing red or white were also removed. Then the Japanese selected five men wearing green to replace the ones who weren't.

Capt. THEODORE BIGGER:

They marched the ten men out in front so they faced us. They were up against a hill. We were all in shock.

Tech. Sgt. JAMES CAIRE :

They were grouped under some coconut palms.

Capt. THEODORE BIGGER:

The Japs wanted them to put on blindfolds. Most pulled them off. Some shouted, "God bless America," or "Tell my people about this," or "Tell the President!" The firing squad was made up of our guards.

Tech. Sgt. JAMES CAIRE:

They were not executed. They were butchered.

Capt. THEODORE BIGGER:

In the first volley most of them fell. But there were probably three or four that were still standing. One fellow shouted, "Why don't you go ahead and kill me?" They fired again. There was a lot of painful groaning. The Japs kept firing until all ten were dead. When the firing was over I noticed I had pulled a clump of hair out of my scalp.

Then the Japs picked a burial detail. Those fellows, when they came back, told me the bodies were pretty well mutilated by the rifle fire.*

Tech. Sgt. JAMES CAIRE:

One of the men witnessing the execution watched his younger brother shot. His name was Betts.

Capt. THEODORE BIGGER:

As far as the Japs were concerned, it was over. They had told us that if one man escaped, ten would be shot. They had shot the ten. We were moved from the theater down into a barrio, near the schoolhouse.

Tech. Sgt. JAMES CAIRE:

The Japanese guards treated us fairly well after the execution. When the bridge was finished we were loaded onto trucks and taken to Manila on the 20th of June, 1942. Then we were driven into the northern part of Luzon, above San Fernando, La Union. Upon arrival at the site, the Japanese had information that the guerrillas were very active, so they took us down to the main POW camp at Cabanatuan.

★ ★ ★

Sgt. RALPH LEVENBERG:

We had "shooting squads" on the detail I was on. We were taken to Nueva Ecija Province to rebuild a fourteen-span bridge which crossed the Pampanga River at Cabanatuan. They put us in a schoolhouse and explained to us that the work was going to be very, very difficult. Then they laid the law down and told us that no one was going to escape. Afterwards we were put in groups of ten. This was the first time I ran across the Japanese offering me a deal that I couldn't pass up. They explained that if anybody escaped out of that ten, the rest got shot. The psychology was obvious—one guy had nine lives on his back. Well, lo and behold, two guys escaped and the rest of us waited and sweated. We sat in the schoolyard for eighteen hours, no food, no water, no bathroom. We sat while the Japs searched

---

* The men executed were Sgt. Bernard Knopick, Sgt. Issac Landry, Sgt. James Turner, Cpl. Stanton Betts, Cpl. David Reas, Cpl. John Wiezorek, Pfc. Oscar Gordon, Pfc. Percival Hallyman, Pfc. Wade Rogers, and Pvt. John Dudash. The American that escaped is believed to be Cpl. George Lichman.

for these guys. Finally a big Jap staff car pulled up and a big shot from Manila got out, dragging on the ground a sword longer than he was. He was very upset, but he told us that the escapees had been found and immediately beheaded. He wasn't going to take his revenge this time, but next time we had no doubts he would. Then they put us back on the bridge and things started again.

Under normal conditions the highway department would have gone out and repaired this bridge in a week. It took us a month. We did everything by hand. We used a pile driver which twelve of us would have to pull up on a rope. I sawed steel beams under water with a hacksaw. It was there that I learned the old "Japanese shuffle." Ten men on a side picked up a huge crossbeam with poles. If you could move in unison it was easier. So we learned to shuffle. Some of the details that I've heard about, the guys had a picnic. The Japs fed them well, would split beer with them. But this wasn't the detail I was on. Many, many men died where I was. The water was very, very cold. The Japs gave us spoonfuls of powdered quinine until it ran out. This was where I had my first experience with dengue fever. Boy, if you want to get something that'll make you feel lousy, get a dose of dengue fever. It just washes you out and every bone in your body feels like there's a torch on it. It was terrible. Of course with malaria you feel bad and you alternate between fever and chills, but with dengue you want to die. I mean you want to die. Fortunately, on this detail we had some guys that were still pretty sharp. They managed this thing right. They told us the sooner we got it over with the sooner we'd get the hell out of there, because this was no picnic. We finished the bridge in thirty days and the Japanese allowed us to form up and cross the bridge first. The word was passed, and as we crossed some of the guys began to hum "God Bless America."

★ ★ ★

Pfc. CLETIS OVERTON:

I'd say I spent thirty days at O'Donnell. Then the Japanese came into the area where I was and picked out about 300 men. We were loaded on trucks with just what we had on. In my case that meant mechanics overalls, shoes, and a hat. The trucks took us to Manila, where we spent the night in Bilibid. Then they moved us by train south. I don't know what towns we went through. They took us off the train and moved us by truck again. Probably ten to twelve trucks. We drove what seems like the biggest part of the day. Then we left the trucks and walked through a hilly jungle forest for several hours. They stopped us at a stream. Although not deep, the water was running through a wide, gravelly bed. This was down in Batangas Province. The detail was named after the nearest barrio, Lipa. The work was to construct a road through the jungle. We understood it was to go from some place over here to some place over there. Through the jungle we had to clear the forest and build the roadbed. We worked with picks and shovels and axes and wheelbarrows. Along the way we passed an American food dump. Just stacks and stacks of canned goods. The Japanese allowed us to carry boxes of canned goods with us. We had no cooking pots. We had an American officer, a first lieutenant, if I recall, who with a sergeant helped organize us. The first thing we did was build ovens from the river stone. Then they put the rice the Japanese gave us into the steel-bottomed wheelbarrows and placed them over the heated ovens. That's how we cooked the rice. We slept on the ground and it began to rain. Seemed like it rained every day. Come time to lay down, you laid down wet on the wet ground. Pneumonia broke out, then dysentery, and the guys began to die. After about three weeks they moved us out of there. When we got back to the trucks, it only took two of them to carry us. Somebody said thirty-five survived—out of 300. I don't know that to be a fact. I was on one truck and there was one other behind mine. None of the road had been completed when we were pulled out.

They carried us back to Bilibid. There the food was better and more plentiful. They even had some limited medical supplies. I understood some American Navy doctors had charge of Bilibid. In fact, they had a sanitary toilet facility. You'd go and sit on a stool outside and there was running water all the time. I remember that because it was the first sanitary facility I'd seen in a long time. I stayed in Bilibid about four weeks. I got sulfa tablets there and the quinine helped knock my malaria down. In July 1942 I was moved with a group to Cabanatuan. When I arrived I learned that the biggest part of the O'Donnell people were also there.

★ ★ ★

Sgt. FORREST KNOX:

This photograph was taken around January 1, 1943. We were in never-never land, which I'll describe. The camera probably belonged to "the Bull," because he was the one who gave us each a copy.

1. Mike Dunn (Mikeoo). 2. Athea. 3. Buckner. 4. Peplar.
5. Lollar. 6. Alva Chapman (Chipper). 7. McKnight. 8. Joe
Erington. 9. Medic (Goosie). 10. Andrews. 11. Piggot.
12. Forrest Knox (Knocky). 13. Mickalo. 14. Dick Walker.
15. Pappy Steen. 16. Owen Sandmier (Sandy). 17. Garland
(GaGa or Gar). 18. Aaron Combs (Curly). 19. Lt. Crosby.
20. Numb Nuts. 21. Son-in-Law. 22. Julian Teadoro.
23. Orderly. 24. Transferred. 25. Colonel's Driver.
26. Nakamura (the Bull). 27. Shit-for-Brains. 28. Mickey the
Rat. 29. Carpenter. 30. Long Tall or Harvard. 31. Kondo.

Each man on this picture has a story. They are a mixture of Army, Air Force, Marines: Mike Dunn was, for the record, an ordnance clerk, but in reality he was corps's code clerk. Athea was a Kentucky hillbilly. You could trust him with your life. Buckner was from California. Peplar, New Jersey, I think. Lollar was a Mississippi hillbilly—never ever washed, but was a top-notch Air Force mechanic. Chipper—Alva Chapman—my best friend. Tank Commander out of A Company, McKnight, from Pennsylvania. He'd worked in an insane asylum. He was the one who told me how to kill with a towel. Joe Erington, California, Salinas tank company. Andrews, first sergeant of C Company, 192d. Piggot, California, a Marine reservist called up and sent to Shanghai. Myself. Mickalo, sergeant out of C Company. He was Andrews's buddy. Dick Walker, Salinas, California. At one time he had been a big-time tennis player on tour with Tilden. Got out of England during the Blitz. A Jap officer who played against him in Japan was in charge of a bridge detail south of Manila. The Jap had him transferred to our detail to keep him out of O'Donnell, where the POWs were dying like flies. Pappy Steen from California, an Air Force crew chief and mechanic. Told me once, "Bad checks got more men into service than any other reason." Owen Sandmier, sergeant out of A Company. This man was friends with the Bull and was the real boss of our detail. Garland came from Maine. Japs called him "GaGa." Seems they could not say Garland. I put his finger back on once when he got it tore off in a belt. I was the unofficial doctor of our bunch. Curly Combs came from Indiana. He had his leg split open with a banca propeller when we were towing logs. Left some bad scars on his leg. I used to dress his leg with two handkerchiefs. Washed them out and used them every other day. Made into cook by the Bull to protect him and give him an easier job. Lieutenant Crosby, Greenwood, Mississippi, P-40 pilot. Learned to talk Nipponese real good. Went from Jap kitchen to kitchen asking for rations. He was good at it, and between him and Curly we ate good. "Numb Nuts" got the name from Curly Combs. Curly said, "Hi, Numb Nuts," everytime he came in the kitchen for tea. When the Jap demanded an explanation, Curly said it meant tomadachí, or friend. So every time he came for tea he called Curly "Numb Nuts." The two Filipinos owned the shoe factory in front of where the picture was taken in Manila. The older one, Julian Teadoro, was part of the collaboration government. A cabinet member, I think. Next, Nakamura's orderly. The next Jap was transferred in and I don't remember who he was. The one next to the Bull was the big-shot colonel's driver. We always felt sorry for him. The colonel was the meanest sonovabitch I ever ran in to. Nakamura was a *gunso*, or staff sergeant. Came from the northern part of Japan. A fishing village. Went to the third grade in school, he said. Weighed about 100 pounds soaking wet. A drug addict. The only one I ever seen in the Jap Army. He was also one of the best soldiers I ever run across. He carried a saber, but he never beat people with it like some did. "Shit-for-Brains" was a pompous bastard who stood around in your way all the time and never made a sensible suggestion. "Mickey the Rat," he was half Filipino and the interpreter. Tried to get you into trouble every chance he got. I think he got his kicks out of seeing if he could get one of us beat. The next one was a Jap carpenter. Can't remember a name for him. The next Jap wears glasses. Mike Dunn named him "Harvard." Said he was a Harvard man if he ever seen one. He had a totally stupid look on his face. Tall and skinny, so we called him "Long Tall" or "Harvard." Harvard was either a driver for the officers or an orderly. He wears a white shirt under his sun tans, same as the colonel's driver. The last man is Kondo. He was a carpenter on the Calauan Bridge detail. Friendly sort, so the colonel made him part of the firing squad when they executed ten POWs. That colonel had a weird sense of humor. Some Japs were sadistic and could be he was one. He treated his own troops the same. They were all scared of him.

The Bull always wore leather puttees and the orderly wore wrap leggings. Kondo and Numb Nuts wore wrap leggings, sort of field-troop dress. The bare legs were rear echelon or head-quarters personnel. Nakamura wears an arm band. He made us all wear one. You can see it on Athea, Poplar, Lollar, and Pappy Steen. It was our permit as drivers. I had driven through guard stops on the highway without a Jap riding with me. Just stop, dismount, bow, show my arm band. They would check their register book and wave me on. Odd? Well, perhaps, but we trusted each other. One man escaped and the colonel would execute the rest. If we did not trust a man, we told Sandmier and Sandy would talk to Nakamura. The next day he would be sent back to Bilibid, or later Cabanatuan. Sandmier's authority superseded any American officer we had. If a man decided he didn't like our group, Sandmier could get him a transfer.

The picture was taken after our New Year's Eve party. The Japs knew we were going to be sent to Cabanatuan, so they had a big party for us. We had about four gallons of green wine which was made from dried fruit. The Japs gave us a couple of bottles of imitation scotch which we poured in. I kept telling Chipper not to drink too much, it'd make him sick. Then I'd drink his share. I got sick. In the photo I have my hat pulled down. The sunlight was like ice picks in my eyes. Just after the camera snapped, Mickalo, who is standing next to me, turned his head and threw up.

The men who died in captivity that I know of are Chapman, Andrews, Piggot, Mickalo, and Garland. The detail was supposed to be twenty men and one officer. Seventeen and Lieutenant Crosby on the picture. Rick Erington, Price, and Cruz are not in the picture. They always kept a couple of men separate. Rotated them, but very careful never to keep twenty-one of us together. I figured that the colonel did not trust us like Nakamura did. So he held some back to shoot. Survival meant quick learners and adaptability. Most of the men in this picture had it.

Perhaps our humor got a bit twisted. The Jap medic on the left of the picture was "Goosie." He traveled up and down this street several times a day, getting chow from the mess hall, or getting fresh tea for the Jap doctors. Cruz used to lay in wait for him and then jump out and chase him. It would make us double up with laughter to see Goosie fly up the street with his slippers flopping, trying to keep the hot tea or soup from slopping out of the buckets and burning his legs. I had a notion the walking guards thought it was funny, too. They never stopped the joke or hollered at Cruz for it. Odd, the things a man remembers. Like Curly Combs's girlfriend who bought him ice-cream cones. We called her "Scabby Legs." She had leg sores. Worked in a eat house across the street. Curly would blow her a kiss and she would send the street vendor around to the back door with his little ice cart. The guards never stopped that either.

I didn't think the Jap was much different than we were. They hated the war and when alone would talk some. That story they all wanted to die for the Emperor was a bunch of bullshit. The Jap Army discipline was a lot tougher than ours, and an officer like the colonel made it smart. Nakamura ran a thriving black-market operation. His partners were the Kempei-tai, or secret police. Mike Dunn was our gas clerk who kept track of the fuel. He was always short. The "Kempeis" would come in the middle of the night and the guard would come in and get Mike to fill their gas tank. So every month Mike would have a big argument with the regiment's gas clerk, to explain where the shortage went. This little Jap was very feminine and to see the two, waving their arms and trying to argue in two languages, was hilarious. If we started to laugh he would get furious and start to scream. Which of course made it that much more hilarious. Finally, he would flounce off. But the next month was the same. We got so we waited for it. Mike never seemed to enjoy the performance, which made it even funnier to us.

With a lack of recreation, I suppose we were easily amused. That's nearly forty years ago and it still makes me laugh when I think of it. Other things as well.

The Grace Park Hotel, which was across the street from where we were billeted, had a large kitchen in the back. The natives in the hotel did their cooking over narrow strips of wood, about like what you'd make a cigar box out of. The Filipinos had hidden a large pile of rice under a mound of this wood fuel. The Japs finally burned enough wood in cooking to find the rice. The bags had been there so long that the rice was full of worms and weevils. So the Japs gave us the whole lot. We couldn't believe our good fortune. We'd put a gallon of rice in a bucket, then add water from a garden hose, swirl it around, and all the bugs and worms floated out. Now we had clean rice. I ate so much I got a rice belly. But we were in never-never land. The other POWs were starving to death in O'Donnell. My turn would come. Anyway, we had so much rice we traded for a little pig. We left it in the back yard next door. A Chinese family lived there. So Curly was over there several times a day feeding our little sow. Now Curly was known before the war as quite a lady's man. He was good-looking. Well, he started working on the Chinese lady to put out. Trouble was they had no common language. The lady knew Curly wanted something, so one day she went and got her husband so he could interpret for them. Curly never did explain how he talked his way out of that.

We knew time in never-never land was running out so we decided to butcher our little porky, even if he hadn't a chance to get very big. Our big pork dinner was all set. Everyone had his piece of meat on his plate. Chipper was late, as usual. He always lollygagged and never got to meals on time. So this time, to teach him a lesson, Curly, who always served the meal, put the sow's pussy on Chipper's plate and covered it with a saucer. Everyone had a good laugh. It was a fine meal. Then we had a tea party afterwards. Probably a little different from any you've heard of before. Along the front of the building we had mango trees. We picked the leaves from the veranda and dried them in our oven. Then every night we made a five-gallon bucket of tea from them. Into this we also added our "P-40 Juice." The Japs had converted the San Miguel Brewery to alcohol production. They used a blend of gasoline, kerosene, and alcohol as truck fuel. By checking a lot of barrels we eventually found one containing clean, pure alcohol. This barrel we rolled to one side. When we found a bottle we would carry it to the fuel yard and fill it with alcohol. Everyone had a couple of quarts of clear 190 proof alcohol—"P-40 Juice." Cut to about one-half, it made a real nice tea. This night we sat around and joked and laughed until lights out. A couple of the guys sat in the dark and drank. I never could see doing that.

P-40 Juice also had other uses. Sandy had a bad case of "Inky," which is what we called a fungus infection that seemed to like the skin of our balls. The skin would swell, turn red, and when it cracked, leak fluid. The Japs thought it was funny as hell. Their medic would have you stand on a short table and paint you with iodine. The guards used to gather to watch us jump and holler. One night Sandy came in drying himself from the shower. Of course he had been into the tea or he would not have thought it, but he wondered aloud whether P-40 Juice would cure the Inky. So, he dipped his finger in and touched himself. He waited and nothing happened, so he poured some more on his belly and rubbed it in. The trouble was he hadn't waited long enough. He was standing there naked, drinking some more tea, when the fire hit. He howled like a raped ape. He ran into the shower, but the cold water did nothing. Then he ran back to gulp some more tea and then back into the shower. He managed to make about three fast trips before the tea caught up with him. He passed out cold as a mackerel on the floor. We ganged around him, trying to lift him up the stairs and get him to bed. But a wet, limp drunk is hard to carry, so it proved very difficult. On the way up the stairs some serious suggestions were made like pouring P-40 Juice all over him so all we'd need to do was steer him to bed. Some of our humor was rough, but no one was that hardhearted. The next day he was sick. Too much tea and he still had his Inky.

I had found an old medic trunk in a pile of stuff in the recreation hall where we were. There wasn't much in there, but I did find a bottle of little, tiny, dark pills. They smelled like creosote. I think they were opium. Cured the shits right well. Put the guts to sleep. If you took too many pills you could fall asleep standing up.

The Japs had a dispensary nearby. Their medics didn't care about us. The Japs assigned to various bridge building details came from engineering units. About half of these guards were stationed near us, so that they were close to the dispensary. They were syphilitic and taking treatment. We could go to this dispensary, but the Japs only treated us when they felt like it. So much of our doctoring was done by me.

Garland tore his finger off at the first knuckle while running it through a fan-belt pulley. The bone stuck out. He took the finger and ran down to the dispensary in the next block. A couple of minutes later he was back, in tears. Said, "The sonovabitch picked up a pair of shears and was going to cut off the bone." "O.K., Gar," I said, "I'll try to fix it." I got two small glasses and poured in each an ounce of 190 proof. Until you've drunk it, it's hard to describe. When Gar threw his head back to drink, I poured the other glass on his finger. He screamed some. I had a good hold of his wrist and I said some real mean things to him. When he held his hand up I just slipped the cut-off part down on the bone. Only had electrical friction tape, so that's what I used. Told him not to touch it, wash it, or look at it. I knew if it didn't take, we would all smell it. After about a week I peeled the tape off and the finger was good. Only complaint from Gar was I didn't get it on straight. For a first attempt, I thought I'd done real good.

One man got what we called beriberi belly. He swelled up and just seemed to get bigger—but high up. I didn't know what to make of it. Then one day he got sick and vomited. Threw up some great big worms. Looked like what we called crawlers or dew worms. I didn't have any medicine for things like that.

The story of how the men in the photograph got together is this. The Japs came into Camp O'Donnell one day and picked 350 men to rebuild bridges blown up by the American Army on its withdrawal to Bataan. All of the Americans in the picture were part of that detail. The first night out we were quartered in a big recreational hall near the north edge of Manila in Grace Park. After dark a Jap *gunso* came to the front door of this recreational hall, or temporary prison stockade, and said he wanted ten drivers. By sheer chance the man he asked whether he could drive, pretending he was turning a steering wheel, was Owen Sandmier. Sandy, as everyone called him, had a bound-less amount of enthusiasm. It was an odd thing, but that little Jap and this big prisoner became friends almost immediately. So Sandy agreed to supply ten drivers. I was one of the ten men. Our own tank colonel picked ten men of his own during the night. Next morning he had them waiting at the front door. Nakamura-san did not see Sandy. He asked for his drivers. Colonel Wickord said these ten men were his drivers. The Jap said, "No." Colonel Wickord said that he was in charge and these were the ten men he had picked. The little Jap recognized a blowhard when he seen one. And the one and only time I knew him to do it—he pulled his saber and said *he* was in charge. He walked around till he seen Sandy and said, "Ten men." Sandy pointed to the American colonel. Nakamura stood at attention, all four foot ten inches, and pointed to himself. Sandy said, "Grab your gear," and we left. I will never love Japs, but this one *gunso* I admire. He was a good soldier. In all the time he was our boss, he never ever mistreated a prisoner. He was simply the Bull, the man in charge.

If the other Japs had been as good a soldier, perhaps things might have been different for Chipper. When we did get abuse, it was always away from the Bull's supervision. We belonged to a Jap engineer regiment. Any Jap noncom could ask for and receive a driver, or four or five if he needed a lot of trucks. We were assigned to a truck. The Jap just went and stood by the one he wanted. The driver went with the truck. You needed only four words in Nipponese—right, left, go, and stop. We turned out to be handy to have around. This increased our size to twenty men with one officer in charge. Our detail was dumping ground for small groups of prisoners on temporary basis. So our strength might vary up to forty men for a short time. Then the Bull would hold muster and sort through the group. A man could request a transfer to Cabanatuan, or we would pick out some man we did not trust and ship him. This same Jap unit had shot ten men at Balanga and five at Culumpit because of men escaping. Our agreement was we all went or no one went. If we thought a man was going to run, we shipped him. By "we" I mean the men the Bull trusted. They were Sandy, Chipper, Mikeoo, and me. By sorting through men we acquired three good mechanics. So we set up our own garage or shop.

Aaron Combs had been injured on a log-towing job. His leg had been badly cut by a propeller blade on one of the tugs. The Bull made sure he was taken care of; he became our cook. He did not have to leave the quarters except to draw rations from the Jap kitchen. Basically we were his slaves, but he never took advantage of the fact. He treated us as men. Perhaps this was what caused Chipper's injury. He never expected it. But when it happened he was not under the Bull's jurisdiction. He had been loaned to another *gunso* in Cervantes. You see, we did several different things. One of our jobs was to haul supplies over the old Spanish trail into Cervantes. This mountain road was quite often an ambush trap set by Filipinos. So the Japs found out their convoy was not shot up if there were Americans riding in it. We, in a sense, became their insurance. Even if our truck was not called to haul a load over the mountain, they made one or two of us ride with them anyhow. I made quite a few trips over and back. Just standing up behind the cab of the lead truck where I could be plainly seen.

The fuel we used in our trucks was a mixture of sugar cane alcohol, kerosene, and low-octane gasoline. It ran all right, but the trucks were hard to start. We used to carry a broom handle in the cab. The first thing you did was take the fuel cap off and stir the tank for five minutes before trying to start the truck. The fuel separated. There was no such thing as a filling station. All fuel was handled in fifty-four-gallon barrels. We had to siphon the fuel out of the barrels with a hose into a pail, then pour it into the tank. The end result was debris in the tank which caused carburetor trouble. Well, Chipper's truck started having trouble running. We were at Cervantes and our mechanics were in Manila, but this gunso seemed to think all Americans were mechanics. The Jap wanted Chipper's truck to cross the mountain. Chipper tried to get his truck running. He removed the carburetor and cleaned it. We used to prime or start a dead truck with clear gas, not the poor mixture the Japs gave us. Now Nakamura understood engines. This Jap did not. All he knew was Chipper was not starting his truck and was holding up the convoy. He also knew it was important to be off that mountain and in a secure place by dark. The Jap had a screaming tantrum. Chipper knew he needed gas to start the truck so he turned around and walked off to get some from the gas barrel. I guess the gunso figured Chipper was insulting him, or maybe refusing to drive over the mountain. Who knows for sure what is in a Jap's mind. We all learned to do a good job of reading minds, facial expressions, and actions. Chipper guessed wrong. That Jap tried to knock his brains out with a rifle butt. Now there are times when no one can help. We thought the sonovabitch had killed him. The convoy rolled and just left him lay. He was inside the guard perimeter at Cervantes, so the guards did not seem to care either, they just left him lay.

Our little joke among ourselves was, we went to the Far East University and majored in psychology! Chipper never talked about it later, because he knew he flunked the course. And who brags about the time he almost got killed? When we came back over the mountain, he was in our sleeping quarters. They most always gave us a separate room to sleep in. Chipper did not want to eat or do anything. That was a bad sign, as we ate every chance we got. His headache lasted a long time, and the sore spot on his head never did go away. We were careful never to bump him if we were horsing around.

Another thing that happened on this detail was that one of the Jap officers had somewhere gotten the bare frame of a truck. Since he belonged to an engineer outfit, he was able to build a fancy flatbed and fix it up so it was really special-looking. He'd sometimes drive it himself, but most times he liked being chauffered, just like the colonel. I mean, when in this truck, this Jap thought he was King Tut. Wouldn't you know, a Filipino stole that truck. The guy that did it was married to a Japanese gal and the word was she squealed on him. They took him to the guardhouse where they tied his hands behind his back and hung him up on a hook. He never, never laid down. Every time the guard changed, they went and got him and beat him. Everybody coming on duty and everybody going off duty took a lick at him. This just became part of the routine. They used braids of old-style telephone wire which they wound around their hands so as to get a good grip. I never saw a man take as much abuse in my life as that Filipino. Regular as clockwork, he was beaten. You couldn't see his features after a while. We were back in a rest area for Japanese troops quartered in Manila. They kept a stable down the street for officers to use when they were resting up. So one day the guards were out there taking turns working this Filipino over, when a real aristocratic-looking Japanese officer wearing riding boots strolled by. After he watched for a while he had the guards stop and asked them why they were doing this. For about an hour this officer haggled with the officer in charge of the guard detail. Finally they untied the Filipino and threw him in a truck, and some Japs drove him off. I figured the game was over, they were taking him to cut his head off. About four months later, when I was driving my truck up in the mountains around Cervantes, I found this Filipino. He was working on a road-building gang. He still looked beat, but I thought, "You lucky bugger, you survived."

The photograph brings back so much that happened on this detail. My problem is my memory runs together. Kind of like a coon dog who won't follow a single scent. I'm amazed at what I remember, though. I can't imagine anyone forgetting. But Sandmier don't even remember being there. He was a big man and the Japs just loved knocking him down. He got so many concussions from being belted, he has almost a total memory loss.

Survival was hard and one point that's never made is that nobody could survive in conditions as bad as the ones we were in, if it had been continuous for three and a half years. Some places had to be better than others. We had our ups and downs. Cabanatuan, where I was sent next, more than made up for the few never-never-land months I spent under the Bull.

About this time the Japs began to need reinforcements in the big battles that were taking place somewhere other than in the Philippines. Our bunch of guards, the Japs in the picture, were ordered south. We were trucked into Bilibid Prison about January 8. The guards, who we knew well by now, told us they were going home. We teased them and said there was no fighting going on in Japan. We told them they were being sent south and that MacArthur would eat them up. Lieutenant Crosby told us to soft-pedal that. Made sense. Could be we'd make them mad, and if they really were going into combat, they didn't have any more reason to be nice to us. We'd catch our lumps. We really did get confident in the Bull's protection. Sometimes I wonder what did happen to those Jap guards. As for us, it's funny how news got around. We knew Cabanatuan was a death camp. So we lived like there was never going to be an end to our work detail. We were not stupid, just a way of not admitting our ultimate end. A man had to be a moron not to know his chances of returning to America were poor. If you sat and worried, it would gradually break your spirit. This mental escape, I thought, was the only way to go.

6
CABANATUAN

Cabanatuan City is located 100 miles north of Manila in Nueva Ecija Province on Luzon's Central Plain. The POW camp there, at first, consisted of three sites. Separated by several miles, the prison camps were numbered 1, 2, and 3. Camp No. 1, which eventually housed all the American prisoners, had, before the war, been the site of a United States agricultural experiment station. Most of the prisoners from Camp O'Donnell were incarcerated here. When the Philippine Army was mobilized, three camps were built for the units of the 91st Philippine Army Division. Designated each to accommodate a regiment, the three camps were divided by two hard-packed dirt roads into three equal-size battalion areas. Each area consisted of a large wooden building partitioned off into small offices; a wooden dispensary building; a guardhouse with a brig at one end; a long shelter used as a garage; and a number of nipa-thatch, swalisided barracks, each sixty feet long and built to accommodate forty Filipino soldiers. As prisoners' barracks they housed 120 men. Across the road from the camps were a number of small buildings which were used for the Japanese guard contingents. To lodge prisoners, the Japanese built around the camps eight-foot-high barbed-wire fences which accommodated, at even intervals, four-story wooden guard towers. The main stockade, known as Cabanatuan POW Camp No. 1, sat on flat, arid land four miles east of Cabanatuan City and was 600 by 800 yards in area.

Some of the American prisoners arrived in late

May. The sick and wounded who had remained behind on Bataan in field hospitals arrived first and were placed in Camp No. 3. The men who surrendered on Corregidor began to arrive there shortly afterwards and its rolls eventually reached 6,066 prisoners. The camp's first American commander was Col. Napoleon Boudreau.

Once Camp No. 3 reached this quota, the remaining 1,500 Corregidor prisoners in Bilibid were shipped to Cabanatuan Camp No. 2, where they arrived around May 31. There being no water in the camp, they were moved to Camp No. 1. On June 2 the Japanese began to transfer the prisoners from Camp O'Donnell to Cabanatuan Camp No. 1. Again, using rough numbers and eliminating the men who had died on the Death March (650), or died in O'Donnell (1,500), or were assigned to work details (2,000), we arrive at 5,850 men coming from O'Donnell. It should also be kept in mind that this figure represents the sickest, weakest, and most disabled prisoners in O'Donnell. Consequently, 740 of these men died in the month of June in Cabanatuan, 130 alone from an outbreak of diphtheria. By the end of 1942 nearly 2,000 more men died in Camp No. 1. By comparison, in Camp No. 3, where the men were healthier to begin with, between June and October 1942, only sixty-one died.

All the Filipino prisoners at O'Donnell remained there until their eventual release in late 1942.

Capt. BENSON GUYTON*:

After Corregidor surrendered, along with everyone else† I was shipped across Manila Bay and put in Bilibid Prison. Most

---

* Captain Guyton of the 60th Coast Artillery (AA) was captured on Corregidor.
† General Wainwright surrendered all forces in the Philippines to the Japanese unconditionally on May 6, 1942. To help assure complete com-

of us were in pretty good shape. We had been eating regularly on Corregidor—not much, but enough—and being on an island, we didn't get malaria, so we were fairly healthy. I'd have to say that the men captured on Corregidor started captivity by being in relatively good condition. Life in Bilibid wasn't too bad, because I had staggered in with a sack of food I'd collected on Corregidor. You couldn't eat a can of corned beef by yourself, so you'd find four or five other guys and split it. Another guy would have something else, like coffee. After about three days in Bilibid it dawned on me that half the guys from Corregidor had already gone. Groups were being lined up and marched out the gate. I never felt it was wise to be the first guy to move out nor the last, so I thought, "Well, old boy, you get in line tomorrow morning and go wherever you're going."

The next morning I meandered into a column, and along with another 500 men I marched down to the Manila railroad station. We were packed into boxcars and moved to the town of Cabanatuan. That first night my group was kept in the village schoolyard and the following morning we marched to the camp. At one of the rest stops I saw one of our guys lying in front of a mudhole, ready to drink some water.* I said, "Man, don't drink that water." He was exhausted. "Captain, I haven't had a drink of water all day long." So I gave him a drink out of my canteen. It hurt. I didn't know when I was going to get more water myself. Ain't like giving a dime in church, when you know you're going to make a dollar tomorrow. Later in the day we arrived in a camp which I learned was called Camp No. 3.

That night I saw men from Bataan for the first time. A few of them had arrived before us, to help get the camp set up for our arrival. Of course on Corregidor we had heard that the boys on Bataan were not faring very well. But now, seeing them for the first time was a shock. We began to notice these guys, a captain and a lieutenant, who'd been on Bataan. And, oh man, these guys had a vacant stare in their eyes. When you started to open a can they would just stare at the food. You could see their mouths watering. Either they couldn't believe you had a can of food, or else they were afraid they weren't going to get their share. They were frightening. I don't believe I'd ever seen anything like that. It was more than I could handle.

---

pliance with Wainwright's surrender order throughout the archipelago, the Japanese kept much of the Corregidor garrison on the island until the last week in May. Most prisoners left Corregidor on Sunday, May 24.
* The monsoon rains had begun on Luzon.

Cpl. HUBERT GATER:

We arrived at the town of Cabanatuan towards the beginning of June.* The orders in O'Donnell were that anyone who could work would be moved. We marched to Capas. Then we repeated the train ride we had from San Fernando, only this time it was longer. Same size boxcars. It was every man for himself. Everyone had lost forty or fifty pounds. In the early afternoon we arrived.† Again we had a short rest to be counted and to empty our shoes. Then we were marched about four miles to the POW camp.

We were not exactly welcomed into camp. There were some that had friends or relations already there. Most of the men in Cabanatuan [No. 1], when I arrived, had not been on "the March" from Bataan. They were from Corregidor. They didn't look to be in as bad shape as we were. Already, however, they had figured out more men in camp, less food, less water; go away. With our arrival new mess halls had to be set up. There were no volunteers. Every man was tired or sick or just didn't care.

Pfc. MICHAEL McMULLEN‡:

A few days after I arrived in Camp No. 1 they started moving in the guys from O'Donnell. I couldn't believe what I was seeing. When they arrived they just laid down alongside each other. All these men had malaria and dysentery. It was completely out of this world. I walked through them, trying to find someone from my outfit. I passed one particular group and I thought I heard someone call my name. It wasn't until the third time that I found the man. He said, "Mac, don't you know me?" I said, "No. Who are you?" I hadn't any idea. Then he told me. The last time I'd seen him he weighed over 200 pounds. Now he weighed closer to 100. He was matted all over with feces. I actually couldn't believe it. The man alongside of him was so still he could have been dead.

Cpl. WILLIAM GARLEB:

The shock of seeing the guys from O'Donnell coming in was like something sticking in my throat. I couldn't believe the

---

* The movement of the prisoners from O'Donnell to Cabanatuan No. 1 occurred roughly during the time that the great naval battle of Midway was being fought, June 3–6, 1942.
† Many prisoners were also trucked to Cabanatuan.
‡ Michael McMullen and William Garleb were in the first group to arrive at Cabanatuan. At the time of the surrender on Bataan, being too sick to make the Death March, they had remained at field hospitals. When Corregidor fell, all the patients well enough to move were shipped to Cabanatuan. It is unclear what happened to the men who were too ill to be moved. There is agreement from the men who left the hospitals that they don't remember seeing these people again.

horror I was seeing. There was Sergeant Nance. He had been a big guy, lifted weights. He was so skinny now that he looked like a skeleton. Everyone looked the same. That thin, everyone lost their facial characteristics. It was like watching a horror movie. These guys from O'Donnell were like walking zombies. Skeletons walking towards you with skin hanging on the bones. You could hide your hand behind a guy's shoulder blades, they were sticking out that far. It was almost impossible to believe. Heads looked like skulls. Then there was the color— yellow, white, grey. Their eyes were just yellow. It was enough to make you want to lie down and die. Everything was so different from what I was brought up with. There was just too much reality at one time.

Pfc. JACK BRADY:

Leaving O'Donnell for Cabanatuan was not seen as anything different. At the point when we were moved, there was absolutely nothing in the way of any kind of hope whatsoever that any of it would ever end. I felt it was going to go on forever. I'm not sure I was conscious of this feeling at the time, but in looking back the only thing I was interested in was just going through one more day. If I did, it was enough.

Cpl. HUBERT GATER:

Because I didn't have malaria or dysentery, I was put in charge of the water faucet. The faucet didn't trickle like at O'Donnell, it dripped. My orders were to fill two five-gallon cans for the mess hall, then to fill canteens for the men. The poor devils, they took turns all night staying in line with six to eight canteens each to help a friend. If an officer tried to pull rank and get ahead in the line, he was told where to go and fast. It rained nearly every day for the first month or so. The mud was terrible.

Cpl. CHARLES McCARTIN:

I was so ill I couldn't move, so they sent me over to the hospital section. I lay there for days. Around me there were men just ready to give up. I decided I was going to help those folks. No one else was doing it, and even though I could hardly walk, I grabbed some canteens and crawled over to the water spigot that was nearby. After I rested a while I went back and filled some more. I was just determined that I was going to help those men all I could. I started doing that type of thing every day. Without realizing it, the exercise each day, of forcing myself to move, gave me a little bit more strength. Gradually I began to recover.

During this period a corpsman would come through our hospital barracks once a day, carrying a stick. He walked up and down the aisles looking at the various fellows. If they didn't have their eyes open he'd hit them real hard on their legs or side. Some responded, some didn't. There were two very sick men on either side of me. When one of them was whacked, he hardly moved. It didn't faze him. He died a day or two later. The other man got angry: "Get away from me! What are you trying to do, kill me?" This man was still alive when I left the hospital. It was done so care could be given to those who still had the will to live.

Cpl. HUBERT GATER:

The first week after working day and night I was so exhausted I fell into my bunk. The next morning four men from my section were dead. That really shook me up. O'Donnell. Cabanatuan. Death followed us.

Pfc. JOHN FALCONER:

Death was easier than life. All I had to do was just lay back and die. I didn't have to worry about that. It was as easy as letting go of a rope. A lot of people quit hanging on.

Pfc. ROY DIAZ:

In Cabanatuan we slept five to a bay, head to feet. One morning I woke up earlier than the others and found the guy next to me dead. I grabbed his mess kit, so I had two rations of rice at breakfast. It was dog eat dog. You had to survive some way.

1st Lt. MARK HERBST, M.D.:

There are people dead who have no right to be dead—medically speaking. You talk about why people decide they want to die, I don't know, but I do have one glaring example. We had a lieutenant in my battalion who was a "number-one" soldier. He led more charges in the Battle of the Points than anyone. He was amazing. It was just a matter of time, but he was finally wounded. He was sent back to Hospital No. 1. Because he was such a valuable man I went back as soon as I could, to make sure he got whatever he needed. I saw him again in Cabanatuan. He had dysentery and was losing ground rapidly. Being such a good fellow, all the men near him tried to help him. They did their damnedest to try to see he got extra rations of rice. He kept going downhill, losing weight, having more and more trouble. One day I thought, "Let's see what's going

on." So I walked over to his section. I didn't see him get his first ration of rice, but I got there when he had a second plate. When he left I followed him. He went into the latrine of another section and dumped the rice down the hole. Now why a guy would do that when everybody and his brother would have given their left ear for another plate of rice, I can't say. This fellow just wanted to die. And he did.

Cpl. HUBERT GATER:

People continued to die. Major Riley died. A good medical officer. He had brought my brother's three children into this world in Albuquerque. In O'Donnell he visited the sick every day, even though he had no medicine. I wondered what wonders he had done with a touch and "I'll see you tomorrow." I'd see him on his sick calls lean against the barracks to steady himself, he was so sick himself with malaria. My good friend Barnes Omsted died. All my close friends died—Brown, Sims, Roberts, Samoni.

Pfc. JOHN FALCONER:

I had a friend, Charles Rockwell, who was a first sergeant in D Company. He was very sick and I took care of him. If he could have gotten a can of tomatoes, he might have pulled through. All Charlie wanted was a can of tomatoes. He never got it. He got so sick that they told him they were going to move him to Zero Ward. Before they moved him he said, "John, will you take care of my blanket for me?" I think he knew he wasn't going to come back. I told him, "Charlie, you know I can't have that blanket." Everything in the barracks was inventoried, and if I ended up with an extra blanket our barracks commander would have charged me with stealing. So Charles found some toilet paper and because he was too weak to write, I wrote his will. "I, Charles Rockwell, am leaving my blanket in the care and keeping of Pfc. John E. Falconer." Then he tried to sign it. Eventually he managed to.

J. J. CARTER*:

In Cabanatuan I was deathly sick and couldn't eat. Some of the fellows who were out on details would smuggle in milk or sugar so that I could put it on my rice, and in return I'd give them half my rice. Then they'd trade my half ration to some guy who was real hungry for the whole of his ration in the morning, or the next morning, or the morning after that. Nobody was going anywhere anyway. So this was one of the things that kept me down. I wasn't eating because I was trading part of my rations for flavor on the other part. Then it got worse. It kept getting more and more expensive. They kept wanting more of the rice because they knew I couldn't get out from under, because I owed more than I had. Then others caught on to this trading and they started doing it. So one day I said, "I got better things to do than die like this. It just don't add up." This whole thing dawned on me and I became very embittered that people had done me this way. I decided if I ever got on my feet, I was going to get even.

Pvt. LEWIS ELLIOTT:

I seen two brothers in Cabanatuan. One was lying in the barracks dying of malaria and his brother's out selling quinine for cigarettes. Can you believe that? I saw it.

Staff Sgt. HAROLD FEINER:

Only once did I believe I was not going to survive. While in Cabanatuan I got very sick with a combination of illnesses. I got malaria and yellow jaundice. Today it's known as hepatitis.

* Pseudonym.

It saps all your strength. I also had several attacks of dengue fever. It was known as breakbone fever and they're not kidding. It feels like somebody's taking your main bones and constantly beating them with a hammer. Then I lost control of my bowels. I was really in bad shape. I began to feel that I couldn't make it anymore. Some major came along. Oh, he chewed me out! "You should be ashamed of yourself! How can you call yourself an American soldier? I understand you have medical problems, but there are others worse off. You've got enough strength. Clean yourself up!" I did. I was at lower points than that later, but never again did I feel I wasn't going to go all the way.

Pfc. ANDREW AQUILA:

At Cabanatuan I hit my low. I had both dysentery and malaria. They wanted to send me down to Zero Ward. The hospital had two parts: one part for patients who could get well and the other part, Zero Ward, where you went just before the graveyard. One of the doctors was from my state of Ohio. I said, "Doc, don't send me to Zero Ward, because if you do I'm going to give up." He kept me in the medical ward. A week later he came back and told me I'd have to go down, so I went to Zero Ward. I was down below 100 pounds. About this time the Japs let us slaughter some water buffaloes. I was fed the liver of these animals every other day for nearly a week. That brought back my appetite and I began to regain my health.

Capt. LOYD MILLS:

You tried to keep alive. Luckily for me I got into a group. That was the only way to survive. Generally, groups were made up of guys out of the same outfit. We tried to help each other. Someone would steal or swap for quinine. When one of us would get a malaria attack, the other guy would help out. I had a friend. We'd come over on the same boat. He was out of the 31st Infantry. One night he came down to my area shouting for me. He said, "You've got to get me over to the hospital." He was really hurting; he had an internal obstruction. I told him, "No, don't go over there." He said that if I didn't do something for him, he'd die right there. I took him over to the hospital and found the doctor. Before I left he gave me his billfold to keep for him. They operated. He never came back. Anyway, back in his billfold there was a 100-peso bill. With it I was able to buy some stuff which I spread around in my group.

Cpl. WILLIAM GARLEB:

At first I prevented myself from making friends. I was afraid to, because they could die tomorrow. You can put up whatever façade you want, but when someone close to you dies, a part of you dies with him. So there was this psychological undermining of the individual going on all the time. And yet, insanity was extremely rare. In my opinion, the reason for this was the environment we lived in was so hostile that you either lived or you died. To have been insane would have meant dependency, and nobody could have been that dependent and lived.

Cpl. HUBERT GATER:

It was surprising what each man was capable of doing. Whatever job needed to be performed, there was always a man who knew how to do it. A foot pedal drill for the dentist. A wind machine to blow the undesired parts from our rice. We made shoe bottoms from two-by-fours and used the old top or heel for a strap. We wasted nothing. We began to discover we depended on one another for survival.

Cpl. BERNARD "CHICK" SAUNDERS:

In Cabanatuan I spent most of my time in the hospital area. We always tried to help each other out, particularly if someone was out of your outfit or from somewhere near where you lived. Some close friendships were formed. If you laid next to someone for months you had to get close, whether you ever heard of him before or not. If he was too sick to get water and you could get around, you'd get it for him. Or if one of you had an extra ration, you'd share it. You would be surprised at the amount of compassion there was.

Pfc. JOHN FALCONER:

I had gotten the midnight gallops and in trying to make a corner, I snagged my leg on a splinter and tore my leg open. The infection began immediately and went right down to the bone. One of the corpsmen from my tank group gave me some very weak antiseptic. He also gave me fifteen inches of one-inch gauze. "Wrap your leg in that." But he added, "I don't want you to throw it away. Wash it and use it again." If I hadn't had that help, I don't know what would have happened to me.

Another thing that was important in surviving was what you thought. While I was in the hospital a doctor came through

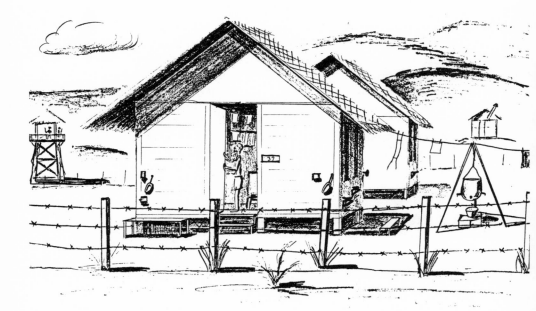

and pointed out certain people who were to receive extra nourishment. There were three days that I got a half a canteen cup
of condensed milk. Just the fact that someone cared about me,
somebody thought enough of me to give me milk, helped me
find the inner strength to go on. The whole idea of mental
strength played a large part in my survival. I was afflicted with
beriberi. My feet were all swollen and my body retained liquid.
I was all puffed up. One man felt that if we got out in the early
morning hours and walked in the dew, that that would help
heal our feet. He probably felt we needed the exercise, and
that was as good an excuse as any other for us to get some.
I would have never gotten it any other way. I'm sure it was
more mental than physical, but those walks helped a great
deal.

But to say that others were the only thing necessary to
survive is overstating the situation. Many times you lived because of something you did for yourself. Some of the people
were too sick to get or eat the rations they were permitted. I'd
go back down to the mess hall and beg them to give me some
of the extra food. Today I couldn't force myself to do that, but
then I did. I had to, because I was hungry. When you're hungry, food is the most important thing in your mind. I still am
very ashamed of one case. If there was any food left over in
the mess hall they would give it to one of the barracks, and
they would alternate the barracks each day. That way each
barracks in its turn received extra rations. One day I slipped
into a barracks other than mine and received a second bowl of
lugaw. I knew I shouldn't have gotten it because it was somebody else's. I rationalized my doing it by believing that someone from this barracks would someday slip into my barracks and
steal my food. But my guilt was still great. Just as I sat down
and began to eat the lugaw, I saw one of my buddies walking
towards me. I felt so ashamed I hid the platter under my legs.
After he left I ate every bit of it. My heels had been in it, but
that didn't make any difference. I was hungry. I was as hungry as my friend who took the meat and fish out of the packages I had given him at O'Donnell.

Staff Sgt. HAROLD FEINER:

There wasn't much stealing because there wasn't much available. But there was a certain amount. I'm sure many a man
who swiped something carries that guilt with him today. I was
in the hospital at Cabanatuan. I should say the hospital site,
because the word was just a figure of speech. It was no more
a hospital than you lay on a sidewalk and somebody walks

around you and doesn't kick you. That's the God's honest truth. The doctors were helpless. All they could do was excuse you from duty, but they didn't do anything for you. "Just lie there until you get well or you die." O.K.? So next to me laid a man, a sailor, young feller. Because he was in a coma, when I got there I never knew whether he was a nice guy or not. He was obviously dying. When someone died, rightfully they would take all his belongings and give them to someone else. There was a common pile of belongings, and when someone needed something it was given to him from this pile. Pants, shoes, whatever. What was the use of burying a man with his clothes? I had lost my belt. It had rotted away. I knew the sailor next to me was going to die, so in the night I stole his belt. I was wrong in a sense, because it should have gone in a common pile. Maybe they would have given it to me, if I had asked. But I stole the belt to insure that I got one. I live with that. You had to be there to understand these things.

Sgt. FORREST KNOX:

Along with stealing, you had to be inventive to survive in prison camp. For example, at Cabanatuan there was always a draining problem, so the camp had a network of small drainage ditches running through it. They were maybe one foot wide and two feet deep. Grass grew along the edge. What you had was communication trenches for the rat population. The medics set a regular bounty on rats. Each rat carcass was worth two cigarettes. So there were men squatting by these little ditches all over camp. They would sit there for hours waiting for a rat to run by, so they could whack it. To see a man so skinny, his arms and legs were not any bigger than the stick he had resting on his shoulder, roosting on the edge of a drainage ditch, staring with total concentration into the fringe of grass—I thought they looked like vultures waiting for the dregs from a jungle kill.

The system worked fairly good and after a while the medics thought the rat population had been pretty well eliminated, because they never had to pay a bounty anymore. The answer was fairly simple: the market price went up. You could get five cigarettes for a rat if you traded to the men with a quan pot.* They swore it tasted like young squirrel. If it was edible, it went to the quan.

---

* In an effort to supplement their meager rations, quans, or small kitchens complete with homemade ovens, were used in addition to the camp kitchens where the issue food was prepared. "Quanning" was the hunting of anything that could be used in a quan.

Pfc. MICHAEL TUSSING, Jr.:

Did you ever try eating unseasoned rice, no salt, no nothing? We ate this during our entire imprisonment—weevily, wormy rice. There were times when we got a better grade of rice, but generally we got the sweepings, the kind of rice the Japanese didn't want and couldn't eat.

We got rice so full of weevils that it looked like it had been heavily sprinkled with black pepper. You ate the weevils, too, thinking there might be some vitamins in them. And there were worms, little white ones with brownish heads. I can still see their eyes. If you'd have picked them out, there wouldn't have been anything left. This may seem like a fairy tale to you, but it's true.

Cpl. BERNARD "CHICK" SAUNDERS:

When they issued us powdered toothpaste, we never brushed our teeth with it. It tasted sweet, so we powdered our rice ration with it.

Pfc. NORMAN MATTHEWS:

We did everything to make the rice taste better. We even tried to make vinegar. It's real hard to start, but once started you could make gallons of it. The problem was, you had to have something to start it with.

Pfc. MICHAEL TUSSING, Jr.:

When you made a lot of vinegar, more than you could use, you'd barter it for something else. Sometimes you'd get someone's rice for a little of your vinegar. By the time we got to Cabanatuan, cigarettes were $100 a pack, if you had the money. Money was no good. It was also nonexistent, so everything was bartered.

Sometimes I could barter or steal raw rice from the kitchen. Then I'd take a round bottle and use it like a rolling pin, and roll the rice so that it was like flour. I'd add water to this and make a batter. Then I'd make pancakes.

Pfc. MICHAEL McMULLEN:

My hot cakes were a total disaster. Not only couldn't I get the batter to rise, but then I tried to fry them in stolen fuel oil.* God, were they terrible!

Pfc. MICHAEL TUSSING, Jr.:

You just can't imagine how you missed the simple things on the table like salt and pepper and butter.

Cpl. CHARLES McCARTIN:

At first we were eating rice and occasionally some kind of greens which we called whistle weeds because they were like a reed with a hollow center. We were getting weaker all the time from that diet. Just before Christmas 1942 we received Red Cross parcels.† One fifteen-pound parcel to four men. Something that could not be divided four ways, like a can of corned beef or Spam, was distributed by drawing straws. Since there were four things of approximately equal value, no one got cheated. Anything else was divided four ways. Powdered milk, for example, we'd spoon out four equal parts. We had American food. As soon as we got a taste of it, the morale of the men just turned completely around. It was wonderful. It was something you could see. The day before you'd talk to some guy who was ready to call it quits. The next day he was

---

* Coconut fuel oil was being used by the Japanese in the diesel engines that furnished power for the camp. When refined, it could be and was used for cooking oil.
† In December 1942 not only were individual Red Cross parcels delivered to Cabanatuan, but also packages containing bulk food and medicine. At the end of November the Japanese also established new and larger ration allowances for the prisoners.

alive and trying to make it home. This was Christmas of '42.

Cigarettes were money. You could get almost anything if you had a pack of cigarettes, and as I didn't smoke I had money in the bank. I traded for soap. I couldn't bring myself to trade for someone else's food. About six months later we did receive one parcel per man and I received twelve packs of cigarettes. I was wealthy. I decided to put them into the black market and receive real food, which would be smuggled in. Of course, the price was exorbitant. There was one boy who was a pretty big operator. He'd bribe a Jap guard and get things like eggs from outside the camp brought in. When he learned about my cigarettes, he approached me and asked if I wanted him to trade them for food. I gave them to him, expecting something in return. He came back the next day and told me the Japanese guard had taken the cigarettes and given him nothing in return. When you have something as valuable as twelve packs of cigarettes, you hate to lose them. I was suspicious that I had been double-crossed, that he had traded the cigarettes and kept the food for himself. I went to my barracks' sergeant, who talked to an American captain, who was responsible for this kind of thing. Then he called for a hearing. Both sides of the case were described and because I couldn't prove I had been crossed, the charges were dropped. My case was one of several the captain heard that day. So the upshot of the whole thing was I lost my trading power. That was unfortunate.

Pfc. JACK BRADY:

When I arrived in Cabanatuan, the prisoners from Corregidor had already arrived and had set up their organization. My experience was that they did their damnedest at first to keep me out of their organization. When I arrived, there was what you might call a black market operating. People were managing to get things in from outside. There was no way that I was allowed to get any of that stuff. If you got on a detail that left camp, you could generally get something in the way of coconuts or bananas or sugar to bring back with you. These, of course, were choice details. I don't know anyone from Bataan who, at first, got on those details. We got the ones inside the camp. We were the most sick, too. That kept many from going out of camp. We paid a price for that.

Capt. MARION LAWTON:

We had a feller, Ted Lowen, who—I hesitate to say, but it's the truth—was sort of an underworld operator in Manila before the war. He was into gambling and the things that go with it, so he had connections. Being the type of operator he was, after he got to Cabanatuan and knowing how to do it, he probed until he found a Jap guard who was on the make. Ted must have come into camp with some money, and he finally found a guard he could bribe. "You get this message to Manila for me, and when the stuff comes in you'll get a percentage." Ted bought his way. First thing you know he has a regular little store set up in Cabanatuan, stacked with canned goods, quinine, and all the other stuff he had coming in. I never saw it, but I was told about it. Ted himself was fat and he had two well-fed, healthy bodyguards to watch after him. It was a natural thing to do because, as hungry as people were, they would have beaten and robbed Ted, had he not had his protection. Well, Ted's business got so good that he set up a subdealer way down at my end of camp, a sergeant by the name of Moe Gardner.

When I got to Cabanatuan, of course, I had been through the Death March and O'Donnell, and consequently had nothing of value left to trade for food with. The Corregidor people who were there were, of course, in better condition then us guys. They had brought with them duffel bags with clothes and food, and because they hadn't been looted as badly, many even had money. Within the compound they had set up their own area. I saw the good condition they were in, and I remembered I had a good friend who had gotten to Corregidor before Bataan fell. I'll call him Mac. He was one of the group of four that I met on the voyage over to the Philippine Islands and who, because we got on so well together, began to pal around with when we arrived in Manila. I had some buddies from the States who had arrived in the Philippines six months before I got there and who met us at the dock. They brought my group, including Mac, out to their quarters at Fort McKinley. While we waited to be assigned, we lived on post and got to know Manila. I felt Mac was just as good a buddy as my best friend, Henry Leitner.

Then the war started and we were finally backed up into Bataan. I may have been the only officer who was not hungry during that period. I was the advisor/instructor to a Philippine Army battalion made up of reservists. When the other American advisor was killed, I was left all by myself with this battalion. On the retreat we came through Olongapo and my battalion was left to guard a mountain pass, while the main battle went on further north. While we were there my Filipino supply officer, who was a pretty good scrounger, made several trips to Subic Bay Naval Base and came back with cases of hams and eggs and canned goods and beer and Coca-Cola. He also confiscated an Al Hambra Tobacco panel truck into which he stashed the loot. He also found, in Subic, a burned-out liquor store from which he acquired a case of scotch and a case of bourbon. So when we got to Bataan, I had a good supply of food. I could have lasted another six months. In early March there was a lull in the fighting and since March 5 was my birthday, I decided to throw myself a party. Of all my friends I could only find Mac's outfit, so I sent a runner over to invite him to spend the evening with me.

Mac was very hungry. Supplies were nil. Alberto, my houseboy, had got a chicken somewhere back in the jungle, so with that and some canned vegetables and pudding we had a real birthday dinner. Boy, Mac just gorged himself. Just the two of us and more food than he had seen in two months. We had some drinks and he couldn't believe it. When he got ready to leave, I reached in the panel truck and pulled out a fifth of scotch which I gave him. At first he didn't want to take something that scarce and valuable, but I insisted, telling him it was a token of our friendship. He went away full and happy. A month later he managed to escape to Corregidor and I surrendered on Bataan.

By the time I got to Cabanatuan I had malaria, jaundice, and I just couldn't eat the horrible lugaw they were giving us. With jaundice, no matter how starved you are, you have no appetite. The Doc said, "Protein's your problem. You need food and you're not getting any. You've got to figure a way to get extra food." I thought, "By golly, Mac! I'll find Mac." I went up to him, all ragged, looking like a tramp. Old Mac, I could see a chill come over him. He knew I wanted something. "Hello, Mac. How ya doing?" Then I got serious. "I'm catching hell, Mac. I'm in a bad way and there's a black market operating, and if I could get some money to buy some canned goods I think I could get straightened out. I wonder if you could lend me some money?" "Manny," he said, "I don't have but a hundred bucks and I'm afraid I might need it." I couldn't believe it! You know, I just couldn't believe it. "O.K., Mac. I understand." And I hobbled away cussing him with every step. I wished the greatest evil would befall him and that the Japs would beat him up.

When I got back to my barracks, several hundred yards away, I was so exhausted I fell asleep. When I woke, I wasn't mad at Mac. I thought this thing is survival, every man for himself. If he gives me what he has, then he's going to have problems. It taught me a lesson. You shouldn't expect anything out of a casual relationship. It's only within a family that people can turn to each other for real help. From Mac I had expected too much. That reasoning satisfied my conscience.

Still hungry, though, I knew I must do something else if

I wasn't going to die, and I hit on another idea. I'd go see Moe Gardner and see if he'd let me have some food on credit. I had nothing to lose. All he could say was no. I found Gardner. He looked like a mean street merchant. "Good afternoon, Captain," he said. "What can I do for you?" I told him my plight. "Moe, you don't know me and I don't know you, but I'm a captain in the U.S. Army and my pay each month is going into the bank. It's no good to me unless I get back there to spend it, so I want to make you a proposition. Will you spell me, on the cuff, for a period of time? Do it for as long as you can and when you go as far as you can, call it off. I'll write you a check then for what I owe you." He thought a moment. "O.K., I'll do it, but it'll have to be at my prices." I told him not to worry about the price. I didn't care what it cost. I wanted to live. I didn't get greedy and I asked for only what I thought I needed. I got a can of corned beef and a can of salmon and I stuffed them in my shirt so nobody'd see and went back to my barracks. When chow time came I went and got my rice and walked on behind the barracks until I was alone. I opened up the corned beef and put half of it in my rice. The other half I saved for suppertime. I strung it out. I saved the salmon for the next day. In several days I went back and got some more. This went on for several weeks. Like I say, I didn't ask for too much and I didn't gorge myself.

At the end of a month Moe said, "Lawton, that's as far as I can go." "O.K.," I said, "that was the bargain. How much do I owe you?" "A hundred and twenty-five bucks." He pulled out a square sheet of paper and I put my bank name on it and the date, and I put down the amount and signed it. I thanked him and, boy, by then the jaundice had cleared up. Thirty days of protein and I was back on my feet. It was uphill for a long time after that.

Now this is where religion comes in for me. This boy was not of my faith. I was an officer and he was an enlisted man. We were strangers. He ran a cutthroat black-market operation. He couldn't spend my check then and he could sell anything he had for real money or valuables. He didn't need to do credit business. There was no competition. So I believe that the hand of God touched that man. Something had to do it. There was no reason for him to trust me or to feel sorry for me. There were too many others in the same plight and he couldn't help them all. But he did help me. And my friend turned me down. How can you account for it?

Moe Gardner died later on the ship that was taking us to Japan. I was told that he still had a pocketful of money until someone rolled him.

Sgt. FORREST KNOX:

The truck drivers on the motor-pool detail were on call twenty-four hours a day. The trip to Manila for supplies was a weekly affair. The Jap *gunso* in charge used to carry a suitcase back and forth. Every week another suitcase full of money came to camp. The money was supplied by the Chinese counterfeiters in Manila. As I understood it, they also took care of bribing the *gunso*. Inside camp the money was kept at the MP internal guardhouse. The head MP slept on a bunk that was lined with money. His mattress was a layer of money. Never seen it myself, but a man told me there was a layer three inches deep in his bunk. The system was you wrote a check and received cash to spend on the black market. The check was sent to Manila on the next trip of the suitcase. You were suppose to redeem your check after the war. If the PW died, it was marked off as a business loss. An unfinished story. Did anyone redeem his paper? The Japs were forever changing their money, trying to outfox the counterfeiter. I think the printers must have been Chinese. Sometimes they had their Mickey Mouse money on the streets before the Japs. Most of the black market was run by the civilians. They had all the native contacts. The carabao cart detail was mostly civilians. Who knew how to drive a carabao? So the carts brought in a large part of it. It was a standard joke. Everyone in the world took bribes and the Japs sold out cheaper than anyone else. It seemed that all the Japanese banks used Chinese clerks and cashiers. Japanese story was they could count faster and more accurately than Japs. We said they couldn't find an honest Jap in the entire country, so they had to settle for Chinks.

Capt. ROBERT TAYLOR, Chaplain:

In the hospital we had a smuggling service which brought us medicine, pesos, and news. Our contact in Manila was a person with the code name of "High Pockets." Receiving these goods through unauthorized channels was the reason that several of us got caught up in this guardhouse business. It began for me innocently enough. I wasn't a major link in the smuggling operation and at first was involved only in distributing some of the stuff to the patients. John Phillips was a sergeant in my outfit and I knew him well. He died later in Cabanatuan. I also met his wife Clara. She and some other ladies formed a welfare group in Manila. One day Chaplain Tiffany, who was the key man in the smuggling situation, told me that Clara Phillips was High Pockets and that she had requested information as to whether I wanted anything. "Well," I said, "I don't need anything more

than anyone else would need." Then on second thought I said, "Chaplain, tell Clara, if she can get her hands on one, to send me a Greek New Testament." Of all the things to request in a prison camp. I'd studied Greek and I thought I'd like to refresh myself.

The package containing my book was the one the Japanese picked up. There, amongst the medicine and letters and whatever, was a Greek New Testament addressed to Bob. Everyone else's package was addressed to a code name like "Mango" or "Everlasting." Mine was in the clear and the Japs put two and two together and decided the only man in Cabanatuan named Bob who wanted a Greek New Testament must be a chaplain, and I was the only chaplain named Robert. I suspect some of the guards who must have been Christian figured this out. That's how I got into it.

At first I thought not having a code name would be in my favor. Anyone with one might indicate they were interested in espionage or something else, you know. In the long run, though, it made no difference, because they treated me just like they did the rest of them. They picked up six of us and took us down to the headquarters close to Cabanatuan and interrogated us.*

---

* Besides Chaplain Taylor there were two civilians, Treatt and Rogers, and Lt. Col. Mack, Lt. Col. Alfred Oliver, and Lt. Col. Jack Swartz, who ran the camp hospital.

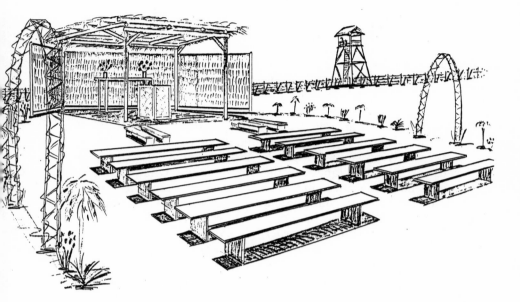

When they came to Chaplain Oliver they said, "You're the senior chaplain in this prison camp. Tell us the names of the people in Manila who are involved in the distribution of medicine and unauthorized communication." He said, "I won't do that. I'll only tell you that they are people who are trying to do something for the camp which you will not do for us. You can take my life, but my Christian conscience will not let me betray them." They beat him until an inch of his life. They kept us and interrogated us three or four times.

At first, maybe the first two weeks, they held the group in a little makeshift place with guards around us day and night. Then they came and got us and marched us around the northern side of the camp and we suspected . . . well, it could have been anything. As we approached the road that led into the prison camp, we discovered that they were taking us into a newly prepared jail. They had rebuilt or remodeled an old house. Inside this building they built six or so small cells measuring five or six feet long, four feet wide, and five feet high. I couldn't stand up straight in it, but I could lie down by kind of crunching up. They put two men into each cell. The cells were windowless and faced a corridor with the door to the outside at one end. Each cell door had a small window which allowed us a little light. It was rather dark all the time, it was hot, and there were flies during the day and swarms of mosquitoes at night.

Fortunately, they permitted the men in the camp to bring us reading material, and by getting up close to the grate in the door and turning our backs to the hallway, we had enough light to read some part of the day. The rest of the time we talked to our cell mates. In my case, Captain Aton.

We were permitted to go to a latrine several times a day, always accompanied by a bayonet-wielding guard. If we had dysentery or any other disease, as some of us did, it was terrible. Fortunately, we didn't get a lot of food, so we didn't have to go to the latrine more than a couple of times a day. Every once in a while they'd come to interrogate us. I couldn't imagine why, at first, we were being so rigorously interrogated for receiving smuggled goods. What I failed to realize was the importance the Japanese put on knowing who High Pockets was. Later I learned that Clara Phillips not only smuggled goods into Cabanatuan, but sent messengers to the guerrillas in the hills as well. The Japs thought we were part of the chain and were very anxious to learn High Pockets' identity.

The worst part for me was not knowing whether it would ever end. We had no way of knowing anything that was happening outside of our jail. One man in with us, a lieutenant colonel, was one of those types who was by nature nervous and jittery. Every time we'd hear the Japanese coming to interrogate us, he'd feel we were going to be executed. We continuously had to talk to him to calm him down. It wasn't, in a sense, real unusual to be scared.

I was treated roughly only once in there. One of our guards we knew by reputation to be a very mean little rascal. In coming through the corridor he heard someone call him an SOB. He wasn't sure from which cell the name had come, but he suspected it had come from Aton and me. We denied it was us. That night Aton and I talked about it and decided, because of this guy's reputation, we would not go to the latrine the next morning if he was our guard escort. It was felt that he could shoot or bayonet us on the way and then claim we had tried to escape. The next morning when the others went out, Aton and I remained behind. It was unwise for us to do this, because the little Jap came back and found us alone in the jail. "Who called me SOB?" Then he opened that little cage door and made us kneel. He took the barrel of his rifle and slammed it into my chest. I did a somersault. But Aton, who he suspected, not only was knocked over, but then made to get up so he could be beaten on the head, neck, and shoulders. It was an awful beating. He was sore and bruised for a long time. Aton later died on one of the ships.

I became ill sometime afterwards. The guards notified one of our camp doctors, who came over. After he examined me, which I don't remember because I was semiconscious, he told the Japanese commander that unless I was allowed to leave I was going to die right there. On the ninetieth day that I spent in this cell, some American corpsmen came and carried me back to the big hospital in the prison camp. The others remained in their little cells another month.*

Sgt. FORREST KNOX:

One of the things PWs were cursed with was what we called dry beriberi. It was starvation, plain and simple. As it was explained to me, every nerve has a pure protein sheath on it, sort of like insulation on an electrical wire. Well, under prolonged starvation the system consumes itself. Like a poorly fed mother loses her teeth to the baby she carries. Our system stripped the protein off the nerves. This left them exposed. In the eyes, ordinary sunlight gave you a flash burn, and you went blind if the exposure was constant every day. Like working in the center of an airfield in bright sunlight. The day the carrier task force hit Manila Bay I could hear the .50-cal.'s firing and

* The two civilians, Treatt and Rogers, and Colonel Mack remained in their cells for approximately five months. They each survived this punishment, but lost their lives on the ship carrying them to Japan.

recognized the American aircraft engines by sound, but I couldn't see the planes. I was going blind.

Well, the other place beriberi showed up was on your feet. As the nerve sheath disappeared, the skin got extremely sensitive. When a man screamed because a fly lit on his toe, he had it bad. One man from our town, Carl, he had beriberi so bad he lost all feeling in his legs. Mother Nature's answer— so you didn't have to scream when a fly lit on your toe. He was in bad shape. Could hardly walk to the latrine. But he had to answer a work call and work the farm. Another man in our town, Phil, had been a barber before service. So he was put on special duty in the officers' area as an orderly. Never had to answer any work calls, got extra rations and small tips for service. Now, Carl hates Phil's guts. After thirty-five years he still won't speak to him. It is damn hard to be a philosopher about what happened when it hurt that bad. No one ever said everything would be fair and equal. But you try and explain that to Carl. Phil, well he found a way to survive and used it. I reckon we all did that, one way or another.

1st Lt. MARK HERBST, M.D.:

The only thing we could do when someone had dry beriberi was to get him on his feet and off the bed. The minute he grew fast to a mattress, he was dead. Anybody that just got too sick to get out of bed was on his way to die. The idea was not to send them to the fields, but to get them to walk around and not be in the hospital moaning, holding their feet. For treatment, if we got a hold of brewer's yeast we gave it to them. Otherwise, we tried to get some vegetables that the boys might have hauled in. Of course what we needed mostly was meat, and our ration of meat was a cubic centimeter of carabao once every three months.

2d Lt. HADLEY WATSON:

My battalion commander during the war told me one day at Cabanatuan, "Watson, there's a detail going south to work on a prison farm. If you can, get on it because you'll have a better chance to get more food. I advise you to go." The word was out that it was supposedly a good detail to get on. I damned near didn't get on it. They were sending only healthy men and I had malaria and beriberi. But I slipped in and ended up at Davao.*

* This thousand-man detail left Cabanatuan on Oct. 24, 1942, the same day the British began their offensive against Rommel at El Alamein. This day also saw heavy fighting on Guadalcanal in a campaign that was already nearly three months old.

Capt. BENSON GUYTON:

In October a 1,000-man detail went to Davao, on Mindanao. This, along with the details going to Japan, made some space, so the Japs abandoned Camp No. 3. The Japs kept consolidating and we kept being crowded together. We were moved to Camp No. 1.* What a mess. Now No. 3 was a clean camp. I don't ever remember latrines overflowing. I can well remember going by a half-full latrine and Colonel Hopkins telling me to start digging another, so that by the time the one was full there was another one already dug. But in Cabanatuan No. 1 there was an acute latrine problem. Many mining engineers in the Philippines had joined the Army and been given commissions. They were good at this type of thing; they knew about soil and drainage. Beecher put one of them in charge of cleaning up Camp No. 1. Mind you, when we came down from Camp No. 3 to Camp No. 1, Beecher somehow or other obtained command of Camp No. 1. I don't know what his relation was with the Jap commander.† I do know Beecher was kind of a strong, burly guy and stayed healthy. I'm sure you can find a story or two that would indicate that Beecher got a little more than his share of food, and that's the reason he stayed healthy. And I would say if he did, it probably was a good thing for everybody. Beecher ran a dad gum good ship, and if he personally had to fudge on his ration a little bit in order to stay strong, it was worth it. It was better to have a strong man representing us rather than a weak, sick one.

Another thing Beecher did was get rid of the mud. Everywhere you went, you tracked mud. We immediately started building walks, good walks, about twice as wide as the little trails they had. Later we surfaced the walks with pea gravel. Also, we built drainage ditches two or three times as deep as the ones we found when we arrived.‡

---

* Due to transfers of personnel to Japan and work details like the one sent to Davao, the remaining 3,000 prisoners at Camp No. 3 were moved to Camp No. 1 between October 28 and 30, 1942. An estimated 8,700 prisoners were now housed in No. 1. Around September 1 Colonel Boudreau, along with all other colonels still remaining in Cabanatuan, had been moved from Camp No. 3 to Tarlac, where the other senior American officers were kept. Lt. Col. Curtis Beecher was appointed Prisoner Headquarters Commander in his place. Colonel Beecher had been the commanding officer of the 1st Battalion, 4th Marines which had come to the Philippines from Shanghai. He was captured on Corregidor.
† Arriving also at Camp No. 1 at this time to replace its commander, Lieutenant Colonel Mori, was Major Iwanaka, who had been the commander of Camp No. 3.
‡ In addition to improving the camps' drainage problems, Colonel Beecher attacked the problem of the flies. They lived and bred in the open latrines and small garbage dumps. Fly-killing campaigns were introduced and prizes of an egg or a few cigarettes were offered to prisoners kill-

I had never been on a burial detail at Camp No. 3. You didn't need to go on one. Maybe one man a day dying. That's no problem for 6,000 men to bury. But boy, at Camp No. 1, even as late as November, December, they were burying 300 a month. One day word came up they needed more people for the burial detail and nobody was there, so here I go. This was during the rainy season, before we put in the gravel walks, so it's muddy. When we got to the cemetery—a big hole, actually— it was about half full of water. When you came up, you just dumped your man in and he splashed away. Carrying him, slipping in the mud, was mean. There was a chaplain. He said some words. I was so doggone uncomfortable and upset that I didn't listen to what the chaplain was saying. I remember looking at a Jap guard standing there with his rifle. I must have had some kind of sad expression on my face. He looked at me and shook his head and said in Japanese, "Yoroshii-nee" (no good).*

ing a hundred flies or more. Eventually, an Engineers officer, Lt. Col. Frederick Saint, by using scrap lumber and salvaged tin, built an experimental septic tank. With its success and the building of these tanks throughout the camp, the fly population was reduced to the vanishing point. After the septic tanks, what flies there were came from the Japanese side of the camp, where similar sanitary conditions did not exist.

* With the organization Colonel Beecher brought to Camp No. 1, coupled with the extra food ration the Japanese began issuing in December and the arrival of Red Cross parcels, the death rate began declining in January 1943.

Sgt. FORREST KNOX:

At one time I worked on the cemetery clean-up detail. You see, the sick were burying the dead and they dug the hole just deep enough to get the bodies in. They didn't dig any damn deeper then they had to and the dogs kept digging them up nights. In the rainy season it was a horrible mess. The rains would wash some of the surface soil away. I worked on a clean-up detail in the dry season. Twenty men were assigned and we'd go out with an American Navy officer. We tried to first find all the loose parts, arms and whatever, and put them back in the graves. Then we covered each of the mass grave sites with more soil and made little flat-topped pyramids of them. The reason there was so many unknown dead at Cabanatuan was because of the dogs. To this day I hate dogs with a passion. My children have dogs, but it was almost a personal insult if they brought them into the house and then expected me to play with them. I wouldn't hold still for that. You get hang-ups from this crap. But it was a good detail because the Japs left us strictly alone. No guard ever went along. The naval officer took us out in the morning, and whenever he felt like it he'd secure the detail and we'd clean off our shovels and go back to camp.

In the Army an officer's word is law. It don't make any difference if he is stupid or just a lily-livered coward. He still has got the hammer and if he wears the ring you can't touch him. Well, in my experience they didn't weigh too good. In fact, it was pretty hard to find one with hair on his ass. In Cabanatuan they had a free ride. If they went on a work detail, they just stood around and did nothing to try and protect a man. We had a Lieutenant Rice with us on the truck driving detail in Manila. Kept trying to pull his rank on us. We had Sandy ship his ass back to Cabanatuan. Well, he pulled the same shit there. He got knocked right out through the side of a grass shack one day. So the colonel had to do the same thing. He shipped Lieutenant Rice on the the next detail out to Japan. Never said a word to the man who nailed him. An officer who measured up, we respected. The rest we just kind of ignored.

It took more than being a lard-ass blowhard to be an officer. Most of them just kept their mouth shut and stayed out of our way. The reason we tolerated Lieutenant Rice at all—well, strange as it may seem, he was a brave man. Just not too smart. He was Air Force and made an instant infantry officer on Bataan when we lost all our planes. When you are on a withdrawal the last man is a sacrifice. Came the moment of truth at "the Points" and Lieutenant Rice said, "Shove off, I'll cover." Well, to the men leaving, a burst of small-arms fire means the last man got trapped. His job was to hold them off long enough for the last squad to get clear. Most died doing it. Lieutenant Rice turned the trick and still got out alive. For that they tolerated him most of the time, but he sure was an obnoxious bastard.

Cpl. CHARLES McCARTIN:

After I had regained my strength and was ready to be returned to the main area of the camp, one of the officers from the kitchen came around asking if there was anybody strong enough to move around some great big cooking pots. I volunteered. Then I was asked if I would like to work in the kitchen as my regular detail. I said, "Fine!"

I was assigned to night duty. The wood choppers would cut and stack the wood. The cooking fires had to be kept going all day and night because we didn't have matches. My job, during the night, was to keep the embers alive. Every hour, when the fire was getting low, I'd throw on another log. Then around 4:00 a.m. I'd start a rip-roaring fire because, within a half hour of my starting that flame, the cooks would come in and begin to cook the lugaw for the morning feeding. Once or twice I fell asleep and the fire nearly went out, but I was able each time to get it going. Those were tight spots. I really was sweating it out until I got the fire going. If I had let it go out, the men in the four or five barracks that were fed out of this mess hall would have gone to work without food. This was a serious offense and I'm sure I would have been severely punished by the American officers in the camp.

Pfc. MICHAEL TUSSING, Jr.:

I was out on a work detail cutting wood for the fires when three officers got separated from the rest of us. When we came back in, they were not in the detail.* Later that day they were found and brought back in a truck. The Japs said they were trying to escape. They stripped them naked and spread-eagled them on the ground. They lay there completely naked in the hot sun. For twenty-four hours they lay there. Before the Japs executed them they were begging to be shot. They made the whole camp watch the execution. They told us it was an example.

---

* Lieutenant Colonels Biggs and Breitung and Lieutenant Gilbert (USN).

Cpl. CHARLES McCARTIN:

They were made to dig their own graves just outside the fence, so the whole camp could see what was going on. The Japanese made the three stand by the hole and when they were shot one man fell in. The other two had to be pushed in. I was standing, watching, next to a Catholic priest. As the men were shot I heard him say, "It's inhumane. Those damn bastards will pay for this." I remember being surprised by his profanity.

Pfc. VICTOR LEAR:

It meant something to us, but it didn't affect us as much as you'd think, because of everything else we'd been through.

Pfc. MICHAEL TUSSING, Jr.:

This was when they started putting us into ten-men groups. Every night we used to count the others and make damn sure they were all there. We began watching each other. You better believe it. Because those Japs weren't playing.

Pfc. VICTOR LEAR:

One of the problems was, people didn't have all their wits about them. Somebody could wander over the fence and not know what they were doing. Those people had to be watched very closely.

Cpl. HUBERT GATER:

A few weeks after we arrived, we heard a rumor that at Lumban ten men were shot because one had escaped. It so affected us that we took our shooting squads much more seriously. At night, if a blood brother went to the latrine another would see that he came back.

A man named Trujillo was shot for an attempt to escape. His nine blood brothers were held in a guardhouse. The man was beat very bad before he was shot. Broken nose and one ear nearly tore off. There's a story behind this "escape." He was selling clothes or medicine or something the Japs wanted. They were almost in as bad shape as we were, even to socks. He was called to the outside of the barbed-wire fence at night by the guard to make a deal. As they were making the deal the Jap officer of the day came up. The Jap guard, to save himself, grabbed Trujillo and knocked him out with his rifle butt. The camp wasn't sorry for him because he was selling to the enemy. He was executed just outside the fence. The blood brothers were released.

2d Lt. FRED GIFFORD:

Two men escaped out of my roster detail of ten. We tried explaining we didn't know who our ten were. They said that it was our problem. We were put in the guardhouse. When the east started to get light I thought, "Well, this will be God's blessing, because I won't have no more of it to go through." When they came, they told us we had received a pardon for a day. So there I was. Twenty-four more hours to sweat out getting shot. Next morning the same thing. This went on for fourteen days. Finally, the Japanese came in and said, because they had captured the two escapees, we got a pardon. That meant going back to the farm. I thought, "Well, boy, what a big deal this is. That's back to torture." I realized there that my prayers had not been answered. I had prayed to die, because going back meant an unknown fate. I felt dying this way was better than being beaten to death. If you ever got beat with a two-by-four, you would take a firing squad first.

Staff Sgt. HAROLD FEINER:

We loafed around a little bit when we first got to Cabanatuan. Then they decided to build a farm.* I went out on the farm details. There were quite a few beatings. I remember chopping down great big gigantic anthills—anthills that had been there for hundreds of years. The ground on which we were to build this farm hadn't been worked in years, if ever. We chopped down the anthills. Snakes had invaded the hills and baby cobras would crawl out. If we had wanted to run for the mountains that was the time, because the Japs had a deathly fear of snakes. We broke up and prepared the ground for planting, and we took the beatings.

Cpl. CHARLES McCARTIN:

We would be awakened before it was light to go down to the kitchen and draw our ration of lugaw.† The Japs would then line us up to be counted, before we went through the gate to

* In December 1942 the Japanese decided to cultivate 300 acres of dry upland near the prison compound. At first a small detail of several hundred men cleared the land. Eventually, 2,000 prisoners were put to work growing rice, egg plant, okra, corn, radishes, beans, carrots, and peppers. Although bringing seeds back into camp was forbidden, smuggled seeds did find their way into the compound, where they were used by the prisoners to grow their own small gardens. This farm detail became the largest single work detail to occupy the time of the prisoners.

† During the dry season the normal schedule in Cabanatuan called for work 7:30–10:30 a.m. and 2:00–5:00 p.m. The men were returned to camp to draw their midday ration. Supper was over at 6:00 p.m. and daylight lasted until 8:30 or 9:00 p.m.

whatever we were going to do that day on the farm. Depending on the season, we did various kinds of farming. One time of the year we'd plant rice and at another *camotes* or big pole beans. You would work in details of ten men. While one group planted, another would weed. You spent the day bending over. At the end of the day it would be difficult to straighten up. We could whisper to each other. You were not supposed to, but there were several guards who, if you weren't talking too loud, would let you get away with it. Around 11:00 a.m. you would be lined up again, counted, and returned to camp for the noon meal. You'd lay around till 1:00 p.m., when you had to return to the farm. In the evening you were allowed to take a bath from water you got in a five-gallon can. That was the best part of the day.

Sgt. FORREST KNOX:

Life at Cabanatuan revolved around the farm and the different work details. Everyone hated the farm, but if we didn't grow most of our food we were going to starve. This old civilian by the name of Jones had lived in the Islands so long he was native. He set out to show us how to farm by hand. No wonder we hated him. To plow 300 acres by hand, call out

2,000 men. First third get pick mattocks. Second third get native hoes. Bigger than ours and heavy. Third group get rakes. Line up. Every man gets about forty inches work space. You start picking at the ground with a mattock blade. Work straight ahead, try to stay in line and even. If you go too fast, you get ahead and everyone else gets whacked to hurry and catch up. Get behind and you get encouragement.

Then the line with hoes starts beating the clods, breaking up the lumps. Same drill—stay even. Then the next line rakes and works the ground smooth. It was ready to plant. You had to see it to believe how well it worked.

We had names for all the guards. There was "Big Speedo," "Little Speedo," "B-17." That sonovabitch was a real air raid with his long hoe handle. We used to call them vitamin sticks. They got more work done than a barrel of vitamins. Once the farm was plowed and planted, it was watered endlessly. We dug a trench native fashion and called it "the Panama Canal." It was pretty deep at the pit end. The creek was diverted and flowed in there. The water carriers were all given a square five-gallon can with a handle nailed in the top. So maybe 300 or 400 men walked all day down the steps to the water in the pit, filled their can, followed the line. When you reached the proper plot, you carefully poured a steady stream of water on the growing vegetables. When your can was empty you kept walking. The next man started where you left off. So around and around you walked all day. Every job had a fringe benefit somewhere. The carriers never got whacked when they had full buckets, 'cause it got spilled. So you only had to be careful going back empty. Funny, huh?

To carry produce off the farms, we had litters. Kind of like oversized stretchers with long two-by-twos underneath. Four men at each end carried it. Now it was very difficult to carry with your hands, because we had lost strength to grip. So, at command, they were lifted shoulder high and carried on our shoulders. Some of the shit-bird guards thought it was humorous to climb on and get carried along too. The extra weight was not impossible, but it did hurt. We were working barefoot. Walking on cinders was no pleasure. But with dry beriberi this was torture.

I was carrying with a Mexican from the 200th Coast Artillery. He was hurting bad and limping. So our guard whacked him on the head from his exalted position. Perhaps I can't read minds, but I was fair at reading faces. The tears were running down his face. He looked at the guard and straightened out his back. He had said it real plain, "I'll never beg." There is no way you can measure courage. What kind of a rule or stick do you measure with? You can only measure against yourself—could I do it? They called him a "spick." He never whimpered and he had as much plain guts as I ever seen. It can still make me cry in sympathy to think how he hurt. Our Far Eastern University taught one thing—color or national extraction didn't mean a hell of a lot. You cannot measure a man till you strip off civilization. Plain courage is a shining thing when you see it.

We had run into rain and had an extra carrying detail from camp. This of course increased our guard quota. What we got was shit birds off the farm. There were three different types of guards. The old regular soldier had China duty. Sometimes mean, but always a soldier. A young Jap, never had seen any war, so he was always trying to impress someone how bad-ass he was. Last, there were the conscripts out of Formosa. They were pretty low on the totem pole and everybody leaned on them and beat them around. We were the only thing lower in the world than they were, so we got the brunt of their displeasure. So our carry group was being harried along by shit birds like they did on the farm. One of our guys, an Indian, was real slow and would not hurry. This Jap squalled at him and made a run for him. When he got up to him he drew back his rifle and made ready to lunge at him with his bayonet. This

Indian stopped and just stared at him. Now I've heard about Apache Indians all my life. But I was where I could see his eyes. It kind of half scared me and he wasn't even seeing me. The Jap hesitated, then backed right down. At least he was smart enough to see death looking at him. Later I asked some of the other Indians, "What's with this blanket ass?" They said, "Don't mess around with him. He's a bad Indian." I believed it. So did that little Jap.

Of course the farm was too soft for much truck traffic, so we had to make a cobblestone road. The carabao cart detail hauled stone from the riverbed for months and dropped it in piles. So, now to lay a road. Line up hundreds of men, shoulder to shoulder. First man picks up a rock, passes it to the second, second to third till it reached the road, carefully laid together. That made a road. Extra men were held ready to add to either end of the line as the work progressed. Everyone stayed awake on this one. We worked barefooted and if a rock was dropped you got a broken toe, plus a whack in the head for being clumsy.

Cpl. BERNARD "CHICK" SAUNDERS:

I couldn't handle the rocks. We formed a human chain and were passing rocks. There were big rocks and if you dropped one the guards would come over to you fast. I kept dropping the rocks as they were passed to me. A Jap came over and pulled me out of the line. He yelled at me and, of course, I couldn't understand him. Then he worked me over. At noontime we went back to the barracks for chow. When we were supposed to go back to the quarry, the American sergeant in charge of my barracks told our group that I couldn't go back out because if I did I'd die. The Japs would have finished me off. So a guy volunteered to go in my place. I didn't even know his name.

Capt. LOYD MILLS:

We had nicknames for all the guards. One guy we called "Laughing Boy" because he laughed all the time. Then he'd come over and just knock the hell out of you. He had to do it, he was a little bitty guy and that's how he overcame his inferiority complex. He worked someone over every morning and there was nothing anyone could do. If you raised a hand, you were dead. Another guy we called "Speedo" because that's all he could think to say. When he said "speedo," you'd better move.

Staff Sgt. HAROLD FEINER:

You'd be working, bent over, pulling weeds or cultivating, and if you picked your head up to look around a guard would scream, "Kura!" We never really did understand what *kura* meant. They'd yell, "Kura, kura, kura," which meant you were either to stop or get going and you better guess correctly which he meant.

We gave all the guards nicknames like "Sailor," "Fish Eyes," "The Pygmy," "Air Raid." Oh, boy, that last one beat the hell out of me once. I carried two pails made from square five-gallon cans. We were irrigating the farm and we carried water from the river to the farm. I was carrying my pails and one of the goddamn wire handles broke. The pail dropped and spilled the water. One of the guards, "Air Raid," that sonovabitch, didn't look to see if the handle had broken or anything like that. He gave me some beating with his stick. Across my back, my head. I had headaches for weeks. He beat the hell out of me because my pail broke.

Cpl. CHARLES McCARTIN:

Some of the guards were more mean than others. About the second or third day I worked the farm, I was working in the rice paddy where I was supposed to massage the roots. In the mud I lost my balance and stepped on one of the rice shoots. A guard saw me. It was an accidental slip, but this guard was pretty strict. He told me to stoop over. He hit me about ten times in one spot. I couldn't sit down for days. They carried this stick which was shaped like a sword that carried a colored string tied to it. This was their symbol of authority. I got beat another time for something the man next to me did.

2d Lt. FRED GIFFORD:

You didn't do nothing and you're still going to take a beating. They'd count you and if the count didn't come up right they'd count again. This time if the count was off they'd beat you with a two-by-four. Then they'd count again, as if that beating would stimulate you to produce somebody else to make the number different. I don't know what their idea was, because that's one mind I could never dig into.

After a while you learned how to put yourself in positions so you took the blows as easy as possible. A man learned how to take a whipping. It hurts you worse to get a beating over the calves of the legs or the thigh than it does to take a beating over the back or over the head. When you get beat on the legs it causes the muscles to contract, and you can't walk and you can't lay down. You can't do nothing. This was really worse than getting beat over the back or head, because when you got beat that way you were plumb out of commission. They can work you as long as your legs are hurting, no matter how bad, but beat over the back or if they broke your neck, then they'd have to take care of you. Also, to get hit on the back didn't hurt as much, especially if you could arch it and let what muscles you had absorb the shock. The thing you didn't want was to get hit by a gun butt, because then they'd get you in the kidneys. That was the worst. If you got hit in the kidneys with a gun butt, you never recovered. I mean never.

Sgt. FORREST KNOX:

The guards in charge of the farm felt what they were doing was important, so they supervised closely. Some of the guards had a little unofficial game they played. A native hoe handle was tapered out like a pick handle. Well, their game—Knock Head Off with Hoe. They'd sneak up behind a man and see how far they could whack his hat. Most of us wore a native sun helmet made out of coconut fiber. Kind of peaked with a narrower brim than our sun helmet. So if you lagged behind your line while weeding on your hands and knees, you could get a whack. It was like golf. If they topped the hat with their swing they didn't get any distance. Swing too low, well the hat would fly and roll quite a ways, but the victim got knocked cock stiff. My friend, Owen Sandmire, got more than one concussion this way. Now he has a total memory loss. There is more than one reason for a man not remembering much about prison camp.

The guards did like to take out their frustrations with a stick. I remember one day, lined up for count by the gate. The guards were sitting on the bank outside the fence waiting. One was whacking the ground between his legs with his pick handle. Guy next to me whispered out of the side of his mouth, "Look at Joe DiMaggio warming up." He had that part right.

Kind of a morning prayer we had. While standing in line everyone would be looking up in the air at the clouds. We were all saying the same thing. "Send her down, J.C." If it started to rain before we went outside the gate, the *gunso* would send us back to quarters. Once outside the gate—what the hell, you were wet already, so you stayed and worked no matter how hard it rained. Of course the guards got wet, too, so we got a couple of extra licks just like it was our fault. Guess it was. If we were in our barracks, so would they be. Being a slave teaches a man a lot about human nature, most of it bad. One of the tricks of survival—laugh no matter what happens.

Pfc. MICHAEL TUSSING, Jr.:

We called Bernie Saunders "Chicken." He was small and everybody liked him. He was simply known as Chicken Saunders all through his whole service career. One particular day out on the farm we were planting corn. Chick was working next to me. One of the guards was always jabbering at us, so we called him "Donald Duck." He was a little guy and he carried a club which was a two-by-four cut in half. In any event, it was a little longer than he was tall. Donald Duck was going along this day, checking the guys to make sure they were planting the corn correctly. Chick was either eating the seed or planting it too deep, or something that didn't suit the guard. So he came up behind Chick, jabbering away.

Cpl. BERNARD "CHICK" SAUNDERS:

When he swung at me, I ducked. Normally I'd never do that, but this time I automatically ducked and the Jap slipped and fell in the mud. Just then the whistle blew, which meant the detail was due to return to camp. I took off, leaving him in the water. Mike just stood there laughing.

Pfc. MICHAEL TUSSING, Jr.:

Chick kept jumping over the ridges, trying to get into a big group of prisoners so he could hide.

Cpl. BERNARD "CHICK" SAUNDERS:

If he had caught me, he would have killed me.

Pfc. MICHAEL TUSSING, Jr.:

Donald Duck was right behind him with the club—quack, quack, quack, "Come backu! Come backu!"

Cpl. BERNARD "CHICK" SAUNDERS:

I got lost in a big group. Either he gave up or just had to get the rest of the prisoners back, but I mingled with the prisoners and lost him. When I came into the barracks, Mike was still laughing. You had to laugh or you'd have cried all the time. It's funny now to me, but it wouldn't have been funny if he'd have caught me.

I'll tell you another funny Donald Duck story. Since we all called him by this name, one day he got curious and asked us who Donald Duck was. We all told him he was a famous Hollywood movie star. The Jap thought that was fine and would strut around thinking he looked like a famous star. In Manila one day he happened to catch a Disney cartoon. When he got back to camp, he beat the hell out of everybody for weeks.

Pfc. NORMAN MATTHEWS:

We called one of the officers "Five O'Clock Shadow." He used to ride a horse and whenever he rode by you had to stop and salute. I got to saluting the bastard with my left hand. The hell with him, I thought. One day he noticed me and when he got off his horse he beat the devil out of me. From then on I saluted him with my right hand.

Pfc. MICHAEL McMULLEN:

We called one guy "You Big Sonovabitch." He'd climb up on top of a bank of soil and with his big old teeth he'd grin like, hell, "Me Big Sonovabitch." That was all fun and for a couple of months we got away with all this kind of stuff. Then they found out what was really going on. After that, why, it was a different story.

Tech. Sgt. MEL MADERO:

I spent my entire childhood trying to avoid a kid named Joe Harrington. At Cabanatuan I worked for a while on the farm detail and on this same detail was Joe Harrington. I'd known Joe ever since first grade. His father owned the slaughterhouse in my home town back in California. Every town has its bully and Joe was ours. I lived just a few blocks from the Harrington house and for years, when walking to and from school, I would plan ways of walking so I wouldn't go near Joe's house. I'd do anything to avoid Joe, so I wouldn't get into it with him. He was just that kind of kid.

Anyway, Joe and I are on this same corn-planting detail at Cabanatuan. The ground had been prepared and we were coming through planting this dried, hard corn. Joe says to me, "Why don't we take some corn back into camp and start a garden?" I thought that was a good idea. So Joe and I filled our canteens with these kernels. I don't know how or why, but as soon as we were lined up in front of the gate to be shaken down, the guards came straight to us. The corn rattled in the canteens, so they had us. With the rest of the farm detail watching, they decided to make examples of us. We were made to stand at attention, with our arms extended, holding the canteens upside down until all the corn had fallen out. Then we were made to kneel with two-by-fours behind our knees. I don't know what kind of torture it is, but it does do the trick. We knelt there with everyone watching us for what seemed like ten hours. I'm sure, really it was for no more than ten minutes. It was towards the end of the day and it was real hot. We felt humiliated. Everyone watching us. Then, since it was not satisfying the guards, they stood us up, facing each other at arm's length. We were ordered to slap each other right across the face with an open hand. We were made to hit each other. First me, then him. It goes on for as long as the guards wish.

At first, every time I hit Joe, instead of a full straight slap, I'd pull my punch. I'm sure the guards were aware of this, so Joe said, "Mel, if we don't get at it these guys are going to have us hitting each other for the rest of the night. They know we're not actually hitting each other." And with that he really hauled off and hit me. This made me mad and we really went at it after that. No punches, just straight slaps as hard as we could swing open hand. This is what the Japs wanted to see. Our faces were bruised and swollen by the time we were told to stop. Here I am. I've gone all through primary school, I've gone all through high school, successfully avoiding Joe Harrington. Now I'm in the Philippine Islands, a prisoner of war out on a farm, and Joe and I are standing in the hot sun pounding on each other.

Sgt. FORREST KNOX:

I worked the woodcutters detail for a while. It was choice duty.* Hard work, but the guards never abused anyone. And you received an extra ration while in the woods for noon break. Detail was fifty men and one officer. Twenty-six axes, one ax for two men. Major had his own. You cut down your own tree, cut it up in small-size pieces, and carried it out to the edge of the jungle and loaded it on a truck. Last trip of the day we rode back to camp. The only change was during rainy season. Then the trucks couldn't get off the road, so we had to carry wood all the way to the road. That was when it paid off to cut small trees. When you had a trunk piece that was notched and carried on two poles and was still so heavy you couldn't hardly breathe, you knew someone fucked up and cut too big a tree. The only excuse for cutting a big tree was the black heart. In some trees,

---

* The wood and carabao details were the chief sources of regular communication between the camp and the civilian population.

I don't know the name, the heart was jet black and without grain. It was traded in camp to the carver. You had to see what a man could sculpt out with nothing but a piece of broken glass to scrape with. It was just beautiful. Again I wondered, did any of it get home? We used to catch native quail in the open field on the way into the woods. The quail would fly for only a very short distance, on account of the hawks. So if you seen one drop into the grass, you could walk right up and slap your hat over it and catch one. They were small, about the size of a meadowlark, and real bright colors. Once we cut down a big wild lemon tree. It was covered with fruit. Well, the lemons were more like green walnuts. Smelled nice, but not one drop of juice. Cut down a bee tree another time. The bees were the size of houseflies. One canteen cup held all the honey and that included all the chips, bark, and rotten wood. Had a real wild taste like it was fermented. The paper-nest wasps were enough to scare a man. Big as your thing. I'll bet a swarm of them could kill a man. You just wouldn't believe how you swelled up from just one sting.

Tech. Sgt. MEL MADERO:

We were trucked out to a wooded area where we chopped wood to supply the cooks with fuel for their fires. The tree would be chopped down, trimmed, cut to size, and then the logs trucked back to camp. The Jap guards always carried bamboo sticks about the size of a samurai sword. It was a natural thing for them to carry. Sometimes they would practice dueling with each other and at other times beat us on the backs. We were working this one day and the roving guard spotted a hornet's nest up in a tree. I guess his curiosity got the best of him and he took his bamboo stick and he hit the hornet's nest. Immediately that thing came off the tree and those hornets started swarming.

I'll never forget this in my life. We were very scantily clad, having only cut-offs or a G-string on. They began biting everyone. We started running or trying to hide to get away from this swarm of really angry hornets. The guards, of course, were no exception. They dropped their sticks or rifles and just ran. About this time the chop truck returned from camp carrying, of all people, the Jap officer in charge of work details. All he found in the area where we should have been were rifles and sticks laying on the ground. No prisoners, no guards. Everybody had taken off or was hiding under leaves. Let me tell you, there was some hell raising that day with the guard. I got bit numerous times and because there was no medicine in camp for these bites, we were all deathly sick. I was in bad shape, even my teeth hurt. We all felt, afterwards, this was a humorous incident.

Sgt. RALPH LEVENBERG:

The ingenuity of the American soldier is something to behold. The Japanese were well ensconced by this time in the Philippines, so they began to get venereal diseases. It was nearly an epidemic. Gonorrhea mainly. Venereal disease became a very serious affair for the Jap military. So the guards around the camp, rather than going to their own doctors for treatment and then punishment, started coming to our medics. Our guys thought, "Hmmm, let's work something out." So they began manufacturing pills out of salt, pressing them in a small home-made mold, and selling them to the Japs as sulfathiazine. It became a real business, even to pressing a pharmaceutical company's brand on the pill. The medics would trade the pills to the Japs for sugar, salt, peanuts, or anything they could get. The medics, in turn, gave the stuff to the kitchens. The comical thing was watching the guards who had bought our pills. Everybody in camp knew what was going on. Pretty soon you wouldn't see a particular guard any more because he had gotten so damn sick that he had to be hospitalized. They never understood why our "sulfa" didn't work on them.

Sgt. FORREST KNOX:

If possible, when not doing anything, we sat and drank tea. Working in the Jap galley we used to steal the tea from the big teapot. It must have held 350 or 400 gallons. It was a big pot built up in the air so we could build a fire under it. Had spigots around the bottom, so several could fill their canteens at once. The men in charge had to change the tea in the oversize tea bag, fill the tank with water, and build a fire so the Nips could have hot tea. Sometimes the tea got pretty weak if we stole too many leaves. Well, it gave us an audience in camp at the picnic table. So, the story: there was a Navy warrant officer sitting with us, sharing the tea. A man strolled up and struck up a conversation. Started talking about school and wanted to know where we had gone to school. The warrant said California State. Well, this guy lit right up and started to jabber. We filled his cup and he talked a mile a minute about California State. The professors. Seemed the warrant officer never had the same ones. He acknowledged he might have heard of some. Then this guy started in on the social life. He mentioned the name of several campus dolls—never rang a bell. Just hadn't run into them. "Well, they went to all the dances." "Nope," the warrant officer said, he'd been pretty much of a grind. "Never did get to go to the dances. Kind of strapped for money. Couldn't afford a girlfriend who expected to be entertained."

This other guy went into detail and had some real fond memories of what went on at parties and afterwards. Well, he rattled on for quite a while. Finally he ran down, said he had to go, and thanks for the tea. Was really happy to meet someone who had been to his school. The warrant agreed it was real nice talking to him. "Stop by again, anytime." They all liked to listen to stories about Stateside. So this guy left. Real happy. Made his day. Empathy, I think is the word. I had gradually got the notion that while they were talking, the warrant and this guy were talking about two different things. The warrant had a half smile on his face while he sipped his tea. I don't know if he noticed my stare while I was speculating, or the joke was too good to keep. He said, "I was talking about California State Reformatory." Finally added, "Wasn't coed while I was there." That got a smile from everyone.

Some guys told real personal stuff. What the hell, we were all going to die. So who could prove anything? Made the stories interesting. I like a story with an odd twist and sometimes I wasn't sure what was the truth.

The officers' barracks started just across the open spot where we lined up for *tenko* [roll call] or count. One morning an officer was out there washing his mess kit and singing at the top of his lungs. Finally, another officer came out and asked him what he was so happy about. Well, during the fighting on Bataan he had been hit in the nuts. He had figured he was fixed for good. Now in the middle of '43 he had just had a wet dream. He was happy as could be. Said, "Well, maybe my wife isn't going to be disappointed after all."

As a gauge to judge a camp, if all we talked about was food, we were starving. If all we talked about was home, we were being treated rough and our minds dwelled on happier times. If all we talked about was women, we were well fed and had a soft detail.

Capt. BENSON GUYTON:

Sometime in 1943 the Japs took two truck loads of POWs to Bataan. We stayed in the schoolhouse in Balanga, I think. The Japs were making a movie called, *Down with the Stars and Stripes,* starring a Filipino actor. We were to act as extras. All the POWs were issued new uniforms, steel helmets, and Enfield rifles. We extracted the oil plus a few parts, so the Japs couldn't use them again, plus a few pieces of metal we could use back in camp. Japs had dynamite buried in the ground. As we ran through the jungle with rifles at port arms in a mock charge, the Japs exploded the dynamite around us. We immediately hit the dirt. Downright dangerous, this life of a POW. Returning to Cabanatuan through flood swollen streams, we had to push the trucks a mile or so. What did I get out of this? A change of scenery, which broke the boredom, a new uniform, and some rifle parts.

Sgt. FORREST KNOX:

Once they asked for men who had shirts. That one turned out to be a movie detail. They took several hundred of us way the hell away from camp. We were told to sit. A Jap came out and told us we were going to be in a movie. He had lived in the States and he spoke English without a trace of an accent. While we were waiting around, I recognized one of the Jap truck drivers who I had been on a detail with up in northern Luzon. He was kind of a fatherly sort of fellow. At night he'd come around to make sure I had enough blankets to keep me warm. I was so glad to see him that I went over and started talking to him. He acted terribly embarrassed and then I realized he was not supposed to have an American friend. I walked back over and sat down again. He'd been real good to me and I wasn't going to put him in a bad light.

　　Finally we were told to line up in columns of four and walk by these piles of rifles where a Jap guard would give us one. Then we were supposed to walk past the camera and drop our rifles into a huge pile and then walk into a nearby valley. They were making a propaganda film and we were supposed to act out our surrender. We all went through the line to get our rifles. Then, while we were waiting for the movie people to get ready, you could look around and see guys playing with them. We hadn't had a weapon in our hands for quite a long time. I had an M-1 Garand. It looked to be in pretty good shape. I pulled the bolt back and it looked like it had been cleaned and taken care of. Then I tightened the sling a little bit, like we used to do for close-order drill. It would pop a little when you hit it. I was sitting there with everyone else, fondling our rifles, and this Jap got up on a thing not much bigger than a card table. He had a megaphone and he said, "Your attention, please. Your attention, please. Please do not pull the triggers on your rifles!" Everyone began to murmur, "What the hell is he talking about?" He continued, "The guards have passed out their own rifles and they're *loaded*." We sat there flabbergasted. This is what happened. It was a day off for the guards as well as us. They were rushing around helping in the movie production and they'd all laid down their rifles. While we were walking past, these goons had passed out their own rifles.

The guards were all standing around looking at us. It was comical as hell. Here we were, way the hell away from camp, and the guards don't have their rifles because we have them. There are hundreds of us. Then all of a sudden several prisoners got up and walked over and handed their rifles to the guards. The Japs bowed and thanked them. It was a day in never-never land. It doesn't seem possible that it could have happened, but it did. So help me, it did.

Capt. ROBERT TAYLOR, Chaplain:

In prison camp it was possible to lose your faith or at least to have it severely shaken. The strange and interesting thing to me was that men under those conditions responded to religion and to God in a very normal way. They didn't flock down the aisle when we were holding services. They didn't panic to get to God. And they didn't panic going the other way either. Prison camp gave them a lot of time to reflect on the important values of life. Consequently, many of them became Christians, not out of fear or because they were suffering, but because they thought it was important to find God. They responded to religion just like they would have in peacetime. The big difference there was that they had plenty time to think about these matters. This ability to meditate, I think, made a difference. Given the time to think, man will find Christ. You find Christ because you feel a need. You know, most people never take or find the time to feel the need. The guy out there that makes $100,000 or $10,000, or even a farmer out yonder worrying about his corn or cotton or whatever, just doesn't stop to think about those things. In prison camp the men were not going anywhere. They had time to think.

Pfc. EDDY LAURSEN:

The thing that really helped me was to lay down on the ground and look up in the sky and try to shut out everything else. If I could look at something that wasn't contaminated by man, it would give me a real uplift. I especially liked the sunsets.

Sgt. FORREST KNOX:

I walked up behind a tough old Marine one day. He was slowly washing his mess kit. He looked hard as nails and tough as a

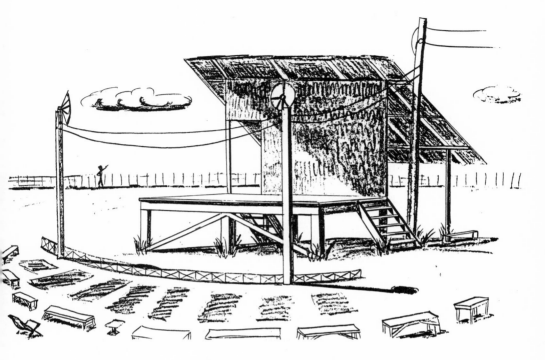

Roman legionnaire and he was softly singing, "I Dream of Jeanie With the Light Brown Hair." For a bass, he carried a nice tune.

Cpl. CHARLES McCARTIN:

I wrote songs in my spare time. I wrote the melody as well as the lyrics. Once we even had an art festival where we displayed the crafts we had made. We held it in the building the chaplains lived in. I displayed my songs. Other guys wrote poetry or drew pictures, some of camp, but many drew pictures from memory of their homes. Many, many men etched designs on their canteens or mess kits. Took me a long time to do mine. I first drew my design on some scrap paper and then tried to scratch it onto the canteen with a nail. My design was fancy and had lots of curlicues. Some men used the same design as their tattoos to put on their canteens. In fact, it gave us a big kick to walk around camp to see what kind of design the fellers were making. It became something to do.

There was one fellow who had evidently been an MC back in the States. I think it was he who instigated the band.* The

* Lt. Col. O. O. "Zero" Wilson.

instruments came from outside the camp, and we had to petition the Japanese to let us bring them in. There was a saxophone, piano, a guitar, and a violin. Although the orchestra practiced at night, they still worked on the farm during the day. They'd give a program once a week, on our day off, and these performances would often include a singalong. One time they had a talent contest and I got into that. Didn't win. But I had a lot of fun. Another time they had an original songwriting contest. There were around five people who wrote songs. The orchestra practiced them and when the night came for the performance, the men out front voted on which one they liked best.* Mine was a love song. So were most of the others. One was humorous. My song came in second, so I was real happy about that.

I've Never Been in Love Before

I love you! Yes, I do! You're the one that I adore.
I don't know what to say. I've never felt this way
I've never been in love before.

I've never known the bliss or felt a kiss
Like they tell about in song.
I always thought that I could pass girls by,
Dear, until you came along.

So, bring your charms to my arms and I'll hold them
    evermore.
I only hope and pray that you'll be mine some day.
I've never been in love before.

Sgt. FORREST KNOX:

I know we really enjoyed the small camp orchestra. Those men were good or we were not critical. Somehow they all turned up with a small piano. There were guitars. The one I remember was the Marine who played the saxophone. He was terrific. We would all sit on the hill. The off-duty Japs came and sat. This once they were accepted. And everyone relaxed. They used to say the Islands had the most beautiful sunsets in the world.

We eventually got lights in the camp. It was generated by a power house operated by Americans. The Japs used the personnel to repair stuff. One brought a radio to repair. Well, one fellow took it apart. The next time the Jap came, he gave him a list of needed parts he would have to get from Manila. Well, parts were hard to get and the ones received never seemed to work, so the defective radio stayed in the power house. By be-

---

* Audiences of 3,000 or 4,000 men were common for the shows.

Come Up And See Me Sometime!

ing very careful, it was only assembled for news broadcasts. The news would trickle through camp. We knew it was straight dope, but to discuss it openly was a no-no because sooner or later the Japs would know we had a private news source. I don't know if the Jap ever got his radio back.

News was the most sought-after thing. And news from home was the answer to a dream. We had a couple of picnic tables. We used to sit there when it was not raining and talk. One man had a letter from home, an almost unheard-of event. He sat there reading. One man couldn't stand the suspense and slipped up behind him and was reading over his shoulder. Suddenly he said, "Gee, I didn't even know you were married." Well, this man was instant mad. He said, "Goddamn it, can't you wait till I've read it?" He looked around the table. The hunger in their eyes. You could almost feel it. His anger evaporated. "O.K.," he said and started at the beginning and slowly read the letter. He was among friends, but it was not often you found a man that generous. You might share your blanket or your food, but a letter, that was personal. The involuntary comment. Well, he had left a pregnant girl. His mother took her in, announced to the town they were married, and was raising her grandson. I had heard decent men came from decent families. How much proof do you need?

Cpl. HUBERT GATER:

In the early part of 1943, the death rate continued to fall. By February my diary recorded only ten deaths. We also saw some movies that month. The first one was a Marx Brothers plus a Japanese newsreel that included scenes of the bombing of Pearl Harbor. We believed some of it was faked. We got electric lights in the camp and grapevine news picked up. The new year also brought wind worse than I remembered in New Mexico. For four and five days at a time we had hard wind and, of course, dust. Then in April, with twenty-four hours' notice, another thousand-man detail was sent to Japan.*

June 1943 brought the rains. Mud, just plain mud, four to six inches deep was everywhere. It rained for twenty-two days straight. The men were ordered to go out to the farm barefooted. Can you imagine 2,000 men going out a gate and leaving what shoes or wooden carved protection they had, and then trying

* In North Africa, Allied Forces had the Afrika Korps on the run in Tunisia. Closer to the Philippines, the Guadalcanal campaign had ended, and with it the Japanese had lost the initiative. An American plan was being devised which would employ a double-pronged advance against the Japanese-held islands in the southwestern and central Pacific. One of these lines, commanded by Gen. Douglas MacArthur, would go from New Guinea to the Philippines.

to sort through this mess when they came back after a day's work?

Sgt. FORREST KNOX:

Sometime early in 1943* we had a big celebration. For the first twenty-four-hour period there wasn't a death. At one time they were burying forty a day. All you have to do is get out a pad and pencil and start adding up, and you got a hell of a lot of deaths in a short period of time. They finally got it down to one a day and then finally the day when no one died. We had a celebration. We'd finally broken it. It was down to what was considered a standstill. Now the medics would fight for those who were sick.

At the present time, unlike Camp O'Donnell, there is no monument or marker at Cabanatuan to indicate that a prison camp existed on the site. The appproximately 5,000 Americans that were buried at Cabanatuan and Camp O'Donnell have been removed and now lie in the Manila American Cemetery and Memorial. The cemetery site is located within the limits of the Army reservation of Fort Andres Bonifacio (formerly Fort William McKinley). It is the largest in area of the cemeteries built and administered by the American Battle Monuments Commission.

---

* On Jan. 18, 1943, it is recorded that not one death occurred in the camp, the first time that had happened.

7
DAVAO

Davao Penal Colony (DAPECOL), a Philippine federal prison, was used during World War II as a POW camp by the Japanese. It lies in a jungle clearing on the island of Mindanao ten miles northwest of the Davao Gulf and twenty-five miles north of Davao City. Here approximately 2,000 American prisoners tended a large farm which grew food for the Japanese Army garrisons spread throughout the Philippine Islands. The first group of Americans who arrived on October 22, 1942, were troops who had surrendered on Mindanao. They were joined on November 6 by a 1,000-man detail sent from Cabanatuan. The prison barracks were made of lumber and covered with wide corrugated steel roofs which overhung half walls. The floors were native mahogany worn down by the feet of thousands of Filipino prisoners.

Nearly two-thirds of the 1,000 hectares under cultivation grew rice. The remaining area grew camotes, black beans, radishes, onions, pechay (Chinese cabbage), tomatoes, hot peppers, sesame seeds, okra, tobacco, and tons of pumpkins. Papayas, mangoes, and citrus fruit grew in groves planted before the American prisoners arrived. There was also attached to the colony a sawmill, a rice mill, a hemp factory which made rope, a chicken farm, a carabao and brahma steer corral and several bodegas (warehouses). From camp the rice paddies were reached by riding on a small narrow-gauge railroad train.

Situated on a gentle rise, Davao Penal Colony was a 100-by-200-yard barbed-wire enclosed com-

pound. It was surrounded by either swamp or nearly impenetrable jungle. Because of its location, it was thought to be escape-proof.

Pfc. VICTOR MAPES*:

We thought we had it bad in Davao until the thousand from Cabanatuan arrived. It was pathetic. The first one I ran into was a feller named Cowan. He was nothing but a six-foot skeleton. Even looked to me like the stick of his butt was sticking through. He said he wanted to buy a can of sardines from me. He offered me five pesos for them. It was the last can I had, but seeing the shape he was in, I told him he could have them. I felt real good about being able to help out a buddy. The next morning here's old Cowan selling my can of sardines for thirty pesos. He knew what he was doing. The old barter system, take a little profit and reinvest it to make more in the black market. All of us who were in Davao learned some things the next few days. We learned these boys from Cabanatuan were desperate and they knew something about surviving that we didn't know, because we hadn't gotten to that point yet. Another thing was, better watch out when you had any dealings with them guys captured on Bataan.

---

* In January 1942 Victor Mapes left Bataan on the interisland steamer Mayan. With a large number of Air Force personnel, he was sent to northern Mindanao to work on the new American heavy-bomber base at Del Monte. He became a prisoner when Brig. Gen. William F. Sharp surrendered this force on May 10, 1942.
    Because of what happened to Victor Mapes in Sindangan Bay nearly twenty-two months later, it is interesting to note how he arrived at Davao. "In May 1942 I was in Brigadier General Fort's 81st Division (PA) Headquarters at Bubong. This hidden mountain camp was several thousand feet up on Butig Mountain. General Fort surrendered his forces on orders from General Sharp. Myself and five others who were at Dansalan, on the edge of Lake Lanao, surrendered on May 30, 1942. There all of General Fort's Philippine and American troops were interned at an old printing plant. A few days later we were moved to the old Philippine Constabulary barracks at Camp Keithly. Around July 1 four men jumped the gun and escaped. The Japs were going to shoot all of us. They began by executing Col. Robert Vesey, Captain Price, and First Sergeant Chandler. Colonel Mitchel argued and pleaded with the Japs to save the rest of us. The Japs finally decided to put us on our own death march. On the 42-kilometer march from Dansalan to Iligan we lost some men. This was July 4, 1942. Then we were sent by small boat to Cagayan and from there trucked to the POW camp at Malaybalay, where the bulk of Major General Sharp's forces had been imprisoned since May 10." On or about October 16, 1942, this group of nearly 1,000 prisoners was shipped to Davao, reaching the penal colony two weeks before the Cabanatuan detail.

Cpl. KENNETH DAY*:

Perhaps the worst thing that had happened to the Cabanatuan men was that their spirits had been broken. They had suffered so much abuse that they seemed to have forgotten there could be a better tomorrow. All they had done for many months was to wait for death. They had seen thousands of their buddies die in battle, starve, burn up with malaria, waste away from dysentery, or literally burst from beriberi. Their own turns were coming; they just wondered when. To cheer them up would be a hopeless task. It seemed to be too late.

We were genuinely sorry for these poor devils. We wanted to help them, but it wasn't easy to buddy up to them. We traded our bananas for their cigarettes; that helped to bridge the gap, but it wasn't enough. They were so much harder and tougher mentally than we were. Our morale had been preserved by the decent life at Malaybalay, but these guys had turned totally bitter in their bare-knuckle struggle for existence. The will to live had taken the place of the Golden Rule.

Not only that, but they were lousy. We hadn't had any vermin until then, and we blamed them for bringing hordes of graybacks into camp. It wasn't their fault, of course, but that's human nature. For a month or more we all went around picking the little bastards out of the seams of our clothing and crushing them between our fingernails. They flourished. We suffered and grumbled.

We boiled water in drums and tried to get all our clothes into the drums within a day or two. That reduced the cootie population, but they came back faster than we could kill them. Some lads went psycho from frustration. They would sit outside the barracks for hours, searching along the seams of their shirts and shorts until they got so nervous they couldn't talk to anyone.

Relief came from an unexpected direction. We were invaded by bedbugs. Bedbugs kill body lice, but they are just as bad and just as hard to eliminate. We tried sousing every building with boiling water on a Sunday morning. That netted us one night's sleep. The Japanese broke out a small quantity of Watkins insecticide. It killed thousands; if there had been enough of it we might have rid ourselves of the little buggers entirely. Two nights of good sleep this time, and then back to normal.

The red devils infested every tiny crack and corner, and they especially liked mosquito nets. It was fun to stir up a nest

---

* Corporal Day of the 5th Air Base Group had been captured on Mindanao.

of red ants outdoors and toss a mosquito net in. The ants would kill the bedbugs, but there weren't enough ants to make any real difference. Those bedbugs got so hungry that they would come out and bite us in broad daylight. We shared our blood with them as long as we were in the Philippines.

One evening the Mindanao Melodeers* gathered in front of the Cabanatuan men's barracks right after supper. We formed ranks facing Major Pritchard. A few stragglers returning from the mess hall stopped, wondering why we were there. Without introduction we simply started to sing. "Honey," "If I Had My Way," "Old Man Noah," "The Rangers' Song." As we sang the veterans from Luzon—men who had forgotten there was anything beautiful left in the world—gathered before us and listened. Those men, ragged and starved physically and spiritually, stood like scrawny statues drinking in the beauty of the music. Many cried. We sang as we had never sung before, inspired by the sight of tears running down the haggard faces of strong men who weren't strong enough to hold them back. They were down, but they weren't out. That singing session did an awful lot for them, if only by reminding them that there was something left to live for. When we had finished we wandered back to our barracks. That was all.

Pfc. VICTOR MAPES:

When we first moved into Davao Penal Colony there were still some incorrigibles being held there. DAPECOL was like a Devil's Island and some of the Philippine prisoners had balls and chains around their legs. Most of the convicts were murderers. One guy I remember told me he had killed a whole family of five people. They became our friends and in a short time we picked up a lot of knowledge from them of how you survive in prison. I mean, if we had gone to Leavenworth after this training, it would have been a picnic. Even though they were hardened criminals, they knew how to survive in a prison system. To them it made no difference who the guards were—Japanese or Filipinos.

I'll tell you what I learned from them. Since I was a Florida boy and knew something about cows, I became a carabao plow jockey. This was a good detail with lots of advantages to it. Trouble was, these carabaos didn't understand English. Didn't know "gee" or "haw," left or right. I'd say, "Whoa!" Damn carabao didn't know what "whoa" meant. I hadn't learned yet to say "Ha ho." I'd say, "Gitty-up." Carabao would just stand there. First day out, I got the hell beat out of me before I

* A chorus formed originally at Malaybalay Prison Camp.

realized what the trouble was. I'd say, "Gitty-up!" and the carabao stayed there in the mud. I said, "Well, if he doesn't want to go, I can't make him." So me and the carabao stayed in the mud all day. Come evening time I got a heck of a beating. That night one of the convicts told me the words the carabao knew. That was one way they helped us. They also knew certain places where you could find vegetables or wild fruits. They also knew all the jungle paths and the black market routes for things like information and contraband. They taught us how to make certain convenient items, like rope. You got to know those things. The Japs finally realized how helpful these convicts were and so they got rid of them. But by then it was too late.*

2d Lt. HADLEY WATSON:

At Davao we lived in eight long one-story bungalows or barracks. Each barracks was broken up into bays. In each nine-by-twelve-foot bay there'd be eight men. Twenty bays on each side lined up against both walls. A bay was similar to a room, except we had partitions separating us, not walls. In each bay were four double-decked bunks. If you were fortunate to have a blanket you made a hammock up on the second deck, or you got banana leaves to pad your bunk if you slept on the bottom. Each barracks had a ranking officer in charge, maybe a lieutenant colonel, and each bay had a bay leader, the ranking guy who would be in charge of the seven others in the bay.

We'd wake up while it was still dark outside. The Japs would come to the barracks door and make sure the colonel in charge of each building was up. He would, in turn, make sure each of the bay leaders was awake. We'd fall out about ten minutes after we were awakened for a count. We'd then go to the mess hall by barracks and each barracks went by rotation to get breakfast. Breakfast sometimes consisted, if we were lucky, of a piece of fish or meat. By the time it was divided around to 2,000 men you might get a piece the size of your thumb. Usually, breakfast consisted of mongo beans or ground corn and occasionally rice. Then we had potatoes that we grew on the farm and we used the potato vines for greens. When the rice crop came in we had more rice.

About 6:00 a.m. we lined up for work details. We were counted again, to make sure all were present and accounted for. This count confirmed the fact that all the prisoners were there and ready to do whatever they were supposed to do that day. Each work section had an American detail leader and an

---

* The Japanese retained a number of convicts who were used to maintain the rice paddy irrigation system and operate the sawmill.

assistant leader. Each leader would call out his group and we'd march out or go and catch the little train that took the details out to the sawmill or rice paddies.

Cpl. KENNETH DAY:

We started to work in the rice field about five miles east of the compound. As many as a thousand men would get on small flatcars of the narrow-gauge railroad and ride to the fields. The ride out to Mactan was long, cool, and beautiful. Monkeys would swing and chatter in the tall jungle trees, and big tropical birds would be stirring. The tracks cut a straight furrow through the jungle. The little diesel locomotive would purr along at low speed. At Mactan we would jump off the train and toss our shirts and mess kits on the hard dirt floor of the bodega—a big shed with a roof but no walls—and line up for detail assignments.

This got to be a frantic, milling scene. They would start picking crews for various jobs from one end of the line. Nobody wanted to be at the end where the plowing and harrowing details were chosen, and many would try to sneak behind the ranks to the other end. Some stupid officers tried to run the operation, but they had no sense of organization. They would stand out in front and bleat orders, while the men laughed at them and did what they pleased. The Japs would get madder and madder and beat us for not understanding what they wanted. Never was leadership in such great demand and such short supply.

Things went from bad to worse until relief came from an unexpected quarter. In what appeared to be a measure of desperation they named our squadron commander, Maj. Herman A. Little himself, to head up the whole Mactan show. We who knew him so well thought this was an unlikely choice, to say the very least. To our amazement he straightened out that chaotic scramble in a day or two.

When we first started to work in the rice fields, our job was to harvest and thresh a crop that was already there. Each man would take a long, curved, serrated knife, and each pair of men would carry a large woven reed basket and a long pole. We would cut the grain heads off the stems and toss them into the baskets, then carry the full basket along the dike, sometimes as far as two miles to the main bodega. Other men would lift it to the top of the threshing machine, dump it, and toss it back down for another trip to the field.

I developed an open sore on the sole of my foot and it wouldn't heal. I showed it to the doctor out there. He sympathized, but could do nothing for it. I didn't want to go back into the paddies where the short, sharp stubble would stab into the ulcer. I lingered around the *bodega* as long as I could, and I struck up an acquaintance with Marine Sergeant "Gabby" Kash, who was in charge of the threshing crew. It turned out that we had both been radio announcers—he while he was in the service in China, I while I was a college student in Seattle. We hit it off right away. He got me assigned to his detail.

I wondered if I had made a big mistake. The work was difficult and primitive. It took thirty men, working as hard as they could, to keep up with the McCormick-Deering thresher, powered by a Caterpillar tractor. Six men handled the baskets of grain; two on the ground, two on a four-foot-high platform, and two more at the top. It took fourteen more to get the chaff away from the back end of the machine, because the blower was missing. Four stood right behind the thresher, and ten more with five baskets ran and dumped them on top of a big pile. It was all they could do to keep up.

The rest of the men worked on the big stack of rice heads that piled up when the machine couldn't keep up with the flow, or carried sacks of threshed grain to railroad cars, sewed up the sacks, etc. Flois Howard had the easiest job, running the tractor. Gabby did nothing but to direct our work and keep the Japanese overseers off our backs.

He did both jobs so well that we didn't mind his apparent aversion to physical exertion. A born organizer, he made things go smoothly, switching us from one task to another every few minutes. He had learned a little Japanese in China, and he kidded the guards into giving us a few cigarettes, a little fruit, and the privilege of swimming in the irrigation ditch every day after work. We also got extra rice, over and above the "heavy duty" ration. The daily dip alone was worth all the extra work. That cool water felt heavenly on the skin, and the carabao turds floating by didn't bother us much. I was in pretty good shape, and I enjoyed matching my strength and endurance with the other fellows. I gained weight and I felt good. The sore on my sole healed over. The harvest lasted about a month. We were greatly relieved, thinking that would be the end of that. It proved to be a bare beginning.

The next little surprise they had in store for us was the introduction to the carabao. We were afraid of them. We had heard that they would go completely crazy at the sight and smell of a white man. There was some truth in that, but it had nothing to do with our race. Those at Mactan, mostly steers, had been worked by Filipinos. They were nervous at first, but they soon got used to us. If we had ever smelled bad to them, we must have got over it by then. Our diet, almost entirely vegetarian, resembled that of the Filipinos so much that the animals couldn't tell the difference. They still smelled terrible to us.

It was still a bit of a trick to ride one of them. Four of us were sent to bring some carabaos from a sort of corral to the working paddies one day. It took us an hour to walk, wade, and stumble across paddies and broken dikes, and we didn't relish the idea of leading those beasts a couple of miles back. An old Filipino showed us how to get on, no simple matter in itself, and how to start and stop the creatures. We lurched up onto their broad backs and started.

The carabaos didn't seem to mind our being there, but staying on top still wasn't easy. This animal's skin is fastened to him very loosely, and it slides all around. His backbone protrudes just enough to give the bareback rider a sore crotch. The beast doesn't know or care how difficult it is to hang on when he is going uphill or down at a steep angle. The carabao can travel through thick, thin, or medium mud of any depth. If there's anything solid beneath him he walks. If there isn't, he swims. When he climbs out of a paddy onto a dike, or vice versa, it behooves the passenger to hold on for dear life. If Mr. Carabao has been wallowing in mud, his whole back will be slippery as we learned on that ride back. There is only one place to hold on when your mount starts down; you reach back and try to grab his little short tail. When he starts up, you lie forward and reach for a horn. Our buddies in the paddies cheered and waved their hats when we rode triumphantly into view. We had proved it could be done.

Working the damnable things was something else. We discovered that the carabao has two speeds: slow and stop. Once stopped, he may not want to start at all, and it may be quite impossible to change his mood. We came to understand this, but the Japs didn't. They would stand on the dikes and yell at us to hurry, and wave their bayonets. It was all very frustrating.

Our plows and harrows were rather primitive. The plows were made of steel, but they were short and had only one handle. The plow jockey was supposed to hold the plow with one hand and guide his beast with the other. That may have worked all right for the Filipinos, but it didn't work well for us. The carabaos, being smarter than we were, sensed that we didn't know what we were doing. They stopped every few steps, and it was a real problem getting them into action again. Sometimes it seemed as if they were laughing at us.

Once in a while one of us could find a stick with which to whack the animal. This might or might not make a difference.

Blows to the head didn't accomplish much; the carabao's frontal skull is inches thick. If we did make an impression, somehow the steer might go crazy and pull the plow or harrow everywhere except where he was supposed to. We learned the Visayan words for gee and haw, and go and stop. That helped a little.

Most of us tried our best to get out of working with carabaos. A few men eventually resigned themselves and became full-time plowmen and harrowmen. They learned which animals were the best to work with, and each morning they would try to get their favorites. That made it still rougher on others of us who only got stuck on that detail occasionally. The old jockeys would hop off the train, stand their *tenko*, and make a dash to the pasture area. The first few would catch their buffaloes early, but their rushing and yelling would stampede the remainder of the herd. Sometimes it took us most of the morning to catch a critter and get it harnessed.

The harness was a crude wooden yoke with ropes tied to either end. Another light rope was tied to a steel nose ring and draped over one horn; this was for steering. Ropes always dragged in the mud and they broke frequently. We spent as much time adjusting and repairing harness as we did actually plowing.

Harrows were square wooden frames with tapered teeth of wood or steel extending down below the bottom crosspiece. This apparatus was dragged across the clods that the plows had turned up. The idea was to bury the clods under a few inches of water. We learned to push most of them under with our feet. One way to get out of working was to run a steel harrow tooth through your foot. I considered this more than once, but I couldn't get up the courage to do it.

In time we worked out an arrangement with our bosses whereby one man with one animal was expected to plow or harrow one paddy in one day. A paddy was one fourth of a hectare, or a bit over a half acre. We found that two men with two carabaos could plow two paddies faster. Maybe the animals liked company, or maybe they were somewhat competitive. One day we happened to get eight paddies assigned in a straight line. We got our heads together before starting work. Why not expand on the concept of togetherness, and maybe get done early?

We lined up the eight monsters and the eight plows abreast along the first dike. The idea was to plow straight along, crossing dike after dike, until we reached the end of the row of paddies. Then we could turn them all around and come back, and so on. We could avoid all those tight turns in the corners, and we could enjoy each other's company. The guards watched with curiosity, but they didn't interfere.

When all was ready, each of us barked a command at his charger. They all started forward, rather smoothly at first, and then things started to go wrong. One of the animals got a little ahead of the others. The one next to him couldn't stand that and he speeded up. The others caught the spirit, and before we reached the first dike the whole thing had turned into a race. Every beast for himself, and the devil take the hindmost.

We had never seen a carabao in high gear before. Now they were all running. We held on to the plow handles and guide ropes as long as we could, but one by one we were dropped off. Mud splashed, plows tore through dikes, guards yelled bloody murder, and we fell down laughing in the stinking muck. It was a grand sight, those wild things galloping off in every direction until they could run no more.

It took us the rest of the morning to catch them again, and a good part of the afternoon to repair dikes, plows, ropes, and flesh. We learned something about the nature of men and brutes that day.

Pfc. LEE DAVIS:

Many of our men came down with high fever and began passing out. The doctors wondered if it was something picked up from mosquitoes. So they asked for volunteers to be deliberately bitten by mosquitoes that had been caught in the rice paddies. The doctors got the volunteers by promising extra food. I know it wasn't any act of mercy that led me to volunteer. It was the extra food that I was anticipating. I remember getting an extra half share of food for doing this.

Cpl. KENNETH DAY:

There may have been thirty or forty doctors at Davao, and a mixed bag they were. The U.S. Army Medical Corps didn't appear to be exactly outstanding anywhere, and it was at its worst in the Philippines. It seemed that doctors who couldn't make a living on the outside accepted commissions in the Army and coasted until retirement time. Enlisted corpsmen must have been selected in an equally negative way. Men found unsuitable for duty in any other branch of the service were shunted off to the Medical Corps.

The Army had a long-established policy of using the Philippines as a dumping ground for ineffective officers in all branches. Those who were too old and/or too stupid were sent there to serve out the rest of their time. Nothing important was going to happen there; they couldn't get in anybody's way, or get in any trouble. We got castoffs from a corps that contained too many incompetents.

Doctors at Davao didn't have to perform any service at all, if they didn't want to. Most of them didn't want to. At least half of the MDs never turned a finger, never took sick call, never saw a patient or rolled a pill or read a medical book. This may have been a blessing. If they had tried to minister to our needs, it might have been worse.

The physicians who did listen to our troubles at sick call took turns in no discernible order of rotation. It became a game of chance for the patients. We might get a doctor who took his oath seriously and did what he could to help, or we might draw some hack who didn't know or didn't care or both. Not that the best of them could do much; they had little to work with and the problem was enormous. All of us were undernourished to some degree, and resistance was low. We were exposed to strange new diseases they could hardly diagnose, much less treat. Nor were they free to prescribe even such a simple remedy as temporary relief from hard labor. The Japanese did not understand, or want to understand. They wanted everybody out working. If it appeared to them that there were too many sick men left in camp, they would give the doctors hell. Worse, they might come through the barracks themselves and roust almost everybody out.

The result was a sort of quota system. No two doctors used the same basis to determine how many men could be held back, or how to select these men. We learned to look first and see which doctor was on duty, before lining up for sick call in the evening. If it was one of the commissioned parasites, we might as well turn back. If it was one of the others, it might be worth waiting that hour in line.

If a man was coming down with malaria, he could just go ahead and have malaria—there probably wasn't any quinine. If it was the onset of amebic dysentery, the patient might be taken off work details and left to lie around the barracks between visits to the latrine—there was no medicine for that, either. If he clearly had scurvy or pellegra or yaws or tropical ulcers, that was too bad. A better diet would have corrected all these things easily, but there was no way to arrange for that.

They did seem to have a limitless supply of gentian violet, a purple liquid that was supposed to have some value against skin infections. It was applied freely to everything from rashes to cuts to infections. There was bandage cloth, but no adhesive tape. The cloth would be tied around and around the body part. A scratch on the chest would be covered by a halter tied over the shoulders. A cut on the ear might lead to a full head turban. Bandages were returned and washed—no, rinsed would be a better word; there was no soap—and used over and over again. After a while they were anything but white.

There were some outstanding doctors. Maj. Jay Tremaine was one of the best; he would always go out of his way to help anybody at any time. I remember Doctors Heidger, Rader, and Deter, but there were others whose names will not come to mind.

And then there was the legendary Doctor Davis, a man so remarkable he is hard to describe. Davis had been operating a hospital on Cebu or Negros island for a sugar company when the war broke out. He had transferred the whole institution, Filipino nurses and all, to a forested location on the highway at a place called Impalutao, not far from Malaybalay and Miramag. He had been commissioned as a major before the surrender, and the Japanese allowed him to run the hospital for some time after. Some stranded American nurses had joined him when their evacuation plane, a four-engined Navy patrol boat, hit a floating log while attempting to take off from Lake Lanao.

Davis's reputation preceded him, and he improved on it in prison camp. He seemed to be capable of performing surgical miracles with his bare hands under the worst conditions. In a "hospital" that was nothing but a big wooden shack jammed full of beds and cots, where germs were free to multiply in the tropical temperature and humidity, and where it was all but impossible to isolate patients or provide nursing care, Davis did appendectomies, amputations, and an assortment of other operations without ever losing a patient. One friend of mine, Doyle Veach, had a kidney removed without undue complications.

"Doc" the man was as common as an old shoe. He enjoyed talking to us, and we admired his wisdom and common sense. Too bad he didn't get back. He was on the wrong ship at a later time.

Pfc. VICTOR MAPES:

I was a plow jockey most of the time until I got sick. They called it rice rash [Schistosomiasis Japonica] or high blood count. What would happen is your legs would become irritated like they'd been bitten by bedbugs. Then you scratched them until they festered and became swollen. Then you got sick and nauseated, your head ached, and you could barely move. It would depend on what stage you were in. Eventually, guys spat blood and felt their heads would pop off their shoulders with the throb.

I got so weak I couldn't keep up with the rest of the people. Even walk. Finally, after a whole year, I managed to get on light duty, a half-day detail. I'd go out and pull weeds out of the vegetables. You really had to be in bad shape to get that detail. I fought being sick. On this detail, I remember, I weeded radishes. I was so hungry, but they wouldn't let us eat the vegetables. If you could only do a half day's work, you only ate half a ration. What I did—others, too—I'd get down on my hands and knees, and weed in the dirt. They'd watch us. When we could, quick, we'd reach down, bite off the bottom half of the radish, and jab it back in the ground so the stem was still showing. Then I weeded like hell to get away from it before it began to wilt. Occasionally, I got caught doing this. Man, they considered that a real bad crime.

We did all kinds of things. Some guys were real ingenious. Like this feller who drove an old antique tractor, the kind that had cleated iron wheels. This feller stayed fat until one day his tractor wouldn't go anymore. When the Japs tried to find out what was wrong with it they discovered, inside the radiator, a little basket where this guy cooked his corn or potatoes while he was driving. Eventually his food clogged the hoses. The boys always had things like that.

Had another one who stayed fat. Old Fitzjohn, who was on the rice mill detail, was a big, rugged, blue-eyed Scandanavian type who kept himself good. He wore civilian-type shoes that he had made from wood and leather. One night, coming through the gate, somebody hit the heel of one of his shoes and it fell off. The rice poured out. He had hollowed out the heel. The Japs beat the heck out of him. Took his shoes and they popped his ears by beating him on the head with them. Then he spent a couple of weeks in a little guardhouse where he couldn't sit or stand. That was the penalty, if you got caught. But the boys, oh, they were ingenious with things like that. Kept them going.

Cpl. KENNETH DAY:

We had thirty-, sixty-, and ninety-day rumors assuring us that the war would be over within that time. Many men lived on these dated projections. Those who believed them were not disheartened when they failed to come true; they would just latch onto the next rumor and ride it out.

Rumors traveled fast. You could start a story at one end of the boardwalk behind the barracks, then walk slowly to the other end and hear the same story being told. There's something supernatural about the "bamboo telegraph." A man at Cabanatuan collected all the rumors he heard and wrote them down. I would like to meet him some day. He had more than 2,000.

Properly handled, rumors can be fun. Our little group of noncoms in the bay in Barracks 9 matured enough to take them for what they were worth and enjoy them. We developed a regular ritual, gathering each night when the lights went out for a final exchange and recap. Each of us would carefully repeat the rumors we had heard during the day, stating where we had heard each one and what the source was supposed to be. It took fifteen or twenty minutes. Often a rumor could be disproved on on the spot: I might have heard that we were to have fish for dinner tomorrow, but Gow, who checked the kitchen regularly, had seen some carabao meat but no fish. Or a story might be verified: McNaughton had heard that there was to be a detail sent somewhere and Miller, who worked at headquarters, knew it to be true. We tried not to believe everything we heard, but it was hard. Our bedtime sessions saved a great deal of disillusion.

Two persistent rumors that ran through all the camps were that (1) Deanna Durbin was dead, and (2) Henry Ford was going to give each one of us a brand new car when we got back. We also believed that we would all be sterile from our prolonged malnutrition. There was no way to trace any of this fiction back to any source—we just believed it.

2d Lt. HADLEY WATSON:

For Sunday's chow we had to wear our classic uniform. Most of the time we wore only a G-string, but on Sundays we wore pants or shorts, if we still had them. One day they got us out there for the 1,000th anniversary of Japan or something, and they made us wear our class-A uniform. We were supposed to salute the Japanese flag. As it went up the mast we were to shout, *"Banzai!"* One wise guy started it and the message was passed down the line. "Fellers, when it comes to *Banzai,* holler 'bull shit.' " So, we were all lined up in our class-A uniforms, skinny devils that we were, and we yelled, "Bull shit!" three times. The Japanese major who was the camp commander sat up on his horse just grinning. He thought it was the best thing he'd heard in his life. The interpreter finally told him what we'd done and he cut our chow rations for several days.

Cpl. KENNETH DAY:

The Japanese word for "count off" is *bango;* their word for toilet is *benjo.* We used both words quite a bit, and more than once a barracks leader would get a laugh by blurting out the wrong one.

The signal for *tenko* was the ringing of a ship's bell that hung on the front of Barracks 5, the headquarters barracks. An elderly lieutenant colonel named Beard had one of the few watches left in camp, and he was assigned the duty of ringing the bell every hour during the day from morning to evening *tenko*. That was his only duty. We called him "the Swedish Bell Ringer." Surely he was the highest-paid bell ringer in the world. He lived to collect his pay, too.

Ranking close to Beard on the pay scale were thirty lieutenant colonels and majors who were given the job of weaving straw hats. There was a serious shortage of headgear in camp, and the Japanese insisted that each man wear a hat when standing outdoor *tenko*. Some Filipinos showed the old men how to make native hats, and they went to work. All day long they would sit in bleacher seats alongside the parade ground and chat of this and that, reliving their good old days in the Army. Their total production for the first month was one hat. Not one hat each—just one hat.

I was one of the bareheaded and had the great good fortune to acquire that prototype straw, a huge thing with a crown easily ten inches high. Wags nicknamed the makers "the Mad Hatters" and tried to compute the cost of that first model. Assuming that the average hatmaker drew $600 per month, my new chapeau cost somebody about $18,000. I would challenge the wealthiest socialite to match that. Later hats came cheaper, at perhaps $500 to $1,000 each, when the Mad Hatters really got their assembly line going. Mine was still the best of the bunch. Holding my head very steady, I could smuggle a whole papaya or a carton of smokes into camp in that high crown.

In mid-January 1943 a shipment of food, clothing, and medical supplies came via the Red Cross. Most of the food was in individual cartons weighing about twelve pounds each. We were dumbfounded. Doyle Veach and I had been working together on a vegetable-gathering detail that day. We found the boxes being distributed when we got back to camp; two South African Red Cross boxes, one Canadian, and one American to each pair of men, to divide any way they chose. Veach and I weren't the ones to hesitate and look for more compatible partners. We grabbed our four boxes, took them to our bunk space, and tore them open right away. I would regret my haste a little. I might not have saved much of my food for very long, but Doyle was an outright glutton. At his urging we gobbled the whole works in a week or two. It was a wonderful binge.

Morale soared as our bodies soaked up the nourishment.

That food wouldn't be considered outstanding here, but there it was heavenly. There was Kraft cheese, crackers, soluble coffee, sugar cubes, powdered whole milk, chocolate, sardines, butter, margarine, corned beef, luncheon meat, prunes, raisins, jam and marmalade, and real U.S. cigarettes. Almost everyone started by eating crackers and cheese. I would say that the two items most enjoyed and appreciated were the two with no food value—cigarettes and coffee. It might have been wiser to stretch this supplementary food out over a longer time, but experience had taught us not to hoard anything. Tomorrow was too uncertain. If it didn't come, something saved might be lost.

A trading market in Red Cross commodities developed overnight. A man who got one brand of cigarettes might prefer another, and he would look for someone who was willing to swap. Someone who didn't care for prunes might exchange for raisins. Nonsmokers would trade tobacco for any kind of food. Before long, everybody was trading something for something else, just to be trading. A price structure evolved quickly, and a medium of exchange appeared to take the place of money. Almost all the popular brands of cigarettes were found in the boxes, but all the boxes had different mixes of brands. There were more Chesterfields than any other brand. For some reason the Chesters had turned moldy in varying degrees: some were all right, some were just a little moldy, and some were far gone. The unit of exchange became one package of not-too-moldy Chesterfields.

Each item found its own price level naturally, based on what the buyer and seller could agree on. The one-pound can of Klim powdered milk went at ten, and never varied. The four-ounce can of coffee was three, butter two and a half, and so forth. Prunes and raisins were "soft," depending on whether someone liked them or not. They might go for three or four, or more or less. There were three cans of corned beef and two cans of luncheon meat—different brands, but we called all of it Spam. Spam stabilized at five, corned beef at four. A year later we would get identical boxes with one exception; the quantities of corned beef and Spam were reversed. Prices immediately reversed, too: beef went to five, Spam to four. Supply and demand, pure and simple.

One brand of smokes was missing altogether from the individual boxes: Lucky Strike. After some weeks the Luckies showed up in a separate shipment. They were distributed equally, and the price was established overnight: one and a half.

A few traders would spend their days wandering from barracks to barracks with offers to buy and sell anything. They would try to buy low and sell high, and make a little edge for themselves. Most of us weren't very good at that. No matter how hard we tried to make a profit, we ended up about where we had started. I did manage to trade for my favorite brand of cigarettes—Philip Morris.

One officer reached for the brass ring. He sold raffle chances on a whole unopened box, collecting more than $1,000 worth of chits from fellow gentlemen to be paid after the war. None of these were ever paid; he didn't make it home.

The Japanese, true to form, reduced our rations while we had Red Cross food.

Pfc. VICTOR MAPES:

We had special "quan details," like if you got with a good first sergeant. He'd know the details where you could get food. If you promised to split with him, he'd send you on the detail. After the split there was always enough to keep and trade on the side.

To the Americans the most serious crime in camp was to be a stool pigeon, whereby in squealing to the Japs you jeopardized some man's life. We did have a few cases of that. The other big crime was stealing somebody's chow. You could almost be killed for that. You couldn't steal it, but you could deal for it. It seemed to me the less you had, the more prone you you were to gamble. We had jokers who were just prone to gambling. I mean they gambled their lives away.

A classic example, and it happened every day, was this. Some guy would say, "I'll gamble my ration of rice against yours. Let's see who's going to eat double and who's going to go hungry." Sometimes they gambled the rice that sat in front of them, or they gambled it before they got it. If you gambled "jawbone," the feller that won would be standing next to you in the chow line and take it from you before you could eat it. Then the guy that lost, since he didn't have that morning's ration anymore, would gamble his next meal, or his next day's meal, or his next three days' morning meals. See, he's broke but he's still hungry, so he gambles what he doesn't have because his credit is all he's got. It was like money in the bank, because he knew he was going to get fed. He was literally gambling his life.

When the decks of cards came in with the Red Cross supplies, the gambling became a big deal. Poker was the game and your chips were a mess kit of rice. Sometimes you'd gamble a can of corned beef or a package of cigarettes. Everything was based on the value of a cigarette. Somebody's issue of rice was worth so many cigarettes. Those were your chips. 'Course, the guy that operated the game took his house cut. If the game went on long enough, well, he ended up with all the stuff.

One aspect of human nature was reflected by gambling. Another aspect was survival. You had to buddy-up with somebody. Sometimes, maybe there would be a group of three or four that would take care of each other. A loner, he had a hard time. A buddy or a group was insurance. You take care of me, I'll take care of you, 'cause neither one knew which one would get the next attack of malaria, or get the hell beat out of him by the Japanese. On a work detail one guy might manage to steal something on Monday. Then on Tuesday the other guy would get something extra and they'd "quan" up a meal together.

Ordinarily, it was almost virtually impossible to stay healthy or survive on what the Japs fed us. It was important to get extra chow, to secure things from elsewhere to help supplement what we were given. Some of the big-time operators, the better thieves, had better techniques and contacts than the rest of us. Oh, I mean they were masters. On the outside they would be the equal of someone like Al Capone. They were professionals and they were successful. Men you tried to stay away from. Once in a while you'd get a country boy, but most of these operators were New Yorkers or men who'd come from Chicago or San Francisco. It was something they acquired in prison. I'm sure they were not that way in civilian life. I knew some of them before prison camp.

Then you had the reverse situation. I saw this from the guys in my own outfit. Some of the boys weren't much on the outside, but when they got in prison camp they made something of themselves. The hardship brought out qualities you never suspected they had. In prison camp all human traits were bared. Some men developed beautiful traits, others developed the worst traits imaginable. In camp you found human nature in the raw.

2d Lt. HADLEY WATSON:

They had these guys that worked over to the Jap kitchen. They got up before daylight and usually come back after dark. They were called "dog robbers," but somebody had to do it. As prisoners you do what the hell you're told to do. One of the good things about this kitchen detail was that you could bring back to camp some tea with sugar. There was a Texan on this detail [Teller] and an Italian boy from the Bronx in New York City [Bennie Santini]. No offense to Italians, but this is one guy that

I wouldn't think had been the best damn soldier in the world. He was a loud-mouth bastard who talked all the time. One day this Nip came in the kitchen to get some of his tea. The Texan had hid a canteen full of it, so he could bring it back to his buddies. The little old boy from Texas tells the Nip guard he didn't have any more tea and that he'd have to make some. This Italian bastard went over to where the canteens were hidden and pulled one out and gave it to the guard. That god-damned guard picked up a piece of fire wood, a big old log, and damn near beat the Texan to death for lying to him about the tea. All the damn New Yorker had to do was keep his mouth shut. The Texan had to be taken to the hospital. But what that Italian Yankee big-shot sonovabitch didn't know was that old Tex had some friends. When they got the message, these Texas boys were waiting for that sonovabitch to get in. You are talking about one guy getting a beating. I've never seen a man beat as near to death in all my life, and here's the whole camp watching. It was all right, he had it coming. Why did he have to go and get his fellow prisoner hurt? Right? I thought he was going to be beaten to death right there on the spot. There wasn't but one guy beating him.* The New Yorker didn't lift a damn hand. He begged them and begged them, "I know I'm wrong. I know I'm wrong." They said, "O.K., you sonovabitch, you're going to take some more of it, too." If the Japs hadn't come in, they would have literally beat the sonovabitch to death. Those Texas boys just weren't going to put up with that crap now. There was talk in the camp for a long time how them Texas boys stuck together. There was still fight in them, you know.

Capt. MARION LAWTON:

At Davao, like other camps, officers and enlisted men were separated by barracks. The senior American became camp commander and then he appointed, by rank theoretically, but more probably by buddy system, barracks leaders or company commanders within the camp. Of course some of the men that were appointed were good at it and some weren't. I didn't like at all my barracks leader, Frank Bridget.† He was a short man who had been a Navy PBY flyer. Flew patrols before the war and things like that. Bridget was also an intensely nervous type and I somehow never liked him. I don't know where he got them, but he used to wear jodhpurs. One morning I overslept, I don't know why or how, because there was always plenty of

---

* "Tex" Arnold, described elsewhere as "a nice guy, but rough as cob."
† Commander Francis J. Bridget of Patrol Wing 10 had organized and commanded the Naval Battalion on Bataan.

noise when reveille came. Our barracks company was the first to file out and line up at the gate for roll call. When Bridget counted off for the Japs, he was one man short. He came boiling into the barracks and yelled at me to wake up! "You sonovabitch! You trying to get me killed? Get the hell out of here!" I thought his behavior was ungentlemanly and unnecessary and I felt he just wasn't very good. Well, I lived to change my opinion!

Pfc. VICTOR MAPES:

Old Colonel Kane had been in the Boy Scouts for a long time and in Davao Penal Colony he formed a Boy Scout troop. He was a real old-timer and a go-getter. There were a number of us there that were Eagle Scouts. If you had gone through that experience you had a feeling for other Eagles. So we got to looking around and heck, here all through the camp of 2,000 men, we found quite a number of Scouts, including men who went through West Point and Annapolis. We even found in there a former Scout Regional Executive.

We never went around broadcasting the fact that we were Scouts, because a lot of people think Scouts are sissies. Maybe some of them are, but I knew a heck of a lot of them, including myself, who weren't. We had meetings right out back of the formation and we even used to give the Scout sign to each other. We had the advantage of Boy Scout training, and knowing some of those things helped me in my survival. Learning, for example, how to take care of yourself in adverse situations, or the techniques of making ropes. The big thing it did for us, though, was help keep our minds off prison camp. We'd pick a man who'd been somewhere. He didn't have to be no great man, just someone with an experience, like he'd been to Alaska. We'd assign guards to each end of the room so the Japs wouldn't happen upon us, and this guy would expound on his experiences in Alaska. That was the only thing we had, 'cause we had no reading material and no outside contact. In these Scout sessions I derived a tremendous amount of knowledge and appreciation of things and places that ordinarily I wouldn't have had a chance to know about.

Eventually, things got so bad that we didn't have time to think much about Scouting or, for that matter, anything else. But in the beginning we were going good.

Capt. THEODORE BIGGER:

Along in the latter part of '43, I was beginning to get concerned whether or not I was going to make it. I would just pass out. What happened was that at this time I was helping take out groups of men. I'd be responsible for taking them out and then checking them back into the compound at the end of the day. The guards counted, but we also tried to keep our people organized. I began, strangely enough, to forget how many men I had out with me. I talked to a senior-grade naval officer about this. He thought something was probably wrong with me and shifted me to another detail. It didn't make any difference to me what I did. Then one morning I started having severe headaches and my ears began ringing. My eyesight also was getting bad. Shortly after that I had something like a seizure. The doctors said it was a build up of fluid in my spine which exploded my nerve endings. Each time I had a seizure the doctors at the hospital at Davao would do a spinal tap. They didn't have any medication to give me. The only word the doctors could use to describe my condition was epileptic. The Japanese thought I was crazy. When they began shipping us to Japan, they kept me in the Philippines.*

Pfc. VICTOR MAPES:

March 4, 1944—I hadn't gotten over this rice rash yet—they got a bunch of us lined up. I had lost a lot of weight, but I was wearing an old pair of fatigues and I looked bigger in them than I was. The Jap doctor, whatever his name was, went by and picked some men and I was left out. Pretty soon he changed his mind and returned one man and came over and felt me. Then he pushed me into the new group. There were about 500 of us who were trucked to a nothing little port somewhere on the Davao Gulf. We worked there building an airstrip. This was called the Lasang Detail.†

Pfc. ROY DIAZ:

When we first got to Davao a Jap lieutenant told us, "If you behave, we'll slack up on the guards." I used to go out on a detail and spend the whole day without seeing a guard. A Jap would take me out and tell me what I was supposed to do. When I'd done it, I walked back to the camp. Once I was out and a Jap sergeant came over to me with a half-gallon of sake. We started to drink together. Him with broken English and me with that Japanese, you know, we was talking to each other. Later, oh boy, I kind of weaved my way back to the barracks. Davao

---

* Theodore Bigger, like many other Americans who eventually became too sick or run-down to work, was taken and kept in Bilibid Prison.
† There was also a detail of fifty mechanics that was sent to Davao City and, in early 1944, 100 men were taken from the colony on a logging detail.

was good for a while until the goddang Colonel Dyess and his group escaped.* The Japs cut the rations to half. We didn't get no more fish. It was like being back in Cabanatuan again. Same damn thing.

Capt. MARION LAWTON:

That first group who escaped worked the coffee plantation and convinced the Japs that they were behind with the pruning. In order to catch up, they volunteered to work on their day off. For two or three weeks they worked on Sundays. Then when they were ready to run, they went out and just kept going. They had all day to go without anybody knowing about it, and when they failed to return at night, the Japs couldn't go out due to the darkness. So the guys had a good start.

Next day, Monday, everything was shut down and everyone was confined to barracks. I don't think we got fed that first day at all. Afterwards everyone's rations were cut for a while, and the guards became more suspicious and meaner. But, the worst thing that happened was we lost Lieutenant Yuki. He was in charge of all work details and it turned out he was a Roman Catholic. Yuki did everything he could to make our life a bit easier. The rules were lenient and we weren't pushed too hard at work. It really was a pretty good camp. When the fellers escaped, they shipped Yuki out and then it got tough. That might have been the worst for us, we lost Yuki.†

2d Lt. HADLEY WATSON:

It's an enlisted man's privilege to escape, but an officer's duty. It's part of the oath you take over a Bible: ". . . you'll defend this country against all enemies, foreign and domestic . . ." That's the oath and it's like a rock, it stays there. As for re-

---

* On Sunday morning, April 4, 1943, ten American prisoners, guided by two Filipino convicts, escaped from Davao by walking away from an unguarded work detail. After several days in the jungle the escapees— Melvyn McCoy, Stephen Mellnik, William Dyess, Austin Shoffner, Jack Hawkins, Michael Dobervitch, Sam Grashio, Leo Boelens, Paul Spielman, Bob Marshall, Victor Jumarong, and Ben de LaCruz—made contact with guerrilla units. Aided by those forces, most of this group was eventually evacuated by submarine to Australia.

Through interviews conducted with these men, the United States received the first accounts of the Bataan Death March and prison camp conditions. In January 1944 the reports of Japanese atrocities written by Lieutenant Colonel Dyess were published in the Chicago Tribune and its news service. Based on this account, Secretary of State Cordell Hull warned Japan in a blunt communique that America would hold Japan accountable for crimes committed against American prisoners.

† Lieutenant Yuki was replaced by the much tougher Major Maeda, who brought with him a sizable contingent of Taiwanese guards.

prisals, I felt we were all soldiers. I thought everything was fair in love and war.

I was at first assigned in camp to the hospital, because I had both wet and dry beriberi. Finally, some Red Cross medicine arrived and I was given pills and medication for my illnesses. When I got able to work a little, they assigned me half day to the rope detail. Six months later I was put to building a fence around the prison camp. I drove a carabao, who pulled a two-wheel cart that hauled fence posts. I thought I was quite fortunate to get that job. I grew up on a farm and had worked mules and horses. Luckily, they had some of the best lemons I've ever eaten around the edge of the jungle where we were building the fence. This helped my scurvy a lot.

A few weeks later, the Japs picked me and several others to go up and take care of their personal gardens. There I met a prewar buddy of mine, Lt. Marvin Campbell. While we were on this detail, he and I decided that we would organize a little group and escape.

Capt. MARION LAWTON:

At Davao, Americans discouraged other Americans from escaping. Each of us debated whether we should escape or not. I wasn't physically able to escape, but I figured the people who wrote the book encouraging prisoners to escape were thinking about Europe, not the Philippine Islands. Most of us were not sure of the attitude the Filipinos would have towards us. Furthermore, what could we accomplish, other than just getting out of prison and roaming around the jungle? Maybe surviving, maybe not. Also, the shooting-squad business had a lot to do with our attitude of preventing escapes. If someone went, he was going to get people killed or he'd get our rations cut and have tougher restrictions placed on the rest of us. The philosophy of the American leadership was that it wasn't fair, because of the extra trouble an escape would cause the camp.

2d Lt. HADLEY WATSON:

Two of Campbell's and my plans to escape were broken up. Americans would rat on us. There were men who did this, I won't call any names, but two of my plans were knocked in the head. The stoolies would rat to the American officers in charge of the camp, to make sure you didn't escape.

The first time, Campbell and I planned to tunnel out through a well to a creek bed that ran under the fence. We were going to dig at night and were still discussing how we would get rid of the dirt, when one day one of the American colonels came out to me. He said, "Come over here a minute." I walked over to him.

"Yes?"

"I hear you're planning to escape."

"I don't know where you got that, sir. I don't know how I'd get away from here, and I don't know where to go if I got away." And I left it at that. The colonel said, "You won't finish that tunnel! We're not going to have any reprisals around here. You'll just stay here like the rest of us." So that was all there was to it. I mean, when a man gives an order, you accept it. You're trained to take orders. The colonel told us we were not going to escape. Anyway, not that time.

Pfc. VICTOR LEAR:

We felt we were better off not trying to escape. We received some medication from the guerrillas in the area. They'd leave it in certain *bodegas,* or supply houses, out in the fields, and the work details would smuggle it back to camp and give it to the hospital. We knew the guerrillas were out there at all times. They got the information to us that if we tried to escape, there was no way they could help us get away. We should sit tight. We were being fed enough to sustain life. We had a little meat once in a while, and fruit from the jungle which we could bring back. If you were on a wood detail, you could get anything you wanted in the jungle. We had been prisoners long enough, and had been out on work details long enough, to know that we were better off in Davao then we were out in the jungle. We knew that was a bad place to be. If you're sick and you don't have medical supplies and you can't feed yourself and you don't have shoes and all you're wearing is a G-string, where in the hell are you going to go? What are you going to do?

Pfc. MICHAEL TUSSING, Jr.:

To escape would have been a tremendous decision. The majority of us had been in the tropics only a short while. Had we been there longer, studied the area to know more about it, learned how to survive in the jungle, taught ourselves Filipino customs and language, then I think my first thought would have been to go to the hills. But here we were on an island, with an ocean to cross, 9,000 miles from home. Would you have escaped? First place, you would have had to depend on Filipinos. Furthermore, you would have been a burden on them. As it was, they had very little themselves. Also, the Japanese threatened that if they were caught assisting prisoners in any way, they would be killed. Some, we thought, might even turn us in for the reward. So the decision to escape was a terrible one to make.

Pfc. VICTOR LEAR:

I don't think anybody who was rational thought escape was worth it.

2d Lt. HADLEY WATSON:

The next time we tried to escape, someone else got wind of our plan and screwed up our route. This time we were going to crawl along a drainage ditch, behind the mess hall, that came out by the latrine. The ditch then went under the bridge that we walked over to get to the mess hall, and we were going to follow it until we got to the creek. From there it was an easy crawl under the fence, and a chance to make a run for the jungle. The day before we were going out, an American detail filled in the creek under the fence with stakes and wire. This of course made it impossible to get out—that way.

PART III

ON THE LOOSE

8
ESCAPE FROM DAVAO

2d Lt. HADLEY WATSON:

Occasionally the Japs would pick two or three men to take care of their own personal gardens. I used to get selected along with 2d Lt. Marvin Campbell. We worked the Jap gardens for a month or so before we got up enough confidence to talk about escape. We decided that we would organize a little group and run for it. I had a good friend who was with a law firm, and he told me once that a group of attorneys could accomplish more than one or two lawyers. In other words, the bigger the force the more strength you've got. Because we figured there would be some action, we wanted people who would fight.

Campbell knew Mickey Wright, who led a fence detail down by the jungle where we wanted to start. Once Campbell and I put our list of men together Marvin went up to Wright, the detail leader, and asked him to select our little group to go out with him. We decided not to tell anyone who didn't need to know, because twice before we had been stopped by our own men. Most of the men were afraid of reprisals, so you couldn't tell anybody anything because, hell, somebody'd rat on you. Supposedly, for every man who escaped, the Japs would kill ten. But this never happened. When McCoy and Dyess and their group escaped in April of '43, the Japs starved us by cutting our rations and tightening security, but they never went so far as to kill anyone. One day not long after that, here went Pease and Brown. Nobody got killed that time either. But fear in the camp was there, so Campbell and I trusted nobody. We didn't even tell Wright we were going. I knew Mark Wohlfeld wanted to escape and that he would fight too, so I decided to tell him, but then only at the last moment.

Capt. MARK WOHLFELD:

About midnight of the 27th of March, 1944, I had to make this visit to the latrine. It was a twelve-cylinder latrine, so I was surprised when another man hobbled up to me instead of sitting at the other end. This ticked me off, because he was depriving me of my privacy. It was Lieutenant Watson. He was there with his red beard and rags, bandage on his leg, bandage over his eye, using a cane when he walked. He looked as though he were ready to piss out right there. I had seen Watson in camp, but I didn't associate with him because he was always hobbling about pretending he was crippled so he would pull light duty. He was also known to understand all the ins and outs of the camp. I also figured he was dangerous because he was a gambler. You see, in the Regular Army before the war it was very much like *From Here to Eternity*. There were operators and there were victims, and Watson was a big-time operator. In the camps none of this changed. Remember, Watson was a former enlisted man. Since he used to be one of them, he commanded more respect from the enlisted men than any of the other officers did. All Watson had to do was to ask for something, and if it was possible to get, he would get it. Also keep in mind that Watson had a high IQ and a command personality.

When he sat down next to me in the stinking latrine, I greeted him. He said right off that he had me on an escape party for the next morning, and that it was too late for me to do anything about it because it had all been arranged with Wright. He told me when I was alerted before roll call, to be sure to have the stuff I was going to take ready to carry out. I thought Watson was off his rocker, so I went back to my plank in the barracks and thought about the idea. I knew that if I didn't make my attempt now, I might never do it because the timing was perfect. In February I had received a Red Cross package, and since I hoped to escape I ate it quickly to gain some strength.

2d Lt. HADLEY WATSON:

After I left Wohlfeld, I went back to my barracks and quietly got my stuff together. I had a buddy in the pharmacy who got me some medicine, and I filled the bottom half of a little Nescafé coffee can with this stuff and covered it with crumbs of tobacco. I also made packages of iodine swabs, medicine, aspirin, and so forth for Campbell and Wohlfeld to carry out. I woke Mark up before roll call and gave him his medicine and told him to wear it out. I also told him to keep his mouth shut.

Capt. MARK WOHLFELD:

During the night Watson poked me and gave me a package, so I knew something was going to happen. I arranged my dummy equipment around my cot. Those of us who were going to try to escape had a dummy set of equipment, so if the Japs would look at our planks while we were out working and saw our mess kit and little trinkets, they'd figure we'd be coming back. We also had another set of odds and ends that we carried with us in the event we did escape. Before the sun was up, the Japs called *tenko*. Everybody had to roll out quickly, because the last man out of the barracks was kicked. We were then told to *atsumare* [fall in], and we moved out in front of our barracks. It was too early yet to be oppressively hot. Once we had counted off, we returned to the barracks, picked up our mess kits, and went to the mess hall to get the morning ration of lugaw.

After breakfast we lined up in thirty-man formations, and the Japanese interpreter had our American clerk read off that day's work assignments. When work detail Number One was read off, those men fell out. We were told that work detail Number Two was to be under the command of 2d Lt. Mickey Wright. The clerk then read off my name, Watson's, Campbell's, and the seven others who were going to be involved. We formed up in columns of fours and marched to the tool shed where we were each given our equipment. We took our shovels, put them at right shoulder arms, and with four Jap guards and a corporal flanking us, marched northward toward the railroad tracks and the jungle beyond.

2d Lt. HADLEY WATSON:

Wohlfeld asked me if anyone besides Campbell knew what we were going to do. I told him I had spoken to no one else. But, I said, except for some of Wright's old cronies who filled out the detail, all the others were on the hot list. This list was made up of potential escapees like me, and was kept by the camp's senior American officers in order for them to watch us more carefully, to make sure we would not make a break for it.*

Capt. MARK WOHLFELD:

It was a game to me. There was nothing to be serious about. I was trying to figure out what the score was, how I was going to do it. Not having a plan was no big deal. My theory was always that overly planned plots, with all their architectural engineering of how many paces a man walks and how many feet

---

* Besides Watson, Wohlfeld, Campbell, and Wright, the fence-building detail that day consisted of Second Lieutenants Andrew Buckovinsky, James McClure, James Hayburn, Fanslier, Warrant Officer Carmichael, and an older naval officer, Lieutenant Boone.

of rope will be required, often go astray. The best way to effect an issue of this sort is to have the proper reflexes and to use surprise.

Our job that day was to strengthen the fence around the agricultural clearing. The Japs hoped that by adding more fence posts, they would prevent the jungle animals from getting to the vegetables. In our two-mile march we passed a sugar cane field and an area in which repairs were being made on the railroad. Later in the morning a sugar cane detail and a railroad section gang would be placed in those areas. They would play their role in our escape attempt.

The best time to alert the others as to what we were going to try was while we were all marching together. After I asked one of our guards for permission I started singing "Mademoiselle From Armentieres," but changed the words to fit the situation. I began loudly, if not musically, "Today's a day we'll never forget, parlez-vous; are you willing to break out with us, parlez-vous; if you're willing to go give us your word, parlez-vous . . ." The others picked up what I was doing and you could see they were beginning to think about it. They all eventually nodded agreement. I kept singing, "At the first rest halt, parlez-vous; stay in a tight circle and we'll make our plans, parlez-vous . . ."

Now one man in the group, a naval warrant officer, was someone we particularly banked on for help. For months he had been telling everyone how he planned to escape. He had all sorts of bizarre methods which he planned on using. We assumed that he would take over the leadership of our group at the first rest. I wasn't going to do anything stupid. I'd already been on several patrols on Bataan, and when I would open fire, all I would hear would be the sound of my own rifle. The rest of my patrol would have taken off or kept their heads down. So I knew that I wasn't going to volunteer to be a hero in this escape attempt.

Watson and I had done as much as we were going to do. We had gotten them all here and set up the situation. At the first *yasume* [rest], we'd all decide how we were going to do it. Everyone had nodded agreement, and an officer's commitment is his bond. Watson and I accordingly assumed everyone would be in on it.

When we got to the fence line where we were going to work, the Jap corporal gave us our orders. We started digging post holes and as the time moved on I noticed that all the other men, instead of watching our presumed leader, the escape artist, were watching me. After an hour, I sort of waved at the Japanese corporal and said, "*Yasume dozo*," or please give us a rest. He said, "O.K., O.K." We stopped work and, as pre-arranged, formed a tight circle so that we could make our plans. With nothing better being said, I told the men that at the next *yasume* we'd form another tight circle, which would mean the four guards and the corporal would be close to us. Then at my command we'd rush the guards, disarm them, try-ing not to hurt them unless we had to. Then to just head west-ward into the jungle, hit the river, and work toward the high ground where we knew we would run into Filipinos.

The guards showed us we had used our five minutes, so we went back to work. It's about midmorning and hot and steamy when I asked the guard for another *yasume*. Now this great leader of ours had gotten the word around to his bud-dies, and instead of forming our circle, he took six of our detail and moved them about twenty-five yards away. That left Campbell, Watson, an officer named Buckovinsky, and myself alone. Now we had to think of something else. We had to break out then because we couldn't go back to the prison camp. Watson's jacket was full of medicine, and I had a small knife made out of corrugated iron which was good for slashing. With our two groups separated, we had two guards watching us and two watching the others with the corporal in between. That meant if we jumped our guards, the remaining three could fire into us. We yelled to the other group. They yelled back, "Fuck you, we've changed our minds."

2d Lt. HADLEY WATSON:

I got real mad. I figured that if they didn't want to fight they'd better lay down and get out of the way, because if they didn't, I was going to treat them just like a Jap.

Capt. MARK WOHLFELD:

After the war these men might eventually be good doctors and lawyers, but right now they were no damned use at all. Before the guards jerked us back to work, I said to our small group, "Look, we're going to have to do this ourselves, it has to be next break or we'll never do it." We went back to work. The scene is this: there's our barbed-wire fence; then a two-foot-deep by two-foot-wide drainage ditch which was needed to drain the rain water from the cucumber mounds; and then about twenty paces beyond, the jungle. I told Watson, who was digging next to me, that one of us should take a guard into the jungle and clobber him. While that was happening, the rest of us would clobber the other one. Then we'd just run into the thicket. At this time the other six men got as far away from us as they could, because they could feel something was cooking.

2d Lt. HADLEY WATSON:

We were going to get Buckovinsky to go into the jungle to pick some fruit for us. The idea was to take a shovel over there and kill the guard to get his gun, and then lay some holes in those other fellows. We weren't kidding around. Mark wasn't volunteering anything, and Buckovinsky said that if I was so damned smart, why didn't I take my shovel and go over there and get the guard's gun. I said, "All right." I had this long red beard and for two years the guards used to pull it to annoy me, and now I was so mad that all I wanted to do was kill Japs.

Capt. MARK WOHLFELD:

Because he understood only a few English words, I began pantomiming to the guard that we wanted to go over to the jungle to get some fruit. When Watson picked up this shovel, the guard stopped him and showed he wasn't to take it with him. I began to argue with the guard in pidgin-Jap, telling him Watson would need the *scoopu*. "He has to reach for the fruit with the *scoopu*." He finally agreed. Watson went between the barbed-wire strands, crossed the ditch, and started for the jungle. One of the riflemen followed Watson while the other one posted himself between the jungle and us. Watson and his guard disappeared into the palm fronds.

2d Lt. HADLEY WATSON:

Those trees are virgin timber with these long, thick roots. I took the shovel and cut my way back into the jungle till I got to a fruit tree. As if to knock some fruit down, I climbed up on one of the roots and thought, "Right here is the best place to do it." I took that shovel, and I was going to just chop the guard's damned head off, but he ducked. I hit him on the arm instead and knocked the rifle out of his hands. The bastard grunted, then jumped me and threw me ten feet through the jungle. I thought I'd never quit going through those thorns. He came after me, and I couldn't find a damned thing to hold on to because the bugger didn't have any hair. Finally, I got my fingers in his mouth and on his throat, and I held that sonovabitch till he was black as black. As I was crawling back to get the rifle, that bugger got up and started to come at me. It was fortunate that the shovel was laying right there. Well, I just took the damned shovel and backhanded him with it, and I cut him five or six times in the head. Finally I got mad, and with the cutting side I just laid his head open from ear to ear. He didn't bother me any more, and I got his rifle.

Capt. MARK WOHLFELD:

Suddenly there was what sounded like a loud *thwack* and the crackling of twigs. Then the Jap guard with Watson began hollering for help. The corporal gave the others the order to open fire. They all fired wildly at the exact point where Watson had gone into the jungle. This meant that they were firing at their own man as well, but it didn't make any difference to them. One of the riflemen was beside me near the fence while Campbell was standing near the corporal. Campbell was depending on me to do something and he yelled, "For Christ's sake, Wohlfeld, you yellow sonovabitch, do something to help Watson." But I couldn't move. I mean, even with all that mental preparation, I was frozen. This Jap guard's about a yard from me, but I couldn't bring myself to do anything. So Campbell hit the Jap corporal in the mouth with the edge of his shovel. When the teeth and blood landed on me I woke up.

My rifleman had fired his full clip and was fumbling around trying to get a new clip into the magazine. I took my shovel and I aimed at his head. I swung as I would at a high, fast ball and missed. I landed on my hands and knees. I stayed there with my eyes closed waiting for him to blow my head off. But he couldn't get his bolt closed. In fact, he was so excited he dropped his ammunition clip next to me. So instead of shooting me, he beat me across the back with the rifle barrel. He did this two or three times when I said, "Enough of this," and I turned around and tripped him. I grabbed my shovel and swung. Again I missed his head, but the blade tore deeply into his left biceps. We were now both covered with blood and flies. I rolled around with him, and because there was so much blood, he slipped away from me and fell into the drainage ditch. With all the mud and the way he fell, he got stuck in the ditch. I rolled towards him until we were facing each other. With the flies in my eyes I couldn't tell whether he had closed the bolt, but he had the rifle in his right hand and was moving it towards me. Meanwhile, about 300 yards away from me were the sugar cane gang and the railroad repair detail. Soon as they knew something was wrong, their guards began firing at us. The bullets bounced around and I got nicked in the arm. The birds flew up in clouds and the monkeys screamed. It was just confusion!

I couldn't see exactly everything that was happening, so I had to piece it all together afterwards. Don't forget, what I'm telling you lasted about sixty seconds. Campbell, I heard later, had taken the corporal's rifle and beaten him with it until he broke the stock in two. In a glance, I remember seeing Campbell break for the jungle. Buckovinsky was nearest me lying flat as possible. I'm still in the ditch, panting, the Jap's arm is spewing blood, and he's moving his rifle towards me. I yelled at Buckovinsky to take his rifle. "I can't," he said. "They're shooting at me." I'm thinking that everybody's being shot at, so I screamed, "Get up, you sonovabitch—move, you dirty coward!" He began to move towards me, and he was so frightened that instead of crawling under the barbed-wire fence when he gets to it, he stands up and climbs over it. He got his pants caught and ripped them getting off the barbs. He ran over to me and said, "Oh my God, my God!" He then reached down, took the rifle, and started to run for the jungle, leaving me in the ditch with the Jap. Before he reached the tree line he got hit and fell. I remember thinking, "Good for you, you Polack sonovabitch." He staggered back up and disappeared into the forest. Now here I'm all alone, covered with teeth and gore and flies, with bullets flying over me. Finally I jumped out of the ditch and before I sprinted for the jungle I remembered to kick the guard's head into the mud.

2d Lt. HADLEY WATSON:

After I picked up the rifle, I went up to the edge of the jungle and a machine gun from the railroad section gang opened up over me. It was just plumb hot in there with all those bullets coming in. Campbell had hit one of the guards, and Mark had knocked the other one down. I emptied the clip of my weapon. Now this next is the funny spot—it's comical. Campbell's corporal had gotten up and was screaming something, moving and hollering and, boy, I hit him with two rounds. I don't know whether I killed him or not, but when I last saw him his eyes were popping out and he was just tumbling. After I emptied my clip, I went back to get the rest of the dead Jap's ammunition, and when I came back out, all the Americans were gone and the guards had scattered. With nobody to shoot at I said, "What the hell? Everybody's out and on their way. I'll meet them at the river."

Capt. MARK WOHLFELD:

The bullets are flying all over, zinging off the barbed wire, and kicking up dust everywhere. I decided to take one last look before I hit the jungle. The rest of the POWs are on the ground lying flat with their hands over their heads, nobody moving. What happened in the confusion after that was that two others from our group also ran off. So that made five altogether that got away. But we were all separated, or at least I wasn't with the others.

2d Lt. HADLEY WATSON:

Because we were surprised by the other details opening up on us, we didn't all get into the jungle the way we were supposed to. Campbell and Buckovinsky got in together, Mark got in somehow, and how the hell the others got in I don't know, but I do know that our leader, the great escape artist, just laid down and stayed there till it was all over.*

Capt. MARK WOHLFELD:

I was exhausted, and my left arm began pulsating. I tried to make a tourniquet out of vines for my arm, but somehow that just made the wound bleed more. In desperation I took some mud and plastered that over the wound. The bleeding stopped.

After running for a while, I came to a big bog. I didn't know if it went on for a hundred yards or a hundred miles, but I knew I had to get across it. I couldn't go around it because that would take me back in the direction I had come from, so I began looking for a way through it. After several minutes of hunting, I came across one of those long Philippine hardwood trees that the natives had knocked down so that it would span one of the worst sections of the swamp. I was so exhausted at this point that I knew before I could continue, I would have to rest. I walked out on this log about twelve steps and then slid over the side into the mud. Although the water was about two feet deep, I sank into the mud up to my waist. It was like going into a vacuum cleaner. I grabbed onto a small branch near me, and I held that with my wounded hand while I covered my head with water lilies. I noticed that the water all around me was clouded up from the mud I had disturbed. Fortunately, it started to rain. I couldn't hear any more firing and the birds started to come back. I felt I would just hang on there and rest for a while. I knew it would take the Japs some time to get a patrol out after us, so I just fell asleep with my head on the log.

When I awoke, there was a cloud of insects around my head and my left hand was clamped frozen around the stump. I heard the Japanese chattering excitedly. They had found where I had

---

* A naval officer, Lieutenant Boone, was shot and killed while trying to climb the barbed-wire fence.

broken through the jungle. They began calling in pidgin-English, "America, come backu, America, come backu!" I didn't know where I was or where I was going. I was tired and my arm was throbbing something awful, so I began to think, "Geez, maybe they'll take me back. They have this code of *Bushido* and maybe because I fought my way out, they'll forgive me and let me go back to work."

"America, come backu!" Then all of a sudden one of the Japs opened up with a machine gun—*rat tat tat tat tat*—and again the birds went crazy. I thought, "Fuck you. Come back, my ass!"

I could see the patrol by the log. They were carrying packs, so I knew they intended on being in the jungle for several days. They came bouncing across the tree trunk right over me and disappeared in the jungle on the far side. They stopped and yelled some more. Then they opened up again with the machine gun. I thought that was the dumbest thing I had ever seen. They're trying to lure me back and here they go firing into the jungle. It didn't make much sense, but it sure was typical. If the patrol went into the jungle I felt I'd be much safer following them, because if I went back the other way, I'd meet them coming around. I remembered from Bataan that the Japs always had small units following their main groups. They'd use them as messengers or as a rear guard, so I waited. Sure enough, about ten minutes later two more Japanese trackers came across the log and followed on after the first unit. The rain began to come down harder—one of those warm tropical downpours.

My left arm was stiff, and I was sitting in a ninety-degree position with my legs covered by thick mud. When I tried to pull myself out, I'd lose my strength and the mud would drag me back. Finally, I found a sunken piece of log. After a struggle, I pushed up on that and with my good arm shoved myself up on the log. When I got to the other side of the bog, I was filthy. I had left my shirt hanging on the barbed wire, but my shorts, socks, and shoes were packed with mud. I used a nearby pool to wash myself. The trail that the Japanese patrol had taken was right in front of me, and I began to walk along it until I found a narrower animal trail running diagonally across the one I was on. I figured that this small trail might be safer for me. I began jogging when suddenly the ground gave way and I crashed down. I managed to kick myself forward and my arms landed on the far side of this hole, but my legs got caught on some pointed stakes. These pits are called *suyoks,* and the Filipino farmers use them to hunt wild pigs. I was too weak to climb out and too tired to think of any other solution. I just lay there, wet and miserable, waiting for a Jap patrol to find me.

2d Lt. HADLEY WATSON:

I kept the rifle and moved down the fence line until I ran into the river. To put the Japs off my trail, I began wading up this stream until I saw a hill. I climbed it, hoping that I would spot other Americans who had obeyed the plan of coming down the fence and going up the river. But instead, I laid down and fell asleep. I'm not telling you that I'm so brave that I went to sleep. I just damned gave out. I woke up later with the Japs hollering and firing. So I kept my position the rest of that day and night. The next morning I started up the river again. Later that day I could hear chickens clucking, but couldn't find a trail anywhere that would lead me to a village. I kept going all that second day until I figured this wasn't going to get me anywhere. I decided then that I'd come back down the river towards the prison farm and steal vegetables at night, until I decided what to do next. I knew this plan would be dangerous, but it was better than starving. I didn't dare shoot any game for fear of letting the patrols know where I was.

Capt. MARK WOHLFELD:

Fortunately, when I fell into the pig pit, I was not impaled on one of the bamboo spikes. After gathering my strength, I crawled out and continued along the trail. Once I spotted a Jap column searching the edge of a bamboo thicket, so I turned north into the densest part of the jungle. I came to a clearing that ran along both sides of the railroad tracks. From where I was I had a clear view of the tracks in both directions. There were some guards posted a short ways off. I was so close to them I could hear them talking. I rested for a while, hoping they were a mobile search party that would shortly move on. The longer I waited, however, the more I realized they were there for the night. I could hear them chopping wood and then I smelled their cooking fires. It was, I guess, about four o'clock in the afternoon. While I waited for dark before crossing the tracks, I heard someone shouting. From the direction of the camp I saw a handcar coming. It was being pumped by POWs and on it were two Jap riflemen and our American camp commander. This commander was repeating over and over into a megaphone, "Americans. Surrender yourselves. Come out of the jungle. You will be able to go back to work if you do." What I am saying are not his exact words, but it approximates his message to us. When I understood what he was saying, a wave of bitterness swept over me. An American officer who fought under the same flag as I did was asking me to surrender. At that moment I developed an intense dislike for him.

After it had gotten dark I dashed across the railroad tracks and found a large tree to lie under. In spite of the insects feasting on me, I went to sleep instantly.

The next day I began moving towards the high country, figuring I would run into Filipinos in that direction. It rained on and off all day. I grew careless and late in the afternoon stumbled into a Jap bivouac. I dove back into a bamboo thicket and by the time they had their search organized, I was gone. I walked until I came to a stream. As it was getting dark, I decided this would be a good place to stop. I laid down in the roots of a big tree, stretched my socks across my face to keep the insects off, and fell asleep. The next day I began walking upstream in hopes of running into some Filipino farmers.

2d Lt. HADLEY WATSON:

Sometime the third day, while backtracking, I heard a rooster. I worked my way through the jungle and finally ran into a village. There, the natives fed me some ground-up bananas and something like hot cakes. The chief motioned me to go to the back of the village, when all I wanted to do was sleep. But he kept prodding me until I moved to a shack behind the village. He put two guards on me, and their job was to get me out of that damned area in case the Japs came. The fear of reprisals was so great that the next day they led me out of the village to a trail crossroads. Then those buggers ran off, leaving me all by myself. I knew those trails were hard to follow if you weren't used to them. I took a rock and stripped a tree a little bit so I'd know where I was if I got lost. It seemed I always came back to where I started. Finally, I had enough of wandering around, so I took me a trail and came back into the village. I took my rifle, cocked it, and told the chief I wanted some of his fellows to go with me wherever we were going or, by God, I was going to start shooting! He got real scared and put some of his buggers with me, and I marched them in front of me with my rifle ready to fire if they so much as looked as if they were going to run off. They escorted me over to a Christian Filipino's place that grew corn, tomatoes, okra, and every other vegetable you can imagine.

The first thing these Christians did was feed me. Then they began to take the damned leeches off. I had so many on my legs that there was no way of pulling them off, so they took their bolos and shaved them off. After they bathed my legs in hot water, I laid down again. When I woke up, it was noon the next day. I ate some more and then went back to bed.

The next day I was taken deeper into the jungle to a Moro

village. I stayed there a week, waiting for the Christian to come back. The Moro family that I stayed with fed me from a common tray. We'd have a little dried meat or some fish and rice. They'd start on one end of the tray and I'd eat from the other. You have northern Moros and southern Moros, and this tribe reminded me of our Indians back home. The girls had on their wrap-around skirts and toted their babies in sacks behind them or in front, so the babies could get their chow. It was as cute as could be. The old chief decided that if I was strong enough to fight my way out of that prison camp, I must be pretty special. Damned if he didn't bring the whole village down—babies, old people, kids, and dogs—just to look at me!

Twice while I was there, the Japs came through looking for me. The first time I hid up in a roof while the Japs searched the cornfields. The next time the chief hid me in the cornfield while the Nips combed the little village. Finally the Christian came back and told me that he had a detail that was going to take me to the headquarters of the local American guerrilla commander. I learned from him then that one of our escape party had been killed by the Japs.

Capt. MARK WOHLFELD:

Early in the morning of what must have been April 1, I began to get very discouraged. I had been following the stream for several days without finding anyone who could help me. My condition was getting worse. I was starved, tired, and sick, and didn't think I could continue much longer. I came around another bend and there, standing in midstream, holding a spear and looking at me was a native fisherman. He reminded me of a cigar-store Indian. I walked closer to him. Someone said, "*Amigo.*" I looked at the river bank and found six or seven other Filipinos watching me. I couldn't speak their dialect, so I motioned that I was hungry. They came over and shook my hand and gave me some rice. I hadn't eaten in so long that I had a hard time swallowing. They helped me over to the shore. From being in the stream so long, my feet were swollen like large potatoes. They gestured as if they wanted to carry me, but I motioned that I could walk. They led me through the jungle for about two hours until we came to their village. There must have been fifty nipa shacks built on stilts in this barrio. I was bearded and in rags, but it made no difference to my rescuers. They placed me in the *teniente's* [mayor's] shack. I lay there the balance of that day and night. The next day everyone from that poor village brought me as much food as they could gather. I had a mountain of fruit, boiled fish, dried fish, and rice. Since

I couldn't eat all of it, the *teniente*'s family thrived on what I left, which was most of it. On account of how bad my feet were, I couldn't climb. This made my going out of the shack to the community latrine impossible. To help me, they cut a hole near where I lay, and I used that to defecate through. Whenever I had to go, the women of the family I was staying with would go out on the porch and wait until I was finished with my business. I found it very embarrassing.

The *teniente* and I could not speak to each other, which was very frustrating. One day he brought to me a little ten-year-old girl who spoke English. I felt wonderful. She was from the east coast of Mindanao, where she had attended a Catholic school. When the war began, her father, who was in the Army, evacuated her to the interior. I asked her if there were any Americans on Mindanao. "Yes," she said, "there are many Americans, but they are bandits. They take our women, they take our food, and they fight amongst themselves." I thought this might be an exaggeration, so I asked where they were. I was told that they were north in the swampland around the Agusan Valley, near the town of Waloe. I asked my little friend if she or her father could take me there. She said that they couldn't, because her father was a deserter, and if the guerrillas found this out they would shoot him. Nevertheless, I had to get to the Americans. I had malaria, dysentery, and leech bites, and if I stayed in this barrio I was going to die. I told the little girl to explain to the *teniente* that I needed a guide, and that if I didn't get one I'd die and the word would get out that it was his barrio's fault that I died. This was evidently a responsibility he did not want to shoulder. As soon as I could walk, I was supplied two Filipino guides, and with them I began my search for the American guerrilla camp.

We marched for two days. Each night we spent resting in whatever barrio we were near. On the third day, as we were going along a trail, we were ordered to halt. About five feet away, behind a bush, I saw two Filipinos. They were both carrying Enfield rifles and they were pointed at me. They seemed nervous and all I could think of was that, having gotten so close, these ignorant farmers were going to blow me off the trail without even letting me identify myself. Fortunately at this moment a Filipino second lieutenant arrived and we identified ourselves. He apologized for the actions of his men.

For the next four hours he led me and his little patrol through the jungle, until we arrived at a clearing in a bamboo thicket that was his company headquarters. While we were on the trail, he explained that one of his duties was to leave supplies for the POWs at Davao. He told me he had left medicine,

Life magazines, C rations, and all sorts of other American things in and around the camp, in places where the POWs would find them. In Davao I heard rumors that the American commanders had confiscated this material and sworn the finders not to reveal the existence of this equipment. These officers felt their actions would minimize the possibility of mass escapes into the jungle. I never found out if this was true or not, but I did learn that the guerrillas were leaving items for the prisoners to find. Logic would indicate that a mass escape from Davao would have been suicidal, so that if the American commanders had decided to hide the existence of the guerrillas from the men, they could not be faulted for their reasoning.

As soon as I had settled in with the guerrillas, my rags were burned and I bathed in a tub of warm water. My arm was attended to with sulfathiazine and I was fed hot broth. Then my hair was cut, along with my finger and toe nails. I was finally given a clean uniform. All this happened on April 6, Army Day. For me, though, what made the day really fantastic was learning that another prisoner had been picked up and would be brought in as soon as the guerrillas could get a party to the village where he was staying.

2d Lt. HADLEY WATSON:

I was still laying up with the Moros when one day a guerrilla patrol came by to collect me. A day later I ended up in a jungle clearing which was being used by the local guerrillas as their headquarters.

Capt. MARK WOHLFELD:

Late one afternoon, who should walk in but Lt. Hadley Watson. Knowing he was coming, I prepared a special greeting. I made sure he couldn't see me and as he walked past I stepped out and said, "Dr. Livingston, I presume." Of course Watson hadn't read that far, so he didn't know what I was talking about.

2d Lt. HADLEY WATSON:

Don't you think I wasn't happy to see him! We didn't hug and kiss, we weren't that close, but it was good to see him. I called him "A dumb New York square head," and he called me "That bastard from North Carolina."

Capt. MARK WOHLFELD:

Eventually a radio message came through from main guerrilla headquarters that Watson and I were to be transported to Colonel

[Wendell W.] Fertig's command post at Talacogon. We moved out with a detachment of guerrillas who were going to drop off at various outposts along the Agusan River. We started out in these long canoes which the natives called *barrotos*. When the river ended, we went on foot. The trip was to last twenty-one days. Along the way I became very ill and we had to stop for me to be treated.

2d Lt. HADLEY WATSON:

We sat around for a couple of days until a Filipino third lieutenant arrived to escort us to Colonel Fertig's headquarters. Fertig commanded all the guerrillas on Mindanao and was quite a big shot at that time. About three weeks after we had escaped from Davao, Mark and I began our journey north to the Agusan River to join up with the main guerrilla band.

We were on the trail a couple of weeks at least. It was a long, hard walk and during it old Mark came down with malaria. The first night we gave him five or six atabrine and put a grass mattress over him so that he could sweat out a little bit of that fever. The lieutenant who escorted us was quite an active little fellow and he got us up early the next morning, but Mark had that malaria real bad. He was six foot, one inch, but he couldn't have weighed more than 100 pounds. He was so sick he had a terrible time climbing over all the fallen trees and vines that clogged the trail. Being a country boy, I was used to these bad trails and I got around pretty good. Mark kept tripping and falling. Once he fell about ten feet down a gully and the Filipino cussed him in Visayan for slowing us down. Finally, at the end of one of these days, with one last hill to climb, Wohlfeld gave out. He said he just wasn't going to go any farther. The guerrilla lieutenant told me we would spend the night in a little grass shack back of a nearby cornfield, and that I'd have to get Wohlfeld over there or we'd leave him. Well, I wasn't big enough to tote old Mark. I only weighed about eighty pounds myself. I figured the best way to get a buddy out of a bad situation is to make him mad. I called him everything I could think of that wasn't polite. Finally I said, "You sorry SOB, just sit there and rot. I've begged and pleaded with you to get moving like any decent Southern boy would. You damn Yankees just ain't got it!" That did it. He picked up a stick and staggered up that hill after me. I ran in front of him just keeping out of range of that club and just kept taunting him. I ran down the other side of that damned hill and jumped across a little stream and landed in the cornfield. Old Wohlfeld just charged on down with his stick, and I'm sitting in the cornfield just dying laughing at him. By the time he got to me, he'd cooled off a little bit, and from there it was an easy walk to the hut. In the morning Wohlfeld was feeling better, and from then on we just kept going till we reached Colonel Fertig's headquarters.

During the trip, our guide told us that there was a big guerrilla organization and that if we wanted to, we could join up and do some more fighting. Mark and I talked about it, and we decided that if we got a chance, we'd stay with the guerrillas, but only if we'd be given a good command and if Fertig would jump us a couple of ranks. Once you decide to stay in the Army, rank is important, and there's no need sitting there with your thumb behind your ear as a second lieutenant, if you could become a captain. I'd been a lieutenant too long, and I thought I'd kind of like to get a promotion.

When we finally limped into battalion headquarters, we went up to report to Fertig in his house. The colonel introduced himself to us and began talking about his command. Meanwhile, back in the kitchen, Fertig's cook was baking a coconut pie, you know, one with frosting and everything, and Mark and I were just sitting there with our mouths watering. Remember we'd been starved since Bataan, and this pie was like heaven to us. Fertig kept talking and explained that if we wanted, he'd ship us back to the States, where the chances were we would become instructors and never have to see combat again, and where we'd get one automatic promotion. However, if we stayed with him, and he began to pump us up, he'd give us two promotions and a good command. So I told Fertig, "Hell, I volunteered to come in the Army, I volunteered to come to the Philippines, I volunteered to go to the Scouts in order to get a commission, and I'm still mad and still want to fight." Wohlfeld told Fertig he wanted to do the same thing, and we both told him we'd stay if he guaranteed us two promotions.

Now Mark and I are looking at each other, and we're watching that pie being baked back there. We thought old Fertig would surely invite us to dinner, and we'd get a piece of that beautiful pie. I mean, at that point, Wohlfeld and I would have taken any of Fertig's assignments, just for a piece of pie. After we agreed on our new ranks, Fertig told us to go over to the officers' quarters, which was nothing but a nipa shack, and have a little rice and meat, and that we should come back after dinner. Well, Wohlfeld looked at me, and I looked at him, and that pie kept on baking. On our way over to the officers' hut, Wohlfeld, who didn't swear very much, said, "You know, I don't know if I'm going to like working for that sonovabitch."

I turned to Mark and said, "Well, I was thinking the same thing, but since you're a captain and I'm just a second lieutenant, I thought I'd let you say it first."

Cpl. KENNETH DAY, Davao Penal Colony:

After the escape, things got complicated inside camp again. This time the Japs made no threat to execute anybody in retaliation, but we were sharply segregated. Those who had been on work details near the escape group that day, or who lived near any of its members in the barracks, were moved to another compound. There was almost no communication with them for a long time. They weren't exactly punished, but they were supposed to feel disgraced. We made up our own joke about all this. We called each other "good boys" and "bad boys." "Bad boys" weren't allowed to work for some time. Some punishment!

There was a small personal loss in this for me, however. One of the escapees owed me a can of Red Cross butter.

As the liberating forces of Gen. Douglas MacArthur closed in on the Philippines, the Japanese, in May and June 1944, moved nearly 1,200 POWs from Davao back to Cabanatuan. The 800 who remained worked on details around Davao City or Lasang. In September these men boarded a Japanese freighter and began a journey that ended in Sindangan Bay. Today, Davao Penal Colony continues to be a Filipino institution for long-term convicts. It has changed very little since World War II.

9
INCIDENT AT SINDANGAN BAY

Pfc. CLETIS OVERTON:

It was about the 1st of August 1944 that the Americans first bombed the airstrip.* The Japs kept us locked up for two weeks so that we couldn't see the damage. Then they cut our rations to practically below starvation diet. About a month earlier a large group of us had been moved from Davao to the coastal port of Lasang and put to work building an airfield.† Our detail was assigned to break up the coral that the Japs were using to pave the runway. Midsummer on Mindanao is brutal. The heat just presses you down.

Pfc. VICTOR MAPES:

I wore nothing the whole time I was at Lasang but a G-string. Like everybody else, I was burned black; my feet were covered with torn calluses; and I weighed about 100 pounds. On account of the glare off the white coral, I couldn't see very well either. Also, I had a three-tone beard: inside, it was coffee color; in the middle, it was the color of raisins; and finally, where it had been bleached by the sun, it was white.

As a matter of fact, I think it was this beard that helped me when I got into the water. I hadn't shaved it off because I had long before traded away my razor blades.

We washed in one of the local mudholes. Actually, all we were doing was throwing dirty water on each other, but at least we moved the dirt from one end to the other, and it made us feel a little better. Occasionally, before it got too tough, they took us down to the river, and we'd use sand to scrape the crud off each other. That was the only way we kept clean, except for once in a while when a good rain would come by. Then we'd get a real bath, just standing underneath the eaves of the hut, letting that fresh warm water fall on us.

After we had been bombed we were locked up for weeks.

---

* The 5th Air Force began attacks on the Japanese airfields around Davao in early August 1944.
† Lasang is a small port ten miles south of the Davao Penal Colony.

There was no way of telling at that time what was going to happen to us. Obviously we knew the American forces were getting nearer. Some even thought we were going to be liberated soon.

Pfc. CLETIS OVERTON:

The guards finally came around and started taking amebic dysentery cultures. We surmised then that they were going to move us somewhere.

Pfc. VICTOR MAPES:

All of a sudden one morning, they gave us a breakfast of carabao meat and told us we were moving out.

Pfc. CLETIS OVERTON:

The rumor was we were going to be taken off. Maybe a Japanese guard had gotten some word and had passed it on to one of our boys. Anyway, after laying around starving for about twenty days, we were lined up in columns of four. Then the Japs ran a rope all the way around the column. They tied half-hitch loops around our arms, and if we weren't careful walking, we got all tangled up. They herded us that way through the town and when we reached the dock, they untied us.

Pfc. VICTOR MAPES:

You couldn't help noticing in our group the boys who had been on Bataan. They were all carrying canteens. They'd been on the March and they knew the importance of water. I envied them —I didn't have a canteen.

Pfc. CLETIS OVERTON:

There was a freighter sitting just off shore. I remember it being a good-size ship. I never knew her name, but she had a big number 86 painted on her side.

Pfc. VICTOR MAPES:

We waded out to her, and then climbed up landing nets to reach the deck. Because we were so starved, we could hardly make the climb. The net gave and bounced, and I just barely made it. Then, down into the hold I went. They were loading 650 men from our Lasang detail and about 150 more from the logging detail into this freighter's two cargo holds. We were just jammed in. We'd hardly gotten in when pandemonium

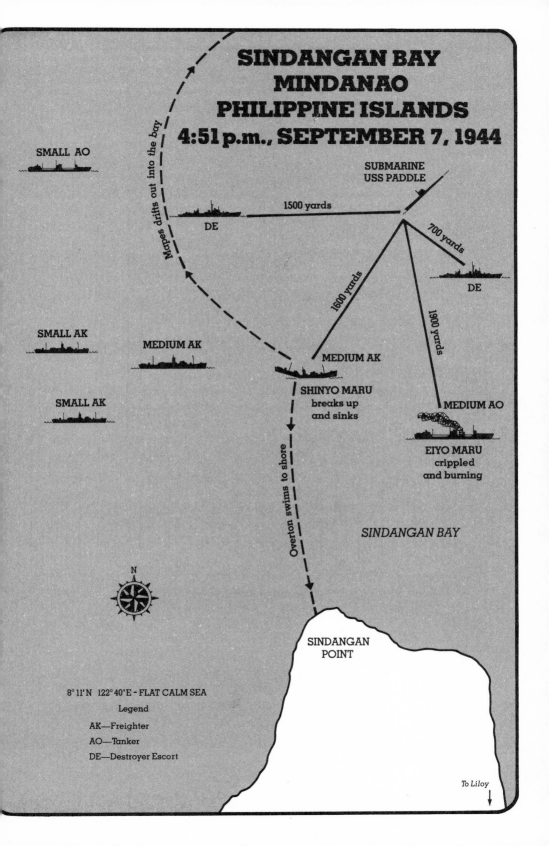

SINDANGAN BAY
MINDANAO
PHILIPPINE ISLANDS
4:51 p.m., SEPTEMBER 7, 1944

SMALL AO

Mapes drifts out into the bay

SUBMARINE
USS PADDLE

1500 yards

DE

700 yards

DE

1600 yards

1900 yards

SMALL AK

MEDIUM AK

MEDIUM AK

SHINYO MARU
breaks up
and sinks

MEDIUM AO

SMALL AK

EIYO MARU
crippled
and burning

Overton swims to shore

SINDANGAN BAY

N

SINDANGAN
POINT

8° 11'N 122° 40'E - FLAT CALM SEA

Legend

AK—Freighter

AO—Tanker

DE—Destroyer Escort

To Liloy

broke loose, and we started fighting like a bunch of wild animals.

Pfc. CLETIS OVERTON:

There was no organization. We were on our own. Guys were hollering for "Joe" or "Bill." Everyone was trying to find his buddy. We just climbed over each other. They stacked us in like sardines. There wasn't even room for all of us to sit down at the same time.

Pfc. VICTOR MAPES:

You might say there were a few leaders—mostly the natural kind. There was a Catholic priest, some West Pointers, and a guy who was a self-appointed bouncer. An officer's rank didn't mean anything. We knew we were on our own. We finally quieted down out of sheer exhaustion, and for a while we were able to keep some semblance of order. It was terribly hot down there, maybe 120 degrees, and you could see steam in the air from our sweaty bodies.

Pfc. CLETIS OVERTON:

Then they put the hatch covers over us.

Pfc. VICTOR MAPES:

Shortly afterwards they got underway. We had one hell of a ride. They had battened down the hatches, and we tore off through some rough water. That old boat was pitching and rolling, and we were thrown every which way. After a few hours, some of the men started passing out from the heat, others were yelling for the last rites. We didn't know if this was going to be the end for us or not. Everyone was screaming and yelling. Finally, the Japanese opened up the hatch, pointed machine guns at us, showed us hand grenades, and told us to keep quiet. Then they closed the hatches again.

Pfc. CLETIS OVERTON:

The toilet facilities in each of the holds were two empty oil barrels. The Japs would raise and lower them on ropes. Four small barrels for 800 men, many with dysentery!

Pfc. VICTOR MAPES:

I was getting dehydrated. At first, when we were able to sweat, steam from our bodies would form on the steel plates of the hold. I got so I could throw my old T-shirt up so that it would absorb moisture from the plates. Then I'd rub myself with the dampness. After they gave us our tiny water ration, we'd perspire a little bit immediately, but that was it. We didn't have a need to urinate but once in a great while.

Once a day, the Japs would lower a five-gallon can of water. We organized ourselves into groups of ten. Each group got to fill up one canteen. From that canteen we each got eight GI spoonfuls of water, then we fought over who got to lick the last spoon or got the last drip from the canteen.

My buddy and I shared his canteen. We'd drink half our water and pour the rest in the canteen, saving some to last us to the next time we got our ration. Before long, there were desperate men everywhere. Once I saw a Catholic priest give his ration away. There were also some phony "desperates" who yelled for water. I knew they weren't in any worse shape than anyone else.

I heard they drank blood in other ships. In ours, they drank urine. I saw it done and it almost caused a murder. When one guy passed out his buddy drank his water. Then he pissed in the empty canteen, hoping his pal wouldn't know the difference when he woke up. When the guy came to, he took a couple of swallows of what he thought was his water. When he realized what had happened, he tried to kill the other guy.

Everybody was having a hard time. Another guy went crazy and kept yelling, "Get thee behind me, Satan!" Some of the men around him were afraid his yelling would make the Japs fire down into us like they said they would. So they tied this poor fellow up. He couldn't understand why he deserved this kind of treatment. Everytime he'd begin to yell, the men around him would hit him with their canteens. You could hear him yell, "Get thee . . ." then *whack!* The next morning I crawled over to take a look at the poor fellow. He was laying there, tied and semiconscious. I don't know whatever happened to him.

We would get our water once a day around noon. We usually got our little dab of rice then, too. I found by experimenting that I could build myself up to use several spoonfuls of sea water in my rice. I saw boys almost die drinking sea water, but I built myself up to it. The salt flavored the rice, and I also got moisture that way. It helped. Occasionally, the Japs would hose us down, to clean up the stench. It felt good for a little bit, but then the salt would dry and cause more dehydration. But that's when I was able to get the salt water for my rice.

Pfc. CLETIS OVERTON:

We were on this freighter for several days when we stopped. The whole works just stopped. We sat there for several days, wondering where the hell we were. The Japs had gotten real nasty and hadn't emptied our crappers for some time. Our honey buckets got so honeyed that when the Japs finally hauled them up, they couldn't bring themselves to empty them. They ordered some of our men to go up and dump them. We got some Navy men to go up on deck, figuring if they could get a look around they might know where we were. That's how we learned we were in Zamboanga Harbor.

Pfc. VICTOR MAPES:

It got quite miserable there in that harbor, in that hold.

Pfc. CLETIS OVERTON:

Suddenly, the Japs gave an order to come on deck. We climbed out on top and were hosed down with sea water. Then they made us walk over a plank onto another ship that was tied next to ours. They put us right in the hold of this other ship and battened down the hatches. I knew that if this ship were bombed, there was no way for us to get out. We got underway that same day.

Pfc. VICTOR MAPES:

About midafternoon of the second or third day, there was a big commotion on deck. Then I heard some rifle fire. Through the slats of the hatch cover, I could see a Jap bugler blowing an alert. It reminded me of Gunga Din. Then some real firing started, and there was lots of panic around me. Next thing I knew, I was under water. I wasn't scared or anything. I felt this was it; I'd given up:*

Pfc. CLETIS OVERTON:

I heard an explosion. Then another. The next thing I knew I was in the water. People were kicking and drowning all around me. I struggled to keep my head above water. I couldn't see how I was going to live. I kept going under and coming up. When I'd come up, I could hear all this screaming. Everyone

---

* On Sept. 7, 1944, the American submarine Paddle (SS 263), during its fifth war patrol, torpedoed and sank the Japanese freighter Shinyo Maru in Sindangan Bay. According to Paddle's log, the attack took place at 1451 hours.

was struggling hard, back and forth. I'd just get my head up when someone would pull me back under—drowning men will grab onto anything.

Two things went through my mind: one was that my parents and friends wouldn't ever know what happened to me; and the other was that I couldn't think of anything I'd done that was of any particular good. I felt that if the Lord saw fit to get me out of there somehow, I'd always give Him credit.

Without my realizing it, the ship had begun to list. The hatch cover had been blown off and the water flooded in from the deck which was now awash. When I floated up to the deck I was flushed over the side. There was a Japanese machine-gun crew still working on the deck. As I floated off, I could hear the rattling of the gun. They were trying to shoot us as we came out of the hold. I was also aware of the ship's whistle. It just kept blowing. I remembered that a sinking ship causes a suction, so I began swimming away. When I turned around, I could see the freighter turned over and sinking from one end. But I couldn't tell which end it was. I also saw that it had been in a convoy and there were other ships around us. When I turned in the other direction, I could see the outline of green mountains. They were about two miles away.

Pfc. VICTOR MAPES:

I was under water, when I got shoved against a pipe that went through the ballast up towards the deck. Above me, frozen to the pipe, was a fellow I knew. I tried to shake him loose but he wouldn't budge. I had to leave him. I was running out of air. Finally, I popped to the surface. It was semidark in the hold. Some barracks bags were floating, and a few men were floundering around, gasping. Some of them were still way back, underneath. There was timber and things like that floating and the water was rising. You could hear the ship's whistle blowing constantly, like a wounded animal. I had to keep shoving debris away from me. There were bodies all around me. I just kept floating upwards. When I reached the deck my leg got caught underneath a girder. The water had reached the deck, but I couldn't move. I just floated there. Then the ship lurched sideways. I heard the crunch of solid bone breaking. I knew I had broken my leg.

This freed me, as my legs hung loose. The ship began to split apart, and the water pushed me in a rush through a crack. As I was forced through by the boiling water, I saw some Japs shooting at us from a lifeboat. The water carried me close to them, and I saw this Jap aiming right at me. I just didn't want to see myself shot, so I turned my head away. He fired, and the guy next to me floundered. He slumped over and slid past me. By the time the Jap could fire again, I was away.

I remember thinking about all kinds of things. I had read Lowell Thomas's *Raiders of the Deep* and about how this character had to avoid the superstructure of a sinking ship. I thought about that and swam as best I could away from the ship. How in hell I would ever remember something I hadn't thought about since high school I can't say.

Pfc. CLETIS OVERTON:

As I began to swim towards the mountains, I came upon two other guys. We decided to build a raft from all the floating debris around us. When we spotted something we thought might be useful, we salvaged it and threw it on our raft. I grabbed a Jap medical kit and a canteen half full of water. A little later I saw a carton about the size of an ammunition box. When I swam over to it, I found it contained fourteen cans of pork and beans and some soap.

Around sunset I heard shots, and we saw a Jap motor launch gathering up survivors and shooting into the water. We concluded they were picking up their own and shooting us. Figuring we had a better chance alone, we split up. Most of the night, I kept kicking towards shore. I could see it in the moonlight. While it was still dark, I got to land. White waves were washing up and down this cliff I was in front of. I eased myself up onto a boulder and sat down. Right about then I heard whistling, but I couldn't see anyone

I realized someone was whistling at me. I couldn't see them but they could see me. I finally made my way towards the sound and found three guys huddled in a cave. They weren't much better off than me. I hadn't had any shoes for months. Years! The Japanese had taken mine at Davao. All I had on when I got on that ship was a pair of blue cut-offs. When I hit the water, I lost everything. In the cave I made a G-string from a life preserver I had picked up.

The next morning we ran into some friendly native Filipinos who told us about the American guerrilla organization in that area. The Filipinos went around gathering up all the American survivors off that ship. We were assembled and then farmed out to different families.

Pfc. VICTOR MAPES:

In the water it seemed I was in a different world. Just coming out of the darkness of the hold into the sunshine made it seem strange. I noticed a floating hatch cover. It was fairly close, and there were about fifteen men draped across it or holding on to it. Some of the guys were yelling. Others had blood coming out of their ears and mouths. A few were having a big time, acting like nothing had happened.

I knew it was impossible for this hatch cover to hold so many men, but I struggled over to it. Someone helped me on board. Then I noticed that my broken leg was bleeding. The ship was about to go under, and my greatest fear was being sucked under. She did, in fact, draw us back when she went down. The whistle blew till the ship was out of sight. Then there were a lot of big geysers and bubbles. The Jap lifeboat which had been firing at us as we floated out of the cargo hold made no attempt to get away and was pulled down with the freighter. They just kept firing until they went down. Suddenly it became very quiet. All I could hear were Americans talking.

On the raft, Captain Cleveland came over to me and looked at my leg. The numbness was wearing off, and it had begun to hurt a little. I noticed there were bones sticking through the skin. Cleveland made a halfway sort of tourniquet out of his belt, then he fashioned a splint from some flotsam and tied it around the leg with my G-string.

There was a freighter nearby which had run aground during the attack on the convoy. They were firing at any American in range. It seemed to me that if we were to get to shore, we would have to float or swim near that ship. I noticed that a buddy of mine, Mike Pulice from the 200th Coast Artillery, also had a broken leg. We talked about what we could do if we were attacked. With our bad legs we knew we couldn't defend ourselves. We also knew that there were so many men on our raft that eventually the grounded freighter would begin to fire on us. About the time Pulice and I decided to go off on our own, I saw this fish face in the water. Floating in his life jacket was a stunned Jap. The men started arguing about what to do with him. Finally, it was decided that we would kill him with his own bayonet. I kept asking him in Japanese to give me some water, *mizu kudahsai*. He just kept shaking his head. Since I was past doing anything like stabbing him, I reached under the water and grabbed his canteen. I didn't think about killing him, all I thought of was his water. I then did the wrong thing. I drank all of his canteen. It was cold, weak tea like they usually carried. I should have saved some to carry with me, but instead I drank it all. Then my buddy Mike, who had the other bad leg, and I grabbed a floating spar and floated away from the raft. I looked back. The maimed and senseless were lying on it, and the rest, including some who were bleeding from the mouth, were holding on to the sides, half in and half out of the water.

Between us, Pulice and I had two good left legs. Figuring that two out of four wasn't all that bad, we began to kick with them. We hadn't swum very far when we found Colonel Colvert floating nearby. He was an old medical doctor from that Davao detail. I figured he had to be from New Mexico because Mike knew him. It was like a blessing from heaven. Here we are, floating around with two bad legs, and we run into a doctor. We asked Colonel Colvert if he was all right. Then we told him about our legs and asked him if he'd stay with us and fix us up when we got to shore. He refused, saying that his job was with all the maimed men we had left back on the hatch cover. He was sorry, but there was more of them for him to help. He continued swimming over to them. About ten minutes later I heard an explosion. The Jap freighter had put an artillery round into the raft. The hatch cover must have disintegrated, because from where I was I couldn't see anything left of it.

About now the sun was going down and it began getting dark. Mike was floating on half a lifesaver he had found. I was using an empty box. Then the Japs on another ship spotted us, and they opened up with rifles. I spun the box towards the Japs and got my head underwater. I could hear the bullets hitting around me. It sounded like nails hitting the water. I tried to submerge my whole body, but because of that damned wood splint, I couldn't get my legs under. They just floated. I was nicked in the ankle of my bad leg. When the firing stopped, there was no more Mike. It started getting real dark.

I made up my mind right then that if I ever had a chance to escape, this was it. But I knew that the worst time in the world to try to get away is when you have a busted leg. I continued to try to float on my box, but it was too small for me, and the darned thing kept bobbing up and down. Finally, I saw a big piece of timber go by. I started after it, but no matter how hard I kicked, I couldn't reach it. A current kept pushing it just out of my reach. No matter how hard I tried, I couldn't catch up to it. Then I noticed the current was moving at an angle from shore, so instead of going right at it, I came round and intersected it. When I finally grabbed it, I climbed on board. I'll tell you I was one happy individual! The night was black. A long way off I could hear gun shots and dogs barking from the shore.

In the distance across the bay, I saw a light on top of one of the mountains [Lanboyan Point]. I kept that as a bearing. At times I could see some stars. I knew I was being carried out to sea by the current.

After a while I heard *chug, chug, chug.* Out of the darkness came this damned Jap motor launch. I started praying. I slid off my board and got behind it, real low. I could see the ears of the Jap riflemen in the bow. The clouds kept moving across the moon. It looked like they were coming right at me. When it was almost on top of me, they yelled and veered off. I don't know how they missed seeing me. Anyhow, I felt lucky as all get out, but I lost my damn timber. The launch went one way and my board went the other. I got very lonesome about then.

I did a little more praying and floundering. Pretty soon a board, about the size of a large table, came by. When I got close to it, I saw it was two sets of boards nailed together with most of the nails sticking out of it. With no alternative, I grabbed it. When I managed to climb on, the damned nails tore my chest. When I couldn't stand that pain, I'd get back in the water where the current would grate my legs back and forth. It was just regular torture, my leg killing me in the water, the nails killing me on the board. Back and forth I went, changing only when I couldn't stand one pain or the other. I kept awake all night that way.

Then it began to rain, and I found a floating palm frond. I stuck it in my mouth and used it to help me catch and swallow some water. I looked like a big bird with that leaf sticking out of my mouth. But I did catch more water with it. Towards dawn, the pain in my leg was so bad that I prayed for a shark to come by and bite it off.

As it got lighter, I made out a small boat a long way away. I began to shout and yell but no one heard me. I knew the current was taking me towards it. Soon I was able to see that it was a native boat. So I began yelling again. Suddenly, it just took off and left me.

As morning broke and the sun came up, the sky became overcast. It must have been around midmorning when the current began to push me toward shore. I knew I was getting closer, because I could see the water turning green. I was still in deep blue water, but I could see where it was getting shallow.

The sun began to break through the haze. I had gone through about three miles of oil the afternoon before, and I had all this oil in my beard. It acted as a buoy and helped me keep my head up. But my butt had been washed clean, and when the hot sun began blazing down, I started to burn. The leg splint was holding me on top of the water, and I was getting a very bad sunburn on my rear.

When I could think ahead, all I wanted was to get to shore,

drink some coconuts, and hide. Then I'd figure out something else. When I got up close and was floating in the green water, I could see a small shack and something moving. It looked like a dog. I began moving towards the breakers when a Jap observation plane with two pontoons began flying in circles not far from where I was. I put on some speed, what little I had, to get into the white water. While I was in the swells, an outrigger canoe with two men came racing out. They came alongside and pulled me over the side. They gave me a holey T-shirt to cover myself up with. Then the Japanese plane found us and gave us a burst of machine-gun fire. My paddlers started yelling like hell. They hit the crest of a large wave like a surfboard, and we flew onto the shore. I didn't know what they were going to do, but I felt they might leave me. As the plane circled round for another run at us, my rescuers picked up the damned outrigger, with me in it, and carried it under a large palm tree. They started jabbering to each other. I knew some Spanish and some dialect, and they knew some English, so we began speaking a little to each other. They assured me that I was still on Mindanao. I had landed at Sindangan Bay, just 300 miles from where I boarded the first freighter. This startled me. I thought I might be in Indochina. They then began to treat my leg with some white powder they told me was sulfathiazole. They said they had gotten it from an American submarine. I didn't believe them. I asked if I could see one of their short rifles. They refused, but showed me "43" on their ammunition. I knew then they must have been telling me the truth about the submarine, because all the ammunition we ever had on Bataan was about 1941 or before. The carbine really interested me because I had never seen one before.

When the float plane lost interest in us, the Filipinos decided to move me into a shack. Man, I was just dying of thirst and pretty soon here comes a coconut shell of water. I wanted that water so bad. They held me in their arms and fed me spoonfuls of it. Then—I could smell it first—they fed me a bowl of cornmeal and chicken gruel. The family that lived in the shack kept peeking in at me, like I was a freak or something.

I began to recuperate a little, when into the shack come a couple of Filipinos telling a wild tale. They'd seen a ghost in a nearby cornfield, and they were all shook up about it. Come to find out, it was one of my fellow prisoners wandering around, a fellow out of the 30th Squadron from Utah. When the Filipinos brought him in, he was stark naked except for a straw hat, and a clay jug of water he was carrying. When he saw me he said, "Hey, Mapes, who am I?" Up to that moment I knew his name like I knew my own, but at that moment I couldn't think of it. He didn't worry about me or ask how I was. The only thing he had on his mind was who he was. I asked him where he was going, and he replied that he was just going to keep going until he remembered his name. I told the natives to watch him and to try to help him if they could. He wandered off down the beach, and I hoped that Jap float plane wouldn't come back and see him. I was very concerned for him. Pretty soon he came back with a big smile on his face, "Hey, I know who I am, I'm Lorton!" Then I remembered, too, and we just started laughing.

That night we got split up when the natives moved us. They gently put me in a burlap bag tied at both ends to a pole which they carried. It was like being in a hammock. My leg was giving me real trouble. They eventually moved me in a big coaster, south, where the guerrillas were gathering us together. I ended up in a schoolhouse in the little barrio of Sindangan. It was there that a man named Pratchard died. He lay on the floor next to me. He had internal injuries, but the natives didn't know how to treat him. He died, just lying next to me.

Pfc. CLETIS OVERTON:

I had landed at Liloy.* When the guerrillas first assembled us, they couldn't feed all of us. And more kept coming in each day. To solve their problem, the Filipinos farmed us out in small groups to different families. I stayed with Francisco Capanong and his wife. After two weeks, a runner arrived telling us that our group was to make its way to Sindangan where Colonel McGee, one of the guerrilla officers in the area, was going to take charge of us and arrange to get us out on a submarine. McGee had been at Cabanatuan and Davao with me and I learned now that he had escaped by jumping off a Jap ship in Zamboanga Harbor.† Then he'd joined Fertig's guerrilla organization. I knew him to be a very fine officer.

Pfc. VICTOR MAPES:

I ended up on top of a mountain with my buddy Mike Pulice, who had the other bad leg and who I was separated from after the Japs fired on us in the water. While we lay in this mountain hut, the Filipinos sent up a boy named Clarence who, with a one-string coconut shell instrument, attempted to entertain us

---

* Liloy, on the west coast of Mindanao, is a barrio at the southern tip of Sindangan Bay.
† In early June 1944, Lt. Col. John Hugh McGee escaped from the ship that was carrying the Davao Penal Colony detail back to Luzon.

while we waited. The natives fed us green bananas, eggs, and carabao milk. Some woman even donated human milk, figuring it might help my leg. I lay there with just leaves packed on it, and it got bigger and bigger and smellier and smellier. When I had to go to the john, I would use half a coconut shell to defecate in, and the Filipinos would throw it out. It was a terrible ordeal up there. Not the worse of the whole deal was my beard. It was so full of sand and oil that I couldn't lift my head. To give me some help, they started to shave the damn thing off. Unfortunately, instead of a razor, they used a dull mess-kit knife. It was torture. Without my beard the bottom of my face was all white. I looked awful.

Day after day I lay there in pain, my leg aching. Each night seemed an eternity. I felt like I lay up on that mountain a thousand years, this thing hurting me so bad. I don't think I got more than two hours sleep in three weeks. Finally, I felt something down there, something crawling. Maggots had gotten in and were crawling all over the wound.

Once in a while we were visited by a doctor. Without supplies he couldn't do much, but he was trying. Finally, he came in one day whistling. In his hand he carried a doggone wood saw. I looked at Mike and he looked at me, and we both wondered whose leg was going to be amputated. We knew that without a miracle, sooner or later, our legs were going to have to be cut off. It was just a matter of time. This day he had the saw, and all I could think of was that he didn't have any anesthesia. In fact, he didn't have anything but this old saw. Pretty soon he sat down and began sawing some bamboo splints. That's how I learned we were going to be moved off the mountain.

The guerrillas came up the next day and put me on a sled attached to a carabao. The whole thing reminded me of an Indian travois. The ground was very rough and I remember, as I went through a coconut grove, watching the coconuts going up and down. Boy, I took an awful beating. My leg drove me almost crazy. The Filipino doctor had given me a cigar just before we started down. He told me it would help me out. I think now it must have been opium because it eventually deadened me, made me real sleepy. As I was lighting up this cigar a Jap fighter raid came overhead. The Filipinos threw some brush over me, unhooked the carabao, and ran into the jungle. The fighters made several strafing runs on the trail, I was told. I don't remember, because I had gone to sleep. The first real rest I had in weeks was right in the middle of an air raid!

The agony of moving went on and on, so that when we finally reached the beach, I couldn't believe it.

Pfc. CLETIS OVERTON:

When we had all been rounded up on the beach, there were just eighty-one of us left. One had died after reaching shore, and another volunteered to stay with the guerrillas as a radio man. At the dock at Lasang there had been nearly 800 of us. Mapes was one of the last to arrive. You could tell looking at him that he had had a tough time. His leg was mangled. Oh, he was in terrible shape.

Pfc. VICTOR MAPES:

Then they got ready to set my leg. Six men got hold of me and pulled that leg. I yelled. You could hear me for miles. I didn't cry. I yelled. They tried to pull it back to where it was supposed to be, to straighten it out so that it would fit on board the submarine.

Pfc. CLETIS OVERTON:

The word got out that a submarine was due. We weren't sure how many of us it could carry, so we drew numbers from a hat, one to one hundred. The lower numbers we knew would get on, and as we went higher we knew the odds got slimmer and slimmer. I drew number seventy-two. I didn't figure my chances were much.

Pfc. VICTOR MAPES:

I finally got some luck. I drew number one. We waited all night and it didn't show. We were moved the next day, north, to Sirai Bay. Again we waited throughout the night for the submarine to appear and again we were disappointed. I began to lose my patience. I thought this whole thing was a bunch of hogwash. We were dreaming, if we thought we were going to get out of here. On September 29, the third night, Captain Thomas, who had taken command of the shore party, lit two big bonfires. Then the guerrillas unfurled an American flag behind the fire so it could be seen. We waited. Pretty soon, the damnedest thing you ever saw, here came this submarine that looked to me like a battleship. I couldn't believe there was a submarine in the whole world that big. I learned later it was the *Narwhal*.*

I was lying on the beach with a splint holding my torn leg together. The doctor was telling me a few last things, and I

---

* The Narwhal (SS 167) regularly operated out of Australia. The night of Sept. 29, 1944, during her fourteenth war patrol, she "received 81 liberated prisoners of war."

was thanking him and giving him a shirt that I had when in comes this yellow boat. Mind you, it was yellow! Seems to me that they'd have picked a darker color. And then I saw the biggest guy I ever saw in my life. He looked like a monster. He was wearing a pair of blues, naked to the waist, and as white as a lily. He looked like a ghost to me. He was so non-chalant about getting on shore. When he walked over to me, he told me he was glad to see me. "Man," I said, "you ain't half as glad as I am! Let's get going."

"Wait a minute," he said, "I've got something to do . . . ," and he walked away. I thought he had to go to the bathroom. You know what that son-of-a-gun did? He went down the beach and wiggled his toes in the sand. Here I'm all shook, thinking that damned sub will sink or something, and he turns to me and tells me how good solid ground feels.

They finally fitted me into this little rubber dinghy and we started. About halfway to the sub we got passed by some native outrigger canoes, like it was Tahiti or someplace. It was a mad house, everybody racing for the submarine. My guy's just going along, paddling real easy. Finally, I asked him if we couldn't get one of these outrigger canoes to give us a tow. He thought it was a good idea. So he threw the lead canoe a rope and that's how I got to the sub before everyone else.

Now they have to get me aboard, and frankly with my leg the way it was, they hadn't any idea how to do it. Their skipper's * first thought was to load me through a torpedo tube. Finally he had a hoist built and they lowered me through the conning tower. These Navy guys tried to be careful, but getting me through and down that narrow opening was terrible. They kept bumping my bad leg. I eventually ended up on a bunk in the forward torpedo room.

Pfc. CLETIS OVERTON:

They moved Mapes and the other guy with the broken leg out first. Then the ensign in charge of the beach party asked our CO how many of us there were. "Eighty-one," he replied. A signalman flashed the sub and they flashed back. I held my breath. The ensign told us that that was fine and they could take all of us. Hearing this was like being born again.

Pfc. VICTOR MAPES:

When everyone was on board, the sailors came around taking food orders. We could have anything we wanted. You know, I

* Commander J. C. Titus.

couldn't think of a thing. Finally, I said, "A peanut-butter sandwich and tomato soup." Of all things! They had everything— steak, ice cream—and I ask for peanut butter and tomato soup. It was just that I was so dumbfounded by the request.

Pfc. CLETIS OVERTON:

These sailors were great big robust fellows. When we started comparing our condition with theirs, we began to realize what really bad condition we were in. When you have only other POWs to look at, you forget what healthy looks like.

Pfc. VICTOR MAPES:

The next morning Jim Green, an old buddy of mine, came around and began to look after me. He told me that there was plenty to eat and that I had to begin eating. I told him I was too sick to eat, that I hurt too much. "Well," he said, "you're going to eat some pancakes." And he fed me by the spoonful. I got so sick. For the next five days I don't remember eating another thing. The gangrene was eating me up, just poisoning me.

The submarine's pharmacist's mate built me a traction splint, but that's all he could do. The guerrillas had sent a young Filipino doctor along so he could treat us while we were on board. He got seasick and stayed sick all the way to New Guinea. He wasn't worth a damn. The Navy boys had to help him, he was so sick. He couldn't even walk.

My leg was all swollen and the smell was so bad that the men in the torpedo room with me hated being there. I knew they hated just having to pass near me. I was alone much of the time. I had a hell of a fever, but I wasn't so sick that I didn't know what was going on. But I was sick enough to get ready to die. I knew I couldn't last too much longer. I just held on.

Pfc. CLETIS OVERTON:

Being in a submarine was a very strange experience. I was very apprehensive about the whole thing. Whenever they had to dive they'd sound something like a model T horn, *ugah . . . ugah,* and then there'd be all this spewing and hissing as the sub dove. The day after we were taken aboard, the sub sounded the *ugah,* there was the usual spewing, and we started going down and the angle got steeper and steeper. We began to slide off our bunks and roll around.

Pfc. VICTOR MAPES:

We were almost vertical. The sailors in the forward torpedo room rolled out of their cots, some feet first, some head first. I was thrown up against a bulkhead. The sailors around me were on their hands and knees, and some of them were crossing themselves. I thought, "Oh oh, this is apparently not normal, even for these guys."

Pfc. CLETIS OVERTON:

We kept diving like this until we finally leveled off. A sailor told us a little later that the systems that controlled the outside diving planes had not functioned properly, and the captain had to use an emergency procedure to stop our dive.* From then on every time I heard *ugah* my stomach hurt.

The rest of the voyage was relatively smooth and six days after we left Sirai Bay we landed at Mios Wendi, Dutch New Guinea [Oct. 5, 1944].

Pfc. VICTOR MAPES:

Some of the guys came by and shook hands with me. They were leaving me there to die.

Pfc. CLETIS OVERTON:

I just didn't think Vic would live. When I left him, his leg was as big as a basketball. It had turned black and it smelled like a rotten horse.

Pfc. VICTOR MAPES:

It was a weird feeling when they left. I knew they knew they would never see me again. I felt I was going to die, too. I really

---

* Commander Titus's report to the Commander of Task Force 72 describes the particulars of this very unusual dive on 30 September.

1518 Radar contact 22 miles, closing to 17, then faded out. Aircraft contact No. 10. Acts like a float plane on A/S patrol.

1522 Contact returned at 12 miles, closing.

1523 Submerged. Lost power on stern planes with planes on 20° dive due to inability of motor to move planes at low voltage. Could not get angle off planes in hand power. The stern planes have been getting progressively worse since last refit (July, 1944) when emergency repairs were made to correct this same trouble. Ship took a 20° down angle. Blew all main ballast and backed emergency, succeeding in stopping her at 170 feet, probably the fastest dive she ever made. This condition <u>must</u> be rectified. Venting all ballast tanks and going ahead emergency was not sufficient to prevent broaching stern first at 1525. Radar obtained a range of 1 mile on the plane, with indications of rapid maneuvers to get into position.

1526 Back to 90 feet, changed course to the right. No bombs so we must have surprised him as much as we did ourselves.

knew I didn't have much longer to live. It was a matter of maybe an hour or two.

They moved me to this Wendi field hospital and a Navy commander took me in hand. The first thing he did was put ice packs on me to start getting the fever down. I still was too sick to eat, though. They say that when you quit eating, you're getting ready to die. My doctor told me I had to eat. I told him I couldn't. "Eat it," he told me, "and throw it up. But eat!" I did this for three or four days. I'd eat and vomit, eat and vomit. After a lot of this, damned if my appetite didn't catch on. Then they had penicillin. I'd never heard of the stuff. That's what really saved me. That and the good Navy doctors down there in Mios Wendi who stayed with me day and night working on my leg. After a week and many medical consultations, it was decided I could keep my leg, at least until I was sent to Australia.

Pfc. CLETIS OVERTON:

At the Naval hospital we shaved and showered, had clean uniforms issued, and were fed all the time. From there, they moved us to another part of the island that had an airstrip. Then they flew us to the 42nd Field Hospital in Brisbane, Australia. Flying somewhere between New Guinea and Australia, we saw a big armada of ships below us. From our height they looked like toys. There was lots of comment about how many ships there were. Several days after we had landed in Brisbane, we picked up a newspaper and read that MacArthur had invaded Leyte.*

* The U.S. 6th Army invaded the central Philippine island of Leyte on Oct. 20, 1944.

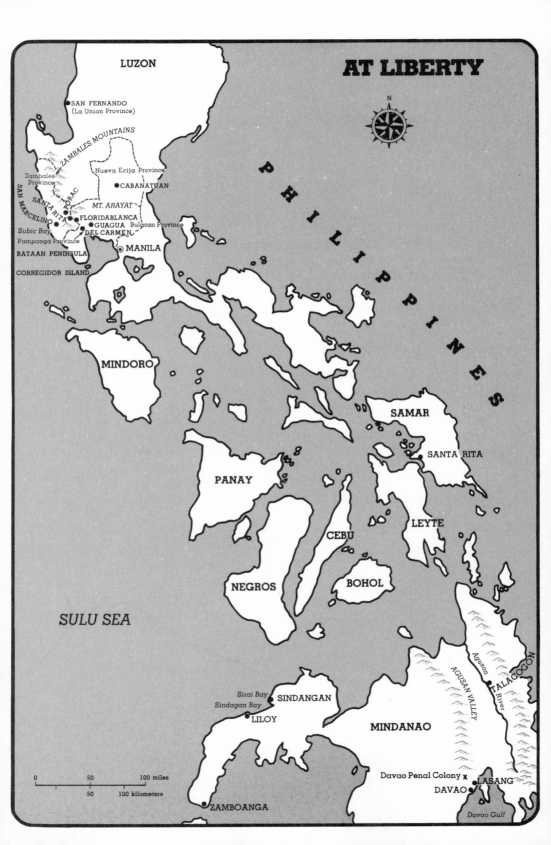

10
AT LIBERTY

During the withdrawal on Luzon in December 1941, many small units of General MacArthur's forces moving into Bataan became separated from their commands. These groups became the nuclei of guerrilla organizations that formed almost immediately. Leon Beck, who had escaped from the Death March at Lubao, became attached to a band of USAFFE Guerrillas that operated in western Pampanga and southern Zambales Provinces. The control of this command, and eventually various other units that operated in west central Luzon, was under General Wainwright's former supply officer, Lt. Col. Gyles Merrill, 26th Cavalry (P.S.).

Blair Robinett of the 803d Engineers escaped the March south of Guagua and joined the Hukbo ng Bayan Laban sa Hapon (People's Army against the Japanese), popularly known as the Hukbalahap or simply "the Huks." This was a politico-military organization, Communist-led and -directed, but attractive to many non-Communists owing to its strong opposition to the Japanese. It was one of the largest and most powerful guerrilla organizations operating in central Luzon. It owed no allegiance to the United States.

Because of problems that Private Beck, late of the 31st Infantry, had with the leadership of his guerrilla unit, he spent much of the war "free-lancing." It was therefore only natural that he and Private First Class Robinett should occasionally run into each other. This is the story of those meetings.

Pvt. LEON BECK:

The first important thing that happened, after I got on my feet following my escape from the Death March, was being sent to another camp where more Americans were hiding out. This camp was up in the mountains on the Pampanga side of the Zambales Mountains.* By virtue of his senior rank Colonel Merrill, who had also escaped and joined my little group, took over our command. In an attempt to consolidate our guerrilla efforts, he sent me with a letter addressed to the officers in that camp. Merrill ordered these men to accompany me back to the lowlands and report to him. I wouldn't say it was a dangerous mission, but it was easier for him to send a private than all those captains I was hanging around with. I was also picked because of my height. I was small like the Filipinos. Walking among a group of Filipinos I blended in, didn't tower over them. Lastly, I was willing to go. I needed something to do.

On the way to the mountains nothing eventful happened. That camp's whereabouts was pretty well-known. So well-known, in fact, that within three weeks of my starting back to Pampanga the Japanese raided the camp. They came in about daylight and raised hell with the men that remained behind. The officers that came down out of the mountains, along with those already with Merrill in Pampanga Province, were assigned different sectors to begin their guerrilla activities in. We became known as the USAFFE Guerrillas.

We rearmed ourselves by going back down into Bataan. We'd go over the battle areas picking up weapons, or scavenging parts to make new ones. We spent a lot of time cleaning and making weapons at first. That's how we got started.

At first we had some pretty good fire fights, if you call getting beat every time pretty good. I remember once being outside the barrio of Mexico when a battle broke out nearby. I got the message that the Huk squadrons engaged at Porac needed help. I ran about fifteen kilometers, double-time, to get into the fight. We did pretty well for about two hours. Then the Japs brought in more infantry and artillery by train from San Fernando. I want to tell you they did a real good job of kicking our butts. It took us all of that day and part of the night to get disengaged. I took a solemn oath right then that I would never again run to another fire fight. If it couldn't wait for me to walk to, it would have to go on without me.

There were about five squadrons in that fight at Porac.

* This camp was run by Arturo and Vicente Bernia and two Americans named Fawcett.

Squadrons were based on the number of automatic weapons we had. For two BARs [Browning Automatic Rifles] we based seventy or eighty men in support. Ideally, we tried to keep a squadron to about seventy-five men. If it got any larger, it would have caused a hell of a problem getting food. When a squadron would go into a barrio, the inhabitants were responsible for feeding it. The exact number of men fed per family would depend on how much food the barrio had. Often we'd just get a handful of rice and a green tomato.

We called our units "squadrons" because of old Colonel Merrill. He'd been a cavalryman all his military career. He had been commissioned on the Mexican border and had chased Pancho Villa with Pershing. Cavalry units are called squadrons. Consequently, our units used cavalry designations.

The Japs began to make things very hot for us around September of 1942, so Colonel Merrill decided to move his USAFFE Guerrilla headquarters from Pampanga Province to Zambales Province. He figured the mountains would afford us more protection than the flat lands we'd been in. Pampanga Province was also the territory of the Hukbalahap. Eventually we had almost as much trouble with the Huks as we did with the Japs, but that was later.

In the move up to the Zambales Mountains I was assigned to look after Colonel Merrill's horse, and it was then that I ran into my first bit of trouble. Even at this time Merrill was an old man and somewhat weaker than the rest of us. So taking his horse was natural, since it was easier for him to ride than to walk. The main reason, though, for Merrill having a horse was that, being a cavalry officer, he just felt better around horses. I don't know exactly how Colonel Merrill ended up with this particular crossbreed mare, but its owner had somehow gotten her out of Manila before the Japs arrived. She was a cross between a native horse and an Australian horse, and she used to race at the big Manila race track.

In our move to Zambales Province, Merrill rode his horse every day, but on one particular day, while we were curling around a mountain trail, we were hit by a torrential rainstorm. It was like a typhoon with all that wind and rain. The track got so bad that Merrill couldn't ride any more. After he dismounted, I was ordered to lead the mare until it stopped pouring. Things went along fine until we started down a particularly muddy trail. Suddenly, the mare and I began to slide. I grabbed for a tree to stop myself. This panicked the horse. She threw her head up and it was like a whip. I got caught on the jaw so hard it split my upper teeth lengthwise. Just split them right through. Of course it knocked me unconscious. When I came to, my eyes were swollen shut, and it was three months before I could turn my head.

Later, I got even with that nag. Over on the Zambales side a little native stud got to her, and in his act of penetration, skinned her. Blow flies got in and laid their eggs. She got all wormy. As I was still responsible for her, I roped and threw her. Then I took a straight razor and split the swelling open where all the infection and worms were. With a stick I scraped and swabbed her out good. Then I sewed her back up. When she healed, that mare looked like she had two snatches on her.

Pfc. BLAIR ROBINETT:

Colonel Merrill was a hell of a nice guy, but he was an old man. He had no business being in the Philippines. He had been in the Cavalry, and his damn hide was made out of saddle leather. He was the only man I'd ever seen who could sit out with his ,arms covered with mosquitoes, reading a book, without being at all bothered. He'd say they weren't biting. Like hell they weren't biting! Merrill was a fabulous individual. I lost contact with him when he went into the mountains. I stayed behind and began running with the Huks.

I didn't go into the mountains with Merrill because I couldn't see locking myself down to one spot and doing nothing. That was the idea Merrill had. He had been ordered by Mac-Arthur to offer only passive resistance to the Japs because of the retaliation possibilities. He was afraid the Japs would come down hard on civilians if the guerrillas began acting up. All MacArthur wanted the USAFFE Guerrillas to do was collect information. The Huks, on the other hand, were fighting for independence. It didn't make any difference to them who they fought, Americans, Filipinos, or Japs. But right then, it was the Japs that had center stage. A militant Communist organization grew steadily stronger in Luzon during the 1930s and when war came they had several hundred men under arms. While we were still fighting on Bataan, the Communist leadership on Luzon formed the Huks. After the Philippines surrendered, they recruited thousands of men. The major difference between USAFFE Guerrillas and Huk guerrillas is that the Huks fought the Japs and the USAFFE Guerrillas didn't. To me fighting was what it was all about. Hell, all I wanted to do was maintain civilian anger against the Japanese, and the best way to do that was for the Japs to beat the hell out of the civilians. I wanted retaliation. MacArthur wanted us to pat the Japs on the back and hold their damned hands. That way it was easier to become friends with them. Another thing, it may not be the proper way to look at things, but in the Philippines my neck was on the line, and as far as I was concerned, keeping my neck was the most important thing I was involved in. Therefore, in order to keep my head on my shoulders, the best thing I could do was keep the Japanese antagonized, and in return they would keep the Filipinos antagonized against them. That way the Japs wouldn't be looking just for me.

The Huks divided their organization into five Military Districts [MDs]. Squadrons made up battalions, battalions made up regiments, and regiments made up an MD. We operated basically in Pampanga, Nueva Ecija, Bataan, Zambales, and Bulacan Provinces. In October 1942 I was assigned to a Huk battalion which consisted of three squadrons or about 400 men which operated in the 1st MD.* We had our own intelligence, communication, ordnance, medical, and maintenance support systems. These units were completely organized. As we would move through the countryside, it was up to each barrio to support us while we stayed with them. To help stockpile our supplies, we taxed each barrio 10 percent. If a man sold a hog and got 100 pesos, the Huks would take ten pesos. If he harvested 100 bushels of rice, the Huks stockpiled ten bushels. Whatever amount of sugar cane ran through the local grinder, the Huks would take their 10 percent. What we gathered was put in storage or sold to buy medicine or equipment on the Manila black market.

We realized that we couldn't operate a successful guerrilla operation without the support of the local people. We found we could get that support two ways—through love or through fear. We worked on the principle that the Japanese were a bunch of bastards and that we would aid the peasants as much as we possibly could. We told them that it was to their benefit to aid the guerrilla movement. If they chose not to help, we were prepared to take out any opposition, tie their damn wrists to the nearest tree, and skin them. We found that all we had to do was skin one and everybody within five kilometers would back off.

I found out the Huks were Communists almost immediately. Once I joined my squadron I found that there would be political instructors coming to talk to us. Quite often it was part of the routine to assemble the squadron and let these organizers talk to the men. I didn't have any problems with this because one, they were killing Japs, and two, their harangues weren't worth a damn. The basic leadership was Communist,

---

* The Huk 1st Military District operated in southwestern Pampanga Province and was commanded by Bernardo Poblete.

but when it came down to that joker sitting out there with a rifle, he couldn't care less whether he was fighting capitalists, Communists, or Japs.

Each barrio had a lieutenant who kept things organized. Every barrio was given a number, like a zip code, and that number was put on all pieces of mail. We ran a pretty good postal system that way. In the Huks you could kiss a girl if you were engaged to her, but if you were caught in bed with her, you'd be staked out bare ass for three days. If you raped a woman, you were executed. We tried to be totally honest with everybody. Justice was quick and simple. Even though the Japs were bastards, the Japanese would not execute a Filipino unless they had overriding evidence that he had collaborated with the guerrillas. They might beat the hell out of him, but they wouldn't always kill him. The Huks, on the other hand, only needed a reasonable suspicion that a suspect had collaborated with the Japanese, or was a member of the Makapili,* for him to have a hell of a hard trip. Suspects were tried before they were picked up.

So many things happened in such a damn short space of time that I can't remember exact dates, but during 1942 and part of 1943 we had a girl named Felipa Culala who headed up the 2nd Military District, which was in the central part of Pampanga. The Japs had picked her up when they first moved in and had raped her. Then for the fun of it, they cut off one of her nipples.† As a consequence Culala didn't have much love for the Japanese, and she ended up being a very efficient guerrilla fighter. She eventually worked her way up from squadron commander to Military District leader, to member of the Military Committee. Her units were particularly aggressive against the Japs and she became something of a legend. But then we started hearing some damn rumors that she had begun to be more of a bandit than a guerrilla. The stories said that she was picking up wealthy individuals and holding them for ransom. Since we were not seeing any of this money, we assumed she was keeping it. The Military Committee decided the charges against her should be investigated. I was asked to pick some DIs‡ and throw them into her area. They found the charges were true. Reco 7 then sent in a special unit that arrested her.§ When

---

* A Japanese-sponsored organization of Filipinos who worked for the Japanese secret police, the Kempeitai.
† This story about Culala has not been verified by any other source and is, perhaps, part of the legend that surrounds her.
‡ Division Intelligence units, sometimes used for assassinations.
§ In late 1943 the Huks reorganized their Military Districts into larger organizational units called Regional Commands (Recos). Reco 7 had jurisdiction in Pampanga Province.

they searched her headquarters, they found maybe a quarter of a million dollars in gold and jewelry. We took all that loot, converted it to cash on the black market, and bought medical supplies with it. Culala was taken out and executed.

We also didn't trust the Philippine Constabulary [PC]. They were probably the world's worst police system. Many of them were also working with the Japanese authorities. They thought nothing of beating the hell out of a peasant and then stealing his chickens, eggs, pigs, or anything else they could use. So the Huks made it a point that everytime they picked up a member of the Constabulary who wasn't one of their people, they'd execute him. It was just that simple.

Once I was in a little barrio about five miles north of San Fernando with my bodyguards. I had about six at that time, and they were all heavily armed. They were there to protect me and they had no allegiance to anyone but me. Major Banal* was my commanding officer, but he didn't command my bodyguards. We'd gotten up to this safe barrio where we had never had any problems before. Most of my bodyguards came from this area, so that night I sent them home to visit their families. The next morning I was sitting having breakfast, when a kid about twelve came in and asked whether he could talk to me. "Sure," I said, "go ahead." "The PC are coming." I didn't get excited, I was having breakfast. "Near or far?" I asked. "Near." That still didn't worry me because I thought he meant about a kilometer away. "How near?" I asked after several more mouthfuls of food. He said, "Maybe 200 meters." Now 200 meters is not very far, especially when somebody's after your head. As quick as he said it, I came to my feet like a red hot cat, smacked my gun belts on, grabbed my submachine gun, and peeled out the back door. I ran into some tall cogon elephant grass and crossed a creek, getting one foot wet as I went. After running for a short while, I came up on the tracks of a small sugar cane railway spur. Here I made a mistake. Instead of stopping and checking out the line before I crossed, I jumped on the tracks and ran smack into about twelve PCs waiting on the rails. They gave out a yell and several of them threw their rifles to their shoulders. With nothing better to do I figured maybe they weren't all that bad and I tipped my hat back, letting them see I was an American. Then I swung my other arm around so they could see my machine gun. My

* Jose Banal was the nom de guerre of Maj. Bernardo Poblete, the commander of Reco 7. He was also known as Tandang Banal, which means old man Banal and refers to his advanced age. Poblete was a veteran of World War I and is said to have fought with Aguinaldo.

message was very direct—don't mess with me. It was, of course, pure bluff. It didn't work. Two of them fired at me. One bullet went past my ear, the other banged off the rails at my feet. I turned the Thompson loose, and I think I hit some of them. The others dove for the cogon grass. As soon as they scattered I doubled back, and this time when I hit the creek nothing touched water. I finally managed to get away. The PC, however, came through the barrio that I had been in, burned some houses, and shot the people they thought I had been staying with. Now this was done by the Philippine Constabulary who knew I was an American and who knew I was on the loose. I don't know if these particular PCs were working with USAFFE units, but I do know many were. It antagonized me no end to think that Americans were playing ball with the PC. To me, this was a bunch of bull. I knew USAFFE personnel that traveled with PC passes. You got to know, of course, USAFFE units weren't too happy with me or the Huks.

When MacArthur passed the word that the USAFFE Guerrillas were to stop fighting and to spend their time collecting intelligence, many USAFFE units had it soft. They wouldn't bother the Japs, and the Japs wouldn't bother them. Some of these USAFFE officers had a nice life, living in large houses out in Pampanga, sitting down each night to dinner served on silver plates with linen napkins. Well, all I had to do was knock off a Jap convoy, and the Japs would immediately begin sweeping the area. This made it very tough on the USAFFE groups. Things got hot for them. Eventually, because of our activity, we booted most of the Americans back into the mountains.

Now, Leon Beck was different. He was sort of a free lancer. Beck came and went as he wished. He was an outstanding individual. He'd back you down the line and he definitely wasn't afraid of a fight. But Leon didn't want to get hooked into any organized resistance, because he felt it would hinder his freedom of movement.

Actually, I don't know exactly when the hell I ran into Beck, but I guess it was early '43. I'm going to say it was the dry season, mangoes were coming on, probably April. We got locked together at Lambac. It's a small barrio, maybe 150 houses. I was running around by myself. The Japs had begun a sweep of the area and I ended up hiding out in Lambac. Beck too had taken cover there and we simply ran into each other.

Pvt. LEON BECK:

Early in 1943 I was in Guagua, Pampanga, acting as Merrill's liaison with some Huk squadrons. I was operating near the big sugar central located at Del Carmen when the Japanese sent out a zone raid to clear the area of guerrillas. I got caught in the net and had to hide out in Lambac. That's where I first met Robinett.

Pfc. BLAIR ROBINETT:

It should have been easy to round up Beck and me. All they had to do was block the damn roads and then, in daylight, sweep the whole barrio. What they did do made no sense then, and none now. They came in and searched eight or ten houses and then left. The next day they came back again and searched eight or ten more. So Beck and I switched houses each night, always moving into a house that had been searched earlier in the day. It was like playing chess. They'd make a move. We'd make one. They'd make another, and we'd counter. We figured we'd eventually outfox ourselves, or the Japs would forget where they had searched and would come back and find us. The villagers were pretty frightened by this time, so, figuring it was just a matter of time before we got caught and they'd catch hell, Beck and I decided to find a better hideout. That's how it happened that one night a villager led us to a small hideout dug into the side of a nearby river bank.

Pvt. LEON BECK:

The cave was situated a couple of feet above the river. If it had been the rainy season, we'd have been under water. We intended to spend only one night there but the Japanese patrol activity was so strong that we spent many days holed up. We tried to make the hole more habitable by enlarging it. We'd only go down to the river at night to wash out our cans, and each time we'd take a different route. If you've ever lived in the jungle you know that it isn't difficult to hide, as long as you don't make a trail to your hideout. So long as you keep your trail covered, you're relatively safe. We were supplied with food by a little boy from the village who was assigned the task. He got into serious trouble over that. Cockfighting was a big sport in the Philippines, and each barrio has its collection of fighting cocks. The old men of the barrio would raise and train them. These birds were constantly having their feathers groomed and their spurs clipped. They were treated like spoiled children. Our little boy, whenever he had trouble getting us food, got to stealing these fighting cocks and barbecuing them for us. This was fine with us since the *pollo* tasted good. But when the old men found out what was happening to their prize fighting cocks, they were ready to kill the boy.

Pfc. BLAIR ROBINETT:

We had covered our path from the village to the cave with dead bamboo. If you know about dead bamboo you know it has thorns on it. One night, after we had been cooped up for days, one of the villagers started to come down to pay us a visit. To avoid the thorns he started running through the bamboo. He sounded like a charging water buffalo and the harder he ran the more thorns he landed on. He finally ran out of path directly above our cave and twelve feet above the water. He just flew out over us all spread out, cursing his damn head off. He looked like a big frog just flying across the moon. It was the funniest thing I'd seen in a long time. I started laughing at the comedy of the damn thing. Beck started swearing and telling me that the Japs would hear me. Maybe I was getting psycho, but the more Beck told me to shut up, the more I laughed! Finally he pulled out his pistols, laid the barrels against my head and racked the hammers back—*click, click.* That stopped the laughing. Even today I don't think he would have fired, but knowing Leon, there's the possibility he might have.

By this time we'd both had enough of the dugout so the next morning, just about dawn, we crossed the river and began working our way along the opposite bank. After a long time we came to an erosion gully which had been dug at a right angle to the river. It was narrow and deep, and because of the heat we climbed in to rest. We both dozed off. The heat woke me up and when I opened my eyes, I was looking straight at a cobra. He had his hood spread and looked like he was going to strike. It scared the hell out of me. I stuttered something like, "L-L-L-Look!" and crawled out at full speed, knocking Beck over as I went. He reached up and grabbed my foot as I left. I just kept going, dragging and bouncing him out of that damn ditch. Soon as we got out, Beck drew his pistols and, looking around, asked where the Japs were. "Hell," I said, "there's no Japs. There's a snake back there." Beck looked at me like I was crazy. I finished my nap under a mango tree. We spent the rest of the day together, but that evening, we went ahead and split up.

Pvt. LEON BECK:

During the next six or seven months I kept running into Blair. I had come down into Pampanga earlier, because I had gotten fed up with the USAFFE Guerrilla unit I was with. I got brown-eyed, like the Texans say. Means the bullshit got eye deep. So I struck out on my own.

I don't know, the time came when I just had to reestablish

my own independence, and going off by myself was the only way I had of doing it on Luzon. You could go off strictly by yourself or go join some other guerrilla unit and operate with them for a while. I just knew I had to get away, had to let things cool down. The group I was with up in Zambales had a lot of officers in it. Besides Colonel Merrill, there was a lieutenant colonel named Calyer, who was also out of the 31st Infantry. There were also two captains, George Crane and Richard Kadel, and Lieutenant Gardner. I also saw a lot of other officers —Volckmann, Blackburn, Ramsey, Moser, Daley, and a priest, Father Duffy,* who was also an officer. There was always that class distinction between them and me, even in the guerrillas. Some of it was subtle, some wasn't. They had their own ways of letting me know that this difference existed. If I'd been submissive, I probably would have wound up as a dog robber for these officers. But I didn't—couldn't!

Once I was even threatened with court-martial. Army says you can't modify weapons, government property, can't destroy it. I modified my rifle to make it lighter to carry. They threatened to court-martial me. They'd lost sight of the fact that we'd just lost the damn war, lost all our personnel, lost all our equipment, and they're going to court-martial me! They got me for cutting the stock off my rifle to make it easier to get to my shoulder, and for removing the stacking swivel off the upper hand guard. I wasn't going to get close enough to a Jap to bayonet him, so I took a hacksaw and cut off the bayonet lug, which eliminated a lot of weight. They threatened me. Colonel Merrill even went so far as to save a sample of the wood shavings, the stacking swivel, and the bayonet lug. He was going to use them as evidence against me when the war was over. Merrill was probably mad at me that particular day. You also can't overlook the fact that the man was getting real old.

There was always chicken shit. I think there always will be as long as there are armies. I can remember specific instances. We'd be moving through the country, and we'd stop and literally have to beg villages to feed and take care of us. I can remember specific officers I've mentioned, insisting that someone get them a spoon to eat with, because they didn't want to use their hands. Well, hell, I never put myself above a Filipino. If he sat down and ate with his hands, I sat down and ate with my hands right with him. I didn't want him to think I was better than he was. I lived at the same level as the Filipinos. Consequently, I never had any problem with them. I was accepted by them. I also like to think that I had their respect and admiration. But I had trouble with my officers. I think that you've talked to other

* Duffy was the same priest who escaped from the Death March with Blair Robinett.

people who knew me during my time in the Philippines and you know I had their admiration. I like to think that I was just maybe a cut above the average. I consider myself a good soldier, always did.

Keep in mind also that when you live every day with a group of people, and you're sick and hungry and frightened that the Japs will kill you, things begin to rub your nerves raw. I remember how the other officers used to pick on Captain Crane and the sucking noise he made when he took a cigarette out of his mouth. They were ready to pull out their hair, it grated on their nerves so bad. Also, some people are more clumsy than others. They'd get up at night to go to the toilet, and they'd stumble all over you. Oh, the grumbling and cursing that went on. Little things like that really grated on our nerves. Some people are envious because, maybe, you're accepted in the group more than they are. One comical incident I remember was coming through Floridablanca. I overheard an American guerrilla officer arguing with a Filipino shopkeeper, "Goddamn it, Beck can come in here and get anything he wants. Why can't I?" So I sneaked into the back of the house and started hollering in Japanese. I laughed for a week.

Anyway, when I got good and fed up running with the same outfit, I'd just leave and go off on my own. After a while I'd run into them or we'd look each other up. When things settled down sufficiently, I'd go back to them again. It was like a marriage. People who tell you they live for years happily married, never arguing, are liars.

So in 1943 I free-lanced for about eight months. I ran with some Hukbalahap squadrons over in Pampanga Province. I taught marksmanship, infantry tactics, arm and hand and whistle signals: "Watch my arm, congregate on me . . . skirmishers through right, skirmishers through left." It was during this time that I kept running into Robinett.

Pfc. BLAIR ROBINETT:

Beck ever tell you about the time he killed the Mayor of Santa Rita? See, Beck just roamed. Sometimes he stayed with me. Then he'd leave, and I might not see him for a couple of weeks. Well, this one time we were together we heard that the Mayor of Santa Rita had a reputation of being pro-Japanese.

Pvt. LEON BECK:

He had been instrumental in having a young boy executed. I don't know how it came about, but I do know the Japanese had taken this kid up to the second story of the *municipio* [City Hall] and had thrown him out a window. He was impaled on a wrought-iron fence. I didn't know what the Mayor's role was, but the townspeople blamed him.

Pfc. BLAIR ROBINETT:

As far as I knew there had been no execution documents issued on the Mayor. Beck and I, however, decided we would neutralize him by sleeping in his house one night. This would jeopardize his position with the Japs because we could always blackmail him with this incident. It was a means of neutralizing him without killing him. I actually didn't think he was all that bad.

We went to his house this one night and knocked on the door. The woman who opened it was an older woman. She peeked out and we could see that the chain was still on. We told her we wanted to speak to the Mayor. "Yes, sir." She closed the door and we waited, and we waited, and we waited. So we tried the door, but it was bolted. Beck pulled out a pistol and began rapping on the door.

Pvt. LEON BECK:

This immediately alarmed the Mayor. He ran to the other side of the house, the side that faced the *población* [public square]. Across the little park was the Japanese garrison headquarters.

Pfc. BLAIR ROBINETT:

We heard the window fly open and the Mayor began yelling, "Help me! Help me!" Well, as soon as he yelled, Beck and I got out of town as quick as we could run. To avoid being captured, we decided to split up. I don't know where Beck went. I can't even remember where the hell I went, but I do know about two weeks later I came back to Santa Rita. As quick as I got into the barrio the people asked what I had done with their Mayor. "Hell," I said, "I didn't do anything with him." They said, "Oh, yes. An American came back and killed him." Well, I knew it hadn't been me and because he and I were the only two Americans in that area, it must have been Beck.

Pvt. LEON BECK:

A few nights after Robinett and I split up, someone actually got to the Mayor. He was taken down to the railroad bridge and executed. I got the credit for it. But I was not the man. I did not do it. I heard Robinett shot him. I've killed people in hot blood, but not in cold blood. There's a difference—a real difference.

You don't have to live with yourself in hot blood. You do have to live with yourself, however, in cold blood.

I sometimes became lonesome during this period, but I don't think I was ever bored. There's always that thought that the next minute can change your whole life. No, I was never bored. But I was lonesome. Oh yeah, lonesome for a lot of things. I was lonesome for milk. When I could find a goat that had her kid running by her side, I'd milk her. The Filipinos thought I was crazy. They drank carabao milk, but I found goat milk a lot richer. It had more nutrients in it. I got lonesome for electric lights. So that I wouldn't be in the dark every night, I'd sneak into a town that was occupied by the Japanese and just sit under an electric light. I was lonesome for different company, different types of people, different classes. I think the average soldier running around in the jungle was about as uneducated as I was. But I always wanted to associate with someone of a little better class. To move up in the world was my goal.

There was always a certain amount of fear, too, that went along with lonesomeness. But there again, that's something you had to learn to control. There was always danger. The danger was just being in the Philippines. I almost got caught a couple of times. Once I was staying with some *compadres* who lived in Santa Rita. Lots of things happened to me around there. This time I was in an apartment above a *botica* [drug store]. Of course, they didn't have any medicine, but it was still called a *botica*. My friends had been playing a piano, and one of them went downstairs to get a newspaper, so we could roll some more native tobacco into cigarettes. The room we were in was long and had lattice work separating the rooms. The house also had an attic. I always made it a practice to stay in a building that had one. To my knowledge, no Japanese patrol had ever searched an attic. So I always felt that if I had enough time to climb into one, I would avoid capture. Well, this Filipino who'd gone out for the newspaper came bursting in whispering, "Japanese! Japanese!" I knew I didn't have time to get to the attic, so I dove for a closet just as two Jap officers came into the room. They had heard the piano from the street and had come in to play it themselves. Those son-of-a-guns must have played for an hour. Of course it seemed like three months to me. I sat there, my heart beating like a jackhammer going ninety miles an hour. 'Course, I was the only one who could hear it, but it sounded that loud to me.

Another time I was running with a unit over in the Zambales Mountains, and some Balugas had killed a wild pig. They had butchered it and given us the head to barbecue. We also got hold of some *basi* wine. *Basi* is made from a stem that

Mount Samat, Bataan, the Philippines, Summer 1980. The Altar of Valor commemorating the men and women who fought in the defense of the Philippines from 8 December 1941 to 10 May 1942.

Freedom! "We were instructed to paint PW on the barracks. American planes began to come over almost immediately. Well, Jesus, bedlam broke out!" American POWs photographed from a U.S. airplane, Yokohama, Japan.

Guards at Fukuoka Camp No. 17. Guard known as One Arm (top left) and the Sailor (next to him) were executed after the war for crimes committed against American prisoners.

Identification photos of American prisoners, Toyama, Japan, Winter 1944–45.

(Top left) Rinko Coal Company gondola, Niigata, Japan. Prisoners would push full car along a trestle to a railroad spur, where it would be unloaded into a larger railroad car. (Top right) Zinc smelters at Camp No. 17, operated by British and Australian troops captured at Singapore. (Middle) Korean miners building a rock pillar in a mine lateral, Camp No. 17. American prisoners worked twelve hours a day and had one day off every ten days. (Bottom) Coal barge, Fukuoka Camp No. 3, Yawata, Japan.

Interior of prisoner barracks, Camp No. 3. Fire-holes in floor were used for heating. Prisoners smuggled coke from steel mill to supplement meager allotment supplied by Japanese.

Eiso (jail) Camp No. 3.

Fukuoka Camp No. 3, Tobata, Japan. The prisoners here worked the steel mills around Yawata. The camp was first occupied in September 1942 by men captured on Wake Island.

Kitchen at Camp No. 3.

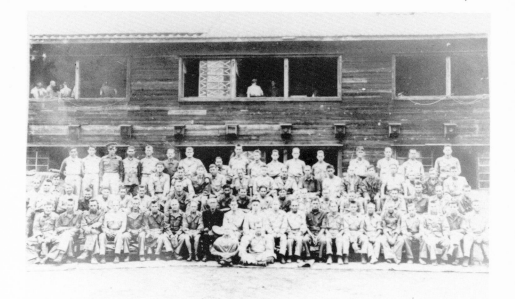

American, British, and Commonwealth POWs at Aomori, Japan, August 1945. "The English CO said to me, 'Trading is not tolerated here.' I thought, 'Boy, you got a lot to learn.' "

Prisoners at Omine Machi, August 1945. Capt. Benson Guyton is fourth from left in front row with hands on his ankles, and Capt. Jerome McDavitt, the camp's American commander, is second from left in front row.

Fukuoka Camp No. 17, Omuta, Japan. Thirty-three barracks housed POWs who worked in mines owned by Mitsui Coal Mining Company. Ninety-five survivors of the *Oryoku Maru* ordeal arrived here in late January 1945. Air-raid shelters are in the foreground.

One of the prisoner barracks at Fukuoka Camp No. 3.

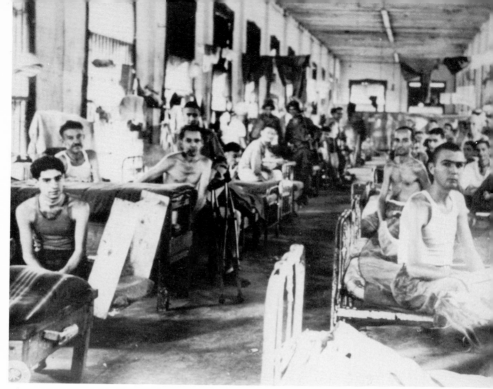

The hospital ward in Bilibid Prison, Manila.

A detail of American POWs in the Philippines.

Pfc. Michael McMullen, Omine Machi (coal mine), Japan.

Pfc. William Wallace, in worn Japanese Army overcoat, Niigata, Japan, Winter 1944–45. "I had amebic dysentery. . . . The Japs put me in isolation."

Pfc. Andrew Aquila, Fukuoka Camp No. 3 (steel mill), Tobata, Japan.

Pfc. Roy Diaz, Yokkaichi (copper smelter), Japan, June 1945. "I got the bulk of the log on my back. Hell, I think, I'm going to be paralized."

Dying of beriberi, Bilibid Prison Hospital.

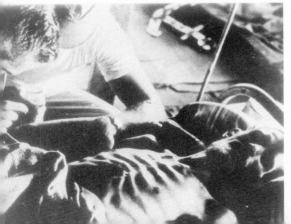

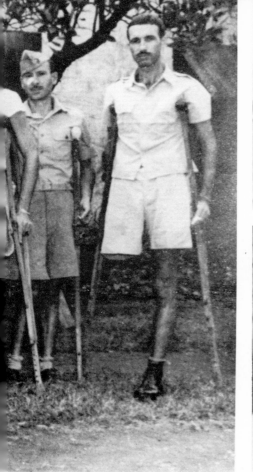

(Top) Pfc. Robert Brown, Harry Hunke, Jr., and Lucien Kocelski, in the Mukden Prisoner of War Camp, Hoten, Manchuria, following liberation. (Middle) Pfc. Wilburn Snyder, 1940. "I didn't want to leave the fellers I was with. Nothing to do with heroics. I was too scared to leave." (Bottom) Sgt. Frank Stecklein, at right, October 1945. "Beatings were repeated. The days went on. I asked them to shoot me."

(Top) American officers liberated from Bilibid Prison, Manila, February 1945. Capt. Theodore Bigger is second from right, kneeling. (Bottom) Officers at Camp No. 17, Spring 1944. Capt. Thomas Hewlett, M.D., is second from left back row; the Japanese camp commander, Urie, fourth from left. The American camp commander, Major Mamerow, is second from left, kneeling, and the camp's mess officer, Navy Lt. Edward Little, is third from left, kneeling.

Sgt. Cletis Overton, December 1944. "I floated up to the deck. The Japs were trying to shoot us as we came out of the hold."

Sgt. Victor Mapes in August 1945. "The ship lurched sideways. I heard the crunch of solid bone breaking. I knew I had broken my leg."

Sgt. Ralph Levenberg, extreme right, and Paddy Clawson, second from left, during a card game at Nichols Field, the Philippines, Summer 1941.

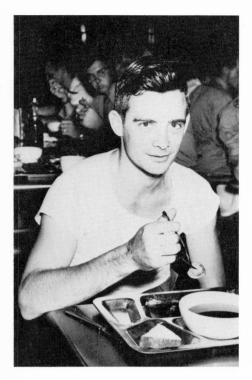

(Left) Pvt. Leon Beck at Fort Sill, Oklahoma, Summer 1946. "Beck came and went as he wished. He definitely wasn't afraid of a fight." (Bottom left) 2d Lt. Hadley Watson, 1941. "Watson had a high IQ and a command personality. Because he was a gambler I also figured he was dangerous." (Below right) Maj. Mark Wohlfeld, October 1945. "I knew Wohlfeld wanted to escape and that he would fight."

(Top left) 2d Lt. John Posten at the auxiliary airfield at Iba, on the Zambales coast west of Clark Field, Fall 1941. (Top right) Pfc. John Falconer, age 20, enroute to the Philippines on the *President Coolidge*, November 1941. (Above) Ten Army nurses who escaped from Corregidor on 3 May 1942, aboard the submarine *Spearfish* in Freemantle, Australia. 2d Lt. Leona Gastinger is second from right. (Left) 2d Lt. Hattie Brantley in front of the Spanish Club, Manila, December 1941. "We went to Bataan in our white starched uniforms. When we arrived we were bedraggled, dirty and dispirited."

grows out of a coconut tree. The stem is recognizable by the cluster of nuts that grow on it. The Balugas cut off this stem and tap it for its juice. Then they add some leaves and berries and sugar and bury the whole mess in earthen jars. When it ferments, it makes some powerful wine. So this night we got hold of some *basi*, and had ourselves a party. One of the fellows in the group was someone I had soldiered with a couple of years before and who I knew didn't drink. But that night he started drinking *basi* and eating this very fat pork. Well, this guy just got so sick. One time he thought he was going to be a B-17 so he dove off some rocks and landed on his head. We all got swacked out of our minds. Fortunately, the Japanese never caught us in a situation like that.

Once some of us were walking down a road at night. When there was a large group, we never walked together. We always split up into smaller units—ones, twos, and threes. That way, if the first group ran into anything, everybody else behind would be alerted. This captain, who I had hollered at in Japanese and who I scared so much, was in front of me. Down the road a way he ran into trouble, but instead of alerting me, he ducked off the road and left me to walk into it. I was coming into a barrio when I heard horses' hoofs on the road. I thought this very strange so I ducked off the road, and sure enough here comes a team of maiden ponies towing a Japanese staff car that had broken down. I came that close to walking into them. The captain who let me walk into this was one of God's most devout cowards. When he got real scared, he'd become violently ill and upchuck. In fact, sometimes he wouldn't have time to bend over. I never missed a chance to frighten him.

This wasn't the only time that Americans turned on other Americans. I found hostile people sometimes, but never hostile barrios. I'll tell you, I had more disappointments from Americans than from Filipinos. For example, I had two men, Americans, who surrendered to the Japanese in 1943, who went so far as to lead a Japanese patrol back to try to pick me up. The only thing I could attribute this to was when we crossed from Zambales back to Pampanga, and we'd been ambushed, one of these men was the only one to escape with a mosquito net. You could sleep two men under it the long way, or if you put it crossways, you could sleep five men under it with only your feet sticking out. Well, I made him sleep five men under it. No way just two men were going to occupy it. There were too many mosquitoes. This guy started crying that mosquitoes were biting his feet. Well, that's tough! He became disillusioned over this and when he and his buddy surrendered a short time later, he led a Japanese patrol back on me. The only thing that kept them from getting us was that they ran into one of our guards. Escaping, we lost all of our equipment. I don't really remember getting away with anything except my side arms.

However, I have no complaints against anyone about helping me when I was sick. In fact, I owe my very life to Bill Gardner. I was out by myself one time. I was staying in a little shack away from everyone; nearest habitation was two or three kilometers away. Why Bill Gardner came to my shack at that time I have no way of knowing. I hadn't had anything to eat in a long time and hadn't been able to walk for four days. I was so constipated. I hadn't had a bowel movement in maybe a week. My stomach was so tender and painful I couldn't even get up, let alone walk. I'd probably have lain there and died if Bill hadn't found me. He set me on his shoulders and carried me as far as he could. Then he stopped, rested, and carried me again until we got someplace where they had an old enema bag. He mixed hot water with lye soap and kept giving me enemas until I moved my bowels and got over it. So I think the Americans really hung tight when it came to taking care of someone who was sick or injured. Of course Gardner himself wouldn't have been alive if it hadn't been for Robinett and myself. This story happened long before I knew Robinett.

Pfc. BLAIR ROBINETT:

Bill Gardner was a first sergeant in the 31st Infantry at the beginning of the war. He'd then been commissioned a lieutenant on Bataan. When Bataan fell, he and several others tried to escape to Corregidor on a homemade raft. Instead, they floated out into the China Sea. They had nothing with them, of course, and by the fourth day they were all in deep trouble, urinating in canteens for something to drink, things like that. Eventually a Jap destroyer picked them up and took them to a small prison compound near Subic Bay. There several prisoners including Gardner decided to escape. Part of the escape plan, besides stabbing a guard, was to swim across a deep river. Ended up that after escaping, the guy who made the plan to swim across the river couldn't swim. It was one of those damned comedy of errors. Gardner did manage to escape and ended up with Volckmann's group of guerrillas that were running up north. To better coordinate their efforts, Major Blackburn and Colonel Volckmann* sent Gardner to Merrill in Zambales Province. Gardner went south with two Filipino escorts from this northern command. After they entered Merrill's zone, they reported to a Filipino guerrilla captain. Well, Gardner told me, one of his escorts

* Maj. Donald Blackburn and Lt. Col. Russell Volckmann.

walked in to deliver a message. He was wearing a very fancy *buscadero* outfit of two Smith and Wesson .38s in tooled leather holsters. The captain told him what a good-looking outfit of guns the messenger had on and when the messenger turned to leave, the captain shot him in the back. A gun fight ensued in which both of Gardner's escorts and the guerrilla captain were killed.

Pvt. LEON BECK:

There was real friction in Zambales between the northern and southern guerrilla sectors. So when Gardner's group came into our area around San Marcelino, some southern guerrillas ambushed and killed Gardner's two Filipino escorts. Gardner, however, managed to kill one of the ambushers. Unfortunately for Bill, the man he killed was the son of the local Filipino guerrilla commander, an officer named Rodriguez. There was also a language problem here. Gardner's two escorts spoke Visayan, while we spoke Ilocano, the local dialect. Well, Rodriguez swore to get the American who had killed his favorite son. I was assigned the responsibility of taking care of Gardner, until we could find a safe time to evacuate him across the mountains.

You see, the guerrillas in each sector of Zambales Province wanted to be the dominant factor. They all wanted to be top man on the totem pole. This caused real friction among each of these Filipino guerrilla units. Nothing went peacefully. Matter of fact, Filipinos killed more Filipinos during the war than the Japs did. They couldn't be controlled. Filipinos will carry a grudge to the grave, just like the Hatfields and McCoys. They're very vengeful people. I'd rather be captured by a Jap, I believe, than a Filipino that carried a grudge against me.

After his oldest son was killed in the ambush, Rodriguez rounded up his entire unit, probably 100 men, and surrounded our camp. They were there to execute Gardner. We tried in vain to talk Rodriguez out of it. It seems silly now, but it was very serious in those days. Matter of life and death, right that quick. We were outnumbered about ten to one.

Pfc. BLAIR ROBINETT:

Gardner says that after the shooting he went down to the shack where the other Americans were and told them his story. Beck was with that group. Meanwhile the Filipinos in the area gathered together and told the Americans to let Gardner go because he had killed a Filipino. They were going to try him for murder first, then execute him.

Beck decided he wasn't going to have any of that, so he drew his two Spanish patent Colt .38s and held the two guards at the back of the hut captive, which allowed Gardner to get his tail the hell out of there. Gardner left. Beck managed to hold Rodriguez for nearly half an hour, allowing Gardner a decent head start. Beck wasn't too worried about himself, because he had the capability of taking care of himself. By the time the Filipinos were able to start after Gardner, he was well into the mountains and on his way to Pampanga. However, Rodriguez sent some Baluga trackers after him. When they finally caught up with him, Gardner killed them, but not before they had wounded him in the back.

One night I was eating dinner, when one of my men reported that they had picked up a collaborator and were about to execute him. I didn't even look up, I just nodded. I told them, however, to make sure they dug a grave for him that nobody would find. After I got through eating dinner, I went down to see if the individual had been executed. The grave had just been dug, and this American was kneeling beside it ready to have his head chopped off with a Jap saber we had captured. He looked up at me and asked if I was going to let these bastards go at him. "Is there any reason I shouldn't?" He explained that he was an American officer. I thought he was too dark to be an American. "You'd be dark, too," he said, "if your mother was a full-blooded Apache." He told me he had come from Merrill. "Who is his executive officer?" "Colonel Calyer."* As quick as that, I knew he knew what he was talking about. In fact he spoke better English than I did, since I had been speaking only Pampango for months. I told my boys to let him loose. That's how I met Bill Gardner.

He asked why we were going to kill him. The answer was simple. We had a standard policy that if we ran any collaborators up into the mountains, the Balugas would kill them, and if they ran any out of the mountains, we'd kill them. If anyone had an arrow in his back, he was obviously running from the Balugas. Therefore we figured that they hadn't completed the job, so we'd go ahead and complete it for them.

Gardner stayed with me a while. He kept asking for things to do. When he was fully recovered, I sent him on an ambush on the Manila north road. First damn crack out of the box he gets shot in the leg. After he got patched up, he wandered over around Santa Rita and began running with Beck. It was months later than I ran into them again. It began simply enough, with

* Lt. Col. Peter D. Calyer, 31st Infantry (US).

an ambush. The normal system of hitting a Jap truck convoy was to set a squad of riflemen on one side of the road and a machine gun on the other. As the trucks came into range the machine gun would sweep their windshields. The normal reaction of the drivers was to swing off onto the other side of the road, right where the riflemen were waiting. We pulled that trick a number of times, and it always worked like a charm. This time the Japs surprised us and put an armored truck into the convoy and when my machine gunner opened, the Jap armored truck started firing back. This shouldn't have bothered us, since our machine gunner was supposed to swap slugs with the Japs until the rest of the squadron got away. This time, however, our gunner became frightened, stopped firing, and ran away. Right then everything went to hell in a basket. A mistake had been made that we couldn't recover from. When I turned to run I stumbled over a damn drainage ditch and sprained my ankle. By the time we all pulled back together, my ankle had swelled up like a football. The squadron was still too close to the road, because we knew the Japs would put some infantry in to look for us. I certainly was in no shape to start running. The rest of that day I was carried. The next morning we decided to pull back farther, towards Mount Arayat. We commandeered a local carabao and I was put on it. Now a carabao walks like he's got four stiff legs. Everytime he put his foot down he jarred my teeth—up and down, up and down. Well, I put up with that critter for several hours until we pulled into a small barrio. It just so happened that Beck and Gardner were also there. I almost didn't recognize Beck at first. He was wearing one of those wide nipa hats that looked like sombreros. Beck thought my riding a carabao was the funniest thing he'd ever seen, so he got in front of this water buffalo and started swinging his hat at him.

Pvt. LEON BECK:

I was only twenty or twenty-one when it happened and I just slapped that carabao until it began to jump. Blair fell off. It scared him more than hurt him. He got all angry and became very abusive.

Pfc. BLAIR ROBINETT:

The carabao wasn't too happy having someone ride him in the first place, and he was even more unhappy when someone started swinging a hat across his nose. The damn animal started doing a tap dance, with me trying to hold on. With no mane or saddle to hold on to, I was at the mercy of the gods. My foot was in such bad shape that I was afraid of hurting it even more. I kept yelling at Beck to stop waving his hat, but he just kept swinging and yelling, "Ride 'em cowboy." I finally tumbled off. I guess all of us had fairly short tempers at that time, so when I got to my feet I pulled out my pistol and cocked the hammer back. "Swing that hat one more time," I told him, "and I'll kill your ass right here." Right there the situation degenerated from comedy to seriousness. Everything had gone down the drain. Beck propped the hat back on his head and told me if that's the way I wanted it, that's the way it was going to be. I didn't trust Beck. I knew too much about him. I went ahead though and dropped my pistol back into the holster and told Beck, "Now, you want to make a damn move go ahead and make it." I knew I could match his draw. Everything was on the line. One of us was going to die right there on that damn dusty barrio road. Gardner and the Filipinos finally realized what the hell was happening.

Pvt. LEON BECK:

They jumped on us and pulled us apart, but I couldn't stop thinking about it. I thought I couldn't let that big devil run over me, I had to do something about it. Nerves were very tight anyway from a lot of things. So I went ahead and hid behind a bush. When Blair came riding up, I stepped out and challenged him again. Everyone piled all over us again. They wouldn't let us settle it. I was so mad by then that I wouldn't stay with them. I left and went out on my own. The next day I ran across some chickens ahead of me on the trail. I decided I'd have them for dinner. I pulled out my pistol and the first two rounds mis-fired. If I'd had the fight with Blair, he'd have killed me deader than hell. Blair and I laugh about it now, but it wasn't funny then. Very serious. Very, very serious.

Pfc. BLAIR ROBINETT:

Having a bad foot was extremely worrisome. The whole idea of being sick and not being able to take care of yourself when you're being hunted preys on your mind constantly. We rarely had medical supplies. The U.S. Government never dropped supplies in our sectors. Matter of fact, whenever you killed a Jap you searched him for three things—quinine, shoes, and cigarettes. Golden Eagle cigarettes were an especially good brand. I never did get a pair of shoes that fit me, and we never found enough quinine to take care of us.

Pvt. LEON BECK:

Finally, in 1944, we began to get air drops. They parachuted in arms, ammunition, dynamite, and medicine. With every carton of rifles there would also be ten carbines, 1,000 quinine tablets, 1,000 sulfathiazine tablets, and one giant jar of sulfa ointment. There'd also be ten olive drab undershirts, ten GI shorts, ten pocket knives, ten boxes of matches and ten pocket books. Of course the ammunition was dropped in separate cases. We needed pocket knives like we needed a hole in the head. The matches were a Godsend, though. They were very rare. You could probably get a prewar peso, that's fifty cents American money, for one match. The pocket books were no good to you except in the daytime and anyway, who wanted to carry a book around? They usually dropped in some junk by Guy de Maupassant and Shakespeare. I didn't think de Maupassant was that great. Now, if they dropped in a good western, well that I would have enjoyed.

The more time I stayed with the Huks, the more trouble I had with them. Once a Huk unit kidnapped the brother of a woman I knew. They just swept through an area, taking all the young boys and turning them into *cargadores* [cargo carriers]. Of course this was a common occurrence with the Huks. Well, I got word about this particular kidnapping, and I decided to set out to rescue the boys. Took me about three days to catch up with the Huks. I had my two bodyguards with me, and we told the Huks that we were going to either take the boys or we'd fight for them. I brought them back to their barrio and turned them loose. A few months later the Huks killed one of my bodyguards when they caught him by himself. Because of this persistent harassment, sometime around August of 1944, I left Pampanga, Robinett, and the Huks, and wandered back into the Zambales and took up residency with my original USAFFE unit. The next month—September 21, 1944, to be precise—we saw our first Allied air strike against Luzon. They were Navy planes. I heard the planes come in and thought they were Japanese, so I paid no attention to them. I was peeking out of a window watching the Japanese load vegetables in this barrio, which they used as a collection point. When the Jap soldiers realized they were being bombed, they quickly canceled their collection and pulled out of town. Needless to say, I was quite exhilarated. For the first time in two and a half years, I began to see there might really be a light at the end of the tunnel. That night several of us dug up some jugs and had a nice *basi* drunk.

● PART IV ●

JAPAN

11
HELL SHIPS

The first American prisoners shipped to Japan left the Philippines during the summer of 1942. During the next two years several more details were sent. These shipments of prisoners took place relatively without incident. However, in July 1944, as the American forces of General MacArthur approached the Philippines, this situation changed drastically. In a desperate effort to get the American prisoners to Japan before they could be liberated, the Japanese were forced to take extreme measures. Without a sufficient number of available freighters, the Japanese authorities tried to make do with what they had. Consequently, between September and December 1944 too many prisoners were put on too few ships. The resulting treatment aboard, coupled with the prisoners' physical and mental condition, earned these freighters the name of "Hell Ships."

By the time the situation was critical enough for the Japanese to move this large body of men to the Home Islands, American submarines roamed the China Sea at will. Not surprisingly, these subs clustered along the major shipping lanes that connected the Philippines with Formosa and Formosa with Japan. The Hell Ships sailed in convoy with other Japanese shipping and carried no markings to indicate to the waiting American submarines that they transported prisoners. The results were catastrophic. The Arisan Maru, for example, when sunk by an American submarine, took down with her more American prisoners than died at Camp O'Donnell. A rough count suggests that more than 5,000 Americans died when their Hell Ships were torpedoed or bombed.

When General MacArthur's liberating forces reached Luzon in January 1945, they found that the Japanese had successfully removed all the able-bodied American PWs. Since the purpose of having these prisoners in Japan was to help make up for the labor force the Japanese were losing to the military, they left behind in the Philippines all prisoners thought to be unfit for hard labor. These sick, weakened, and incapacitated prisoners remained either in Cabanatuan or Bilibid. They were liberated in early 1945. Freed also at this time were approximately 5,000 civilians and the military nurses captured on Corregidor, who had been interned since May 1942 in Manila's Santo Tomas University.

Sgt. FORREST KNOX:

How do I describe a packed, hot, filthy, stinking ship's hold that turned slowly into a mad house? We called them "Hell Ships." They were. Most of the guys won't or can't talk about them. When I force myself to think of my trip, I can't put it in chronological order. What I tell you is all different incidents stitched together in no particular order. There was just too much, too many things happened.

Before we left the Philippines, truck loads of winter clothes came into Bilibid. I received a winter trench coat with English buttons and a pair of hobnailed shoes. Right size, even. The perimeter guard was doubled. We were trucked to Pier 7. More trucks kept coming in. When we marched out of the pier shed, we could not believe the size of the ship for the number of men who were waiting to board her. They put 500 of us in one hold and 500 in the other. In the hold with me the Japs put about fifty English troops who had survived the building of a railroad in Burma.* They were put right in the center, under the hatch, and during the entire voyage not one of them died. They

---

* The great majority of English POWs in Siam (Thailand) worked on the construction of the Bangkok-Moulmein railway alignment between Ban Pong, Siam, and Ye, Burma. This was the spur that crossed the River Kwai (Khwae Noi). Thousands of British soldiers died in the building of this railroad. The prisoners Forrest Knox refers to were survivors of this ordeal who had been loaded on a ship in the Straits Settlements, presumably for transport to Japan. As a result of engine trouble their

were what they mean when they say "survivors." They didn't look any different than us—skinny, beat. But I don't guess you could have killed one of them with an ax. One I remember, he tried later to sing to quiet the mad men.

After the ship was loaded, tugs pulled us away from the dock and moored us to a buoy in the harbor. Tropical sun on a steel deck. Body heat from 500 men packed together. All around men began passing out. They just slid down out of sight, where men stepped or stood on them. Wearing heavy clothes on the dock got us warm and we drank our water. Somehow it never crossed our minds what was going to happen to us.

As a guy goes crazy he starts to scream—not like a woman, more like the howl of a dog. We were locked in a hold together, 500 of us. We're in there solid, wall to wall. Tight, so you couldn't put your feet between people when you tried to walk. I don't know how to describe heat, there was no way we measured temperature. We were all practically naked by that time, because we had taken off everything in order to cut down on the heat. It must have been 120 or 125 degrees in that hold. The Jap's favorite trick was to cut off our water. It was bad enough in other places when they did this, but there, in this oven, when they cut it off, guys started going crazy. People running, people screaming. An American colonel was on deck. There were always some Americans topside who were used to raise and lower the honey buckets and food tubs. The Japs told the colonel to tell us to be quiet. He shouted down, "Be quiet or the Japs will completely cover over the hatch with canvas."

At this time we were nearly completely covered by hatch planks that had been lashed together with steel cable. I walked across that hold, stepping on people, to where the officers were. I tried to get them to answer me. Face to face with a major; "What are you going to do?" He wouldn't answer me. I knew he was conscious 'cause his eyes were open. I grabbed him and shook him, "What are we going to do?" The guy couldn't talk. I looked around. They were all the same—zombies. The medical officer had a kit in which he carried capsules we called Blue Heaven. I don't know for certain what the hell they were, and I don't know whether they'd been passed out, but I do know these officers were zapped out. I couldn't get an answer to what we were going to do to quiet the men. I went back to my group and told them the officers were all gone and would be no help. We were on our own.

The Navy chiefs trying to talk to the men got drowned out.

freighter put into Manila Harbor, where it was damaged during an air attack. Those Englishmen who remained alive were placed in Bilibid, where they joined American details also destined for Japan.

The Englishman's singing held them only for a short time. The chaplain tried to preach a sermon. Finally, he shouted for the men to join him in a group prayer. He never finished, or at least on our side he was drowned out by the bedlam. The screaming and running got worse. The colonel topside hollered down, "They're going to do it. They're going to cover you with canvas!" With the temperature we were in, if they'd closed off that little air we got, I don't know how many of us would have been alive by morning. I had picked up the habit of wearing a small sweat towel around my forehead like the off-duty Japs did. You could knock a man senseless with a full canteen swung by the chain. Our canteens were empty. The next guy that went by screaming they caught and killed. I can remember the first guy's name and he wasn't even a soldier. He was a civilian, one of those that was working for the Navy at Cavite when the war began. He was strangled with my little towel. A guy that had worked in a mental institution in Pennsylvania knew how to do it. Several others were also killed. The crazy ones, they howled because they were afraid to die—but now the ground rules changed. If they howled, they died. The screaming stopped. The running stopped. Men realized that if they ran one more time, they were going to be killed. Just one man near us questioned what was done. When he was invited to come a little closer to discuss it, he stopped talking and turned his head the other way. The Japs didn't cover the hatch.

Later in the night I began talking to a friend of mine whose name was Garland but who was called "GaGa." Because it sounded babyish he didn't like the name, but that's what the Japs called him and it stuck. He asked me to make sure his wedding ring got back to his wife. "I got it hid here in the binding of this Bible." I told him sure I would, but that if he hung on, "By morning they've got to give us water. Things have got to get better." It was as black in that hold as if we'd been in a mine. He said, "Oh, shit, Knocky, it just isn't worth it." He quit right then. He was dead by morning. The ability to survive is mostly mental. The little New Testament he had his ring hid in was at an absolute premium. Not because anybody wanted to read it, but because the pages were made of rice paper and that made the best cigarette paper. So these New Testaments were stole like crazy. Wouldn't you know in the morning Garland's damn book was gone. I knew it had to be pretty close to me, so I started explaining to the guys, "Now, look, this was his Bible and he gave it to me personally to deliver to his wife. I'm not about to use it for smoking and I made this promise to a dead man." I never got it returned.

We made Olongapo probably the next night. That was the

naval base above Bataan, so it was protected. Each night we stopped. We'd come in real slow and stop practically on the beach. The Jap escort destroyers would stay out beyond the convoy and drop depth charges in an attempt to keep the American submarines at a distance. One of these nights, it must have been at the upper end of Luzon, I was standing in line on the deck in order to use the *benjo,* the shit house they'd rigged over the side of the ship—just platforms you could squat on. It was sundown, and I looked out and saw this beautiful little tropical island we were anchored next to. The next day we made a dash for the Formosa Strait and that's where the subs really nailed us. It was like being in a shooting gallery.

One of these nights the subs got three hits. You could hear the explosions right in a row—*pow, pow, pow.* The one that should have hit us ran right alongside. Everyone was quiet, listening. I was just several men away from the bulkhead. In the quiet you could hear it coming. Sounded like a motor boat. The guy next to me was off a submarine. "What the hell is that?" I said. He says, "It's a torpedo." I didn't think to ask him how he knew. I quick took the cap off my canteen and gulped down the little water we'd been given earlier. One of the survival techniques everyone had to learn was to always keep at least one drink of water. As long as you had a swallow left, you could keep from going crazy. If your canteen was empty, you could blow your top. I took this sailor's word and if it was a torpedo I didn't want to die thirsty. I listened to that *whirrr* and she just buzzed by. The guys who were on deck said later they could see it coming. It was porpoising along in a long curve and just missed the ship. Of course the Japs got frantic every time something like that happened.

This wasn't the only time I got really scared, though. One night some guy stole my canteen. It was something you never lost. It was impossible to stay awake forever and one night in the hold someone snitched my canteen. I'd spent hours etching a design on its aluminum surface, so I knew I'd recognize it if I ever saw it again. Our water was given to us in our canteens, which were filled on deck. Then they were lowered back down and distributed. The next time that rope came down I was watching it and I saw my design. The guy down with us gathered up all the canteens and began passing them out. I followed mine right along till a guy took it. I just held out my hand and said, "That's my canteen." "Oh," he said, "I thought it was mine." I said, "No!" I expected a fight, 'cause there's no mercy in a situation like that and the most common method of killing a man was with a full canteen. You took the chain in your hand and swung. I was ready for him; by then I was a tiger. If he tried to hit me, I was going to do my best to kill him first. I mean, on this ship, in this place, there was no mercy. But instead of fighting, the guy handed it back. Later, on another ship, I saw some compassion, but not on this one.

Above our heads there was a small space where the hatch planks had been left spread apart. Just wide enough to let a man through. Up and down through that hole a rope went continuously. Everything was passed on it—piss buckets, strings of canteens, rice buckets, dead men. It was our only connection to the outside world. This little hole was watched any time we were not doing something. Any story about this voyage would be incomplete without the background sound that never stopped twenty-four hours a day. "Pass the bucket." We slept when we could. So between midnight and morning it was generally quiet. Except for "Pass the bucket." That was endless.

One man who passed out was pulled out of the hold. Some time later the colonel sent him back down, so someone else could take his place on deck. Well, he worked his way across the hold till he figured he was back where he started from. Naturally, there was no room for him. It was like pulling your foot out of water. The space instantly filled up. He demanded his space. Well, the loudest debate I ever heard developed over this. These two men were close buddies, so it never quite came to blows. They were chin to chin, shouting at each other. One part sticks in my mind yet. One man yelling at the other, "Why you must be completely and totally insane."

It was not unusual to want to kill someone. The Japs were too far away and we were packed together in an oven for twenty-eight days. So we went after each other. This one guy, I didn't know why, kept scratching at the steel bulkhead. For hours he scratched and scratched. This noise infuriated me immensely. No matter how I tried to isolate my mind from it, the noise cut through to me. "What the hell are you doing?" He said, "I'm trying to make a hole."

"A *hole*? For what?"

"There's water out there. I can hear it."

This one feller, I can remember he was real tall and lanky and he might have been a big man once, but now he was pretty skinny. When he slept he had his legs all doubled up and he looked like a grasshopper. His legs kept falling on me. All night long I pushed his legs off of me. Any little thing eventually got irritating. So I scrounged around and I found my belt. With it I tied his legs up by the knees. When he woke up he was madder than hell and wondered who had tied him up. I told him I had and that I wanted my belt back.

Our nerves were worn raw. There was no such thing here

as being case-hardened. Stress is a funny thing. I can remember a kid from Arizona or New Mexico. I don't know what, but that sonovabitch irritated me to the point where I almost killed him, just because he wouldn't keep his mouth shut. He kept talking about water, about how he'd go up to the mountains where the water bubbled out of the ground in cold clear streams, and how you could see the trout through the water. Endlessly he talked about this cold water. Take a man that's dying of thirst and keep talking to him like that and eventually you're going to get to him. Because I didn't have a full canteen I couldn't belt him, and somehow or another I couldn't strangle him. He wasn't howling, he was just talking, and that didn't seem like reason enough to kill him. In the hold of that ship you executed those that were an absolute danger to you. This guy wasn't an absolute danger to me. He was just driving me crazy.

We eventually ended up in Hong Kong and stayed there for ten days. I figured later that the bombing on Formosa was so heavy that they shuttled us off to wait until we had a better chance of getting into one of them Formosa harbors. While we were in Hong Kong we got bombed anyway.* When we were anchored, the Japs let us out in batches to walk the deck. Our convoy was sitting there with the mountains all around us, and it reminded me of being in a giant bowl. Above I could see the bombers, oh I don't know, maybe at 15,000 feet, and the Japs were firing at them with everything they had. My eyes weren't all that good, but I was curious about where all this flack was coming from. I looked around and in the distance I see these two little ones coming down off the mountain. I can remember them real plain. The pair of them were practically flying at sea level, sliding straight at us. I didn't move. All the guns I could see were concentrating on the bombers above us, and I didn't want to draw their attention to the planes coming at us. I nudged the guy alongside me and told him where to look. They were getting closer and really coming in hard. When he saw them all he said was, "Jesus Christ!" I thought, "Here it comes," and I stood up and faced them. Alongside me the guy turned away and crunched himself in a ball. When they were almost on top of us they turned slightly and finished their run on a tanker. They hit that bugger square—*bang!* Then they pulled up and when the water and smoke settled, the tanker was gone. That fast. I couldn't believe it, something that big couldn't sink that fast, but she was gone.

After laying over ten days in Hong Kong, we joined a

* The only raid on Hong Kong in October came on the 15th, and was flown by the 14th Air Force from Kunming, China.

convoy and headed back out into the China Sea to see if this time we could make Formosa. We had that small work detail on the deck, about ten men, who worked the ropes. Everything went up or down on these ropes, including the bodies. On deck all the Japs cared about were the dog tags. Once they had been collected, the bodies were tipped over the side. We called it "water logging." I remember one time the Japs emptied the hold. They had pulled up a corpse which didn't have a set of tags on. The Jap captain told us he was going to come off with the same number that he had started with. He knew how many he had begun with back in Manila, and when we landed in Formosa he was going to have the same number of either warm bodies or dog tags. Now he had one unidentified dead American on his deck. We climbed on deck and were counted and were asked if we recognized the body. In the emaciated condition it was in, I don't see how in hell anyone could have identified it. Looked like a mummy. With his mouth wide open he hardly looked human. Whether the captain ever got his name I don't know. Maybe someone made up a name just to end the charade.

Men who had gone crazy in the dark and heat and who had not recovered were tied to the hatch cover, and they spent the last part of the journey lashed to the deck. We finally made port in Formosa about twenty-eight days after we had sailed from Manila, a short 500 miles away. One thing happened, I remember, while we were still in the harbor at Takao, waiting to go to Japan. In the next convoy after ours that left Manila, one of the ships carrying 1,800 prisoners was torpedoed and sunk.* Martin Binder, one of the few survivors—a boatswain off the *Canopus,* if I remember right—was put aboard our ship. After the Japs picked him off a raft he was taken to Formosa, where he was dumped on us. At first the Japs wouldn't let us talk to him but later, of course, we all got a chance to hear his story.†

---

* This was the Arisan Maru, which sailed from Manila on Oct. 10, 1944, with 1,800 American prisoners, mostly officers. She was sunk by the USS Snook on Oct. 24 while crossing the South China Sea, 200 miles south of the Formosa Strait (20° 31′ N, 118° 32′ E). It is estimated that not more than ten prisoners survived the sinking.

† In a statement made a year after the war ended, Boatswain Binder told the following story. After his ship was torpedoed the Japanese removed all their own civilians and soldiers. Before they left they cut the rope ladder leading out of the Number 1 hold, which held prisoners. Binder, who was in the other hold, managed to get topside and into the water, where he clung to a raft. The sea was moderately rough. He noticed many prisoners in the water around him and they waited for the circling Japanese destroyers to come in and pick them up. No help, however, was offered. The Arisan Maru took about four hours to sink. The next day no ships were in sight, and he climbed aboard a raft which held four other survivors. The nights were freezing cold and the days burning hot. Most of the time the raft was awash. When he awoke on the third day, three of the men were missing. The fourth man that day drank salt water and went out of his mind. The last Binder saw of him, he was swimming away from

He was badly sunburned and in bad shape. We questioned him endlessly about who had been on board with him. Amazing the number of men he could recite. It was from him I learned about the Luther twins who were from my home town, Janesville.

I was then kept in a prison camp on Formosa where I worked in a sugar cane field. Three months later I was taken by train to the port of Takao, and when we got out there, here waiting for us was a great big clean freighter. It was much nicer than the first ship. On this one we were given water and food and no more ropes or ladders. We walked out of the hold on regular stairs. But then, nothing could ever be like that first ship.

I've forced myself at times to think about that experience. It broke me as a soldier. I was a good soldier until then but that ship ruined me. Afterwards I could no longer make a decision. How I survived it I can't really tell. Some survived it because they were kids and never realized just how rotten the situation was. Others survived day to day—bullheaded stubbornness would be a good explanation. But when you got into bad shape, like in the hold of that ship, the ones that got out were the ones that hated. Love never kept anyone alive. You could do your flat best for someone and they'd lay there and die. But if you hated, whether a Jap or those medics or an officer, it seems strange but those that did—I mean hated real hard—they lived. Those that started begging for their mothers, then you'd better start digging a hole for them. Once you felt sorry for yourself, you were an absolute gone bastard.

I think you also had to have faith, faith that there was a God, faith in your country, because it was going to be the U.S.A. that was going to have to get you out of this situation. If you didn't believe that, then you believed it would never end.

I looked at it that I had been paid good money to kill Japs, and now I had been put in a position where they were getting paid to kill me, and no way in hell was I going to make it easy for them. They were going to have to work to earn their pay. Everybody has their own philosophy of why they survived and you won't always get the same answer. I felt as long as I could stand on my own feet they wouldn't kill me, and strange as it may seem, in extreme danger I stood up. This business about being a psycho when I got back to the States, it started a long time before then. Maybe it started when I stood and watched that pair of fighters in Hong Kong harbor. There must be some

---

the raft. Four days and four nights later a passing Japanese transport picked Binder up and carried him to Formosa. He was first put in a jail and then transferred to a freighter. When this ship was unable to leave port he, along with Forrest Knox and many of the other prisoners aboard, was placed in a prison camp on Formosa.

insanity in taking outrageous risks. I used to read a lot as a kid, and something that I remembered reading was about how every Spanish boy dreams of being a bullfighter, but how there's only about twenty-five in all of Spain that can keep their feet still. A point of honor with me was that I could keep my feet still. On this last leg of the trip to Japan I stood on the deck of this big freighter and watched an American dive bomber drive right down my throat, and I never flinched. I stood there and looked at him. There was only one other man that I saw who could do it, and that was this bo's'n off the *Canopus* who had survived his ship sinking.

It was right after we got aboard this new freighter in Takao, Formosa, that the dive bombers hit the harbor. We were moored next to a pier and there were two destroyers a little aft of us. The hold was open, so many of us were sitting on the deck when the raid began. The first thing I knew, all the AA guns in the harbor and on the destroyers opened up. All the guys began to run, looking for cover. I couldn't imagine where they were going to find cover on a ship. I stood up and watched the battle. These planes kept diving and the ack-ack was as thick as soup. Out of the corner of my eye I noticed this chief bo's'n also standing up, watching the action. One of the planes came right down alongside us and dropped his bombs short of the pier. It felt like our ship jumped several feet every time the bombs landed. I kept watching this damn chief out of the corner of my eye. I thought, "This bastard Binder has got to chicken out. He can't stand this." It was one-upmanship. From the con-cussion of the bombs, the coal dust and dirt in all the cracks on board the freighter shook loose. Smoke blew across us. I was sure that bugger wouldn't last. But he stood right there and never turned a hair.

That evening we got underway and were moved towards the mouth of the mole. I thought, "Well, boy, this is kind of a lousy place to be." In the middle of the night I heard a plane circling. The guy next to me said, "What's it sound like to you?" I thought it sounded like an American engine and told him so. We listened some more. "Nope," he said, "that's Japa-nese." He circled over us again. Your ears got like radar after a while and you could tell right the hell where anything was by its sound. This plane went out to sea and then came in down low and zeroed in on the mouth of the harbor. You could hear him good. Everyone sat up. I said to the guy next to me, "I think you better be right this time rather than me." That sonova-bitch came right over us so low I thought he'd hit the mast. He dropped a torpedo and took a tanker out right behind us. He pulled away and the Japs never fired anything at him. That was a spooky night.

A day or so out of Takao we got caught in a typhoon. This freighter rolled like crazy, but oh, man, were we happy. In a storm like this we knew we didn't have to worry about submarines or bombers. It closed down the shooting gallery. The only disadvantage was we weren't allowed on deck. The honey bucket was in one corner, so guys with dysentery real bad would get up and run for it. Some wouldn't make it all the way and they'd begin to squirt as they ran. Fellers lying down would wipe the shit off themselves and roll over. You got used to being shit on.

We had an old guy with us and he seemed ever so much older than the rest of us. He was dying. We all knew that. One of the guys got up and went over to him and brought him some chow. He sat next to him and began to feed him. He'd put something in the old guy's mouth and then try to wash it down with a little water. But the guy was so far gone he couldn't even take food this way. So the feller feeding him put his mess kit down next to him and told him that if he got hungry during the night, he could eat the food that was left. In the morning when we checked, the old man was dead. So the feller picked up his mess kit and then stood and looked at the body. Then he walked over to the honey bucket and dumped the chow in it. We never threw food away, I mean you ate even when it was rotten. When he came back nobody said anything. Finally, he felt he had to apologize to everybody for what he had done. He said, "If I thought the sonovabitch was going to die I would have eaten it myself." It was so rare for a man to act as he had. Usually you helped yourself.

We landed in Japan a day or so later.

★ ★ ★

When the Davao detail arrived back at Cabanatuan, they were at first kept in isolation and away from the other prisoners in Camp No. 1. Several weeks later the detail was moved into camp. By September 1 Cabanatuan was down to about 4,000 prisoners, most of whom were officers. Two details left Cabanatuan for Bilibid and Japan early in September. The voyage of the Oryoku Maru, which is described here, carried the last detail of prisoners

shipped from Cabanatuan. Remaining behind in Camp No. 1 were approximately 500 Americans who the Japanese considered too sick or disabled to make the trip to Japan. On January 30, 1945, these men were liberated by a daring raid on the camp made by American Rangers and Filipino guerrillas. Ironically, the survivors of the last detail from Cabanatuan who had been on the Oryoku Maru arrived in Moji, Japan on the same day.

Capt. MARION LAWTON:

We didn't know it at the time, but while we were still in Davao Penal Colony American planes bombed Davao City. As the American forces started moving on the Philippines, the Japanese made a desperate effort to get as many American prisoners as they could out of the Philippines and on to Japan. I guess it was a matter of pride with them that they didn't want us retaken. They moved us in June '44 out of Davao back up to Manila and Bilibid. After a while most of us were moved back to Cabanatuan.

We saw the first planes about September 20. They were a long way away, over the mountains. Then a flight came near our camp and went on in and hit Clark Field, and oh, what a beautiful sight! There were several groups of bombers covered by the fast fighters. Boy, were we joyous! When they came back from the raid, one of the American fighters peeled off and as he came over Cabanatuan he wagged his wings.*

American planes made appearances then for about three or four days in a row. Then they didn't come back for a while. Shortly afterwards the Japs moved 1,600 of us out of Cabanatuan. Everyone not bedridden or too ill or not mobile enough to walk was moved to Bilibid.† The Japs knew they were running out of time. We sat in Bilibid for nearly a month. American planes came over again and again and bombed Manila Bay. You couldn't see out of the ground floor cells because of the wall, but if you got up in the upper story of Bilibid you could see out fine. Boy, those dive bombers when they came down sounded like their wings were going to come off. They'd release their bombs on some Jap shipping and then climb back out of the

---

* Air strikes on Luzon were carried on at this time. The planes were from Vice Adm. M. A. Mitscher's carrier forces of Halsey's 3d Fleet. The raids were part of the American preparation for the invasion of the Philippines.
† This detail of 1,600 men consisted mainly of officers. It left Cabanatuan during the middle of October, several days before General MacArthur's forces invaded Leyte.

smoke. They hit for about two days in a row and then they disappeared. We said, "Now the Japs will never get us out of here."

Two weeks went by. Then the Japs finally got a ship into Manila which they could use to move us to Japan. We left our sick in Bilibid. One of the men left behind, David Hardee, was a lieutenant colonel from North Carolina who I had gotten to know well in Davao. As we were lining up to march out of Bilibid I stopped by his bed to say good-bye and ask him to scribble a note to my mother. "I know you'll get home before I do, so please write my Mom and tell her I'm O.K." He promised he would.

Pfc. LEE DAVIS:

We were marched out of Bilibid and down through the streets of Manila to the Port Area. This was very humiliating because the Filipinos were watching us from both sides of the street. We crossed over the Quezon Bridge and then onto Pier 7, where we were loaded onto a large Japanese ship.* Having sat in the tropical waters for some time, the hold of the ship, where I was put, was excessively hot. We were jammed in so tight that when we laid down, it had to be on our sides. The honey bucket was in the center of the hold, so anyone trying to get to it had to leave his place and step over people before he reached it. Shortly after we got underway the Japs put the cover on the hatch.

Capt. MARION LAWTON:

The Japs gave us a light ration of rice and some water. We were packed into the ship's hold so tightly only a few men could sit down at a time. The Japs gave us a light ration of rice. Then they lowered some water. The distribution in my hold was not easy and probably not equal. Some men got a lot, some none at all. The stronger fellers controlled the distribution. Nothing prevented the healthy from going back more than once, and no one aided the sick and weak in getting their share.

Pfc. LEE DAVIS:

I left Bilibid with all my possessions in a shoe box. I had my canteen in there, a little bit of salt that someone had scrounged

---

* In the early afternoon of Dec. 13, 1944, 1,619 American prisoners boarded the <u>Oryoku Maru</u>. Three holds were assigned to the prisoners, large ones forward and aft, and a smaller one amidships. The detail was divided into three groups, with Commander Portz (USN) in charge of the first, Lieutenant Colonel Beecher (USMC) the second, and Commander Maurice Joses, a Navy doctor, the third.

for me, and a couple of pair of socks. Once I had to crawl over to the honey bucket to relieve myself, and when I returned to my space I found someone had defecated in my shoe box. I promptly put the lid back on and passed the whole business out. I heard some colonel say, "Who the hell sent this up this way?"

Capt. MARION LAWTON:

That first night in the hold of the *Oryoku Maru* in Manila Harbor there was madness. Claustrophobia and total darkness created a terrible, terrible feeling. There was the heat. The desperate need for air. The temperature must have been near 120 degrees. There was thirst. Many of the men, those that had gotten some water, gulped it right down. They sat there in that oven in their own sweat. When all the liquid was gone, men became desperate. They went mad. Some drank urine. Some turned vampire. They tried to drink the blood of the sick men who couldn't resist. Men were murdered on that ship. The next day I was next to an old college classmate of mine. His arms were badly scratched. I asked him what had happened. He told me it was nothing. "It's more than nothing," I said. "Who did this to you?" "Well, I fought off a feller for half the night who was trying to cut me so he could drink my blood. He was mad. Finally two fellers next to me realized what was going on. One of them grabbed this guy while the other one beat him on the head with his canteen."

Pfc. LEE DAVIS:

That night it was like being in the Black Hole of Calcutta. The men went literally mad. I saw Americans scrape sweat off the steel sides of the ship and try to drink it. One person near me cut another person's throat and was holding his canteen so he could catch the blood. This night was something very terrible. I was told later that I went out of my head. I was screaming and cursing the Japanese. Men around me told me if I didn't shut up, they'd kill me. I didn't listen to them. I didn't know what I was doing. Somebody knocked me unconscious.

Capt. MARION LAWTON:

That first night men became irrational. Many were tormented by the heat and thirst. Not knowing what to do, they roamed in the darkness. Not knowing what they were looking for or what they could do, but sure they couldn't sit still or calm themselves, they roamed. Men screamed. And in this madness, Frank Bridget came onto the scene.

I hadn't seen much of him after we left Davao. My run-ins with him when he was my barracks commander were enough to keep me away from him. Bridget got up on the ladder in the hold of that ship and began to exercise command. He shouted at first until men began to hear him. He spoke soothingly and calmly later. "We're in this thing together. If any of us are going to live, we are going to have to work together." However he said it and whatever he said, his approach worked and the situation became more calm. Make no mistake, Bridget was not the American commanding officer in that hold. He took that responsibility. People, I found, rise to greatness when the occasion comes. You never can predict who will. It was impossible to guess who was going to be a hero and who a coward. It's a spur-of-the-moment thing. You can't rehearse it. You either run away or you perform. Bridget hit the right key. He talked until he was hoarse. Then someone else took over for a while. Then Bridget would come back on. He was still wearing his jodhpurs. He came into prison camp with them and he was wearing them that night in the hold of the *Oryoku Maru*. He was wearing them a few weeks later when he died.

Henry Leitner, a good school friend, and I made a pact. I knew things were going to be rough and that it would be necessary for us to stick together. I hadn't been close to Henry in college; he was a class ahead of me. It was in the Army that I got to know him well. We had a lot of fun together before the war. He was an intellectual who wrote poetry in prison camp. He was a feller that I really vibrated with emotionally. I was glad I had him with me now. We were going to need each other if we were going to survive.

At times during the night Henry would go out of his head. There was not enough oxygen and there was all that heat. I hung on to him, just hung on to him. "Come on, Henry, just hold on now." I'd encourage him and he'd settle down. Not that he was getting violent, but he wanted to roam. He was lost inside himself. Then at one time I got that way and he looked after me. I don't think anyone survived that first night who didn't have somebody to buddy with.

During this period of time, this night, the *Oryoku Maru* had been sailing north. We had started up the coast of Luzon. The convoy we were in was moving very slowly and we were hugging the shore. In the morning following the first night, this is December 14, the planes found us.

They strafed us first. Then they bombed. Henry and I were on the upper bay, a sort of shelf that hung out off the ship's bulkhead, in the forward hold. Henry was sitting to my left and a feller I didn't know was sitting on my right. We felt pretty safe from the strafing because of the decking over us. But several bullets began bouncing off the steel bulkheads. There was some ricocheting. One of the slugs hit the shoulder of the feller on my right. It knocked a hole the size of a half a dollar in his shoulder. It burned and then numbed him. He didn't yell. But a bullet hit that close to me.

One of the bombs knocked a hole in the side of the ship just above the water line and got a number of guys with shrapnel. Then a bomb hit the aft hold, knocking down some steel beams. This killed nearly 100 men. By then we had run aground. We stayed where we were and took air raids the remainder of the day. That night the insanity began again. Many died of suffocation. Some were murdered by Jap guards as some of the prisoners tried to crawl out onto the deck.

In the morning (December 15) the Japanese spent a great deal of time getting their own people off. In the first-class area of this vessel the Japanese had packed civilians—women, children, diplomats, and business people—who they were evacuating before the expected American invasion. As soon as the sun was up, our planes returned. Because they were above decks the Jap civilians were really chopped up in the strafing and bombing.

Pfc. LEE DAVIS:

The American planes came back and one of their bombs hit the back end of the ship. The ship immediately started listing and it gradually settled lower and lower. Some Americans climbed the ladder to the deck and managed to remove the cover. I don't know how I managed it, but I climbed out with some others. It was a mad scramble, sort of like a bunch of rats trying to get out of a hole. When I reached the deck, instead of jumping overboard and to safety, I ran for the dining room to look for food. Just before I reached it, a Japanese guard came out of a door near me and began to spray the area with his machine gun. I turned and jumped overboard. Almost at once I grabbed a plank and started paddling for shore. I noticed an officer swimming. The only way I knew he was an officer was by his age. He had a long white beard which was floating over his shoulders. I offered to give him a ride. "Would you like a little help in getting into shore?" He was dog paddling along. "No, thanks," he said, "the water's fine." Right then the American planes came in again and everyone in the water started waving. The first fighter recognized us and wigwagged his wings. We began screaming with joy. When I reached shore the Japanese were waiting.

Capt. MARION LAWTON:

When the fighters came back, our guys waved them off. Seeing white bodies, they must have understood there were prisoners aboard, because they flew away and did not return until late in the afternoon.

The guards told us to take off our clothes, and since we were only about 300 or 500 yards from shore, we were made to swim ashore. I don't know of anyone who drowned. Several prisoners, Ken Wheeler for one, and a guy from Utah, made several trips back and forth helping people who were in difficulty.

Henry and I kept our clothes and shoes. We figured if we saw any indication that the Japs were going to jump us, we'd duck under the water and take our clothes off. In the swim I lost my shoes.

Once on shore we were herded onto a fenced-in cement tennis court located near the officers' quarters in the old American Navy base. There were probably 1,300 of us gathered there.* I recognized we were at Olongapo in Subic Bay.

The first night most of the men without clothes were cold from the wind. The next day we roasted and blistered in the sun. We went without food this first day.

Pfc. LEE DAVIS:

There were many, many wounded men lying about. They had been wounded either in the strafing runs or when the bombs landed. Most of these men died quickly as their wounds turned gangrenous. I assisted one of our doctors in bandaging a small-arm wound one of the men had. When we looked at the arm in the morning, it had turned angry green and yellow. It looked very bad. The doctor† said we had to try to save his life by amputating his arm. We picked the guy up and carried him into the tennis court and found some place where we had enough room to operate. The only surgical tool the doctor had was a pocketknife. He told the young man what he was going to do, then, "Anything we can do for you? Would you like to bite on

---

* The American leadership counted 1,320 men making it to shore. They estimated that fifty of the missing 300 had died due to the conditions on the ship during the nights of Dec. 13 and 14. The others died in the bombings or had drowned. In the tennis court the men were organized into lines of 100 men each. Eleven of these lines stretched across the concrete playing surface. An American officer was placed in charge of each line, and he in turn broke his line into squads and appointed squad leaders. An additional 200 men were in a sand and gravel sick-bay area which lay behind one of the base lines.

† Lt. Col. Jack Swartz, who had been the hospital CO in Cabanatuan. The Marine who lost his arm was named Speck.

a piece of wood?" The guy said, "Do you have a cigarette?" Someone had half of one and he gave it to this man to smoke while his arm was being cut off. He lived but a few hours.

Capt. MARION LAWTON:

The second day they brought us a sack of raw rice* I ended up with about three level mess spoons of uncooked rice each day spent in the tennis court. There was a water spigot outside the fence where we would go to get water. Sometime in the next day or so they brought down some truck loads of Salvation Army-type clothes, all Filipino sizes. Someone would get a pair of socks, someone else tennis shoes, or a shirt or a pair of pants. We stayed on the tennis court for what I remember to be four or five days.

Around December 20 they loaded us on trucks and took us to San Fernando, Pampanga, which was along the Death March route. Half the group was put in the provincial prison and the other half in the local movie theater. We stayed there until Christmas Eve.

Pfc. LEE DAVIS:

Before we were put onto the trains at San Fernando, they separated the Americans who were too sick or wounded from the healthy ones. I got in the line with the sick. I told them I was too sick to make the journey to Japan. They shoved me back into the line of healthy prisoners. The men they removed were supposed to be returned to Bilibid. I never learned if they got there.†

Capt. MARION LAWTON:

Christmas Eve we were crowded again into trains, the same trains that had taken us to Camp O'Donnell, and early on Christmas morning we arrived above Lingayen Gulf at San Fernando, La Union.‡ We were marched down to the Port Area, where we stayed for a couple of more days. We were hot and

---

* Thousands of miles away in Belgium, where it was Dec. 16, the Germans launched their greatest counteroffensive of the war in the west. Eight days later, American forces broke through the Bulge and aided the forces trapped in Bastogne.
† Inquiries into what happened to these fifteen men have shown that they never arrived at Bilibid or Cabanatuan. Whether their truck was caught on the road and bombed, or whether they were murdered by the Japanese, is a question that has not yet been answered.
‡ Into each railroad car the Japanese put 150 men with another thirty-five or so riding on each of the cars' roofs. The train arrived around 2:00 a.m. on Christmas morning, after a seventeen-hour trip.

thirsty the whole time. On the beach, however, they let us cool off in the China Sea.* Many of the men were not fed.

Several days later we were lined up and packed into two Jap freighters. The *Enoura Maru* housed almost 1,000 of us. The rest, approximately 250, were loaded on the *Brazil Maru*. The ship that I was on (the *Enoura Maru*) had just unloaded horses, and the flies were just like bees. The floor of the hold was covered with horse manure and urine and smelled terribly.

The convoy sailed by day and anchored by night, always hugging the west coast of Luzon. When we left the Philippines we made Takao, Formosa. During the voyage food was scarce again. The flies were constant. We would have lowered to us a tub of rice. The flies were like hornets coming out of their hive. When the tub got to the bottom you couldn't see the rice for the flies. We were so hungry it didn't make any difference. At first we groveled through the horse troughs searching for any grains of barley which had not been eaten. Probably twenty men died on this stretch. We accumulated eight or ten bodies before they would let us bury them over the side.

When we arrived in Formosa, around December 31, we anchored in the harbor and tied up alongside another freighter. For several days we sat there. Then one morning we heard a plane coming in. We knew it was American by the pitch of the engine. Jap planes had sort of a rattly sound, but this one whined. I told Henry to get going and we worked our way to the front of the hold, which was where it was the narrowest. Smaller target, you know. I had figured the plane would attack midship and I wanted to get as far away from there as I could. We had scrambled forward when that damn bomb hit.† One plane, one bomb. It hit along the edge of the deck. It broke loose timbers which crushed many of the men. It knocked down the girders holding up the deck, and all of this steel fell down amongst the men who were packed under it. Everyone was dazed by the concussion. I looked around when I could and saw about a dozen fellers crushed by a beam. They were in agony. I couldn't move at first. People all around were pleading for help. Men were pinned across the legs or chest or back. Henry and I finally rounded up about twenty people and we started to help these poor fellers. There were just a few of us, but we

---

* Groups of 100 each got to spend about ten minutes in the water. That day two rations of one rice ball per man were issued. The distribution of this food was not organized properly, so that some men received neither food nor water.

† Jan. 9, 1945. Five hundred miles south, on Luzon, four divisions of Gen. Walter Krueger's 6th Army began landing on the shores of Lingayen Gulf. The air attacks on Formosa that day in support of the Luzon invasion were flown by carrier planes of Task Force 38 and B-29s from the 20th Bomber Command.

were impelled to help. We confronted a mangled eighteen-inch steel H-beam. We would have needed a steam crane to pick it up. We couldn't budge it. We sat there with those men underneath that beam for three days before the Japs ever did anything.

There were about 600 of us in the hold and I'd have to say nearly half were killed outright. Many more died later from wounds.* I got hit in the hand with some shrapnel. Our own corpsmen and doctors did all they could. They made splints out of smashed boards, they tore up shirts to wrap wounds. 'Course, there were flies on all the wounds. There was no sanitation, and it was merely a matter of stopping the bleeding or putting splints on broken limbs.

At the end of three days the Japs lowered a net into the hold in order for us to load our dead. When the net was full, they emptied the net into a barge standing next to us. Then they lowered the net again. That's how we got our dead out.

Finally some Jap medics came in with Mercurochrome and dabbed a few wounds and that was the extent of the medical treatment.

We sat in the smashed hull for several more days before we were transferred to the *Brazil Maru*. This took place about January 12, 1945.† It had been nearly a month since we left Manila and we had only made Formosa. Shortly after we were moved to the other freighter, we sailed in convoy for Japan.‡ Nearly as soon as we left Formosa we hit cold weather. The *Brazil Maru* was carrying sugar as well as prisoners, and it wasn't long before the fellers got into it and gorged themselves. Diarrhea arrived.

We were crowded and thirsty. There was never enough food. Many had diarrhea and then, with the cold weather, pneumonia hit us. Now we ran into snow and ice storms. A tarpaulin had been put over the hatch, but the freezing wind whipped through the hold. When it rained, the dirty water from the deck would pour down on us. Men drank it—filthy, dirty water. The diarrhea and pneumonia just started wiping us out.§ We buried an average of twenty-five a day.

Pfc. LEE DAVIS:

On our way through the East China Sea we were packed in terrible. Dead bodies were stacked like logs against the bulk-

---

* Approximately 270 were killed and another 250 wounded.
† The Enoura Maru was bombed again and sunk at Takao by B-24s of the Far East Air Force on March 26, 1945.
‡ An estimated 975 prisoners began this voyage.
§ Comdr. Frank J. Bridget was one of those who died of diarrhea during this leg of the trip.

head. Many had died of malnutrition and exposure. The bodies were sunk at sea. It was so cold the deck was covered with ice. We had no clothes. We had just left the tropics, so we were unprepared for the cold. The Japs had hung a box over the side of the ship which we used as a toilet. One day we were in line waiting to use this *benjo*. I was shivering and feeling miserable. A man in front of me dashed over to fill his canteen with some brackish water that had collected on a canvas covering. He ran down to the hold before the Japanese could catch him. Instead, the guard hit the man who was standing next to him, who happened to be me. I was knocked down to the deck with a cruel blow from his rifle stock that caught me between the shoulder blades. I guess I should be ashamed of it, but I began crying.

Capt. MARION LAWTON:

For more than a week we sailed, arriving on Kyushu in late January.* I've seen the figure that 500 of us arrived alive. Somewhere else it says 375. Out of more than 1,600.† After we got to Japan we lost about 100 people who were just about gone when we arrived.

When we were taken on shore there was snow on the ground. The Japanese split us into three groups of 100. Some clothing was issued.

Henry and I had stuck together all this time. We were terribly run down. We were given three blankets each. From them, Henry and I made a sleeping bag. Like a cocoon, we tucked in the sides and bottom and we could slide into it and keep fairly warm. My stomach was all right, but I was terribly dehydrated and in right low condition. The doctors gave me intravenous injections of saline which helped. The stuff came out of Red Cross packages the Japs had there. We were finally moved into barracks. In moving, Henry and I became separated. I noticed when we bedded down that he was two or three cots from me.

I knew he was ill and when I caught the corpsman I asked what his trouble was. He told me Henry had pneumonia and that he was a very sick man. The next morning I looked up

---

* The morning of Jan. 30, 1945, the Brazil Maru arrived in Moji, Japan, a major port and industrial center on the Shimonoseki Strait. In the evening of this day, American troops recaptured Clark Field and Fort Stotsenburg on Luzon. In addition, heavy air strikes continued against Iwo Jima in preparation for the invasion of that tiny Japanese-held island just 700 miles from Tokyo.

† No accurate figures exist as to how many men survived this ordeal. Lieutenant Colonel Beecher recalls that out of his original group of 588 there remained only 160.

and there was Henry in his undershorts, nothing else on, strolling towards the door. I called to him and asked him where he thought he was going. He said, "I'm going to get some of that snow. I'm thirsty." I said, "Henry, please come back. There's plenty of hot tea here." "No," he said, "I'm hot. I've got to have something cool." His fever was burning. He strolled on out. That night he died.

You know, you go through battle and through this Death March and prison camps and thousands of people die and you get hardened to it. If you didn't, you'd crack up. So it got that death didn't upset me. This bothered me really. I couldn't get used to knowing that I had become indifferent to death. I thought no more of a man dying than an animal thinks of it. When Henry died, I cried.

It saddened me and tore me up, but you know, it did something for me. I'm selfish in this, but Henry's death contributed a lot to me. From him I regained a tenderness, a real concern, an emotional feeling for my fellow man. It was sad and yet, selfishly, it was a beautiful thing for me. I don't think that's unreasonable either, that even in his death he gave me something.

12
HARD LABOR

As the war rolled forward, the Japanese military machine ground up more and more of its country's economy. Signs of austerity appeared in every facet of Japanese life. The American submarine blockade seriously affected the amount of raw material shipped into the country. Industrial centers, packed next to each other, made ideal targets for American bombers. Industrial production began to lag and food became particularly scarce. The shattering defeats of 1943 required that millions of Japanese factory workers be drafted into the military. Japan's industrial foundation began to crack.

In an effort to replace some of the labor force lost through conscription, the Japanese transported its war capitives to the Home Islands. More than 175 camps were established in Japan to house this newly arrived prisoner work force. For thousands of men, places with exotic names such as Shinagawa, Fukuoka, Oyama, Tobata, and Toyama became places of hard labor, hunger, and despair.

American prisoners of war found the work they were required to do hard, the hours long, the days off infrequent, the food inadequate, the living conditions harsh. They went and did whatever manual labor the Japanese ordered them to do. They shoveled coal and repaired railroad track, they pushed dump cars and chipped paint, fed and cleaned blast furnaces, unloaded and loaded ships and barges. They worked in coal, lead, and nickel mines, rolling mills and foundries, steel plants, dry docks and piers. Daily amounts of work

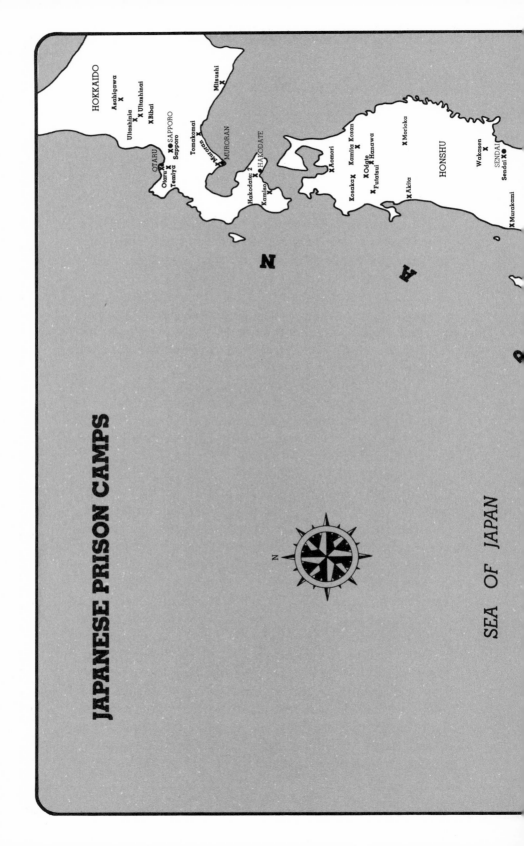

JAPANESE PRISON CAMPS

HOKKAIDO

Asahigawa
X

Ultaahinia
X   X Ultaahinai
X Bibai

Mitsushi
X

OTARU
Otaru X   X ● SAPPORO
Yamiya   Sapporo

Tomakomai
X

MURORAN
X Muroran

Hakodate 2
X   HAKODATE
Kamijo ●
X

X Aomori
Kamita Kozan
X
Kosaka X   X Odate   X Morioka
X Futatsui   Hanawa

X Akita

HONSHU

Wakasen
X
SENDAI
Sendai X ●

X Murakami

N

SEA   OF   JAPAN

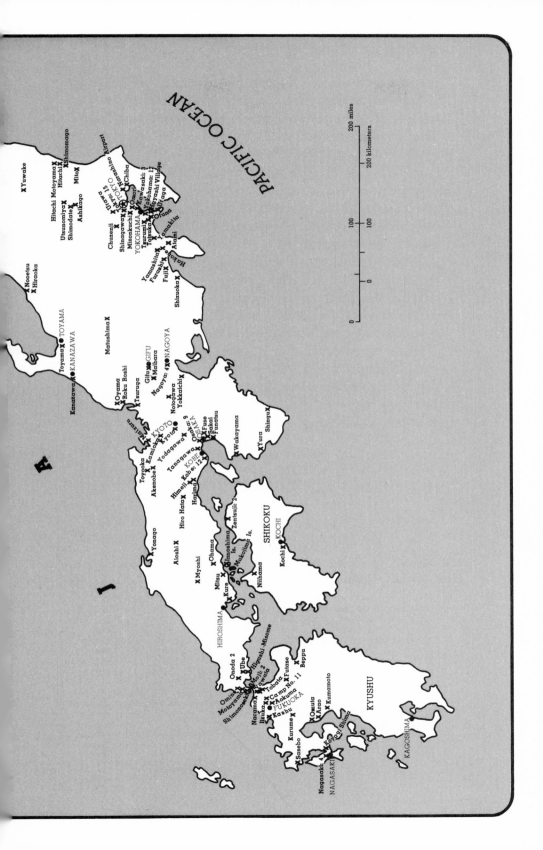

PACIFIC OCEAN

X Yuwake

Hitachi Motoyama X
Utsunomiya X   Hitachi X
Shimodate X   X Shimomogo
Ashikago   Mito X

Nooetsu   Chuzenji X   Narashino Airport
X Hiraoka   Ureo: 15 S   O Narashino ?
                                    Shinagawa X X TOKYO   X Chiba
Hitachi   Shimodate X X Omori
Toyama X   KANAZAWA   Mitonkuchi X X X X Kawasaki: 2
Kanazawa X   YOKOHAMA X X X X Yokohama: 12
                              Tsurumi X X X X Ariyoshi Village
                          Toguka X X X X Uraga
                          Matushima X   X Ofuna
                                    Yamashita X X Kamakita
                                    Fuwaki X
                                    Fuji X   X Ha jo?   X Atami
Toyama X TOYAMA   Shizuoka X

Gifu X GIFU
X Oyama   Gifu X X Maibara
X Roku Roshi   X NAGOYA
    Tsuruga   Nagoya: X X
                Notogawa X
                Yokkaichi X
X Maizuru
Toyooka   X KYOTO
X Akenobe X Kamikawa X X X Yura X Yura
Toyooka X Yodagawa X X X Osaka: 9   X Shingu
Tanagawa X X OSAKA
Himeji X KOBE Kobe: 12 X Fuse
Harima X   X Fundtsu   X Wakayama
Hiro Hata X   X Sakai

Aioshi X   Zentsuji: 2
X Myoshi   Shimoshima
Mitsu   Is.
Kure X X X Mukojima Is.
                X Nihama   X Kochi   KOCHI
HIROSHIMA   SHIKOKU   Kochi X

Onoda 2   Higashi-Misome
X Ube   Iwata X
Ominato X   Moji: 2
Motoyama X X X Tobata X Futase
Shimonoseki X X X X   Beppu
Iizuka X X X X X X X Camp No. 11
Nagasaki X X X X FUKUOKA
X Kasui   X Kumamoto
Kurume X   X Omuta
X Sasebo   X Arao
Nagasaki X X X X Gogai Shima
NAGASAKI

KYUSHU

KAGOSHIMA

0   100   200 miles
0   100   200 kilometers

required of each prisoner were often established. If these quotas were not met, the men were punished. When reached, the quotas were increased. The prisoners worked in rain and snow, they worked when it was hot and when it was below zero. Unable to properly feed their own civilian population, the Japanese gave the prisoners only enough food to guarantee they would work another day. For the men captured on Bataan, 1945 began their fourth year of chronic starvation.

More important than their slow physical deterioration, the treatment they received in Japan began to work on the minds and spirits of the prisoners. The threads which precariously laced this captive community together began to unravel. Unable to prevail, the human spirit now endured and hoped only to survive. Under the Japanese, life had always been flint hard. Now, in Japan, it became more and more difficult, and by the summer of 1945 it verged on the impossible.

Cpl. HUBERT GATER, Fukuoka Camp No. 3 (Yawata/Tobata)*:

We arrived in Kobe. Because of the heat at Manila Bay, almost all had taken off their shoes and shirts. Most of us dis-

* Fukuoka Camp No. 3 was first located in a suburban section of the city of Yawata on the island of Kyushu. Yawata was one of Japan's major steel-producing areas, and the camp there was first occupied in Sept. 1942 by American civilians captured on Wake Island. A large steam electric plant was located within 500 yards of the camp installation; surrounding it were steel mills and steel rolling mills, all producing Japanese war essentials and relying substantially on prisoner labor to operate them.

To protect the prisoner personnel, as far as possible, from anticipated bombing raids, a new camp was erected in a suburb of Tobata. The prisoners of war continued to work in the Yawata plants throughout the war, and were transported to and from the camp in open flatcars even during the bitterly cold winter weather. Of the total prison population of 1,200, nearly 500 were American. The working day was nine to ten hours long, and did not include the time it took to get to and from the camp.

Camp locations appear in parentheses. All the camps, except where otherwise noted, were in Japan.

embarked missing some type of clothing we were certainly going to need.

There were very few civilians around the dock area, which was probably restricted. We had another long wait while we were counted again. We were led to electric streetcars. Each car was filled properly, two men to a seat. The blinds were closed. In about an hour, after a few stops, we were ordered out. Fukuoka, Japan. Prison Camp No. 3. There were eight barracks, 150 men to each. Half of them were occupied by mostly Javanese Dutch, East Indians, and English from the fall of Singapore.

We were given cards to fill out. The important question was our civilian occupation. I put down cook. Not my occupation, but what I had done for two years at Cabanatuan. We were then issued wooden dog tags to be worn around our neck. On one side was my Japanese POW number. On the other side, in Japanese, the classification of my future job. About thirty were classified as cooks. After we got our new dog tags, we asked the Japanese interpreter what the Japanese words on them meant. I'll never forget it. He said, "Electric furnace." We were elated. We would probably bake bread and pastry for the camp.

Then came the issue of clothing. Pants and coats. No underwear and no socks. It's easy to describe. They were burlap, green in color, and you could read a newspaper through them.

We were issued a *bento* box, built like our cigar box, but about half the size. This was to be our lunch pail from now on. In this you would get three rations a day, day after day, rice only. Now and then the evening meal would have some dried minnows, uncleaned, or a piece of sand shark that was so rank you swallowed it because you needed to go another day.

During the day we marched in twos to the electric train track. We were green. The old-timers knew the tricks. Whoever jumped in first got the back rest against the side of the flatcars. Those little guys from India could run between our legs and get the best seats. We went through a long tunnel built by the Japanese and English in World War I. When you left the tunnel you were suddenly in a twenty-square-mile steel mill. When we got off the flatcars there was a Jap civilian to take charge of each group. We were again counted before going to our work area. My group of thirty cooks was taken to a huge building about a mile from the tunnel. I don't think our cooking experience helped us much on this new job. They figured we could stand the heat, so we were assigned to the electric steel blast furnaces.

Thirty of us started out. Within a month there were twelve of us left. They didn't all die. Some were sick enough to stay in camp, and others were put on other jobs. When I say sick, the only way you could remain in camp was to have a temperature of 102 degrees or over.

I started each day by going down a line to fill tubs of iron ore, sand, and lime. These were taken away by crane to the furnaces. That first week ended with my hands blistered and bleeding.

Staff Sgt. HAROLD FEINER, Fukuoka Camp No. 17 (Omuta)*:

This camp was as tough as they came. It was mean. If there was nothing else that had gone wrong, the work itself would have made it bad. We mined coal twelve hours a day, had a thirty-minute lunch break, and were given one day off every ten days. We weren't represented by the United Mine Workers, that's for sure. You can't describe the conditions. Some of the coal veins American miners wouldn't even consider working, the Japanese were working. We would have to wade in rivers. We'd drag beams and cross members seven feet, eight feet, nine feet long while crawling on our knees through little tiny laterals. They didn't want to know how it was done. Just do it.

We worked many days until we almost fell. It was indescribably hard work, especially with those maniacs. They were all hyped up. This little Jap puppet would get on a stand—they loved to elevate themselves—and he'd tell the overmen how much had to be dug that day. He spoke too fast for us to understand all of it, but we figured it out because we knew the numbers. You'd hear this *woosh, woosh, woosh,* all this bowing up and down.

---

* Omuta is located forty miles south of the city of Fukuoka, on the island of Kyushu. The camp site for No. 17, located in a compound built by the Mitsui Coal Mining Company, was operated by the Japanese Army. A group of 500 American prisoners, the "A" Detail sent from Cabanatuan, arrived and opened the camp in August 1943. Another group of 200 arrived in Sept. 1944. British, Australian, and Dutch prisoners were also housed in No. 17 and worked in the mines. The total population of the camp was 1,721. Three shifts a day worked in coal mines and zinc smelters. Each shift worked twelve hours a day; every tenth day was a day off.

The last detail of Americans assigned to Fukuoka No. 17 were ninety-five survivors of the Oryoku Maru. The 497 prisoners who survived this ill-fated voyage reached Moji, Kyushu, on Jan. 29, 1945. These prisoners were at first divided among the Fukuoka area camps. One hundred went to No. 3 (Tobata), 193 to No. 1 (Kashi), ninety-five to No. 17 (Omuta), and 110 to the Japanese military hospital in Moji. Of this last group, thirty-four were eventually moved in Feb. and Mar. 1945 to No. 22 (Aokuma). The remaining seventy-six prisoners died in Moji. The final count of dead on this voyage is 1,198. For many of the 421 survivors there still remained one more trip. In April 1945 survivors helped make up a detail which was sent to Korea and Manchuria.

We didn't wear clothes in the mine. It was generally very hot. In the winter this was sometimes good. But we had sores over our bodies and the sweat would burn the hell out of us. Our eyes would burn and it would get into our genital area, and we'd scratch all over. Burn. Your feet, everything.

Our faces were black. We used to always say, "Jesus, will we ever get the coal dust out of our bodies?" It was ingrained everywhere. All black. Our eyes were black, our ears. Any crevice would be black. We were given baths, but we never got clean.

Capt. BENSON GUYTON (Omine Machi)*:

When we landed at Moji a Jap guard there was telling us about planes they called Bee-Nijoo-Koo. I got the gist of it, from some of the other boys that understood Japanese better than I did, that the B-29s had bombed the steel works at Yawata. Then we were put on a train with the shades pulled down, and probably after a forty or fifty-mile train ride we arrived at the little coal mine village of Omine. We walked a mile or so up a steep grade to a fenced-off village consisting of two-story barracks in which our people were to sleep four to a room. The rooms were tiny and the straw mattresses touched each other. Being a captain, I had a room to myself, which was nice for a guy that had been sleeping on bamboo slats at Cabanatuan.

We found when we arrived nearly 200 British prisoners, mostly from an AA artillery battalion, who had first seen service in the air battle of Britain. They had been captured on Java and brought to Omine in 1942.

The mine was a big one. We were just 256 American prisoners of more than 1,000 that were needed to work this particular mine. There were maybe 1,000 Koreans, perhaps as many Japanese, and a lot of women.

I went into the mine after the war was over just for my education. The British officers had worked in the mine when they first arrived. I guess I ought to be grateful to them, because at some time before we arrived they had finally gotten a kind of agreement with the Japanese that officers would not work in the mine. I much preferred sitting on my butt to mining coal.

What always played on my mind, however, was the feel-

---

* The coal mine at Omine, on the island of Honshu, is said to have been the largest coal mine in the Hiroshima district. The first occupants of this camp were 180 British prisoners who arrived in Nov. 1942. The American detail, numbering around 250 prisoners, reached Omine on Sept. 6, 1944. Able-bodied prisoners worked in the mines, drilling, mining, and loading. The coal cars were filled and pushed by hand. The mine was operated on two shifts, 5:30 a.m. to 6:00 p.m. and 4:30 p.m. to 5:30 a.m., with shifts alternating each ten days.

ing that here I was drawing officer's pay for supposedly being in command of a group, and I wasn't really doing anything. It was obvious from the first that the men were being worked in the mine longer hours than were good for them. It was also evident that a lot of men were going to the mine who really were sick, or in some other way unable to work—sore feet or afflicted with hideous boils. We also got insufficient food. We hadn't been there, I guess, over a few days before Jerry Mc-Davitt, the American commander, and I went over to the English major to talk with him about conditions. You know, "What do we do?" He was a good officer and had been to the Japs before to complain. He said, "I'll go with you and we'll ask for more food. It won't do any good, but we'll go." It turned out exactly as he predicted.

First off, getting to see this snotty little Jap captain proved difficult. He had a corporal who was his next in command. Corporal Kiniyama was a pretty mean guy and you had to get past him before you saw the captain. and this wasn't easy. So we went in.

"What do you want to see him about?"

"We want to talk to him about improving conditions in the camp."

"What do you want to improve?"

'Course, he doesn't know much English, so we have to go over this a dozen times before we see any light on his face, indicating he's understanding what we're saying. He growls at us and threatens to whack us with his wood sword.

Eventually, he agrees for us to see the captain. Mind you, all Americans had to salute Japs. American captains had to salute Jap privates. At any rate we are being coached, and he shows us how to bow. I never did learn to bow to Kiniyama's satisfaction, but eventually we get into see this Captain Saka-moto. We are allowed to knock on his door. He of course pays no attention. We're confused: if we knock again do we make him mad? Eventually we go through with it, we walk in and bow, and he kind of half nods back. He turns out to be edu-cated in California and speaks English with a mean accent. He never once showed any indication that he had any good feelings toward Americans. My evaluation of him was that he was a smart-aleck type. We then make our plea. "A lot of our men that are in the mine really are unable to work. They're sick. Could you possibly allow . . ."—I mean, we're damn near begging—"would you be able to let a few more of our sickest men stay in? Would you let our doctor tell you which ones are unfit? These men are working long hours, they don't have any safety equipment, they don't have shoes, they are not being fed properly." What we get back from him as an answer is a long, hard stare. That is all.

1st Lt. MARK HERBST, M.D., Mukden Prisoner-of-War Camp (Hoten, Manchuria)*:

The reason we saved so many men, so far as I'm concerned, is that we learned about soybeans. When I first went into this camp, being the senior medical officer, I was in on the conclave with the Japanese when we explained to them the terrible dysentery, beriberi, and malnutrition our fellers were suffering with. The Jap commander asked, "What do you need?" I said, "Ordinary food." "Do you want rice?" I said, "No. We gotta have protein." "What's protein?" "Meat, fish, milk, cheese," I answered. "Cheese?" "Yeah." He went out and came back with two little Edam cheese wheels. "Well," I said, "that's pretty good for my hollow tooth, but what do we do for the other 1,399 men?" We bandied around a while. I thought, then asked, "You got a lot of soybeans around here, haven't you?" "Yes. Do you eat soybeans?" I said, "I told you, we'll eat anything. We prefer meat, but we will eat soybeans." So he very carefully experimented and brought in a few soybeans. We got to the point where we'd count the number of beans in each bowl of soup we dished out. Five beans one time, maybe nine the next time. If one guy got five, while someone else get six, all hell would break out. Finally, since the Japs didn't eat them, we got quite a few soybeans. We baked them, we boiled them, we fried them, we even crushed them and made bean curd. See, soybeans

* The men that occupied this camp were in the detail that left Cabanatuan in late summer of 1942. A group of thirty-one officers and 1,962 enlisted men left Manila Oct. 8, 1942, on the Tattori Maru. It is reported that this ship also transported Japanese soldiers who had been captured by the Americans during the fighting on Bataan. These soldiers were seen to be in chains. When the American detail arrived in Kobe, nearly 600 were transferred to a Pusan hospital. The remaining PWs, when joined by 100 Englishmen, were sent to Mukden, arriving on Nov. 11, 1942. They were first placed in a temporary camp located about a mile north of the Mukden city limits, and occupied barracks built at the time of the Russo-Japanese War. Conditions at this temporary camp were very unsatisfactory due to the winter weather, inadequate housing, and insufficient medical service. During the first winter approximately 200 died of malnutrition, exposure, and the poor condition the men were in when they left Cabanatuan.

On July 19, 1943, the entire camp was transferred to a new facility especially constructed for the prisoners of war. Most of the stories related in these chapters took place in this new camp. The camp was located on a fertile plain on the outskirts of the city of Hoten (called Mukden, until the Japanese changed its name in 1931). It was approximately three miles northeast of the Walled City, on the railroad line to Harbin. It faced the MKK (Manchukuo Kaubushiki Kaisha) factory where many of the men worked. Prisoners also worked in a tannery, a textile factory, and a lumber mill. The working day was eight hours long and no work was required on Sundays.

have protein, they have minerals, they have carbohydrates, and they got vitamins. They helped us get through.

Capt. THOMAS HEWLETT, M.D., Medical Corps,
Fukuoka Camp No. 17 (Omuta):

Deficiency diseases were a continuing medical problem, and despite repeated pleas to the Japanese command, we were never able to obtain any dietary improvement.

The Japanese soldier of World War II appeared well-nourished throughout the conflict. Basic items of his diet were rice, fish, and a multiplicity of vegetables and fruits in season. Since this was the traditional diet of Japan, the soldier fared well and at worst might be faced with a ration of decreased volume. The diet of the prisoner of war was based solely on rice, without any other source of protein, carbohydrate, or fat. Fish and fresh vegetables were never made available in amounts significant enough to be considered of nutritional value. Rare issues of dog meat or whale blubber served only to aggravate the digestive problems of men in a state of chronic starvation.

In our continuing survey of the food at Camp 17, we were aware of the dilutions of the two major rice rations served to the prisoners. Prisoners serving in the mess facility of the Japanese guard detail kept us advised of the difference in the food served in the Japanese mess. Doctor Murao, the first Japanese doctor assigned to the camp, informed us that millet was used to increase the volume of the ration. It had no true food value.

Our individual rations were based on individual work status, the larger rations being served to those on full-work status, lesser amounts were served to those on light duty or patient status. The latter two groups being basically unproductive in the war effort.

Cpl. ISHMAEL COX, Temporary Camp (Hoten, Manchuria):

When we first got to Mukden it was winter and we were very hungry. We cleaned the villagers out of their dogs. I'd eaten nearly everything else—cats, rats, snakes. We'd be on a detail in the Philippines and see a damn snake go across the road. He didn't have a chance. That snake might just as well have said, "Here I am, take me." You know how strong an eel tastes like? Well, a snake is three times as strong and tastes like mud and dirt, but it was something to eat. On Bataan, of course, we ate monkeys. Skinned and cleaned, they look like little newborn babies. To me they tasted like liver. Now I was going to eat dog. To stay alive, mister, a man will do almost any damn thing.

I didn't want to get the first dog. I thought, "How can you

kill man's best friend?" But I learned they make damn good meat when you're hungry. Some of the fellers set a snare and placed it out one of the windows. The guys would all yank and drag the poor dog into the barracks. Once they got him inside they beat it to death. I thought, "What a hell of a way to do it." That night, when we got to cooking up the meat, I said, "Boy, that smells like walking by Joe's place back home." It smelled so good. We got to killing so many dogs that, because it was winter and cold enough inside the barracks so that you could write your name on the frost formed on the walls, we hung their carcasses up just like in a butcher shop. When we left the area the villagers couldn't find a damn dog.

Pfc. WILLIAM WALLACE (Niigata):

It was just unbelievable how little food we were given in Niigata. Once a week, usually, we were given some type of fish, usually stewed. Most every day we got boiled soybeans in a soup. Then we got three cups of steamed rice, about as much as a normal coffee cup would contain.

I was assigned to the Rinko Coal Company, and our group was responsible for unloading all the coal boats coming down from Manchuria. There were two details: shoveling coal from a ship's hold, or loading railroad cars. Which job you did depended on how you arrived at the coal yard. We would march five miles each day from camp, four men abreast. When we arrived, the Japs would take the first 100 and send them into the hold of the ship, and the last 100 would work on the railroad. The next day you'd say to yourself, "I don't want to push no railroad car, so I'll get in the front of the column." That day they'd reverse the details. So you never knew what job you'd get by your place in the line.

The hold of the ship meant filling large steel nets with coal. A hundred men would work filling three nets. One would be going, another coming, and another being filled. There was always one net which needed filling. The nets then unloaded the coal on a barge where it would be shoveled onto a conveyor belt, which carried it twenty feet into the air to a railroad trestle. There the coal was loaded into small coal cars. Then a prisoner would push this car several miles to the railroad spur, where it would be dumped in a large railroad gondola car. We did this work all day. We would leave camp at 5:00 in the morning and we would never return before 8:00 at night. Once a week they would take us into a large bathhouse. Everybody took baths at the same time—coolies, women workers, and prisoners.

The hardest work detail was pushing the coal cars. The track was uneven. The wheels on the cars had not been greased for years and years and years. The Japs would put two coolies or two women on one car, but when it came to prisoners they assigned one. Each of these little cars held about a ton and a half of coal.

When you got to the railroad you would load a freight car. If you got there and there were no gondolas waiting, you'd dump the coal on the ground and return to the ship with your empty car. The first priority was to get the coal ships unloaded, so they could get out of the harbor before there was an air raid.

When railroad cars were available, there would be a detail which took the coal from the pile that had been dumped, and loaded it into the freight cars. Four guys made up a detail. We used *yea hoe* poles which had baskets at each end and were carried across our shoulders. Two men would shovel the baskets full, and the other two would dump the baskets into the railroad car. Our quota was to fill two gondola cars a day: one by the lunch break, the other before we left at night for camp. We found that the railroad cars came in different sizes. If you got a small car it was an easy assignment. If you got one of those huge ones, you'd just have to take a beating that day, because no way under the sun could four people fill it. To the Japs, a car was a car. If one held ten tons and another twenty-five tons, it was still a car as far as the loading was concerned. You always prayed you would draw a small car.

Two men would be on the shovels and two men on the *yea hoe* poles. Every twenty minutes you were supposed to swap positions. Shoveling was considered easier than carrying, because you had to walk up a wood ramp ten or twelve feet to get to the top of the car. If the Japanese were not around to enforce the switch of jobs, it was harder to do. If the guys on the shovels were bigger than the fellers on the baskets, then the guys on the shovels stayed on the shovels. If you weren't big enough to take that shovel away, you stayed on the baskets.

There wasn't anything you could do if you had a really weak guy in your foursome. If you didn't fill your car by the appointed time, you took a beating. In the morning when you went out to work, you tried to locate where the weak people were and then tried to get as far from them as you could.

Sgt. H. G. TYSON (Osaka):

I went to work in the Yodagawa steel mill. The first detail I was put on was making molds in wet sand for castings. I could never get the form out without tearing up the mold. The next job they put me on was breaking pig iron. There were these long ingots that needed to be broken up with twenty-five-pound sledgehammers. I weighed so little that it ended up the sledge-hammer swung me, instead of the other way around. The last job I had in Osaka before being transferred to Oyama was really the hardest and that was working in a rolling mill. I handled sheets of red-hot steel. Using large tongs, I had to feed the sheets through a series of rollers. Although the guards left us alone in this operation, I worked with a Jap civilian who took an instant dislike to me. He tried to feed the hot stuff through the rollers so fast that I wouldn't have time to get my tongs up in time. If I was slow, the hot steel would catch me on the arm and burn me. Made this job particularly difficult.

Sgt. FERRON CUMMINS, Camp 10-D
(Innoshima Island, Onomichi):

Hiroshima was only twenty-five kilometers south of us. My camp was located on an island near the port of Onomichi, and as camps went, this was a small one. There were seventy-eight British and 100 Americans. I hauled anything the Japanese needed hauled—rice, coal, sand, foodstuffs—all around a dry dock area. It wasn't a bad camp. We didn't lose but one man in that camp. He died of a heart attack.

We had learned by this point that we couldn't go any-where, so to survive you kept your nose clean and goofed off as much as you could when you got a chance. This was an art in itself. We slowed down just enough so that it looked like we were still doing something. If something needed two men to lift it, we'd use three. We learned to sense what the guards would let us get by with. At first, it was done by feel. One time we were told to carry some very heavy boards. We de-cided we needed four men to carry them. They wanted one man to do it. Just flat, we told them one couldn't do it. We got our heads cracked a few times, but finally they permitted three men. It was worth the beating, because what was at stake was the amount of work we would have to do. They were al-ways inclined to give us more work. If we didn't draw the line, we'd have been in trouble.

My main job was working with four other fellers pushing a long-tongued two-wheel cart all over this island. One of the men on my detail wasn't able to pull his end of the load, be-cause he was real sick. Since we couldn't change him, we had to carry him. We gave him the easiest part of the job. He was just a weakling.

We hauled pig iron, another time ashes. Always liked to get a detail of hauling rice. Each of us carried a piece of bamboo about six to eight inches long. Stuffed it in our leg wrappings and when we could we'd steal rice by filling up the tube. Our guard was a civilian who treated us real good. He knew what we were doing. When we were loading rice he'd tell us what to do, then he'd go somewhere else. As soon as he went away we'd see what we could get our hands on. If it was edible right there, we consumed it.

I think we got two days off a month, maybe three. Worked sunup to sundown. Every day was the same. Rain or cold. In the winter we pretty near froze. No fire in the barracks. When it rained, we hung our wet clothes at the end of the sleeping bays. In the morning we put them back on. If they were still wet, you went to work with wet clothes.

Pfc. JOHN FALCONER, Fukuoka Camp No. 3
(Tobata):

In the bitterly cold winter of 1944–45 we were transmitted to and from the Dai-ichi Seiko steel mill in open flatbed railroad cars. Often when we got to the pickup point, if the cars hadn't arrived yet, we were able to go over to the giant melting pots that were sitting on a siding and warm ourselves.

In the barracks we had small fire holes which were supposed to keep us warm at night. They never gave us enough fuel to do that, so whenever we could we stole coke from the mill and smuggled it back.

We had a bath there where nearly 1,000 men would wash. It was equipped with two large cement tanks about ten feet square and three feet deep. We'd bathe thirty or fifty at a time and by barracks. If you were the first or second barracks to wash, it would be fair to say you got a little cleaner. If you bathed after that, you'd come out dirtier than you went in. You'd wet yourself first and soap up, then get into the tub. The hot water felt good. One time I got in there and it felt so good I passed out. That was one of the most wonderful feelings I can remember in prison camp. Oh, it was beautiful. A couple of friends hauled me out and I came to. But oh, what a wonderful feeling it was to pass out. Then, nothing troubled me. I thought, Death can't be that bad if it feels like this. After that I thought of this many times.

Staff Sgt. JAMES CAVANAUGH, Subcamp No. 2
(Kawasaki):

On the bay, between Tokyo and Yokohama, is the port city of Kawasaki. Our first job there was to build warehouses down in the port area. One afternoon, this was 1943, they came into camp and plucked me right out of my group and put me in a small room all by myself. Shortly after that, escorted by two guards, I was taken by train to the Shinagawa Camp Hospital in Tokyo, where I was placed in solitary confinement. They told me I was a diphtheria carrier. Now when I was a kid I had diphtheria, but I have no idea how the Japs learned that. They put me in a small room without a window. The only person I ever saw was a Jap medical sergeant. This was really the low part of my life. I was given some reading material, but I was so lonesome and low I didn't use it. I did a lot of thinking. I was there by myself for six months. I thought of my mother and father, and believe me, I prayed a lot. I used to have terrible bouts of depression. After months I got some funny, funny feelings. I had suicidal thoughts. I'd remember about guys that had been killed and I couldn't figure out why I was still alive. I really got low. I think sometimes I was off my rocker. Then, without explanation, they released me and returned me to Kawasaki.

Back in camp I met a British Navy doctor who, on his way to join an aircraft carrier, was captured in the Indian Ocean and wound up in our prison camp. He saved a lot of lives. He saved mine several times. Dr. Anthony Curtin was, and is, his name. He used to actually steal quinine for the men who had malaria. When they'd catch him, they would beat him mercilessly. They'd take him into a rice storage area which was like a cement vault, and two or three guards would work him over. I've seen him beaten so badly that just after it was over he couldn't tell me his name. But they never broke him. He would fight for us, do everything possible to save our lives. One afternoon, in a bombing raid, when a load of steel fell, I broke my left leg at the ankle. After it had been set, a Jap guard who didn't believe I had broken it came over to me and, to make his point, twisted my ankle and oh, Jesus! Doctor Curtin stole some morphine and gave it to me while he reset it.

1st Lt. MARK HERBST, M.D.,
Mukden Prisoner-of-War Camp (Hoten, Manchuria):

Our 1,400 PWs were joined by 600 British prisoners, and this camp had three American and one Australian doctor. Of course we had a Japanese doctor assigned to us. I was the senior American doctor. I had several nicknames. I was "Handlebars" because of the wingspan of my mustache. I was also known as "Breathe Steam Herbst" for my prescription of what the fellers should do for upper respiratory infections. Our surgeon, Elmer

Shabart, was a Chicago Polack. Before the war he had been an alcoholic. Drunk, you wouldn't recognize him, but sober, he was the finest guy in the world. The other American doctor was an introvert who didn't associate with anybody.

Most of the time when we had no medicine we would just talk to the fellers. Talking to them was important. It's the old chiropractic type of thing. You could do something for them, if you got them doing something for themselves. I learned there that I could lay my hands on them and give them a gift of gab and they'd go away happy.

One time I had one of the local Japanese doctors go on sick call with me. Everyone had the same story, diarrhea. Most of the time we had Korean-grown oranges or tangerines around. So my prescription for all these men was an orange, an aspirin, and three tablets of brewer's yeast. We found that just five grains of this compressed Japanese brewer's yeast, called *ebios*, would be enough vitamin B to turn things around. We, maybe, also had a little sulfathiazine. Finally this Japanese doctor said to me, "Are you fortune-telling, doctor?" "What do you mean?" I said. "Don't you examine them?" I said, "No need. They're all alike."

Pfc. EDDY LAURSEN, Temporary Camp
(Hoten, Manchuria):

Doctor Herbst did a lot for me and was a good person. The story I'll tell you is not about him. It happened while we were still in the temporary camp up in Mukden that first winter. My attack happened in the evening and it was terrible. I was lying in bed and it felt like someone had suddenly put a stiletto in my back and was twisting it slowly. I started curling up. About six guys jumped on me to keep me from going too far. One of the fellers went out immediately to get some help, because I was screaming bloody murder. One of our doctors said to this soldier, "Can't you see I'm busy playing cards?" Even today this gets me infuriated. We didn't even have a deck of cards, but he had one. So the soldier came back and told the barracks. Several said, "Let's go!" They went to the officers' quarters. They didn't even knock. They went right in and said, "You come and see Private Laursen right now. Or else!" He threw his cards down. "All right. Bring him up to the dispensary." They came back and six of them picked me up on a rice-straw mattress which was going every which way, and carried me through a narrow hallway, around a sharp turn, then half a block to the dispensary, where they laid me down on the dirt floor. When I say dispensary, don't think of something you see in this country. This

looked like a chicken coop. It was dirty. The doctor came in.
He looked clean to me, and even under those conditions he was
a handsome man with a clear complexion. He towered over me.
I was still groaning and carrying on. "All right," he said, "I
know how you guys are. Speak up. I can't hear you." I just
choked up. Finally he squatted down. I was in a knot. He
grabbed my legs and pulled. I let out a scream. This is the
God's truth, so help me. He ended up diagnosing my problem
as kidney stones. I mean, he didn't have the equipment to do a
proper diagnosis, so I forgive him for that. He finally admitted
me to the so-called hospital and I slowly got a little better, until
they moved us to the new camp. Then I was put in that hospital
for a short time. Eventually, I went to work in the MKK factory.
I stayed there several weeks, until one day I had to run back
to the camp during an air raid.

Pfc. ROBERT BROWN, Mukden Prisoner-of-War Camp
(Hoten, Manchuria):

When I got into camp, I worked in the dispensary with the
doctors. I spoke a little Japanese, so I helped out with the
interpreting. I began to learn Japanese on the *Tattori Maru*.
When you get bumps on your head and then bumps beat off
because you don't understand the language, it behooves you to
learn, doesn't it? I started by listening for words, by using my
ears. If you're paying attention and if they say something
enough times, you begin to pick it up. At one time they encouraged us to try to learn and gave us a phrase book. I found
a copy of this book and passed that right away. What was
strange, besides counting off, which is something we had to
do all the time, the men wouldn't have any part in learning
Japanese. At Mukden I worked with another boy, he was out
of the 31st Infantry, by the name of Hunke, Harry M. Hunke.
He and I tried to learn Japanese together. He'd learn from his
side, and I'd learn from my side, and then we'd compare notes
and practice on each other. We tried to learn ten words a day.
I learned all the parts of the body. Then the words for the
medicine we had, and then the words for all the sicknesses.

While most of the men worked across the road in the MKK
machine-tool factory, Harry and I became interpreters in the
camp infirmary for the Japanese doctors. Every man that came
into sick call, or anything like that, had to go through us.
I would take the men's temperatures and then write a short
narrative of their physical complaints. Then we'd all go through
the daily ritual. All the men who had turned in on sick call in
the morning would sit in the outer office waiting for the Jap

doctor to see them. When the doctor would arrive we'd all get up and bow and then, in Japanese, I'd tell the doctor how many people were there for sick call. Then we'd bow again and the doctor would go back into his office. I'd bring the sick men in, one at a time, and I'd tell the doctor what the man's trouble was. Then, after sick call, Harry and I were janitors. We'd clean the office and scrub the floor or do whatever they wanted.

I didn't allow myself to be caught in the middle of any situation. Also, there wasn't any tug of war going on here between what we wanted and what the Japs wanted. It was all going one way. I was on the bottom, and whatever they said was going to be was the way it was. Whatever you said to them didn't mean a damn thing. You wouldn't dare, anyway, unless you wanted to get a beating. The American doctors tried. They had their professional jealousies. They thought they were much better than the Japanese, and they were. But goddamn it, you didn't try to be arrogant to them. Our doctors tried it and it didn't work with them either, because the Japs kicked them out of the hospital.

I played the game honestly. If a man was sick, I got him in to see the doctor. If he was faking, I made sure he went to work. We had an Englishman once, and it didn't make any difference whether he'd been British or American, I'd have done the same thing, who tried to cheat so he could be hospitalized. What he did was steal another man's stool specimen that was infected with an amebic bacilli. As a result of this he was placed in the dysentery ward of our hospital. The Jap doctor couldn't understand this situation. Here was this Limey, who looked as healthy as a horse, but who had amebic dysentery. The doctor kept shaking his head and saying, *"Okashii, okashii"* [that's odd]. The word finally filtered down to us what this guy was doing, how he was switching stool specimens, so I turned him in. He got the hell beat out of him, but I'd do the same thing tomorrow. He was taking a bed, he was taking our medicine, and he was taking our time and effort, and we didn't have enough of any of these things even for men who were really sick. I was there trying to work the best I could for my fellow prisoners. Sometimes I could influence the Jap doctors into putting a real sick man into the hospital. I certainly didn't want my position compromised by someone who was lying and cheating. If I wasn't square in my dealings with the Japanese, I could never change anything. I had to be in their confidence, if I was going to be the go between. They had to rely on me. It's like the time that this Jap doctor, Kawajima, who was officer of the day, caught me playing poker in the barracks. Hell, if I'd have been somebody else, he'd have beat the hell out of me and the other guys. Fortunately, he didn't want to kill our relationship or my ambition or whatever.

Capt. THOMAS HEWLETT, M.D., Fukuoka Camp No. 17 (Omuta):

Originally, the medical care in Camp 17 was to be handled by Japanese civilian doctors employed by the Mitsui Corporation. Members of the original 500 requested care by fellow Americans and such was started about October 1943. Throughout the two years, medical efforts were severely restricted by the labor quotas established by the Japanese Army. The guard detail demanded so many men in each duty shift, thus our efforts were aimed at protecting the men whom we judged most ill. A medical officer was on clinic duty for each shift that returned from a work detail, thus it was possible to offer some protection to those we found most ill as a shift returned to camp.

As the camp increased in population, doctors who joined us were assigned to work in their field of interest. We were young and not fully trained. As an example, Doctor Bras, interested in laboratory work, arrived in camp with a crude microscope constructed of bamboo tubing and field-glass lens. Thus we gained an additional capablity in diagnosis and it became possible to cross-match blood.

Medical supplies for the camp was a joint responsibility shared equally by the Mitsui Corporation and the Army. Eventually, hospital space increased from a combined dispensary and ward building to one adequately large clinic building and six ward buildings; one isolation ward of nine beds; three medical wards of thirty beds each; two surgical wards, one of thirty beds, one of fifty-eight beds, to a total of 187 beds or mats. Through the humaneness of Baron Mitsui, a 1919 Dartmouth graduate, we did have bed space for the sick and wounded.

Address
You have fulfilled your duties to your countries. It is for you to tender in a clean sheet, to work in harmonious concord, to obey and to lead a life of neat, orderly discipline under our leadership. I profess, on the other hand, to extend you my love and am in everyday prayer for the ever betterment of your conditions here. You are to understand though, that any breach of discipline, any disobedience will court only drastic punishment for you in its most prosaic and military sense.

Colonel M. Matsuda
Commandant, Mukden Prisoner-of-War Camp

2d Lt. FRED GIFFORD, Subcamp No. 5 (Niigata):

The guards would fray the middle of a six-foot-long bamboo pole, leaving both ends solid. They'd stand you at attention, bareheaded, and walk up behind you, hold that stick about six inches from your head and bring it down hard. It didn't hurt bad, but the shock of it and the noise of the broken bamboo gave you the same feeling that an awful beating gives you, only this way it went right into the center of your mind. It just felt like your whole world was caving in.

They punished you that way because they said you had been disobedient. You might have been disobedient in the sense that you didn't understand what they said. They might say "right turn" and you'd turn left or go straight ahead. That was disobeying an order. That's how easy it was to get a beating.

Sgt. H. G. TYSON (Oyama):

It wasn't funny to him, but it was funny to a lot of us. One of the guards came up to a Marine in our camp and said "Wakaru," which means, "Do you understand?" The Marine thought he said, "Walk or run," so he walked a piece and then ran. The guard caught him and beat him.

Being beaten was something you understood would happen to you daily. You were either going to get slapped or you were going to get beaten on the head with a sledgehammer handle. Daily, each and every man could assume that sometime during the day he was going to get beat some way or another. It just got to be an accepted fact. Once you went to work and the guards came out and started checking, you'd be lucky if you weren't picked on. Usually they picked on everybody, so there were no exceptions.

The Japanese mentality was something you tried to figure out, because if you could, you would avoid some punishment. Not too many figured it out, however. I'll give you an example. Let's say nails and pencils are two things on the camp list of items you can't have. One day they suspect there are nails in the camp, so they come through looking for them. If you have any you're in deep trouble. You could, that time, have had a gross of pencils and they wouldn't pay any attention to them. Now the next time they suspect there are pencils in the camp, so they come through looking for pencils. If they found nails, it wouldn't make any difference, because they're looking for pencils.

When they gave us punishment, a lot of times they would say it was on account of our superior attitude. I always used to think, "Well, if you didn't feel inferior, you wouldn't think we had a superior attitude."

Pfc. JACK BRADY (Omori):

I somehow got the impression that he thought he should apparently be God's righthand man. Anything he said was law and if someone forgot, the wrath of God was going to fall on him in the form of "Wily Bird." He was absolutely the most sadistic man I ever met. He used his saber as a club sometimes with, sometimes without the scabbard.

On several occasions he had prisoners lined up so the guards could go to work on them for half an hour with tool handles, broomsticks, or anything that was handy. Once he got me good. Our barracks at Omori were arranged in such a way that his office looked down the row of prisoner barracks. Anybody who came out of the barracks at any time was supposed to bow to his office, whether he was there or not. In my case, as I came out of my barracks, I spotted him in front of me. So instead of bowing to his office, I bowed to him. That was wrong. 'Course it could have been just as bad the other way, if I bowed to his office and not to him. The first thing he did was to take me to the area where the benjos were emptied. Naturally, as the pails were dumped some of the slop spilled on the ground. Over this foul earth he made me do push-ups. Using that damn saber, he made me do push-ups until I collapsed. For days afterwards my arms were useless. I couldn't use them. That's what he did to me. But he was more famous for his beatings, which in some cases put guys out for a week or more.

Not all the guards were miserable characters, though. In fact, we had one we called "Gentleman Jim." While he was camp commander there wasn't a thing that went on that was out of line. But as soon as he left, oh man, it got miserable again. Whereas some of the camp commanders lasted only six months, Wily Bird stayed on forever. His real name was Watanabi. We also, sometimes, called him "Animal."

We had some real characters. One doctor we called "Doctor Fujiyama" because he was constantly blowing his stack about something. Our interpreter we called "the Black Bastard." He was invariably dressed in black. The last half of his name was also accurately given. He was the one who constantly told us the camp rules. He always ended up his speeches, "Anyone who disobeys this law will be shooted to death by a bayoneted guard." It was impossible to keep from laughing, no matter how often we heard him say this. He'd get madder and madder, the more we laughed. He wasn't too easy to get along with, but then it could have been our fault. Another guard had a sweet expression so we called him "Kewpie Doll" or "Cutie Pie" or "Baby Doll." He was a sadistic sonovabitch. Then, there was "George." He was a good guard. He had lived for some time before the war in the States. We asked him why he was a guard and not an interpreter. "Hell," he said, "I don't speak Japanese that well."

What made a good guard? If you and he stuck by the same rules. That made a good guard. Predictability. With the bad guards you couldn't tell what they might do. I might be doing something exactly according to the rules and, suddenly, I'd get a terrible beating from behind with a club. Another time I'd do something that was at variance to the camp rules and absolutely nothing would happen. Most of the guards were unpredictable in their reaction to something you'd do. It made life hard. Wily Bird, though, was always bad. If he couldn't find something wrong, he'd order you to do something absolutely against all the rules, just so he'd have an excuse to jump you.

J. J. CARTER* (Tanagawa):

I told myself, "If they want to beat you, they're going to beat you." I felt like they were traffic cops. Those guys have to give so many tickets, so they're going to give them to somebody. The same with Jap guards. I felt sometimes like they just had to beat so many people a day, and if you came handy you was going to get it.

And unpredictable. One day you go out there and this guard gives you a cigarette. Boy, you think, you're making some time with this Jap. Next day you think you'll get him to buy you a pack of cigarettes. "Here, buy two packs and keep one for yourself." Pow! Pow! Pow! He'd just beat the fire out of you.

I learned early never to trust a Jap. The day I surrendered, I have my hands over my head and a Jap comes down the line and in perfect English says to me, "You want a cigarette?" "Yes," I say. He picks it out of my pocket, puts in in my mouth and lights it. He reaches up, jerks it out of my mouth and puts it out on my face. And they said I was crazy. Yes, they were very unpredictable.

Staff Sgt. HAROLD FEINER, Fukuoka Camp No. 17 (Omuta):

The overmen and guards were a mixed lot. Some were good. One of the overmen, I don't know his name, we called "Seattle." He'd been a merchant seaman before the war and the only thing he could say was, "Me go Seattre." With no *l* in the

* Pseudonym.

Japanese language it would crack us up. We'd ask, "Where did you go?" He'd say, "Seattre." He was short and very mild. Now, Yatoji was a bastard. I tried to kill him once.

Two of the guards we had were real bad. We called one "the Sailor" and the other "the One-Armed Bandit." If you want to get more information about them, ask Frank Stecklein. Yeah, you ask Stecklein about what they did to him.

Staff Sgt. FRANK STECKLEIN, Fukuoka Camp No. 17 (Omuta):

We had names for all the Japs we worked with. "The Duck Hunter" and "the Rabbit." The Duck Hunter was beaten many times by the Japs because he stood up with the Americans. He was an old guy who worked with us when they opened up the mine. He'd do anything for us. The Rabbit was also just one hell of a guy. When the overseers weren't around, he'd shovel as much coal as we did. There was others that always brought food for the prisoners, onions or little buns or things like that.

Then there was "Billy the Kid," "the Screamer," "the Wolf," "Riverside," "the One-Armed Bandit," and "the Sailor." God, that Billy the Kid! The bastard would be sitting there behind you in the mine. And you'd look—you had the light—and he'd be nodding off. So we'd slow up. I mean you had to, when you could. So God, he'd wake up and see us loafing on the job. He'd have that club and he'd just beat the hell out of us.

The Wolf was a bastard. One day he beat me up so bad it was pitiful. We got done early and one of these easy Japs, maybe it was the Rabbit, let us take off early. Usually there were three trains after each shift and I was gonna catch the first one. Doggone, when I passed the Wolf, he caught me. He was always on the job.

He used to walk around with a wooden rod about forty inches long that had a point so he could test the coal face. He knew me and the minute he caught me he beat me all over the goll dang backs of my legs and butt. Not hard, like with two hands. Just one hand, swinging. Then, after he got through beating me like that, he had me pick up a rock and hold it straight out. Then he began hitting me with that damn rod on the elbows. I went down. Shoot, I couldn't hold it up. So he had me pick up a smaller one. I held it while he beat me some more. I couldn't hold that one either, so he had me pick up a third one. I stood there and held it out at arm's length till the next train. Then he let me go. I thought at the time this was bad. I'll tell you, it weren't nothing compared to what the Sailor did to me a couple of months later.

Cpl. BERNARD "CHICK" SAUNDERS (Oyama):

We worked in an open-pit nickel mine. We were allocated so many cars a day that needed to be filled. If you didn't make your quota, you'd be beaten. Often you couldn't make it because it was too high, or you'd be assigned to work with a weaker man who wouldn't be able to keep up. At times the guards were more lenient. It depended on their attitude that particular day. Some days were rougher than others. We had guards who had served and been wounded on Bataan. They'd ask where on Bataan you were. If you were smart, you wouldn't tell them.

Cpl. ISHMAEL COX, Mukden Prisoner-of-War Camp (Hoten, Manchuria):

My mouth got me in more trouble than anything. Shit, I was quite a man at one time. When I was young I could bump two men's heads together. I hated taking crap from the Japs. I took more than one beating because of that. The one with the sand was the worst. I don't know if you've seen people in pain, I mean seen pain written all over someone. Blood running out their nose and mouth and ears. That's the way it was. They beat the holy hell out of me. And I stood there and prayed to God, "Let me live to get out of here. Let me live to get out of here." Some of the best friends I ever had didn't make it. You know, some people take a beating better than others. I bit my fist many times to keep from hollering. I always prayed to never fall down from one of those beatings. When you fell down they'd say, "Oh, he's a damn weakling. Let's work on him good."

As I said, my mouth always got me in trouble. We was all standing, listening to "Bully of the Woods." That's what we called him—cock of the walk in other words, a Jap lieutenant. He was telling us through the interpreter, "We got good Japanese. Isn't that right, *san hachi-ju hachi?*" That was my number, 388. I decided to answer him. "Yes, sir. All the good ones are still laying on Bataan and Corregidor." And, goddamn, he showed me how good they were. Ooooweeee, man, they showed me. After stomping me, they took me into a room. You know what a bicycle tube is? They filled one with sand and tied off both ends. It don't leave no scars on the outside, only the inside. I lay nearly paralyzed for weeks, maybe months. I lost track of time. They thought I was going to die. Every morning they'd come around to see if I was still breathing. I'd say, "Not today you ain't going to get me." One buddy from Lackawanna, New York, told me, "Hold out. We're working on it. We can't get no doctor, but we're trying to get you something for the pain." They brought me some pills two or three days later. The boys said, "Whatever you do, don't tell anybody where you got these. If you have to, die with it." I took the whole bunch in a day and a half. Talk about trips, but it eased the pain. I always had a bad back from that, but eventually I got back on my feet.

As far as the Japs were concerned, I was a fuck-up. So they transferred me to work in a lead mine in Osaka. There I got a chance, and with some other guys, I got even. I got real even.

13
STAYING ALIVE

Address

As matters stand now, the factory work detail is still proving far from satisfactory. Factory regulations permit two rest days a month, in spite of which, numerous cases of non-attendance on days other than those prescribed have occurred for no reason whatsoever. This condition is extremely unsatisfactory.

The stealing and theft of company goods and materials while at work is of the basest of human nature and is a blemish on the uniforms you wore. Of course, the number of miscreants has not been many, but it is a disgrace to, and the responsibility of, the whole to see that there is a stop put to it all. Theft and stealing is unheard of in Japanese military circles. Not an article, however small, will escape the eyes of the guards. Punishment will be dealt out more strictly and severely. All future cases and individuals should watch themselves to see that there is no overstepping of the mark.

Colonel M. Matsuda
Commandant, Mukden Prisoner-of-War Camp

Pvt. LEWIS ELLIOTT, Mukden Prisoner-of-War Camp (Hoten, Manchuria):

We got the alcohol down at the forge factory. We was going to celebrate Christmas. We'd received footballs and basketballs from the Red Cross. From them we removed the bladders, which we filled with alcohol. When the Japs would pat us down at the forge checkout, they felt like our bellies. Once we got back to the camp, we poured the alcohol into a can and hid the can under some floorboards in the center barracks.

If there was something wrong inside the camp, the guys back there would hang white sheets out one of the windows. When we'd come marching back to camp and see the sheet, we knew something was wrong. It meant get rid of your contraband. One day, coming in from the factory, we didn't see no white sheets, so we brought back more alcohol. The Japs were waiting. They told us to strip to the bare skin and here a lot of us guys had them damned bladders strapped to our waists. If you looked sharp you'd see a guard turn his head or look the other way, and the bladders went sailing over the wall.

The day before Christmas the Japs walked right over to the barracks, didn't use no hammer or nothing, picked up the loose boards, and got that alcohol. Everything we done they knew about before we ever done it. We had a white rat in there, but we never found out who it was.

Sgt. CHARLES COOK, Mukden Prisoner-of-War Camp (Hoten, Manchuria):

I met one of the finest men I've come across. He was my boss when I worked in one of the factories. A civilian, he watched over our small group. He told us, "Don't get in trouble. If you do, come see me before the Army gets you. Once they get you I can't do anything. As long as you're in the factory and the Army hasn't got you, I'll get you out of trouble." And he did. 'Course we were a bunch of eight balls. Even though he was our friend, he was our enemy. He would get a little Chinese boy to go out and buy cigarettes for us. We smoked all we wanted. "Don't take them back to camp with you. You can have as many as you want. Just don't steal them." Well, we stole anyway. We took more cigarettes than we needed and smuggled them into camp.

Staff Sgt. HAROLD FEINER, Fukuoka Camp No. 17 (Omuta):

They raise mandarin oranges in the southern part of Kyushu. When the Japs ran out of gasoline, they transported food in horse-drawn wagons. One morning it was still dark and the sections were walking by the side of the road going to the mine. A wagon full of oranges passed us going the same way. They were mounded six feet high. The word got passed, "Eat the skin and all. Don't leave any traces." We cleaned the wagon out. I grabbed four oranges myself. I shoved them in my mouth, mmmmm, like a baby eating, stuffing them down my throat with all five fingers, as fast as I could. The driver never turned around, we were that quiet. I imagine when he got where he was going and delivered three or four oranges instead of hundreds, there was hell to pay.

Capt. BENSON GUYTON (Omine Machi):

What worried me a lot was that I was drawing captain's pay to do something for the men. I won't say I was there to look after them. These guys were pretty good at looking after themselves. They'd been prisoners of war as long as I, and some had been in much tougher straits. So they looked after themselves pretty good. Be that as it may, you did whatever you could whenever you could. There were times when people got in trouble and you felt you ought to help them. Here you had to use some judgment as to when you would try to help out, because if you picked the wrong time you wound up getting the beating instead.

Another thing you'd have to judge was how deep in trouble the guy was you felt like helping. Should you go down every time, you ended up diluting your effectiveness when that important time came. So it was a mean thing and it worried me.

One day, shortly after we got to Omine, a feller came up to me and said, "Hey, you better go down to the guardhouse. One of our guys is getting the hell beaten out of him." So O.K., I go down. Here's the Jap guard drawing back to hit our feller with a six-foot-long two-by-two. He's already hit him a time or two. The guy hadn't been beaten to a pulp yet, but mentally he was about gone. I walk up to this guard and just gently take ahold of his two-by-two. Of course the guard turns around, but I don't let go of his club and I quick ask him what the trouble is. Well, he hadn't saluted this guard. I feel him relax a little bit, so I eventually turn loose his stick. Now, I begin to get mad as soon as I realize I'm not going to take the whipping. To be called down because this guy had failed to salute a guard. I had cussed out a group earlier for failing to salute. I'd said, "Salute the bastards. It won't hurt you. Why get beat for something as stupid as not saluting?" These guys just flat wouldn't do it and this feller here was one of the guys. I actually began to get mad at one of my own men. I mean *mad*! I turn to him and dress him down. The Jap can tell I'm really, really getting on this guy. I ask the guard to turn him over to me, "I'll beat the hell out of him." I would have, too, if I had a stick. So this guy and I start walking off because I'm going to beat him. I'm feeling, though, like that Jap's going to change his mind later and start on both of us. He didn't. By the time we get to the barracks I've cooled off a little bit and I grab a broom. "Now, you sweep off this porch." While he swept, I leave to cool off more. I get to thinking. You know, boy, we really got away with murder.

From then on, when a guy got in trouble and I figured I ought to go down and get involved, I replayed this scene. With this first guy it was real as far as I was concerned, but every time after that I acted out my anger. I played dumb and tried to find out what the problem was, and then I'd explode and really chew the guy out. Then I'd get him back up to the barracks and give him the broom. Had the cleanest porch in the whole camp.

J. J. CARTER* (Aomori):

One place I was in we were digging this huge drydock, and we had a quota each day of six cars per man that had to be filled with rocks. I said, "If they want six, I'll fill four." So I put out four, sometimes three. The guys that did six, at the end of the day got a bowl of noodles. I never got that bowl of noodles. I'd get whipped instead. I tried to tell the fellers, 'course I was just a kid, I wasn't any smart feller, "It only makes sense that if you get through six cars, they're going to ask you to fill more." Sure enough, they moved the quota up to eight. Didn't make any difference to me. I stayed at four and took my beatings. I minded the beatings a lot, but I knew I could physically handle them better than I could handle the exertion of energy. I knew I had to conserve my strength. Food's just like gasoline. If you drive a car real fast, real hard, it's going to burn up more gasoline. That's the way I felt about the work I was given by the Japs. Some guys got wise on eight cars and didn't turn them out, but there were others who did eight—all for an extra bowl of noodles. I took the beatings. I didn't like them, but the beatings weren't going to kill me—working too hard would.

Capt. BENSON GUYTON (Omine Machi):

We had a sit-down strike once. One of our boys who was as skinny as a rail, about six foot two, stole a Jap guard's lunch. Boy, all hell broke loose! I was kind of slow to catch on what had happened. All of a sudden they have everybody out there and they have two or three roll calls. Japs had an awful time counting men. We didn't help, of course. We stood at attention, I suppose for twenty minutes. Seemed like a couple of hours. Finally, they let the British go. Then all the Americans, except my barracks. All of a sudden I heard a commotion behind me and in this rear rank the Japs are beating on this thin kid, Johnson. They'd figured he was the thief, and after roughing him up they threw him in the eiso [jail].

Two or three days later, here came a Jap guard to tell me I should go down to the eiso. I get down there and find Johnson sitting on the throne and he won't get up. Sit-down strike. He won't leave. I duck my head in there and say, "You better get out of here and go to work. They'll beat the hell out of you if you don't." "Naw," he growls. I reach in and as I begin to pull

* Pseudonym.

him by the hand he swings back at me. I walk back up to the Jap guard and say, "You put him in there, you get him to work." And I got away with it. This guy Johnson did, too. The Japs are more superstitious about mental illness than anybody. They figured that anyone who wanted to stay in the *eiso* had to be crazy. So the Japs wouldn't get within ten feet of him. He winds up sweeping out the Jap commandant's office. So he outsmarted the Japs. You going to put a thief in the commandant's office? Johnson starts fattening up. You can tell he's stealing from the Japs. He steals more. The Japs have a problem. They solve the problem exactly like our Army would. Transfer him out of our camp and into another.

Pfc. ROY DIAZ, Copper Smelting Plant (Yokkaichi):

We had a good scam going. The Japs would bring into the saw-mill all this lumber that still had nails and spikes in it. This would be big stuff and we had to remove the metal before it was sawed. Sometimes we'd forget and leave a railroad spike in. They'd run that log through—*zzzzzzz, crunch, crash!* No more cutting for that day.

Of course some of the scams didn't work. There was a guy by the name of Sheehan. How in the hell this guy made it back I don't know. During B-29 raids the rifle guards would herd us down to the beach, where we would wait out the raid. I hated to go because the sand was alive with fleas. One particular bombing raid, Sheehan managed to stay behind and while we were all down at the beach being eaten alive, they went into the guards' mess and stole some rice balls and sake. Sheehan and a Polack.

We got back after the air raid and we don't know anything about what's been happening. Twenty minutes later they call us out again. "What's going on?" We're lined up. Jesus, they come down the line and they pull out the Polack and then they pull out Sheehan. The next morning we go to work and we see they have Sheehan hanging by his wrists off the roof of a building. When we come back at noon, he's still there. Go and come down to the line and they pull out the Polack and then bamboo rod behind his knees which he had to kneel on with a bucket of rocks in both hands. How in the hell they survived I don't know. Sheehan came back home. I don't know about the Polack.

Sgt. H. G. TYSON (Osaka):

As I told you, when I was in the Yodagawa Steel Plant rolling mill, I worked with a civilian who disliked me intensely. He tried to burn me often by feeding red-hot steel sheets through the rollers before I could catch them with my tongs. He never was successful, but he tried often enough.

One night we were working and I was coming off of the cold roller with a slab of red-hot steel, when I saw this Jap civilian come around from behind the hot rollers. To this day I don't know whether my tongs slipped or I just turned them loose, but they opened and onto the steel floor slid my sheet of red hot metal. It caught the Jap just above the ankle. Nearly severed his leg in two. 'Course, they had to rush him to the hospital. I got beat up over it, but I felt good.

Staff Sgt. HAROLD FEINER, Fukuoka Camp No. 17 (Omuta):

I was working in a lateral putting up supporting walls with whatever rock was available. There's a lot of rock in a coal mine which is separated from the coal before it's thrown on the conveyor. This rock can be any size. We had a guy working with us, Rose, who wasn't a very likable guy. He'd been a tough sergeant and a loner and now he was quite sick. He was losing his strength and his will. Yatoji, our overman, was an exceptionally mean Jap. He told Rose to pick up a rock. Rose tried, but dropped it. The Jap began slamming him with a stick. I butted in, "Leave the man alone. Don't hit him again. We'll do the work for him." Yatoji turned around and started to work me over with his stick. I grabbed this sonovabitch and I just about killed him. I dragged him out of the lateral, out to where this endless conveyor belt was running, and I took him and held his neck against the belt like I was going to cut his head off. The guys let me do it to a point, then stopped me. I worked the rest of the night.

On my way out of the mine a Japanese guard called my number, "*ni hachi-ju ni, koi*" (282, come forward). They took me before the camp sergeant major and I was put in a small cell. It was cold in there. Finally the Japs told me I would be tried for striking a Japanese civilian, and then I'd be found guilty and executed. I was taken to Tokyo. They gave me a new pair of clothes to wear.

In Tokyo I was taken to a room in a building and given some tea. Who the hell did I find there but Yatoji. In looking around I also saw several other overmen, and a foreman for these men. They were very respectful to the man sitting on the bench. There were some uniforms, but most of the men were civilians from Mitsui Mining. My story of what had happened to Yatoji, about how he had stumbled and fallen against the conveyor, was pretty flimsy, so I felt I had no chance. These guys in the room, yak, yak, yak, with no interpreter. I was found not guilty. The overmen had supported me and the camp sergeant major had investigated and thought I had told the truth. So this time, I got away with it. The next time I wasn't as fortunate.

Cpl. ISHMAEL COX (Osaka):

In the mine we worked with Jap supervisors. We'd blow a rock surface, then shovel all the ore and stuff into a basket, carry the basket to the ore cart, dump it in, and then push the cart to where we dumped the ore. If you could have gotten in your car one more piece of ore, they'd make you push it all the way back to the lateral so you could fill it as high as they wanted. They'd do this just for orneriness. One day I caught one of the supervisors and killed him. He made a mistake and got caught between the chute and our ore car. We pushed the car real hard and knocked him down like he was a tackling dummy. *Bam,* down he goes, squawking and falling. We emptied our car on top of him.

'Course I don't say what I did next I did alone. All of us together helped and at one time we got thirty-seven of them. The Japs got to trusting us and figured we knew something about explosives. We'd drill and pack, drill and pack. When we were ready to blow a surface, all the Japs would get behind a splinter-proof barricade. We had to find cover the best way we could. When it was time for a *yasume*, all the Jap foremen and supervisors would gather in a large vault that had been excavated for that purpose. During this time we were unwatched, so for weeks and weeks, just a little bit at a time, we drilled holes for dynamite around a lateral that led to this *yasume* room. It took about seventy or eighty days to get all the holes drilled and packed. We wasn't sure it would all go off, because some of it had to be packed days before we were ready to blow the whole thing. See, we had to pack as we went, to keep the holes from being discovered. We just, by God, drilled and got everything set, and figured we had nothing to lose. Come the day, thirty-seven went in for a morning break and they didn't come out. We just blasted the hell out of them. We got some dust and gravel and rocks throwed on us, but hell, that was all right. We'd done our work.

They beat the hell out of us that day, trying to get us to tell what happened, but nobody told and they couldn't prove nothing. About four days later, we had to go in and clean all that mess out. How about that? Clean them out. Boy, they was rotten and stinking and we dug them out. That was sick. We killed just as many in the deep black as we killed on the Abucay Line. I bet you on that!

Pfc. JOHN FALCONER, Fukuoka Camp No. 3 (Tobata):

For my birthday I thought I'd get my gut full of rice. I had some cigarettes which I decided to use. I wasn't going to use them to pay off guards, but I did decide to trade them for food. I went all down our barracks, and when I couldn't find any takers I walked over to the other barracks. "Cigarettes for rice?" Fortunately, nobody was dumb enough to take me up on my offer.

A number of times I traded a half portion of my rice for salt. People with the salt would say, "I'll salt your rice if you'll give me the other half." I thought that was O.K., since it was the only way to make the rice palatable. I know it was a state of mind, but it was one of the ways I was able to eat rice.

J. J. CARTER (Tanagawa):

When I was in the Philippines I was sickly all the time. These guys would come in off work details with sugar and cigarettes and say, "Give you a piece of sugar here for your meal." Good. Another guys comes in, "What'll you give me for cigarettes?" "I don't have anything." "How about your evening meal to-morrow?" That was O.K., too. May not be alive tomorrow. Well, finally it dawned on me that this was all wrong and that I'd never come back this way. I also got bitter. People doing this to me.

In Japan I decided to get even. When I got well enough to get out of camp, I started bringing in potatoes and fish. The fellers back in camp needed these. "What'll you give me?" "My next issue of cigarettes." Just like that I was head over heels in the business of trading. And from then on I had nothing to worry about.

In Japan it wasn't just the fact of being able to get out. It was a matter of here's an old boy who can't control his appetite or his craving for nicotine. You did business with the weak. One end was the weak guy and the other end was the strong guy, the businessman. A guy who had helped me, named Dyer, and I went into business and this is business I'm talking about. We didn't call it trading, it was loaning meals for other meals.

A breakfast was never as valuable as an evening meal. You might have to make a quick change because you couldn't keep rice, and you didn't want to have more coming in than you could eat or loan out for the future. Then the best you could do was trade it for an evening meal. You might also trade it for two breakfasts down the way. The usual exchange rate was two for one. Some places it was three for two.

Another thing, we got ten cigarettes a month. All right, I get up in the morning and I can't eat all the breakfasts I have coming in this day, so I trade one of them for the next issue of ten cigarettes. "Hey! Hey! Right here. Right here." I'd write the transactions down in my book. Cigarette rations come out, all right, and I get my extra ten. All I have to do now is hold this ration for five days. Then, I turn it back around, and you're not going to believe this, but it's the truth, I trade one cigarette for one ration. What was ten for one becomes one for one. I trade not just one guy, but the guy next to him and the guy down the way and the guy at the furthest end of the barracks. I know in five days guys will have smoked their ration or traded them off. So I've cornered the market and I get whatever I can for them.

What you didn't do is walk up to some guy and say, "I'll give you one cigarette and you give me one meal." That's not the way. It was like the payment plan. You don't walk up to a car dealer and give him $7,500 and drive the car out. The $7,500 would scare you off. What you look at is only the $200 payment once a month. So that's the way you traded in camp, always in the future.

The last rule in the game was not to have too many rations coming in at one time. If you couldn't eat them and you couldn't save them because of spoilage, you didn't want to barter them out under pressure. You lost that way.

To start with I probably got in the business to get even with the fellers that dealt me that way in Cabanatuan. Then it took on its own life. What was so strange to understand is that men would starve themselves to death, paying their debts. The whole business dealt in the idea that some people could cope with a situation and some couldn't.

Capt. BENSON GUYTON (Omine Machi):

You done got into a headache sure enough now. Goll dang, that gambling drove us up a wall. You wouldn't find out that a guy was in trouble until he was just about dead. And you would find out that, in one or two instances, the guy had gotten a pretty good beating from our own boys. And what you would find out is that this guy had been swapping food two for one. Tonight he comes in and he's so hungry and so gone mentally that he goes down to a guy, "If you will give me a half of your ration tonight, I'll give you all of mine tomorrow." So the first thing you find out is that a guy owes about twenty rations, and a guy doing without twenty rations is going to die. Particularly bad on cigarettes, swapping two for one. We got an issue of cigarettes every ten days. We didn't celebrate Sunday, but every ten days the night shift and the day shift in the mine would swap. You would have anywhere from a day to a half a day off, depending on which shift you came off. On that day they would issue three cigarettes for a private and on up the line to about twenty for a captain. So the poor guy that's hooked on cigarettes, he'd smoke his three up that first day. Then he'd go and bum a cigarette from somebody else. "I'll pay you back two next payday." So here comes next payday and the guy's so hooked and he's got his three, and he tries to smoke them before somebody comes and takes them away from him. Then he goes around and borrows from somebody else. Man, a guy might owe fifty or sixty cigarettes. And he'd get beat for it. Of course they'd also trade food rations for cigarettes, too, and that's where they'd get in trouble health-wise. They'd be trading food to get enough cigarettes to pay back what they owed.

So, what're you gonna do? We came up with a system of declaring a guy bankrupt, and when a guy was bankrupt we'd put him on "the table." And in our camp, Sgt. Robert Jones was in charge of "the table." If anybody deserves a medal, Bob Jones does and he volunteered for this job. These bankrupt individuals were just about done mentally. Most of these guys recovered because of Jones. He would carry around in his musette bag these guys' soap, because that was valuable and could be traded. He'd carry around their cigarettes whenever they were issued. We arranged to pay back what they owed in cigarettes, about one tenth of what they owed. We wouldn't let them pay back any food. They'd sit at a separate table and Bob would make them sit with their hands on the table. This was to avoid them slipping any buns or crumbs into their pockets, which they would then try to trade. These guys would pull every trick in the book to try to pull something on Bob Jones. I'm sure somebody slipped a crumb off the table now and then and traded it off. But not much. Bob Jones was good. He'd go down with the bankrupt guys to the bathhouse and he'd pass out their soap and they'd take their baths together. Then he would collect the soap and bring the men back to the barracks.

J. J. CARTER (Aomori):

It wasn't really a big problem, if a man who owed you went bankrupt. That was part of it. It was the way it was. It meant he couldn't get back into the game. Unless he went to another camp. Then it started again. At another camp people didn't know him so he could go again.

It is unrealistic to think that the American camp commanders could have stopped the trading. I think the officers accepted that this enterprise system was part of the American way of life. Not only that, see, the officers didn't have to go out to work. Every once in a while us guys out of camp would get something the officers wanted. How were they going to get it? We weren't just going to hand it to them. They were going to have to trade for it. So if they banned trading, how were they going to get their little extras? They couldn't say, "You can't swap food or cigarettes," because what else did they have to trade except food and cigarettes?

Let me put it this way. I was in six camps and I was never in a well-run one. I doubt they existed. I mean, how were our officers going to lead and what were they going to lead with? The Japs owned and operated everything. These officers, I don't care what rank they carried, were trying to live, too.

Pfc. MICHAEL TUSSING, Jr., Fukuoka Camp No. 3 (Tobata):

In my experience the American leadership varied, depending on which camp you were in. We had good officers who showed leadership, were for the men, worked with the men, and tried to do things for the men. Then there were others who in order to make things easier for themselves, bent over backwards trying to please the Japanese. This would, of course, be at the expense of the men.

Pfc. MICHAEL McMULLEN (Omine Machi):

There were American officers who didn't have the initiative or the guts to stand up to the Japanese. They'd decide they would have their men do anything the Japanese wanted. Others wouldn't. That was the key.

Pvt. LEWIS ELLIOTT, Mukden Prisoner-of-War Camp (Hoten, Manchuria):

The officers and the enlisted men fought like cats and dogs. It started out, as best as I can tell, on Corregidor, when we were captured. They took us all out there on Monkey Point and we sat there on the little old airstrip in the hot sun. There wasn't no water, no food, no nothing. The Japs wanted a work detail, so five of us volunteered. We spent a whole day taking all that food out of the Tunnel [Malinta Tunnel] and loading it on Japanese boats. While we was doing this, we was eating. When they sent us back to the strip we had stole enough to take with us. The first night all hell broke out. Officers come over to us, "O.K., there's five of you guys. We'll give you ten cans of this food and we'll take the rest." Boy, that guy got hit right in the snoot. We said, "Goddamn, if you want to eat, you do like the rest of us, get out there and work."

The last part of our time in Mukden, when we got a lot of officers in there, we had guys who stayed in camp to guard our barracks. Because the officers didn't work, they'd come over to our barracks and steal our stuff. Every morning we got a biscuit and a bowl of cornmeal mush. Sometimes we'd decide to save the bun for supper ration, and we'd put it on the shelf above the bed. Maybe, when you come back from work, the bun was missing. We couldn't prove it was the officers until they caught one guy, a major.

So we talked the Japs into us leaving a guard in each of our barracks. They let us do it. And they put out an order that the officers stayed in the last barracks all during the day. They weren't let out until us factory workers came home.

Pfc. ROBERT BROWN, Mukden Prisoner-of-War Camp (Hoten, Manchuria):

The officers worked for a while in different places in the camp. They got so involved in that, they began to take advantage of the situation for their own greed. They began stealing food whenever they were in the kitchen or the bakery. If they weren't, then their dog robbers were doing it for them. Now, damn it, you don't take food from a man. So the men went to the Japanese and told them to remove the officers from these jobs. Eventually, the Japanese did.

Capt. THOMAS HEWLETT, M.D., Fukuoka Camp No. 17 (Omuta):

Just prior to the departure of "A" Detail from Cabanatuan, instruments were requested from the senior American medical officers. Having spent a year on Corregidor with a 500-man labor detail, I was well aware of the need for surgical instruments for use on prisoners.

My requests were refused by the senior American officers. They were naive enough to believe that all essentials would be supplied, once we reached Japan. The instrument kit that I had put together on Corregidor was minimal, at best. My friendship with certain enlisted men working in medical supply at Cabanatuan made it possible to supplement my kit, to the point that at least we would be able to handle emergency surgery while en route to Japan. The individual instruments were placed in the baggage of a number of prisoners, thus they escaped detection during the inspections we were subjected to. The instruments were reassembled after we were settled in Camp 17.

Our only available anesthesia consisted of several vials of dental Novocain tablets. Two of these tablets dissolved in a small amount of the patient's spinal fluid and injected into the spine gave about forty-five minutes of anesthesia, giving us time to perform most operations that had to be done. Dutch torpedo technicians, who eventually came to Camp 17, were able to make surgical knives out of old British table silverware.

September 17, 1943, a prisoner named Vaughan suffered a broken back when trapped in a mine cave-in. He was admitted to the mine hospital, but treatment was not started as the senior surgeon at the hospital considered the situation hopeless. I was taken to the hospital and permitted to examine the patient. My findings indicated that if treatment was instituted, we might be able to correct the total paralysis of his legs and return him to activity. So the mine surgeon agreed to transfer him to Camp 17 hospital to die. Vaughan was a very reasonable young man with an intense desire to live. It was explained to him that, if the planned treatment worked, he would suffer extreme muscle spasm and pain. We had no morphine or similar drugs to give him any relief. He agreed to follow our plan and the pain it entailed. A hinged traction table was constructed and placed in the small isolation building, and Vaughan was placed in traction. It was hoped that by using the isolation building, we could muffle the sound of his screams from the other prisoners. However, I am sure that those who were quartered in the area of the isolation building can recall the nightly screams of this man as he endured the treatment. Eight weeks after his torture was begun, we walked him into the camp commander's office. This convinced Lieutenant Uri that the American doctors knew their business. Lieutenant Uri ordered the mine surgeon to come to camp and see our results. Unfortunately, Vaughan committed suicide in the first year after his recovery from Japan.

As a general rule, if a prisoner suffered an injury in the mine, some physical punishment was administered underground before he was brought to the surface. This punishment was handled by the civilian Japanese overmen. If the patient suffered a broken bone in the mine, X-ray examination might be carried out at the mine hospital. We might get to see the films two to three weeks later, so we treated fractures without X-rays.

Japanese surgeons operated in cotton gloves, since rubber

gloves were not available. We operated barehanded. The fingernails of the surgical team stayed black as a result of our using
bichloride of mercury and 7-percent iodine in preparing our
hands before surgery. Despite our primitive equipment and environment, our infection rate in surgical patients never exceeded
3 percent.

During our first two months in Japan, several prisoners
underwent surgery in the mine hospital. These operations were
done either without anesthesia or with very weak local anesthesia, and the patients were returned to us in rather severe
shock.

Hand injuries, which were repaired at the mine dispensary,
required thorough exploration as soon as the patient returned
to camp. Usually such wounds were filled with coal dust, and
severed tendons had to be repaired. Eventually, after a number
of these mismanaged wounds were demonstrated to the camp
Japanese Army doctor, he ordered that injured prisoners be
returned immediately to the camp hospital.

1st Lt. MARK HERBST, M.D., Mukden Prisoner-of-War
Camp (Hoten, Manchuria):

The number-one Japanese doctor, the one who thought himself
a surgeon, was Kawajima. I believe he had gone to Pusan for
two weeks of surgery and he came back to us ready to operate.
This, of course, didn't sit very well with any of us. We managed, by hook or crook, to know whenever he scheduled some
surgery. These would be simple jobs like hemorrhoids or hernias
or appendixes, simple operations, but still botchable. Whenever
he scheduled his surgery we'd get up around 5:00 a.m. and do
the necessary work. He'd come in about 9:00 a.m. "Please get
So-and-So ready for surgery." I'd say, "What for?" "Hemor-
rhoid." "Oh, we did that already."

We did quite well with practically nothing. We had fellows
who would get their hands caught in a gear over in the factory.
They'd come with a mangled hand loaded with grease and dirt.
Normally, you and I would expect to get stuck full of anti-
biotics. All we could do was give these guys pans of hot water
and tell them to soak it. They'd come out with hands as good
as mine just from soaking them in hot water and having the will
to move them around to regain the use and strength in them.

Another feller got hit in the bombing raid.* My buddy,

* A strike of ninety-one aircraft hit the Mukden area Dec. 7, 1944. Eighty
planes attacked the MKK plant and adjacent area. Although there was a
less successful, smaller raid two weeks later on the same target, it was no
doubt the first raid which hit the prisoner-of-war camp.

Shabart, was amputating his arm, which was hanging by a thread. I was assisting, and had noticed this boy also had some scratch marks around his head. I was giving him some chloroform, which I had never used before. All of a sudden I noticed blood dripping on my shoe. Here's a cauliflower of brains sticking out through one of the scratch marks. He'd been hit with a piece of shrapnel, and under the pressure of the anesthetic on the cerebrum, the brain came out of one of these holes. I looked at the surgeon, he shrugged and finished the arm. Then we didn't do anything else for the kid except keep a dry sterile dressing on the head wound. As the anesthetic wore off, the brain pulled back in where it belonged. The guy never had a bit of trouble with the head marks. Now he did lose his arm.

Pfc. EDDY LAURSEN, Mukden Prisoner-of-War Camp (Hoten, Manchuria):

They decided I was well enough to work, so I went to the factory to mend coveralls. In about three weeks I could tell my back was getting worse again. I asked to get off the detail, but was turned down. I asked several times. The American doctors told me I was a goldbrick and I had to work. I told them, "All right. I'll work till I drop. Then you can carry me out and do with me whatever you want."

During an air raid we were forced to run from MKK into the camp and I collapsed somewhere between. I folded up. They carried me to camp. That was the last time I worked. I've been in a hospital virtually ever since.

I spent nearly twenty-four months in the hospital at Hoten. There wasn't a great deal of treatment. I was fed less, oh yes. You had to work to get a full ration. Doctor Herbst took over my case. He decided to put me on a curved frame which he hoped would straighten me out. I was humped over like an old man. So the carpenters built me this frame in the same place where they built the coffins for the guys who had died the winter before. It did straighten me out, so that I was able to get on my feet again.

1st Lt. MARK HERBST, M.D., Mukden Prisoner-of-War Camp (Hoten, Manchuria):

We had a catatonic. He scared the daylights out of the Japanese. They're scared to death of anyone crazy. Sometimes when he'd come back from MKK the boys would have to push him, because he was in one of his catatonic seizures.

Once in a while "Bull of the Woods," the Jap adjutant, would tiptoe slowly up behind him. Everyone in the changing room would know what was going to happen. The Bull would creep up to where he was right behind this guy's ear and then let out one of the most terrific roars imaginable. The rest of the boys, even though they knew it was coming, would jump a foot off the ground. The catatonic stood there and never batted an eyelash. Eventually, we got him over to the hospital. One day he stole the Jap doctor's samurai sword. We chased him down the hall and beat the daylights out of him ourselves, to get the sword back before the Jap found it missing. I visited him later in the hospital and found him alert and normal, except he had a black eye. "How'd you get that?" Scrawny little guy next to him said, "He spat at me, so I let him have it." He went back to the factory shortly after that.

Pvt. LEWIS ELLIOTT, Mukden Prisoner-of-War Camp (Hoten, Manchuria):

See, in the barracks we had double decks with six guys sleeping below and six above. We had an old master sergeant who was all crippled up with beriberi, so he didn't work in the factory. He didn't do much because we thought he was in pretty bad shape. One morning Bull of the Woods came through the barracks. If he caught you where you weren't supposed to be, he'd give you a good whipping. To get out of his way, everyone who slept in the top bunks made a dash for them. A kid started to scramble up the ladder and this crippled old sergeant moved so fast he climbed right over him to get up there first. He was forty-five years old and the kid was like the rest of us, twenty or twenty-one. He went over the kid in a blur. I thought he couldn't even move.

Staff Sgt. HAROLD FEINER, Fukuoka Camp No. 17 (Omuta):

The egos of the Japanese had to be seen to be believed. They used to always go around flexing their muscles and telling us how strong they were. One day I was working with a gang headed by "Seattle" making rock columns, which held up the ceiling. He was a gentle guy, but he talked real rough. One day he gave me an order, "Pick up that rock and put it here!" I looked at that stone. I knew I could lift it, but I decided I wasn't going to pick that sonovabitch up. I looked at Seattle and said, "I can't pick that up. I'm sick, I'm weak American. We don't get enough food. I'll tell you what we do. You strong *Nipponese otoko* [Japanese man]. With your help we could pick it up together." You could see his chest swelling with pride. "O.K., O.K.," and he bent down on one side, with me on the other and he counted "*ichi-ni-san*" and one, two, three, we picked it up. I began to puff and strain. All the effort was in my neck and head. With the force I was using in my arms, I couldn't have picked up a pack of cigarettes. That little sonovabitch lifted that thing all by himself and he didn't know it. The guys watching were rolling on the ground, laughing. They kept saying, "You so strong!" Seattle loved it.

1st Lt. MARK HERBST, M.D., Mukden Prisoner-of-War Camp (Hoten, Manchuria)

I made a point of having nothing medical to do with the Japanese. With one exception. One of the little Japs wanted me to pull his tooth. I refused: "You have a dentist downtown." "No, no," he says, "he's no good." I figure I start on this Jap's tooth and something goes wrong and whack! He persisted, "I want you to do it." I finally agree and he tells me he's going to get some anesthesia. I said, "I don't know how to use it. You want your tooth out, we take it out now." I did everything I could to prolong the agony, being just as mean and ornery as I could. The Jap kept saying, "Aaah!" When I was through he said, "Very good. Much better than downtown. Pull this one, too." Can you imagine what the guy downtown was like?

Pfc. LEE DAVIS, Divisional Camp (Jinsen, Korea):

The Japanese commander gave orders that we had to go to the latrine with our shorts on. Although it was only a few steps from the barracks, he was offended by our running naked. One hot day one of our officers came out naked, heading for the latrine, holding on to the end of his swollen jigger. The Japanese officer saw him and ordered him to stop. The Jap was wearing the most elegant pair of leather riding boots I'd ever seen, and he ordered the guy to attention. When our guy didn't come to complete attention, he pointed down to the hand that was keeping the man from urinating. Then he hauled off and slapped him. When he did, the man's hand came off his hose and his urine went up and down the riding boots. A Jap guard and I managed to get around a corner, and we laughed so hard he had to put down his rifle. The American officer was slapped severely.

Pfc. ROBERT BROWN, Mukden Prisoner-of-War Camp (Hoten, Manchuria):

The Japanese commander in our camp bought some sows and kept them in a pen on the camp grounds. After a while, he sent them out to where there was a stud boar. After they had been serviced, they were returned to camp where they had their piglets. After a while, sending the sows out to be serviced became too big a hassle, so the Jap commander brought in a stud. So into camp came this young boar. The Japs expected him to grow. We discovered, somehow, that if we took a stick and rubbed his side he'd lay down, get an erection, and shoot his sperm—*wham, wham.* So when we had nothing to do we'd say, "Let's go down and whack off the pig." Well, this happened ten or twelve times a day, enough anyway to where we stunted his growth. The Japs could never figure out why he never grew to full size.

Staff Sgt. HAROLD FEINER, Fukuoka Camp No. 17 (Omuta):

Every morning before we went down in the mine we would line up and count off in Japanese. Number 55 in Japanese is *go-ju go* and number 55 in camp belonged to a sergeant who was a big Jewish boy from Detroit. Each morning when it came time for him to call off his number he would yell, "Go-ju go, so why don't you let me?" Sometimes Sid would get walloped and sometimes he wouldn't.

Pfc. LEE DAVIS, Divisional Camp (Jinsen, Korea):

By the time I arrived in Korea I was a walking skeleton. On top of being skinny, our crotch crickets were very prevalent, and the bedbugs were everywhere. Because of our condition, many of us were put to sewing buttons onto Jap uniforms. We were told that each four-hole button had to have four stitches through each button. So we took each button and sewed four stitches through each hole, then we took the button and sewed it on the garment with one stitch.

1st Lt. MARK HERBST, M.D., Mukden Prisoner-of-War Camp (Hoten, Manchuria):

The feller in charge of the camp kitchen was the cousin of a friend of mine back in Canton, Ohio. So if there was anything a little extra to be had, why, Andy would see to it that Shabart and I got it. Of course whenever Andy got sick, which was normal, we would take good care of him.

Our men would sometimes be served sand shark. I don't know if you've ever smelled any sand shark or not, but if you wanted a description of what it smelled like take a bucket of urine and sit out in the sun for a day or two. Shabart and I got to the Japanese side and found some nice yellow fin tuna. We chunked off a couple of pieces and smuggled it back to the kitchen, so Andy could bake it for us. We never got caught.

Capt. BENSON GUYTON (Omine Machi):

One of the boys, a corporal, got his finger run over by a coal car, so the Jap doctor amputated it. This old Dillon was a pretty smart boy. He picked at this stump for the next six months, and it never did get well. So Dillon came up to me and attached himself to me as an orderly. I said, "I don't need no orderly." He said, "The hell with you, Captain. You're always going around here doing something that an officer ought not to be doing." So, talk about a guy living the life of Riley now. From then on, here'd come old Dillon up the stairs: "Ah, Captain, time for you to get up"—and he'd have a canteen full of hot water. The one thing we got all the time we were in Japan was good black tea. The drinking water was not good, it had to be boiled. So if you're gonna boil it, you just as well made tea.

If there's anything in camp that wasn't tied down, Dillon could get it, particularly with my twenty cigarettes. So Dillon got a straight razor. So this here captain had tea to sip each morning between the lather and razor.

Staff Sgt. JAMES CAVANAUGH, Subcamp No. 2 (Kawasaki):

One summer's day in 1943 they picked out a bunch of guys from a line-up and beat them mercilessly. We couldn't understand why. They just picked them out, took them to the yard, and beat hell out of them.

Shortly after that, the Japs put in our camp about fifty Italian Marines who had been stationed in the Italian Embassy in Shanghai. They were big, tall guys in good shape. Some of them were blond. Their commander was a doctor in botany and prior to the war had been the Navy attaché in the Italian Embassy in Tokyo. They were thrown in with us. They told us when Mussolini had been overthrown, the Japs had disarmed and imprisoned them. Then the light dawned. Someone remembered that the guys that had been mysteriously beaten a few weeks before all had Italian names. This was the Jap way of taking out their frustrations on us when Italy tried to surrender.

Pfc. JACK BRADY (Omori):

When we joined the British, we worked like coolies. In this detail I ran across Englishmen who were absolutely the finest people you could meet anywhere, and there were others who were as crummy as you could meet anywhere. We had a real honest dispute with them just once.

Suddenly, someone discovered one of the buildings was burning. The Japanese pulled us off the sand-carrying detail and put us to hauling buckets of water. The English jumped right in and started helping the Japs put out the fire. That was on one side of the building. On the other side, we Americans discovered a big stack of lumber and, since we couldn't see any reason not to, we began tossing the lumber into the fire. When the British found out what we'd done they got upset. We were upset with them as well. We couldn't see them helping to put the fire out. Of course, when the Japs caught us, they too were a little upset. They cut our rations. And the British ration. That's another reason why the British were so unhappy. This is also when we got Wily Bird.

Pfc. MICHAEL McMULLEN (Omine Machi):

There were 400 Americans and 200 English in camp. I didn't dig coal with the British because they had to eventually separate us. In the Philippines we had officers who were men enough to refuse to have us bow to the Rising Sun. We'd salute the Japanese, but not bow to their flag. We had them convinced that was what we'd do. When we arrived in Japan, the story was altogether different. The British in camp had come from Singapore and we found them breaking their backs bowing to the Japanese. When we arrived, whenever we saw a Jap we'd just give him an eyeball. He'd stop us, call us back, and then slap hell out of us. Naturally we tried to convince the British prisoners that our system of not bowing was the correct one. Our officers even talked to their officers. Naturally, after a while, we got tired of being beaten, and since the British did not change their position, we began fighting amongst ourselves. Finally, a line separating the two factions was drawn across the camp. In the final analysis we balanced the question of bowing, because we got tired of being slapped and beaten every time we didn't.

J. J. CARTER (Aomori):

A lot of people, when they saw *The Bridge on the River Kwai,* said it was way out, unbelievable. It wasn't too far out for me. I believed it. I'd been with these Limeys. They had this achieving thing. It was as if some of them felt they almost owed the Japanese something. I never could understand it.

We worked with the British in this one camp up in a rock quarry. We had to load our handcar and get it down the incline, so we could dump the rock in one of the crushers. We had a quota of cars that the Japs wanted us to fill each day. So my buddy and I were working up on the quarry and, as usual, we're behind on our quota. We'd pushed our car up, and we noticed on one of the spurs a pair of Englishmen who were already about two cars ahead of us on the quota, digging like crazy, filling another car. So I said, "Let's go in there and have some fun." Once we got in the spur, they had to wait until we were finished loading before they could come out. We just pushed our car in next to theirs. "Y'all move down a bit. We're making our quota and we don't lack a whole lot ourselves."

We were up on this mountain, so whenever we went down to the crusher we had to hold back on the car, in order to prevent it from running away from us. So we put this big wood chock up on our front wheels, which prevented the car from rolling.

We're working on the rock and, of course, the Limeys have their car all loaded and they're impatiently waiting for us to finish. "You chaps hurry up. Hurry up!" "O.K.," I said, "if you guys are really in such a big rush, you'll come over here and help us." They aren't about to do that, but they do go over and get the guard. He came over and told us to hurry. *"Isogu! Isogu!"* The secret to this thing was not to be defiant and not to say anything. Just keep on working steady. If you once speeded up when they hollered, you were done for. So we kept working at our normal slow pace, so the Limeys go over and get the guard again. This time he comes over and knocks my buddy down, then he starts looking for something to hit me with. He's grabbing at anything, and he pulls out the wood chock from under our car and knocks me down with it. And here goes the car down the track. Then it dawns upon him what he's done. Here's this runaway, picking up speed. I tell you, even though he'd whipped up on me, I was just laughing, watching him running down the track, trying to catch that car. It wasn't no chance of catching it. It went right on through the scales, right through the winch, and bang, into the crusher, just throwing rocks everywhere. I about died laughing.

Staff Sgt. HAROLD FEINER, Fukuoka Camp No. 17 (Omuta):

When we first arrived in camp, we agreed amongst ourselves on the amount of coal we'd dig a day for the Japanese. I don't remember the exact figure, but say the Japs wanted us to dig ten carloads. We told them we couldn't do that many, we'd do five and that was it. Let them beat up a couple of guys, but that's it, five. We finally settled on digging seven carloads a day. That was our quota and it was agreed on with the Japs. We dug this much for quite a while. Then the English came into camp. Before the Japs sent them down in the mine we told them, "Look, fellers, we've been loading seven cars a day, but these bastards are going to ask you to dig ten. They'll promise you more food if you load more coal, but don't believe them. They won't give it to you. We've fought this battle, so dig your seven carloads."

As soon as the Limeys went down into the mine they started digging twelve cars a day. Now man for man, Americans are bigger people than the English, so the Japanese immediately began to tell us, "The English are smaller, but they're loading more coal than you." Bang, they started to again whip the hell out of us. After that, every time we caught a group of Englishmen, we beat the hell out of them. In the camp or down in the mine, we worked them over good. They really loused up our good deal.

The next round in this story is the British getting even. The only way we ever got at the Japanese was cussing at them. But we did it with a smile, so we could get away with it. A guy would go up to a Jap and with a big grin, say, "You dirty bastard, can I take a *yasume*?" Whenever we talked to them, we'd smile and curse them. They couldn't understand what we were doing and we thought it was so funny. Well, the slimy Limeys turned around and explained, in detail, what a son of a bitch or bastard is. They explained to the guards the exact meaning of words we were calling them. The next time one of our guys, smilingly, called a Jap a "bastard," the guard replied, "Bastard? I'm a bastard? I don't know who my father was?" Bingo, he started beating up on the guy. So, we took more whippings. O.K. 'Course, we worked the English over again, but that wasn't the answer.

Finally, a little guy from Detroit, a pretty smart guy, figured out the answer. "I'll tell you what," he said. "I'm Jewish. You're a Polack, you're a Lithuanian, you're a Greek, you're a Swede. The next time we curse a Jap, curse him in your parent's language." And that's what we did. We taught each other all the curse words we knew in foreign languages. So we got back to calling the Japs rotten bastards, but in Swedish or Spanish or Yiddish. The Japs never figured out what we were doing and the Limeys didn't either.

Sgt. FORREST KNOX, Group Camp
(Osaka-Kobe Area):

I admired some of the Limey sergeant majors. They were probably some of the finest soldiers I ever saw. But the ordinary

English soldier was a difficult guy to live with. Our egos had a little bit to do with how we felt. They used to brag all the time about being English soldiers. We all felt they were in no position to brag, since they had nowhere near put up the fight we had. We found them insufferable.

Their language was really funny. The one incident that really sticks in my mind was one day some of these Limeys were goofing off and hiding around the corner of a warehouse. They should have been in the line carrying things. All of a sudden, a guard starts down the line and this Limey in front of me warns his mates, who are dogging it. What he said really amused me. "Guyferkinyaferkinferkers." That meant, "Get fucking, you fucking fuckers."

Individually, some of the Limeys were damn good soldiers. I got a boil on my leg once, from pushing carbon sticks. I went to a medic and he told me it had to be lanced. That was all right with me. So I dropped my pants and sat down. With his lance he made a quick X slash, which laid the boil open so the stuff could run out. I was ready to go when he said, "Wait a minute, I have to trim it. Hold still." And he jammed a pair of scissors into the boil and trimmed off the four flags of skin. Just cutting a boil without any painkiller will make you jump, but wiggling a scissors in the tender area, I mean . . . The medic said, "You aren't going to throw up on the floor and make a mess in this bay, are you?"

The next day I went back to the dispensary to get a clean bandage and I saw something I couldn't believe. A Limey soldier was laying on the table, and he had a boil seven or eight inches across one cheek of his butt. It was so big and purple, they couldn't find the head. The doctor said, "Well, O.K., this is going to hurt some," and put his scalpel, I mean the whole goddamned thing, into the boil, just zip. Then he put a drain tube in the hole he'd made, which drained the pus out of it just like milking maple sugar from a tree. I wouldn't lie and say that Limey didn't whimper a little when they were working on him, but he made damn little sound, considering what they were doing to him. The doc finally said, "O.K., pull up your pants." He straightened up and walked out real slow. I wondered how long it would take before he could bend over again.

Pfc. JOHN FALCONER, Fukuoka Camp No. 3 (Tobata):

In Japan we didn't have much and so it required some luck to live. Each morning in the steel mill, we had a ceremony which began the day. All the workers would bow to the East and pledge allegiance. We had a very understanding interpreter. He told us, "We pray that we're going to be victorious and that everything's going to come out all right for Japan. Our people are praying to their God. Why don't you pray to yours that the war will soon end and that men on the battlefields won't die today." He told us, "I was educated in Pennsylvania and happened to be caught here when the war broke out. Do what they tell you to do and you won't get into trouble. You know, when the war's over you're going to be on the first ship back to the States. I'm going to be on the second one." He was a very good guy.

Occasionally our foreman would let us go up to the shack where the Japanese laborers ate. He was an old civilian and we called him Pops. He took us from camp to work, and he was good to us. In this shack they'd give us a canteen of something like buttermilk. It wasn't, but it was good and it was warm. For me this was important, because it proved someone cared. We weren't entirely unwanted. So important. So important.

Pfc. ROBERT BROWN, Mukden Prisoner-of-War Camp (Hoten, Manchuria):

Something I realized about staying alive was that you could not survive and be pining for someone back home. That's why I felt so sorry for men who were married. Time can play many tricks on your mind. It killed a lot of men in prison camp, not knowing what their sweeties were doing. Being as young as I was, most of my thoughts were of my mother and father. Not until fourteen days before the war ended did I receive a letter from them, and then it was two years old. It seemed like there were people all around me who got letters every other day. What I did to survive, rather than pine for my parents—I knew it was a fictitious feeling and certainly not a lasting one—I made myself hate them. It was easier there to hate than to love. Whenever they came into my mind, I'd kick them out. "I'm mad at you. You're back in the States and you're not writing me." It was just one method to endure the anguish. When I got home I told my folks what I'd done, and they sat there with their eyes open; "I don't believe what you're saying." I said, "Don't take it that way. I had to. You were back here. You had access to food. I had to take care of myself. I couldn't have you in my heart and be pining over someone like that."

You know, it takes a lot to survive as a prisoner of war, because you're treated lower than whale manure on the bottom of the ocean. The thing that was so discouraging, disgusting, was the justice. There was none! If a Jap caught you violating a rule or regulation, and they had one for everything, or if they thought you were violating one, and they beat you into the ground, what were you going to do about it? I never once saw one of my American officers try to defend anybody. Maybe they thought they didn't have a chance. I saw the British officer go over to the Japs and raise hell with them. He got knocked on his butt, but he got up and started all over again. Maybe our method of not saying anything was a better one. I don't know.

The thing that really hurt was to take a man as big and strong as an American could be, and have this little half-pint Jap, who you know damn well he could kill, come up and beat the Jesus Christ out of him. Now that dims the candle. That burns out the light inside of you real fast.

Maj. JOHN MAMEROW, Fukuoka Camp No. 17 (Omuta):

We were then on an eight-hour schedule for three shifts, with ten days between *yasume* days [rest periods]. The Japanese officials informed us that since they did not recognize Christmas as a holiday, and since New Year's Day was a national holiday, we would celebrate a combined holiday on our usual *yasume* day. We were told that an extra special ration would be given us, and we would be permitted to hold a religious ceremony in the afternoon. All men except hospital patients would attend the noon meal. There was no Catholic priest in the camp, but a Dutch chaplain, J. C. Hamel, who spoke perfect English if you discounted his Chicago accent (having spent several years in Holland, Michigan), was interned with us.

On the morning of New Year's, the Japanese interpreter asked me to accompany him to the hospital, where he would present a gift to each patient. We went, and each patient was presented two cigarettes. The interpreter then gave a speech, stating that the Emperor was pleased to present them with this gift, and, "While this is a small gift, you must appreciate the generosity of His Majesty." After we left the hospital I was given a package of ten cigarettes for being a good camp commander. I went back into the hospital and asked the men what they thought of their gift. I was given the royal razzberry.

At the beginning of the noon meal each man was given a cup of sake, another gift from the Emperor, and their noon meal consisting of rice, vegetable soup, and some beef, the best parts being removed before we got it. Several of the men traded their food for sake, resulting in some becoming intoxicated with the usual results. The Japanese camp commander, Fukuhara, gave a short speech acclaiming the glory of Japan and the generosity of the Emperor.

That evening the Japanese allowed us to present a program in the mess hall of songs, dances, and recitations. The Japanese military and civilian guards also presented a couple of skits. This was to be our last celebration as prisoners of war.

14
END OF THE ROAD

Early in the summer of 1944 huge new American bombers, the B-29 Superfortresses, began to raid the Japanese mainland. Flying from central China, they made a handful of raids on the southernmost island of Kyushu. Because of immense logistical problems encountered in trying to equip these planes, as well as the vast distances between base and target, the raids were viewed as inefficient and were discontinued.

The American air offensive against Japan could not become effective until bases closer to the islands were secured. With this in mind the Marianas, just 1,300 miles from Tokyo, were taken in mid-1944. On November 1 a lone F-13, flying a photo reconnaissance mission, became the first U.S. plane over Tokyo since April 1942. Twenty-three days later 111 Superfortresses, flying from the newly won island of Saipan, attacked the Japanese capital. With this assault began a sustained offensive which, in just eight months, was to totally devastate Japan.

J. J. CARTER* (Aomori):

The Japanese commander called us into the compound and told us that if the war did not end by October (1945), three-quarters of the Japanese population would die. There was no doubt in any of our minds that we would be in that three-quarters.

* Pseudonym.

Staff Sgt. JAMES CAVANAUGH, Subcamp No. 2
(Kawasaki):

American planes started coming over the Tokyo area around
the first of November. After this, the bombing raids began to
increase in intensity and frequency. Located where I was, between Tokyo and Yokohama, I got a chance to see many of
these raids. They were really interesting to watch. Evidently
our bombers, which were big babies—we knew they weren't
B-17s, I learned later they were B-29s—used Mount Fuji as
their gathering point. They'd rendezvous before making their
run on Tokyo. We weren't allowed to watch, but when the
Japs hit the ground we sneaked little looks.

At first, every afternoon a high-flying plane—we called him
"Photo Joe"—came in at about 30,000 feet and circled around
and around. The Jap flak wasn't reaching him, so he just casu-
ally made his reconnaissance and then flew away when he was
done. Once in a while, on his way out he'd wag his wings. A
day or two later, there'd be a big raid! Many of the raids happened at night. The Japs had a lot of searchlights in the area
and in the lights you could see the bombers. You could also see
the Jap tracers going up towards the planes. Every night there
was a raid, it would be the same. Then, several weeks later, the
planes began firing at the searchlights. I watched the tracer bullets coming down and the lights would go off, one at a time,
until they were all out. All you could see then was the light
from burning buildings.

When the guards weren't around, you could sometimes get
to talk to some Japanese civilians. Some of them had worked
on ships and had picked up some English. I learned from one of
these Japs that up in the mountains, around Mount Fuji, there
were several thousand men being trained in individual aircraft,
and when the American ships came into Tokyo harbor, these
men were going to dive their planes into them. The name they
used for these men was *kamikaze.*

Maj. JOHN MAMEROW, Fukuoka Camp No. 17 (Omuta):

We got information many ways. The best way for me was to
listen to the Jap camp commander. "We have wiped out so
many of your troops," and he'd tell me where. When I got back
to camp I looked at a little pocket map we had, and I'd notice
that every time we got wiped out, it would be some place closer
to Japan. They were always sinking our Navy. They'd sink it
one day, and the next it would bounce back up. We called it the
"rubber Navy."

Capt. THOMAS HEWLETT, M.D.,
Fukuoka Camp No. 17 (Omuta):

The weather in Japan begins to cool in October, and the nights can be most uncomfortable. It is during this month that the Emperor, in his benevolence, decides to issue blankets to the Japanese Army. In October of 1944 we had received rumors that Allied Forces were beginning to close in on Japan. Tracking movement of these forces on the maps in a small pocket atlas published as an advertisement in England, our hope of rescue was beginning to come alive. The small atlas was completely *verboten,* as the Japanese had even forbidden astrologic maps. Thus our atlas was protected at all costs.

In our moment of increasing hope of eventual rescue, the medical officers decided to demand an increase in rations from the Japanese command. We drafted an official-type letter demanding an immediate improvement in the camp rations, intimating that if rations were not improved, the prisoners would be unable to meet the work demands. This document was signed by all the medical officers and hand-delivered to Japanese headquarters. Just prior to the delivery of our letter, we had been advised that the camp and hospital would be inspected by the International Red Cross.

The day after the communiqué was delivered to Lieutenant Fukuhara, I was walking in the barracks area. I had forgotten that I was carrying the treasured atlas in my pocket. Two guards joined me and demanded that I accompany them to the *eiso.* I did not see any Americans in the vicinity as we started toward the *eiso.* On arrival, in front of the sergeant of the guard, I was booked without undue ceremony. I was searched and relieved of my pocket possessions—fountain pen, cigarettes, watch, and the Kolynos Atlas. My possessions were quickly put together in a rag, tied up, and the package placed in the safe. My efforts to learn the charges against me were to no avail, and I was locked in a small cell with no view of the outside.

The first night I heard returning work details, as they were checked back into camp with the usual screaming of the guards. Late in the evening my cell was visited by a guard who had been annoyed with me for a period of several months. He entered the cell carrying a baseball bat. As was the custom, he ordered me to attention as he got ready to swing the bat at me. In his rage and eagerness to punish me, he was oblivious to the small size of the cell, which so limited his swing that the beating was little more than a rough massage with the bat. I moaned and feigned pain for about thirty minutes, when he became exhausted and departed, locking the cell door. Why the hell he did not take me out to an open area I'll never know.

Days were spent pacing the cell and wondering what was going on in camp. The second night one of the guards was friendly, since I had done a minor operation on him. He realized that I had not been permitted to smoke, so when he had a short break he moved me to another cell and had me rapidly smoke three Kenchi cigarettes. If you knew Kenchis, you will appreciate my nauseated, stunned state for the rest of the evening. The late shift returning from the mine that night shouted several remarks in English, which made me believe that the other prisoners knew I was confined in the *eiso.*

The third night was one to remember. Another guard on whom I had done a minor operation informed me that the charge against me was very serious. I was charged with inciting a riot. In prolonged questioning I finally learned that the charge arose because of the recent letter to Lieutenant Fukuhara. He concluded that the letter demanding a ration increase was instigated by me, and that as senior medical officer I had forced the other doctors to sign the document. This was controlling group thought and therefore inciting a riot. Any prisoner with even a few marbles knows that inciting a riot is a sure, quick way out of life. So I really started to sweat, despite the coolness of the evening. I was still awake, trying to adjust to my eventual fate, when the early morning hours were disrupted by two civilian trucks arriving in front of the guardhouse. These trucks were delivering the October blessing from the Emperor. The famous paper blankets that were supposed to warm soldiers, and prisoners as well, through the long winter. The shouting and counting that went on during the exchange of blankets from civilian distributors to the Army was like watching a comedy. Finally, the count was correct. The numerous papers were signed and the trucks departed. Almost immediately after the departure of the trucks, one of the guards took three blankets from one bundle and threw them into my cell. For the first time since confinement in the *eiso* I did have body warmth.

On the fourth day I watched a two-hour repeat of the blanket-counting exercise, as issues were delegated to the guard barracks, each prisoner barracks, and the hospital buildings. Repeated checks failed to disclose the three blankets in my cell and the error in total count was covered in the paper work. During the fourth evening my concern was partially relieved when the sergeant major visited and informed me that I would soon be released from the *eiso* and resume my duties at the hospital.

During the fifth day I began to worry about the atlas locked up as one of my possessions. At 5:00 p.m. Lieutenant Fukuhara strutted into the *eiso*, adorned with sword and pistol. He ordered my immediate release. I was ordered to stand in front of the sergeant of the guards' table to receive my possessions. The safe was opened and the cloth in which my valuables were stored was placed on the table and opened. The contents were intact. One guard immediately picked up the atlas and opened it to a specific map. He started a loud discussion with one of his comrades. The few minutes of their discussion seemed to last hours and Fukuhara was still present. Finally, the discussion was concluded, the atlas was closed and handed to me. I instantly jammed it into a pocket. The watch, pen, and cigarettes were also returned. I turned to head for the hospital area, when a guard called me back to pick up the blankets in my cell. I returned to the hospital with three nonexistent blankets and the atlas. My friends were overjoyed that the atlas was still intact and immediately used it to check recent rumors. The next day the International Red Cross inspectors showed up, and we went through with a display of patient care planned to assure the inspectors of the benevolence of the Imperial Japanese Army.

Pvt. LEWIS ELLIOTT,
Mukden Prisoner-of-War Camp (Hoten, Manchuria):

I got in the *eiso* at Mukden and everything changed for me. Because they were made of wood, we had fire guards in the barracks every night. Each guy would pull one hour, then wake the guy next to him so he could pull his hour. Well, this kid's laying next to me and he says, "You might as well go to sleep. I'm going to read this book and I'll stand your fire guard for you and then I'll wake that other guy up." After I went to sleep, a Jap sergeant named Nara walks into the barracks. He'd been to school in Berkeley and used to tell us, "You guys called me a little slant-eyed sonovabitch. So now, if you mess up, I'll get you." He goes up to this damn kid, this Willard, who's sitting there reading a book, and asks, "Where's the fire guard?" The kid says, "There he lays."

Well, they took me in front of the commander and gave me seven days in the *eiso*. It was the dead of winter. I got a can of water and a biscuit every day, and two blankets every other night. When I didn't have my blankets I'd run all night to keep warm. The guardhouse was sunken and I could only see the guard's boots as he walked by. It was dark most of the time. I spent seven days in there on account of that kid.

I got to thinking, "Elliott, you're going alone from now on.

Don't depend on them assholes." Because I got a history of pneumonia, I didn't think I'd get out of the jailhouse. No sir, I wasn't going to depend on none of them bastards.

When the guys brought me my water at night, it would be boiling hot. To keep warm, I'd put it next to my body. I'd use every bit of that heat before I drank it. The last day or so the guys slipped me two extra blankets, camouflaged in the two they were giving me. The next morning, when the Jap guard came in to pick up the two blankets, I'd hidden the other two. That way I kept warm an extra night. The Japs never caught on.

When I got out, they put a red ribbon on my back. Then they took a hair clippers and went right down my head. Had to wear my hair that way, and that ribbon, for thirty days. Then I was assigned to the "eight-ball section." This group was guys who'd all been in the guardhouse for one reason or another. This submarine sailor was in it with me because he'd been caught drinking down at the factory. Another guy was in there for stealing cigarettes.

If the Japanese had any extra work details that needed to be done like loading or unloading trucks, they'd come and get this eight-ball section. By being in that group I couldn't write home, and I wouldn't receive no mail. I kept trying to get back to my regular outfit and an officer helped, but he couldn't hack it. I stayed in this section for the rest of the war.

Whenever I saw any of the other guys, I'd tell them they was pro-Jap. They'd always kid me about being an eight ball. I told them I was the only goddamn non-pro-Jap in the camp. Big joke.

2d Lt. FRED GIFFORD (Niigata):

Each time the Japs moved us we had to adapt to different conditions. Niigata was entirely different than any other place I'd been, because in the wintertime it was extremely cold. I've seen it as much as twenty-five degrees below zero and no heat in the barracks.

The last winter I was there, I got the dysentery. They put me in solitary. I got out on February 2, and it was well below zero. I weighed less than 100 pounds. They gave me a scoop shovel. I didn't know what I was going to do with it. I didn't have enough strength to carry it, so I dragged it. They told me to chop ice off the railroad tracks. The snow was about twenty feet deep. I didn't dig much and I didn't chop much. I just moved around enough to keep from freezing to death.

I had a friend who couldn't resist that trading. I shared my cigarettes with him, but they wasn't enough. He needed more. He also never took a bath, and he got lousy and it was kind of unsafe to hang around the feller. So he got sick somehow, probably from not having enough food to eat. They took him to the dispensary, which they called a hospital. It was necessary to give this guy a bath, so they stripped him down and bathed him. It was very cold. He never survived no more. He died of pneumonia a short time later.

J. J. CARTER (Aomori):

When I came into this last camp the English camp commander, Abbott, said to me, "See here, trading is not tolerated in this place." I said to myself, "Boy, you got a lot to learn."

When I left Tanagawa, everything that anybody owed me was clear. If someone went with me, he would still owe me. A guy who fell behind endeavored not to beat you out of anything he owed, because he knew he'd have to come back to you again. He needed a way to get it and he knew you'd always have it. When I left camp I left my partner, Dyer, in great shape. Many of the guys that owed me stayed behind, so I said, "Boy, it's yours, go and collect it."

Moving to a new camp and losing all I'd traded for wasn't really a concern for me. It's kind of like being a millionaire. If a millionaire goes broke he don't worry a whole lot about it, because he knows he can be a millionaire again. To get back into business in a new camp meant merely taking the initial plunge. All I did to get in business was to go without a meal or two. I could start off with a breakfast, which was not difficult to do without. "I'll loan this meal 'til tonight." "Oh, great! I'll take it." That night, when that meal came in, "Who wants a supper?" "I do." "When you going to pay it back?" "Tomorrow morning." "Two for one." "O.K." Next morning I'd say, "I've got a meal here for next issue of cigarettes." I'd be off and running. It was that simple.

Pfc. JOHN FALCONER, Fukuoka Camp No. 3 (Tobata):

It was awfully hard to live. I hated to see the night come. That darkness was terrible. Every night seemed like an eternity. I never knew whether the sun would rise the next day, because in the morning they'd come through and pick up the guys. I don't know his rank, but his name was Pickle. Sounds funny, but that was his name. I took care of him. He could barely make it down to the hole in the ground where the latrine was. I took him down one night and brought him back. I knew that you had to challenge a person. He couldn't make it up the ladder to his bay. I told Pickle, "Now climb up that ladder." The next morning he was dead. Our barracks commander knew I had been taking care of him, so he told me, "John, if there's anything of Pickle's here that you want, go ahead and take it. I knew Pickle had a GI handkerchief of bran which he was saving for a time when he really needed it. I thought, "Boy, I can use that." When I opened it, I found it crawling with maggots.

Pfc. WILLIAM WALLACE (Niigata):

The last winter conditions became terrible, especially with the snow. But I learned how to use snow to make my life easier. Sometimes, at night, it would snow three feet. In the morning, when we lined up in the compound for the count, I'd fall over into that fresh snow, *blook!* I'd hold my breath and it would look as if I'd lost consciousness. This would get me four or five days of rest. If I'd been caught, they would have killed me. But to stay away from that coal yard, to stay out of the snow and freezing rain, and to still be fed, I was willing to take any risk. I got away with it six or seven times. It always got me several days. I never told anyone about this trick. It was my secret. To pull it off properly, I needed enough snow to fall in.

I had amebic dysentery that last winter. The Japs put me in isolation. The first day I was able to go back to work it was cold, windy, and raining heavily. Later in the day the rain turned to sleet. I caught double pneumonia. On April 1, 1945, I was back in the hospital. It was Easter Sunday. That day was also my birthday. I turned twenty-two.

Staff Sgt. JAMES CAVANAUGH,
Subcamp No. 2 (Kawasaki):

As long as our bombers stayed at 25,000 feet they could fly over the Jap antiaircraft fire. Then suddenly, they started coming in at 5,000 or 6,000 feet.* Right off the deck. It was like you could reach up and touch them. The Japs had a field day. Right in our area alone we counted fourteen B-29s that went down in one night. They really got creamed! Before the men bailed out, they'd put their planes on automatic pilot. These planes would

---

* Throughout the winter months of 1944–45 heavy cloud cover over the Japanese mainland and strong winds diminished the effectiveness of American high-altitude precision bombing. In March, the decision to scratch these raids in favor of low-level area bombing was made. This new tactic made the B-29 more effective in hitting smaller industrial targets. On March 9 the B-29s began a run of incendiary attacks against Japanese cities which drastically changed the strategic nature of the air war.

then fly around and around. Finally, they'd go *splat* out in the bay.

Pfc. JACK BRADY (Omori):

We had figured out in our camp that we would never be able to go through another winter. We had a little slogan: "Frisco dive in '45 or stiff as sticks in '46." They had cut down the food allowance so much we figured that, if we weren't home by Christmas of '45, we would simply fade away.

We gained some emotional strength from the great Tokyo fire raid. It was a hell of a big fire. And it was very beautiful. The raid began in the middle of the night. The sky turned reddish orange and was bright enough to read by. The burning was right across the canal from us. The flames shot as high as some of the planes. The planes came in low and you could see them drop those big bundles of incendiaries. The feeling in the camp was of pure jubilation, knowing Tokyo was being burned and that our forces were close enough so they could put on that kind of show.*

A few days later it wasn't so nice. They cut our food to nothing. The guards also were very unhappy because they'd lost a large number of people in that raid. Suddenly, everything tightened up to the point where everything you did, didn't make any difference what, ended up with a beating. "Frisco dive in 45 or stiff as sticks in 46." No doubt about it!

Sgt. RALPH LEVENBERG,
Narumi Subcamp No. 2 (Nagoya):

Nagoya was devastated with fire bombs in March of 1945.† It seemed that the bomb run was right over our camp. All night they came over. Music to our ears. They must have been no more than 500 feet off the ground. The city was burned to the ground. We didn't go to work for a long time because the steel mill had been crippled. They also didn't want us to see the destruction. And oh God, the stench of all those dead bodies was horrible.

---

* A raid consisting of nearly 330 Superforts attacked Tokyo on the night of Mar. 9–10, 1945. Sixteen square miles of the capital were burned to the ground. It is estimated that 85,000 people died in the inferno. The following days saw fire raids on major industrial centers. By Mar. 19 the B-29s had dropped 10,000 tons of incendiary bombs on Japan's industrial heartland. The pounding continued as the tempo and size of the raids increased. The destruction widened as spring blazed into summer.
† The day after the first Tokyo fire storm, a giant incendiary raid of 285 bombers struck Nagoya. Going in at altitudes from 5,100 to 8,500 feet, the B-29s dropped 125 more tons of incendiary bombs than had been dropped on Tokyo. This raid was less spectacular than the one on Tokyo; it destroyed two square miles.

Capt. THOMAS HEWLETT, M.D.,
Fukuoka Camp No. 17 (Omuta):

The philosophy of the prisoner of war is a strange one, individually developed to make survival possible in a most hostile environment. He first learned to laugh at the tragedies that comprised the everyday life. He completely obliterated the pangs of hunger. The starving man would willingly trade his meager ration for a few cigarettes. In many instances he would risk his rations, gambling with professionals who pursued their trade without compassion for any life except their own.

The language problem was ever present. Interpreters, either Japanese or English-speaking, tended to put themselves in a command position, so they created an atmosphere of distrust. One prisoner of the "A" detail was executed for attempting to learn to read Japanese.

Early in the course of starvation, hunger is overwhelming and the theft of food by such a person is not a criminal act. The Greek, Pavlockus, was starved to death in the guardhouse for stealing food. It took them thirty-eight days to accomplish this execution; benefit of trial was denied.

For a minor infraction of rules, a nineteen-year old Australian soldier named David Runge was forced to kneel in front of the guardhouse for thirty-six hours. During the period, he developed gangrene of both feet. Bilateral amputation was carried out March 10, 1945. He was carried on the backs of comrades, to keep us reminded of the benevolence of the Japanese.

In camp, the prisoner's life was subject to the individual whims of the guard on duty. The prisoner could be aroused from rest to undergo punishment or humiliation, whichever met the sadistic needs of the guard.

Underground, the prisoner was faced with falling walls and ceilings, blast injuries and entombment. He lived each day with the possibility of sudden death or permanent disabling injury.

In such a situation malingering was anticipated. However, with our mission to protect the prisoners we felt were the sickest, we had to constantly fence with malingerers. Daily we saw chronic ulcers that were prevented from healing by the application of lime, which was available in the latrines. I never learned the name of the "Bone Crusher" but he could, for a price, inflict a broken arm or leg. Such breaks were unlike those accidentally incurred, so his work was recognized immediately. Usually his patients ended up on the honey-bucket detail within the camp.

On so-called *yasume* days the prisoners were subjected to formal inspections or sporadic shakedowns. It was extremely difficult to obtain permission for any organized entertainment.

Homosexuality was present in all nationality groups. This reached a point that Doctor Proff conducted a weekly marital relations clinic, in an effort to keep the couples happy in our tight society.

Staff Sgt. HAROLD FEINER,
Fukuoka Camp No. 17 (Omuta):

We had several kleptomaniacs in camp. Everyone could have stolen. There was that kind of need. A crumb of bread could be left lying around and, being hungry, you could think about stealing it. But when you did, you were stealing from someone who also was hungry. One of the men in camp, a sailor, turned out to be the worst thief. Nothing was sacred to this guy. One day I was laid up in the barracks with an injured ankle. We slept in little rooms which had sliding doors. I started to hear, *ssswish, sswish*, the sound our doors made when they were opened and closed. "What the hell is this?" I said. So I decided to take a peek out and I saw this sailor coming and going from the deserted rooms. I knew immediately what he was doing. When he came and looked into my room I pretended to be asleep.

That night, when the section came back from the mine, I went up to the section leader and said, "Sergeant, ask the guys if they're missing anything." When he did, guys began to speak up: "Hey, who's been in here? I'm missing a butt." I says, "O.K. The sailor grabbed them. I've been here all day and I saw him do it." We could have turned him over to the Japanese and no question about it, they would have killed him. But we had an alternative. We gave him a kangaroo court. Nothing formal, just a hearing. When we found him guilty, we sent him through a line. There were fifty men in a barracks and every man took a swat at him. We couldn't hit him with a weapon, only our hands or belts. He had to walk that line. Some guys would slap him, but other guys were mean. Especially guys that were missing things—you know, a piece of soap or something of equal value. It might have been half a damn cigarette. We had some very mild thieves. Guys who let their hunger overpower their good sense. But they weren't real thieves like this sailor.

As bad as this character was, we had an American in camp who was worse—far worse. The most vicious individual in that camp was an American, a Navy lieutenant, Edward Little. He was an overbearing, arrogant bastard who was in charge of our mess. He wasn't a stool pigeon in the classic sense. I'll give you examples of this man's behavior. Little came up to a good friend of mine and addressed him in Japanese. My friend said, "I am a sergeant in the United States Army and you, Lieutenant Little, are an American officer. I want you to address me in English." Little turned him in to the Japanese and they beat hell out of him.

There were other incidents which I remember very well. I had just gotten back from a shift in the mine when I was called out with others to help tie things down, because we were expecting a typhoon. Because this was an extra detail, we were going to be given an extra meal. The evening was dark, windy, and it poured. As I went through the line, Little came up to me and said, "You've been through this line twice," and he pushed me. I spilled the food all over myself. I went for him. A guy yelled, "Feiner, you stupid bastard, don't hit him." If I had, I would have been killed. They stopped me in time.

I know Little directly caused the deaths of two men. A soldier named Knight* was caught stealing some *pahn* (bread). He shouldn't have done it, no question about it, but this dirty bastard, Little, turned him in to the Japanese. He also turned in a Marine named Pavlockus who he caught trading food. Little certainly knew the Greek would be in grave danger, since he had been in confinement for refusing to mine coal for the Japs. The Japanese put Pavlockus in a little cell and there they starved him to death.†

Pfc. WILLIAM WALLACE (Niigata):

Things happened in Japan amongst the men that can only be explained in light of the conditions we were exposed to. What happened? In O'Donnell and Cabanatuan people helped each other. When we got to Japan, this changed. Everyone came close to dying, so as Mr. Darwin said, it became survival of the fittest. In my camp the biggest and healthiest took the easiest jobs.

At the end there was very little decency or human dignity left. Humanity had long since departed from camp. Human worth had disappeared. We were just animals and that's all it amounted to.

Men began to steal from each other. When the Red Cross parcels were given out, cigarettes that had not been smoked or traded were stolen. So was sugar and coffee. When someone was caught, we wouldn't turn them over to the Japanese. The men who were so weak and couldn't do anything about it, we

---

* Pvt. William Knight, of Warsaw, New York, was beaten for nearly a week and died on May 20, 1945.
† Marine Cpl. James Pavlockus was put in the guardhouse without food or water. Thirty-eight days later, on Jan. 28, 1944, he was dead of starvation.

disciplined ourselves. The strong disciplined the weak. In our camp there wasn't an organization which defended the weak from the strong. If you were strong, you could defend yourself.

For example there was the problem of food distribution. The same two men always distributed our food. One man would give out the rice, and the other one the beans. They were in cahoots with each other and were able to defend themselves physically against accusations made about the amount of food they were putting in our bowls. If you were these men's enemy, you got a loosely packed bowl of rice. If you were their friend, you got a bowl so tightly packed it would be hard to get out.

I would stand in line and watch it. Of course I'd say, "You're really packing that one." They'd ladle the rice in with a measuring paddle, and depending on how hard they pushed the rice down into your bowl, this would be how much you got.

The whole time I was there no work was rotated, which would have been the fairest way of doing it. These kitchen people, who had the choicest jobs in camp, never went out and shoveled coal. The American officers never suggested to the Japanese that the jobs be changed. Of course the officers didn't have to do manual work. If you're ever captured, make sure you're an officer, hear? That way you're a gentleman by an act of Congress.

There were three labor details in Niigata. Lots of us were working for Rinko Coal Company. Others worked in a foundry. Then we had a bunch of stevedores down on the docks, loading and unloading ships. We all lived in the same barracks, but the jobs didn't circulate. Working in the coal detail was the hardest. But foundry never worked coal, and coal never worked on the docks. Of course this situation created jealousies and fights. Most everyone was jealous of the men who worked on the docks. Stevedores had the best opportunity of anyone to steal. When they were unloading cases of apples or oranges, they always managed to break into them. When they'd smuggle these fruits back into camp, they'd swap them for extra rations of rice. They'd never just give them away. It was dog-eat-dog.

Pfc. ROBERT BROWN,
Mukden Prisoner-of-War Camp (Hoten, Manchuria):

I had a sergeant from my original squadron who wanted something, but who didn't have the nerve to ask for it himself, because he knew I would refuse him. He worked in the kitchen. It was a corrupt job, set up for him by our officers. They would assign their stooges, and in return for this favor they would get extra food. This sergeant was being transferred to one of our branch camps, and he wanted to take some medication with him. He had the audacity to send someone to ask me for this medication. I told the man, "You go back and tell him if he doesn't have guts enough to come on his own and ask for it, he's not going to get it. I'm not giving it to you and I wouldn't give it to him, either."

You needed to live by principles. I was called out, for example, many a night to a barracks where the Japanese had caught one of our men doing something, and asked to translate. Now that was tough. I'd walk into the situation and here'd be a Jap officer nailing a prisoner for some rule violation, and he'd want this guy's explanation. I told our fellers, and I think anybody who ever tried to translate would tell you, I wasn't about to change anything they said to help them out. If I did, then I'd become part of the problem. There ain't no way that I should have to make excuses or modify some guy's answer in an interrogation. If I was going to interpret, I better damn well put across accurately what each side was saying. But you'd stand there, in this barracks at night, and know the American was lying. I mean, it was survival. If you can tell a story and get away with it, O.K. What can you do? I mean it was part of life.

J. J. CARTER (Aomori):

I had a real trick pulled on me in the last camp I was in. We used to get grain which would be ground up into flour and be used to make doughballs. They'd steam these doughballs and then issue them. In that high, dry climate of northern Honshu, boy, you could stuff them away, and the longer you saved them, the more filling they were.

I had this buddy of mine there, Irving, who was a Jew boy from New York. He and I just hit it off great. You know how you've always heard of what good business people Jews are? Well, strangely enough, Irving was a sorry businessman. If it hadn't been for me, he would have starved to death. I caught him when he was just really getting hungry. So just like I did for old Dyer, I took him in and showed him how to trade.

On my birthday I decided I was going to throw a little party for Irving and myself. I told him we were going to put back a doughball or two every day till the 25th of January, which was my birthday. Then we were really going to chow down. 'Course we were eating good all along. We weren't missing our meals, we were just saving doughballs that were coming in, you know, owed to us.

On the 25th, I came in from work and I was all set for our feast. I took my bath and when I came to our bunk I didn't see any doughballs laid out. I said, "Come on, Irving, let's get them out." He said, "We don't have no doughballs." "What in the world are you talking about?" He said, "I've been eating them all along." He'd eaten up all the profit. He'd eaten us out of business. In other words, some people can discipline themselves and some can't. Some people can deal with hunger and some can't. I don't know when I was so mad at a feller.

2d Lt. FRED GIFFORD, Subcamp No. 5 (Niigata):

The hardest part of this detail was the inadequate food we were given. You never had nothing to eat and hunger was your biggest problem. The work could be done, providing you had the energy to do it. To get that energy, you had to have food. The Japanese didn't have food themselves. So they couldn't give it to us. Some officer once said, I believe it was Napoleon, "If you can't take care of a prisoner, don't take a prisoner." The Japanese evidently never heard of that because they starved us.

Sgt. RALPH LEVENBERG,
Narumi Subcamp No. 2 (Nagoya):

We were eating very badly at the end. Gruel in the morning, an eight ounce loaf of rice bread for lunch, and rice in vegetable stock, some stalks, and very occasionally some meat or fish in the evening. Along with the constant craving for food, the camaraderie began breaking down. Hunger and imprisonment were getting on our nerves. Three years of it. Guys began to steal from each other.

Our Red Cross parcels had come in Christmas of 1944, but we didn't gobble them down. We tried to make them last as long as we could. Then things began disappearing. Our chaplain was made King of the Kangaroo Court, you know, the Judge. We had a big feller from New Mexico who had formerly been a highway patrolman, who managed to keep in pretty good shape. The Japs liked him and he used to wrestle with them. He was a big guy and it was he who meted out the Judge's sentences. If bread had been stolen but not eaten and could be returned, then the thief was slapped. Now, when this New Mexican hit you, he did it in front of the whole barracks. That was enough to humiliate anyone. Secondly, when he hit you, you were hit. If what was stolen could not be returned, then the thief took a more severe beating. This big guy used to know how to beat someone and never leave a mark.

One guy worked in the Japanese commandant's office, and because he learned he would get extra rations if he ratted on us, turned into a Japanese informer. The stolen newspapers, which were the only way we got information, stopped coming into camp. That made it rough on us. When he finally got caught, the chaplain decided the best punishment we could give this feller was the silent treatment. We almost drove the guy out of his mind. Nobody, but nobody, in that whole camp talked to him until Liberation, and then he was turned in. It was a terrible, terrible punishment.

Cpl. ISHMAEL COX (Osaka):

I got beat once by an American, too. A lot of times in the lead mine you didn't feel like doing anything or eating anything. I hadn't given up, but it was just one of those days that I felt that a cigarette would do me more good than some food. I thought that if I just had something to relax me, I'd be fine. So I traded a chow ration for two cigarettes. Because we had a stoolie in the place, the Japanese found out what I'd done. They came in and got the American who they'd selected to do the punishment, and he beat me. I took down my britches and was made to bend over a table. Then, while the Japanese stood there, this American took a webbed pistol belt and gave me ten whups across the butt. Of course I didn't have much of a butt then. But I got my ten licks.

The way the Japs used this American was just like the Mafia. No damn difference. He probably got a little extra from them, and he also avoided being beaten himself. But that was his job in camp. Because he seemed like he enjoyed his work, all of us boys called him a sadist. We all told him that at the end of the war we were going to get him and fix him like he'd fix us. I thought of killing him, but shit, I doubt that if I had wanted, I could have killed myself. After we were liberated I never saw this American again. I wish I knew where he went. I sure wish I knew.

Pfc. ROBERT BROWN,
Mukden Prisoner-of-War Camp, (Hoten, Manchuria):

We had night sick call when the guys working in the factory would come back. If something couldn't be done right, then one of our doctors would pick out the guys that needed to come back the next day and see the Japanese doctor. My job was to process this night sick call, much as I did the morning call. One time I was a minute or two late coming down to the office, because I'd been playing cribbage. We had a good old American officer who was trying every way in the world to make himself important. My position, apparently, began to become an irritant to him, so when I came down late he reported me to the Japs and recommended I be punished. As this was in the winter, and pipes in the factory had frozen, there was no work that day and the men, to have something to do, were being given close-order drill out there on the playground. So as punishment I was sent outdoors to help drill the men.

Staff Sgt. HAROLD FEINER,
Fukuoka Camp No. 17 (Omuta):

We had been on an exceptionally long shift. The Japanese were pushing very hard and we had worked fourteen or fifteen hours in a row. We were in a very deep part of the mine, and had to literally crawl back to the waiting area where the cars picked us up. The cars arrived, finally, and we collapsed onto the benches. Just then a detail of Korean miners, who had been working somewhere else, came up and began to push us out of the cars. One of them came up and hit the feller next to me and I tumbled out of the car. I banged my head on the rocks. I got up and climbed back through the cars till I got to this Korean. I pulled him out and beat the living hell out of him. I busted his nose and I knocked some teeth out of his head. I really worked that bastard over. I thought, "He'll remember Americans for a long time." I thought I might also get away with it. I'd done it once before, so I'll see what happens.

When I got upstairs, the Japanese guards were waiting for me. They almost killed me. They knocked me down, but I'm too damn stubborn to stay down or cover my head. I kept getting up saying, "You sonovabitches, knock me down again—I won't stay down!" I had enough brains not to strike at the guards, because they would have killed me right then and there. They kicked me and busted my ear drums.

Pfc. ROY DIAZ (Yokkaichi):

I did a lot of work repairing a railroad until the accident. We were told we had to carry a log about three feet in circumference and eight feet long. I tell the Japs, "No, we can't lift that." The kid that's with me: "Sure, we can do it." I say, "Look, you drop this thing, you let me know before you do." "Hey-yup," and we stand up with this log between us. We actually get it off the ground before the kid drops it. I got the bulk of it on my back. Hell, I think, I'm going to be paralyzed. No more work for me.

Pfc. JOHN FALCONER, Fukuoka Camp No. 3 (Tobata):

The Japanese would allow just so many people to be sick. No matter how many were actually sick, only a certain number got taken care of at sick call. And you see, those that were the sickest weren't the fastest to get down to the hospital in the morning. I was so sick that I couldn't ever beat the healthier men to the doctor. One of the doctors told me, "Now Falconer, I want to see you tomorrow. But if you don't get here within the quota of allowable sick, all you got to do is fall down. Just faint." So at the risk of being beaten, the next morning on the way to the factory, out on the road, I pretended to fall down, unconscious. That's how I began to avoid going to work. This was all part of the million-dollar education I got in prison camp. But if I had a million dollars, I'd give it to you right now not to have had that education.

Pfc. ROBERT BROWN,
Mukden Prisoner-of-War Camp (Hoten, Manchuria):

In February sometime, 1945, about 300 men came in that had been on a ship.* The Japanese made them walk into camp under their own power, we weren't allowed to help them in any way. I was standing there, watching them come by, to see if I recognized anyone. This guy looked up at me, "Hi, Bob." I said, "I'm sorry, I don't recognize you." He was so damn skinny and sick, I didn't know him. He was one of the pilots out of my own squadron, the 17th Pursuit. We agreed amongst ourselves that these men were a hell of a lot worse off than we were, so we decided to cut back on our own rations to increase the rations these men received.

1st Lt. MARK HERBST, M.D.,
Mukden Prisoner-of-War Camp (Hoten, Manchuria):

When that group came into camp, they were in very poor condition and very much put down mentally and physically. I found my own colonel and I offered him some of my tobacco. He said, "Oh, I have some." He had a little coffee can with about half an inch of tobacco at the bottom, and he went to give me some. "No," I said, "I want to give you some." I had traded a broken watch for a kilo of what we called Purple Death, which was a very black, very, very strong tobacco. It was the damnedest stuff. You would roll a bit of that, take a drag, and your head would get knocked back. On the second one, your eyes popped. I gave

---

* Around May 1, 1945, 236 American prisoners were moved to Mukden Prisoner-of-War Camp. Although this detail was made up mainly of men taken from camps in the Fukuoka area, there were also an unknown number of men included in this group who had survived the Oryoku Maru sinking. Seventy-one survivors, who had first been sent to Fukuoka Camp No. 3, were placed in a larger detail and moved to Korea on April 24. There the group was divided. Half remained in Korea, while the remaining prisoners completed their journey to Hoten. The exact number of men who'd been on the Oryoku Maru and who arrived in Hoten is unknown.

the old colonel some of this. "My God," he said, "what are you trying to do, kill me off so early?"

Staff Sgt. JAMES CAVANAUGH,
Subcamp No. 2 (Kawasaki):

Our Navy bombers came in one day and finished off all the buildings that were more than two stories high and still standing. You could hear them assembling and then, *zing*, in they came. Some of the bombs landed out in the bay, a little north of where we were. Later, we wondered what all the sea gulls were so excited about. There were dozens of them flying around. The Italian Marines figured out what had happened. There weren't too many guards around, and the next thing we knew these Marines were out swimming around, throwing dead fish in to us. It was like the miracle of the loaves and the fishes. The rest of us cleaned out some tar buckets and made a fire and we all had a grand fish fry. For miles around, everything was bombed out, there was no electricity and no running water, but huddled around in a group were Italian Marines, American prisoners, and Jap guards all having an old-fashioned fish fry.

Staff Sgt. FRANK STECKLEIN,
Fukuoka Camp No. 17 (Omuta):

I had a rash on my legs, so I was excused from going down into the mine. But since I was a senior sergeant I had to work in the camp, and I was put in charge of some men. I don't remember no more how many, could have been eight or ten. We was gonna build a fence around this warehouse which the Japanese had filled with American Red Cross parcels. One of the men assigned to my little detail was a bad character in the camp, a sailor by the name of Yoder. He even gave Mamerow and Little trouble. He got a chance and, goddamn, one way or another he broke a window and got into those parcels. When I found out about this I said, "Oh, God, we're all gonna get in trouble here. You've done wrong." But oh hell, we were all so hungry, what the heck. So Yoder gave me a can of salmon. I took it back to the barracks.

Me being in charge of this detail, when they discovered the break-in, I was the first one they came after. They searched my place and found the salmon. Right away they took me up to the camp commander [Lt. Fukuhara]. Then they brought in Yoder and two other guys. The Jap asked what we were doing. I told him we were hungry.

He took this bamboo stick—three inches thick maybe, two feet long—which had one end split into tails and the other wrapped with tape so he could get a good grab; he had me take off my shirt and kneel in front of him, and he beat me to hell. I was all bloody. After he beat the other three, they took us to the Japanese guardhouse right alongside the gate where the prisoners went in and out. The ground was covered with rocks. They made us kneel there with sticks behind our knees.

This happened in May 1945. We got nothing to eat, nothing to drink. Every so often they took a bucket of water and threw it on us. Sometimes when a guard wanted to pee, he'd pee in our faces.

After a while the Japs gave us sticks about a foot long and an inch thick, and we had to beat each other on the head. I'd beat Yoder, Yoder would beat the guy next to him, and so on. Sometimes we let up on each other and barely tapped the head, other times one of the meaner guards would come over and tell us to hit harder. We did this for a long time. Then about six o'clock the sergeant of the guard came out. He had us get up one at a time. With a pick hammer handle—you know, heavy— "Unnnnh," he slammed it into our lower backs. Both hands, like swinging a baseball bat. When he hit me, I went down and out.

They poured water on us, and during the night we resumed the position of kneeling on the rocks with the sticks behind our knees. The only night we didn't kneel on the rocks was the night the B-29s came over. Then they tied us up to a post. For three days and three nights this treatment went on.

The second day, the Sailor took me into a small cell. He had this thick leather strap which he doubled and then doubled again. He stood in front of me and he just beat me, beat me, beat me. I cried. I prayed. I prayed, I'll tell you—"Hail Mary" and "Our Father." He beat the others the same. This became a routine. Beatings were repeated. You'd holler for water. The days went on. I asked them to take us out and shoot us.

Around the second day a guy by the name of Knight joined us. He'd been caught stealing buns. Little turned him over to the Japanese. Now there were five of us. The ordeal was routine. The sergeant of the guard beat us with that pick handle. Not so much me, but Yoder and Knight really got it. There was just a few guards that always beat on us. There were others who wouldn't touch us and who even tried to help us. At night they'd give us water.

After the third day the camp interpreter, who was one of the finest men I ever met, came up and said, "I got you out. I'm going to take you over to the commander." Knight was not included and he stayed behind.

The commander beat us again with his stick. Then he told the interpreter to take us down to the kitchen and get us a double ration. When we got down there, Little gave us one ration. I know the interpreter asked for double rations, but he only gave us one. That night I went back to the mine. I was in the mine about two hours and I passed out. My legs were in terrible condition. I was taken out on a litter and put in what they called the hospital. Two days after our ordeal ended, Knight died. Right there in front of the prison.

Maj. JOHN MAMEROW,
Fukuoka Camp No. 17 (Omuta):

We had four men executed while I was there. We had a couple of stealing incidents where the guys went in and stole food out of the Japanese galley. One man [Knight] was caught and executed for it. Another man was accused of stealing Red Cross parcels. The Japanese brought him out to the middle of the parade ground. We were told the officers had to watch the execution. Then they changed their minds and we were sent back to our barracks. My headquarters barracks overlooked the parade ground. I was able to watch through my window. Before he was made to kneel, they tied his hands behind him. The Japanese formed a circle around him. I saw the bayonet go up and down three times.*

I had another man [Pavlockus] who was starved to death. He was kind of a troublemaker. The Nip commander told him that if he was brought in front of him one more time, he'd never come out of the jail house. He was caught causing more trouble, so we had to take him in again. He died of starvation in the jail.

And there was one more. He had a constant habit of talking to the Japanese civilians in the mine. He had a Japanese book and was always running around with it. We tried to tell him he would get into trouble. Two minutes later he'd be right back doing it. Finally he got caught talking to someone he wasn't supposed to talk to and they brought him out of the mine. They made him kneel on a bamboo pole while holding rocks in each hand. I was too far away to hear anything, but I was told he screamed a lot. I got his body after he was dead. He'd been beaten to death.†

Staff Sgt. FRANK STECKLEIN,
Fukuoka Camp No. 17 (Omuta):

You could hear Johnson screaming. This guy, Walter Johnson, he thought he could speak pretty good Japanese. He got pretty friendly with the Koreans down in the mine and from them he

---

* Pvt. Noah Heard of Salinas, Calif., was bayoneted to death on Mar. 31, 1944.
† Cpl. Walter Johnson of McPherson, Ka., was beaten to death in April 1945.

got a lot of information. The Japs accused him of being a spy. So, the Sailor took him and, Jesus, he was beaten. I knew old Johnson before the war. We used to play the accordion together. God, you could hear him all over the camp, screaming. And goddamn, the Sailor and the One-Armed Bandit and the others beat him to death. I mean, he died. Johnson died.

Staff Sgt. JAMES CAVANAUGH,
Subcamp No. 2 (Kawasaki):

May the 29th, 1945, I'll never forget it. There was a big raid which pounded Yokohama.* I mean pounded. They came in first with the incendiary bundles, then they switched to the heavy stuff. Pounding, pounding all day. We were a little north and the wind was blowing towards us. The next day at nine o'clock in the morning it was like nine o'clock at night. The sky was black with smoke for nearly three hours. Fire and smoke. I watched. It was like a tornado of flame. You could see the heat. It was all blowing our way. You could faintly make out people screaming. It was a terrible experience. But I'll tell you, it got to this stage, we figured the more aircraft that came over, the sooner we were going to get out. We'd been prisoners for three years. Live or die, you know.

Pfc. JOHN FALCONER, Fukuoka Camp No. 2 (Tabata):

My body was breaking out with boils and my mental condition was beginning to deteriorate. I mean you can only survive so much. I had reached the breaking point. I didn't give two hoots about what the Japs did to me. I had a cloth hat like an aviator's hat, and in the barracks at night I put it over my head. The Japanese and the other guys would talk to me. I wouldn't hear them. I blocked them out of my mind. In my bunk at night, in the dark, it was just me. It was all me. I couldn't go any further. I had seen others reach this point. I had reached my limit.

I couldn't work regularly anymore. I wasn't strong enough. I'd lie up in my bunk for maybe a week. When you didn't work the Japs gave out only half a ration of food. Some men, in order to get off work, would drop a beam or a rock on their feet. I couldn't do that. I had enough pain without inflicting more on myself. What they did wasn't all that different from faking unconsciousness, as I did.

I miss a lot in my memory about this time. I feel kind of ashamed. You'd think a guy would remember, but I don't. It's

---

* This was a daylight incendiary mission. Escorted by P-51 fighters, 454 B-29s dropped 2,570 tons of incendiary bombs and destroyed a third of Yokohama.

like I had put that cap over my memory as well as my ears. The easiest thing to do was just lay back and let death come in quickly and quietly. I wasn't eating anymore. The fellers were thinking of putting me on the trading table. When you were at the trading table, people told you what to do. I still had my pride. I wanted to be independent. I didn't want someone telling me what to do. I had had enough of that already.

Sgt. FORREST KNOX (Toyama):

Towards the end of the war, just to survive, I had to gradually and simply wall my mind off from what was happening around me. I could still function, I was there and I did what I was told to do, but my defense mechanism created a situation which permitted me to insulate my mind from my surroundings. When I did that, I felt they really and truly couldn't hurt me.

We were so automated at the end that we did whatever the Japanese told us to do, regardless of what it was. There were a few guys that never seemed to be completely dominated, but most of us were zombies. I thought that was what was wrong with me when I came home. We called it "stir crazy." 'Course, I had those hallucinations, too, and that was the scary part.

Staff Sgt. JAMES CAVANAUGH,
Subcamp No. 2 (Kawasaki):

In late July we took a bad bombing, the one where we lost twenty-five guys. The bombings had gotten so bad that the Japs moved most of the guys up to the copper mines in northern Honshu. There were possibly thirty of us left in Kawasaki that last summer. We'd help the Japanese fill in craters, or dig out of the rubble civilians who had died during a raid. One raid we must have found 300 or 400 dead. Then we got hit bad ourselves. We had twelve guards with us—well, actually they weren't military, more like civil defense people who volunteered to guard us. The night of the raid, eleven of these people hid in a shelter. It was pretty well built because I'd help build it. I was in a small group that was away from the camp and we hid in a large cement sewer pipe. The bombers really turned our camp over. They came in first with incendiary bombs. Then they hit us with the heavy stuff. During a raid you could hear the bombs whizzing and you'd count to sixteen. If you reached sixteen, the magic number, you were safe. If you didn't get to sixteen it was all over. That night our camp took a direct hit. We lost twenty-five Americans. It was so close to the end of the war, we felt so bad. The shelter where the eleven Japs were hiding also took a direct hit. Killed all of them. The one guard who was with us was the only one left. When he learned what had happened to his buddies he went haywire. He put a bayonet on his rifle and began to wildly stab at us. He cut quite a few men. He went out of it. I stayed out of his way.

Earlier, during the raid, I had been knocked unconscious by the concussion of a bomb that had landed close to the sewer pipe. When I finally made it back to what had been our camp, I found some water in a fire barrel and tried to clean off the dirt. A Jap caught me and beat hell out of me. Most of the men who escaped being killed that night were badly beaten by the Japs.

The next day came and it was like the calm after the storm.

Capt. BENSON GUYTON (Omine Machi):

When we first got into camp, this British major came to us and said, "For goodness sakes, chaps, don't let anybody steal a newspaper out of the mine." "Gosh dang, man," we said, "these guys we've got are professional thieves. There's no problem in getting . . ." "No," he said, "you'd only bother our system. We've got two blokes here that are bleedin' experts, and we don't want to get too many papers around so the Japs will find them and shut off the supply. Our chaps are trained and they know what to look for—maps and those sorts of things." Now mind you, these Limeys, all they were interested in and worried about was London. They didn't care about the war in the Pacific. Man, when they smuggled out a newspaper with news that the war in Europe had ended, it was all we could do to keep them from going out shouting and celebrating. As far as they were concerned, the war was over. I never seen people so happy.

Well, the British continued to bring up the stolen newspapers. It's easy to exaggerate how good they were in getting them out of the mine, so let me put it this way, they never got caught. From these newspapers we knew we'd taken Okinawa. Somehow we missed Iwo Jima. But man, you knew the war was getting close. At night you could hear the bombs. Probably a month or two before the war ended, we saw a raid of 250 B-29s go over. We celebrated when we saw that.

I was always thinking of things and Jerry McDavitt, the American camp commander, was dang good at doing things. I'd sit and think of something out loud, "You know, we oughta do this. I don't know how we'll do it, but it sure would be a good idea if we could." Man, old Jerry'd jump up and do it. Anyhow, when we started seeing the signs that the war was coming to an end, I thought, "You know, the first team's going to be put in against the Japs. There's no place to fight but Japan." I said to McDavitt, "It's sure gonna be hot for us. In fact, I just don't see how the Japs are gonna let us live. But there might be a chance to run for it. What do we do if we start seeing parachutes pouring down around here?" So we started working on that and came up with a scheme for taking over the camp.

From then on we knew exactly where every Jap guard was. There were fourteen rifles in that camp and we knew exactly where every one of those rifles were all the time. We always had enough men in camp, hopefully, to take over. A lot of times we were down to just two men for one Jap guard and he got the rifle. I don't know if we got down to what the signal would be when we were going to take over, but we figured we could grab these guards, cut the telephone lines, and then run for it.

We didn't have Doc Immerman in on it at first. In fact, the plan scared the daylights out of us because if the Japs found out about it, man, we were in trouble. So we limited the number of men who knew about it. Doc's the only one found out about it. "Hey, what's this you're planning to take over the camp?" "How the heck did you hear about it?" "My gosh," we thought, "if he heard, who else has?" Doc said, "Well, you dang sure better count me in." "No," we said. "With that Red Cross arm band you're a noncombatant." "The hell with that," he said. Immerman was put on the team. He said, "What about the Limeys?" So we went over to the British officers and told them about it. As soon as we mentioned it, a couple of them exploded. No way were they going to take part in anything like that. This British major, he riled up, said, "By gosh, if you don't . . . If I have to shoot you, I will." So he made them go along. They were pretty good as far as discipline.

So the plan was in place. Now we waited for the American paratroops. I'm glad we never had to put the plan to a test.

Staff Sgt. JAMES CAVANAUGH,
Subcamp No. 2 (Kawasaki):

At the end I weighed 120 pounds, soaking wet. If you bent over, it would take half a minute to straighten out. You'd make all kinds of funny noises as your bones creaked. We worked during the days and hit the bomb shelters at night. We were raided practically every night. But we had to work or we didn't eat. Sometimes we cared less, really, about living or dying.

You'd see one of your best buddies—this was our great humor—and you'd say, "Jeez, you don't look very good today. You're good for only about three more months." This was very harsh comedy. Instead of saying to someone who was really down, "Keep up the old spirit," we'd say, "You're all finished. You'll never make it home." Actually, this was very true at this time. Our resistance was so low that if anyone got dysentery he would last only four or five days. We had, just before the surrender, very little medical treatment. The Japanese, if the truth be known, didn't have it for themselves. It's hard to explain to people, but the poor in Japan were also going hungry. They didn't have cigarettes. They didn't have clothing or shoes. How were they going to give us things they didn't have themselves? Their ration system gave them only enough to subsist on. What you have to remember, the Japanese people, the civilians, took a terrible beating.

Sgt. RALPH LEVENBERG, Narumi Subcamp No. 2 (Nagoya):

Fourteen days before the war was over, we had a big air raid while we were in the plant. It was the Jap policy, in cases like this, to get us the hell out of there and back to the barracks. With my job in the kitchen, I was always the last man to leave. Consequently, I was the last man to get to the electric streetcar which took us back to the camp. On this particular day the warning came late and there was a lot of panic in the streets with people running to get out of the way. The sirens were wailing and I couldn't get onto the streetcar. I hung off the side. Well, this Jap hit me across the back with an ax handle, *vroom!* That was the end of me. I didn't know much of anything after that. I was paralyzed and out of it until the war ended.

Pfc. LEE DAVIS, Divisional Camp (Jinsen, Korea):

One of my best friends was a relative of Doris Duke, who was known as the world's richest girl. He and I had become very close while we were still stationed in California. In Korea we were wearing real heavy coats. One night he went to the latrine and because he was so weak he fell into the honey bucket. He managed to crawl out and come back to the barracks with his pockets full of it. He died that night. With all his wealth, and all the wealth of his relatives, he died in this manner.

Pfc. ANDREW AQUILA, Fukuoka Camp No. 3 (Tobata):

Towards the end of the war, each night we were getting more and more air raids. One guy in our barracks made a wager with someone in another barracks of a half ration of rice that a raid would take place at a certain time. When he won the wager he went over to the barracks to collect his half ration. On his way back, a Jap guard caught him. He explained what he was doing. Since one of their rules was that we couldn't trade rice, the guard beat hell out of this guy. When he came into the barracks he was bleeding badly around the head. The next day he had his head bandaged. They wouldn't permit him to stay in the hospital, but returned him instead to work. Finally, when he got worse he was permitted to go to the hospital. No more than two weeks before we were liberated, he died.

Sgt. FERRON CUMMINS,
Camp 10-D (Innoshima Island, Onomichi):

I watched them drop the atomic bomb. At the time I didn't think too much about it. We had seen raids before, big ones, with 500 planes in the air, so we were used to them. A bombing raid was just an everyday occasion. We knew it had to be a big explosion because of the smoke. The billows just went higher and higher. We saw the mushroom cloud over the top of the mountains. A big white cloud, the outer edges were blue gray. I seem to remember feeling some concussion, but by the time it had come that distance and rolled down the canyon, it didn't bother us. We barely felt the heat. At the time we thought they had hit a big ammunition dump.

The next morning we learned differently. My supervisor told us that the Americans had dropped one bomb and had killed "*takusan* people. *Nito.*" [Many people]. He sure was beating his teeth about it. Next, we saw a newspaper, so we knew he wasn't exaggerating. It was kind of hard to believe that one bomb would take care of everything they were describing.

Three days later a plutonium bomb was dropped on Nagasaki. Emperor Hirohito informed his country of their surrender in a radio message broadcast Aug. 15. The formal instrument of surrender was signed Sept. 2, 1945, aboard the battleship Missouri in Tokyo Bay.

PART V

FREEDOM

15
LIBERATION

Staff Sgt. JAMES CAVANAUGH, Subcamp No. 2 (Kawasaki):

In August our guards got very bitter. We didn't know why. We knew something was up because we had heard from a few of the Japs that something terrible had happened. They wouldn't tell us what. All they'd say was *"Boom!"*

Staff Sgt. HAROLD FEINER, Fukuoka Camp No. 17 (Omuta):

When we came up from the mine it was hot. The air was stifling because Nagasaki was still burning. We weren't close enough to see flames, but the whole area was smogged over. When we got topside the camp commander, an arrogant little bastard, got the whole camp together. He says, "Today the Emperor has declared a day of mourning for the brave Japanese and the brave Allied soldiers." "Bullshit," I thought, "Bullshit!" The war was ending, but he wouldn't tell us that.

Capt. MARION LAWTON, Divisional Camp (Jinsen, Korea):

Right around the middle of August our medical officer, Jack Swartz, noticed the young Jap doctor, who was assigned to our camp, to be terribly nervous and upset. He watched him for a while and recognized that the fellow was frightened. They had developed a very good relationship, so he asked this youngster what was bothering him. He told Jack that the Americans had dropped a terrible bomb that wiped out a whole city, a quarter of a million people. "We've lost the war and now I'm going to be killed. I was only serving my country." Jack counseled him, "Don't you worry. Americans don't do business like that. You've been very decent to us and, if necessary, I'll vouch for you." Of course as soon as Jack got into camp he spread the word and by noon the whole camp knew the war was nearly over. But we were reluctant to do any celebrating, for fear that when the end really came the Japs would panic and become irrational and shoot us. We controlled our happiness and just talked amongst ourselves.

Pfc. JACK BRADY (Sendai):

They told us about a big blast, but we didn't believe them. We thought it was more propaganda about how cruel Americans were. After that, though, they were much too frightened whenever there was an air raid, so we knew something really big must have happened. Tokyo had taken such a plastering that we'd been moved from Omori to up north on Honshu. One day we were all called back from the steel mill. The next morning we lined up to listen to a radio which had been set up in the compound. We knew it was the Emperor talking, but we didn't know what he said, except some of the guys picked up something about *senso,* "the war," and *owari,* "end." We were stunned by this, and a little confused. For the next two or three hours we wandered around and talked to each other. We didn't pay attention to much else. The next thing we noticed was all the guards had gone. There wasn't a Jap anywhere in that camp.

Cpl. KENNETH DAY (Toyama):

One morning—I think it was August 15—the day shift at the smelter was ordered to return to the *kukei* shack. We left our jobs and assembled inside. Strict orders were given that we were not to step outside for any reason. No, not even to go to the latrine across the road. Stay in the building.

Curious, but pleasant. We lolled about and smoked and talked. It was a poorly built structure, with slits here and there between the horizontal siding boards. We could peek out. About 100 yards up the road a number of Japanese workers had gathered around a small radio. Someone was talking, but the set was so scratchy we couldn't catch any words.

All at once all the Japanese took their hats off. We could guess what that must mean: the Emperor was talking. They listened quietly for a few minutes, then put their hats on and went back to work. It was around 11:00 a.m. They came and got us, and we went back to our jobs.

Capt. MARION LAWTON, Divisional Camp (Jinsen, Korea):

A Jap colonel requested a formation so he could make an announcement. He told us the war had ended, that Japan had lost, and that he had orders to surrender the camp to the senior American officer.* As he handed over his sword we burst loose, yelling and carrying on. We went into the Jap storehouses and took the rest of the day to feed ourselves.

---

* The officer was Lt. Col. Curtis Beecher, USMC, who had commanded at Cabanatuan and who had also survived the Oryoku Maru ordeal.

Sgt. RALPH LEVENBERG, Narumi Subcamp No. 2
(Nagoya):

I remember suddenly the interpreter coming in and calling
everyone to attention, to tell us that the Emperor of Japan and
the President of the United States had decided to cease hostilities. Well Jesus, bedlam broke out. Then he told us that they had
been ordered to turn the camp over to our officers. Then he got
just as nice as peaches and cream. He wanted everyone to know
that he was going back to the Royal Hawaiian Hotel as a desk
clerk where he had been before the war, and before the Japanese forced him to return to Japan.

Capt. JEROME McDAVITT (Omine Machi):

I was called into the Japanese commander's office. Captain
Omura, a former farmer from Shikoku, told me, "I have been
instructed by the Imperial Japanese Army to turn this camp over
to the senior American commander. That is you. What do you
want me to do?" Just as plain as that. I had no knowledge that
this was going to happen this way, so I had to do some pretty
fast thinking. My brain wasn't too sharp, but I said, "Captain
Omura, the first thing I want is for you to remove all the Japanese and Koreans who have been supervising my men and forcing them to work. I want them taken someplace where they
cannot ever again be seen by my men. Second, I want you, Captain Omura, to start bringing food into this camp, the kind and
quantity that I designate, including fresh meat, even if it's on a
rope. I want you to bring it until I tell you to stop. Next, I want
you to report to me for further instructions every morning at
8:00 o'clock until we leave this camp." He said, "Is that all?"
Then he unbuckled his samurai sword and handed it to me by
the handle. "No, Captain Omura," I said, "I know what that
sword means to you and your family, and I hereby give you
another direct order. Take that sword home with you and don't
ever give it to any American." Right then, for the first time in
my life, I saw tears in a Jap's eyes. I knew then I had him on
my hip. Anything I asked for I knew I'd get, and it turned out
exactly that way.

Cpl. HUBERT GATER, Fukuoka Camp No. 3 (Tobata):

We were lined up as usual. This time no guards, just the major,
Yaichi Rikitake. His message was brief: the war is over, you are
the victor.

Just to be free we slept outside, away from the bedbugs, and
attempted to return from animal to man. The Jap guards drifted

off. Only Major Rikitake stayed; he was a whipped old man. When we arrived in Japan, Major Rikitake offered our Colonel Dorris his sword, to commit hari-kari with, to save face. He refused—it wasn't our custom, he said. At the surrender Colonel Dorris returned the sword to Major Rikitake so he could do the same. He refused—too old, he said.

Capt. THOMAS HEWLETT, M.D., Fukuoka Camp No. 17 (Omuta):

The night of August 15, Chaplain Hamel borrowed my bible to use in a memorial service which he planned to conduct the next day for Allied war dead. The Japanese guards listened to the service in silence, and departed the scene shortly afterwards. That Hamel was permitted to hold such a service assured us that the war was indeed over.

To start the service, the Chaplain read the 90th Psalm. Two verses seemed most applicable: "9. For all our days are passed away in thy wrath: we spend our years as a tale that is told. 10. The days of our years are threescore years and ten; and if by reason of strength they be fourscore years, yet is their strength labor and sorrow; for it is soon cut off, and we fly away."

Staff Sgt. FRANK STECKLEIN, Fukuoka Camp No. 17 (Omuta):

Guys found me in camp. "Geez, Stecklein, where were you? They've been hollering for you down in the mine. They have the Screamer in one of the *benjos* and they're shoveling shit to him." I'd already left, so I missed that.

Some of the men went downtown and looked for Billy the Kid. They would have killed him if they'd found him, but he hid someplace.

Read to POWs, Fukuoka Camp No. 17

I am pleased to inform you that we received military orders for stop of warfare. Since you were entered in this camp you have doubtless had to go through much trouble and agony due to the extension of your stay here as prisoners of war but you have overcome them and the news that the day for which you longed day and night, the day on which you could return to your dear homeland where your beloved wives and children, parents, brothers and sisters, are eagerly awaiting you has become a fact, is probably your supreme joy.

I'd like to extend to you my most sincere congratulations but at the same time I sympathize most deeply with those who have been unable due to illness or some other unfortunate reason to greet this joyous day.

By order, we the camp staff have done all in our power towards your management and protection but owing to the disturbed external conditions here we regret that we were unable to do half of what we wanted to do for you. But I trust in your great understanding in this point.

Several days ago at one camp the prisoners presented the camp staff and factory foreman with part of their valuable relief foodstuffs and personal belongings while at another camp prisoners have asked for permission to present civilian war sufferers with their personal belongings. This I know is an expression of your understanding, open hearted gentlemanliness and we the camp staff are deeply moved.

Until you are transferred to Allied hands and at a point to be designated later you will have to wait in this camp: therefore, I sincerely hope you will wait quietly for the day when you can return to your loved ones behaving according to camp regulations holding fast your pride and honour as people of a great nation and taking great care of your health.

Sig. Fukohara Tai Dona

Cpl. ROBERT WOLFERSBERGER, Branch Camp No. 1
(Hoten, Manchuria):

We were loaded into trucks at the tannery and taken back to the main camp. No one knew what was going on. When we got into the big camp someone said an atom bomb had been dropped. I thought he said, "Adam." I said, "An Adam bomb! What the hell sort of bomb is that?" The word had it that it was highly explosive. We also found an OSS team had arrived.*

Pfc. ROBERT BROWN, Mukden Prisoner-of-War Camp
(Hoten, Manchuria):

Because of the overcast, we couldn't see the plane. We heard it, though, and it wasn't Japanese. Four engines is four engines, and American engines are American engines. Off in the distance we saw about twelve parachutes. Some were white and some red. Right on the heels of this, all the men working in the factory were brought back to camp. Oh boy, the rumors began flying. In prison camp you live on rumors. They started on Bataan and never ended.

---

* Six OSS men were sent from China by Maj. Gen. Albert Wedemeyer. Their mission was to effect the release of the American prisoners in Mukden. They were dropped near the main camp late on the morning of Aug. 16.

We weren't working after the parachutes landed and nobody was saying anything. Hunke and I were by the main gate when we saw some guys out in front of the guard shack.

I thought they were British. Their uniforms were green and clean. They didn't look like us. "My God, who are they?" Some thought they were pilots from a plane that had crashed. That made sense because behind the camp we had a small prison that held the flyers the Japs had knocked down during the December 1944 raids. These strangers were taken by the Japs into the headquarters building. We looked through the windows and saw a guy pull out a cigarette and light it with a lighter. I knew then they weren't prisoners. A prisoner would never have had a cigarette lighter, let alone cigarettes. We were close enough to hear: "Well, we'll contact our headquarters in the morning." "Oh, oh, this is it. This is it!"

A couple of nights later, while we were having a celebration, the Russians got there.* They lined us up and ordered the Japanese to bring in all their arms and ammunition. Then they told the American officers that they were going to shoot the guards. Of course General Parker talked them out of it.† We were told by our officers that there would be no retaliation and as far as I know, except for one guy who busted a Jap in the mouth, there wasn't any.

Sgt. CHARLES COOK, Branch Camp No. 3
(Hoten, Manchuria):

We climbed up on the mess hall roof and saw the Russians going down the road, riding on tanks and trucks. We hollered and waved. They waved back and kept rolling. Because there were still Jap guards around us, we didn't know what the hell was going on. When were we going to be liberated?

The next morning the Japanese had their normal morning ceremony of chanting, bowing, and praying for the Emperor. A Russian soldier, riding by on a bicycle, saw what was going on and came tearing through the gate with his pistol drawn. All our guards still had their rifles, but it didn't make no difference to him. Right quick he let us know he was a Polack and not a Russian. I don't know how they call theirselves, but that's what

---

* The Soviet Union declared war on Japan Aug. 8, 1945 (Moscow time) and immediately drove into Manchuria with three Army Groups. Russian forces reached Mukden August 20, the same day that a Japanese delegation left Manila for Tokyo with instructions about the occupation of Japan and the signing of final peace terms.

† Maj. Gen. George M. Parker, Jr., the former commander of II Corps on Bataan, was in the group of senior officers who arrived in Hoten on May 21, 1945.

we called them. One of the men in our group could speak a little of his language, so he told him what the score was. Right then, the Polack cocked his pistol and put it next to the Japanese officer's ear. Everybody thought he was going to kill the Jap. We told him not to do it. There was no reason for that. It's funny how a situation can change in an instant. Here was our tormentor of a minute ago now at our mercy. Yet this particular officer had done nothing to us. Even though we had ill feelings towards the Japanese, this individual was just like us and we didn't want anything done to him. He hadn't hurt us, so why should we hurt him? That's how quick it changed. We told the Polack soldier to get one of his officers. And glory be, if a Russian officer didn't come in a truck to our main gate. O.K., but we didn't want to leave behind these Jap guards, since we thought the Russians would kill them. The Japanese were scared to death. The only ones left were the poor soldiers who never touched any of us. The mean ones, see, had already left and were hiding. We finally got the message through to the Russian that he needed to go back and get another truck to take all of us, including the Japanese. to our main camp. He said he'd be back. That was the last we saw of the Russians.

After a few more days an armed detail from our main camp came over to escort us back. We marched the whole way. We went through Mukden all the way back. I don't know how far we walked. It didn't matter. Lord, we was free. The distance meant nothing. I mean, how fast you can recuperate, when you feel like you can fly?

Capt. THOMAS HEWLETT, M.D., Fukuoka Camp No. 17 (Omuta):

A medical report, compiled by the medical staff, was completed August 25, 1945, while we were still together and in a complete state of recall.

This report was accepted into the Australian Army Museum. However our meager records, including the death list, were not acceptable to U.S. courts-martial since they were not typewritten. I was young and inexperienced with the system in those years, so at this late date I apologize for not keeping a typewriter with me.

Our mortality, I might comment, was lower than Doctor Proff and I predicted it might be after our first two months in Camp 17. One hundred and twenty-six men died, of all nationalities, in the two-year period. Forty-eight deaths attributed to pneumonia, thirty-five to deficiency disease, fourteen to colitis, eight to injuries, six to tuberculosis, five to executions, and ten to miscellaneous diseases. Of the original "A" Detail of 500 men from Cabanatuan, twenty-one died.*

Following the exodus of the guard detail, we set out to scavenge the city of Omuta. Early in the exploration we found several warehouses packed with Red Cross food and medical supplies. The dates of receipt and storage indicated that these items had reached Japan prior to August 1943. Thus while we suffered from lack of food, essential medicines, surgical supplies, and X-ray equipment, these items were hoarded in warehouses during our two years in Japan.

Pfc. LEE DAVIS, Divisional Camp (Jinsen, Korea)

Playfully, we went downtown. I must have looked like a mangy dog. I saw a Korean woman barber and on the spur of the moment I decided to get a shave and haircut. We hadn't seen a woman for a long time. I also hadn't been in a barbershop and it seemed, oh so wonderful, to lie back in that chair. When I saw her razor I was a little hesitant. It was a hacksaw blade which had been fashioned into a razor. But the guys urged me on, so I let her get at me. She shaved between my eyebrows, my cheeks, and my chin. Afterwards, my face was one sore mess. It was awful, but I was happy.

Pfc. ROBERT BROWN, Mukden Prisoner-of-War Camp (Hoten, Manchuria):

General Wainwright was put in a camp a little north of us.† When he left Manchuria to attend the surrender ceremony on the deck of the *Missouri,* he sent us a note in Mukden which was read to all the men. It said he had wanted to come by and see us, but since time didn't dictate that trip, he wanted us to know that he wished us all the best.

Cpl. KENNETH DAY (Toyama):

We were instructed to paint the letters "POW" on the roof in a bright color. We did, and soon we were rewarded by a visit from Navy fighter planes. There must have been a carrier nearby. The small planes dropped a few little packages containing American cigarettes, newspapers, and magazines. One pilot dropped a note telling us to open the kitchen door. He made another pass and bounced a rolled-up newspaper through it. Show-off!

* This detail arrived at Camp No. 17 in Aug. 1943.
† At Sian, Manchuria, which is northeast of Mukden.

Pfc. LEE DAVIS, Divisional Camp (Jinsen, Korea):

The planes began to come over almost immediately. They were real low and we saw the crew members waving out of the bomb bays. We thought they were waving at us. They really wanted to get us out of the way, but we were too happy to even think right. Next run they started dropping supplies in twin fifty-gallon drums, which had been welded together. One of these drums fell and broke an officer's leg. While we were taking care of him, I remember going through the dining area where one of the drums had gone through the roof and burst. One barrel had been filled with jam and the other with gum. There was all this spearmint gum floating in an ocean of apricot jam.

Sgt. RALPH LEVENBERG, Narumi Subcamp No. 2 (Nagoya):

First off, planes from a carrier found our camp. They came in low, wagging their wings, and dropped notes and cigarettes. Then, with the help of a light, they flashed to one of the guys who'd been a signalman, asking what we needed most. Our doctor said, "Tell them we need medication for the TB cases we have. Also tell them I could use some good bourbon whisky. For medicinal purposes." A little later a plane came over and signaled for us to clear out of the area because they didn't have any parachutes. Wrapped in two GI mattresses was the medication and a case of bourbon. Not one of the bottles was busted. Then another little guy came over and flashed us to show him our kitchen. When it was marked, he dropped two cases of corned beef through the roof. He wrote a note on one of the boxes: "Needs to be cooked. Bon appétit!"

Cpl. ROBERT WOLFERSBERGER, Mukden Prisoner-of-War Camp (Hoten, Manchuria):

Along with the food and medicine, the planes dropped a projector and lots of movies. We watched cartoons, lots of combat newsreels and travelogues. We put a sheet up on one of the buildings and everybody just crowded around watching. We hadn't seen a movie in three and a half years. We ran them for hours.

Cpl. KENNETH DAY (Toyama):

One of the great treasures from the sky was a pair of current magazines, *Reader's Digest* and *Coronet*. It was clear that there wouldn't be time for 250 men to read either of them all the way through, so it was decided that someone should read them aloud. The British started with *Coronet* and we kept the *Reader's Digest*. When they had been read, we switched.

I was chosen to do the reading on our side. It took several sessions of an hour or so each, and my voice was worn out. Much of what we read we didn't understand. They spoke of things we had never heard of and people we didn't know. Who were Halsey, Mitscher, Eisenhower, Patton, and Spaatz?

Capt. JEROME McDAVITT (Omine Machi):

About two or three minutes to twelve o'clock everybody was out to watch the drop. Off to the east, in a beautiful blue sky containing two huge white fleecy clouds, someone saw a speck. As it got bigger and we heard the buzz, we saw there were two planes coming directly toward us between the clouds. As they crossed overhead, they waved their wings. Their bomb bays, I noticed, were still closed. They went on over and made a big left-hand turn and came back between those two clouds again; this time the bomb bay doors were wide open. From them they kicked out, each of them, twenty-four double-deck fifty-five gallon drums, welded and stacked. They floated down to us on sixteen red parachutes, sixteen white parachutes, and sixteen blue parachutes. No reason I can think of, except it was a show which the Air Force unit that made the drop wanted to give us. I stood there amazed, and whatever words you want to use would describe my feelings.

Several of the men ran over to me. "Captain, sir." I didn't fuss at them, but I thought, "You know, that's the first time you've referred to me as 'sir' in three and a half years." I said, "Yes?" "Captain, sir, can we make one?" I didn't want them to think I'd already figured it out, so I paused. Finally, I said, "Yes, but be careful you don't tear the parachutes."

The next morning an American flag was flying over our camp.

Pfc. JOHN FALCONER, Fukuoka Camp No. 3 (Tobata):

From the parachutes our camp tailor made a giant flag. They hung it in one of the barracks and it went from the ceiling to the floor. I hadn't seen our flag for three and a half years. When I first saw it, I just automatically snapped to attention. It was terrific.

A day later another guy and I went out. He was from Ohio and we called him Pinky. A streetcar line ran right in front of our camp and Pinky walked out and stood in the middle of the tracks and held his hand up and stopped that car. We got on and rode it up into the hills. Then we walked some more until we came upon another camp holding American prisoners. Pinky probably knew where we were going, but I certainly didn't. In the camp, which was a small one of maybe 300 men, we found that our planes had been making food drops to them as if they'd been 1,500 men there. In our case, in a camp of nearly 1,500, they'd been making drops for 300 men.

In this camp I found an old friend of mine who had shelves full of food. "John," he said, "what can I give you?" We started opening cans. I ate a can of butter, a can of jam, a can of Spam, and I sampled many more. I got so full. When it was time to leave I couldn't find Pinky, but I was given a bag of canned foods to take back to my camp. I decided that day you could get just as intoxicated on food as you could on drinks. I didn't know where my camp was and it was dark, and when I saw two headlights coming down the road I stood out in the road and stopped what I found to be a truck. It was an English lorry carrying C-rations down to our camp, so I hitched a ride. I slept amongst all that food. I didn't care what happened to me or where we went, as long as I could stay with the food.

Sgt. RALPH LEVENBERG, Narumi Subcamp No. 2 (Nagoya):

Of course it was in our camp that we purchased the bull from the "Honeydipper." The Honeydipper being the guy who used to empty our latrines so that he could sell it as fertilizer. He had the most massive bull you ever saw to pull his cart. Once we found out how much money we had earned from the Japanese, we pooled it and offered to buy the bull. The owner wasn't really part of our camp. He only came and collected and never bothered us, so we figured what the hell, let's buy the bull from him. Oh Jesus, how he didn't want to sell to us. But we'd watched this bull come and go for eighteen months, so we weren't going to be disappointed.

Well, then came the Texans who could do anything, and they were going to be the butchers. They took this monster bull into the communal bathhouse and they tied its legs and they threw a lasso around its neck and the whole time all you could hear was *mmmoooooo*. Then one of the Texans came up to the bull and with a two-by-four started hitting it between the horns as hard as he could. The bull just groaned. A little Jap cook who had been a pretty nice guy—wasn't part of the guard force or anything—stood there watching this, shaking his head and muttering *baka*. You know, crazy Americans. Then he got an idea. He went away and returned with a butcher's knife and it was he who cut the neck veins.

We diced the meat and cooked the bull for three days.

When we ate it, it was terrible. Oh Christ, you could bounce the meat on the floor, it was so tough. But that didn't seem the point. More importantly, we accomplished something on our own.

Pfc. ROBERT BROWN, Mukden Prisoner-of-War Camp (Hoten, Manchuria):

Not until the 24th, my birthday, were we really turned loose to go into Mukden. Unofficially we had men out every night. Sometimes 100 or more men would go over the wall. It was real confusing for a while. Here would be these guys coming back in the morning and the main gate would be closed, so they couldn't get back in.

I made two trips into Mukden, which I'll tell you about. We went in the colonel's carriage. Matsuda had this real plush horse-drawn carriage which we expropriated. We filled it with food and beer and, like big shots, we went downtown. We just gave the food away. If we saw something we wanted we just took it. The Chinese were petrified of the Russians, so most of the stores were boarded up. We went up to the big hotel in the city and spent the night. The next morning the Russians made it their headquarters and kicked us out.

The next time we went in we went looking for girls. We went down in the same damn carriage and we took with us one of the interpreters who the OSS had parachuted in. In town we seen some gals run into one of the buildings, so we figured that must be the place. When they found out we were Americans everything was fine, so we unloaded our food and beer and went in. Because we weren't supposed to stay out overnight, we arranged for the interpreter to come back in the carriage and pick us up. There was lots of women, so we all wound up with one. When it began to get dark, we started looking for the guy that was going to pick us up. Well hell, we kept waiting and waiting and he never showed up. None of us knew where we were or where the camp was, so without any other choice we decided to stay the night. We just got all settled for the evening, when all of a sudden we heard a big commotion outside and here were these three drunken Russians, also looking for girls. There weren't any for them, so one of our guys, Eddie, he's all drunked up, he says, "I'll give them mine." Well she, nor any of the others, wanted any part of the Russians. So Eddie took a Jap pistol that he carried and started shooting up the hallway. Drunk, drunk, drunk. When that happened, all the girls took off and went out a back window as the Russians broke in the front door.

When they found there were no girls with us, they started shooting at the walls and the plaster went flying and I thought, "Oh, Jesus Christ, I'm going to die here." Finally Eddie and the Russians passed out. The rest of us went to sleep. In the morning we found a Chinaman and told him to take us back to the camp. When we arrived, we knew we'd be in trouble. As soon as the Japs left, the American officers, because there were so many of them, turned the camp into an American base. When we walked through the gate we got a big chewing out from this major, and then we were put under arrest. No big deal, they let us go right afterwards.

Cpl. ROBERT WOLFERSBERGER, Mukden Prisoner-of-War Camp (Hoten, Manchuria):

Four of us decided to go over the fence. One of the guys knew where there was a ladder. We decided to cross the wall by one of the wooden gates, because there was a two-foot gap between the top of the wall and the electrical charged wire that ran above it. I was the last one to climb up and over. I did something stupid and got a jolt of electricity which knocked me out and down on the other side. The impact of hitting the ground brought me to. I could hear the other guys running, so I got up and followed after them. We stopped to rest opposite the MKK factory, and when I reached for some cigarettes I found I couldn't hardly lift my left arm. I told them it was killing me. They wanted to take me back, but I told them I'd go alone. No sweat. I went up to the gate and kicked the stupid thing. When they opened it, our guards wanted to know why I was on the wrong side of it. I told them I was coming back from a detail. When I reported to the hospital, they found I had fractured my clavicle. Of course they put me in a T-splint and wrapped me up like a mummy.

Several days later a B-24 landed at the airport several miles away to take out the men who were seriously sick or disabled. Since I was all wrapped up with a broken collar bone, I ended up getting air evac'd out.

Pfc. JOHN FALCONER:

I had to take a train which took me down near Hiroshima. It was just like the ripple effect you get when you drop a stone into water. First there were trees. Then the leaves were missing. As you got closer, branches were missing. Closer still, the trunks were gone and then, as you got in the middle, there was nothing. Nothing! It was beautiful. I realized this was what had ended the war. It meant we didn't have to go hungry any longer, or go without medical treatment. I was so insensitive to anyone else's human needs and suffering. I know it's not right to say it was beautiful, because it really wasn't. But I believed the end probably justified the means.

Cpl. KENNETH DAY, (Toyama):

Our departure from Toyama on September 6—one year to the day since we had landed in Japan—was by rail, with a whole train to ourselves. I have no idea how all this was organized, but it came off very smoothly. We had to travel a long way south and then across the island of Honshu to the east coast and then back north, to get to where we were going. It took two or three days.

On the first day we saw towns that had been leveled by fire. We cheered. We could look all the way from one edge of a town to the other and not see one thing standing. Just flat areas of ashes, like a beach bonfire that burns all the way out. Here and there a pathetic figure might be seen searching for anything of use. In some places there were low piles of corrugated-steel roofing sheets, rusty and charred. That was about all.

Miraculously, the railroad system appeared to be untouched. The rails and rights of way were intact. Trains moved at full speed. In every town the depot still stood. Why didn't they burn, too?

By the time we had passed a dozen such cities and towns, we stopped cheering. The devastation was so total that it overpowered our senses. We did not go near Hiroshima or Nagasaki, but those cities could not have been razed more thoroughly than the places we did see. By the second day we said little, but just stared out the windows. I had come to loathe and despise these people, but this was almost too much. I began to feel sorry for them, I still wanted to kill them, but a feeling of sympathy crept in alongside the hatred.

Staff Sgt. HAROLD FEINER, Fukuoka Camp No. 17 (Omuta):

A few days later a few of us decided to go into Omuta. We hit the *kempeitei* [police] station. We took all their guns, I grabbed a pistol like a Mauser, and then we beat the living shit out of them. Then we went to the train station, and for the next couple of days we rode trains all over Kyushu. The Japanese civilians tried to give us food and were very nice to us. We were skeptical about taking anything that was given to us, for fear that it would be poisoned. Instead, we got off the train wherever we were to take anything we wanted from any store that was open.

Once we went to Moji. People were laying all over the streets. They must have gotten away from Nagasaki. Hundreds of people just laying around. Later we were in Kagoshima, and I spoke enough Japanese to be understood, and I asked a young kid, did he know where there were any Americans? He said, "I've heard that Americans are in Kanoya." Several days later four of us, plus some Dutchman, got on another train and went to Kanoya. When we got there, standing on the station were these seven-and-a-half-foot-tall, 350-pound Americans.* Oh, geez, we just walked off the train and there they were drinking beer. They gave us some. Boy, one beer and I was drunk.

Pfc. ANDREW AQUILA, Fukuoka Camp No. 17 (Omuta):

We knew the Americans were in the southern part of Kyushu, but as yet had not come to release us. We waited about a week. I told a buddy of mine, "If they're not here by tomorrow, I'm going to take off by myself and go down to where they are." When no Americans appeared the next day, I gathered my few belongings and went to the railroad station. I'd been told it would take about ten hours to get to the part of the island where our troops were. The first day I went just two hours and spent the night in another camp. The next day, when I got on the train, I felt I'd make it while it was still daylight.

The train moved very slowly because the tracks had been heavily bombed. I traveled all by myself, in a train full of Jap civilians and soldiers. What a nut I was to do such a thing, but it was something I just had to do. I felt I wanted to get out. When the train stopped that second night, I still had not reached the American forces. At the station where I got out, I was met by some Jap MPs, one of whom spoke perfect English. He told me that there wouldn't be another train I could take until the next morning, and that I would be welcome to spend the night with them. "No," I said, "I'm at the station and I'll wait here." One of them went out and made a phone call. When he came back he told the one who spoke English something, and he told me, "You're going to have to come with us." I was alone and I couldn't do anything. "O.K. Let's go." We walked around in the pitch dark for what seemed an hour. Finally, we arrived in a building where there were other Jap soldiers. They started questioning me, "They treat you all right?" I had in my bag notes on the treatment I'd received, but I sure wasn't going to tell them that. "Oh, the treatment was fine." "What unit were

* The occupation began as an advance party of Americans arrived in Japan on Aug. 28. Two days later the occupation began in force with the arrival of American units in Tokyo and the Yokosuka Naval Base, south of Yokohama at the entrance to Tokyo Bay.

you with?" I told them I'd been with a tank outfit. They asked where I was from and other things that I can't remember any longer. At last they asked me whether I was hungry. "No," I said, because I didn't know what they'd feed me. They came in later with some tangerines and tea which I finally broke down and ate.

Then they placed three chairs together and told me I could sleep on them. Who was about to go to sleep? I lay on those chairs wide awake. Finally later, of course, I fell asleep. At around sunrise they woke me up. "Time for you to catch your train." When they escorted me down to the station, it was only a five-minute walk. They'd walked me around the night before, and to this day I don't know why. They turned me over to a Japanese officer who was traveling on the train and instructed him to take me to where the Americans were.

For several hours I sat just opposite this officer who stared at me. He was gripping his sword so tightly his hands were white. I pretended not to notice and struck up little conversations with the civilians who were sitting with us in the coach.

Finally we arrived at a station where I ran into some American MPs. "Boy, am I glad to see you," I said. He looked at me, "I thought you were a Jap." I still had my Jap clothes and my head was shaved. I explained about the Jap officer and he said to him, "Get going, Mac. We'll take over now."

I was told to eat in the American officers' mess. The first thing I noticed was the table linen and the silverware and the dishes. To this day I remember not being able to get over the tablecloths. They were so white.

Pfc. JACK BRADY (Sendai):

We were told to get down to Sendai where there would be a ship in the harbor that would carry us to Yokohama. One of the characters in the camp claimed he knew how to run a train. We found he did know how to run it. Trouble was he didn't know how to stop it. We took some sake on board the train and when we arrived in Sendai, the bottles were empty. We banged into the station and were jolted a little. When we got off the train, we were ready to start the war all over again, because we were met by people dressed in funny helmets, wearing green uniforms, and carrying short rifles. When we surrendered we had soup-bowl helmets, wore khaki, and used long Springfield rifles. The lieutenant, who went down to make contact, came up and explained to us the world had changed since we'd last been in the Army.

Pfc. LEE DAVIS:

I was put on a hospital ship. Just as I got into the barge which was going to carry us out, I saw our Japanese commander standing near the wharf. He was wearing one of these long-handled swords, and to this day I wish I'd gone back and taken it from him as a souvenir.

Aboard ship we were told to drop our clothes and to take a shower. When we came back, our clothes had already been burned, so we were given Navy pajamas and robes. A Navy nurse came in and said, "Well, boys, what's the scuttlebutt?" Those were the happiest words I'd ever heard.

Sgt. RALPH LEVENBERG:

A lot of guys flew out of Japan, but the bad cases like myself were taken out on a hospital ship. They had me in a wire basket and I was put in an LST, or whatever it was, that carried me out to the big ship. Every time we hit a wave, I passed out. I was in pretty bad shape. The next thing I remember is smelling this wonderful perfume, and when I opened my eyes I was looking into the baby-blue eyes of this gorgeous American nurse. I passed out again. What the hell.

Cpl. ISHMAEL COX:

When I was liberated I couldn't walk. My legs were swollen and I couldn't wear any shoes. You know, when you get a balloon blowed up so tight that just a touch will pop it? That's the way I looked. My testicles were swollen as big as my head. I wrapped my legs and feet in rags and straw and rope, anything I could get, to keep the gravel from hurting. We took a train to Osaka.

Some men say they couldn't have gone on much longer if the war hadn't ended. I'm going to tell you there ain't nobody, and I mean nobody, can tell me the limits the human body can stand, till it's put to the test. There ain't no piece of machinery that can outdo the body God gave us. A man will live seventy-five years and in that time he'll wear out ten or fifteen pieces of machinery. When a man keeps his mind on God, God's going to sustain him, buddy. I don't know whether you believe in God or not. Doesn't make any difference to me, because you got to be responsible for your own soul, not me. But when a man allows God to sustain him, he can go through hell if he has to. I mean, he can go right down and fire the furnaces of Satan and still come out, if he keeps God in front of him. That's what I did. Yes sir, I refused to die.

J. J. CARTER* (Aomori):

My fantasy was that as soon as the war ended the Americans would drop some paratroops into our camp and they would escort us to freedom. What actually happened was very different.

Along toward the first part of September our British camp commander organized us, and the 400 of us walked to the train station and waited for a train that would take us to Tokyo. Around 5:00 in the afternoon, we boarded a train just full of Japanese, civilians and soldiers. Of course we're not talking about sitting down. We were packed in the aisles and spent all night riding this train. Midmorning we pulled into Tokyo and found out we were supposed to go to Yokohama.

We caught another train and rode in to Yokohama. Again, there was no one to meet us. We all grouped up and wandered out of the station and found a typical GI in the middle of an intersection. He had a cigarette hanging out of the side of his mouth while he directed traffic. Our Limey commander went up to him, "Say, old chap, where are the British forces?" The GI, never missing a move: "Friend, that's what we've been wondering ever since the war began." One of our own officers went over to him and explained who we were and what we were looking for, and was told where we should go. So much for my fantasy of being escorted to freedom. I began to feel a little bitter about the whole situation. I got the feeling that they just rather not have us there.

Finally we were taken to the harbor where we boarded the hospital ship *Marigold*. We had all our clothes throwed away and then they dusted us. We needed it. Afterwards, I was called in to a small room where an American officer, he might have been a doctor, questioned me. He asked what kind of work we'd done in camp and what our rations were. When I began to tell him, he interrupted me. "I'm not interested about back yonder, what were you eating the last few months?" I told him. "How many hours did you work?" I told him. He said, "Now, before we go any further, let's understand, I don't want to hear war stories. We're after information. I have sense enough to know you can't work those hours on the food you say you were given and live."

"Well, let me tell you something," I said. "You're going to hear a lot of things that you won't believe. I don't need war stories either. I have my own. I have all the war stories I want. But what I'm telling you is facts. You don't want to sit over there and call me and the others liars. Let me warn you about something. You better be awful careful. Some men here are not all

* Pseudonym.

together. They've been beat and starved and have had to live in their own excrement. They're not going to let you sit there and call them liars. They're not going to warn you, but they're going to try and kill you." He shouted, "Let me stop you right there. You're talking to an American officer and that kind of talk could get you court-martialed." I laughed right in his face: "Would you please tell me what you, as an officer, or this whole Army could do, that hasn't been done to me in the last forty-two months?" He said, "Get out of here. Just get out."

Finally, after we were interviewed several times, they began to know who we were and what we'd done. Then they told us that they were going to fly us to the Philippines. I wasn't interested in going to the Philippines. I was interested in going to America.

16
HOME

J. J. CARTER:

Then, we got on a C-54 and went down to Okinawa. We were there several days. To be honest with you, I don't know what we were waiting on. We lived in a tent city just like a bunch of refugees, with nothing to do but eat and wait.

One day it was time for us to go and we landed at Clark Field, old Fort Stotsenburg, and were taken and put in tents again. I'm not complaining about sleeping under canvas. It was just all this messing around that was getting to me. From the time I was liberated, I had a terrible fear that I was not going to get home. In the Philippines I was so fearful the furthest I would go from my tent was to the PX and chow hall. We were offered tours. Filipinos came in and took some of the fellers to their homes.

Sgt. FORREST KNOX:

Chipper and I hitched a ride into Manila to see a Filipino family who had befriended us when we were on the Jap truck-driving detail. Knowing we were living in a tent city, there was no way they were going to let us return that night. After we ate a big meal, with Filipino beer and everything, who should walk into the house but the Filipino I told you about, who after his wife turned him in for stealing a Jap truck, was beaten for weeks. He still looked like he'd been branded with an iron, and he'd come out of that experience kind of lumpy like. I asked him, "Just for my own curiosity, did you steal that truck?" He says, "Yes, I stole it. I sold it for 3,000 pesos." It was on the tip of my tongue, but I stopped in time, but I wanted to know what had happened to his wife. Knowing Filipinos, I think I knew.

Cpl. KENNETH DAY:

Somewhere south of Manila we became part of a huge tent city. It must have been a replacement depot or staging area for assault troops during the fighting. A fellow could get lost there. We had to memorize the numbers of our streets.

We hadn't seen our last Japanese yet. In the morning a

crew of chattering workmen came around and picked up litter between the tents and along the company streets. We realized that they were prisoners of war. Our prisoners. Another odd feeling. We listened to them talking, and we could make out a few words of what they were saying. It was not complimentary. We let them yak for a while, then laid into them in their own language. They were shocked. They had not known who we were. They were much quieter after that.

We were going to be there for a while. Shots, records, pay, and all the many little pieces that fit together under the heading of processing. Hurry up and wait—the Army hadn't changed. They told us it was O.K. to go to Manila and I hitched a ride in. I had not known the city before the war, except for one fast trip through in a covered truck, so I didn't recognize the landmarks. There was a lot of rubble around, but there were many people on the streets and a few shops open. I had a good lunch of *pansit canton* and took a walk around. There were little tables set up along the downtown curbs, offering a pathetic collection of merchandise. I remember that they had used nails, partly straightened, for a few *centavos* each. Those that had not been burned cost more.

I found a movie theater running and I went in. It was a pretty good picture—Humphrey Bogart in *Sahara*, I think—but I couldn't take it. A lot of shooting, and I had had enough of that. I didn't stay in town long. Got a ride back to the camp, and didn't go out again.

J. J. CARTER:

We got on a boat in late September. They'd kept promising us planes, but when they couldn't get any we were put on a troop ship. Lo and behold, it went straight from the Philippines to New Zealand. Then we left for Frisco. We slept in bunks four or five high. And whenever the guy above you got seasick, you still got your face full. We became so bored we even volunteered for KP. Still had all this anxiety and frustration.

Cpl. KENNETH DAY:

We stopped in Hawaii for a few hours, tied up alongside the narrow channel at Pearl Harbor. While we were there an entire Navy task force steamed in, passing no more than 100 yards from our port rail. We were enormously impressed by this parade of big ships, noting the battle emblems on their stacks. As each ship came abreast of ours, the entire crew stood in formation on deck as if saluting. We assumed that they were passing in review for some high official somewhere, but we couldn't see any reviewing stand. There were no other ships docked near ours. I think now that they may have been paying their respects to us.

Our orders were changed just after we departed Hawaii. New destination: Seattle. How about that! They were going to take me straight back to my own home town.

We stopped next at Vancouver, B.C. Fireboats came out in the harbor and shot streams of water in the air. We navigated our way down through Puget Sound in the night. I went to bed, unable to see anything and wanting to be ready for the big event the next morning.

The *Gosper* anchored out in Elliot Bay in thick fog. I wanted to show my buddies the beauty of Seattle, but we couldn't see a thing. We lay to for hours and finally inched into a pier. Well as I knew that waterfront, I couldn't even tell which pier it was. There were no signs, and piers look pretty much alike. The guys kidded me quite a bit.

Three women appeared. We looked them over, of course, but had no idea who they were. My eyesight had failed more than I realized. Then one of the ladies made a move that looked familiar. I stared at them again, and saw that one was my fiancée, another her sister.

I didn't know what to do. I walked away from the rail and sat down with Heimbuch and Grill. They mentioned the women, and I told them one of them was my girl. Had I been talking to them? No. "What's her name?" George asked. "Lola," I told him. He muscled his way to the rail and shouted at the top of his voice, "Hey! Lo-o-o-la!" She looked up and spotted me. We carried on a brief shouted conversation, and everybody on ship and shore knew that the whole greeting committee was for me. It was a grand feeling.

J. J. CARTER:

I had called my parents from Manila, so I just knew that whenever I got to Frisco my folks would be there to meet me. When we pulled alongside the dock, there was just a sprinkling of people waiting for us. Come to find out, some of the people waiting were ex-wives who had remarried, thinking their husbands were dead. They'd come to San Francisco to get the thing straightened out.

When I got off the boat, no folks were there to meet me, no friends, nobody. We lined up, were checked off, boarded a bus, and were carried to Letterman (General Hospital).

I could never figure out why nobody was on that dock waiting for us. Everyone gathered on the rail and looked for someone. I figured that people would, at least, be curious enough to come and watch us—fellers, you know, who'd been in prison camp for three and a half years. I remember before the war, on our way to the Philippines, in Hawaii, when we docked, there was a band playing. I wasn't no hero now, and I didn't expect no hero's welcome, but I expected the government to pay my folks' way to Frisco. I had no doubt they'd be there. My mother told me that she called and the Army told her not to come, because I'd be home shortly. But I didn't get right home. I stayed in the hospital, began to drink, and my weight hit 173, which is more than I weighed in my entire life. When I was allowed to go into San Francisco on a pass, I thought, I've come to the wrong country—they've dropped me off in the wrong place.

Capt. MARION LAWTON:

When I got back to Letterman Hospital in San Francisco there was Hadley Watson. He'd come in to greet us. I didn't even want to see him. He'd been home six months, was a big hero and all that stuff. I remembered his escape from Davao had caused us a lot of misery. The Japs had cut back on our rations. But by gosh, they did get out and they joined the guerrillas and went back into battle.* This is what a soldier's supposed to do. I think now it was all right, but in 1945 I didn't feel so kindly.

Pfc. JACK BRADY:

I tried to go back to UCLA by using the GI Bill, and found I had nothing to talk about with my classmates. I sat in classes just as they were experimenting with these new jet planes, and UCLA seemed to be a favorite place for the damned jets to fly over. Every time a plane came over close an ex-Marine captain and I would duck. We were the only ones in class who would. A couple of characters kept making snide remarks about our reaction. Finally the Marine said to me, "The next time anyone gets on us, you take the guy behind you and I'll take the guy alongside of me, and we'll finish it." When we did, we were invited into the Dean's office and told it would probably be advisable to drop out, until we were a little more settled down.

I couldn't talk to people. I couldn't even talk to my parents. They had an entirely different outlook on things. I had to move out. I couldn't talk to any of my old friends. They were en-

---

* Both Hadley Watson and Mark Wohlfeld played active roles in Col. Wendell Fertig's guerrilla organization on Mindanao. Their many adventures fighting the Japanese and Colonel Fertig could readily fill another book.

tirely different. I shouldn't say they were, I was. I couldn't get along with anybody, so I went back into the service. I found I couldn't get along with anyone there, either. I got real moody. I guess it took about two years, something like that, before I finally snapped out of it a little bit.

Pfc. ROBERT BROWN:

Coming home was very confusing. I couldn't stand anyone to give me a hard time. I'd shake and go to pieces. It happened once at Camp Beale when I went up for discharge. I went on over and I was treated like everyone else, which was all right with me. I went over on the 14th of March, 1946, and I was the only ex-POW turning in my uniform. I didn't have any civilian clothing, all I had was the uniform that was on my back. I saw all these discarded uniforms piled up and having been a prisoner I just automatically thought, "Well, Jesus Christ, I'd like to have some of those." So I asked this guy, "What do you do with all those clothes?" He said, "Turn them in. You want something?" I said, "God, yeah!" I started putting pants and shirts in my barracks bag when a second lieutenant comes up and nails me. "What are you doing!" He began to give me a real hard time. I stood there, with my knees shaking, my heart going a hundred miles an hour. My God, I about fell to pieces. I didn't know what the hell to do. I really didn't. The lieutenant just kept giving me all kinds of razzmatazz. Finally, I did what the British call an about wheel and walked over and got in my car, leaving this lieutenant yelling after me. I went straight up to General Jones's headquarters.* I steamed in and here's an old, bald-headed major sitting there. He looked at me like, "What the hell are you?" I said, "I'm Brown and I want to see General Jones." He says, "What for?" "Well," I said, "I was in prison camp with him in Mukden and I have to see him!" General Jones heard me through his door and he told the major to let me in. I went in all wound up. He settled me down and asked, "What's the trouble?" I began explaining about taking the clothes, and then how this goddamn second lieutenant jumped all over me. I said, "I didn't know what to do, so I came to see you." He said, "O.K. You go back down to where you were and take whatever you want." We sat a while and chatted about Mukden.

That's an example of what happened. It took a long time to get over it. It wasn't anger as much as it was fear. I was nervous. There had to be something wrong with my nervous system. There were no psychiatrists waiting for us when we

---

* Maj. Gen. Albert M. Jones, who had commanded I Corps on Bataan.

got off the boat in San Francisco. As a matter of fact, coming home was very low key.

My mother got a telegram from the War Department saying I'd arrive in Frisco on the 21st of October. We docked on the 20th. There were no more than fifty people waiting. When I left home in 1939 my parents didn't have a phone, but I checked the telephone book for my area and found their number and told them I was in San Francisco. They said they'd be down next day.

I was put in the hospital and as I lay there I began to think. I'd gotten home and the next day I was going to see my family. I'd waited four years for this, but then what? I didn't know where I was going, because I had run out of stepping stones. I was at the end of the line. It was like I'd been put in an airplane and, at 30,000 feet, dumped out.

My parents came the next day. I was supposed to be quarantined for a week but I said, "The hell with that," so we all jumped in their car and drove over the Oakland Bay Bridge to visit a cousin. All these cars speeding around me. We were in the middle of it. I hadn't been in a car for three and a half years and I was petrified.

When I come home to Marysville, because of the thousands of troops in Camp Beale there was a curfew in place, 11:00 p.m., if I remember correctly.

The first night my Dad wanted to take me out and have a drink. I'm twenty-one years old and my father wants to take me downtown to look the town over. I'm in my uniform, because that's all I have that fits. We walk down the main street. A big, fat 4-F'er in uniform out of an MP unit tells me because of the curfew to get off the street. That rattled me good. My dad told him, "My kid just come back from a POW camp, and you better move your fat butt out of our way or I'm going to whip you right here." By God, he left us alone.

I came home, but I was still in jail. I bought a car. I also drank a fifth of booze a day, but couldn't even get drunk. I was so goddamn nervous. I couldn't sit still. I'd drive my car between Marysville and Yuba City. I had to keep moving. I couldn't sleep. My mother put me in a bed with a mattress and everything. I'd been used to sleeping on a little straw tick. I couldn't sleep. I wound up in the living room, lying on the rug. I couldn't converse with anybody. I spoke some Japanese and knew some Chinese cuss words. But I couldn't talk to anyone. I'll bet my mother thought, "What the hell did I get home?"

There were no jobs. I was uneducated, for all purposes. I knew I could survive in a prisoner-of-war camp, but what else could I do? I sat down and talked to a friend of mine, and then

I discussed it with my mother. I said, "I'm going back in the service." Some of the people I knew thought I was nuts. But by God, I knew I wasn't getting anywhere in Marysville. What could I do? So, I reenlisted.

Sgt. FORREST KNOX:

I came into Janesville on a train. The closest phone was the corner bar. When I tried to call my folks, I learned they'd moved out of town. Finally got my cousin. He said, "Stay right there, we'll pick you up." While I waited, the bartender poured a drink and set it on the bar in front of me. Without knowing it, I made local history. Curt Grant had one hard-and-fast rule in his bar. He was in business to sell liquor, not give it away. It was also the last free thing I got in that town.

Pfc. JOHN FALCONER:

Back home I found all kinds of people who had prayed for me. I honestly feel that saved me. My mother was a God-fearing woman and she said to me, "John, how bad was your leg hurt?" "I was never hit by a bullet," I told her. "I know," she said, "but I dreamed you hurt your leg." I pulled up my pant leg and showed her the scar that I got when I tore my leg on the splinter, trying to get to the latrine in Cabanatuan.

Staff Sgt. JAMES CAVANAUGH:

When I got home I learned Colin Kelly had been made a big hero. Someone told me he had crashed his B-17 into a Jap battlewagon. This was news to me. I had been on the crew which on the third day of the war loaded Captain Kelly's bomber at Clark Field. On the return leg of Kelly's flight he was jumped by a Jap fighter near Mount Aryat, and while the crew bailed out, Captain Kelly stayed with the plane and was killed when it crashed.

2d Lt. LEONA GASTINGER:

I saw the movie *So Proudly We Hail!* and I knew it wasn't true. It was taken from the story of the nurses on Bataan. We weren't zonked out from being in love like Claudette Colbert, and I knew no one was like Veronica Lake, who blew herself up with a hand grenade. Those things just didn't happen.

After the war I was out in San Diego and I was standing in the hotel lobby, and a feller came up to me and said, "I remember you. You were my nurse on Bataan." I looked at him and I said, "Don't tease me like that. You couldn't possibly remember me." He vowed he did. I just didn't expect people to remember me, there was so much going on then.

Probably the time after the war that astonished me most took place in Kansas City in November 1945. I heard from a friend that General Wainwright was going to be in town. I got to the hotel where there was going to be a reception for the general. When I first saw him my knees started to shake, because the last time I'd seen him was on Corregidor. Kind of shyly, I went up to him and said, "General Wainwright, I'm sure you don't remember me, but . . ." He spoke up: "Of course I remember you, Leona." He called me by my first name. He told me I was the only nurse who had come to say hello to him since he'd been back in the States. I was so glad then that I'd gone to see him.

Pfc. VICTOR LEAR:

I hold my country responsible for being uneducated as to the type of people the Japanese are. I hold them responsible for anything they do for those people 'cause they're not human. You give them the same chance today and they'd treat us the same way again. Anyone who buys a Japanese automobile is as un-American as a traitor.

Cpl. ISHMAEL COX:

I got back to Letterman General Hospital and four of us POWs were walking down a corridor and we saw this fat, greasy . . . "Look, look, a dirty goddamn Jap!" We took out after him and chased him all over that damn hospital. He finally ran into the Surgeon General's office. "What's going on here?" We said, "That's a dirty goddamn Jap. We got to get him." "Whoa, whoa," he said, "something's the matter here. There's a lot here that you people don't know." "Yeah," I said, "and a lot you don't know. He's a damn Jap, that's what he is." To me it wasn't no such thing as a good one. The colonel said, "Well, I'm gonna tell you, that boy fought right along with our boys. He probably helped you get liberated." "The hell, you say," I said, "he's a damn Jap!" He explained the situation to us like a father. He said, "Now, you went through hell, boy, you don't want to come back and mess yourself up." So that's how I found out about good Japs.

Capt. BENSON GUYTON:

At the war's end I did not go back for the war trials, but I did write up Kiniyama. So did some of the British. Several years later I got to thinking about Corporal Kiniyama and decided to see if I could find out what happened to him. I wrote the Adjutant General, who told me I should write the State Department. Then the State Department told me to write the Adjutant General. So I wrote a letter to both of them, which mentioned that I'd like an answer and that I'd prefer not to have to go to my Senator for it. I got a nice letter back from the Adjutant General saying that Kiniyama was tried and convicted of inhumane treatment of Allied prisoners of war and was sentenced to, I believe it was, twenty years at hard labor. He served seven years of this sentence, at the end of which time he was paroled to take care of his aging mother. At the next reunion I read this letter to about twenty Omine Machi people. I would say, judging by the expression on their faces, that they figured this was justice. Kiniyama had not beaten anyone bad and had not killed anyone.

Staff Sgt. FRANK STECKLEIN:

When I returned to Tokyo they took me out to Sugamo Prison so I could talk to the Sailor and the One-Armed Bandit. The lawyers warned me before I went, "Frank, don't touch them. It would be bad at the trial if you did. Talk to them, but don't touch them."

In the interrogation room at Sugamo there was a Japanese-American interpreter and several MPs. The Sailor and the One-Armed Bandit sat across the table from me. I spoke a little Japanese, so I asked the Sailor whether he remembered me. He kind of nodded his head yes. I says, "Well, do you also remember the beating you gave me?" No, he said, he don't ever remember giving anybody any beating. Goddamn! I screamed at him, *"What!!* You mean to tell me you don't remember when you took me in that cell and beat me?" I just let him have it with my voice. "You don't remember taking that strap and beating on me all the time, and how I begged and prayed? How about you?" I turned to One Arm. "How about when you went around beating me, when I was kneeling there at the front gate?" Both began to shake. The sons of bitches were shaking like mad. The interpreter said to the Sailor, "You did beat the sergeant, didn't you?" He said, "Yes." One of the MPs, a tech sergeant, came over to me, "This is the first time anyone has confessed to beating a prisoner. We don't know anything and we won't see anything. Take them. They're yours. We're leaving the room. You do with the sons of bitches what you want." I remembered the lawyer's warning, so I refused the offer.

When I got on the stand, their attorney was trying to

prove that Knight died of starvation. He said to me, "Do you know why Knight was starved to death?" "Starved?" I said. "Starved nothing. He was beaten to death." Afterwards my lawyer told me that when I testified Knight had been beaten to death, I put the rope around the Sailor's neck.*

Once I finished testifying, I decided to go back to the Mitsui Mine and Camp 17 to look up some of the other Japs I'd known there. They brought the overmen into a room after each shift and I recognized all of them—the Screamer, the Wolf, and Billy the Kid. They'd heard I was in camp, so they hadn't shaved and done other little things like that to change their appearances. I pointed them all out. They knew me real well. I said to them, "You know what I could do, if I wanted to?" I'd been told that if I wanted to testify against them, they would have them arrested and charged. But hell, I didn't want to stay over there that long. It would have meant another year. The lawyers wanted me to, because those lawyers were always anxious to get more Japs. But my mother felt I'd been over in Japan long enough. When I told these Jap overmen I wasn't out to get them, they treated me like I was one of their brothers.

Then, of course, I also saw the Duck Hunter. He was one of the good ones. He even invited me out to his house. I didn't want to go, but he'd invited his whole family for this big dinner. I told the interpreter, "Jesus, the man's poor. I don't like to go there and eat the little he has." He said, "Frank, you would hurt him worse if you didn't go."

Maj. JOHN MAMEROW:

I was ordered to go from March Field in Riverside to San Francisco, so I could appear before a board investigating the behavior of Commander Edward Little, who had been my mess officer at Camp No. 17. I knew that when we went through the Replacement Depot in the Philippines every man spoke against Little, and several of the men had come to my tent to discuss the matter. As a result of these complaints, court-martial charges were preferred and preliminary investigations were held at various points in the United States. I sat in front of the San

---

* Following the war many Japanese were tried for war crimes committed against Allied prisoners of war. From Camp No. 17, for example, Asao Fukuhara, the camp commandant, and the two guards known as the Sailor and the One-Armed Bandit were tried in January 1946 and executed.

The commander of Japan's 14th Army was also brought to trial. Lieutenant General Homma was charged with crimes against American and Filipino soldiers during the forced evacuation of these men from Bataan in mid-April 1942. Four years to the day from the start of the Japanese Good Friday offensive Masaharu Homma was executed by an American firing squad at Los Banos, Luzon, on April 3, 1946.

Francisco board and answered questions for three days. Then a general court-martial was convened in Washington, D.C., and I was there for almost a month waiting to be called. When I finally testified, I spent some four or five days in the witness chair.

Little was universally detested by everyone. I think the whole thing boiled down to just one word—attitude! Edward Little was one of the original 500, and when the selection of a camp mess officer was discussed with the Jap commander, I chose Little over all the other officers. I felt at the time he was the best qualified man for the job. He dealt with our most precious commodity, food, and I felt he would carry out my order that each man receive his honest share. Everyone was always hungry, and Little did evolve a system which insured that each man received his fair share. Everyone tried to beat his system. While he was efficient in his job, his display of arrogance and lack of courtesy to the men caused their dislike of him. Although he never did it to me, most everyone else who disputed his word or tried to make a complaint got his standard answer, "Get the hell out of my kitchen!" On several occasions I had to act as mediator between him and the men and once, to prevent a riot, I had to tell him to get out of the mess hall. A lot of the things he was accused of doing, like turning in Knight, happened after I had left the camp. While I was still there, Little had threatened he would turn some men over to the Japs. This I forbid him to do, but there were always rumors. Little denied to me that he had turned anyone over to the Japs while I was commander in the camp.*

Capt. MARION LAWTON:

I just suppressed the experience when I got home. I closed the book. It was a chapter in my life and I was through with it. I married in February of 1947, and involved myself in community affairs. When my wife Peggy saw a mention in the local paper of a reunion of Bataan and Corregidor survivors, she suggested we attend. I refused. I'd seen other veterans' reunions which were made up of rowdy bunches of drunk veterans who tried to act like young people, throwing toilet paper out hotel windows, and who generally made asses of themselves. I didn't want any part of that. I also felt I might find

---

* The American mess officer at Fukuoka Camp No. 17, Edward Little of Monrovia, Calif., was brought to trial Mar. 10, 1947 on charges of conduct unbecoming an officer and a gentleman. At the end of a four-month secret court-martial held in the Navy Gun Factory in Washington, D.C., Lieutenant Commander Little was acquitted of all charges.

a bunch of drunks feeling sorry for themselves and wanting to be pitied. No thanks, I didn't want that either.

Next year Peg read another notice about a reunion. "I know you'll see some of your friends there." I knew my close friends had all died. But she gently worked on me until I reluctantly agreed to attend a reunion. When I got there, the experience hit me immediately. It was so important to see people who had gone through what I'd been through, who had turned out to be decent and proud human beings, people I was glad to see. I just felt a brotherhood and a love I didn't know existed.

Staff Sgt. HAROLD FEINER:

The first day we got into O'Donnell, a very close friend of mine died in my lap. I decided then that I'd get back, and when I did I'd tell Ed's parents how he died. On my honeymoon I stopped off to see his parents, who lived outside of Buffalo. I was still in uniform and I drove out to this farm. The parents were quite old. I told them that Ed had died in my arms, peacefully, which was true, and that he had received the last rites from a Catholic chaplain. I received a Christmas card from that family for years. They never believed me, though. They just didn't want to believe that their baby was dead.

Sgt. FORREST KNOX:

I met all the gold-star mothers. I was on the honorary firing squad or was a pallbearer for every casket that came home. Some were empty boxes. The mother wanted a grave and marker she could see and mourn over. I closed my mind at those times. I was hard as nails when I came home.

Because my brother was an officer in our National Guard company, when he first came home he visited every family who had lost a son to offer his condolences. I used to go around with him and act as his moral support. His sense of duty made him suffer through a hard job. The day came when he said we would go out to see the Sheas.

Bernard Shea. "One Horse" was all we ever called him. His mother brought him to the armory one day in 1941. She said she was undecided whether he should join the National Guard or the Boy Scouts. Poor Bernard never, ever lived it down. His mother was a good woman, with good intentions. She knew he had to get away from the farm. If you've ever read Beetle Bailey in the comics, you'd recognize Bernard Shea as Zero. He tried real hard, but never quite understood what went on. He never laughed, because he didn't understand the intricacies of a joke. I felt a little sorry for him and tried to

protect him from some of the hazing. So I automatically became his buddy and listened to all his little confessions. Fort
Knox and basic training was tough on him. He was away from
home. When he started to drink beer, he couldn't drink much
without becoming violently ill. He also had some monumental
hangovers. I tried to tell him to quit, but he wanted to be like
everyone else. Some of the jokes played on him were cruel,
but on the other hand he asked for some of it.

They made him an officer's orderly. The perfect job. He
always did his best to do exactly as he was told. One of the
funniest jokes, to me at least, pulled on him was during his
trip to Lexington, Kentucky. The whole company was a part
of it. It takes time and organization to spring a good joke, and
we all really worked on this one. The idea was to first indoctri-
nate him with the fear of being rolled in Lexington for his
money, and then to arrange a mock situation in which he thought
he was being rolled, while the rest of us watched. It involved a
long, convoluted story to get him in a house of prostitution just
before curfew went into effect and the lights in the town went
off. We watched the scene from across the street in a bar which
faced the house he'd been taken to. Everything depended on
timing, which had to be tight and perfect. It was. When the
squad car went down the middle of Lexington's red-light district and flashed its lights, it meant the town was closed. With
One Horse still in the house when the madam turned off her
lights, his paranoia of being rolled took over. All he wanted
was out. The girls in the house had a tiger on their hands. Four
of them jumped on him, the madam got a belt in the mouth for
her troubles, and as far as she was concerned that was the
end of the joke. Enough was enough and she unlocked and
opened the front door. One Horse came came through it like a
bronco out of a chute. Monday morning he was at reveille. No
one knows how he got back to camp. I quizzed him about his
night on the town, but all he did was swear at me and tell me
I wasn't really his friend. By and by he got over it. But it was
hard for him to learn, don't trust anyone. He asked someone
where in Louisville could he buy rubbers. Of course he was
sent into a woman's fancy lingerie shop. Once again he had to
flee down the street, leaving a woman screaming behind him.

Sometimes he was real confused by what happened to
him. It was comical as hell to see him doing close-order drill
by himself. He was always making mistakes and getting chewed
out. But he persisted and practiced by himself. He never made
mistakes when he was giving the commands. His problem was
that, because his comprehension was slow, he never was quite
in time.

We finally shipped overseas to the Philippines. I thought it was a dirty trick. Bernard should have been sent home. That Philippine *balót* duck egg we had him set to eat the day the Japs bombed Clark Field is an example of the jokes that were played on him in the Islands. When the war came, One Horse was very military. Wore his steel hat at all times plus his pistol belt, canteen, and gas mask. He'd been told he must never be without them, and somehow he never noticed he was the only one who wore them.

The war bewildered Bernard. The surrender left him dazed. I made a mental bet that he would never get out of Bataan. When we gave up, I made an estimate of who I thought would survive the war from our company. I made a few mistakes. How could I take the torpedoes fired from our subs into my figures? One Horse, well I knew he would never make the mental adjustment.

I was surprised to see him at Camp O'Donnell. He came in late, weeks behind the rest of us. I went to welcome him. He was terribly depressed. I tried to talk him back up. A man wears several cloaks. This one was the oddest for me. I'm an atheist, but I was also Bernard's father confessor. He told how the Japs took him off the March and made him drive one of their trucks. So Bernard joined the Jap Army. He became a driver and an orderly. Strange how they knew it was the only job he was trained to do. He lived, slept, and ate with the Japs. At this point in the story he began to weep. To cut down on the smell, the Japs began to bury the dead around their camp. This, of course, became One Horse's job. One day he dug another grave and the native he was putting into it, he realized, was still alive. The Japs forced Bernard to kill him with a shovel before he covered him up.

Bernard's mother had done a good job raising a Christian son. Now, in O'Donnell, his guilt was crushing him. I tried to explain that he was only a victim, the Japs were guilty—he wasn't. He was my friend. I tried real hard to justify and explain what happened. But his conscience would not give him any slack. He had committed an unpardonable sin. "God will never forgive me for killing an innocent, helpless man." I ran out of words and arguments. He finally got up and walked away. His head was hanging. I had failed him and I had been his last chance. His soul was crushed. As he walked away I knew he would die. To survive you must want to. He no longer wanted to.

My brother and I, after the war, went out to tell the Sheas what had happened to their son. What could I tell Bernard's mother and father—that his strict religion had destroyed him? I could not explain to them what had happened, so kept his final confession to myself. This is the first time I have ever told the story. People keep asking, "What happened?" Perhaps this will explain, in a small way, why some men answer, "I can't remember."

The record says Bernard Shea died in O'Donnell of dysentery.*

Pfc. ROBERT BROWN:

On the hike out of Bataan I ran into a guy I'd been to high school with. His name was George and his leg was split from the knee all the way down to his ankle. I helped him for I don't know how many miles. After a while I left him because he was dragging me down. I saw him again in Cabanatuan. When I left the Philippines for Manchuria in the fall of 1942, I knew George was going to die.

The first thing my mother said to me when I got home, "George came around to see you." I said, "Mom, you gotta be kidding. Couldn't be."

J. J. CARTER:

I talked to a psychiatrist in Letterman. He asked me a lot of things that I didn't understand. I did some paper tests, punched holes. He asked me if I'd been having headaches, how I felt, what I thought, and if I was anxious to get home and lots of other silly questions. Then I was told to report to Brooks General Hospital in "San Antone" and granted a ten-day delay en route. I started home.

With the orders I got the train tickets. First, Los Angeles. Then on to Cisco, Texas, wherever that's at, Cisco to Waco, Waco to "San Antone," and "San Antone" to Houston. I got on the train in Frisco one night and got off the next morning in L.A. There I sat. That night I got on another train and we slowly crossed the desert. I finally arrived in this little old place and when I looked out the window I saw it was Cisco.

I got off the train and walked into the little depot. I went up to the ticket window and asked the man when the train for Waco left. He said, "You can't catch a train from here to Waco.

---

* Company A of the 192nd Tank Battalion was a Wisconsin National Guard unit formed in Janesville, a small farming community a half-hour drive from Madison. After the war Janesville put on its Corn Exchange Building a Memorial to The Dead and Living Who Fought at Bataan. The plaque lists the ninety-nine men of Company A who went off to the Philippines in 1941. As is the way in rural towns, these men were either related to each other by blood or marriage, had gone to school with each other, dated each others' sisters, shopped in their fathers' stores, played ball together on the town team. Sixty-five of these men died in service.

There's a train that comes through here tonight, but it's a milk train." So I asked again, "Well, when does the train through here that goes to Waco stop and pick up passengers?" "There's no train," he repeated, "that you can get on here that will take you to Waco. You just get off here. You don't get on." I said, "When the milk train comes in tonight I'll get on it." He said, "You can't do that." "Well," I said, "you make sure you have all the officers that you have here tonight, because it'll take all of them to keep me off that train. I'm going to Waco."

That night, when the train pulled in, sure enough, they started loading milk, but there was one passenger car. I got on. When the conductor came by he wanted to know where I came from. "I got on at Cisco."

"Nobody gets on at Cisco."

"Nobody till now got on at Cisco."

"Well, you can't stay on this train."

"The American Government has given me orders to get on this train and I have those orders right here. If you want to defy the American Government you go right ahead. Whenever you do, you'll still have the problem of putting me off. Here is my ticket. When I get to Waco, I'll get off."

In Waco I asked the station master when I could catch a train to San Antonio. "Tomorrow. We don't have no trains through here until then." Then, by some miracle, he asked me where I was headed. He saw I was a serviceman and this was evidently something that happened to other men. I told him I wanted to end up in Houston. "You don't want to go to 'San Antone.' You can go direct to Houston and that train leaves in thirty minutes." He took my ticket, issued me a new one, gave me some money back, and I was on my way again.

When I got to Houston I grabbed a bus which let me off close to my home. When I arrived I hardly recognized it and my parents weren't home. Some neighbors spotted me and ran across the street. "Didn't you see your parents? They're at the depot." Then they explained to me that the trains from Waco get into Houston in a different terminal than the trains from San Antonio. I, of course, arrived at the other depot. When my folks arrived, I felt really home.

I asked my mother a few days later how she felt when she heard Bataan had fallen. "I didn't feel anything," she said, "because I thought you were on Corregidor." But my mother suffered through my captivity. She didn't understand, though, what really happened and why the same boy that left her in 1941 didn't come back in 1945. Until I got married, she kept trying to make that 1945 person into the boy that left in 1941. There was no way!

One of the first things we did was celebrate the Christmases of 1941, '42, '43, and '44. All together, at one time. Every present that I would have received was right there.

I continued to drink. The first drink I had was on the dock in San Francisco. One of the guys went across to a liquor store and bought a bottle. I spat the first drink out. Then, I held my nose just to get it down. But I kept trying until I succeeded. At home I increased my drinking.

My leave was very short and almost before I realized it, I had to report to San Antonio. The deadly fears which I had after liberation remained. I asked my parents to take me to the hospital. When I got there, the doctor immediately placed me in the psychiatric ward.

I knew there was something wrong with me, I won't argue that part, but I don't believe I should have been put in this ward. The conditions were terrible. Just terrible. The door was always kept locked. I couldn't understand why they did this. That night I found out why. I was in with some dangerous fellers. I mean, they were just out of it. One feller next to me got to screaming. Others were down manning machine guns, holding off the enemy. It was wartime again. They were suffering terribly from battle fatigue.

The next morning the doctor came in to see me. I always had heard that if you put up a whole lot of struggle, arguing, it would only make the situation worse. He had my chart in his hand. "Your name Carter?"

"Yes."

"You just came in, didn't you?"

"Yes."

"How's it going?"

"Oh, it's going all right. Another night or two I'll be just like all the rest of them here. I'll be down by the side of my bed repelling a Japanese charge."

So he said to the nurse, "Take Carter here up to my office."

When I went there he said, "Do you know why you're here?" I had no idea. He explained that in the last camp I was in, Aomori, a record was kept of me and that record was turned in when I got to Yokohama. It stated that I was suffering badly from a mental something or other that had a long name.

I said, "I'm glad to hear about that. Now I'm going to tell you something that might sound strange to you." I remember the officer on the *Marigold*. "As soon as I found out the Japs suspicioned me of being crazy, I played it up to the fullest. The first place they began to suspicion me was at Osaka. If I hadn't played crazy, I wouldn't be here today. This came about when

I wouldn't cooperate with them in meeting my work quotas. Even when the quota was practically nothing, I didn't do it. They beat me, but I didn't do their work."

In a couple of days I was moved out of the locked-door section and into another ward. They began to see what I needed was to be put in circulation and not penned up. I had the idea that if I didn't get out of there, if they found something wrong with me, I'd never get to go home.

On my convalescent furlough I was home only three days and I told my dad, "I'm going to go to work." I started out shoveling dirt in a labor gang. My dad finally got me an apprentice's card so I could learn the pipe-fitting trade. One hundred and twenty days later I was out of the Army.

When I left in 1941 I was supposed to come back and marry a girl. I had the idea that everything stood still while I was gone. Nobody got older and nobody changed. On my first day home I chatted with my folks a while, then, "I guess I better run down and see Mavis." My mom said, "Son, Mavis is married." "No," I said, "she can't be." That was quite a blow. "When did she get married?" Then the blow really came. "She got married in March of '42." I said, "You're joking. I hadn't even been captured yet!" I felt pretty bad. I felt rejected. Strange thing happened then. I tried to marry every woman I saw. I felt like, if I could just get married, that would prove I was worth something. I was feeling sorry for myself. I guess I still am. I got cheated out of four years of my life. I felt like I'd never fit in until I married.

I got married in March of '46. Then I neglected my wife miserably. I went running with a gang and fooled around. I've asked my wife many times since those days how come she kept on. She said, "I just felt like sometime it would change." She is one of the few people who understood what I'd been through. She's a remarkable woman. No other woman would have stayed with me. It's a miracle that I found her. She helped me so much.

I still get captured about once every month. Actually, it's harder on my wife. I never wake up, but she does. She doesn't know how to cope with this nightmare. I'm always captured in different places and the circumstances are always different. But it's always by the Japanese. Sometimes in these nightmares I say, "You know, this is strange, but I was captured once before."

In prison camp I got to the point when I didn't think I was going to make it home. It really didn't make any difference either way. This fear that I got about not getting home didn't come on me until the goal came in sight. The thought struck me, what if, after all this, I don't make it home? I fought and struggled, connived, cheated, lied, and once almost murdered, and now, being so close, what if now I don't make it? That pressure affected me. I'd venture to guess that there's something wrong with all of us, each and every one of us who survived. A human mind can't go through what we went through without something being wrong. You can't go through the suffering, the agony and harassment, the humiliation of being on a Hell Ship, living ankle deep in human feces, to get off in Moji and be sprayed down with fire hydrants on a cold Thanksgiving Day, and not have something wrong with us. Mark this down. The Government better find it out. There's still something wrong with us. I've got sense enough to know that I'm not all I ought to be. That's why I watch myself very carefully and warn people, "Don't do certain things."

I took a test for something some time ago and the psychiatrist said I was a potential suicide. He felt I cared so little for human life. I said, "Man, I fought for three and a half years to hold onto life." He said, "But you'd never hold on to it again like that." Something else I'd never do again. No question in my mind that I'd go right back and fight again for our flag. I wouldn't, however, go through what I went through, because I'd die before I let them capture me again.

Pfc. ROBERT BROWN:

You know, when we got home there wasn't a damn thing done for anybody. In my case they asked me if I wanted to apply for disability. I said I certainly do. After I reenlisted in '46, the VA came through with 50-percent disability, temporary, based on the sicknesses I had—malaria, dysentery, scurvy, and all the rest of the junk. Some of the fellers didn't do that. They just got home, got discharged, and said, "Good-bye." Today they're hurting bad. I mean, these guys are sick. When we got back, we weren't given any real counseling of any type. A lot of guys needed psychiatric help. They needed to be reindoctrinated or debriefed, something to ease them back into the mainstream of America. The guys have problems. I can't sleep at night. My feet burn. They drive me crazy. I got hit by a rifle butt back here on my shoulder. My whole neck is sore up to my ears. Sometimes I pop aspirin or Tylenol all day long. Don't do a damn bit of good. We go to the VA and they won't do a damn thing for us. That's what gets me right in the pit of the stomach. They tell us that we have to prove that our ailments are service-connected. Why should we have to prove it? The records are missing, if there ever were any. Think the Japs kept records of the beatings given us in Cabanatuan? Goddamn it, we were there! Just being there is enough! To try to prove something to some quack American doctor with the AMA saying, "We don't understand anything about malnutrition. We've never seen what you have. We don't believe you." How in hell would they know—they weren't there and they don't even try and find out. If we get ten minutes with one of these doctors, any damn doctor, we're lucky.

Pfc. WILLIAM WALLACE:

When I came back to the States I still had five or six stitches in the top of my head. I'd been working on a coal barge when, for no reason, a Japanese civilian threw a large chunk of coal at me. It knocked me cuckoo and cracked my skull. A Limey doctor and a Navy corpsman stitched it up. The scar is still there. Although I mention it every time I go, no VA doctor has ever looked at my head. I drew a 10-percent disability, $44 a month (1979). I know of men who never left the States who are drawing 100-percent disability. This is one of the things which has made me angry with the VA, their inconsistency in the way they treat people. But you don't want to hear about that.

Staff Sgt. HAROLD FEINER:

Maybe it was a humanitarian thing to do, but it was also a stupid idea. When I got out of Camp 17 I weighed just more than 100 pounds. When my parents met me a few weeks later, they didn't recognize me because I was like a balloon. The Army fed us as much as we could eat. Many of the men came back looking so good, they began to believe that they were healthy again. They were running on euphoria or prosperity or whatever you want to call it. Just putting on weight, they said to themselves, "Hey, I'm better. I'm well." Guys actually thought they had died and gone to heaven. They were in paradise. Guys were hungry for women, they were hungry for life. They wanted to start families, they wanted to go to work. Many guys were frightened to admit to the Army doctors who examined them just how sick they were. They felt that if they told them something was wrong, the Army would keep them in the hospital for a long time. So the guys hid things. And let's face it—I'm not knocking all Army doctors, that would be unfair—but there were a lot of stupidos in there. There were a lot of doctors who were disgusted because they'd been drafted and had to leave a good practice and, instead of taking care of Mrs. Rich, were now taking care of some poor POW. Many of them couldn't have cared less. Coupled with men who wanted out, the doctors caused a situation which is haunting many of the men now. I know guys that got back in October 1945 and were out by December. They weren't in a hospital more than six weeks before they were out. And boy, I want to tell you, the ghost of that brief stay is haunting them today.

Another thing that's happening is that things that didn't show up before are showing up now. Some doctors don't understand this. Here's a situation where a guy got out of the service thirty-five years ago and he seemed then a fairly stable individual. Why is he, now, suddenly having nightmares? That shouldn't be questioned. The thing is, whether he had them thirty years ago or not, he is having nightmares now. Then he didn't complain about them, but I'm sure he had them. I know I climbed the wall and was drenched, when my wife would shake the hell out of me to wake me up. The children would come running into the room because they could hear me screaming. Everybody who was a POW of the Japanese goes through this.

Sgt. FORREST KNOX:

I spent a year in an Army hospital in Battle Creek, Michigan. I thought I got an education overseas, but in that hospital I got a refresher course. I spent a lot of time telling the doctors all the things that had happened to me. Every time I had another complaint I would get another exam. I felt rotten all the time. I took the hookworm cure ten times. Because the treatment was worse than the worms, everyone else called it quits. The results of every exam were the same—I was perfect. There was not a thing wrong with me. I complained about my eyes. I got another eye test. Perfect. Only one problem—I couldn't read the menu posted in the mess hall. When I had a cold and blew my nose, I could blow air through my left ear drum. Got it busted one day when a Jap slapped me around. I kept asking, "What did you say?" The medics got exasperated: "What the hell's the matter? You deaf?" So I had another ear exam. Must have had a dozen doctors look at it. Nope—perfect again! I used to sleep walk at night and had those hallucinations.

While a prisoner, you never relaxed or dropped your guard. Now I was free and safe. The nightmare began and I started to walk in my sleep. Some slight noise would wake me up and I'd find myself out of bed, standing, shivering, not knowing where I was. I would tell the doctor the next day I didn't feel good. The answer was always the same: "There isn't anything wrong with you." In the hallucinations I would meet dead men walking down the street. It always happened the same way. I would be walking along, not really thinking of anything. There would be someone walking towards me that I recognized. I would get a sudden happy feeling at seeing him. Then, the sick shock. I knew, I mean I *knew* suddenly he was dead. I would turn away and just stand there. If it happened once, it would have been nothing. But it kept happening, in broad daylight, as I walked on the street. I couldn't just up and bring myself to tell the doctors that I was crazy. I knew I had flipped out on that Hell Ship. Now again, I was sure I was going crazy. The Army always had the joke about the guy who pretended to be nuts to get a Section 8 discharge. How did I prove to them I wasn't pretending? I couldn't. How do you get over something like that? All kinds of people take credit. No one helped. I felt utterly trapped. It was the toughest battle I fought and I fought it alone.

Finally, they ran out of patience with me in Battle Creek. They told me there was nothing more they could do for me, that I was cured of everything and that now I should go home. I said I wanted to be cured first. "Stay as long as you like," they told me. "You got a bunk and the mess hall. We'll feed you, but we're through treating you." After sitting and staring at the wall for two weeks, I finally gave in and asked to be sent home. I seen a copy of the medical report at discharge time. Everything I had talked about or reported was listed. Then the bottom line—*Denied.* What I learned: the Army Medical Corps is set up to get soldiers back into combat. Repairs are only incidental. The war was over and they didn't need me. Besides, they all knew I was goofy. Not a soul told me what to do. "Just go home." Yes, the war was over and wasn't peace wonderful? My discharge date was November 11, 1946. I was a year late and everyone had already forgotten the war.

On my first leave I was told, "Don't talk to anyone." I was confused: "Why?" "If you say anything at all about what happened overseas, Red will get court-martialed." Red Lawson, because he was blind and had beriberi so bad that even a fly landing on his feet made him cry, was left behind by the Japs in Cabanatuan. When he was released by the Rangers early in 1945, he got home to our little town before everyone else. There was a big City Hall meeting. Everyone asked questions about what happened to their sons or husbands. Red never lied. The War Department had never told the mothers anything about what Red was now telling them. This was the first time. Some of the mothers threw a fit. Washington, D.C., got a flood of indignant letters, "Why haven't we been told? What are you hiding?" The chair-bound brass in the Pentagon were there for glory, not lip. Red got an airline ticket to Washington. Message said, "Urgent!" For one week they took turns screaming at Red. Court-martial papers were drawn up, "Revealing secrets in time of war." A Jap's favorite pastime was to stand you at attention and then slap you silly. In Washington, Red found the same game, but with a different opponent. The generals said Red could go home and they would hold his court-martial papers in his file. Just one more letter from Janesville and they would activate them. He still will never talk about what happened. They really made a believer out of him. He remained a prisoner in his own home. He never went out because people demanded the truth of what happened.

All the survivors of Company A, 192d Tank Battalion finally made it home to Janesville. "Chipper." We were on the truck-driving detail when a Jap tried to part his skull with a gun butt. The rest of his life he had a tender spot on the back of his head and terrible headaches. He told his wife once what happened to him and then never spoke about it again. I tried to get Chipper to go down to the local Tank Company memorial service one year. He said no one, including the gold-star mothers, was going to make him feel guilty because he came home and their kids didn't. He drank to kill the headaches. The VA said he developed all his medical problems after he came home. There were no records, medical or otherwise. Problems were not service-connected and he couldn't prove anything. The years passed. He died of a stroke.

Wes. Could write a complete medical book on what happened to him overseas. He is blind in one eye and deaf. Diabetes. Leg is dead and walks with a cane. VA gave him 40-percent disability.

Red. Mother nature cured him of beriberi. He's been dead from the knees down since 1944. He can't see and he can't feel the ground. He falls down a lot. People always say, "Red's drunk again." He falls when he's sober, too. The VA says there is no connection with his being starved in Cabanatuan.

Bud.* Alcoholic, divorced. Has cancer. Doctors said he would die two years ago. He was a good man when we needed one. Being a survivor means you never quit. So he hangs on.

Boyd. My tank driver. Died of a stroke the first year home. I always suspected schistosomiasis, but stateside doctors never heard of it—and I'm not entitled to a guess.

Orvis. Wound up in Mukden. When he came home he was skinny as a rat. Like most, he never fattened up. When discharged, he had an X-ray that proved he didn't have TB. Sick

* Pseudonym.

all the time. They got live germs on a spit test. Took another X-ray with the same results as the one taken at his discharge. They finally found TB with oblique X-rays. It was hidden by his collar bone and shoulder blades. They operated and took off the top of both lungs. This wasn't service-connected because they had X-rays which proved he didn't have it in 1945 and 1950. He developed emphysema. He lived with an oxygen tube down his throat for one and a half years. He died with 20-percent service-connected—10 percent nerves, 10 percent feet.

Howard. My special buddy. He wore a name tag around his neck on a string that said *"BLIND,"* so the Jap guards would stop beating him for not bowing when they walked by. The VA fought him tooth and nail for twenty-five years before they finally admitted he was blind. There is no such thing as starvation.

John. Was on the Hell Ship with me. When the killing started I remember hearing John say, "What the hell are you doing?" A voice answered, "I'm trying to help." John said, "Well, let go. That's my leg and you're not helping." Not once, when we returned home, did John ever mention that ship ride. He talked to me at funerals, but never looked me in the eye. He died of emphysema.

Sandy. I was with him for nearly two years. He asks me, "What happened?" He has almost a total memory loss. It is one way to stand the pain of remembering.

My own story is simpler. I went to every place I knew around town looking for a job. Answer was always the same, "We aren't taking any applications today." At General Motors, the big employer in town, I got the same answer. I had been a classmate of the interviewer, so he told me real confidentially, "Now look, GM can't hire you. You're a wreck. There is no way you could do a day's work, and we can't support you just because you're a veteran." Just two weeks before the Army had told me I was in perfect condition and didn't need any help. I was still learning my new lessons.

I really wanted to be an electrician. The union had it sewed up tight. I couldn't even hire out as an apprentice. That would cut into the overtime the journeymen could make. Outside looking in again. I even checked in on reenlisting. They told me they were already top heavy with NCOs, so I couldn't get my staff-sergeant rating back if I re-upped.

My mother couldn't understand what was the matter with me. I was home, wasn't I? For four years I had clawed and fought and killed just to get back home. Now, no one wanted me or gave a shit if I had a place to live or a job to support a family. I was crazy enough to finally go back to the VA. Same story. There was nothing the matter with me. When I came through Fort Sheridan, getting my discharge, one of the desks I had to go past to get myself stamped had a sign "Psychologist." The officer was bored with his tedious job. He played with a cigarette. "Are you afraid of crowds?" I answered "No," and waited for him to ask me what I *was* afraid of. He picked up his rubber stamp, slapped the paper, signed his name, and sent me on my way. And they got the goddamn gall to complain I don't have any records. By 1948 I was ripe to explode. I started going to a mental clinic in Madison. An old doctor there talked to me. He answered the phone more than he talked to me, but at least he didn't call me a liar. After a year I had explained all the things which happened. His advice: "Stop hiding at home, get out, and talk to people. What had happened could not be changed: till I could talk about it I would never get over it. I have taken his advice. I'm afraid I shock people at times. I still wonder why I talked to you in St. Louis. But I was alone and felt lost again. It don't matter now. Does it?

Pfc. WILBURN SNYDER:

Just the other year I went to one of the reunions that's held in the Philippines. On the bus that drove us old veterans around was a banner saying we belonged to the Defenders of Bataan and Corregidor. When the Filipinos saw this, even the little tots, they held up their fingers in the V for victory sign. I asked the driver about this. "What do those little kids know about that sign?" He said, "Joe, they may not know how to read and write, but they know about Bataan."